The King Arthur Flour Baker's Companion

THE **ALL-PURPOSE**
BAKING COOKBOOK

THE COUNTRYMAN PRESS

WOODSTOCK, VERMONT

AN INVITATION TO THE READER
If you like this book, you'll love King Arthur's bimonthly baking newsletter, *The Baking
Sheet*. For information or to subscribe, call *The Baker's Catalogue* at 1-800-827-6836.
Also, if you have questions about the recipes in this book, call our baker's hotline at
802-649-3717, 8:30 AM–8 PM Monday–Friday, 9 AM–5 PM Saturday, 11 AM–4 PM Sunday
(EST).

LIBRARY OF CONGRESS CATALOGING-IN-PUBLICATION DATA
The King Arthur Flour baker's companion : the all-purpose baking cookbook / King Arthur Flour.
  p. cm.
  ISBN 0-88150-581-1
  1. Baking. I. King Arthur Flour (Firm)
TX765.K55 2003
641.8'15—dc21

                                                            2003046253

COVER AND INTERIOR DESIGN BY Vertigo Design, NYC
RECIPE AND INSTRUCTIONAL ILLUSTRATIONS BY Laura Hartman Maestro
FOOD PHOTOGRAPHY BY H/O Photographers, Inc., Hartford, Vermont
TOOLS PHOTOGRAPHY BY Brenda Hickory
COPYEDITING AND INDEX BY Joan Whitman

Published by The Countryman Press, P.O. Box 748, Woodstock, Vermont 05091

Distributed by W.W. Norton & Company, Inc.,
500 Fifth Avenue, New York, 10110

PRINTED IN THE UNITED STATES OF AMERICA

10 9 8 7 6 5 4 3 2 1

Acknowledgments

This book is the realization of a decade-long dream by baking visionary P. J. Hamel, senior writer and editor at King Arthur Flour. This book, these recipes, the patiently described techniques, and the friendly take-you-by-the-hand tone are in large part her handiwork. P. J. was ably accompanied by her team of bakers and writers in Norwich, Vermont, and by Brinna Sands, another visionary, inveterate baker, and prolific writer on all things baking related. Brinna has been a part of the King Arthur family since 1976, and in 1990 authored *The King Arthur Flour 200th Anniversary Cookbook*. P. J. and Brinna's dedication to the gentle art of making someone a homemade loaf of bread, or cookies, brownies, pie, muffins, cake, or other piece of love, is a true inspiration.

The book you hold in your hands was a true company-wide project, and recipes flowed from all corners. It is a testament to the hard work and contributions of all of King Arthur's 150+ employee-owners. After the recipes were chosen, they were tested, and tested, and tested yet again in King Arthur's kitchens. Baker/writer Susan Reid, with the assistance of Robby Kuit and Teresa Griffith, tweaked, and massaged, and refined the recipes until they were just right. Susan took up the slack all along the way, doing whatever needed doing—from writing headnotes, to compiling and checking lists of ingredient weights, she smoothed what often seemed a bumpy road. Publications manager Toni Apgar coordinated this year-long effort and, in the process, gently rode herd our stable of baker/writers. In addition, the following peo-

The bakers at King Arthur Flour

ple made invaluable contributions: Test kitchen director Sue Gray; artisan bakers Richard and Stephanie Miscovich; Master Baker Jeffrey Hamelman; Susan Miller, who runs our Baking Education Center; Cindy Fountain, who runs The Baker's Store in Norwich, Vermont; Michael Jubinsky and Judy Ulinski, who over the years have taught a quarter-million students through our national baking classes; Shannon Zappala, who has tirelessly worked to elevate King Arthur Flour's position on the food world map; Janet Matz, our art director; and Robyn Sargent, Ali Scheier, Jen Korhonen, Starr Kilgore, Emmy Zietz, Jane Korhonen, Robin Rice, and Brenda Hickory. Thanks are also due to President Steve Voigt, for encouraging us along the way, and for allowing us the time and resources to develop this manuscript.

And to our editor at The Countryman Press, Kermit Hummel, we also say a great big thanks, because his enthusiasm for this project from day one saw us through the inevitable tough times. He always believed this would be the wonderful book it is. We now count him as a friend as well as an editor. We appreciate the sage advice of W.W. Norton editor Maria Guarnaschelli, who assisted us in developing this book's outline.

Finally, we'd like to dedicate this book to John Sheldon, our long-time catalogue photographer and colleague. His pictures grace these pages; his talent carries us ever upward; his friendship enriches our lives.

We wish you all warm bread from the oven whenever you want it.

THE KING ARTHUR FLOUR COMPANY, INC.

Contents

Introduction

Why, in today's fast-paced world of food-at-your-fingertips and instant gratification, would anyone want to bake? Packaged cookies and boxed crackers at the grocery store taste pretty good and are well within most people's financial reach—why bake your own? Artisan bread bakeries have opened up on every other street corner; the bakers there produce fresh bread daily. Why bake bread at home? A stroll into the bakery section of the local club store will yield you a personalized birthday cake, instantly, for less money than it takes to feed a family of four at a fast food chain— why take the time to make and decorate a birthday cake for a child?

Because store-bought is, at best, a shallow substitute for homemade. Do you like fudgy brownies (*not* cakey!), with a thin, shiny crust, a hint of espresso, and a swirl of raspberry icing? You can't buy them; you have to bake them. Do you want less salt, or more? Do you like your coffeecake less sweet? Your chocolate chip cookies crunchy or chewy? Tailor these recipes to your own nutritional needs and tastes, without making them taste like cardboard. Do you dislike the long list of multisyllabic additives and chemicals on the label of that frozen chocolate cake you buy for the kids? You are what you eat; take control of your life (and theirs), and let them eat cake— your cake. The scent of hot yeast bread gently wafting through the kitchen, a comforting aroma as old as time itself, is reason enough to bake your own bread.

But what if you never learned to bake? Or you learned, but haven't been totally satisfied with the results? You may not have had Grandma gently guiding your hands as you rolled out your first pie crust; and even if you did, perhaps you've forgotten most of what she showed you. That's where *The King Arthur Flour Baker's Companion* comes in. In this book you'll find the recipes and solid information you need to become a top-notch baker, one who makes the lightest, most tender pancakes, a dark, gutsy chocolate cake, and an apple pie that'll bring a grown person to tears. You'll make oatmeal cookies better than any you've ever tasted, even those from that fancy cookie shop at the mall; your yeast breads will rival those of the local bakery, at one-tenth the price. In short, you'll learn (or realize once more) the pleasure of baking for your family and friends, and the satisfaction that comes from using your imagination and skill to create baked goods that feed not just the body, but the soul.

Let this book be your companion as you walk a path followed by bakers from hundreds of cultures for thousands of years. You're a link in a limitless line of bakers: the sticky bun recipe you pass along to your son or daughter today will continue to be shared long after you're gone. And the guiding hand you place atop a friend's, as she kneads her first batch of bread dough, will in turn be placed atop her grandchild's someday. We here at King Arthur Flour take our responsibility to the bakers of America seriously; as America's oldest flour company, founded in 1790, we are committed both to preserving our country's baking heritage, and helping to forge its future. You are an integral part of that future.

Come with us now into the kitchen, and let's bake.

P. J. HAMEL, BRINNA SANDS, TONI APGAR,
and THE BAKERS at KING ARTHUR FLOUR

A Note on Measuring

Butter the size of an egg? A cup of flour or 100 grams of sugar? Measuring is one of those things we don't think about until we're slightly stymied, or until we open a British cookbook, or perhaps one from Europe, or maybe our grandmother's. There are, of course, a number of systems for measuring, some pretty out of date, some unique to the United States, and one that's pretty universal. Measuring has always been somewhat of an interpretive business.

But measuring goes beyond the devices you use to determine how much of what goes into a recipe. Thermometers, both in your drawer and in your oven, are measuring devices. So is your timer, and the thermostat in your kitchen. So is a barometer, hygrometer, and altimeter. When you're aware that bread rises quicker when the barometer is falling (it's good to bake on a rainy day), that flour "shrinks" in the winter because it's dry so you may need less of it (flour absorbs or sheds moisture depending on humidity), or that you'll need less yeast and baking powder if you live at 8,000 feet, you'll begin to understand all the variables you need to consider when you bake. You may find that you can make something successfully at home, time after time; but take the same recipe and try it in another kitchen with other equipment and you may have a very different result. Measuring cups and spoons, scales, humidity, altitude, and temperature all have an impact on the results of your efforts.

Our System of Measuring

Our American system of weights and measures was based originally on the British system, but they have developed differently from each other in the past two centuries. Although in 1959 English-speaking scientists agreed to use the metric system for scientific and technological purposes, that's been of little use to bakers.

In the early 1800s, Americans began to substitute volume measurements for weight, probably because a "teacup" or an "egg" as bases for measurement were easier to come by than an accurate scale, especially on the trail west. A "knob" of butter, "butter the size of an egg," even "alum the size of a cherry," are measurements that are sprinkled through old cookbooks. In earlier times, "receipts" for baked goods were based on these fairly rough ingredient guidelines that led to very individualized results. Baking success was dependent on an accumulation of experience.

Today we try to re-create recipes accurately, without eliminating an individual's touch. Just as your speech has a personality of its own, so should your baking. But as we try to become more accurate, our tradition of volume measuring can leave us short because volume measurements are prone to wide variations (a "cup" of flour can weigh anywhere between 4 and 5½ ounces, and the measuring cups themselves can legally vary up to 12 percent). Measuring by weight is much more consistent and accurate.

Measuring Flour

At King Arthur Flour, we've held a long debate about what a "cup" of flour weighs. In the past, for simplicity's sake, we called it 4 ounces. You can, in fact, create a 4-ounce cup of flour by sifting the flour first. The sifting process incorporates a lot of air into the flour, which is the first source of leavening. Scooping flour, which can produce a much heavier cup (up to 5½ ounces), will obviously contain less air and more flour. You can also fluff up flour in your flour bag, sprinkle it gently into your measuring cup, scrape the top with a straight edge, and get close to 4 ounces, but you probably will get a little bit more.

Our preferred weight for a cup of flour is 4¼ ounces, and that's what we've used throughout the book. This is closer to the standard weight that bakers use. It makes calculating total ounces a little more difficult, but in all of the recipes we've done the calculating for you. This discussion would be much easier if we'd stop relying on measuring cups and start using the scale. But since the old volume system of measurement is still pretty standard, we're using it along with weight measurements.

Measuring Devices

- Our first plea is that you buy and use a scale (see Tools, p. 601).

- For volume or weight measuring, have on hand a couple of sets of measuring spoons. It's easier to measure small amounts—a teaspoon, a tablespoon—with spoons even if you have a scale. There are some sets available that measure from ⅛ teaspoon through ½ to 1 tablespoon. There are also sets containing odd sizes. It's useful to have more than one set (see Tools, p. 599).

- Have two kinds of measuring cups, one that measures flush at the top edge for dry ingredients and one that has a lip at the top for liquids. There are some liquid measures available that also have metric measurements on one side. These can be useful when using cookbooks from other parts of the world.

- Other important measuring devices are thermometers and timers (see Tools, pp. 600 and 601). Because ovens have their own personalities, a thermometer that helps you know what's going on inside is important. Oven temperatures can vary considerably as can oven thermostats, which drives how long your oven "cools" before the heating element kicks in again. Thermometers can also measure the temperature of a dough, batters, syrups, and finished goods.

- Even with the most accurate of measurements, such variables as humidity, altitude, the fat content of the milk you use, the mineral content of your water, all are going to affect your baking. Ultimately your eyes and hands, when they have had enough experience, will make many of your measuring decisions.

Measuring Hints

Make sure that you know what you're supposed to be measuring, for example, 1 pound of apples, chopped, or 1 pound of chopped apple. The former is apples weighed before they've been chopped—with skins and cores. The latter is skinned, cored, chopped apple.

Measuring by Volume

- When measuring flour by volume, fluff up the flour, sprinkle into your dry-cup measure (the one that measures exactly a cup at the top), and scrape off the excess with a straight edge (a metal flour scoop with a straight edge allows you to scoop and sweep with one hand). This will get you approximately 4¼ ounces. (See illustrations on next page.)

- When measuring other dry ingredients such as sugar by volume, overfill your dry-cup measure and scrape off the excess with a straight edge.

1

Stir the flour to fluff it up . . .

2

. . . sprinkle it into the measuring cup . . .

3

. . . and sweep off the excess with the straight edge of the scoop.

• Measure light or dark brown sugar by packing it into your measuring cup.

• To measure a solid fat (butter, vegetable shortening, or lard) in a measuring cup, use one that is significantly larger than the amount you want to measure. For example, to measure 1 cup of butter, fill a 2-cup liquid measure up to the 1-cup mark with *cold* water. Push butter into the water until the water reaches the 2-cup mark, which will give you 1 cup of butter. Drain the fat thoroughly. Alternatively, use a measuring cup specifically designed for measuring sticky substances (see Tools, p. 599).

• If you need to measure a liquid sweetener or peanut butter, spray the inside of your measuring cup lightly with a vegetable oil spray first. That will make it easier to get the sweetener out of the cup. (If the recipe calls for a vegetable oil or other liquid fat, just measure that in the cup before you measure the sweetener, you'll get the same result.)

Measuring by Weight

Weighing ingredients is a more accurate way of determining amounts than measuring by volume. When it comes to volume measurements, there are many variables that can affect actual amounts. Measuring cups and spoons can vary significantly, as we've discovered over and over in our test kitchen. Cooks everywhere use varying techniques, and one person's idea of "full" or "packed" is usually different from the next person's.

Ingredient weights can vary significantly, also. Flour weighs less in some climates where the air is drier, than it does in others, where it's humid. It also varies from summer to winter. Raisins from an opened box that's been in the pantry or refrigerator for months won't weigh as much as fresh ones. Vegetables and berries can have a wide range of water contents, so they may weigh different amounts at any given time. You get the idea.

This chart gives average weights for commonly used amounts given in recipes. It can help you plan your shopping, as well as being handy if you want to convert recipes to significantly larger amounts.

Weights in Ounces for Recipes

28.35 grams per ounce

ITEM	MEASUREMENT	WEIGHT IN OUNCES
Almonds, sliced	½ cup	1½
Apples, dried, diced	1 cup	3
Apples, peeled, sliced	1 cup	7
Apricots, dried, diced	½ cup	2¼
Baking powder	1 tablespoon	½
Berries, frozen	1 cup	5
Butter	½ cup, 1 stick	4
Buttermilk, yogurt	2 tablespoons (⅛ cup)	1
Bread crumbs (dried, seasoned or plain)	¼ cup	1
Caramel, 14–16 individual pieces	½ cup	5
Carrots, grated	1 cup	3½
Cheese, cheddar, grated	1 cup	4
Feta	1 cup	4
Ricotta	1 cup	8
Parmesan, grated	½ cup	1¾
Chocolate, chopped	1 cup	6
Chocolate chips	1 cup	6
Cocoa, unsweetened	2 tablespoons	⅜
	¼ cup	¾
	1 cup	3
Coconut, grated, unsweetened	1 cup	4
Coconut, sweetened flakes	1 cup	3
Coffee powder	2 teaspoons	⅛
Cornmeal	1 cup	4⅞
Corn syrup	1 cup	11
Cornstarch	¼ cup	1
Cranberries, dried	½ cup	2
Cranberries, fresh	1 cup	3½
Currants	1 cup	5¼
Dates	1 cup	5¼
Dough Enhancer	2 tablespoons	⅝
Dough Relaxer	2 tablespoons	⅝
Egg white, fresh	1 large	1¼
Flour		
Unbleached, all-purpose flour	1 cup	4¼
Bread flour	1 cup	4¼
Cake flour	1 cup	4
Pastry flour	1 cup	4
Potato flour	¼ cup	1½

ITEM	MEASUREMENT	WEIGHT IN OUNCES
Pumpernickel flour	1 cup	4
Semolina	1 cup	5¾
Whole wheat/graham flour	1 cup	5¼
White whole wheat flour	1 cup	5
Garlic, minced	2 tablespoons	1
Garlic, peeled and sliced	1 cup	5¼
Ginger, crystallized	½ cup	3¼
	⅓ cup	2¼
Ginger, fresh, sliced	¼ cup	2
Honey	1 tablespoon	¾
Instant Clearjel®	1 tablespoon	⅜
Jam or preserves	¼ cup	3
	⅔ cup	7¼
Lard	½ cup	4
Maple sugar	½ cup	2¾
Maple syrup	½ cup	5½
Meringue powder	¼ cup	1½
Milk	1 cup	8
Milk, dry	¼ cup	1¼
Molasses	¼ cup	3
Mushrooms, sliced	1 cup	2¾
Oats, rolled or thick flakes	1 cup	3½
Oil, vegetable	1 cup	7
Olives, sliced	1 cup	5
Onions, baking (french-fried)	½ cup	1⅜
Onions, fresh, chopped	1 cup	5
Peanut butter	½ cup	4¾
Pecans, diced	½ cup	1⅞
	1 cup	3¾
Pineapple, dried	½ cup	2½
Pine nuts	½ cup	2½
Praline or pistachio paste	½ cup	5½
Pumpkin, canned	1 cup	9½
Raisins, loose	1 cup	5¼
Raisins, packed	½ cup	3
Rhubarb, fresh, medium dice	1 cup	4¼
Sesame seeds	½ cup	2½
Scallions, sliced	1 cup	2¼
Shallots, peeled and sliced	1 cup	5½
Sour cream	1 cup	8
Sugar, granulated white	1 cup	7
	⅔ cup	4¾
Sugar, confectioners', unsifted	2 cups	8

ITEM	MEASUREMENT	WEIGHT IN OUNCES
Sugar, dark or light brown, packed	1 cup	8
Sugar, Demerara	1 cup	7¾
Sun-dried tomatoes (dry pack)	1 cup	6
Sunflower seeds	¼ cup	1¼
Tapioca flour	¼ cup	1¼
Tapioca, quick-cooking	2 tablespoons	¾
Vegetable shortening	½ cup	3¼
Walnuts, whole	½ cup	2¼
chopped	1 cup	4
Water	⅓ cup	2⅝
	⅔ cup	5¾
	1 cup	8
Yeast, active dry or instant	2¼ teaspoons	¼
Zucchini, shredded	1 cup	8¼

- A number of scales are available for a variety of prices (see Tools. p. 601). You'll want a scale with a "tare" function so you can add ingredients to your bowl, zero out what you've just weighed, and add and accurately weigh the next ingredient. Also, if you have a scale that converts from our American system of measurement to metric measurements (grams), you'll have access to the recipes in cookbooks from all over the world.

- Get to know your scale. Make sure it will accommodate both the weight of your ingredients and the weight of the container. Lightweight mixing bowls are a good choice for weight measurement.

A Translation of Old-Fashioned American Measurements

We shouldn't give up our old measurements entirely. There's too much history and sentiment tied up in them. "Butter the size of a walnut" stirs a chord that "28.35g butter" just can't. But where there are no walnuts, we need the other measurement as well.

Butter the size of a walnut (or a "lump") = 2 tablespoons
Butter the size of an egg = ¼ cup
Coffee cup = 1 cup

Dash = ⅛ teaspoon
Dessert spoon = 1½ teaspoons
60 drops = 1 teaspoon
Gill = ½ cup
Pinch = 1⁄16 or ⅛ teaspoon
Salt spoon = ¼ teaspoon
Teacup = ¾ cup
Tin cup = 1 cup
Tumblerful = 2 cups
Wineglass = ½ gill or ¼ cup

At King Arthur, we've made a commitment, for the foreseeable future, to include both traditional volume measurements and weight measurements in all our printed recipes. Eventually we'd like to include metric measurements because those are the door to the rest of the world and its history, as well as to our common future. There are so many of us around the world who would love to share the things we love to bake with each other. But because we're all speaking different measurement "languages" we can be somewhat stymied.

Using Cookbooks From Outside the United States

With the exception of the other English-speaking nations, cookbooks are written with metric measurements. Should you run into a metric cookbook, here are some conversions of our basic measurements, which are difficult to translate exactly. Small amounts will not make much difference so metric amounts are usually rounded. (You use milliliters [ml] when speaking of liquids, and grams [g] when speaking of solids.) For baking purposes, a gram is the same as a milliliter.

1 teaspoon = 5 ml/g
1 tablespoon = 15 ml/g
1 ounce = 28.35 (or 30) ml/g
1 cup = 227 (or 230) ml/g
1 pound = 450 ml/g
2.2 pounds = 1 kilogram

And should you be faced with an overseas oven, here are some temperature conversions from Fahrenheit to centigrade, with the gas marks, used in some countries, as well.

225°F = 100°C or Gas Mark ¼
250°F = 130°C or Gas Mark ½
275°F = 140°C or Gas Mark 1
300°F = 150°C or Gas Mark 2
325°F = 170°C or Gas Mark 3
350°F = 180°C or Gas Mark 4
375°F = 190°C or Gas Mark 5
400°F = 200°C or Gas Mark 6
425°F = 220°C or Gas Mark 7
450°F = 230°C or Gas Mark 8
475°F = 240°C or Gas Mark 9

High-Altitude Baking

It's a scientific fact: The higher the altitude, the lower the air pressure. While this is an excellent environment for training athletes, it's a difficult one for baking. Baking depends on the specific interactions of several kinds of ingredients, including flour, leavening, fats, and liquid; throw in the wild card of atmospheric pressure, and all bets are off, if you've been used to baking at sea level. To complicate things further, individual microclimates vary greatly in the mountains, so the adjustment that works for you may not work for your neighbor down (or up) the road.

If you're baking at an elevation of 3,000 feet or greater, this chart is meant as a starting point, to help you convert recipes. Different types of baked goods need different adjustments, some suggestions follow. It may take a few tries to get results you're happy with; if possible, try to adjust only one ingredient at a time, so you can isolate the effect it has. Be sure to keep notes on what you've done, and try the smaller adjustments first when a range is given.

Leavening

When using baking powder and baking soda, the chart on page xx can help you adjust amounts. When making a recipe that calls for both baking powder and baking soda plus an acidic ingredient, like buttermilk or sour cream, try switching to all baking powder, and using regular milk in place of the acidic ingredient.

WHAT TO CHANGE	HOW TO CHANGE IT	WHY
OVEN TEMPERATURE	Increase 15 degrees F to 25 degrees F; use the smaller increase when making chocolate or delicate cakes.	Since leavening and evaporation proceed more quickly, the idea is to use a higher temperature to "set" the structure of baked goods before they over-expand and dry out, or rise too quickly and then collapse.
BAKING TIME	Decrease by 5 to 8 minutes per 30 minutes of baking time.	Baking at higher temperatures means products are done sooner.
SUGAR	Decrease by 1 tablespoon per cup.	Increased evaporation also increases concentration of sugar, which can weaken the structure of what you're baking.
LIQUID	Increase by 1 to 2 tablespoons at 3,000 feet. Increase by 1½ teaspoons for each additional 1,000 feet over 3,000. You can also use extra eggs as part of this liquid in recipes with a tender crumb, like muffins and cakes.	Extra liquid keeps products from drying out at higher baking temperatures and accelerated evaporation rates.
FLOUR	At 3,500 feet, add 1 tablespoon per recipe. For each additional 1,500 feet, add 1 more tablespoon. In quick bread and muffin recipes, flour with a higher protein content may yield better results.	Additional flour helps to strengthen the structure of baked goods.

CAKES: To increase liquids, use extra eggs; if only part of an egg is needed, use the white.

COOKIES, CRACKERS AND PIECRUSTS: Won't be dramatically affected; will usually need extra water to help the dough come together.

FRIED DOUGHS: Lower the frying temperature by 3 degrees F for every 1,000 feet above 3,000, and increase cooking times.

High-Altitude Changes

BAKING POWDER OR BAKING SODA IN ORIGINAL RECIPE	3,000– 5,000 FT.	3,500– 5,000 FT	5,000– 6,500 FT	ABOVE 6,500 FT
1 teaspoon	⅞	¾	½	¼
1½ teaspoons	1¼	1	¾	½
2 teaspoons	1½	1¼	1	¾
2½ teaspoons	1¾	1½	1¼	1
3 teaspoons	2	1½	1¼	1
3½ teaspoons	2½	2	1½	1
4 teaspoons	2½	2	1½	1

QUICK BREADS: No additional adjustments necessary other than those suggested in the tables.

YEAST BREADS: Decrease the amount of yeast in the recipe by 25 percent, and make water/flour adjustments as necessary to get a dough with the correct texture. Make sure your bowl has plenty of room for the dough to rise.

Since rising times are much shorter at higher altitudes, and the dough won't have sufficient time to develop its optimum flavor with one rise, you have a number of options to improve flavor:

• Give the dough one extra rise by deflating it and letting it rise an additional time before forming it.

• Try covering the dough and placing it in the refrigerator for its first rise, to slow the action of the yeast and give the dough more time to develop.

• If you have sourdough starter, use some of it for some of the liquid in the recipe.

• Make a sponge by mixing the yeast and liquid in the recipe with 1 to 2 cups of the flour. Cover and let the sponge work for a few hours in the refrigerator, until it becomes bubbly and rises, then continue with the recipe.

For More Information

Because high-altitude baking is a complex subject, we recommend that you acquire a set of booklets that covers all aspects of baking at 3,500 feet and up from the Colorado State University Cooperative Extension Resource Center, 115 General Services Building, Fort Collins, CO 80523-4061. For questions, call toll-free 1-877-692-9358, or e-mail them at cerc1@ur.colostate.edu.

Breakfasts

"Wake up and smell the coffee!" Often tossed out as a good-natured nudge to dreamers, in reality the phrase could be a siren's song to start the day. Is there anything so satisfying as gradually surfacing from the depths of sleep to the soft light of day and catching a whiff of brewing coffee? Someone has been up ahead of you; coffee is made, and if you close your eyes and snuggle into the blankets just a bit longer, breakfast might be made, too.

The simplest, most nutritious breakfast of all is probably whole-grain cereal, hot or cold, skim milk, fresh fruit, and juice. But when you eat hot oatmeal or cold cereal day after day after day, it does lose its luster. That's one of the reasons weekends were invented—to break the chain of monotonous breakfasts.

On Saturday, out comes the griddle, the old mixing bowl, the flour, buttermilk, and eggs. Gently whisking pancake batter, seeing it suddenly become creamy-smooth, watching it spread into a perfect round when it hits the griddle with a sharp sizzle, seeing it bubble, smelling the cakes—this is relaxation; this the reward for a week of work well-done.

Pancakes are only one of the special treats we designate as weekend fare. There are waffles and French toast too, of course; being bread-bakers, we've found many interesting breads to bathe in a milk-and-egg bath and sauté in butter. When we're feeling even more ambitious, and have actually planned ahead, we might make crêpes, filling them with spinach and cheese when a hearty breakfast is in order, or making cheese blintzes with fresh berries on top if something a bit lighter is desired.

So give yourself a break from the hectic pace of Monday through Friday and its plodding everyday parade of cereals. Weekends are for baking, and for enjoying breakfasts that take a bit of planning and preparation.

Pancakes

Griddle cake or fry cake, flannel cake, flapjack, or hoe cake, the pancake—flour, milk, butter, a touch of leavening, and eggs, stirred together and cooked on a griddle—has been an American staple since the eighteenth century. An old tradition in England, where Pancake Tuesday is celebrated the day before Lent begins, and in Holland, where buckwheat is the grain of choice, pancakes made the journey to this country with the earliest settlers. Using everyday ingredients, easy to stir together and cook, pancakes were a workingman's staple as this country grew up, from the logging camps of Maine to the wagon trains heading west.

Why Should Pancake Batter Rest Before Using It?

Pancakes (like muffins) rely on both fat and gentle handling for their tenderness. Once flour is combined with a liquid, it forms a network of proteins that, if handled roughly (e.g., beaten vigorously) will become tough by bonding together. This toughness will evidence itself in a tendency to become rubbery. When making pancake batter, whisk together the dry ingredients, whisk together the wet ingredients in a separate bowl, then gently combine the two, stirring just until everything is moistened. Let the batter rest for 5 to 10 minutes, to allow the leavening to start working and to let the flour start absorbing the liquid. If you have the time, refrigerate the batter for an hour or so, which allows any lumps of flour to slowly dissolve, and makes for a more fluffy, flavorful batter. When you're ready to cook the pancakes, give the batter a quick stir and you're good to go. (In recipes where you beat the egg whites separately and add them at the end, don't beat and add them until the end of the batter's resting period.) For ultra-tender pancakes or waffles, try using pastry flour.

The Simple But Perfect Pancake

SIXTEEN 3-INCH PANCAKES

2 large eggs

1¼ cups (10 ounces) milk

2 teaspoons vanilla extract (optional)

3 tablespoons (1½ ounces) butter, melted, or vegetable oil

1½ cups (6¼ ounces) unbleached all-purpose flour

¾ teaspoon salt

2 teaspoons baking powder

2 tablespoons sugar, or ¼ cup malted milk powder*

Beat the eggs, milk, and vanilla until light and foamy, about 3 minutes at high speed of a stand or hand mixer. Stir in the butter.

Whisk the dry ingredients together to evenly distribute the salt, baking powder and sweetener. Gently and quickly mix into the egg and milk mixture. Let the batter relax while the griddle is heating (or overnight in the refrigerator). The batter will thicken slightly while resting.

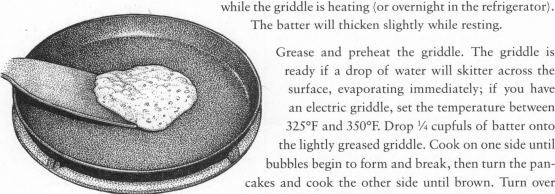

Grease and preheat the griddle. The griddle is ready if a drop of water will skitter across the surface, evaporating immediately; if you have an electric griddle, set the temperature between 325°F and 350°F. Drop ¼ cupfuls of batter onto the lightly greased griddle. Cook on one side until bubbles begin to form and break, then turn the pancakes and cook the other side until brown. Turn over only once. Serve immediately.

The pancake is ready to turn when the edges begin to look dry and bubbles form and start to break.

NOTE For waffles, reduce the milk to 1 cup and 2 tablespoons, and increase the fat to 5 tablespoons.

*Malt, rather than sugar, is what sweetens most commercial pancake mixes. For that typical "diner" taste, try malt in your pancakes instead of sugar.

nutrition information per serving   **four pancakes, 104g**

199 cal | 7g fat | 6g protein | 24g complex carbohydrates | 4g sugar | 1g dietary fiber | 19mg cholesterol | 450mg sodium | 124mg potassium | 81RE vitamin A | 1mg iron | 192mg calcium | 101mg phosphorus

Zephyr Pancakes

TWENTY-FOUR 3½-INCH PANCAKES

These pancakes come from the Midwest and are a true celebration of what dairy products can do. They are incredibly light and tender and literally melt in your mouth.

2 cups (8½ ounces) unbleached all-purpose flour

2½ tablespoons (1¼ ounces) sugar

1½ teaspoons baking powder

1 teaspoon baking soda

½ teaspoon salt

3 large egg yolks

1¼ cups (10 ounces) heavy cream

1¼ cups (10 ounces) buttermilk

2 tablespoons (1 ounce) butter, melted

1 teaspoon vanilla extract (optional)

In a medium-sized mixing bowl, whisk together the flour, sugar, baking powder, baking soda, and salt. In a separate bowl, whisk together the egg yolks, cream, buttermilk, melted butter, and vanilla. Whisk the wet ingredients into the dry, just until combined—it's okay if there are a few lumps.

Preheat and lightly grease a heavy skillet or griddle. Scoop the batter onto the griddle with a ¼ cup measure or a large spoon. Make sure the heat is slightly less than medium. The pancakes will puff up very high. When the first side is golden brown and the edges start to look dry, turn pancakes over to finish cooking the second side. Remove the pancakes from the griddle and keep them in a warm serving dish until you have enough to feed everyone.

nutrition information per serving   3 pancakes, 88g

227 cal | 14g fat | 4g protein | 18g complex carbohydrates | 3g sugar | 1g dietary fiber | 104mg cholesterol | 223mg sodium | 94mg potassium | 165RE vitamin A | 1mg iron | 94mg calcium | 98mg phosphorus

An Easy Way to Scoop Out Pancake Batter

For nice, round, evenly sized pancakes, use an ice cream scoop to scoop the batter from bowl to griddle. A scoop holding about ¼ cup of batter will make a familiar 3- to 4-inch pancake.

Gingerbread Pancakes

TWELVE 3½-INCH PANCAKES

These pancakes are a quick and easy way to have warm gingerbread in just minutes. All the things that team well with gingerbread make sense with these pancakes: warm applesauce, sliced peaches, or warm custard sauce. Naturally, some lightly sweetened whipped cream can only enhance this treat.

1 cup (4¼ ounces) unbleached all-purpose flour

¼ cup (1¼ ounces) yellow cornmeal

2 tablespoons (⅞ ounce) sugar

½ teaspoon cinnamon

¾ teaspoon ground ginger

⅛ teaspoon ground cloves

½ teaspoon salt

1 teaspoon baking powder

½ teaspoon baking soda

¼ cup (1¾ ounces) chopped crystallized ginger (optional)

2 tablespoons (⅞ ounce) vegetable oil

¼ cup (3 ounces) molasses

1 cup (8 ounces) buttermilk

1 large egg, lightly beaten

In a large mixing bowl, whisk together the flour, cornmeal, sugar, spices, salt, baking powder, baking soda, and the crystallized ginger. In a separate bowl, mix together the oil, molasses, buttermilk, and egg. Add liquids to dry ingredients all at once, stirring until just combined.

Preheat a griddle and lightly grease it. Drop the batter, ¼ cup at a time, to make a 3½-inch pancake. Cook until the edges look dry and some of the bubbles that come to the surface break. Turn the pancakes over to finish cooking, then remove them from griddle to a warm serving dish.

nutrition information per serving   **3 pancakes, 147g**

324 cal │ 9g fat │ 7g protein │ 31g complex carbohydrates │ 23g sugar │ 2g dietary fiber │ 55mg cholesterol │ 623mg sodium │ 270mg potassium │ 33RE vitamin A │ 1mg vitamin C │ 3mg iron │ 172mg calcium │ 156mg phosphorus

Lemon Ricotta Puff-Pancakes with Vanilla-Scented Sauce

TWENTY-FOUR 3½-INCH PANCAKES

We love to make these light, eggy pancakes when berries are in season, as they're especially good garnished with fresh strawberries or blueberries, and served with a side of smoky bacon or sausage.

BATTER

3 large eggs, separated

1½ cups (12 ounces) buttermilk

3 tablespoons (1¼ ounces) sugar

1 cup (8 ounces) ricotta cheese

1½ cups (6¼ ounces) unbleached all-purpose flour

1 teaspoon baking soda

1 teaspoon baking powder

2 tablespoons lemon zest (from 2 large lemons), or ½ teaspoon lemon oil

¼ teaspoon nutmeg

½ teaspoon salt

SAUCE

1 cup (8 ounces) ricotta cheese

½ cup (2 ounces) confectioners' sugar

1 teaspoon vanilla extract

¼ teaspoon salt

BATTER In a medium-sized mixing bowl, beat together the egg yolks, buttermilk, sugar, and ricotta cheese. In a separate bowl, whisk together the flour, baking soda, baking powder, lemon zest, nutmeg and salt. In a third bowl, beat the egg whites until stiff but not dry. Mix the dry ingredients into the buttermilk mixture with a few quick strokes. A few lumps remaining are okay. Fold in the egg whites.

Heat a lightly greased griddle or skillet over medium heat until hot enough to evaporate a drop of water immediately. Drop the batter by ¼ cupfuls onto the heated griddle. Cook for about 2½ minutes on the first side; bubbles should rise and burst on the first side before you flip the pancakes. Cook for about 1 minute on the second side. They should be a very light golden brown when finished. Serve with sauce.

SAUCE Mix all of the ingredients until smooth in a small mixing bowl. For an ultra-smooth sauce, blend in a blender or food processor. Refrigerate until needed. Thin with 1 tablespoon milk or cream if sauce is too thick.

NOTE The pancakes may be made a day ahead, cooled on a wire rack, then wrapped tightly and refrigerated. To reheat, preheat the oven to 375°F, place the pancakes on a lightly greased baking sheet, and heat for 5 minutes.

nutrition information per serving   3 pancakes, with 1 tablespoon vanilla sauce, 193g

314 cal | 8g fat | 15g protein | 25g complex carbohydrates | 20g sugar | 1g dietary fiber | 115mg cholesterol | 648mg sodium | 228mg potassium | 125RE vitamin A | 3mg vitamin C | 2mg iron | 306mg calcium | 251mg phosphorus

Warm Strawberry Puff

ONE 8-INCH PUFF, 1 TO 3 SERVINGS (THIS RECIPE IS EASILY DOUBLED)

When strawberries come into their own in early summer, this is the perfect way to show them off. At other times of the year, sliced apples will substitute nicely.

BATTER	FILLING
3 large eggs, separated	1 tablespoon (½ ounce) butter
2 tablespoons (⅞ ounce) sugar	1 tablespoon (¾ ounce) corn syrup
½ cup (4 ounces) light cream	¼ cup (1¾ ounces) sugar
⅛ teaspoon salt	1 pint (10½ ounces) fresh strawberries, washed, hulled, and sliced in half
1 teaspoon vanilla extract	
1 tablespoon (½ ounce) butter, melted	1 teaspoon lemon juice
⅓ cup (1⅜ ounces) unbleached all-purpose flour	¼ teaspoon cinnamon
	1 to 2 tablespoons crème fraîche or sour cream, for topping

Preheat the oven to 350°F.

BATTER Place the egg whites in a clean, grease-free bowl and whip them until frothy. Add the sugar and whip until soft peaks form. Set this mixture aside.

In a medium-sized mixing bowl, whisk together the egg yolks, sugar, and cream, then add the salt, vanilla, melted butter, and flour. Whisk until smooth.

Heat a 10-inch pan with a heatproof handle over medium-low heat (an omelet pan or cast iron skillet works well). Spray the pan with nonstick vegetable oil or rub it with a bit of vegetable oil.

Gently fold the egg whites into the batter. Pour it into the heated pan and swirl the pan gently. Continue to cook for 3 to 5 minutes, until the bottom is light brown. Place the pan in the oven and bake for 10 to 12 minutes, until the pancake is puffy and set.

FILLING Melt the butter in a small skillet. Add the corn syrup and sugar, then bring to a boil. Add the strawberries, lemon juice, and cinnamon. Stir to coat the strawberries with the sauce, then remove the mixture from the heat.

Remove the cake from the oven and slip it onto a serving platter. Spread the strawberries over half the cake, then fold it over to cover the filling (as you'd fold an omelet). Dust the edges with confectioners' sugar. Garnish with a dollop of crème fraîche or sour cream and serve immediately.

nutrition information per serving   ⅓ of pancake and filling, 236g

375 cal | 22g fat | 8g protein | 9g complex carbohydrates | 29g sugar | 2g dietary fiber | 263mg cholesterol | 173mg sodium | 285mg potassium | 255RE vitamin A | 57mg vitamin C | 1mg iron | 84mg calcium | 146mg phosphorus

Welsh Cakes

FIFTY 3½-INCH CAKES

These cakes are a cross between a pancake and a baking powder biscuit, but much richer and sweeter. Sturdy enough to be eaten out of hand, they can be served plain, sprinkled with sugar, or spread with butter and gilded with sugar or jam. In addition, they're excellent the next day, warmed in the toaster, as you'd warm toaster cakes.

3 cups (12¾ ounces) unbleached all-purpose flour

1 cup (7 ounces) sugar

2 teaspoons baking powder

½ teaspoon nutmeg

¼ teaspoon salt

1 cup (2 sticks, 8 ounces) butter, cut into pieces

¾ cup (4 ounces) currants*

2 eggs beaten with enough milk to yield ¾ cup liquid

In a medium-sized mixing bowl, sift together the flour, sugar, baking powder, nutmeg and salt. Cut in the butter until the mixture is a coarse, even consistency. Add the currants, then add the egg and milk. Stir until the mixture forms a soft dough.

Divide the dough in half and, working with one half at a time (keep the other half covered and refrigerated), roll the dough into a circle ¼ inch thick. Using a biscuit cutter or other small (2½- to 3½-inch) round cutter, cut circles of dough.

Heat an ungreased skillet over medium heat (an electric frying pan, set at 325°F, works well, too). Fry the cakes for about 2 minutes on the first side, and an additional 1½ minutes on the second, or until both sides are golden brown. As with pancakes, you'll have to adjust the heat if you find the cakes are browned on the outside before they're thoroughly cooked in the middle. Repeat with the remaining dough. Keep the cakes warm in a 200°F oven until ready to serve. Sprinkle with granulated sugar or cinnamon-sugar, if desired, before serving.

*Because the cakes are thin, it's important to use currants rather than raisins; raisins are too big.

nutrition information per serving   **2 cakes, 43g**

166 cal | 5g fat | 2g protein | 14g complex carbohydrates | 8g sugar | 1g dietary fiber | 38mg cholesterol | 68mg sodium | 68mg potassium | 82RE vitamin A | 1mg iron | 34mg calcium | 38mg phosphorus

Oatmeal Pancake Mix

10 CUPS OF DRY MIX

This mix is exceptional for several reasons: it is remarkably easy to use and the proportions couldn't be simpler—1 cup of mix, 1 cup of buttermilk, 1 egg. If you're not in the habit of having buttermilk around, we can say it's worth the investment. You can freeze leftover buttermilk for future batches of pancakes. These pancakes taste wonderful, puff up beautifully, hold in a warmer for half an hour without getting tough or rubbery, and they're more than willing to act as a vehicle for any kind of fruit addition. A partial list of combinations that have made successful appearances so far: peach, raspberry, banana-walnut, cheddar-apple, blueberry, and cranberry-apricot pancakes. We think you will find this mix a great staple in your pantry, and it makes a great gift. We will only insist on two things: that your syrup be genuine maple (we do live in Vermont, after all), and it must be warm.

3½ cups (12¼ ounces) old-fashioned or rolled oats

5 cups (21¼ ounces) unbleached all-purpose flour

3 tablespoons (1½ ounces) sugar

3 tablespoons (1½ ounces) baking powder

1 tablespoon salt

1 tablespoon baking soda

1 cup (7 ounces) vegetable oil

Grind the oats in a food processor until they are chopped fine but not a powder. Put the flour, oats, and all other dry ingredients into a mixer with a paddle. Mix on slow speed, drizzling the vegetable oil into the bowl slowly while the mixer is running. When all the oil has been added, stop the mixer and squeeze a clump of mix in your hand. If it stays together, it is just right. If it is still crumbly, add another tablespoon of oil at a time until the consistency is correct. Store in an airtight container for up to two weeks at room temperature, or indefinitely in refrigerator or freezer.

BATTER Whisk together 1 cup of mix, 1 cup of buttermilk (a combination of half plain yogurt and half milk also will do), and 1 egg. Don't worry if it seems thin at first: the oats will soak up the milk and the mix will thicken a bit as it stands. Let stand for at least 5 to 10 minutes before cooking. Heat a griddle, lightly grease it, and drop the batter onto it by heaping tablespoons to make a 3-inch diameter pancake. When the edges look dry and bubbles come to the surface and don't break, turn the pancake over to finish cooking on the second side.

NOTE A batch using 1 cup of the mix will make twelve 3-inch pancakes.

nutrition information per serving   **3 pancakes, 103g**

169 cal │ 8g fat │ 6g protein │ 19g complex carbohydrates │ 1g dietary fiber │ 55mg cholesterol │ 444mg sodium │ 150mg potassium │ 29RE vitamin A │ 1mg vitamin C │ 1mg iron │ 138mg calcium │ 144mg phosphorus

A Quick Mix and What to Do with It

This basic dry mix, the base for a variety of baked goods, is great to bring along in the RV or camper, on the sailboat, or to your vacation home. It's an easy way to make biscuits or pancakes in just a few minutes.

THE BASIC MIX

9 cups (2½ pounds) unbleached all-purpose flour*

5 tablespoons (2⅜ ounces) baking powder

5 teaspoons (1 ounce) salt (extra-fine, if you have it)

1½ cups (7¾ ounces) nonfat dry milk, or dried buttermilk powder (we like to use ¾ cup each dry milk and buttermilk powder)

⅓ cup (2½ ounces) sugar

1½ cups (9¾ ounces) vegetable shortening, butter-flavored if you like

Measure all the dry ingredients into a large bowl, whisking them together to blend. Cut in the shortening until well-blended, using a pastry fork or blender, your fingers, or a mixer. An easy way to do this is to put about a third of the flour mixture and all the shortening into the workbowl of a food processor and pulse to blend; it'll take just a few seconds. Then stir in the rest of the flour. Or place about a third of the flour mixture and all the shortening into a mixing bowl and mix at low speed, adding the remaining flour mixture when the flour and shortening have formed very fine crumbs. Store the mix in plastic bags or an airtight container for up to 1 month (up to 3 months in the refrigerator or 6 months in the freezer).

*Substitute 100 percent white whole wheat flour for up to half of the unbleached all-purpose flour, if you wish. However, this substitution will cut into the mix's storage time. Whole wheat flour deteriorates quickly when stored at room temperature, especially when it's warm out. So a mix made partly with whole wheat will keep only for a week or two at room temperature, though it'll last much longer when stored in the freezer.

Notes for Using the Quick Mix

- When measuring the mix for a recipe, be sure to fluff it up first. It will compact as it sits, and therefore it's easy to use too much. Each cup of mix should weigh 4½ ounces. Luckily the following recipes are very forgiving; if the dough ends up feeling dry, just add a bit of extra water or milk.

- For real ease when camping, measure the amount needed for various recipes into bags. Include dried eggs for any eggs called for, as well as any flavor powders or dried fruits. Use a marker to write on the bag exactly what needs to be added, as well as the baking instructions (to save you searching for a recipe that's most likely at home on the counter). Also, when you're ready to bake, use the bag as a bowl. Use a wide-mouth bag, one that can be placed in a bowl to steady it at the campsite. Open the bag, place it in a bowl, add liquid ingredients, mix, and when you're done, throw the bag away—there's almost no cleanup. Remember to bring along a small bag of flour for flouring your work surface (crude as it may be) as well as a can of nonstick baking spray.

Quick Mix Pancakes or Waffles

ONE DOZEN 3-INCH PANCAKES OR 3 TO 4 LARGE WAFFLES

1 to 1¼ cups (8 to 10 ounces) water or milk, depending on how thick you like your pancakes

1 large egg
1 teaspoon vanilla extract
2 cups (9 ounces) Quick Mix

In a small bowl or measuring cup, whisk together the water or milk, egg, and vanilla. Mix these liquid ingredients into the Quick Mix and stir gently until just a few small lumps remain. Don't try to get rid of all the lumps, as this will mean you've stirred too long and the pancakes will be tough; the lumps will disappear as the pancakes or waffles cook.

Heat a griddle or cast iron pan over medium heat. Brush it with oil or melted butter; this is usually only necessary for the first pancakes you cook. When the griddle is the proper temperature, a drop of water will bounce across the surface. Use a ¼-cup measure or muffin scoop to ladle the batter onto the griddle. Turn the pancakes over when the bubbles that appear on the surface remain open. Cooking the other side of the pancakes will take a much shorter time, perhaps only 30 seconds, depending on the heat of the griddle and the thickness of the pancakes. Remove the pancakes from the griddle and serve them hot.

To make waffles, add a tablespoon of vegetable oil to the batter for a crisp waffle. Be sure to grease the waffle iron and preheat it.

nutrition information per serving　　3 pancakes , 135g

276 cal | 10g fat | 8g protein | 33g complex carbohydrates | 3g sugar | 1g dietary fiber | 56mg cholesterol | 691mg sodium | 168mg potassium | 41RE vitamin A | 3mg iron | 225mg calcium | 169mg phosphorus

Waffles

Waffles are a step up the fancy scale from pancakes. They take specialized equipment to produce—an iron—and just plain look as if they take more effort, even if they really don't. There are two basic styles of waffle: American-style, the relatively flat, baking powder–leavened waffle we all grew up with, shaped in squares, rounds, or hearts; and Belgian-style, a thicker, more deeply indented square waffle, often made with yeast, and first introduced to this country at the 1964 World's Fair. These days, Belgian waffles are the type most often found on restaurant menus, often accompanied by whipped cream and strawberries along with maple syrup and butter.

Pancakes vs. Waffles

The major difference between most pancake and waffle batters is that waffles need to have more fat in them than pancakes. Waffles without sufficient fat will remain somewhat flabby even when toasted to a dark brown; they also have a tendency to stick to the waffle iron. Pancakes are also more tolerant of having extras thrown in—a handful of blueberries, some cornmeal, slices of banana or strawberry. Waffles are usually prepared plain, with any additions served on top or alongside, because "add-ins" often prevent them from becoming crisp. Also, the ins and outs of the waffle grid are prone to stick to a slice of peach or a nugget of crystallized ginger.

Waffles weren't always a breakfast food, and they haven't always been served with a sweet topping. In the 1930s, waffle suppers consisting of waffles with a savory topping—most often creamed chicken—were standard entertainment. They enjoyed a particularly favored place in the Franklin Roosevelt White House, whose thrifty head housekeeper saw them as an economical way to entertain heads of state. These days, you're more likely to encounter waffles that have veered the other way—say, chocolate-pecan waffles with ice cream and hot fudge sauce. Still, there are few breakfasts so satisfying as a crunchy-tender waffle, butter melting into its crevices and gilded with syrup; a side of country ham or thick-cut bacon takes it over the top.

Waffles are more likely than pancakes to be made with different grains, particularly down South, where cornmeal (for added crunch) and rice flour (for extra tenderness) are sometimes added to the wheat flour.

Help! My Waffles Stick to the Iron!

What a pain, digging stuck-on waffles out of the grids of your waffle iron. To avoid this particular challenge, make sure there's some fat in the batter; fat not only will make waffles crisp on the outside and soft within, it will help them separate from the iron.

Before spooning batter into the iron, make sure it's thoroughly greased with vegetable oil or melted shortening applied with a pastry brush, or with nonstick vegetable oil spray. Finally, when the steaming slows down and you think the waffle's done, open the iron just a bit; if the waffle clings to the top grid, give it a gentle tug to see if it will let go. If not, try giving it a minute or so more in the closed iron. A waffle that's not fully baked tends to stick.

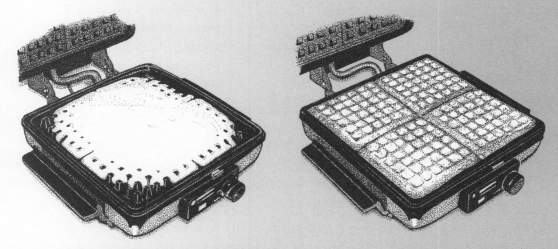

Spoon in enough waffle batter to not quite fill all of the space, as shown. The batter will fill in the empty space when the top is lowered for baking.

Classic Buttermilk Waffles

ABOUT TEN 8-INCH WAFFLES

When we think of brunch, we think of waffles. This first recipe is for a plain waffle, crisp and golden, perfect with maple syrup and butter or berries and whipped cream. When made with pastry flour it will be extra crispy and light as air inside. When made with all-purpose flour the waffle has a bit more body—still light, but chewier on the inside. Waffles are best consumed as soon as they're baked, but in a pinch you may place them on a wire rack to cool, wrap tightly to store in the refrigerator, then reheat for 6 minutes in a 350°F oven. The optional pecan meal adds a nutty flavor.

2 large eggs

1¾ cups (14 ounces) buttermilk

½ cup (1 stick, 4 ounces) butter, melted and cooled to room temperature

2 teaspoons vanilla extract

2 cups (8 ounces) unbleached pastry flour, or 1¾ cups (7¼ ounces) unbleached all-purpose flour

2 tablespoons (⅞ ounce) sugar*

2 teaspoons baking powder

1 teaspoon baking soda

1 teaspoon salt

½ cup (1½ ounces) pecan meal (optional)

In a medium-sized mixing bowl, beat together the eggs, buttermilk, melted butter, and vanilla. In another bowl whisk together the dry ingredients; combine the wet and dry ingredients just until smooth.

Spray the waffle iron with a nonstick cooking spray before preheating it. For an 8-inch round waffle iron, use about ⅓ cup batter. Cook for 2 to 3 minutes, until the iron stops steaming.

*Omit the sugar if you want savory waffles, such as a base for creamed chipped beef or chicken.

nutrition information per serving   one 8-inch waffle, 82g

360 cal | 15g fat | 19g protein | 34g complex carbohydrates | 3g sugar | 1g dietary fiber | 110mg cholesterol | 604mg sodium | 684mg potassium | 127RE vitamin A | 1mg iron | 564mg calcium | 440mg phosphorus

Why Buttermilk?

Many of our pancake and waffle recipes call for buttermilk rather than regular milk. The reason? The acidity in buttermilk tenderizes the gluten (protein) in flour, plus it works with baking soda better than plain milk by both neutralizing the flavor of the soda at the same time it is activating it, providing wonderful leavening.

Crunchy Cornmeal Waffles

ABOUT TEN 8-INCH WAFFLES

This recipe makes a very tasty, crunchy cornmeal waffle for breakfast. It can also appear as an unusual and savory appetizer at a party, when dressed up with herbs and spices, and topped with the warm cheese sauce that follows on next page.

1¾ cups (14 ounces) buttermilk

2 large eggs

5 tablespoons (2½ ounces) butter, melted and cooled, or ⅓ cup (2 ounces) vegetable oil

1½ cups (6¼ ounces) unbleached all-purpose flour

1 cup (4⅞ ounces) yellow cornmeal

2 tablespoons sugar

2 teaspoons baking powder

1 teaspoon baking soda

1 teaspoon salt

FOR SAVORY VERSION

2 tablespoons minced fresh or 3 tablespoons dried chives (optional)

2 to 3 teaspoons ground cumin (optional)

1 teaspoon ground chipotle pepper, or ¼ teaspoon hot pepper sauce (optional)

3 tablespoons dried tomato or bell pepper flakes (optional)

In a medium-sized mixing bowl, whisk together the buttermilk, eggs, and melted butter or oil. In a separate bowl, blend together the dry ingredients, then quickly and gently combine the wet and dry ingredients. Let the batter sit for 10 minutes to allow the cornmeal to soften.

Drop the batter by ⅔ cupfuls onto a hot waffle iron and bake until the waffle iron stops steaming. For a savory treat make the savory version and serve with Chili Con Queso Sauce (recipe on next page).

nutrition information per serving   one 8-inch waffle, 75g

266 cal | 3g fat | 18g protein | 40g complex carbohydrates | 2g sugar | 2g dietary fiber | 30mg cholesterol | 588mg sodium | 686mg potassium | 47RE vitamin A | 1mg iron | 551mg calcium | 436mg phosphorus

Chili Con Queso Sauce

2 CUPS

½ cup (4 ounces) prepared salsa

8 ounces cream cheese

1 cup (4 ounces) grated Monterey Jack cheese

1 bunch scallions, sliced (about ¼ cup, about 2 ounces)*

10-ounce package frozen, chopped spinach, defrosted and squeezed dry

Heat together, over low heat, the salsa, cream cheese, and grated cheese, stirring until the mixture is smooth. Stir in the scallions and chopped spinach. Spoon the sauce onto hot waffle sections. Refrigerate any leftover sauce; it makes a wonderful dip for tortilla chips, or a spread for a wrap sandwich.

*Use the white part and some of the green, about 4 inches total of each scallion.

`nutrition information per serving` **2 tablespoons sauce, 62g**

116 cal | 9g fat | 5g protein | 3g complex carbohydrates | 2g dietary fiber | 31mg cholesterol | 257mg sodium | 119mg potassium | 288RE vitamin A | 7mg vitamin C | 1mg iron | 125mg calcium | 89mg phosphorus

Fudge Waffles with Ice Cream and Chocolate Sauce

TEN 8-INCH WAFFLES

Is it a brownie with tire tracks or a waffle that took a wrong turn at breakfast and ended up on the dinner table? This festive dessert may have an identity problem, but you won't have any problem when you serve it to your family or guests—they'll enjoy every chocolaty bite.

2 large eggs, at room temperature

¼ cup (2 ounces) butter, melted and cooled, or ¼ cup vegetable oil

1 teaspoon vanilla extract

1 cup (8 ounces) buttermilk

1 cup (4¼ ounces) unbleached all-purpose flour

¾ cup (5¼ ounces) sugar

½ cup (1½ ounces) unsweetened cocoa powder

½ teaspoon baking powder

½ teaspoon baking soda

¼ teaspoon salt

¼ teaspoon nutmeg

½ cup (2 ounces) chopped walnuts

½ cup (3 ounces) chocolate mini-chips

In a large mixing bowl, combine the eggs, butter or oil, and vanilla. Beat until light, about 2 minutes. Blend in buttermilk, then flour, sugar, cocoa, baking powder, baking soda, salt, and nutmeg. Gently fold in nuts and chocolate chips.

Bake waffles in a preheated well-greased waffle iron until done (following directions for your own waffle iron). Serve with the ice cream of your choice and chocolate sauce (recipe follows). Waffles can be served immediately, or wrapped in plastic wrap and served the next day. Warm them in a toaster oven if you wish.

nutrition information per serving   **1 waffle, 82g**

243 cal | 12g fat | 5g protein | 11g complex carbohydrates | 19g sugar | 1g dietary fiber | 56mg cholesterol | 233mg sodium | 120mg potassium | 64RE vitamin A | 1mg iron | 57mg calcium | 84mg phosphorus | 7mg caffeine

Chocolate Sauce

ABOUT 1 CUP

½ cup (3½ ounces) granulated sugar

¼ cup (¾ ounce) unsweetened cocoa powder

½ cup (5½ ounces) light corn syrup

¼ cup (2 ounces) half-and-half or evaporated milk

2 tablespoons (1 ounce) butter

½ teaspoon vanilla extract

In a small saucepan, combine sugar, cocoa powder, corn syrup, and half-and-half or milk. Stir to blend. Cook over medium heat until mixture comes to a full boil, then reduce heat to medium-low and simmer, stirring occasionally, for 3 minutes.

Remove sauce from heat and add butter and vanilla, stirring until butter melts. Cool to room temperature, then store in the refrigerator. Serve warm or at room temperature; this sauce reheats easily in a glass cup in your microwave.

nutrition information per serving   **1 tablespoon, 19g**

70 cal | 2g fat | 1g complex carbohydrates | 14g sugar | 4mg cholesterol | 14mg sodium | 24mg potassium | 14RE vitamin A | 3mg calcium | 11mg phosphorus | 3mg caffeine

Potato Waffles

TEN 8-INCH WAFFLES

This is a waffle that can help you use up leftover mashed potatoes for breakfast, or can make an appearance as a side dish in the evening. The potatoes give a wonderful, tender texture and earthy flavor to the waffles.

1½ cups (12 ounces) riced, cooked potatoes, or leftover mashed potatoes*

1 teaspoon salt

2 large eggs, separated

¼ cup (2 ounces) butter, melted or 3 tablespoons (1¼ ounces) vegetable oil

2 cups (16 ounces) buttermilk

1½ cups (6¼ ounces) unbleached all-purpose flour

1 teaspoon baking powder

1 teaspoon baking soda

3 tablespoons minced chives or scallions (optional)

6 slices bacon, cooked and crumbled (optional)

In a medium-sized mixing bowl, combine the potatoes, salt, egg yolks, and butter, mashing and mixing until lump-free. (A blender or food processor will do the job in a few seconds if your potatoes are very lumpy.) Beat in the buttermilk.

In a separate bowl, whisk together the flour, baking powder, baking soda, chives, and crumbled bacon. Add these dry ingredients to the liquid mixture and mix quickly just until most of the lumps are incorporated.

Beat the egg whites until stiff but not dry, then fold them into the potato and flour mixture. Bake the waffles immediately (so they remain light). Waffles may be made ahead, wrapped tightly when cool, then reheated in a 375°F oven for approximately 5 minutes just before serving.

*If using leftover potatoes that have already been seasoned, cut back on the salt in this recipe.

nutrition information per serving   **one 8-inch waffle, 105g**

301 cal | 7g fat | 20g protein | 39g complex carbohydrates | 1g dietary fiber | 48mg cholesterol | 463mg sodium | 841mg potassium | 77RE vitamin A | 2mg vitamin C | 1mg iron | 602mg calcium | 466mg phosphorus

Pumpkin Praline Waffles

TWELVE 8-INCH WAFFLES

What is more warm and homey than the scent of baking pumpkin? These waffles are redolent of spices and would pair well with lightly sweetened whipped cream.

1 cup (4¼ ounces) unbleached all-purpose flour

1 cup (5¼ ounces) whole wheat flour

2 teaspoons baking powder

½ teaspoon baking soda

1 teaspoon salt

2 teaspoons ground ginger

1 teaspoon cinnamon

½ teaspoon nutmeg

½ teaspoon ground cloves

1½ cups (14¼ ounces) cooked fresh pumpkin or canned pumpkin

½ cup (4 ounces) brown sugar, packed

6 tablespoons (¾ stick, 3 ounces) butter, melted

4 large eggs, separated

2 cups (16 ounces) buttermilk

½ cup (1⅞ ounces) chopped pecans

In a large bowl, combine flours, baking powder, baking soda, salt, and spices, stirring to mix. Stir in pumpkin, brown sugar, butter, and egg yolks. Add buttermilk and mix until thoroughly blended.

In a large bowl, beat the egg whites until stiff. Fold the whites into the batter and gently stir in pecans.

Scoop batter into a preheated waffle iron. Bake waffles until golden brown. Serve with butter and warm maple syrup.

nutrition information per serving   one 8-inch waffle, 133g

250 cal | 12g fat | 7g protein | 22g complex carbohydrates | 9g sugar | 3g dietary fiber | 89mg cholesterol | 362mg sodium | 255mg potassium | 2mg vitamin C | 2mg iron | 129mg calcium | 158mg phosphorus

Sourdough Waffles

TWELVE 8-INCH WAFFLES

This recipe uses the acidity of sourdough in reaction with baking soda for leavening. It makes the lightest, crispest waffles in the world with a flavor that you won't find anywhere else. (You also can use this batter for pancakes.) When you use white whole wheat flour, the flavor remains light but you get the advantage of the vitamins in the wheat germ and the fiber in the bran.

For best flavor, make up the sponge the night before. Making waffles also creates an easy excuse to feed your starter without getting into anything very time-consuming. But knowing how waffles can be a spontaneous sort of thing (and having in desperation done it this way), you can also make these without waiting for the sponge to work.

This will make enough for a family of four moderate eaters. If you don't fit into that category, double it or cut it in half. Traditionally these waffles are served with butter and maple syrup, but their unique flavor combines well with things savory as well.

SPONGE	BATTER
1 cup (4¼ ounces) unbleached all-purpose flour	2 large eggs
1 cup (5 ounces) white whole wheat flour	¼ cup (½ stick, 2 ounces) butter, melted
2 (⅞ ounce) tablespoons sugar	¾ teaspoon salt
2 cups (8 ounces) buttermilk	1 teaspoon baking soda
1 cup (16 ounces) sourdough starter* (p. 273), fed and ready to use	

SPONGE   Mix together the flours and sugar in a medium-sized ceramic mixing bowl. Stir in the buttermilk. (If you're doing this at the last minute, take the chill off it; a microwave does this nicely. Don't worry if it separates a bit.) Add 1 cup (or 2, if you're doubling the recipe) of your refreshed sourdough starter and cover loosely with plastic wrap. Let sit at room temperature overnight, or for whatever shorter time span is practical.

BATTER   Beat together the eggs, butter, salt, and baking soda until light. Blend this mixture into the sponge, and see dramatic chemistry begin to happen.

Spray your waffle iron with a bit of vegetable oil pan spray. (This is probably necessary only for the first waffle.) Pour ½ to 1 cup batter onto the iron, depending on its size, close, and cook for approximately 2 minutes, or until the iron stops steaming. Remove gently with a fork.

Waffles are best eaten as they come off the iron; they don't take well to stockpiling. This makes for serial eating, but it builds anticipation and probably contributes to general squabbling about who deserves the next one.

nutrition information per serving   **1 waffle, 92g**

161 cal | 5g fat | 6g protein | 20g complex carbohydrates | 2g sugar | 2g dietary fiber | 47mg cholesterol | 292mg sodium | 132mg potassium | 55RE vitamin A | 1mg iron | 93mg calcium | 104mg phosphorus

French Toast

French toast, true to its name, originated in France, where it is called *pain perdu* ("lost bread"), because it is made with leftover stale bread. Many of the world's countries boast some variation on the theme in their culinary cultures; after all, what could be a simpler combination than bread, milk, and eggs?

This is an instance of the sum being more than its parts; French toast is up there with some of the classic comfort foods. Soft, moist bread with a thin layer of hot butter-crisped crust, just begging for an application of more butter, and syrup—we can't imagine anyone but the most curmudgeonly culinary snob not entertaining a lifelong love affair with French toast.

French toast is customarily made with plain white bread, though there are those who swear by day-old challah or whole-grain breads and those who think French toast made with cinnamon-raisin bread is just about as close to breakfast heaven as you can get. There are two basic methods used to prepare French toast: the typical soak and sauté, and the fairly recent innovation of cutting the bread thicker (or layering two slices), stuffing it with cream cheese and/or fruit, laying it in a pan, pouring the soaking liquid over it, and letting it rest overnight before baking in the oven. This "French toast" is closer to a strata, but, nomenclature aside, it does taste wonderful.

Finally, did you know that you can make French toast in a waffle iron? After the bread has been soaked in egg and milk (or, even better, cream or melted vanilla ice cream), simply place the slice of bread in your square waffle iron. The result is an interesting combination of two breakfast favorites.

Rich French Toast

6 SERVINGS

When we tested this recipe, it met with universal acclaim. The difference between this and everyday, run-of-the-mill French toast is the quality of the ingredients. Start with a high-rising, golden-white, tasty white bread; you'll find our favorite recipe, simply titled White Bread 101, on page 198. Slice it thick; we found ⅝ inch just about right. Bathe it in cream and eggs accented with nutmeg, vanilla, and a touch of rum. Sauté it gently in butter; keep it warm in a hot oven, then serve it on warmed plates with sifted sugar and maple syrup. (Because it's been fried in butter, you won't need to butter it further when serving.) Crispy on the outside, toothsome/tender within, this is the French toast of which dreams are made.

1 tablespoon butter	¼ teaspoon nutmeg
1 tablespoon vegetable oil	2 teaspoons rum (optional)
3 large eggs	1 teaspoon vanilla extract
¾ cup (6 ounces) cream	6 slices bread, frozen and thawed or
¼ teaspoon salt	several days old*

Preheat the oven to 250°F. Line a baking sheet with parchment or grease it generously and set aside.

Place the butter and vegetable oil in a heavy skillet and set it over medium heat.

In a small bowl, whisk together the eggs, cream, salt, nutmeg, rum, and vanilla. Stir until smooth but not foamy. Pour the batter into a shallow casserole dish large enough to hold two pieces of bread snugly.

Place two pieces of bread in the soaking dish, turn them over, and turn them over again. The entire process should take about 15 seconds; you want the bread to absorb some of the liquid but not to become thoroughly saturated.

Place the bread in the skillet and fry it for 3 minutes before turning. Turn the bread; it should be golden brown. If not, raise the burner heat slightly. Fry the bread on the second side for about 2 minutes. Again, it should be golden brown. Transfer the French toast to the baking sheet and place it in the preheated oven. Allow it to remain in the oven while you cook the remaining pieces.

When all the pieces are cooked, serve the French toast on heated plates, dusting it with confectioners' sugar or non-melting white sugar or cinnamon-sugar (our favorite choice). Serve maple syrup or maple cream on the side.

*The bread needs to be somewhat stale, otherwise it will fall apart in the batter.

NOTE Ordinarily you'd consider two to three pieces of French toast a single serving, but this particular recipe is so rich, and each slice of bread is big and thick enough, that we consider one piece a serving, particularly if you are serving something else with it, such as a breakfast meat.

`nutrition information per serving`   **1 slice, 87g**

223 cal | 15g fat | 5g protein | 13g complex carbohydrates | 1g sugar | 1g dietary fiber | 147mg cholesterol | 249mg sodium | 92mg potassium | 175RE vitamin A | 1mg iron | 50mg calcium | 98mg phosphorus

Banana Bread French Toast

14 SLICES, ABOUT 7 SERVINGS

This version of French toast works equally well as a breakfast treat or the warm base for a scoop of vanilla ice cream as dessert. The flavors of banana and coconut are a natural together.

3 large eggs

1 cup (8 ounces) eggnog*

½ teaspoon nutmeg

1 package (10 ounces) shredded sweetened coconut

3 tablespoons (1½ ounces) butter

1 loaf (about fourteen ½-inch slices) banana bread

Whisk together the eggs, eggnog, and nutmeg until smooth. Pour the batter into a shallow pan or bowl with a flat bottom. In a separate shallow dish, pour out the coconut. Slice the banana bread.

Heat the griddle to medium, until a piece of butter swirled on top of it bubbles. Put the slices of banana bread into the batter, let them sit for 30 seconds, then turn them over. You may want to have a slotted spatula handy to lift them out of the batter once they become soaked through. Let the excess batter drip off the bread, then place the bread onto the coconut. Turn over, then transfer coated bread onto griddle. Turn down the heat to medium low and let the French toast cook for 2 to 3 minutes on the first side. Turn over to finish cooking on the second side, then transfer to a heated plate or serving platter to keep warm. Serve with syrup or ice cream, as you prefer.

*If you are in the wrong season for eggnog, use 1 cup half-and-half and 2 teaspoons of dark rum or ½ teaspoon butterscotch flavor.

`nutrition information per serving`   **2 slices, without syrup, 112g**

355 cal | 18g fat | 5g protein | 22g complex carbohydrates | 23g sugar | 1g dietary fiber | 89mg cholesterol | 257mg sodium | 188mg potassium | 131RE vitamin A | 1mg vitamin C | 1mg iron | 45mg calcium | 95mg phosphorus

Stuffed French Toast

ABOUT 6 SERVINGS

Think strata. Think bread pudding. Think how busy you'll be Christmas morning, and how little time you'll have to whip up a suitably fabulous breakfast to have on the table, piping hot from the oven, once the early morning frenzy abates. Think stuffed French toast, a "casserole" made from layers of bread, cream cheese, and strawberry jam, moistened with egg and milk, and baked to soft-crisp perfection.

You can fill the French toast and make up the custard in advance, then dip and bake when you are ready to go. Spread the filling on the slice of bread about ¼ inch thick, then top with the second slice of bread. Wrap and keep in the refrigerator until you're ready to bake. If you are thinking about a breakfast buffet, this is a dish that will hold warm for quite a while. Cut each sandwich into quarters and shingle them on a serving platter so that your guests can try several smaller pieces.

One of our colleagues swears by her husband's French toast. The secret? He melts vanilla ice cream, and soaks the bread in it. We tried it, and there is no doubt that the French toast dipped in ice cream was very tasty—even more rich than usual. As usual, one good idea breeds another, and P. J. chimed in: "What about eggnog?" Meanwhile, here is our tried-and-true custard for French toast.

BREAD
Twelve ½-inch-thick slices white sandwich bread (or the bread of your choice)

FILLING
4 ounces cream cheese (half of an 8-ounce bar), softened

1 tablespoon confectioners' or glazing sugar

½ cup (5½ ounces) strawberry jam, or the jam or preserve of your choice

1 teaspoon vanilla extract

¼ teaspoon cinnamon

CUSTARD
8 large eggs

3 cups (24 ounces) milk (or two 12-ounce cans evaporated milk)*

¼ cup (1¾ ounces) sugar

¾ teaspoon salt

2 teaspoons vanilla extract

First, select the pan you want to use, one that best fits the size of your bread slices. We used a 12 x 12 x 2-inch sticky bun pan and cut some of the slices to fit the pan. The point is to try to leave the bread as intact as possible, as lifting out and serving whole pieces is nicer than dealing with smaller pieces. Lightly grease the pan, preferably with butter.

In a small bowl, beat the cream cheese until soft, then blend in the remaining filling ingredients. Spread 6 slices of bread with the filling, top them with the remaining 6 slices, and lay these "sandwiches" in the pan, cutting to fit as necessary.

In a medium-sized mixing bowl, blend together the custard ingredients and pour the mixture over the bread in the pan. Let it sit for 30 minutes total, so the bread can soak up the custard.

Preheat the oven to 350°F.

Sprinkle freshly grated nutmeg atop the French toast and bake it for about 20 minutes. Turn over the pieces and bake for another 20 minutes, until the bread is puffy and lightly browned. Transfer the French toast to individual plates and serve it warm, with maple syrup, or one of the syrups that follow.

*Obviously, with milk being such a large part of this dish, the richer the milk you select, the richer the final dish will be. Let your taste (and waistline) be your guide.

nutrition information per serving   1 stuffed French toast, 295g

451 cal | 17.7g fat | 57g complex carbohydrates | 30g sugar | 18g protein | 2g dietary fiber | 313mg cholesterol | 748mg sodium | 363mg potassium | 280RE vitamin A | 4mg vitamin C | 3mg iron | 243mg calcium | 310mg phosphorus

Filling Variations

Use these variations as idea-generators for creating your favorite filling. To finish the French toast, follow the instructions above until the soaking process. For these variations, we suggest letting the assembled sandwiches sit in the custard for 5 minutes total, a minute or more on each side, to really soak up the custard mixture. Lay the drained slices on a lightly greased baking sheet. When a topping is called for, sprinkle with about half the appropriate topping for your filling, bake for 20 minutes, turn the slices over, and sprinkle with the rest of the topping. Bake for another 20 minutes, or until the toasts are brown on each side.

Banana Walnut Filled French Toast

1 ripe banana (4 ounces), diced
4 ounces cream cheese, softened
½ cup (2 ounces) chopped walnuts

½ teaspoon vanilla extract
Crushed walnuts, for topping

Mix together the banana, cream cheese, chopped walnuts, and vanilla, reserving the crushed walnuts for the topping. Spread about ¼ inch thick on one slice of bread, and top with the other. Dip in custard and finish as noted above, adding the topping one side at a time.

Cinnamon Raisin Filled French Toast

½ cup (3 ounces) raisins

4 ounces cream cheese, softened

2½ tablespoons (1 ounce) sugar

1 teaspoon vanilla extract

½ teaspoon cinnamon

Pinch of nutmeg (optional)

Cinnamon-sugar, for topping

Mix everything together except the topping. Spread about ¼ inch thick on one slice of bread, then top with the other. Dip in the custard, add topping, and bake as noted on page 25.

Butter Pecan Filled French Toast

4 ounces cream cheese, softened

2 tablespoons (1 ounce) brown sugar

1 teaspoon dark rum or butter-rum flavor

½ cup (1⅞ ounces) chopped pecans

Crushed pecans, for topping

Mix everything together except the topping. Spread on one slice of bread about ¼-inch thick, then top with the second slice. Dip in the custard, add the topping, and bake as noted on page 25.

Bacon or Apple and Cheddar French Toast

½ cup (1¼ ounces) crumbled cooked bacon, or ¾ cup (3¾ ounces) grated apple

¾ cup (3 ounces) grated cheddar cheese

3 ounces cream cheese, softened

Spread the mixture on one slice of bread about ¼ inch thick, then top with the second slice. Dip in the custard and bake as directed on page 25.

Flavored Syrups

If you know your audience has a weakness for, say, butter pecan or strawberry rhubarb, you can indulge them easily with these syrups. They're very quick to put together (about 15 minutes) and are a simple way to make breakfast a special event.

Three Berry Syrup

3 CUPS

1½ cups (7½ ounces) frozen mixed berries

2 tablespoons (1 ounce) lemon juice

¼ cup (1¾ ounces) sugar

1½ cups (16½ ounces) light corn syrup

¼ cup (1 ounce) cornstarch

2 tablespoons (1 ounce) cold water

Put berries, lemon juice, sugar, and corn syrup in a 2-quart saucepan over medium heat. Bring everything to a simmer, stirring to dissolve the sugar. While you are waiting for the berries to come to a simmer, put the cornstarch in a small bowl or cup and add the cold water. Stir until the cornstarch dissolves. When the syrup is simmering, add the cornstarch slurry all at once. Stir continuously until syrup comes back to a simmer and goes from cloudy to clear again. Serve warm.

nutrition information per serving ¼ cup, 77g

143 cal | 6g complex carbohydrates | 32g sugar | 1g dietary fiber | 45mg sodium | 44 mg potassium | 4RE vitamin A |
6mg vitamin C | 7mg calcium | 5mg phosphorus

Butter Pecan Syrup

3½ CUPS

This syrup will thicken at room temperature, so it should definitely be served warm. If you're using the microwave to reheat it, do so at medium power and be sure to cover the container.

1 cup (8 ounces) brown sugar, firmly packed

½ cup (4 ounces) water

¼ cup (½ stick, 2 ounces) butter

1 cup (4 ounces) chopped pecans

1 cup (11 ounces) light corn syrup

2 tablespoons (1 ounce) dark rum, optional

¼ teaspoon butterscotch extract,
⅛ teaspoon pecan flavor, or 1 teaspoon vanilla

Put brown sugar, water, and butter in a 2-quart saucepan. Cook over medium heat, stirring, until the sugar dissolves and the butter melts. Add the pecans, corn syrup, and flavoring of your choice. When everything is evenly combined and heated through, remove from heat and serve.

nutrition information per serving ¼ cup, 59g

193 cal | 6g fat | 1g complex carbohydrates | 35g sugar | 10mg cholesterol | 37mg sodium | 77mg potassium |
33RE vitamin A | 18mg calcium | 18mg phosphorus

Apricot Syrup

3½ CUPS

A little bit of orange juice gives this a subtle citrus tang.

1 10-ounce jar apricot jam or preserves
1½ cups (16½ ounces) light corn syrup
½ cup (2¼ ounces) diced dried apricots

2 tablespoons cornstarch
½ cup (4 ounces) orange juice

Place jam, corn syrup, and diced apricots in a 2-quart saucepan. Place over medium heat and bring to a simmer, stirring occasionally. While the jam is heating, dissolve cornstarch in the orange juice in a small bowl. When the syrup comes to a simmer, add the orange juice mixture to it all at once and stir until the syrup returns to a simmer. It will go from cloudy looking to clear, and thicken slightly. Remove from heat and serve warm.

nutrition information per serving   ¼ cup, 76g

161 cal │ 5g complex carbohydrates │ 37g sugar │ 42mg sodium │ 82mg potassium │ 22RE vitamin A │ 9mg vitamin C │ 4mg calcium │ 8mg phosphorus

Strawberry Rhubarb Syrup

3½ CUPS

This is a lovely way to keep a taste of springtime around no matter what time of year it is.

1 cup (4¼ ounces) diced rhubarb
1 cup (7 ounces) sugar
2 tablespoons (1 ounce) lemon juice
½ teaspoon cinnamon, or 1 cinnamon stick

1 cup (5 ounces) frozen sliced strawberries (unsweetened)
1 cup (11 ounces) light corn syrup
¼ cup (1 ounce) cornstarch
2 tablespoons (1 ounce) water

Place the rhubarb, sugar, lemon juice, and cinnamon in a 2-quart saucepan over medium heat. Bring to a simmer and cook until the rhubarb is tender (about 5 minutes). Add the strawberries and corn syrup, and while the mixture comes back to a simmer, combine cornstarch with water in a small bowl. Once these are dissolved, stir into simmering rhubarb mixture. Stir continuously until syrup comes back to a simmer, goes from looking cloudy to clear, and thickens. Remove the cinnamon stick, if you were using one, and take syrup off the stove to serve warm.

nutrition information per serving   ¼ cup, 72g

146 cal │ 4g complex carbohydrates │ 34g sugar │ 1g dietary fiber │ 28mg sodium │ 57mg potassium │ 1RE vitamin A │ 11mg vitamin C │ 12mg calcium │ 5mg phosphorus

Blini

ABOUT 2 DOZEN 4-INCH BLINI

These buckwheat pancakes are Russian and were eaten at the revelrous pre-Lenten feast known as Maslenitsa, or "butter week," from the Russian word *maslo*, butter. No meat was allowed during this week, thus the relish with which they consumed dairy products and fish, preferably caviar.

SPONGE

1⅓ cups (5⅝ ounces) whole buckwheat flour

1½ cups (12 ounces) warm water

2 tablespoons (⅝ ounce) non-instant dry milk, or ⅓ cup instant dry milk

1½ teaspoons instant yeast

BATTER

2 large eggs, separated

½ cup (4 ounces) milk

1 teaspoon sugar

½ teaspoon salt

¼ cup (½ stick, 2 ounces) butter, melted

FOR THE SPONGE Mix all the ingredients together in a medium-sized mixing bowl, cover, and set aside. Depending on how much sour flavor you like in your blini, the sponge can ripen for a few hours, all day, or overnight, so plan ahead when preparing it. The more time you give it, the more tang you'll taste.

FOR THE BATTER Beat the egg yolks until light, then beat in the milk, sugar, and salt.

Blend the batter into the sponge and let it rest for 30 to 45 minutes. Set aside the egg whites and let them warm to room temperature.

While you're waiting, get together the things you want to serve with the blini. We suggest any (or all) of the following: melted butter, sour cream, caviar, thinly sliced smoked salmon, pickled herring, kippers, chopped onion or scallions, chopped hard-boiled egg, capers, or for something sweet, jam.

Just before you're ready to cook the blini, whisk the melted butter into the batter. Beat the egg whites until they form medium peaks and fold them into the batter. Use a heavy, well-seasoned cast-iron griddle, if you have one. If not, use any heavy frying pan or griddle. Heat the pan over low to medium heat and wipe it with butter. (You shouldn't need to grease the pan again once you start cooking.)

Pour 2 to 3 tablespoons batter onto the griddle for each blini. They should be about 4 inches in diameter. Cook them as you would pancakes, until bubbles appear that break and don't fill in. Flip over and cook until lightly browned. These can be stacked on a warm plate in a warm oven until serving.

nutrition information per serving   **1 blini, ungarnished, 38g**

66 cal | 2.7g fat | 3g protein | 8g complex carbohydrates | 1g dietary fiber | 29mg cholesterol | 86mg sodium | 80mg potassium | 37RE vitamin A | 34mg calcium | 65mg phosphorus

Crêpes

Crêpes, a thinner, larger, unleavened version of pancakes, are a staple street food in Paris, where they were born. There, vendors with pushcarts and special large, flat crêpe irons make crêpes that are a full 12 inches in diameter. Spread with the customer's choice of filling (ranging from simple butter and sugar to ham and cheese to hazelnut-scented chocolate), the crêpes are folded for ease of handling and eaten with gusto.

In this country, crêpes are more often thought of as ladies' lunch fare, tidy little wrappers for creamed chicken or hot buttered crabmeat. In the '50s, as crêpes suzette, they were the star of many a flamboyant restaurant dessert finale, lit brandy adding an element of excitement to what might otherwise have been perceived as simply pancakes with orange sauce.

Now, crêpes have made a breakfast comeback—of sorts. With breakfast fajitas all the rage, crêpes stuffed with meat-, cheese-, or vegetable-enhanced scrambled eggs are an approximate substitute for the stuff served at the local fast food joint. We prefer them as blintzes, rolled around a rich, creamy cheese filling and topped with sour cream and fruit. However you choose to serve them, they're suitable for making ahead, then assembling and heating just before serving.

Parisian Street Vendor Crêpes

ELEVEN 10-INCH CRÊPES

In Paris, the crêpes sold by street vendors are big, a real meal and a half. You can use any size pan you like, however. Crêpe batter is a cinch to make. You just need to make it enough ahead so it can sit at room temperature for an hour or so. This resting time really changes the nature of the batter and makes for a much better crêpe. This recipe can be easily cut in half. Or make the whole recipe and freeze the extra crêpes for later.

2 cups (8½ ounces) unbleached all-purpose flour

½ to ¾ teaspoon salt

1½ cups (12 ounces) milk

4 large eggs

¼ cup (½ stick, 2 ounces) butter, melted but not bubbling hot

In a mixing bowl, combine the flour and salt. In another, smaller bowl, beat together the milk and eggs. Make a well in the flour mixture and pour in about half the liquid mixture. Blend well, then add the remaining liquid and stir until fairly smooth; a few lumps can remain. Stir in the butter. Cover and let sit for at least 1 hour.

The best thing to cook these crêpes in is a 10-inch cast iron pan (or, for smaller crêpes, a neat little crêpe pan). Heat the pan until it's medium-hot. Wipe the bottom of the pan with a bit of butter (a paper towel works well). Pour a scant ⅓ cup of batter into the bottom of the pan, pick up the pan, and tip it in a circle so the batter covers the bottom of the pan. Cook until the bottom begins to brown and you can slide a spatula under the crêpe. It will hold together quite well, so you can flip it over pretty easily. Cook briefly on the other side and place on a warm plate. Cover until the remaining batter is cooked.

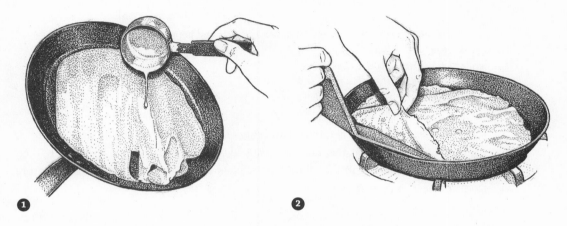

1. Tilt the pan toward yourself at a 45-degree angle while you pour the batter on it. Tilt the pan from side to side to finish covering the surface.   **2.** The crêpe is ready to flip when the top looks dry and the edges are just beginning to curl. Don't let it take on a lot of color.

THE FILLING This can be anything from sliced ham and cheese to butter sprinkled with sugar with (or without) a bit of Cointreau. A Parisian favorite is crêpes lightly smeared with Nutella, which is a smooth chocolate paste flavored with hazelnuts. After that, diced banana goes on top. The crêpes can be folded in quarters to eat on a plate, or rolled, burrito-style, for a walkaround snack.

nutrition information per serving   **1 crêpe with 1 tablespoon Nutella and 1 banana, 207g**

291 cal │ 6g fat │ 8g protein │ 44g complex carbohydrates │ 12g sugar │ 4g dietary fiber │ 81mg cholesterol │ 173mg sodium │ 595mg potassium │ 68RE vitamin A │ 11mg vitamin C │ 2mg iron │ 78mg calcium │ 141mg phosphorus

Savory Spinach-Filled Crêpes

14 FILLED CRÊPES

Crêpes aren't just for sweet breakfasts or desserts; they're the perfect foil for a savory filling. The following is very nice used in crepes either rolled, folded, or to make two crepe cakes (below).

1 tablespoon vegetable oil	2 tablespoons (1 ounce) butter
4 cups (10 ounces) sliced fresh mushrooms	¼ cup (1 ounce) unbleached all-purpose flour
1 cup (5 ounces) peeled and chopped onions	1½ cups (12 ounces) milk
1 cup (5½ ounces) chopped ham (optional)	Salt and pepper to taste
3 pounds fresh spinach, stemmed and chopped, or three 10-ounce packages frozen chopped spinach, thawed and drained*	3 large eggs

In a large pan, heat the vegetable oil and sauté the mushrooms, onions, and ham until the liquid has cooked off the mushrooms. Add the chopped spinach, stir quickly, then cover the pan and cook just until the spinach has wilted. Remove the spinach mixture from the heat and set it aside.

Melt the butter in a small saucepan. Add the flour and cook, stirring constantly, until the flour is golden. While whisking, add the milk a little at a time. Bring the mixture to a boil and cook until it's thickened; add salt and pepper to taste. Remove from the heat and cool for 15 minutes, then stir together the cream sauce, spinach mixture, and eggs. Use this mixture to fill crêpes (see p. 30). You can sauté them in butter until heated through, or place in a buttered baking dish, sprinkle with grated cheese, and bake them in a preheated 350°F oven for 20 minutes, until heated through.

*If you use baby spinach, there's no need to stem it. Baby spinach is very fragile and wilts down quickly, so be sure not to overcook it.

nutrition information per serving   2 filled crêpes, 290g

372 cal | 19g fat | 19g protein | 32g complex carbohydrates | 4g dietary fiber | 230mg cholesterol | 749mg sodium | 975mg potassium | 884RE vitamin A | 35mg vitamin C | 6mg iron | 206mg calcium | 302mg phosphorus

Variation   CRÊPE CAKES: To make crêpe cakes, place one unrolled, unfilled crêpe in the bottom of a lightly greased 8- or 9-inch round cake pan. Fan five crêpes around the perimeter of the pan, allowing about a quarter of each crêpe to overlap the one next to it. Spread half the filling evenly over the crêpes and fold in the edges. Place one crêpe on top. Repeat with the remaining crêpes and filling in another lightly greased 8- or 9-inch round cake pan.

Brush the top crêpe in each pan with melted butter or oil and bake the cakes in a preheated 350°F oven for 35 to 40 minutes, until the tops are slightly brown and crisp. Let the cakes sit for 10 minutes before cutting them into wedges. Serve hot. Makes about 12 servings.

Cheese Blintzes

14 BLINTZES

Even if you're from apple country rather than the Big Apple, you've probably enjoyed some version of cheese blintzes at your local pancake house or breakfast spot. A thin, buttery crêpe, wrapped around a mild, smooth, ricotta or cottage cheese–based filling is the perfect palette for the spoonful of fruit sauce that will complete the picture.

This dish may be made well ahead, either in total or in part. The crêpes may be cooked, cooled completely, then stacked, wrapped well, and either refrigerated or frozen. Stuff them one day ahead, then hold in the refrigerator overnight; or stuff and freeze for up to a month.

We offer two types of filling: a creamy ricotta filling, slightly runny when baked, and a firmer, less sweet, more traditional filling. Serve with blueberry compote (see recipe on p. 35).

The Crêpes

1 cup (8 ounces) water
¾ cup (6 ounces) milk
3 large eggs
5 tablespoons (2½ ounces) butter, melted

½ teaspoon salt
1½ cups (6¼ ounces) unbleached all-purpose flour

In a medium-sized mixing bowl, whisk together everything to make a smooth batter. Place the batter in the refrigerator for 1 hour or longer, to relax the gluten.

Heat an 8-inch (or slightly larger) crêpe or omelet pan until a drop of water skips across the pan. Lightly grease the pan and pour a scant ¼ cupful of batter into the middle. Tilt the pan and swirl the batter to completely coat the bottom with batter (see illustration on p. 31). Cook until the crêpe is opaque and set. Transfer the crêpes, uncooked side down, to a sheet pan or rack to cool. You cook the crêpes on only one side; this is sufficient to cook them all the way through. When you stack them, stack them "uncooked" side down, so that this side will be on the outside when you roll them.

Creamy Ricotta Filling

1 3-ounce package cream cheese

1 large egg, lightly beaten

2 teaspoons lemon zest, or ¼ teaspoon lemon oil

2 teaspoons vanilla extract

¼ teaspoon salt

3 tablespoons (1¼ ounces) sugar

2 (15-ounce container) ricotta cheese

In a medium-sized mixing bowl, beat the cream cheese until soft. Add the beaten egg a bit at a time, beating until smooth after each addition and scraping the sides of the bowl often. Add the lemon zest, vanilla extract, salt, and sugar and mix until well combined. Fold in the ricotta cheese.

Traditional Filling

1¾ cups (16-ounce container) cottage cheese*

2 cups (15-ounce container) ricotta cheese

1 large egg

1 teaspoon vanilla extract

1 teaspoon lemon zest, or ⅛ teaspoon lemon oil

2 tablespoons (⅞ ounce) sugar

Place the cottage cheese and ricotta cheese in a colander lined with cheesecloth, or in a yogurt cheese maker. Let them drain for 1½ to 2 hours, pressing down lightly occasionally.

With some brands of cheese you'll remove only 1 or 2 tablespoons of liquid, while others may give up ¼ cup or more.

For a smoother, creamier filling, blend all the ingredients in a food processor. For a more traditional, grainier filling, simply mash the cottage cheese with a fork and stir in the remaining ingredients.

ASSEMBLY Use approximately 3 rounded tablespoons filling for each 8-inch crêpe. Place the filling about 2 inches from the top of the crêpe, fold the sides in, fold the top down, then loosely roll the crêpe into a log. This is the same procedure used to make egg rolls; the point is to contain the filling.

Heat a medium-sized frying pan and melt about 2 tablespoons of butter in it until it's sizzling. Sauté the blintzes until they're lightly browned and heated through.

Alternatively, nestle the blintzes in a buttered 13 x 9-inch pan and bake them in a pre-heated 350°F oven for 25 to 30 minutes, or until they're thoroughly heated. Serve hot with blueberry compote.

*If you can find farmers cheese, substitute it for the cottage cheese and skip the draining step.

nutrition information per serving 2 blintzes filled with creamy ricotta filling, 188g

381 cal | 23g fat | 15g protein | 23g complex carbohydrates | 6g sugar | 1g dietary fiber | 184mg cholesterol | 326mg sodium | 204mg potassium | 290RE vitamin A | 1mg vitamin C | 2mg iron | 227mg calcium | 228mg phosphorus

nutrition information per serving 2 blintzes filled with traditional filling, 220g

374 cal | 18g fat | 23g protein | 25g complex carbohydrates | 4g sugar | 1g dietary fiber | 171mg cholesterol | 541mg sodium | 247mg potassium | 232RE vitamin A | 2mg iron | 258mg calcium | 309mg phosphorus

Blueberry Compote

2 CUPS

½ cup (3½ ounces) sugar

1 tablespoon cornstarch

¼ cup (2 ounces) cold water or fruit juice

1 teaspoon lemon zest, or ⅛ teaspoon lemon oil

1 teaspoon lemon juice

A pinch of salt

2 cups (10 ounces) fresh or frozen blueberries

In a medium-sized saucepan, whisk together the sugar, cornstarch, and cold water or fruit juice. Add the remaining ingredients, except the blueberries, then bring the mixture to a boil over medium heat, stirring constantly; this will take only a few minutes. Remove the mixture from the heat and cool it to lukewarm. Stir in the fresh or frozen blueberries just before serving.

nutrition information per serving 3 tablespoons compote, 61g

85 cal | 8g complex carbohydrates | 14g sugar | 1g dietary fiber | 1mg sodium | 26mg potassium | 4RE vitamin A | 2mg vitamin C | 4mg calcium | 6mg phosphorus

Popovers

12 POPOVERS

We like the following recipe because it's easily made, doesn't require a popover pan (although these are helpful), and makes an even dozen popovers. A teaspoon of dried mixed herbs is optional.

3 large eggs

1½ cups (12 ounces) whole milk

scant 1½ cups (6¼ ounces) unbleached all-purpose flour

½ teaspoon salt

¼ cup (½ stick, 2 ounces) unsalted butter, melted

1 teaspoon dried mixed herbs (optional)

Preheat the oven to 450°F.

Place all of the ingredients in a blender in the order indicated above. Blend for 30 seconds, stopping midway through to scrape down the sides of the blender. Allow the batter to rest for 15 minutes.

Using solid shortening or a nonstick vegetable oil spray, thoroughly grease 12 muffin cups (or 6 popover or 12 mini-popover cups). Be sure to grease the area around the cups as well as the cups themselves. Fill the cups about two-thirds full with the batter. Bake for 20 minutes, then reduce the oven to 350°F and bake for an additional 10 minutes. Resist the urge to open the oven door at any time during this process. Remove the baked popovers from the oven, pierce the tops with a knife, and allow them to cool in the pan for 5 minutes. Then gently turn them out of the pan onto a wire rack. Serve warm.

nutrition information per serving   1 popover, 52g

112cal | 5g fat | 4g protein | 12g complex carbohydrates | 64mg cholesterol | 11 mg sodium | 61mg potassium | 71RE vitamin A | 1mg iron | 34mg calcium | 55mg phosphorus

Why Do Popovers Pop?

Popovers are one of the few baked goods that rise from eggs and steam rather than from a leavener or yeast. Popover batter has a larger proportion of liquid to flour than most other baked goods. It's the steam created by the liquid in the batter that raises popovers to their astounding heights.

The protein in the eggs and flour combine to form a matrix that's soft enough to expand with the steam but strong enough to contain it. We've had our most consistent results with popovers when we made them using flour with at least 11.7 percent protein, rather than a lower-protein pastry flour, which you might be inclined to use for tenderness. Popovers will expand until their crust finally hardens. When you remove them from the oven pierce them with the tip of a knife, so any leftover steam can escape quickly. This keeps the popovers from becoming soggy.

Fried Doughs

Is there another American confection that has as long and storied a history as the doughnut? Starting at Plymouth Rock, where America's first English settlers stepped ashore carrying doughnut recipes from Holland, through pioneer days and the Industrial Revolution, up to today's "grab it and run" breakfast, doughnuts have been there. From the lumber camps of Maine to the sidewalk cafés of New Orleans, and at every lunch counter and diner booth in between, these deep-fried, sugared treats have been a mainstay.

All fried breads are a revered tradition in American cuisine. Everyone has an opinion on them—most based on how Mom or Grandma used to make them. During our research, our King Arthur coworkers flocked to the test kitchen, bringing recipes, frying equipment, and doughnuts or fried dough or fritters they'd made at home, to demonstrate their particular recipe or methodology. The test kitchen was crowded with pans of bubbling oil, dough, cutters, skimmers, bags of sugar, jugs of maple syrup, plates of golden-brown fried breads, and people—people everywhere, talking, laughing, sampling. The fried bread project was a true communal effort, a throwback to the "work bees" of old, equal parts labor and socializing.

Despite the doughnut's reputation as a dieter's no-no, we still enjoy them. And crullers. And fried dough and fritters and beignets. A properly made doughnut or other fried bread will absorb only about 1 teaspoon of fat, which is just over 3 grams. And many fried breads are made from plain, almost-fat-free yeast doughs, which means eating one is less fat-intensive than consuming a serving of most any kind of cookie, cake, pie, or pastry. Even richer doughs, those containing milk, eggs, and butter, won't bring the Fat Police knocking on your door (as long as you eat just one; not an easy task when you're confronted with a plate of beignets and maple syrup).

With all of the modern frying equipment available to home bakers these days, and armed with the knowledge that deep-fried food doesn't have to mean fat-laden, may we suggest a foray into fried breads? We guarantee, the experience will take you right back to the fried dough booth at the county fair, and the smell of cinnamon doughnuts in Grandma's kitchen on Saturday morning.

Deep-Frying Tools and Techniques

Tools to have on hand include a spatula, slotted spoon, deep-frying/candy thermometer, a pair of tongs, and a plate or baking sheet lined with absorbent paper (such as paper towels). Flattened brown paper grocery bags are absorbent, and you can put a layer or two of paper towels on top.

For doughs that are flat in shape, like Navajo Fry Bread or fritters, an electric fry pan is ideal. The thermostat will help to maintain a consistent temperature. For doughnuts or funnel cakes, you need a heavy pan (cast iron works well) with sides that are at least three inches high. The fat for frying doughnuts should be at least two inches deep.

The temperature of your oil is the most important factor in the quality of your finished product. Too low, and your dough will be heavy and greasy. Too high, and the outsides will overcook before the insides can catch up.

This is where your thermometer comes in. Clip it to the side of your pot, with the bulb a half inch from the bottom of the pan, and leave it there while you cook.

When placing your dough into the oil, be careful to place one edge of it into the fat, then let go. Don't drop it in from above the surface—you could splash hot oil straight up if you do. Turn your doughnuts over carefully, away from you, and use tongs or a fork and spoon to keep them from splashing as they flop over.

Be careful not to overload the pan—you want to leave enough space for each piece of dough to float freely. You'll also see the temperature of the oil drop after putting in a number of pieces of dough. After frying one batch, let the temperature of the oil recover (this is where the thermometer comes in). It's better to be patient and let the oil come back up to the proper frying temperature than to turn up the heat.

The distinctive "doughnutty" taste of bakery doughnuts comes from lard. Many people look askance at lard, but honestly, it's not poison. It's lower in saturated fat and cholesterol than butter. (By the way, don't try frying dough-

nuts in butter; its smoke point is too low.) If you fry doughnuts correctly, they'll absorb only about a teaspoon of lard each; and they'll have that flavor that your tastebuds will immediately identify as *doughnut*.

Doughnuts

Buttermilk Doughnuts

ABOUT 30 DOUGHNUTS

The recipe for these traditional doughnuts, which is probably at least one hundred years old, was passed down to us from a farm wife in Wisconsin. They are both comforting in their simplicity, and delicious.

1 cup (7 ounces) sugar

2 large eggs

1 teaspoon baking soda dissolved in 1 cup (8 ounces) buttermilk

3 tablespoons (1½ ounces) butter or margarine, melted

1 tablespoon vanilla extract

1 teaspoon baking powder

3¾ cups (15¾ ounces) unbleached all-purpose flour

¼ teaspoon nutmeg

6 cups (3 pounds) lard or vegetable shortening (2½ pounds), for frying

Confectioners' sugar

In a medium-size bowl, beat together the sugar and eggs until smooth. Beat in the baking soda/buttermilk, butter, and vanilla. Add baking powder, flour, and nutmeg, stirring until well combined. Refrigerate overnight.

Next day, remove the dough from the refrigerator and place it on a well-floured surface; the dough will be sticky. Roll into a large circle ¼ inch thick (you can divide dough in half first, if you wish). Cut the doughnuts with a doughnut cutter, or with two biscuit cutters—a large for the outside, a small for the hole.

In a large, deep kettle, melt the lard or vegetable shortening and heat it to 375°F. Fry the doughnuts for 1½ to 2 minutes on each side, or until golden brown. Drain on absorbent paper. When cool, put confectioners' sugar in a paper bag, add a couple of doughnuts at a time, and shake to coat the doughnuts with sugar.

NOTE To form crullers, cut strips of dough ½ inch wide by 8 inches long with a pizza wheel or knife. Bend the strip into a horseshoe shape, then twist the sides together (see illustration). Pinch the ends together before frying.

nutrition information per serving   **1 doughnut with confectioners' sugar, 45g**

151 cal | 6g fat | 2g protein | 11g complex carbohydrates | 11g sugar | 23mg cholesterol | 68mg sodium | 35mg potassium | 1mg iron | 45mg calcium | 29mg phosphorus

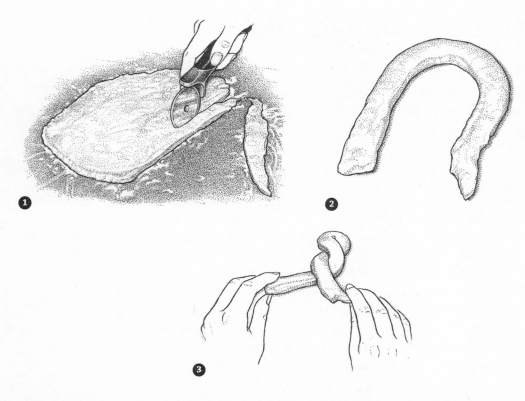

To form crullers, **1.** cut ½-inch strips of dough, and **2.** bend them into a horseshoe shape.

3. Twist the two ends of the dough around each other, then pinch them together to form the cruller shape.

Fats in Frying

When you cook something in fat, especially something porous like a doughnut, some of the fat winds up in what you're cooking, between 3 and 5 grams per doughnut (in calories this means somewhere between 27 and 45). If you have the fat at the right temperature and can keep it that way when you're cooking, you can minimize the total amount.

The reason fats are an efficient cooking medium is that they can be heated to a much higher temperature than water. When it's at the right temperature, a dough will sear and become crisp, which prevents it from absorbing all of the fat. Some fats are better than others for this, based on their "smoke points." Just as fats become liquid at different temperatures (melting points), the point at which they begin to break down and begin to smoke also differs. Since most doughnuts need to be cooked at about 365°F, knowing the smoke points of various fats and/or oils can be useful. You'll find them on page 552.

There are some things that will lower the smoke point of fats. Oxidation is the first. As soon as fat or oil is exposed to air, it begins to "oxidize," or break down. At room temperature, this happens very slowly. As soon as you begin to heat a fat, oxidation accelerates, so be sure to preheat your oil for as short a time as possible.

Because it is the oxygen in the air that is the culprit, a taller rather than a wider pot is a better choice for deep frying. That means less of the oil is exposed at the surface. Here's one more consideration. The iron in a cast iron kettle will also speed up oxidation unless it's well seasoned. An optimal choice would be a fairly tall, stainless-steel pot, as stainless steel is non-reactive and won't act as an oxidation catalyst. This doesn't mean you can't use others. They'll do fine; don't let the lack of a stainless steel pot discourage you from this adventure. You just may need to change your fat or oil a little more frequently. And if you're making doughnuts just once a year, it won't make any difference anyway!

Once you start cooking and begin to "contaminate" the fat with foreign material, its smoke point is also lowered. A fat or oil can be used more than once, five or six times if you keep it clean. Strain it through cheesecloth or a clean dishtowel to remove as much foreign matter as possible each time you use it. Once the fat has darkened, it has oxidized to the point where it will begin to give your doughnuts an "off" flavor. Then it's a good time to start fresh. Oils that are predominantly polyunsaturated or are unrefined and cold-pressed are not good choices for deep frying, as excessive heating deteriorates them rather quickly.

The best way to keep track of the temperature of the fat or oil in your pot is with an appropriate thermometer. The easiest type to read is an alcohol thermometer with a long, clearly marked rectangular scale rather than an expansion thermometer with a round dial. Either kind comes with a clip to hold it on the side of your pot. If you have enough fat or oil in your pot, at least 3 to 4 inches deep, it will take a minimum of adjustment to keep it at a fairly stable temperature. That's the key to making doughnuts that are crisp without being greasy.

Beignets

18 BEIGNETS

Baking powder beignets are made from a quick dough—the consistency of a thick pancake batter—that you drop by spoonfuls into hot oil; no rolling out or overhandling of the dough to worry about. After frying, serve them sprinkled with confectioners' sugar and a generous pool of maple syrup.

We made our beignets with white whole wheat flour, but unbleached all-purpose flour will do just as well.

6 cups (2 pounds) vegetable oil, vegetable shortening (2½ pounds) or lard (3 pounds), for frying

1 cup (8 ounces) milk

1 large egg

¼ cup (2 ounces) vegetable oil or melted butter

2 cups (10 ounces) white whole wheat flour or unbleached all-purpose flour

1½ tablespoons baking powder

1 teaspoon salt

2 tablespoons (⅞ ounce) granulated sugar

¼ cup (1 ounce) confectioners' sugar, to sprinkle on beignets

½ cup (5½ ounces) maple syrup, for dunking

Heat at least 2 inches of oil to 350°F in a large, deep pot.

Mix the milk, egg, and oil together. In a separate bowl, mix together the flour, baking powder, salt, and granulated sugar. Stir together with a whisk until evenly incorporated. Add the milk mixture and stir until smooth.

When the oil is the correct temperature, drop the batter by large spoonfuls into the hot fat. Fry four or five beignets at a time, making sure that there's plenty of room for them to expand. Fry the beignets for 2 minutes on each side. Use a slotted spoon to remove them from the oil and drain them on paper towels.

Serve beignets hot with a sprinkling of confectioners' sugar and a pool of maple syrup.

nutrition information per serving 1 beignet, 49g

156 cal | 8g fat | 5g protein | 10g complex carbohydrates | 8g sugar | 2g dietary fiber | 1mg cholesterol | 237mg sodium | 86mg potassium | 1mg iron | 89mg calcium | 79mg phosphorus

Flash Points

There are two other temperatures that are fairly consistent for all these fats and oils that you should know about before you embark upon deep-fat frying. Most fats and oils will reach a "flash point" at about 600°F. This means you'll see little flamelets jump from the surface, not a good sign. Beyond this is the "fire point," or the temperature at which the fat will ignite and begin to blaze. This happens just shy of 700°F for most fats. Most thermometers won't approach these temperatures, so your cue for the time to be concerned is when the fat begins to smoke, at the smoke points listed on page 552.

Should you ever run into a situation where, for whatever reason, you wind up with flaming fat or oil, cover your pan to shut off the supply of oxygen. Don't ever try to put it out with water. Water will just splash flames all over the place and make a bad situation worse. If things do get that bad, use baking soda to extinguish the flames. In fact, it's a good idea to keep a box at hand when you're deep-fat frying. The chance that you'll need it is remote if you're careful. If you have a fire extinguisher in the house and know how to use it, that's even better. Many people have them but have never gone through a fire drill with them so aren't going to know what to do if they're in a panic.

Paczki

8 PACZKI

Paczki (say, "pooch-key," "poonch-key," or "punch-key") are, quite simply, deep-fried sugar-dusted jelly doughnuts native to Poland. But there's more to the story than that. Paczki were traditionally eaten on the Tuesday before Ash Wednesday—Shrove Tuesday, Fat Tuesday, or Mardi Gras—in order to use up all the eggs, butter, sugar, and other good things in the larder before the lean days of Lent, when sweets were often foregone as a form of penance. Now, all of a sudden, paczki have become big business, particularly in the Midwest. Billboards trumpet the arrival of Paczki Day, and parades are held in honor of the paczki.

Here in Vermont, though we've read about paczki, we've never actually seen them for sale in any local bakery. We decided that, in order to understand what all the fuss was about, we'd just have to make them ourselves. The National Paczki Promotional Board was kind enough to send us a recipe and lots of information—including words and music to "The Paczki Polka."

Make your paczki on the Monday evening before Fat Tuesday, then serve them the next morning as a kick-off to the culinary festivities. Even if you're not in an area of the country that celebrates Paczki Day, by eating a paczki you become part of the celebration—at least in spirit.

4½ teaspoons instant yeast

⅓ cup (2¼ ounces) sugar

2 tablespoons (⅝ ounce) nonfat dry milk

½ teaspoon salt

1 teaspoon baking powder

1 large egg

½ cup (4 ounces) water

3 tablespoons (1¼ ounces) shortening

2¼ cups (9½ ounces) unbleached all-purpose flour

6 cups (2 pounds) vegetable oil or shortening (2½ pounds), for frying

1 cup (about 8 ounces) jam or jelly (we like raspberry), for filling

Granulated sugar or confectioners' sugar, for topping

In a medium-sized mixing bowl, or in the bowl of your electric mixer, combine yeast, sugar, dry milk, salt, baking powder, egg, water, shortening, and flour. Knead the dough until it's smooth and supple, adding additional flour as needed. Cover the dough and allow it to rise for 1 hour; it won't rise very much, if at all. Transfer the dough to a lightly greased work surface.

(You can also place all the ingredients in the pan of your bread machine, program the machine for manual or dough, and press start. When the machine has completed its cycle, transfer the dough to a lightly greased work surface.)

Divide the dough into eight pieces. Round each piece into a ball, then flatten each ball slightly. Place the balls on a lightly greased or parchment-lined cookie sheet, cover them with greased plastic wrap, and allow them to rest for 2 to 2½ hours. Again, they won't rise much.

About 10 minutes before the end of the rising time, heat the oil in a deep fryer or in a deep saucepan. If you're using a deep fryer, follow the directions for frying doughnuts. If you're heating the oil in a saucepan, pour oil into the pan to a depth of about 3 inches and heat it slowly to 375°F.

Fry the paczki, two to four at a time (depending on the capacity of your pan), for 3 minutes on each side, or until they're a very deep brown but not burned. Transfer them to paper towels to drain.

When the paczki are cool enough to handle, fill them with about 2 tablespoons of jam or jelly each. The easy way to do this is by using a cookie press equipped with a filling tube, or use a thin spoon, such as an espresso spoon, to make a small hole in the doughnut and spoon the jelly into the middle. Roll the paczki in sugar.

NOTE The traditional method for making paczki involves rolling out two flat rounds of dough and sealing them, jam inside, before frying. We found the above method much easier.

nutrition information per serving   **1 paczki, 85g**

297 cal | 14g fat | 6g protein | 26g complex carbohydrates | 10g sugar | 1g dietary fiber | 35mg cholesterol | 207mg sodium | 116mg potassium | 19RE vitamin A | 2mg iron | 115mg calcium | 91mg phosphorus

Chocolate Doughnuts

16 DOUGHNUTS PLUS DOUGHNUT HOLES

These delicious cake-style doughnuts feature a thick chocolate glaze.

⅓ cup (2 ounces) chopped semisweet chocolate or chocolate chips

4 tablespoons (½ stick, 2 ounces) butter

3 large eggs

¾ cup (5¼ ounces) sugar

1 tablespoon baking powder

½ teaspoon baking soda

½ teaspoon salt

3½ cups (14¾ ounces) unbleached all-purpose flour

½ cup (1½ ounces) unsweetened cocoa

1 cup (8 ounces) buttermilk

1 teaspoon vanilla extract

6 cups (about 2 pounds) vegetable oil or shortening (2½ pounds), for frying

GLAZE

3 ounces unsweetened chocolate

5 tablespoons boiling water

2 cups (8 ounces) confectioners' sugar, sifted

In a small heatproof bowl, combine the chocolate and butter. Cover with plastic wrap and melt over simmering water or at medium power in the microwave. Stir to combine and set aside.

In a large mixing bowl, combine the butter/chocolate mixture with the eggs and sugar and mix until light. In a separate bowl, whisk together baking powder, baking soda, salt, flour, and cocoa. Add to egg mixture and stir to moisten. Add buttermilk and vanilla, mixing just enough to bring the dough together. Gather the dough into a ball and wrap with plastic wrap. Refrigerate for at least 1 hour before rolling out.

To make the doughnuts, heat the oil or shortening to 350°F in a pan that will hold at least 1½ inches of oil. On a lightly floured surface, roll out the chilled dough to a ½-inch-thick circle. Cut into doughnut shapes with a doughnut cutter, or with two biscuit cutters—a large for the outside, a small for the hole. Fry the doughnuts two or three at a time; cook for 90 seconds on one side, turn, and cook for 90 seconds on the other. Remove doughnuts from the oil with a slotted spoon, and drain on paper towels.

To make the glaze, chop the unsweetened chocolate and put it in a medium-sized heatproof bowl. Pour the boiling water over the chocolate and stir to melt it. Stir in the confectioners' sugar to make a smooth glaze.

To finish the doughnuts, dip them (flat side down) into the glaze, then turn over onto a rack to let the glaze finish dripping down.

nutrition information per serving　1 doughnut, with glaze, 83g

244 cal | 7g fat | 5g protein | 20g complex carbohydrates | 21g sugar | 2g dietary fiber | 43mg cholesterol | 196mg sodium | 149mg potassium | 41RE vitamin A | 2mg iron | 73mg calcium | 107mg phosphorus | 17mg caffeine

Yeast-Raised Glazed Doughnuts

16 ROUND DOUGHNUTS PLUS DOUGHNUT HOLES

What could be better than a warm, tender, vanilla-glazed doughnut? This recipe results in just such a cloudlike confection. The dough needs a number of hours to grow to its full potential, so be sure to plan ahead. You can complete this recipe through the first rise the day before, refrigerate the dough overnight, then roll, cut, and cook them the next morning for a very special treat.

½ teaspoon salt

¼ teaspoon nutmeg

¼ cup (1¾ ounces) sugar

2¼ teaspoons instant yeast

3 cups (12¾ ounces) unbleached all-purpose flour

1 large egg

1 cup (8 ounces) milk

2 tablespoons (1 ounce) butter, melted

½ teaspoon vanilla extract

6 cups (2 pounds) vegetable oil or shortening (2½ pounds), for frying

GLAZE

¼ cup (2 ounces) milk

2 cups (8 ounces) confectioners' sugar

¼ teaspoon vanilla extract

Whisk together the dry ingredients. In a separate bowl, combine the egg, milk, butter ,and vanilla and stir into the flour mixture, mixing until well combined. Let the dough rest for 5 minutes, then knead for 6 to 8 minutes by hand or mixer until you have a smooth, soft dough. Place the dough in a buttered bowl, turn it over to grease the top, and let it rise, covered, in a warm place for 1½ to 2 hours, until doubled in bulk.

Deflate the dough and turn it out onto a lightly floured surface. Gently roll the dough out to ¼-inch thickness and cut with a round cutter (or, using a pizza wheel, cut into strips to make crullers, see p. 40). Cover loosely with greased plastic wrap and let rise again for about 1 hour, until doubled again.

Place oil or shortening in a heavy pan or deep skillet and heat to 350°F. Place the doughnuts in the oil, two or three at a time, and fry until golden brown. Turn over and cook the second side. This should take no more than a minute for each side. Overcooking will make the doughnuts tough. Drain on paper towels.

To make the glaze, stir the milk into the confectioners' sugar until it is smooth, then add the vanilla.

When the doughnuts are cool enough to handle (but still warm), dip the tops of the doughnuts in the glaze, then place on a rack or plate to let the glaze drip down.

nutrition information per serving 1 glazed doughnut, 54g

138 cal | 2g fat | 3g protein | 17g complex carbohydrates | 9g sugar | 1g dietary fiber | 18mg cholesterol | 80mg sodium | 67mg potassium | 30RE vitamin A | 1mg iron | 24mg calcium | 48mg phosphorus

Sweet Cheese Puffs

These puffs are a snap to make, and have a delicate, light texture. Because of the ricotta and deep-frying, they remind us of Italian cannolis. While this isn't the traditional formula for Chanukah jelly doughnuts, these could very well have a tiny bit of jelly piped into them with a cookie press (equipped with the small tube tip), or with a pastry bag. You could also use a small cappuccino or espresso spoon to spoon a bit of jelly into them before shaking on sugar and serving.

5 large eggs

15 ounces (1⅞ cups, 1 small container) ricotta cheese

2 tablespoons (1 ounce) melted butter

5 tablespoons (2⅛ ounces) sugar

¼ teaspoon salt

1 to 2 tablespoons lemon zest or ¼ teaspoon lemon oil (optional)

2½ teaspoons vanilla extract

4¼ teaspoons baking powder

2 cups (8½ ounces) unbleached all-purpose flour

3 to 4 cups (1 to 1½ pounds) vegetable or salad oil, for frying

Confectioners' sugar, glazing sugar, cinnamon sugar, or non-melting white sugar, for coating

In a large bowl, beat the eggs until foamy. Mix in the ricotta cheese, butter, sugar, salt, and flavorings. Stir the baking powder into the flour, then quickly and gently stir into the ricotta mixture.

Heat the oil in a deep pan to 350°F. Drop the batter into hot oil by the rounded measuring teaspoon, or (best method) using a small (1 teaspoon) cookie scoop. Fry the puffs for 2 to 3 minutes. They should turn themselves over when one side is cooked, but if they're browning too quickly on one side, use tongs or a chopstick to turn them over.

Remove the puffs from the hot oil and drain them on paper towels. Toss in a paper bag with sugar. They're best served immediately, while still warm.

nutrition information per serving **2 doughnuts, 40g**

102 cal | 5g fat | 1g complex carbohydrates | 5g sugar | 4g protein | 65mg sodium | 44mg potassium | 37RE vitamin A | 1mg iron | 65mg calcium | 72mg phosphorus

History of Doughnuts

Although October has been designated "Doughnut Month" by the powers-that-be in Washington, February seems infinitely more appropriate, as it is traditionally the month that Lent begins. In Europe, the week before Lent is when all the rich food that is in the house is used up in preparation for forty days of fasting.

There are a number of delicacies that traditionally have been made in Europe for pre-Lenten feasting. And it is these that are the ancestors of what we think of, in this country, as the doughnut. In Germany, there are Shrovetide pancakes—ballen, fastnachts, berliners, or bismarcks. In France are beignets viennois, or viennese fritters, which the Dutch appropriated and called appelbeignet. The Dutch made their own olie-koecks, or, as they have been called more recently, olie bollen.

Many of our original colonists, having been persecuted in England for their religious persuasions, sought temporary refuge in Holland. They were there for well over a decade before leaving to find freedom in the New World. While they were there, they acquired many Dutch ways and words and culinary inclinations. So one of the predecessors of the doughnut came with them. The Dutch are also responsible for the cruller, made from an egg-rich dough that they twisted into the elongated shape we are familiar with today, but which they also tied into "love" or "matrimony" knots.

Farther south, Germans came to farm the rich lands of Pennsylvania. These Pennsylvania "Dutch" (so called because they were from Deutschland, or Germany) brought with them the predecessor of the jelly doughnut, the fastnacht, or fossnock. These farmers believed that if fastnachts were not eaten on Shrove Tuesday, the crops would fail that year.

The French version of the doughnut, the beignet viennois, first appeared on this side of the Atlantic in Canada, having come with the Acadians, French settlers in the Canadian Maritimes. Doughnut making in these northern climes was seasonal. Rather than being a pre-Lenten treat, they were made right after fall butchering, which was the only time that there was enough fat to make them. Typically, Acadian doughnuts are sweetened with molasses, making them similar to the cake doughnut recipes you find in early New England cookbooks. Another Canadian version of the cake doughnut is the croquignole, which is incredibly rich, light, and airy and probably related to the cruller, as it too is twisted.

Louisiana is now famous for the beignet, brought there by those same Acadian (Cajun) settlers. Today you'll find them as a delicious expression of a culture that celebrates the pre-Lenten season with unusual (in this country) gusto. This is Mardi Gras, which literally means "fat Tuesday" and which turns New Orleans into a rollicking carnival.

This is not the end of the doughnut evolution in this country. In the Southwest you'll find churros, bunuelos, sopaipillas, fry bread, and on and on. The doughnut, with its European antecedents, has found fertile ground on this continent and has burst forth in many forms with many names. The common threads that weave them together are a few ingredients—flour, sugar, and some kind of leavening—and the deep fat that they cook in.

Rolling Sticky Doughnut Dough

Sticky, moist doughs are more easily handled if they're refrigerated for an hour or so, or even overnight. A doughnut dough that seems absolutely unworkable may be just fine after it's had a chance to "seize up" in the refrigera-tor. Also, using lots of flour (if necessary) when rolling out doughnuts won't hurt the finished product. Roll gently and quickly, and the flour, for the most part, won't be absorbed.

The Sugaring Party

In mid- to late February, as northern New England begins to tilt more and more toward the sun, the temperature in the middle of the day soars above freezing to the ethereal heights of 40°F to 50°F. The chickadee begins to sing her "sweetie" song, and we begin to hear the raucous call of the red-wing blackbird who's come back home to his cattails. But the winter-weary earth is still so cold that, as the sun drops below the horizon, so does the temperature.

This is a magical time in northern New England. Even though you can't see it happening, those lifeless-looking maple trees are beginning to pump gallons of water out of the ground, mixing them with nutrients and sugars and sending them up and out to nourish buds that have been waiting patiently in the frozen landscape. That's when sugar farmers "tap" the trees to intercept some of this spring liquor. It takes 35 to 40 gallons of it to make 1 gallon of maple syrup, which is why it's so precious.

To celebrate this momentary bounty, many folks have "sugar parties." If you're lucky enough to be the recipient of some of this year's syrup, here's how to have a party of your own.

- If you don't have any homemade sour cucumber pickles, find some at your local store.

- Then make Buttermilk Doughnuts, page 39.

- Next, take a quart of maple syrup and boil it down until two or three drops form a ball when dropped in a cup of cold water.

- Finally, cover a baking sheet with fresh, clean snow (or crushed ice if snow is not to be had), and pour the hot syrup over it, where it will stiffen like taffy. Eat it with a doughnut. Or dip your doughnuts directly into the hot syrup and skip the snow. When you think you can't eat any more, have a bite of sour pickle, and off you go again.

Fritters

Fritter is a word that encompasses a fairly wide range of comestibles, whose only common thread seems to be frying. A fritter may be made by chopping fruits or vegetables into small dice, combining with a pancakelike batter, and frying on a griddle. Or it can mean dipping pieces of fruit or vegetable in batter and deep-frying them, the Western equivalent of tempura. A fritter can also mean any small deep-fried cake, made from yeasted dough or choux paste (cream puff dough), sometimes filled with jelly or jam.

Our favorite fritters are the pancakelike kind; when made with vegetables, they're a hearty complement to a bowl of soup, or a supper side dish that goes outside the pale of vegetables/starch/salad. Fritters made with diced fruit or berries are the opposite side of the blueberry pancake coin: they're fruit bound together with a bit of batter, rather than batter enriched with a bit of fruit.

Deep-fried fritters can be made with whole pieces of fruit or vegetable, or with mashed or puréed fruit (or cheese) mixed into batter and dropped by tablespoonfuls into hot fat. Even hush puppies, that ubiquitous Southern supper side dish, are a kind of fritter.

Carrot Fritters

ABOUT 20 FRITTERS

These little gems, reminiscent of silver-dollar pancakes in size, are a little sweet, a little crunchy, and buttery-good. They're a wonderful, simple variation on that old lunchroom favorite, carrot sticks. They're also a very nice way to use some of those big, knobby carrots you pull from your garden in the summertime.

5 to 6 medium-sized carrots (3¾ cups, 14 ounces) finely chopped or grated, not puréed	1 tablespoon sugar
	⅛ teaspoon cumin (optional)
2 large eggs	¼ cup (1 ounce) unbleached all-purpose flour
½ teaspoon salt	4 tablespoons (½ stick, 2 ounces) butter

Mix carrots, eggs, salt, sugar, cumin, and flour in a medium-sized mixing bowl. Set aside.

Melt enough of the butter in a medium-sized skillet just to cover the bottom of the pan. Drop the batter by tablespoons into the hot butter. Fry fritters for a couple of minutes on each side, or until they're set and golden brown. Cool on paper towels.

nutrition information per serving   **2 fritters, 62g**

90 cal | 6g fat | 2g protein | 6g complex carbohydrates | 1g sugar | 1g dietary fiber | 56mg cholesterol | 134mg sodium | 151mg potassium | 1225RE vitamin A | 4mg vitamin C | 1mg iron | 18mg calcium | 40mg phosphorus

Blueberry Fritters

24 FRITTERS

These fritters are tender, with a touch of lemon and a bright burst of blueberry flavor. If you want them to be rounder in shape, cook them in oil that's 2 inches deep so they'll float. They're very good with a dusting of confectioners' or cinnamon sugar. Maple syrup also complements them quite nicely.

1 cup (4¼ ounces) unbleached all-purpose flour	2 large eggs, separated
½ teaspoon baking powder	1 teaspoon lemon juice
2 tablespoons sugar	⅛ teaspoon cream of tartar
½ teaspoon salt	1¼ cups (6¾ ounces) blueberries
¼ teaspoon allspice	1 to 3 cups (7 to 21 ounces) vegetable oil, for frying
½ teaspoon cinnamon	Confectioners' sugar or cinnamon sugar, for dusting

Whisk together the flour, baking powder, sugar, salt, and spices. Whip the egg yolks with the lemon juice and stir into the dry ingredients. Whip the egg whites with the cream of tartar until medium peaks form, and fold these into the batter (it will be quite stiff). Fold in the blueberries.

In a large skillet, heat half an inch of oil until the air an inch above it feels quite warm to the palm of your hand (365°F). Drop the fritter batter into it by scant tablespoons and cook until golden brown on the first side. Turn carefully with a slotted spatula to cook the second side, then drain on paper towels. Dust with confectioners' sugar or cinnamon sugar and serve warm.

nutrition information per serving   **1 fritter, 23g**

47 cal | 1g fat | 1g protein | 5g complex carbohydrates | 5g sugar | 18mg cholesterol | 19mg sodium | 19mg potassium | 9RE vitamin A | 15mg calcium | 17mg phosphorus

The fat for fritters should come halfway up the side of each one. Carefully turn them over with a spatula and a fork.

Corn Fritters

One of the late-summer treats many of us grew up with were corn fritters, on the rare occasions that there was leftover corn on the cob. A great partner to ham, they were a special treat, because they meant we could have butter and maple syrup at dinnertime. For a more savory version, you could add chopped herbs or scallions.

1 cup (4¼ ounces) unbleached all-purpose flour

1 teaspoon baking powder

1 teaspoon salt

2 large eggs

½ cup (4 ounces) milk

1 teaspoon butter, melted

3 to 4 ears (1 cup, 4¾ ounces) corn kernels

1 to 3 cups (5½ to 16½ ounces) vegetable oil, for frying

In a large mixing bowl, whisk together the flour, baking powder, and salt. In a separate, smaller bowl, whisk together the eggs and milk. Add to the dry ingredients and stir until smooth. Whisk in the melted butter, then stir in the corn kernels.

In a large skillet, heat ½ to 1 inch of vegetable oil over medium heat. To test the oil's temperature, drop in a small cube of bread. If it fries up golden brown in three minutes, you're ready to cook. Drop the fritters by tablespoons into the oil and fry until tops puff up. Turn over and finish cooking on the second side. Drain on paper towels and serve warm as a side dish or with butter and maple syrup.

nutrition information per serving   **2 fritters, 65g**

96 cal | 2g fat | 4g protein | 16g complex carbohydrates | 1g dietary fiber | 55mg cholesterol | 352mg sodium | 86mg potassium | 43RE vitamin A | 1mg vitamin C | 1mg iron | 59mg calcium | 72mg phosphorus

Hush Puppies

ABOUT THIRTY-SIX 1½-INCH HUSH PUPPIES

These little spheres of fried cornbread have humble origins, according to Southern lore. They are said to be born of leftover egg and cornmeal used to bread fish that fishermen would mix together, fry up, and toss to the hounds to keep them quiet. From there hush puppies have evolved to be a staple on many dinner tables, and there is no limit to how you can dress them up. The most consistent garnish one finds is some chopped onion, but you can tuck some bacon, cheese, even crabmeat into the batter with wonderful results.

1 to 3 cups (7 to 21 ounces) vegetable or corn oil, for frying

1¼ cups (5¾ ounces) yellow cornmeal

¾ cup (3 ounces) unbleached all-purpose flour

½ teaspoon salt

1 tablespoon sugar

½ teaspoon baking soda

¼ to ½ teaspoon ground black pepper

2 tablespoons (1 ounce) butter, melted

1 cup (8 ounces) buttermilk

1 large egg

½ cup (2 ounces) finely chopped onion or scallions

¼ cup (1 ounce) finely chopped bacon, or ¼ cup (2 ounces) shredded cheddar or pepperjack cheese (optional)

Heat 1 to 2 inches of oil in a large, heavy skillet to 375°F. In a large bowl, whisk together the cornmeal, flour, salt, sugar, baking soda, and pepper. In a separate bowl or large measuring cup, whisk together the melted butter, buttermilk, and egg. Add all at once to flour mixture, and stir in the onion and bacon or cheese, just until evenly combined.

Drop the batter by teaspoonfuls into the oil and cook for 2 to 3 minutes, turning once to ensure that they brown on all sides. Remove from the oil with a slotted spoon and drain on paper towels.

nutrition information per serving   3 hush puppies, 57g

116 cal | 3g fat | 3g protein | 18g complex carbohydrates | 1g sugar | 1g dietary fiber | 24mg cholesterol | 169mg sodium | 79mg potassium | 34RE vitamin A | 1mg vitamin C | 1mg iron | 29mg calcium | 47mg phosphorus

Fried Doughs

There seems to be a thin line between doughnuts and other fried doughs. But dough for doughnuts is noticeably sweet; if a fried dough begins with an unsweetened dough and it's served unsweetened, or if its sweetness is added later in the form of a dusting of sugar or drizzle of syrup, you'll find it in this section.

Navajo Fry Bread

FIVE 5-INCH ROUNDS

Fry bread, whether savory as an accompaniment to meals, or sweet, expressed as sopaipillas (little pillows), is a rich, warm, and comforting experience. The dough is easy to assemble and handles very nicely after its rest. The people you make it for will remember it (and you) with great warmth.

2½ cups (10½ ounces) unbleached all-purpose flour

4 teaspoons baking powder

1¾ teaspoons salt

1 tablespoon nonfat dry milk powder

3 tablespoons (1½ ounces) lard or vegetable shortening

¾ cup plus 2 tablespoons (7 ounces) ice water

1 to 3 cups (6½ to 19½ ounces) vegetable shortening or lard (½ to 1½ pounds), for frying

In a large bowl, whisk together flour, baking powder, salt, and dry milk. Cut in the lard or shortening with a fork until the dough looks like coarse meal. Pour in the ice water and stir together until dough forms a ball. Gather dough together with your hands and knead lightly to bring it together. Wrap the dough and let it rest at room temperature for at least 1 hour.

After the resting time, roll out the dough until it's ⅜ inch thick and cut it into 5-inch circles. In a large, heavy skillet, heat 1 inch of vegetable shortening to 350°F. Cut two ½-inch slits in the center of each circle of dough, then place in the oil to cook. Turn over frequently to keep the dough nice and puffy, and fry to a deep golden brown on both sides, 3 to 5 minutes. Drain on absorbent paper and cut into wedges to serve.

nutrition information per serving   ½ round, 57g

138 cal | 4g fat | 3g protein | 22g complex carbohydrates | 1g dietary fiber | 572mg sodium | 50mg potassium | 4RE vitamin A | 2mg iron | 118mg calcium | 73mg phosphorus

Sopaipillas

40 SOPAIPILLAS

1 to 3 cups (6½ ounces to 1¼ pounds) vegetable shortening or lard, for frying

1 recipe fry bread dough (see preceding recipe)

½ cup (3½ ounces) granulated sugar mixed with ½ teaspoon cinnamon

½ cup (6 ounces) honey (optional)

In a large heavy skillet, heat 1 inch of shortening to 350°F.

Roll the dough ¼ inch thick and cut into 2-inch triangles or rectangles. Fry the dough in batches, turning once, to make "little pillows" that are golden brown and puffy. Remove from the oil with a slotted spoon, drain on paper towels, then dredge the pieces in cinnamon sugar, or drizzle with honey. Serve warm.

`nutrition information per serving` **2 sopaipilllas, dusted with cinnamon sugar, 33g**

88 cal | 2g fat | 2g protein | 11g complex carbohydrates | 5g sugar | 286mg sodium | 25mg potassium | 2RE vitamin A | 1mg iron | 60mg calcium | 37mg phosphorus

Zeppole

16 ZEPPOLE

Here's a dish that appears in just about every Sons of Italy community cookbook you run across —and no two recipes are alike. Zeppole (ZAY-puh-luh), a fried dough, can be sweet, savory, or both; served hot, warm, or at room temperature, at any time of the day; and can come from a dough that is as runny as pancake batter or as stiff as firm bread dough. Just as every American has his or her own special apple pie or chocolate chip cookie recipe, so does every Italian have his or her own zeppole formula.

To many folks, zeppole should be fried without filling, then shaken in a bag of granulated or confectioners' sugar. To others, a zeppole isn't a zeppole unless it's stuffed with an anchovy to make it savory, not sweet. Or anchovy, raisins, and pine nuts, for a little savory, a little sweet.

3 to 4 cups (1¼ to 1½ pounds) vegetable oil or shortening, for frying

DOUGH

3 cups (12¾ ounces) unbleached all-purpose flour

1½ teaspoons salt

2 teaspoons instant yeast

1 tablespoon nonfat dry milk powder

1 tablespoon sugar

2 tablespoons (¾ ounce) olive oil

1 cup plus 2 tablespoons (9 ounces) water

1 2-ounce can flat anchovy fillets, rinsed and separated*

⅓ cup (2 ounces) golden raisins

¼ cup (1¼ ounces) pine nuts (optional)

In a large mixing bowl, or in the bowl of an electric mixer, combine all of the dough ingredients, mixing to form a shaggy dough. Knead the dough, by hand (10 minutes) or by machine (5 minutes) until smooth. Place the dough in a lightly greased bowl, cover, and let it rest for 1 hour.

You can also place all the dough ingredients in the pan of your bread machine, program the machine for manual or dough, and press start. About 10 minutes before the end of the second kneading cycle, check the dough and adjust its consistency as necessary with additional flour or water; the finished dough should be soft and supple, but not sticky.

To assemble, transfer the dough to a lightly oiled work surface and divide it into 16 pieces, about 1⅜ ounces (40g) each. Working with one piece at a time, flatten the dough into a rough 4 x 2-inch rectangle. Lay an anchovy piece lengthwise over the dough and space 5 to 6 raisins and a sprinkle of pine nuts along the anchovy. Fold the short edges of the dough over the ends of the anchovy, then pinch the long edges together to completely enclose the filling. Roll the dough to make a smooth log about 4½ inches long. It's important to seal the log as well as possible, otherwise the zeppole will split open during frying. Repeat with the remaining pieces of dough and filling.

While you're working with the dough, heat the vegetable oil in a deep fryer, a wide saucepan, or in an electric frying pan to a temperature of 375°F. (The zeppole can be fried in oil as shallow as ½ inch, but ¾ to 1 inch is easier.)

Transfer the zeppole, one by one, to the hot oil. Don't crowd them; using a 12-inch skillet, we were able to fry five at a time without the temperature of the oil fluctuating too wildly. Fry the zeppole for about 5 minutes, turning once; they should be a medium-golden brown. Transfer the zeppole to paper towels or to a flattened brown paper bag to drain. Serve warm or at room temperature.

*You should have 16 anchovy pieces. If not, divide one or more of the larger pieces in half.

nutrition information per serving   **1 zeppole, 60g**

207 cal | 12g fat | 4g protein | 19g complex carbohydrates | 1g sugar | 1g dietary fiber | 2mg cholesterol | 333mg sodium | 96mg potassium | 3RE vitamin A | 1mg iron | 53mg calcium | 52mg phosphorus

Funnel Cakes

ABOUT EIGHT 6-INCH CAKES

These odd-looking, lumpy disks with their dusting of powdered sugar are a staple at county fairs all over the country. Surprisingly easy to make, they are truly satisfying in their warm crunchy sweetness. Note: You'll need a funnel to make these delicacies.

6 cups (2 pounds) vegetable oil or shortening (2½ pounds), for frying

1½ cups (12 ounces) milk

2 large eggs

2 cups (8½ ounces) unbleached all-purpose flour

1 teaspoon baking powder

2 tablespoons (⅞ ounce) sugar

½ teaspoon ground cinnamon

½ teaspoon salt

¾ cup (3 ounces) confectioners' sugar

Heat oil to 375°F in a deep, heavy pan with at least 3-inch-deep sides. In a large bowl, beat together the milk and eggs. Combine the flour, baking powder, sugar, cinnamon, and salt. Stir into the egg mixture until smooth. While covering the funnel hole with one hand, pour in 1 cup of batter. Start from the center of the frying oil and, in a swirling motion, pour batter in concentric and overlapping circles to make a 6- or 7-inch round.

Fry on both sides until golden brown. Remove and drain on paper towels. Sprinkle with confectioners' sugar and serve warm.

1. Pour the batter for funnel cakes in overlapping circles to fry. **2.** Dust funnel cakes with powdered sugar.

nutrition information per serving   1 cake, with sugar, 98g

175 cal | 2g fat | 6g protein | 24g complex carbohydrates | 9g sugar | 1g dietary fiber | 55mg cholesterol | 233mg sodium | 123mg potassium | 51RE vitamin A | 2mg iron | 98mg calcium | 105mg phosphorus

Fried Dough (Frogs)

New Englanders have been enjoying fried dough since the first Colonial housewife dropped a piece of bread dough into some bubbling lard. In our annual pilgrimages to various state fairs around New England, we've sampled lots of fried dough, sometimes called frogs. It's inevitably made one of two ways—with yeast dough, which produces a flat, saucer-shaped disk akin in texture to a raised doughnut, or with baking powder dough, which makes an extremely light, highly puffed pocket, crisp on the outside and with just the thinnest layer of soft dough on the inside. Occasionally, we've seen fried dough served with tomato sauce or honey. But most often it's simply dusted with cinnamon sugar, and maple syrup aficionados can add that condiment from a pump dispenser at the end of the counter.

The following recipe is for fried dough, baking-powder style. Making these is a real visual treat: wafer-thin disks of dough are lowered into hot fat and immediately brown and puff up to astounding proportions. The kids will love to watch, but be sure to give them a vantage point a good distance away from the stove; bubbling fat is extremely dangerous with little ones around.

2 cups (8½ ounces) unbleached all-purpose flour

2 teaspoons baking powder

1 teaspoon salt

2 tablespoons (⅞ ounce) shortening

⅓ cup (2⅝ ounces) warm water

6 cups (2 pounds) vegetable oil, for deep-frying

In a large bowl, mix flour, baking powder, and salt. Cut in shortening until well combined. Stir in warm water to make a soft dough.

Turn out dough onto a well-floured surface and let rest for 15 minutes. Divide into eight pieces. Roll each piece into a 5-inch circle.

Heat oil in a deep skillet to 375°F. Pick up one dough disk with a spatula and gently lower it into hot oil. Cook for 30 to 45 seconds on each side, turning once. Remove from oil and drain on paper towels or a brown paper bag. Keep warm in a slow oven until ready to serve. Serve with melted butter and cinnamon sugar or maple syrup.

nutrition information per serving | 1 fried dough, 65g, no toppings

212 cal | 12g fat | 3g protein | 22g complex carbohydrates | 1g dietary fiber | 374mg sodium | 35mg potassium | 1mg iron | 112mg calcium | 46mg phosphorus

Churros with Chocolate Dip

ABOUT EIGHTEEN 1½-INCH BY 4-INCH CHURROS

This fried confection from Spain uses a batter that is similar to éclair dough, with a little more egg in it. When piped into strips, it makes a churro that is wonderfully crisp outside, slightly custardy inside, and just plain delicious all around. They can be sprinkled with sugar or cinnamon sugar, and dunked in chocolate sauce before eating.

6 cups (2½ pounds) oil, for frying	1 cup (4¼ ounces) all-purpose flour
1 cup (8 ounces) water	3 large eggs
8 tablespoons (1 stick, 4 ounces) butter	¼ cup (1¾ ounces) sugar
¼ teaspoon salt	¼ teaspoon ground cinnamon (optional)

Heat the oil in a deep skillet to 375°F.

Heat water, butter and salt to a rolling boil and add the flour all at once. Stir vigorously over low heat until mixture forms a ball, about 1 minute. Remove from heat. Beat in the eggs all at once and continue beating until dough is smooth. Spoon mixture into a pastry bag fitted with a star tube with a large (½-inch opening) star tip. Squeeze 4-inch strips of dough into hot oil. Fry 3 or 4 strips at a time until golden brown, turning once, about 2 minutes on each side. Drain on paper towels. Mix sugar and cinnamon, roll churros in sugar (they need gentle handling if you do this), or sprinkle the sugar over the pile on your plate.

Chocolate for Dunking

3 CUPS

⅔ cup (4 ounces) dark semisweet chocolate	1 tablespoon cornstarch
2 cups (16 ounces) milk	¼ cup (1¾ ounces) sugar

Place the chocolate and half the milk in a pan and heat, stirring, until the chocolate has melted. Dissolve the cornstarch in the remaining milk and whisk into the chocolate with the sugar. Cook on low heat, whisking constantly, until the chocolate is thickened, about 5 minutes. Add extra cornstarch dissolved in water if it doesn't start to thicken after 5 minutes. Remove and whisk smooth. Serve warm in cups or bowls for dunking churros.

nutrition information per serving   1 churro sprinkled with sugar, 37g

93 cal | 6g fat | 2g protein | 5g complex carbohydrates | 3g sugar | 50mg cholesterol | 41mg sodium | 20mg potassium | 66RE vitamin A | 1mg iron | 6mg calcium | 22mg phosphorus

Malasadas

24 MALASADAS

Folks all over America enjoy doughnuts, or the local variation thereof. The Northeast has its fried dough, the Pennsylvania Dutch their funnel cakes, New Orleans its beignets, and Hawaii has its own fried treat: malasadas.

Malasadas were brought to those islands by some of their earliest settlers, the Portuguese. A variation on Portugal's *filhoze,* malasadas (literally, "badly cooked") are small, eggy-rich balls of yeast dough, deep-fried to golden brown and coated in sugar. Just as mainland America seems to have a Dunkin' Donuts or Krispy Kreme outpost on every corner, so it is in Hawaii with malasada shops. And, far from being limited to a fast food treat, malasadas also appear on upscale restaurant menus, enclosing vanilla custard or cappuccino cream, strawberries or chocolate, and drizzled with guava sauce or caramel.

Because Hawaii's original agriculture was based on sugar, with the great majority of the land planted in cane fields, dairy products were hard to come by; most milk consumed came in cans, shipped from the mainland. Thus many traditional Hawaiian recipes call for evaporated or condensed milk, rather than fresh. Feel free to substitute light cream or half-and-half for the evaporated milk.

2½ teaspoons instant yeast	½ cup (4¼ ounces) evaporated milk
3½ cups (14¾ ounces) unbleached all-purpose flour	2 tablespoons (1 ounce) soft butter
¼ cup (1¾ ounces) granulated sugar	6 cups (2 pounds) vegetable oil, for deep-frying
1 teaspoon salt	½ cup (3½ ounces) sugar and a dash of nutmeg
3 large eggs	

In a large mixing bowl, whisk together the yeast, flour, sugar, and salt. In a separate bowl or large measuring cup, stir together the eggs, evaporated milk, and butter. Add liquid mixture to flour mixture and mix well. The dough will be sticky. Turn out onto a lightly oiled surface and knead for 5 to 6 minutes, until the dough becomes smooth and silky. Cover and let the dough rise for 1 to 1½ hours. Punch down the dough and let rise a second time until doubled in bulk. The texture of the dough will smooth out noticeably from the first to second rise.

Heat oil in a deep, heavy skillet or deep fryer to 365°F. Dip your fingertips in a bowl of oil or softened butter, then pinch off ping pong ball-sized pieces of raised dough. Drop into heated oil and cook until golden brown on one side, 3½ to 5 minutes. Turn over the malasadas and fry until golden on the other side. Use a slotted spoon to scoop them out of the oil and drain on paper towels. Roll in sugar-nutmeg mixture. Serve immediately.

nutrition information per serving

106 cal | 2g fat | 3g protein | 13g complex carbohydrates | 6g sugar | 1g dietary fiber | 30mg cholesterol | 103mg sodium | 55mg potassium | 28RE vitamin A | 1 mg iron | 19mg calcium | 42mg phosphorus

Quick Breads

Banana bread, staple of the bake sale table. Blueberry muffins, a classic breakfast treat. Baking powder biscuits, the perfect foil for a bowl of savory stew, sausage gravy, or a pot of homemade preserves. Scones, the biscuit's first cousin, highlighting the late afternoon tea break. Coffeecake, pulled warm from the oven on Sunday morning. What do all of these delicious treats have in common? They fall under the mantle of quick breads, a bread leavened with baking powder, baking soda, or eggs (rather than yeast), and put immediately into the oven, rather than rising on the counter first.

They're the answer when you want baked goods in a hurry.

Quick breads fall into two basic categories. The first is batter breads, those breads whose initial dough texture ranges from pourable to gloppy, and that are baked in a shaped pan of some kind; breads in this category include muffins, coffeecakes, batter loaves, steamed breads and puddings, and some soda breads.

Quick breads made from dough, including biscuits, scones, and traditional soda breads, usually bake free-form, without a pan to provide their shape. Some breads can go either way: scones and biscuits can be made either as dough or as a stiff batter, in which case they're called "drop" biscuits or scones (since you drop the batter from a spoon onto the baking sheet). Drop biscuits or scones are characterized by their craggy shape and slightly moister texture.

A bowl, a spoon, and your hands are all the tools you need for quick breads.

Muffins

There's nothing so soul-satisfying, so comfortingly familiar as a warm muffin, spread with sweet butter or preserves, enjoyed with a cup of coffee or tea.

Muffins are versatile players in the baking field. Add nuts; add fruit; add cinnamon, nutmeg, pumpkin pie spice, or ginger. Chocolate and other flavored chips are nice, too. Savory muffins can include chunks of cheese, dried or fresh vegetables, or even meat (sausage or bacon are both appropriate). Just remember not to be too heavy-handed with the additions; 1 cup of fruit, nuts, or other addition per cup of flour is just about the outer limit of what you can add and still expect the muffin to hold together and rise. Beyond that, there's simply more filling than muffin, and you've moved into fritters. We highly recommend a muffin scoop (see Tools, p. 605) to deliver your batter to the pans with minimal mess.

Sifting Dry Ingredients in "Stir" Recipes

There are good reasons for the dry ingredients to be sifted or whisked together before you add them to the wet ingredients. First, there's nothing quite so unappetizing as biting into a muffin or cookie and tasting a big lump of either baking powder or baking soda. Second, sifting or whisking aerates the flour, and when you add it to the wet ingredients in its aerated state you're more likely to have a light finished product.

Beaten vs. Stirred

There are two basic ways to prepare a muffin: the easy formula that barely marries the dry ingredients with the wet ingredients, and can be completed with a few simple swipes of a spoon; and a more complicated, cakelike technique that makes a more tender, finer-grained muffin.

When using the simple method of muffin preparation, the key phrase to remember is "fast and gentle." Whisk together the flour and other dry ingredients until you've created a veritable kitchen dust storm; beat the wet ingredients together until they're absolutely smooth. But once liquid meets dry—tread softly. When the protein in the flour meets liquid it forms gluten, a tough, elastic matrix of proteins whose structure traps carbon dioxide and allows bread to rise. Gluten also allows muffins to rise, but muffins don't need to rise nearly as far as bread,

and their structure sets much more quickly. Thus we want to keep gluten development to a minimum when making muffins, which means mixing muffin ingredients gently and quickly once they've combined to form a batter—just barely enough to moisten the flour is sufficient. Don't worry about any small lumps as they'll disappear during baking.

The second muffin preparation method, creaming, relies on thorough beating of the butter and sugar in the recipe, which fills it with tiny air bubbles. The resulting batter makes a fine-grained, tender product, because each of those tiny air bubbles expands as it's heated during the baking process, creating a fine rather than coarse texture in the muffin. You'll find this preparation method no different than that used for cake-making.

All-Star Muffins

16 LARGE MUFFINS

This all-purpose, basic muffin does very well with any number of garnishes (see suggestions below). The batter will keep, once mixed, for up to a week in the refrigerator. It's nice to wake up, turn on the oven, make your morning coffee, scoop two muffins, pop them in to bake, and by the time you've fetched the paper and let the dog back in, you're ready to settle down for a wonderful, warm, fresh-baked treat.

3½ cups (14¾ ounces) unbleached all-purpose or cake flour (14 ounces)

2 teaspoons baking powder

½ teaspoon baking soda

1 teaspoon salt

8 tablespoons (1 stick, 4 ounces) butter

1 cup (7 ounces) sugar

3 large eggs

2 teaspoons vanilla extract

1 cup (8 ounces) sour cream

Preheat the oven to 400°F and lightly grease 16 muffin cups or use paper liners.

In a medium-sized bowl, whisk together flour, baking powder, baking soda, and salt, then set aside.

Scoop muffin batter into greased tin, filling ¾ full.

In a large mixing bowl, cream the butter and sugar together with a handheld or stand mixer until light and fluffy and almost white in color. Scrape down the bowl to make sure all the butter is incorporated, then add the eggs, one at a time, beating well after each addition. Add the vanilla and sour cream and mix until incorporated. Add the dry ingredients and mix on low speed just until the batter is smooth. Fill muffin cups and bake for 18 to 24 minutes, until a cake tester inserted in the center comes out clean. Remove them from the oven, cool in the pan for 5 minutes, then remove the muffins from the pan to finish cooling on a rack. (Muffins left in the pan to cool will become tough from steaming.)

nutrition information per serving   **1 muffin, 73g**

274 cal | 15g fat | 4g protein | 19g complex carbohydrates | 12g sugar | 76mg Cholesterol | 254mg sodium | 57mg potassium | 148RE vitamin A | 2mg iron | 59mg calcium | 63mg phosphorus

Variations   APPLE CINNAMON: Peel and grate 3 to 4 tart apples, such as Granny Smiths or Jonathans. Fold into muffin batter with ¼ cup cinnamon sugar. Top muffins with more cinnamon sugar before baking, if desired.

APRICOT, CHERRY, CRANBERRY, DATE, RAISIN: Soak 2 cups of any of these dried fruits in ⅓ cup orange juice, water, rum, or bourbon, then fold into the muffin batter. Garnish muffin tops with chopped nuts if you like.

APPLE, BANANA, NECTARINE, PEACH, PLUM: Dice 3 cups of any of these fruits and fold into batter before baking. Garnish muffin tops with granulated sugar.

BLUEBERRY, RASPBERRY, BLACKBERRY: Fold 3 cups berries into batter before baking; sprinkle the tops with cinnamon sugar or streusel (see Muffin Tops, p. 74, for streusel) before baking.

CARROT-GINGER-RAISIN: Add 2 cups shredded carrots, ½ cup crystallized or minced fresh ginger, and 1½ cups raisins to batter before baking.

CHERRY CHOCOLATE CHIP: Add 1¼ cups dried sweet cherries (soaked in ¾ cup liquid for 20 minutes, if they're very hard) and 1¼ cups chocolate chips to batter before baking.

PEANUT BUTTER CHOCOLATE CHIP: Add 1½ cups creamy peanut butter (it helps to soften the peanut butter in the microwave before combining it with the batter) and 1½ cups chocolate chips to batter before baking.

TOFFEE CHOCOLATE CHIP: Add a 10-ounce bag of Heath bar bits or 1½ cups of your favorite buttercrunch and 1½ cups chocolate chips to batter before baking.

APRICOT ALMOND: Add ½ teaspoon almond extract, 1½ cups diced apricots, and 1 cup sliced almonds to batter before baking.

BANANA COCONUT: Add 2 diced bananas and 1½ cups shredded sweetened coconut to batter before baking.

DATE NUT: Add 1½ cups each dates and pecans to batter before baking.

MAPLE WALNUT: Add ½ cup maple sugar and 1½ to 2 cups chopped walnuts to batter before baking.

WALDORF: Add 2 tart apples, grated and peeled, ½ cup chopped dates, and ½ cup chopped walnuts to batter before baking.

Banana Chocolate Chip Muffins

12 MUFFINS

This muffin treats you to the ever-popular banana and chocolate combination, with just enough whole wheat to salve your conscience.

8 tablespoons (1 stick, 8 ounces) unsalted butter

1 cup (7 ounces) granulated sugar

1 large egg

½ teaspoon nutmeg

½ teaspoon allspice

2 medium-size ripe bananas, mashed (about ¾ cup, 5½ ounces)

⅓ cup (2¾ ounces) milk

1 cup (5 ounces) white whole wheat flour or traditional whole wheat flour (5¼ ounces)

1 cup (4¼ ounces) unbleached all-purpose flour

1½ teaspoons baking powder

½ teaspoon baking soda

½ teaspoon salt

¾ cup (4½ ounces) chocolate chips

1 cup (4 ounces) walnuts, chopped

Preheat the oven to 350°F.

In a medium-sized mixing bowl, cream together the butter and sugar until they're smooth. Scrape the bowl down, then beat in the egg, spices, banana, and milk. In a separate bowl, whisk together the dry ingredients, then gently stir them into the butter-sugar mixture.

Spoon the batter into 12 lightly greased muffin cups. Bake the muffins for 20 minutes, or until a cake tester inserted in the center comes out clean. Remove from the oven, and after 10 minutes turn them out of the pan to cool.

`nutrition information per serving`   **1 muffin, 103g**

358 cal | 18g fat | 6g protein | 21g complex carbohydrates | 23g sugar | 3g dietary fiber | 42mg cholesterol | 224mg sodium | 223mg potassium | 95RE vitamin A | 2mg vitamin C | 1mg iron | 76mg calcium | 143mg phosphorus | 2mg caffeine

Chocolate Breakfast Muffins

12 MUFFINS

Chocolate for breakfast? After all, you used to drink hot chocolate when you were a kid. And if you were in Paris right now, you might be standing on the corner outside the local *boulangerie*, a steaming cup of *café au lait* in one hand and a fresh *petit pain au chocolat* in the other.

The following muffins are rich and tender, high-rising, and deep, *deep* chocolate, both in color and flavor. Warm from the oven, spread with butter or raspberry jam, they're a totally decadent way to greet the day. We recommend them anytime you feel like treating yourself to something really special. They don't need to be relegated to the breakfast table; frosted with fudgy icing, they double as a cupcake.

⅔ cup (2 ounces) cocoa, Dutch-process or natural

1¾ cups (7¼ ounces) unbleached all-purpose flour

1¼ cups (10 ounces) light brown sugar

1 teaspoon baking powder

1 teaspoon baking soda

¾ teaspoon salt

1 cup (6 ounces) chocolate chips

2 large eggs

1 cup (8 ounces) milk

2 teaspoons vanilla extract

2 teaspoons vinegar

8 tablespoons (1 stick, 4 ounces) butter or margarine, melted

Preheat the oven to 425°F.

In a large mixing bowl, whisk together the cocoa, flour, sugar, baking powder, baking soda, salt, and chocolate chips. Set aside.

In a large measuring cup or medium-sized mixing bowl, whisk together the eggs, milk, vanilla, and vinegar. Add the wet ingredients, along with the melted butter, to the dry ingredients, stirring to blend. There's no need to beat these muffins; just make sure everything is well combined.

Scoop the batter into 12 lightly greased muffin cups. Bake the muffins for 15 to 20 minutes, or until a cake tester inserted in the center of a muffin comes out clean (watch them closely, as they'll burn around the edges if they bake too long). Remove the muffins from the oven, and after 5 minutes remove them from the pan, allowing them to cool slightly on a wire rack before serving.

nutrition information per serving   **1 muffin, 101g**

335 cal | 13.8g fat | 6g protein | 18g complex carbohydrates | 28g sugar | 3g dietary fiber | 69mg cholesterol | 273mg sodium | 265mg potassium | 101RE vitamin A | 3mg iron | 108mg calcium | 117mg potassium | 18mg caffeine

Cinnamon Puffs

12 LARGE MUFFINS

In clothes, in design, and in baking: Simple and classic go hand in hand. If it were possible to say that a breakfast muffin could personify understated elegance, this recipe would serve as proof. There is just a nuance of nutmeg to perfume the muffin, and it's a perfect foil to the cinnamon sugar on top.

MUFFINS

3 cups (12¾ ounces) unbleached all-purpose flour

1 cup (7 ounces) sugar

2½ teaspoons baking powder

1¼ teaspoons ground nutmeg

¾ teaspoon salt

2 large eggs

1¼ cups (10 ounces) milk

5⅓ tablespoons (⅔ stick, 3¼ ounces) butter, melted

TOPPING

¼ cup (1¾ ounces) sugar

½ teaspoon ground cinnamon

4 tablespoons (½ stick, 2 ounces) butter, melted

Preheat the oven to 350°F.

FOR THE MUFFINS In a mixing bowl, whisk together the flour, ½ cup of sugar, baking powder, nutmeg, and salt. Make a well in the center of the dry ingredients. In another bowl, beat the egg slightly, then add the milk and melted butter. Add the wet mixture to the well in the flour mixture. Stir just until evenly moistened (the batter may be lumpy). Lightly grease muffin cups. Fill cups about three quarters full. Bake for 20 to 25 minutes, or until muffins are golden.

FOR THE TOPPING While the muffins are baking, combine sugar and cinnamon in a small, shallow bowl until evenly blended. When muffins come out of the oven, let them cool just enough so that you can pick them up. Immediately dip the tops of the hot muffins into melted butter, then into the cinnamon sugar mixture until coated. Serve warm.

nutrition information per serving　1 muffin, 93g

278 cal | 11g fat | 5g protein | 23g complex carbohydrates | 17g sugar | 1g dietary fiber | 64mg cholesterol | 187mg sodium | 5mg potassium | 124RE vitamin A | 2mg iron | 96mg calcium | 90mg phosphorus

Classic Blueberry Muffins

12 MUFFINS

If you're a pre-1980s vintage Boston-area resident, you may recognize these muffins: they're a variation on the ones served in the cafeteria at Jordan Marsh, which was for years in fierce competition with Filene's for Boston's department-store trade. Tired shoppers, footsore and in need of comfort, could trek to the top of the Jordan Marsh building, there to enjoy a cup of tea and a king-sized blueberry muffin as they compared hat and glove and silk scarf purchases.

This is a cake-type muffin, very tender, sweet, and fine-grained. We use it whenever we want a more delicate than usual muffin; for that reason, it's one of our favorite mini-muffin recipes. We prefer to use tiny Maine blueberries when they're available, as we find them much less prone to "leaking" and breaking during the baking process. We also like to use dried blueberries, or for that matter any dried fruit—cranberries, currants, snipped apricots, apple cubes, and so forth.

8 tablespoons (1 stick, 4 ounces) butter or margarine

1 cup (7 ounces) sugar

½ teaspoon salt

2 large eggs

2 teaspoons baking powder

2 cups (8½ ounces) unbleached all-purpose flour

½ cup (4 ounces) milk

1 teaspoon vanilla extract

2½ cups fresh or dried blueberries

2 teaspoons sugar or cinnamon-sugar, for topping

Preheat the oven to 375°F. In a medium-sized mixing bowl, cream together until light the butter, sugar, and salt. Add the eggs one at a time, beating well after each addition. Add the baking powder, then add the flour alternately with the milk, beating well after each addition. Mash ½ cup of the blueberries and add them to the batter. Stir in the vanilla at the end, along with the whole blueberries.

Mound the batter into 12 lightly greased or paper-lined muffin cups, filling each completely to the top (actually, over the top; the batter is thick enough that it'll hold its shape). Sprinkle with sugar or cinnamon-sugar, if desired.

Bake the muffins for 30 minutes, or until a cake tester inserted in the center of one comes out clean. Remove the muffins from the oven, and after 5 minutes remove them from the pan to cool completely on a rack, or gently flip them sideways in the pan. (Muffins left in the pan will steam, creating a tough crust.)

nutrition information per serving   **1 muffin, 85g**

231 cal | 10g fat | 3g protein | 18g complex carbohydrates | 16g sugar | 1g dietary fiber | 59mg cholesterol | 59mg potassium | 97RE vitamin A | 1mg vitamin C | 1mg iron | 77mg calcium | 121mg phosphorus

Hot Cross Muffins

12 MUFFINS

These muffins give you the distinctive taste of hot cross buns in a quarter of the time it would take to make a sweetened yeast bread.

2 tablespoons (1 ounce) rum or water

1 cup (6 ounces) golden raisins

3 cups (12¾ ounces) unbleached all-purpose flour

1 tablespoon baking powder

⅓ cup (2¼ ounces) sugar

½ teaspoon salt

½ teaspoon cinnamon

½ teaspoon nutmeg

¼ teaspoon allspice

½ cup (3 ounces) candied citron or mixed candied fruit (optional)

2 large eggs

1½ cups (12 ounces) milk

8 tablespoons (1 stick, 4 ounces) butter, melted

FROSTING

1¼ cups (5 ounces) confectioners' sugar

2 tablespoons (1 ounce) soft butter

1 teaspoon vanilla extract

1 tablespoon milk or cream

Preheat the oven to 400°F.

In a small bowl, pour the rum or water over the raisins; set aside while you assemble all of the other ingredients.

In a large mixing bowl, whisk together the flour, baking powder, sugar, salt, and spices. Make a well in the center. Add the soaked raisins and candied peel or citron. Beat together the eggs and milk, add the melted butter, and add, all at once, to the dry ingredients. Stir until everything is evenly combined. Scoop into greased muffin cups, filling each three quarters full. Bake for 20 to 25 minutes, until a cake tester inserted in the center comes out clean. Remove from the oven and cool on a rack while you combine the frosting ingredients. When the muffins are cool, frost with a cross over the tops.

`nutrition information per serving`   **1 muffin, 115g**

321 cal | 11g fat | 6g protein | 34g complex carbohydrates | 15g sugar | 1g dietary fiber | 63mg cholesterol | 240mg sodium | 203mg potassium | 124RE vitamin A | 1mg vitamin C | 2mg iron | 122mg calcium | 113mg phosphorus

Morning Glory Muffins

12 LARGE MUFFINS OR 15 MEDIUM-SIZED ONES

Anyone who reads the recipe-swap food section of their local newspaper knows that one of the most frequently requested recipes is for Morning Glory Muffins. They're a cross between a granola bar and a carrot cake, full of all kinds of good things to get your day started. This is a muffin that holds well and will also reheat well. You could top it off with cream cheese, if you need a spread, but they're quite nice all by themselves. If you have kids that can't be talked into sitting down to breakfast, send them out the door with one of these and you know they'll have a decent start to their day.

½ cup (3 ounces) raisins

2 cups (8½ ounces) unbleached all-purpose flour

1 cup (7 ounces) sugar

2 teaspoons baking soda

2 teaspoons cinnamon

½ teaspoon ground ginger

½ teaspoon salt

2 cups (7 ounces) peeled and grated carrots

1 large tart apple (6-7 ounces), grated

½ cup (1½ ounces) sweetened shredded coconut

½ cup (2 ounces) sliced almonds or chopped walnuts

⅓ cup (1½ ounces) sunflower seeds or wheat germ (optional)

3 large eggs

⅔ cup (4¾ ounces) vegetable oil

2 teaspoons vanilla extract

Preheat the oven to 375°F and lightly grease 12 muffin cups. Put the raisins in a small bowl and cover them with hot water; set aside to soak while you assemble the rest of the recipe.

In a large mixing bowl, whisk together the flour, sugar, baking soda, spices, and salt. Add the carrots, apple, coconut, nuts, and sunflower seeds or wheat germ. In a separate bowl, beat eggs, oil, and vanilla together. Add to the flour mixture and stir until evenly combined. Drain the raisins and stir into the batter. Divide the batter among the muffin cups and bake for 20 to 25 minutes, until golden brown. Remove from the oven, let cool for 5 minutes, then turn out of the pans to finish cooling.

nutrition information per serving   1 large muffin, 106g

334 cal | 17g fat | 5g protein | 25g complex carbohydrates | 17g sugar | 2g dietary fiber | 53mg cholesterol | 339mg sodium | 202mg potassium | 541RE vitamin A | 3mg vitamin C | 2mg iron | mg calcium | 75mg phosphorus

Oatmeal Muffins

12 GENEROUS-SIZED MUFFINS

This muffin is tender, not too sweet, and very grown up in its way. If you aren't overzealous with your stirring, you'll discover little nuggets of melted brown sugar hiding within when you take your first bite. The flavor of the oats, sturdy and comforting, is right up front. Perhaps best of all, this is a low-calorie treat without tasting like one. You'll need to plan ahead, just a little, since the oats need to soak in buttermilk overnight.

1 cup (3½ ounces) quick-cooking or rolled oats

2 cups (16 ounces) buttermilk

½ cup (4 ounces) brown sugar

4 tablespoons (½ stick, 2 ounces) butter, melted

1 large egg

1 teaspoon baking powder

¾ teaspoon baking soda

¼ teaspoon salt

1½ cups (6¼ ounces) unbleached all-purpose flour

1 cup (6 ounces) raisins (optional)

In a small bowl, combine the oats and the buttermilk. Cover and refrigerate overnight.

Preheat the oven to 425°F. In a large bowl, combine the buttermilk and oat mixture, brown sugar, butter, egg, baking powder, baking soda, and salt. Gently stir in the flour and the raisins. Scoop into 12 greased muffin cups and bake for 20 minutes, until the tops are light golden brown and a cake tester inserted in the center comes out clean. Remove from the oven, let cool for 5 minutes on a rack, then turn out of the pans to finish cooling.

nutrition information per serving   **1 muffin, without raisins, 81g**

169 cal | 5g fat | 4g protein | 17g complex carbohydrates | 9g sugar | 1g dietary fiber | 30mg cholesterol | 176mg sodium | 141mg potassium | 50RE vitamin A | 1mg iron | 62mg calcium | 92mg phosphorus

Raisin Bran Muffins

12 MUFFINS

Dark brown, moist, and sweet from the brown sugar and raisins, these muffins keep well. And each one provides you with 4 grams of fiber, a lovely way to start the day.

1 cup (8 ounces) milk or buttermilk

⅓ cup (2⅜ ounces) vegetable oil

2 large eggs

¼ cup (2¾ ounces) molasses

½ cup (4 ounces) brown sugar

¾ cup (1½ ounces) wheat bran

½ cup (1¾ ounces) old-fashioned rolled oats (thick-cut oats)

1½ teaspoons cinnamon

½ teaspoon salt

1¼ cups (6½ ounces) whole wheat flour or unbleached all-purpose flour (5¼ ounces)*

1 tablespoon baking powder

½ cup (3 ounces) raisins

In a medium-sized mixing bowl, whisk together the milk, oil, eggs, molasses, and brown sugar. Add the bran and oats. Set this mixture aside for 15 minutes to give the oats and bran a chance to absorb some of the liquid and become soft. Preheat the oven to 425°F.

Whisk the remaining dry ingredients together thoroughly, making sure there are absolutely no stray lumps of baking powder remaining. Add the dry ingredients to the wet ingredients, stirring just until blended.

Spoon the batter into 12 lightly greased or paper-lined muffin cups, filling each cup almost to the top. Bake the muffins for 14 to 18 minutes, or until they spring back when pressed lightly in the middle, and a cake tester inserted in the center comes out clean. Remove the muffins from the oven, and after 5 minutes remove them from the pan (or gently flip them sideways) to cool completely on a wire rack. (Muffins left in the pan will steam, creating a tough crust.)

*Use either flour, or a combination; muffins made with 100 percent unbleached all-purpose flour will be lighter both in color and texture, but we prefer those made with whole wheat. After all, who'd expect a bran muffin to be light?

nutrition information per serving   1 muffin, 74g

203 cal | 9g fat | 5g protein | 20g complex carbohydrates | 9g sugar | 4g dietary fiber | 38mg cholesterol | 204mg sodium | 232mg potassium | 22RE vitamin A | 2mg iron | 124mg calcium | 248mg phosphorus

Spiced Peach Muffins

16 MUFFINS

These are big, high-crowned muffins that seem to explode right out of the muffin cup. We make them in our Vermont kitchen with peaches, but they're also delightful made with blueberries, blackberries, or raspberries. This is a big recipe, but once you taste one of these, you will be happy to have more than the usual dozen on hand.

4½ cups (19 ounces) unbleached all-purpose flour

1 teaspoon salt

4½ teaspoons (¾ ounce) baking powder

2 cups (16 ounces) dark brown sugar

½ teaspoon ground allspice

½ teaspoon ground nutmeg

1 teaspoon ground cinnamon

2 large eggs

¾ cup (5¼ ounces) vegetable oil

1¼ cups (10 ounces) milk

3 large peaches, diced (not peeled), or 3 cups small whole berries or other fruit, diced

Granulated sugar or cinnamon sugar

Preheat the oven to 400°F.

Combine the flour, salt, baking powder, brown sugar, allspice, nutmeg, and cinnamon in a large bowl. Whisk until brown sugar is evenly distributed and there are no lumps. In a separate bowl or large measuring cup, beat eggs, vegetable oil, and milk together, then stir into dry ingredients. Gently stir in the fruit. Grease 16 muffin cups and heap the batter into the cups; they'll be very full. Sprinkle the tops with granulated sugar. Bake for 25 to 30 minutes, or until a cake tester comes out clean. Remove from the oven, let cool for 5 minutes on a rack, then turn out of the pans to finish cooling.

nutrition information per serving   1 muffin, 130g

340 cal | 11g fat | 5g protein | 29g complex carbohydrates | 27g sugar | 2g dietary fiber | 27mg cholesterol | 298mg sodium | 237mg potassium | 40RE vitamin A | 2mg vitamin C | 3mg iron | 130mg calcium | 97mg phosphorus

Zucchini Lemon Muffins

12 MUFFINS

These muffins are light and tender, with a clean lemon flavor shining through and just a little crunch from the walnuts. Once you've made them, you won't be sorry about your zucchini plants being quite so prolific.

2 cups (8½ ounces) unbleached all-purpose flour

½ cup (3½ ounces) granulated sugar

1 tablespoon baking powder

1 teaspoon salt

Grated peel of 1 lemon, or ¼ teaspoon lemon oil

½ cup (2 ounces) chopped walnuts

½ cup (3 ounces) raisins

2 large eggs, beaten

½ cup (4 ounces) milk

½ cup (3½ ounces) vegetable oil

1 cup (8¼ ounces) packed shredded unpeeled zucchini

Preheat the oven to 400°F.

Combine the flour, sugar, baking powder, salt, and lemon peel in a large bowl. Stir in the walnuts and raisins. In a smaller bowl (or a 2-cup liquid measure), combine the eggs, milk, and oil. Make a well in the center of the dry ingredients and add the wet ingredients. Stir just until barely combined and then gently fold in the zucchini.

Spoon the batter into a greased 12-cup muffin tin and bake for 20 to 25 minutes, or until the muffins spring back when you press them with your fingertips. Remove from the oven, let cool for 5 minutes on a rack, then turn out of the pans to finish cooling.

nutrition information per serving   1 muffin, 82g

238 cal | 13g fat | 4g protein | 22g complex carbohydrates | 8g sugar | 1g dietary fiber | 307mg sodium | 171mg potassium | 14RE vitamin A | 3 mg vitamin C | 2mg iron | 92mg calcium | 82mg phosphorus

Apple Streusel Muffin Tops

9 MUFFIN TOPS

If you're one of those people who wants the top of the muffin, the whole top and nothing but the top, you probably have a pan with large shallow wells that gives you just the treat you crave. Truthfully, any muffin recipe will work to make muffin tops; all you need to do is measure out ⅓ cup of your favorite muffin recipe into the greased wells of your muffin top pan. If you want to use your quarter-cup measuring cup for a scoop, that will work fine, too. This recipe matches tart apples with the smooth sweetness of honey, and then tops it all with a crunchy, brown sugar streusel topping. These are deliciously light.

½ cup (2¼ ounces) unbleached all-purpose flour

6 tablespoons (3 ounces) brown sugar, firmly packed

Pinch of salt

½ teaspoon cinnamon (optional)

½ cup (2¼ ounces) chopped walnuts

3 tablespoons (1½ ounces) soft butter

MUFFIN TOPS

2 cups (8½ ounces) unbleached all-purpose flour

1 tablespoon baking powder

½ teaspoon salt

1 cup (5 ounces) peeled, finely chopped apples

2 large eggs

⅓ cup (4 ounces) honey

½ cup (4 ounces) milk

¼ cup (2 ounces) brandy (or an additional ¼ cup milk)

¼ cup (1¾ ounces) vegetable oil

Preheat the oven to 375°F.

FOR THE STREUSEL Mix together the flour, brown sugar, salt, cinnamon, walnuts, and butter in a small bowl, until the mixture is crumbly. Set aside.

FOR THE MUFFIN TOPS In a large bowl, combine the flour, baking powder, and salt, then stir in the apples. In another bowl, beat together the eggs, honey, milk, brandy, and vegetable oil. Gently stir the wet ingredients into the dry ingredients, mixing just until blended. Spoon muffin batter into a greased muffin top pan. Sprinkle each muffin with topping, dividing it evenly among the cups. Bake the muffins until they're golden brown, 21 to 25 minutes. Remove from the oven and let sit for 5 minutes before taking the muffins out of the pan and cooling them completely on a wire rack.

nutrition information per serving   1 muffin top, 113g

355 cal | 16g fat | 6g protein | 27g complex carbohydrates | 18g sugar | 1g dietary fiber | 59mg cholesterol | 307mg sodium | 158mg potassium | 68RE vitamin A | 1mg vitamin C | 2mg iron | 130mg calcium | 120mg phosphorus

Toaster Corncakes

9 CAKES

Here's a recipe for which we've had quite a few requests—English muffin-sized, sort-of-sweet cornbread rounds that can be split, toasted, and slathered with butter and jam. We've seen these in blueberry and cranberry versions; in the plain corn formula we offer here, the corn flavor really shines through. Serve these cakes with softened butter (they're no match for ice-cold butter and a strong knife) and strawberry jam. Other flavors can be used, but somehow strawberry is just right.

One caveat: In order to make these corncakes in their traditional shape, the shape and size that makes them ideal for splitting and toasting, you must have the proper baking pan.

An old-fashioned corncake pan, a pan with cups about 3¾ inches across and 1 inch deep, is ideal, as are English muffin rings or 3¾ by 1 inch paper crumbcake cups. Alternatively, you may bake this in a parchment-lined 9 x 13-inch pan, then cut the resulting flat loaf into nine pieces, more or less, depending on your appetite and the size of your toaster slot. What you're after is a finished cake approximately 3½ to 4 inches across and ¾ to 1 inch deep.

1½ cups (6 ounces) unbleached all-purpose flour	6 tablespoons (2⅝ ounces) sugar
¾ cup (3¾ ounces) yellow cornmeal	3 large eggs
2¼ teaspoons baking powder	⅔ cup (5½ ounces) milk
¾ teaspoon salt	8 tablespoons (1 stick, 4 ounces) unsalted butter, melted

Preheat the oven to 350°F.

In a large mixing bowl, whisk together the flour, cornmeal, baking powder, salt, and sugar. In a separate bowl, whisk the eggs and milk until thoroughly combined (we like to use a hand blender for this type of chore).

Pour the milk-egg mixture and the melted butter over the dry ingredients and stir just to combine; don't beat this mixture or the cakes will be tough.

Using a spoon or muffin scoop, scoop a generous ¼ cup (or scant ⅓ cup) of batter into nine 3¾-inch lightly greased corncake cups. The cups should be about half full, maybe a bit less. Wet your fingers and spread the batter to cover the bottom of the cups, smoothing the top at the same time. If you're using a 9 x 13-inch pan, grease it lightly (or line it with parchment) and spread the batter into it, smoothing the top.

Bake the cakes for about 18 minutes, or until the bottoms are golden brown but the tops aren't colored yet, or just barely beginning to color (since they'll be going into the toaster, you don't want them to brown too much in the oven). Remove the cakes from the oven and let them cool for 15 to 20 minutes before removing them from the cups. If you've used a 9 x 13-inch pan, let the cake cool, then cut it into nine rectangles, each approximately 3 inches wide and 4¼ inches long. Split and eat warm, or cool to room temperature, split, and toast.

nutrition information per serving   1 cake, 71g

255 cal | 11.9g fat | 5g protein | 24g complex carbohydrates | 8g sugar | 1g dietary fiber | 118mg cholesterol | 309mg sodium | 62mg potassium | 112RE vitamin A | 2mg iron | 105mg calcium | 79mg phosphorus

Corn Muffins with a Kick

12 MUFFINS OR 24 CORNSTICKS

These corn muffins, studded with vegetables, spices, and hot pepper, are a good partner for chili.

1 cup (8 ounces) milk

1 cup (4⅞ ounces) cornmeal

1½ cups (6¼ ounces) unbleached all-purpose flour

1 tablespoon baking powder

1 teaspoon ground cumin

¼ teaspoon cayenne

½ teaspoon ground black pepper

½ teaspoon salt

2 large eggs

½ cup (3½ ounces) vegetable oil

¾ cup (1⅞ ounces) minced scallions

3 tablespoons jalepeño peppers, minced

1 cup (4 ounces) shredded pepperjack cheese

Preheat the oven to 425°F and heavily grease 12 muffin cups or 2 dozen cornstick molds.

In a small bowl, pour the milk over the cornmeal and set the mixture aside to soak while you assemble the dry ingredients.

In a medium-sized bowl, whisk together the flour, baking powder, spices, and salt. Beat the eggs and add them to the cornmeal mixture with the oil. Add the cornmeal and milk to the dry ingredients, stirring until just blended; don't beat this batter or your muffins will be tough. Fold in the scallions, jalapeño peppers, and ¾ cup of the grated pepperjack cheese. Spoon the batter into the pan, filling each muffin cup ¾ full. If you're using a cornstick mold, fill each mold about ½ inch deep, spreading the batter so it completely covers the bottom of the mold. Sprinkle the remaining cheese atop the muffins, and bake them for 18 to 22 minutes, until they're golden brown.

nutrition information per serving   1 muffin, 80g

230 cal | 13g fat | 7g protein | 21g complex carbohydrates | 0g sugar | 1g dietary fiber | 45mg cholesterol | 314mg sodium | 101mg potassium | 63RE vitamin A | 1mg vitamin C | 2mg iron | 172mg calcium | 126mg phosphorus

A Sticky Situation

Crumbled muffins are surely not one of life's greatest tragedies, but aggravating nonetheless.

First, a nonstick muffin pan helps to prevent crumbling. Even if it's nonstick, however, we recommend greasing it lightly with shortening or a nonstick vegetable oil spray. This both protects the pan's finish and increases its effectiveness. If you're using a muffin pan that's not nonstick, grease it a bit more heavily and be thorough; cover every inch of the inside of the pan (and the top, too, in case muffins crown and mushroom over) with shortening or pan spray.

An alternate solution is to use paper muffin cups. If you can find cups labeled "parchment," they're your first choice; unfortunately, they aren't commonly available. Regular paper or foil muffin cups, usually printed in seasonal patterns or bright solid colors, are a good choice when you're taking the muffins somewhere—a bake sale, potluck party, or anyplace where their festive appearance will be appreciated. In addition, a paper muffin cup seems (and is) more hygienic when muffins will be shared among a group of people.

To keep muffins from becoming soggy, as well as to help them out of the pan, wait a couple of minutes after you've taken them out of the oven, then gently tip them sideways in their cups. If you pull (gently!) and the muffin doesn't budge, run a knife around the edge of the cup to help it along. If you pull, and the muffin starts to crumble, give it another 5 minutes before attempting to move it. Muffins taken out of the pan (at least partially) while they're still hot, without having had a chance to cool and harden, have less chance of sticking to the pan.

If you've baked muffins in paper, don't try to eat them right away, while they're hot; they'll probably stick to the paper. Give them a chance to cool to lukewarm, at least, before tearing into them.

So what if you've done everything right, and your muffins still stick? Low-fat muffins, without the self-lubricating quality of their higher-fat siblings, do tend to stick; it's a fact of life. Either accept it or add a bit more fat to your recipe. The flip side to this coin is that muffins very high in fat are so delicate that they have a tendency to crumble, no matter how careful you are. So experiment with the level of butter, oil or shortening in your muffin batter until you're pleased with the results.

Loaves

Stir it, spoon it into the pan, and bake—it's not surprising that the term *quick bread* often refers specifically to a loaf of bread that can be mixed together and popped into the oven in a matter of minutes. Banana bread, the dowager queen of quick breads; pumpkin bread, zucchini bread, lemon-poppyseed, cranberry-orange, date-nut —these are all familiar examples of the genre.

In fact, this is such a popular type of baking that quick bread loaves have their own special pan: the 9 x 5-inch loaf pan. While often used interchangeably with its slightly smaller sibling, the 8½ x 4½-inch loaf pan, the 9 x 5 pan is perfect for most quick bread recipes (while the smaller pan is the ideal size for most yeast bread recipes). Quick loaves are also a good candidate for bundt-style or tube pans; a 9- to 10-inch tube pan can take the place of a loaf pan when you want a more sophisticated presentation for your quick loaf. A 12 x 4 x 2½-inch pan is another choice; we like it because loaves take a bit less time to bake, assuring that your loaf doesn't get too brown on the outside. The resulting slices are also more calorie-friendly.

PDQ Apple-Date Bread

ONE LOAF, ABOUT 16 SERVINGS

This PDQ (pretty darned quick) bread is so rich and tender it's almost a coffeecake.

2½ cups (10½ ounces) unbleached all-purpose flour

1 cup (3½ ounces) oats, rolled or quick-cooking

½ cup (3½ ounces) sugar

1 tablespoon baking powder

1 teaspoon salt

¾ cup (4½ ounces) cinnamon chips

¾ cup (2¼ ounces) dried apple nuggets

½ cup (2½ ounces) chopped dates

1¼ cups (10 ounces) apple cider or juice

3 large eggs

¼ cup (1¾ ounces) vegetable oil

1 tablespoon granulated sugar or coarse white sugar (optional)

Preheat the oven to 350°F.

In a medium-sized mixing bowl, whisk together the dry ingredients and the fruits. In a separate bowl, whisk together the cider, eggs, and oil. Add the liquid mixture to the dry ingredients, stirring to moisten thoroughly. Pour the batter into a lightly greased 9 x 5-inch loaf pan. Smooth the batter into the pan and let it rest for 10 minutes. Sprinkle with sugar, if desired.

Bake the bread for 60 to 65 minutes, until a cake tester inserted in the center comes out clean. Let it cool in the pan for 15 minutes, then turn it out onto a rack to cool completely before slicing. Wrap it well for storage.

nutrition information per serving   **1 slice, 88g**

226 cal | 7g fat | 5g protein | 25g complex carbohydrates | 10g sugar | 2g dietary fiber | 40mg cholesterol | 252mg sodium | 141mg potassium | 19RE vitamin A | 2mg iron | 80mg calcium | 90mg phosphorus

Banana Bread

ONE 9-INCH LOAF, 12 THICK SLICES

This recipe produces a very moist version of banana bread. Make it with or without nuts, according to taste (kids generally prefer the nutless version). It's especially good smeared with double Devon cream or cream cheese. A friend of ours is such a banana bread aficionado, she had it served at her wedding. The bread was sliced thick, toasted, topped with vanilla ice cream, drizzled with rum-spiked caramel sauce, and sprinkled with toasted coconut. The combination of warm bread, cold ice cream, and aromatic caramel sauce was incredible; we never missed the usual white tower of a wedding cake.

2 large eggs

1 cup (7 ounces) sugar

⅓ cup (2⅜ ounces) vegetable oil

1 cup mashed banana (2 to 3 very ripe, large bananas, 7 to 9 ounces)

2 teaspoons vanilla extract

1 teaspoon baking soda

1 teaspoon baking powder

1 teaspoon salt

1 teaspoon cinnamon

½ teaspoon nutmeg

2⅔ cups (11⅜ ounces) unbleached all-purpose flour

1 cup (8 ounces) yogurt, buttermilk, or sour cream

1 cup (4 ounces) chopped walnuts

Preheat the oven to 350°F.

In a medium-sized bowl, beat together the eggs, sugar, and oil. Blend in the mashed banana and vanilla. Whisk together and then sift (it's important that these be thoroughly combined) the baking soda, baking powder, salt, cinnamon, nutmeg, and flour. Add all at once to the banana mixture. Mix quickly but thoroughly, then stir in the yogurt, mixing until just combined.

Pour the batter into a greased and floured 9 x 5-inch loaf pan. Bake the bread for about 1 hour, until a cake tester inserted in the center comes out clean. If the bread begins to brown too quickly, tent it with aluminum foil after 40 minutes in the oven.

nutrition information per serving   ¾-inch slice, ¹/₁₂ **of bread, 100g**

249 cal | 6g fat | 6g protein | 27g complex carbohydrates | 15g sugar | 2g dietary fiber | 1mg cholesterol | 305mg sodium | 207mg potassium | 5RE vitamin A | 2mg vitamin C | 1mg iron | 116mg calcium | 94mg phosphorus

Cranberry-Orange Nut Bread

ONE LARGE LOAF

Whoever decided that cranberries and oranges belonged together was so obviously right that we can only thank them and enjoy the results of their good judgment. The combination of the two flavors evokes family gatherings, brisk weather, a fire in the fireplace, and cozy mornings together.

2 cups (8½ ounces) unbleached all-purpose flour

¾ cup (5¼ ounces) sugar

1½ teaspoons baking powder

½ teaspoon baking soda

¾ teaspoon salt

1 orange, zest and juice (or ⅛ teaspoon orange oil and ¾ cup orange juice)

¾ cup (6 ounces) buttermilk, sour cream, or yogurt

1 large egg, beaten

3 tablespoons (1¼ ounces) vegetable oil

1 cup (5 ounces) cranberries: fresh, frozen, or dried, roughly chopped

½ cup (2 ounces) chopped nuts (optional)

Preheat the oven to 350°F.

In a large mixing bowl, whisk together the flour, sugar, baking powder, baking soda, and salt. In a medium-sized bowl, combine the orange juice and zest, buttermilk, egg, and vegetable oil. Add the wet ingredients to the dry in the bowl and mix until evenly combined. Stir in the cranberries and nuts, then pour the batter into a greased 9 x 5-inch loaf pan. Bake the bread for 55 to 65 minutes, until a tester inserted in the center of the loaf comes out clean and the bread starts to pull away from the edges of the pan. Remove it from the oven and cool on a rack for 15 minutes, then turn it out of the pan to finish cooling. This loaf will slice better if wrapped when cool and left to rest overnight before serving.

nutrition information per serving 1 slice, 61g

126 cal │ 3g fat,2g protein │ 13g complex carbohydrates │ 9g sugar │ 1g dietary fiber │ 14mg cholesterol │ 209mg sodium │ 69mg potassium │ 9RE vitamin A │ 7mg vitamin C │ 1mg iron │ 43mg calcium │ 41mg phosphorus

Date-Nut Bread

ONE LARGE LOAF (16 HALF-INCH SLICES)

You might think that we at King Arthur Flour never stoop to buying store-bought bread. But there are some breads that we really, really like, and this is one. The Arnold Bakery used to offer a date-nut bread that was small, really a tea–bread size, so moist and gooey that it came in its own little paper cradle. It has been one of our quests to re-create this bread, since it's a sumptuous flavor treat, especially with cream cheese. It makes wonderful little three-bite sandwiches.

¾ cup (6 ounces) boiling water

1½ cups (8 ounces) chopped dates

1 tablespoon butter

¼ cup (2¼ ounces) brown sugar

¼ cup (2¾ ounces) molasses or corn syrup

2 large eggs

1 cup (4¼ ounces) unbleached all-purpose flour

1½ teaspoons baking powder

¼ teaspoon baking soda

½ teaspoon salt

1 cup (4 ounces) chopped walnuts

Preheat the oven to 350°F.

In a medium-sized bowl, pour water over the dates and butter. Stir and let the mixture sit until lukewarm. Purée one-third of the mixture in a food processor or blender to make a paste, then stir it back into the date mixture. (This step can be left out, but it really adds to the texture of the finished product.) Add the brown sugar, molasses, and eggs. Stir until everything is thoroughly combined.

In a separate large bowl, sift together the flour, baking powder, baking soda, and salt. Make a well in the center and pour in the date mixture. Mix until all the ingredients are combined. Pour the batter into a greased 9 x 5-inch loaf pan. Bake for 60 to 65 minutes; loaves are done when the top has risen and a cake tester inserted in the center will have some dates clinging to it but no batter. You'll also see the loaf start to pull away, just slightly, from the sides of the pan. Don't overbake or you'll lose the gooey factor. Remove the bread from the oven and cool it on a rack for 10 minutes before turning it out of the pans to finish cooling.

nutrition information per serving   1 small slice, 39g

107 cal | 4g fat | 2g protein | 13g complex carbohydrates | 5g sugar | 1g dietary fiber | 18mg cholesterol | 103mg sodium | 103mg potassium | 11RE vitamin A | 1mg iron | 33mg calcium | 40mg phosphorus

Pumpkin Chocolate Chip Bread

TWO 9-INCH LOAVES, ABOUT 16 SLICES EACH

Whenever we have a company gathering this pumpkin bread is sure to be one of the first things to disappear. This makes two loaves; you can keep one in reserve and be a real hero when the first loaf is gone.

⅔ cup (4⅛ ounces) shortening or 1 cup (5½ ounces) vegetable oil

2⅔ cups (18½ ounces) sugar

4 large eggs

2 cups (or one 15-ounce can) pumpkin (not pumpkin pie filling)

⅔ cup (5¼ ounces) water

3⅓ cups (13¾ ounces) unbleached all-purpose flour

½ teaspoon baking powder

2 teaspoons baking soda

1½ teaspoons salt

1 teaspoon nutmeg

1 teaspoon vanilla extract

1 cup (4 ounces) chopped walnuts or pecans

1½ cups (9 ounces) chocolate chips

Preheat the oven to 350°F.

In a large bowl, cream together the shortening or oil and the sugar. Beat in the eggs, pumpkin, and water. Add the flour, baking powder, baking soda, salt, nutmeg, and vanilla, stirring to blend, then mix in the nuts and chips.

Spoon the batter into two lightly greased 9 x 5-inch loaf pans. Bake the bread for 1 hour, or until a cake tester inserted in the center of one loaf comes out clean. Remove the bread from the oven and cool it on a rack. When it's completely cool, wrap the loaves well in plastic wrap and store it overnight before serving.

If desired, just before serving, drizzle with icing made of 1 cup confectioners' or glazing sugar, 2 tablespoons melted butter, and 1 tablespoon milk.

nutrition information per serving   1 slice, 72g

245 cal | 12g fat | 3g protein | 11g complex carbohydrates | 21g sugar | 1g dietary fiber | 28mg cholesterol | 200mg sodium | 93mg potassium | 306RE vitamin A | 1mg vitamin C | 1mg iron | 21mg calcium | 58mg phosphorus

Lemon Bread

ONE 9-INCH LOAF, ABOUT 16 SLICES

This bread is moist, with a clean lemon flavor that lingers gracefully. If you can't get enough of that sunny flavor, brush the top with the lemon glaze while the loaves are still warm and serve with lemon butter.

BREAD

1 cup (7 ounces) sugar

½ cup (3½ ounces) vegetable oil

3 tablespoons lemon zest, or ½ teaspoon lemon oil

¼ cup (2 ounces) lemon juice

¾ cup (6 ounces) buttermilk

2 large eggs

1½ teaspoons salt

1 tablespoon baking powder

1 tablespoon poppyseeds (optional)

2½ cups (10½ ounces) unbleached all-purpose flour

LEMON GLAZE AND LEMON BUTTER (OPTIONAL)

½ cup (4 ounces) lemon juice (about 2 lemons)

⅔ cup (4⅝ ounces) sugar

8 tablespoons (1 stick, 4 ounces) butter, at room temperature

¼ teaspoon salt (if using unsalted butter)

Preheat the oven to 350°F and grease a 9 x 5-inch loaf pan.

FOR THE BREAD In a large mixing bowl, combine the sugar, oil, lemon zest, and lemon juice, beating until thoroughly combined. In a separate small bowl or large mixing cup, beat together the buttermilk and eggs. Combine the dry ingredients in a medium-sized bowl and whisk together to mix evenly. Add the dry ingredients to the sugar and oil alternately with the buttermilk mixture, scraping the mixing bowl at least once. When everything is incorporated, pour the batter into the prepared pan. Bake until a cake tester inserted in the center comes out clean, 50 to 60 minutes. Remove the bread from the oven and place it on a rack.

FOR THE LEMON GLAZE Combine the lemon juice and sugar in a microwave-safe container and microwave on high for 30 seconds to dissolve the sugar. Brush half of this mixture on the bread as it cools, if desired.

FOR THE LEMON BUTTER Take the other half of the lemon glaze and heat it in a small saucepan set over medium heat. Simmer the liquid until it has a syrupy consistency. Remove from the heat and cool to room temperature. Mix the syrup with the softened butter and salt. Chill; spread on lemon bread or your favorite fish or vegetables.

nutrition information per serving   **1 slice, not glazed, 61g**

184 cal | 8g fat | 3g protein | 14g complex carbohydrates | 12g sugar | 1g dietary fiber | 27mg cholesterol | 311mg sodium | 54mg potassium | 13RE vitamin A | 3mg vitamin C | 1mg iron | 69mg calcium | 57mg phosphorus

Maple Cornbread

9 SERVINGS

Increasingly, King Arthur Flour's loyal customers communicate with us via e-mail, and we love it. It's thrilling (albeit somewhat eerie) to sit and read e-mails, in succession, from bakers in Alaska, South Carolina, Texas, and Maine on www.bakingcircle.com. The following message came from Carol Stevens, who wrote as follows:

"I'm sending you a recipe for maple cornbread. Even though you're in Vermont and have probably put maple syrup into everything imaginable, I thought you might like this recipe. I made it for my Mardi Gras 'thing' of red beans and rice for dinner. Of course it was King Arthur Flour as well as Vermont maple syrup that made it so yummy!)"

We found this dense, sturdy cornbread to be just slightly sweet, with a bare hint of maple. For you Southerners who decry the Northern use of sugar in cornbread, read no further; we confess, this is a north of the Mason-Dixon line aberration. But to those of you who don't object to sweetened cornbread, read on; we think this is just the ticket with a bowl of chili or stew.

1 cup (4¼ ounces) unbleached all-purpose flour	1 cup (8 ounces) milk, whole, skim, or 2 percent
1 cup (4¾ ounces) yellow cornmeal	¼ cup (2¾ ounces) maple syrup
1 tablespoon baking powder	4 tablespoons (½ stick, 2 ounces) butter, melted
½ teaspoon salt	2 large eggs

Preheat the oven to 425°F. Lightly grease an 8 x 8-inch square or 9-inch round baking pan.

In a medium-sized mixing bowl, whisk together the flour, cornmeal, baking powder, and salt until thoroughly combined. In a small bowl or a large measuring cup, whisk together the milk, maple syrup, melted butter, and eggs. Add the liquid mixture to the dry ingredients and stir just until moistened.

Pour the batter into the prepared pan and bake the cornbread for 20 to 25 minutes, until it's lightly browned and a cake tester inserted in the center comes out clean. Remove it from the oven and serve it warm with butter and additional maple syrup, or with a main dish—red beans and rice would be nice.

nutrition information per serving 1 piece made with whole milk, ⅑ of recipe, 83g

203 cal | 7g fat | 5g protein | 23g complex carbohydrates | 6g sugar | 2g dietary fiber | 65mg cholesterol | 372mg mg sodium | 115mg potassium | 84RE vitamin A | 2mg iron | 136mg calcium | 105mg phosphorus

Walnut-Strawberry Quick Bread

ONE LOAF

We love this bread no matter which way we make it: all strawberry, all rhubarb, or a combination of the two. We also used half a cup of applesauce in one recipe with great success when we ran short of strawberries.

½ cup (2 ounces) chopped walnuts

1½ cups (6¼ ounces) unbleached all-purpose flour

1 cup (7 ounces) sugar

½ teaspoon baking soda

¼ teaspoon salt

¼ teaspoon nutmeg

1 tablespoon lemon zest, or ¼ teaspoon lemon oil

2 large eggs

1¼ cups (10 ounces) mashed strawberries

½ cup (2¾ ounces) vegetable oil

Preheat the oven to 350°F. Grease and flour (or spray with nonstick vegetable oil spray) a 9 x 5-inch loaf pan.

In a medium-sized mixing bowl, whisk together the walnuts, flour, sugar, soda, salt, and nutmeg. In a separate bowl, whisk together the lemon zest, eggs, strawberries, and vegetable oil. Combine the wet ingredients with the dry ingredients, whisking until well-blended.

Pour the batter into the prepared pan, and bake for 55 to 60 minutes, until a cake tester inserted in the center comes out clean. Cool the bread in the pan for 15 minutes, then remove it from the pan and transfer it to a rack to cool completely, 1 hour or longer. For best flavor and easiest slicing, wrap the bread while still slightly warm and let it sit overnight.

Rhubarb Variation Use 1¼ cups cooked rhubarb in place of the strawberries, to make a slightly tart bread. Start with 2½ cups sliced rhubarb. Cook over medium heat (or in the microwave) to make about 1¼ cups unsweetened rhubarb sauce. If you use only rhubarb (no strawberries) in your bread, increase the sugar to 1¼ cups. You may also substitute rhubarb for just some of the strawberries, to make strawberry-rhubarb bread. No need to increase the sugar in that case.

nutrition information per serving ¹⁄₁₂ **of loaf made with strawberries, 65g**

242 cal | 13g fat | 3g protein | 13g complex carbohydrates | 16g sugar | 1g dietary fiber | 35mg cholesterol | 108mg sodium | 93mg potassium | 17RE vitamin A | 14mg vitamin C | 1mg iron | 12mg calcium | 48mg phosphorus

Bacon Cheddar Cornbread

9 SERVINGS

This recipe uses the spice cumin, which has a warm, toasty flavor. Cumin is popular in chili recipes, but it isn't hot at all. Fresh or frozen corn will work for this recipe, and both are equally good. So don't wait until summer to make it.

1½ cups (6¼ ounces) unbleached all-purpose flour

¾ cup (3⅝ ounces) yellow cornmeal

1 tablespoon baking powder

½ teaspoon salt

3 tablespoons (1¼ ounces) sugar

1½ teaspoons cumin

1 large egg, beaten

1 cup (8 ounces) milk

¼ cup (1¾ ounces) vegetable oil

1 cup (4¾ ounces) cooked or thawed corn kernels

6 ounces (6-7 slices) bacon, cooked and crumbled

1 cup (4 ounces) grated cheddar cheese

Preheat the oven to 400°F and grease an 8-inch square pan.

Whisk together the flour, cornmeal, baking powder, salt, sugar, and cumin in a medium-sized bowl. In a separate bowl, whisk together the egg, milk, and vegetable oil and add to the dry ingredients. Stir in the corn, bacon, and cheese.

Spread the batter in the pan and bake for 30 minutes, or until it's golden brown and a cake tester inserted in the center comes out clean. Remove it from the oven and cool on a rack.

nutrition information per serving   one 2½ inch square, 105g

232 cal | 8g fat | 10g protein | 29g complex carbohydrates | 4g sugar | 2g dietary fiber | 42mg cholesterol | 457mg sodium | 164mg potassium | 74RE vitamin A | 2mg vitamin C | 2mg iron | 222mg calcium | 202mg phosphorus

Herbed Beer Bread

ONE 9-INCH LOAF, ABOUT 16 SLICES

Beer can't happen without yeast, and the carbonation produced by both yeast and beer is a nice touch in a quick bread. The aromatic quality of beer, the flavor of herbs, and some sunflower seeds for crunch make this a tasty loaf.

2 cups (8½ ounces) unbleached all-purpose flour

½ cup (2⅝ ounces) whole wheat flour

½ cup (2⅞ ounces) semolina

1 tablespoon baking powder

1 teaspoon salt

2 tablespoons (1 ounce) sugar

1 12-ounce bottle of beer

3 tablespoons (1 ounce) vegetable oil

¾ cup (3½ ounces) hulled sunflower seeds

1 teaspoon each: dried parsley, sage, rosemary, and thyme

Preheat the oven to 350°F and grease a 9 x 5-inch loaf pan.

In a large bowl, mix together the flours, baking powder, salt, and sugar. Add the beer and oil and stir until the batter is evenly moistened. Stir in the sunflower seeds and herbs, then pour the batter into the prepared loaf pan. Bake the bread for 45 minutes, until a tester inserted in the center comes out clean. Remove it from the oven and cool it in the pan for 15 minutes on a rack. Run a dull knife around the edge of the bread and turn it out of the pan to finish cooling.

nutrition information per serving   1 slice, 59g

166 cal | 7g fat | 4g protein | 20g complex carbohydrates | 2g sugar | 2g dietary fiber | 226mg sodium | 86mg potassium | 1RE vitamin A | 2mg iron | 59mg calcium | 138mg phosphorus

PDQ* Onion Rye Bread

ONE LOAF, ABOUT 12 SERVINGS

*As in pretty darned quick. It's almost an oxymoron: rye bread, traditionally made with a starter and treated to a long, slow rise, being quickly made. But you can mix up the baking powder–leavened batter for this tender, moist bread in just a couple of minutes. A hot, delicious loaf will be on your table in less than an hour, start to finish. We love to serve this toasted and buttered, with eggs at breakfast or with stew or soup later in the day. It also makes a tasty open-faced Reuben or pastrami sandwich.

1¾ cups (7¾ ounces) medium rye flour

¾ cup (3 ounces) unbleached all-purpose flour

1½ teaspoons salt

1 tablespoon sugar

1 teaspoon caraway seeds

1¼ cups (3½ ounces) French fried onions or baking onions, crushed

2 teaspoons baking powder

¼ teaspoon baking soda

3 tablespoons (1¼ ounces) vegetable oil

1 tablespoon vinegar or dill pickle juice

1 large egg

1 cup (8 ounces) water

½ cup (4 ounces) sour cream

Preheat the oven to 350°F and grease an 8½ x 4½-inch loaf pan.

In a medium-sized bowl, whisk together the dry ingredients, setting aside ¼ cup of the onions to sprinkle on top of the loaf before baking. In another bowl (or in a liquid measure), whisk together the oil, vinegar, egg, water, and sour cream, then stir the liquid ingredients into the dry ingredients, mixing just until blended. The mixture will look a bit lumpy.

Pour the batter into the prepared pan and sprinkle with the onions. Bake the bread for 50 to 55 minutes, or until a tester inserted in the center comes out clean. Remove the bread from the oven, wait 5 minutes, then turn it out of the pan and cool it on a rack.

nutrition information per serving | 1 slice, 68g

157 cal | 6g fat | 4g protein | 24g complex carbohydrates | 1g sugar | 3g dietary fiber | 21mg cholesterol | 386mg sodium | 186mg potassium | 24RE vitamin A | 24mg vitamin C | 1mg iron | 79mg calcium | 90mg phosphorus

Rosemary Cheddar Cheese Bread

TWO LOAVES, 12 SLICES PER LOAF

We love the combination of rosemary and cheddar cheese, so we combined them here in a marbled quick bread. Our recipe calls for making two batters, one with whole wheat flour, and the second, lighter-colored batter, with cheddar cheese. While this two-batter bread requires an extra step, it's very easy to put together and the results are well worth it. The loaf is very pretty and tastes great.

ROSEMARY WHOLE WHEAT BATTER

1 large egg

1¼ cups (10 ounces) milk

4 tablespoons (½ stick, 2 ounces) softened butter

1 tablespoon baking powder

1 tablespoon dried rosemary

½ teaspoon salt

2 cups (10½ ounces) whole wheat flour or white whole wheat flour (10 ounces)

CHEDDAR CHEESE BATTER

1 large egg

1 cup (8 ounces) milk

4 tablespoons (½ stick, 2 ounces) butter, melted

1 tablespoon baking powder

½ teaspoon salt

¼ teaspoon cayenne

½ teaspoon ground black pepper

2 cups (8½ ounces) unbleached all-purpose flour

1¼ cups (5 ounces) grated cheddar cheese

Preheat the oven to 350°F. Grease two 8½ x 4½-inch loaf pans.

FOR THE ROSEMARY BATTER Beat the egg and add the milk and the softened butter. Stir well. Mix together the baking powder, rosemary, salt, and flour. Stir with a whisk to incorporate all the ingredients. Add the egg mixture and stir just until combined. Put half of the batter into each of the two prepared pans.

FOR THE CHEESE BATTER In a medium-sized bowl, beat the egg, then stir in the milk and butter. In a separate bowl, whisk together the baking powder, salt, cayenne, black pepper, and flour. Stir in the cheese, then the milk mixture, stirring just until combined.

Pour half of the cheddar batter into each pan on top of the rosemary batter. Use a table knife and stick it, point down, all the way through the batter to the bottom of the pan. Keep the tip touching the bottom of the pan and drag the knife through the batter in curving motions until the loaf is marbled. Repeat with the second loaf.

Bake the loaves for 50 to 60 minutes, or until nicely browned and a cake tester inserted in the middle of a loaf comes out clean. Remove from the oven and let them rest for 5 to 10 minutes before turning out onto a cooling rack.

nutrition information per serving   **1 slice, 55g**

114 cal | 3g fat | 5g protein | 16g complex carbohydrates | 2g dietary fiber | 25mg cholesterol | 264mg sodium | 102mg potassium | 41RE vitamin A | 1mg iron | 142mg calcium | 132mg phosphorus

Savory Christmas Bread

ONE 10-INCH LOAF, ABOUT 16 THIN SLICES

Red, green, and gold: the colors of Christmas. And what nicer way to show the colors than in a tasty loaf of bread? This easy-to-make baking powder bread handles surprisingly like a yeast bread. It bakes as a free-standing loaf, and can even be braided if you're feeling fancy. Sun-dried tomatoes (or pimientos) and finely chopped green pepper (or chives) sprinkled throughout give this loaf a festive appearance

3 cups (12¾ ounces) unbleached all-purpose flour

2 teaspoons baking powder

1 teaspoon salt

8 ounces provolone cheese, grated (approximately 2 cups)

4 large eggs, beaten

½ cup (4 ounces) evaporated milk

3 large garlic cloves, minced

¼ cup (½ ounce) finely chopped green pepper (or fresh chives or green part of scallions)

¼ cup (1½ ounces) finely chopped sun-dried tomatoes (or drained pimientos or red bell pepper)

Preheat the oven to 350°F.

In a medium-sized bowl, mix together the flour, baking powder, salt, and cheese. Add the beaten eggs, reserving 2 tablespoons for glazing the bread before baking. Mix in the evaporated milk, garlic, and vegetables, stirring to make a soft dough.

Turn out the dough onto a well-floured surface and form it into a smooth ball. Roll the ball into a log shape about 10 inches long. Place it on a greased cookie sheet. Brush with the reserved beaten egg.

Bake for 30 to 35 minutes, or until the loaf is golden brown. Cool thoroughly. To serve, cut into very thin slices, fanning slices onto a plate. Bread is delicious as is, or can be spread with butter.

Just a Hint

Use a good-quality pair of shears to chop many kinds of herbs and vegetables. Snip parsley, chives, or other fresh herbs; use the part of the scissor blade closer to the handle to cut tougher items, like scallions, celery stalks, or sun-dried tomatoes.

nutrition information per serving | **1 slice, 60g**

154 cal | 5g fat | 8g protein | 18g complex carbohydrates | 1g dietary fiber | 63mg cholesterol | 359mg sodium | 121mg potassium | 73RE vitamin A | 2mg vitamin C | 2mg iron | 171mg calcium | 144mg phosphorus

Turning Quick Bread Batter into Muffins (and vice versa)

A typical quick bread recipe using 1½ to 2 cups of flour will fill about a dozen regular-sized (about 2½-inch diameter) muffin cups. Prepare the quick bread batter, grease the muffin cups, fill them to nearly full, and bake in a preheated 425°F oven for 18 to 22 minutes, or until they're puffed, set on the top, and a cake tester inserted in the center of one comes out clean.

Or try the reverse: take a favorite 12-muffin recipe and make it into a quick loaf. If the recipe calls for about 2 cups of flour, use a 9 x 5-inch loaf pan; for 1½ cups of flour (or less), use an 8½ x 4½-inch pan. For amounts in between, well, use your best judgment; the batter should fill the pan about two-thirds full. Bake the bread in a preheated 350°F oven for 50 to 70 minutes (though generally around 55 to 60 minutes); times may vary depending on the exact amount of the batter, and the composition of any "add-ins"; juicy additions such as berries will make for a slightly longer bake.

Coffeecakes

Coffeecake is a weekend treat, when you actually have the time to bake a cake and take the time to enjoy it. Open the Sunday paper and serve yourself a square of cake from the corner, where big, sweet nuggets of streusel gather and melt. Go ahead, lick your cinnamon-buttery fingers.

Apricot Butter–Almond Cake

ABOUT 12 RICH SERVINGS

This cake started out as Sticky Toffee Pudding, a traditional English cake made with dates. (The word *pudding* in English cuisine refers to desserts in general.) While we really like the original cake, this incarnation, a moist, rich, tender, and buttery cake/coffeecake, is suitable for dessert or brunch.

CAKE
5⅓ tablespoons (⅔ stick, 2⅔ ounces) butter
¾ cup (5¼ ounces) sugar
2 large eggs
¾ cup (9 ounces) apricot preserves, preferably unsweetened

1⅛ cups (4¾ ounces) unbleached all-purpose flour
2 teaspoons baking powder
Heaping ¼ teaspoon salt
½ cup (4 ounces) milk

TOPPING

¾ cup (6 ounces) brown sugar, packed

6 tablespoons (3 ounces) butter

Heaping ⅛ teaspoon salt (if using unsalted butter)

¼ cup (2 ounces) heavy cream or evaporated milk

½ cup (1½ ounces) sliced almonds

2 teaspoons vanilla extract or 2 to 3 drops vanilla-butternut or butter-rum flavor

FOR THE CAKE Preheat the oven to 350°F.

In a medium-sized mixing bowl, cream together the butter and sugar until light. Beat in the eggs one at a time, beating well after each addition. If the mixture looks curdled at any point, don't panic; it'll straighten itself out as you go along. Stir in the apricot preserves.

In a separate bowl, whisk together the flour, baking powder, and salt. Add the dry ingredients to the egg mixture alternately with the milk, beating to combine.

Pour the batter into a lightly greased 9-inch round or 8-inch square baking pan. Bake the cake for 25 to 30 minutes, until a cake tester inserted in the center comes out clean. Remove the cake from the oven and allow it to cool for about 10 minutes while you preheat your broiler.

FOR THE TOPPING While the cake is baking, make the topping. In a small saucepan, heat over low to medium heat the brown sugar, butter, salt, and cream. Simmer the mixture gently over low heat, uncovered, for 15 minutes; when you see ½-inch bubbles forming and breaking with a snapping sound, remove it from the heat and stir in the almonds and the flavoring.

TO ASSEMBLE Spread the warm topping over the cake. Broil it 1 inch from the heat for just about 1 minute; the topping will bubble and become golden brown. Watch it carefully. If you're nervous, broil it for a longer amount of time a bit farther from the heat. Remove the cake from the oven and allow it to cool for 20 minutes before slicing.

Coffeecakes and Variations

What's the difference between coffeecake and just plain cake? Not much. Generally, coffeecakes aren't frosted (though they may be drizzled with icing); are made into a sheet or bundt-type cake, rather than layered; and don't range quite as widely through the flavor spectrum.

nutrition information per serving   1 slice, 103g

351 cal | 16g fat | 4g protein | 11g complex carbohydrates | 38g sugar | 1g dietary fiber | 69mg cholesterol | 194mg sodium | 164mg potassium | 136 RE vitamin A | 5mg vitamin C | 1mg iron | 94mg calcium | 95mg phosphorus

Banana Split Coffeecake

12 TO 16 SERVINGS

This is a dessert coffeecake we created when faced with an overabundance of very ripe bananas and no sour cream for a traditional coffeecake recipe. This moist, chocolaty marble cake with its ultra-rich chocolate glaze is a winner.

CAKE

¾ cup (4½ ounces) semisweet chocolate chips

1 large or 2 small (8 ounces) very ripe bananas (to make ½ cup purée, about 4 ounces)

3 large eggs, at room temperature

1½ cups (10½ ounces) sugar

3 cups (12¾ ounces) unbleached all-purpose flour*

1½ teaspoons baking powder

1 teaspoon baking soda

½ teaspoon salt

1 cup (7 ounces) vegetable oil

1 cup (8 ounces) buttermilk, at room temperature

2 teaspoons vanilla extract

GLAZE

¾ cup (4½ ounces) semisweet chocolate chips

3 tablespoons (1½ ounces) butter

¼ cup (2 ounces) light cream or half-and-half

1 tablespoon light corn syrup (optional, but keeps the sauce easier to pour, like hot fudge sauce)

Slivered almonds, to garnish

FOR THE CAKE Position a rack in the middle of the oven and preheat the oven to 350°F. Grease and flour a 10-inch bundt-style pan.

Place the chocolate chips in a medium-sized bowl and melt them over simmering water, or in the microwave. Set aside. Place the bananas in a bowl and mash them with a fork; set aside.

Place the eggs in a large mixing bowl and beat them on high speed of an electric mixer, using a whisk attachment if you have one, until they're light and foamy. Gradually add the sugar and beat until the mixture is thick, about 5 minutes on high speed.

While the eggs are beating, sift the flour, baking powder, baking soda, and salt onto a piece of parchment paper and set aside.

Gradually add the vegetable oil to the egg mixture, scraping down the sides of the bowl. Continue to beat for another minute. Stir in the buttermilk and vanilla.

Remove the bowl from the mixer and fold in the dry ingredients. Pour approximately 1½ cups (14½ ounces) of the batter over the melted chocolate and gently mix until the chocolate and batter are well-blended. Fold the mashed banana into the remaining batter.

Pour half the banana batter into the prepared pan. Pour the chocolate batter over this, and top with the remaining banana batter. Swirl the two batters together with a short-bladed knife.

Bake the cake for 65 to 70 minutes, or until a cake tester inserted in the center comes out clean. Allow the cake to cool for at least 15 minutes before removing it from the pan. Glaze it when it's completely cool. This cake keeps for several days in an airtight container.

FOR THE GLAZE Place the chocolate chips, butter, cream, and syrup in a heatproof bowl. Heat in the microwave or over just-simmering water until most of the chips and butter are melted. Stir until the remaining chips and butter are melted and the mixture is smooth. Allow the glaze to cool to approximately 90°F, or until it's only slightly warm.

Pour the glaze over the cake, allowing it to run down and cover the sides. It's not essential that the entire cake be covered; don't be fussy. Sprinkle the top of the cake with slivered almonds. Refrigerate the cake, or set it somewhere cool until the glaze is set. (The glaze that has run off the cake may be scooped up with a rubber spatula and kept in the refrigerator for several weeks; it's delicious over ice cream.)

*For a lighter, "sandier" texture you may substitute cake flour for unbleached all-purpose flour.

nutrition information per serving   ¹⁄₁₆ **of cake, glaze made with light cream, 110g**

409 cal | 23g fat | 5g protein | 18g complex carbohydrates | 27g sugar | 2g dietary fiber | 65mg cholesterol | 191mg sodium | 155mg potassium | 48RE vitamin A | 1mg vitamin C | 2mg iron | 89mg calcium | 87mg phosphorus | 5mg caffeine

Classic Cinnamon-Nut Coffee Ring

ABOUT 18 SERVINGS

This cinnamon streusel coffeecake is a tender, crumbly butter cake shot through with whorls and chunks of cinnamon-sugar.

CAKE

5 tablespoons (2½ ounces) butter, or 5 tablespoons (2 ounces) butter-flavored shortening

⅓ cup (2⅜ ounces) vegetable oil

1 cup (7 ounces) sugar

3 large eggs

1 teaspoon salt

1 teaspoon ground cinnamon

2 teaspoons vanilla extract

2¼ cups (9½ ounces) unbleached all-purpose flour

2 teaspoons baking powder

½ teaspoon baking soda

1 cup (8 ounces) sour cream (light or regular, or substitute yogurt)

FILLING

½ cup (2 ounces) chopped walnuts or pecans

½ cup (3 ounces) chocolate chips (optional)

½ cup (3½ ounces) sugar

½ cup (2¼ ounces) unbleached all-purpose flour

1 teaspoon cinnamon

3 tablespoons (1½ ounces) butter, melted

Preheat the oven to 350°F.

FOR THE CAKE In a medium-sized mixing bowl, beat together the butter, oil, and sugar until fluffy. Add the eggs one at a time, beating well after each addition. Add the salt and flavorings and beat until evenly incorporated.

In a separate bowl, whisk together the flour, baking powder, and baking soda. Add the flour mixture to the butter-egg mixture alternately with the sour cream, mixing on slow speed just until blended.

FOR THE FILLING In a small mixing bowl, combine the nuts, chocolate chips, sugar, flour, cinnamon, and butter.

Spoon half of the cake batter into a lightly greased 9- or 10-inch tube or bundt-style pan. Smooth the batter to level it and sprinkle on two thirds of the filling. Top with the remaining batter and sprinkle with the remaining filling.

Bake the cake for 45 to 55 minutes, until a cake tester inserted in the center comes out clean. The smaller (9-inch) pan will take the longer time to bake. Remove the cake from the oven and let it cool in the pan for 15 minutes. Turn out onto a wire rack. Cool it completely, then sprinkle with confectioners' sugar before serving, if desired.

nutrition information per serving ½-inch slice, ¹⁄₁₈ of cake, 75g

291 cal | 16g fat | 4g protein | 16g complex carbohydrates | 19g sugar | 1g dietary fiber | 55mg cholesterol | 265mg sodium | 73mg potassium | 87RE vitamin A | 1mg iron | 58mg calcium | 108mg phosphorus | 4g caffeine

Cranberry Almond Coffeecake

SIXTEEN ¾-INCH SLICES

Thanksgiving: a day of thanks. The day after Thanksgiving: a day of leftovers. Is there any holiday that rivals Thanksgiving for producing a refrigerator stuffed with half-full plastic containers and knobby foil-wrapped bundles of food?

The turkey usually disappears quite easily. The pies eventually vanish, too. The vegetables get thrown into soup, or are reborn as potato bread. Eventually, the refrigerator empties and things get back to normal.

But that lonely bowl of cranberry sauce gradually works its way to the back of the refrigerator, where it's forgotten and eventually grows old enough to throw away.

Here's the solution. While the leftovers are being dealt with Thursday night, scoop out a cup or so of cranberry sauce and put it in a special spot in the fridge. Sunday morning, make the following coffeecake. You'll have it on hand to serve holiday-weekend visitors, or the straggling remnants of your visiting family.

CAKE

8 tablespoons (1 stick, 4 ounces) butter

1 cup (7 ounces) granulated sugar

2 large eggs

1 cup (8 ounces) buttermilk or yogurt (nonfat is fine)

1 teaspoon almond extract

1 teaspoon baking powder

1 teaspoon baking soda

2 cups (8½ ounces) unbleached all-purpose flour

½ teaspoon salt

1 cup (7½ ounces) cranberry sauce (whole berry is preferable)

½ cup (1½ ounces) blanched slivered almonds, toasted

GLAZE

¾ cup (3 ounces) confectioners' sugar

2 tablespoons (1 ounce) milk

½ teaspoon almond extract

Preheat the oven to 350°F.

FOR THE CAKE In a large bowl, cream together the butter and sugar. Beat in the eggs, buttermilk, and almond extract. In a separate bowl, mix together the baking powder, baking soda, flour, and salt. Add all at once to the wet ingredients, stirring just to blend.

Grease and flour a 9- or 10-inch tube pan. Spoon half the batter into the pan. Spread half the cranberry sauce evenly atop the batter, then spread the remaining batter over that. Top with the remaining cranberry sauce and sprinkle toasted almonds evenly over the sauce.

Bake the coffeecake for 55 minutes, or until a cake tester inserted in the center comes out clean. Remove it from the oven, and cool it in the pan for 5 minutes.

While the cake is cooling, make the glaze by mixing confectioners' sugar, milk, and almond extract. Turn the cake out of the pan and dribble the glaze over the warm cake. Let the cake cool completely before serving (or serve it warm if you don't mind it crumbling a bit).

nutrition information per serving   1 slice, ¹⁄₁₆ of cake, 85g

240 cal | 9g fat | 4g protein | 13g complex carbohydrates | 23g sugar | 1g dietary fiber | 43mg cholesterol | 211mg sodium | 93mg potassium | 68RE vitamin A | 1mg iron | 54mg calcium | 74mg phosphorus

Crumb Coffeecake

SIXTEEN 2-INCH WEDGES, TWENTY-FOUR 2-INCH SQUARES, OR SIXTEEN 1½-INCH SLICES

This coffeecake is the culmination of a longtime quest to recapture a certain kind of moist, pick-up-with-one-finger, clean-the-plate-coffeecake crumb. After a lot of trial and error, we discovered what was missing was a simple technique: to melt the butter before combining it with the sugar and flour. It made all the difference. This coffeecake is downright irresistible.

The recipe will make two 8-inch round coffeecakes, or fill a 9 x13-inch pan, or a 9- or 10-inch tube pan.

CRUMB

2½ cups (8½ ounces) unbleached all-purpose flour

1¼ cups (8¾ ounces) sugar

½ teaspoon salt

1½ teaspoons cinnamon

1 cup (2 sticks, 8 ounces) butter, melted

1 teaspoon vanilla extract

¾ teaspoon almond extract

CAKE:

8 tablespoons (1 stick, 4 ounces) butter

1 cup (7 ounces) sugar

2 large eggs

1 teaspoon vanilla extract

1 cup (8 ounces) sour cream

2 cups (8½ ounces) unbleached all-purpose flour

½ teaspoon baking soda

½ teaspoon salt

1 teaspoon baking powder

Confectioners' sugar, for dusting

Preheat the oven to 350°F. Grease the preferred pan(s).

TO MAKE THE CRUMB In a medium-sized mixing bowl, whisk together the flour, sugar, salt, and cinnamon. Melt the butter in the microwave or small saucepan and add the extracts to it. Pour the butter into the flour mixture and mix until all the butter is absorbed and you have a uniformly moistened crumb mixture. Set aside while you make the cake batter.

TO MAKE THE BATTER In a large mixing bowl, cream the butter and sugar until light and fluffy. Add the eggs one at a time, and beat between additions. Scrape down the mixing bowl, then beat in the vanilla and sour cream. In a medium-sized bowl, whisk the flour, baking soda, salt, and baking powder together. Add to the butter/sour cream mixture, mixing until evenly combined. Pour the batter into the greased baking pan(s). Crumble the crumb mixture over the top, until the batter is completely covered. Bake for 20 to 25 minutes for 8-inch rounds, 30 to 35 minutes for a 9 x 13-inch pan, or 35 to 40 minutes for a 9- or 10-inch tube pan. Bake until a tester inserted in the center comes out clean. Remove the cake from the oven and cool on a rack; dust the top with confectioners' sugar, if desired.

nutrition information per serving   2-inch square, 58g

242 cal | 14g fat | 2g protein | 9g complex carbohydrates | 18g sugar | 54mg cholesterol | 154mg sodium | 36mg potassium | 135RE vitamin A | 1mg iron | 28mg calcium,33 mg phosphorus

Almond Puff Loaf

TWO LOAVES, 10 SLICES EACH

This recipe seems as if it can't be right—there's no sugar in the dough! But just follow the recipe and you'll be rewarded with a pastry that is remarkably elegant. The buttery crust supports a tender, almond-scented layer of airy pastry, which in turn is dressed up with a luxuriant layer of preserves. The glaze is the crowning touch, and when eaten all together, the results are simply captivating.

PASTRY

1 cup (2 sticks, ½ pound) butter

2 cups (8½ ounces) unbleached all-purpose flour

1¼ cups (10 ounces) water

3 large eggs, at room temperature

1 teaspoon almond extract

TOPPING

1 10-ounce jar of jam

½ cup (2 ounces) chopped walnuts or almonds

ICING

1 cup (4 ounces) confectioners' sugar

2 to 3 tablespoons (1 to 1½ ounces) milk

½ teaspoon vanilla extract

Preheat the oven to 350°F.

Cut 1 stick of butter into 1 cup of flour until the mixture forms coarse crumbs. Blend in ¼ cup cold water. Form the dough into a ball and divide it in half. On a greased cookie sheet, pat each half into a 3 x 11-inch rectangle, spacing the rectangles 4 inches apart. Slide a spatula dipped in cold water alongside and over the top of the rectangles to smooth out their surfaces.

Put remaining 1 cup of water in a saucepan and add the remaining stick of butter. Bring the mixture to a rapid boil, stirring until the butter melts completely. Remove from the heat and pour into a mixing bowl. With your mixer or by hand, immediately add remaining 1 cup of flour and stir vigorously until thick. Add the eggs one at a time, beating well after each. Beat in the almond extract. Divide this batter in half. Drop by spoonfuls on top of each pastry base, covering completely, top and sides. Bake for 1 hour, or until golden brown. Remove the pastries from the oven and immediately frost with your favorite jam or preserve (raspberry or apricot are particularly good). While the puffs are cooling, stir together the confectioners' sugar, milk, and vanilla to make a thin icing. When completely cool, drizzle the puffs with the icing. Sprinkle the tops with chopped nuts, if you like.

nutrition information per serving　　1 slice, 55g

211 cal | 12g fat | 3g protein | 11g complex carbohydrates | 11g sugar | 1g dietary fiber | 57mg cholesterol | 12mg sodium | 56mg potassium | 101RE vitamin A | 1mg iron | 11mg calcium | 38mg phosphorus

Steamed Breads and "Puddings"

If you're a northern New Englander of a certain age, one of the food constants in your childhood was probably the Saturday night supper, consisting of beans, franks, and Boston brown bread. The beans, small navy or pea beans sweetened with brown sugar or molasses, flavored with onion and mustard, and enriched with bacon or salt pork, were baked for eight to ten hours in an earthenware pot set in a slow oven. The franks were cooked in minutes atop the stove, just before supper. And in between those two extremes was the brown bread, a cylindrical, molasses-brown, raisin-studded loaf, moist and tender from its three hours of steaming. For most kids, the beans occupied one side of the plate; the frank acted as a dividing line across the middle; and the bread, cut in a substantial inch-thick slice and spread with melting butter, rested in solitary splendor, untouched by beans, on the remainder of the plate. A piece of frank dipped in beans, followed by a bite of brown bread, was a much-anticipated weekly treat.

Brown bread, though arguably the most familiar of the steamed breads, certainly isn't the only one. With a long British tradition (think plum pudding, with its similar preparation method), steamed breads came to this country along with the original colonists. At a time when most homes didn't have an oven, steaming was the only available way to make bread (without waiting for the community oven).

Though generally out of favor in the frenetic lives most of us lead now, steamed breads bring to the table the same attributes they've always possessed: they're moist and tender, usually sweet and, served hot from the steamer, a perfect vehicle for melting butter.

What's the difference between steamed bread and steamed pudding? Nothing, officially; it's just a matter of nomenclature. We've noticed, however, that steamed puddings may be a bit sweeter, and are usually made with fruit, while steamed breads don't necessarily include fruit, and may be savory.

Boston Brown Bread

ONE 2-POUND LOAF, SIXTEEN SLICES

This is traditionally served with baked beans because the combination of grains and legumes (beans or peas) produces a complete protein, but one held together with fiber rather than fat. It is a cinch to put together, is moist and delicious, and can be eaten with beans, or pea soup, in any form, or even by itself. The ingredients can be mixed up very fast; the steaming takes about 2 hours.

1 cup (4⅞ ounces) yellow cornmeal

1 cup (4 ounces) pumpernickel

1 cup (5¼ ounces) whole wheat flour

1 teaspoon baking soda

1 teaspoon salt

1 cup (6 ounces) raisins (optional but good)

2 cups (16 ounces) buttermilk or nonfat yogurt

¾ cup (9 ounces) dark, unsulfured molasses

Mix the cornmeal, flours, baking soda, salt, and raisins together. Combine the buttermilk and molasses and stir them into the dry ingredients.

Place the mixture in a greased, 2-quart pudding mold or other tall, cylindrical heat-proof container, filling it about two-thirds full. Grease the inside lid of the pudding mold as well. Secure the lid.

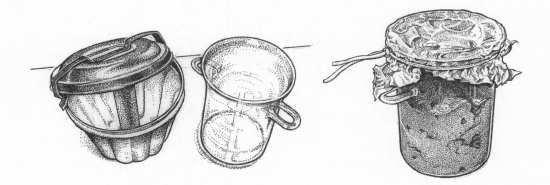

You can steam quick breads in a pudding mold with a lid, or a lab glass container, with foil tightly tied on top.

Place the mold in a kettle or saucepan on top of something (crinkled aluminum foil or a stainless-steel vegetable steaming insert will do nicely) to keep the mold off the bottom of the pan. The kettle should be deep enough so its lid can cover the pudding mold.

Fill the kettle with boiling water two-thirds of the way up the mold. Cover, bring the water back to a boil, then lower to a simmer. Steam for about 2 hours, adding water if necessary. Remove the mold and undo the lid. Give the bread a tap on the bottom to encourage it to slide out. Remove the bread while it is still warm and let it cool on a rack.

Variation TO BAKE THE BREAD INSTEAD: Spoon the batter into a lightly greased 8½ x 4½-inch loaf pan and cover it with buttered aluminum foil. Leave room at the top of the foil for ballooning in the center, so the bread has room to expand without hitting the foil. Fasten the foil tight to the edges of the pan so the bread will steam a bit.

Bake the bread in a 325°F oven for 1 hour. Remove the foil (the middle may be slightly sunken) and bake for an additional 10 minutes.

nutrition information per serving   1 slice, without raisins, 71g

146 cal | 1g fat | 4g protein | 18g complex carbohydrates | 13g sugar | 3g dietary fiber | 1mg cholesterol | 268mg sodium | 230mg potassium | 6RE vitamin A | 2mg iron | 57mg calcium | 132mg phosphorus

Chocolate Steamed Pudding

SIX SERVINGS

This recipe comes from friends who took the ingredients for this pudding on cross-country skiing treks. When the time seemed appropriate, they made a campfire and created a steamer out of a one-pound coffee can (no longer an easy thing to come by), a piece of aluminum foil for a lid, a piece of string to hold it on, and an empty tuna can to keep the coffee can off the bottom of the lobster pot in which they steamed the pudding.

Because this pudding is ethereally light, it takes only 1½ hours to steam, just enough time for a good snowball fight or a side trip over the next hill. It is really very cakelike, but, because it's steamed, is incredibly moist despite being virtually fat-free.

2 ounces (squares) unsweetened baking chocolate	1 cup (4¼ ounces) unbleached all-purpose flour
1 teaspoon butter, melted	½ teaspoon salt
1 teaspoon vanilla extract	1½ teaspoons baking powder
1 large egg	½ cup (4 ounces) milk
¾ cup (5¼ ounces) sugar	

Melt the chocolate with the butter in a small saucepan and add the vanilla. In a mixing bowl, beat the egg until light and lemon-colored. Add the sugar and beat until fluffy. Combine the flour with the salt and baking powder. Add this, alternately with the milk, to the egg mixture. Then add the chocolate mixture and stir just to blend.

Place the batter in a greased, 1-pound coffee can or a 1-quart pudding mold. If you're using a can, cover with aluminum foil and secure it with a string or a large rubber band. Steam the bread over simmering water in a covered kettle for 1½ hours. Remove the mold or can from the kettle and undo the lid. Give the bread a tap on the bottom to encourage it to slide out. If it doesn't come out easily, run a dull knife around the edge of the mold or can. Remove the bread while it is still warm and let it cool on a rack.

nutrition information per serving   **1 slice, 80g**

220 cal │ 5g fat │ 8g protein │ 17g complex carbohydrates │ 23g sugar │ 1g dietary fiber │ 7mg cholesterol │ 318 mg sodium │ 101mg potassium │ 1mg iron │ 124mg calcium

Date Pudding

12 SERVINGS

Like many old recipes, we thought this was somewhat plain, so we dressed it up a bit with spices. The resulting dark, moist, dense cake (it's really more cake than pudding) is nice just as it is, warm from the oven, or add some whipped cream.

1 cup (5 ounces) pitted, chopped dates

1 tablespoon (½ ounce) butter, melted

2 teaspoons baking soda

1 cup (7 ounces) sugar

¼ teaspoon salt

½ teaspoon cinnamon

¼ teaspoon ginger

1 cup (8 ounces) boiling water

½ cup (2 ounces) chopped walnuts or pecans

1⅓ cups (5½ ounces) unbleached all-purpose flour

Preheat the oven to 350°F.

Combine the dates with the butter, soda, sugar, salt, and spices. Stir in the boiling water and allow the mixture to cool. Add the nuts and flour, stirring just to combine. Pour the batter into a greased 9-inch round pan and bake the pudding for 25 to 30 minutes, until it's set but still very moist.

nutrition information per serving   1 slice, 63g

179 cal | 4g fat | 2g protein | 19g complex carbohydrates | 16g sugar | 2g dietary fiber | 3mg cholesterol | 361mg sodium | 118mg potassium | 11RE vitamin A | 1mg iron | 10mg calcium | 32mg phosphorus

Creating a Steaming Rack

It's not a good idea to set a pudding mold or other steaming pan directly on the bottom of the large saucepan you'll use to steam the bread or pudding; the bottom of the bread may cook too quickly or, if the mold is glass, it may crack if the water level gets too low. If you don't have a rack that will fit inside the pan, take a big piece of aluminum foil and gently crumple it into a circle that's about 2 inches thick and a bit wider than the diameter of your pudding mold or other steaming pan, as shown in the illustration at right. Your mold or pan will happily sit atop this foil "throne" as it steams.

Down East Pudding

ONE 2-POUND PUDDING, 16 SLICES

The following recipe is typical of a pudding that was made in the late-summer days of early New England. This version is made with whole wheat flour, which old-timers were apt to use. It is full of wild Maine blueberries that have ripened on the scrublands of Maine from time immemorial, and it's sweetened with those old-fashioned sweeteners, brown sugar and molasses. Because our energy needs have diminished somewhat in this century, we've made this version without suet or fat of any kind so it will fill you up without filling you out.

2 cups (10½ ounces) whole wheat flour

1 teaspoon baking powder

½ teaspoon baking soda

¾ teaspoon salt

1 teaspoon ginger (or cinnamon, nutmeg, allspice, or a blend)

2 large eggs

½ cup (4 ounces) brown sugar (or for a lighter taste, use 1 cup brown sugar and no molasses)

½ cup (6 ounces) dark, unsulfured molasses

1 cup (8 ounces) buttermilk

2 cups (8 ounces) wild Maine blueberries (or blackberries or raspberries, etc.)

Mix the flour, baking powder, soda, salt, and spice together. In another bowl, beat the eggs and add and beat in the brown sugar, molasses, and buttermilk. Stir the blueberries into the dry ingredients and mix these quickly into the egg mixture. Pour the batter into a greased 2-quart pudding mold (it should be about two-thirds full). Secure the lid and place it in a kettle or saucepan that is tall enough so you can put a lid on it. It's important to put something on the bottom of the pan so the steamer isn't directly in contact with it. Crinkled tin foil or a vegetable steamer will do (see sidebar on p. 103).

Fill the pot with boiling water about two-thirds of the way up the pudding mold. Cover, bring the water back to a boil, and lower the heat to a simmer. Steam for about 2 hours, adding water if necessary.

After the pudding is done, remove it from the water and let it stand for a few minutes. If it seems to be sticking anywhere, loosen it gently with a knife. Then take a serving plate, upend it over the mold, and turn the pudding out, giving the mold a tap if it's reluctant to let go.

This pudding makes a delicious (and healthy) dessert or snack as is, but you can dress it up by spooning a bit of yogurt sweetened with a little maple syrup over it.

nutrition information per serving   1 slice, 66g

114 cal | 4g protein | 22g complex carbohydrates | 7g sugar | 3g dietary fiber | 27mg cholesterol | 197mg sodium | 131mg potassium | 15RE vitamin A | 1mg vitamin C | 1mg iron | 46mg calcium | 93mg phosphorus

Biscuits

Biscuits, like pie crust, seem enrobed in an aura of mystery to beginning or unconfident bakers. Both involve a few basic ingredients and a couple of key (but not difficult) steps. If you use the right ingredients and follow the directions carefully, either should be within anyone's realm of expertise.

While you can use entirely all-purpose flour for biscuits, we like using pastry flour for a tender crumb. (See p. 517 for more on pastry flour.) Your key to success, as with any biscuit recipe, is using a gentle hand and a sharp cutter. By just barely coaxing the fat and flour together, then patting the dough together as lovingly and gently as you'd towel-dry a baby, you're keeping the flour's gluten from toughening as you handle it. And by cutting the biscuits with a sharp blade, you're leaving "side-walls" that will freely expand as the biscuit bakes, allowing them to rise to their full height. The edges of a biscuit cut with a drinking glass or dull tuna can will be squashed down and the biscuit won't rise as well.

1. Cut biscuit dough with a straight-sided metal cutter. **2.** A biscuit cut with a glass won't rise as high as a biscuit cut with a metal cutter. The dull edge of the glass compresses the layers in the dough.

Serve biscuits with butter or double Devon cream; serve them with jam or jelly; slather them with lemon curd or honey or (golden or cane) syrup or even maple syrup. But whatever you do, serve them hot from the oven. A cold biscuit, while still good, can't hold a candle to one plucked hot from the oven, broken open to reveal a steaming interior, and topped with a pat of cold butter.

Beaten Biscuits

3½ DOZEN 1¾-INCH BISCUITS

Beaten biscuits, a very old, very traditional Southern bread, are most often mentioned as the best vehicle for country ham. But float these buttery nuggets atop your favorite soup; they retain their crunch for quite a while before finally yielding to the soup's warm embrace. Because of their hint of sweetness, they go better with a bland, creamy soup, or one that's a bit sweet anyway—such as corn chowder—rather than with a very spicy or acidic (tomato-based) soup.

The following recipe (to which we've made some slight changes) comes from the message board on bakingcircle.com. Here's what the contributor says: "The best biscuits for country ham are beaten biscuits, not breakfast-style biscuits. Beaten biscuits were made by preparing a dough, then beating the dough with a rolling pin (usually outdoors on an old tree stump!) until the dough blisters (around 500 licks). There are several recipes around, but I like this one as it reduces the work a lot by using the food processor to do the beating. (And yes, I did make them the traditional way once to see if all of the effort was worth it—the answer is no.)"

Note: In order to replicate the "500 licks," we suggest a food processor. If you don't have a food processor, it would probably be best if you didn't try this recipe.

2 cups (8 ounces) unbleached pastry or unbleached all-purpose flour (8½ ounces)*	¼ teaspoon baking power
2 teaspoons sugar	6 tablespoons (¾ stick, 3 ounces) soft unsalted butter or lard (or a combination)
½ teaspoon salt	½ cup (4 ounces) whole milk

Preheat the oven to 325°F.

Place the flour, sugar, salt, and baking powder in a food processor equipped with the metal blade and process for 5 to 10 seconds, just until blended. Add the butter and process until the mixture resembles coarse crumbs, 10 to 15 seconds, or slightly more.

Add the milk and process for at least 3 minutes. The dough will be soft and putty-like, almost like melted mozzarella.

Remove the dough from the processor, transfer it to a clean, very lightly greased work surface (a light spritz of vegetable oil cooking spray works well), cover it, and let it rest for 15 minutes; this gives the gluten a chance to relax, making the dough much easier to roll.

Roll the rested dough into a rectangle about 12 x 17 inches; it will be about ⅛ inch thick. Fold it in half crosswise and roll lightly to bind the two layers together.

Using a very small, round biscuit cutter—between 1½ and 2 inches—cut out as many biscuits as you can, placing them on a parchment-lined or ungreased baking sheet close together, but not quite touching. You can reprocess the scraps from the first cutting us-

What Makes Biscuits Flaky?

The technique for making biscuits is quite similar to that for making piecrust, as is the goal, a tender, flaky final product. In both cases, fat is cut into the dry ingredients, then liquid is added to make the dough cohesive. The fat is there to create tenderness, which happens two ways. First, fat coats the proteins in the flour, preventing them from forming long gluten strands, and thus creating a fine-grained texture. Second, fat acts as a temporary buffer between layers of the flour-liquid matrix; as the biscuit bakes, the fat eventually melts. But it's done its job, creating a structure in the biscuit that we perceive as flaky.

ing the same method (wait 15 minutes, roll out, fold over, roll to bind). But the best-looking biscuits will come from that first roll-out, so try to use as much of the dough as you can the first time around.

Lightly prick the biscuits with a fork. Bake them for about 20 minutes, until their tops are a very light golden brown and their bottoms a deeper brown (but not burned). (The biscuits will cool in the oven, and will continue to bake after you've turned the heat off, so don't over-bake them. In fact, some Southern recipes say that the trick of beaten biscuits—and the sign of a really good biscuit baker—is that they be thoroughly cooked, crisp and dry, but a pale creamy-white color, with no hint of browning.)

Turn the oven off, crack the door open, and allow the biscuits to stand in the oven until they're totally cooled (or just barely warm). Store them in an airtight container at room temperature, where they'll keep for two weeks. To serve with country ham, use room temperature biscuits, or lightly heat them in a low oven for a few minutes.

*You want to use a "soft" flour here, with a lower protein level. If you're using all-purpose flour, put ¼ cup cornstarch in the bottom of a measuring cup and fill the remainder with flour.

nutrition information per serving   **3 biscuits, 33g**

113 cal | 6g fat | 2g protein | 13g complex carbohydrates | 1g sugar | 15mg cholesterol | 90mg sodium | 36mg potassium | 51RE vitamin A | 1mg iron | 17mg calcium | 27mg phosphorus

Biscuits for Breakfast

NINE LARGE SQUARE, OR 16 2-INCH ROUND BISCUITS

If you're a Southern baker with any basic skills at all, you can skip right past this recipe. In fact, we'd appreciate it if you'd turn the page immediately—we don't want to shock you with this Northern version of one of the South's most revered breads. This is the way we learned to make biscuits, and they are tender, high-rising, the perfect foil for a pat of melting butter. The added egg gives these biscuits a touch of golden color, a hint of richness, and just a bit more structure, and they hold together better than the eggless version.

To make a decadent strawberry shortcake, layer these biscuits with sliced fresh strawberries and lightly sweetened whipped cream.

2 cups (8½ ounces) unbleached all-purpose flour

1 teaspoon salt

1 tablespoon sugar

2½ teaspoons baking powder

4 tablespoons (½ stick, 2 ounces) cold butter

¼ cup (1⅝ ounces) cold shortening

½ cup (4 ounces) milk, cream, or half-and-half*

1 large egg

Freezing Biscuits and Scones Before Baking

Here's one cool thing: For light fluffy biscuits or scones, shape the biscuits (or scones), place them on a baking sheet, and freeze for 30 minutes or longer. Baked goods that rely on the combination of flour, liquid, baking powder, and solid fat for their structure will rise slightly better when frozen. Why? Because the fat stays solid longer in the oven, holding together the structure of the biscuit as it rises. Eventually the fat melts, but by that time the flour/liquid matrix has developed and set, and what you've got left is layers of bread interspersed with thin air pockets where once resided solid fat—a flaky, tender biscuit!

In a medium-sized mixing bowl, whisk together the flour, salt, sugar, and baking powder. Cut the butter into pats and work the butter and shortening into the flour, using a pastry blender, mixer (you can also use a food processor, up to this point), or your fingers. When thoroughly combined, the mixture should resemble uneven, coarse crumbs; don't keep working it until it's perfectly homogeneous. The point is to work the cold fat into the dry ingredients fairly evenly, but you don't want the fat to become one with the flour. The uneven, tender texture of biscuits comes from pockets of cold fat in the dough, which in the baking process don't melt until after the dough is set, leaving butter-catching fissures in the baked biscuit.

Measure the milk into a liquid measuring cup, add the egg, and whisk until smooth. Add this to the flour-fat mixture and stir just to combine; as soon as you no longer

The Difference Between Biscuits and Scones

Biscuits contain little or no sugar, and usually no additions of any kind. The classic baking powder biscuit, a plain white roll, is best served hot, with butter or honey, along with a meal. Scones, on the other hand, are usually sweetened; very often contain fruit, nuts, or spices; and are not generally served hot with meals, but more often alone, or with tea or coffee. So, while the basic breads may be quite similar, they take different paths as they're baked and served.

see areas that are very obviously wetter than other areas, stop mixing and dump the dough onto a lightly floured work surface. Knead it a couple of times to bring it together, if necessary; remember, every time you push, pat, or shape the dough from now on you're toughening the gluten, and therefore the biscuit, so try to handle it as little as possible. With the help of a dough scraper, shape the dough into a 6 x 6-inch square, about ¾ inch thick. Run a rolling pin over the top once to even it out. Wrap it in plastic wrap and place it in the freezer for 1 hour.

Preheat the oven to 400°F. Remove the dough from the freezer, unwrap it, and set it on a work surface. It will be very stiff but still soft enough to cut with a sharp knife, sharpened dough scraper, or pizza cutter. Cut the dough into nine 2-inch squares and place the squares on a lightly greased or parchment-lined baking sheet. Make sure to cut out the biscuits with something sharp; if you use a dull knife, you compress the biscuits' edges and they won't rise as high.

Bake the biscuits for 16 minutes, or until they're a light golden brown. Remove them from the oven and serve hot, warm, or at room temperature.

*You can use any kind of milk, from skim right up through whipping cream. The richer the milk, the richer and more tender your biscuit will be. Making biscuits with skim milk instead of half-and-half reduces calories per serving to 205 and fat grams to 11.4.

nutrition information per serving   1 biscuit, made with half-and-half, 62g

218 cal | 13g fat | 4g protein | 20g complex carbohydrates | 1g sugar | 1g dietary fiber | 50mg cholesterol | 370mg sodium | 57mg potassium | 74RE vitamin A | 1mg iron | 132mg calcium | 69mg phosphorus.

Cheddar and Black Pepper Biscuits

ABOUT TWENTY-FIVE 1½-INCH BISCUITS

The tang of black pepper teams up with the rich flavor of cheddar cheese in these biscuits. We suggest you adjust the amount of black pepper to suit your taste—¾ teaspoon gives a nice warm touch, 2½ teaspoons is spicy but wonderful.

3 cups (12¾ ounces) unbleached all-purpose flour

2 tablespoons baking powder

½ teaspoon baking soda

1 teaspoon salt

1 tablespoon granulated sugar

½ cup (1 stick, 4 ounces) butter

1 cup (4 ounces) grated cheddar cheese

¾ to 2½ teaspoons coarsely ground black pepper

¾ cup (6 ounces) buttermilk or plain yogurt, for glaze

In a large bowl, sift together the flour, baking powder, baking soda, salt, and sugar. Cut in the butter and cheese. Stir in the black pepper. Refrigerate the dough for half an hour. Meanwhile preheat the oven to 400°F.

Gently stir the buttermilk into the chilled dough. Gather the mixture into a ball with your hands, and on a well-floured surface, roll or pat the dough into a 12 x 8-inch rectangle approximately ¾ inch thick.

Grease a baking sheet. Using a large spatula, or a couple of spatulas, transfer the dough to the baking sheet. Use a dough scraper, baker's bench knife, or a knife to cut dough into 1½-inch squares. Separate the squares slightly on the baking sheet. Brush each square with a little buttermilk or yogurt.

Bake the biscuits for 15 to 20 minutes, or until they're very lightly browned.

nutrition information per serving   **1 biscuit, 32g**

105 cal | 5g fat | 3g protein | 11g complex carbohydrates | 15mg cholesterol | 264mg sodium | 36mg potassium | 49RE vitamin A | 1mg iron | 108mg calcium | 68mg phosphorus

Herbed Cream Cheese Biscuits

TWENTY 2-INCH BISCUITS

When it's finally warm enough in the morning to eat breakfast on the porch or deck, why not celebrate with something really special? Our test kitchen director Sue Gray says a favorite brunch dish of hers is these herbed biscuits with smoked salmon and scrambled eggs. "Chives are one of the first plants I harvest from my herb garden," she says. "They're perfect when they're young and still tender. And even though this recipe is one I can make year-round, it's one of those things that tells me summer's almost here. Just the colors on the plate—the green chives in the golden biscuits set next to the orange salmon and bright yellow eggs—are wonderful."

2½ cups (10½ ounces) unbleached all-purpose flour

1 tablespoon baking powder

1 teaspoon salt

½ teaspoon ground black pepper

3 tablespoons (¼ ounce) chopped fresh chives, or 2 tablespoons dried chives*

1 teaspoon dried thyme

1 cup (4 ounces) grated sharp cheddar cheese

4 tablespoons (½ stick, 2 ounces) butter, or ¼ cup vegetable shortening

4 ounces (half a large package) cream cheese

¾ cup (6 ounces) milk

Preheat the oven to 425°F. In a medium-sized bowl, whisk together the dry ingredients, including the grated cheese, until everything is evenly distributed. Using a pastry fork or blender, your fingers or an electric mixer, cut in the butter and cream cheese, mixing until crumbly; some larger chunks of cheese and butter can remain. Pour in the milk while tossing with a fork; the dough should remain a bit crumbly but hold together when squeezed. Add an additional 1 to 2 tablespoons of milk, if needed.

Turn out the dough onto a lightly floured work surface and fold it over a few times so that you can be sure it's totally cohesive. Pat it into an 8-inch square, ¾ inch thick. Cut it into 2-inch squares, or use a 2-inch round cutter. Place the biscuits on an ungreased baking sheet.

Bake the biscuits for 16 to 18 minutes, until they're lightly browned. Serve them warm or at room temperature.

*Substitute chive cream cheese or herbed cream cheese for the chives, thyme, and cream cheese, if desired.

nutrition information per serving   1 biscuit, 37g

99 cal | 4g fat | 4g protein | 11g complex carbohydrates | 13mg cholesterol | 236mg sodium | 47mg potassium | 51RE vitamin A | 1mg iron | 99mg calcium | 72mg phosphorus

Sour Cream Rye Biscuits

16 BISCUITS

These pair well with any kind of hearty soup or stew. In the unlikely event you have some, reheat any leftover biscuits briefly, and use them to make ham and cheese biscuit sandwiches.

2½ cups (10½ ounces) unbleached all-purpose flour

½ cup (2 ounces) pumpernickel or medium rye flour

1 tablespoon Bakewell Cream* plus 1½ teaspoons baking soda, or 1 tablespoon baking powder plus ¼ teaspoon baking soda

1 teaspoon salt

1 tablespoon caraway seeds (pulse in spice grinder if you would rather not have the whole seeds)

4 tablespoons (½ stick, 2 ounces) butter or vegetable shortening

½ cup (4 ounces) sour cream

¾ cup (6 ounces) milk

Preheat the oven to 400°F.

In a medium-sized mixing bowl, whisk together the dry ingredients. Using a pastry blender or fork, your fingers, or a mixer, cut in the butter or shortening.

Measure the sour cream into a 2-cup liquid measure and add the milk, stirring to combine. Add these liquid ingredients to the dry ingredients, stirring until everything is evenly moistened. Turn out the dough onto a lightly floured surface and fold it over a few times to make sure it's cohesive. Pat it into an 8-inch square about ½ inch thick.

Use a 2-inch cutter to make round biscuits, or cut the dough into 2-inch squares. Place the biscuits on a lightly greased baking sheet, brushing the top of each with milk (or an egg mixed with milk), to make them shiny and a deeper brown, if you like.

Bake the biscuits for 12 to 14 minutes, until lightly browned. Serve them hot or warm.

*For information on Bakewell Cream, see page 546 of the Ingredients chapter.

nutrition information per serving | 1 biscuit, 44g

119 cal | 5g fat | 3g protein | 17g complex carbohydrates | 1g dietary fiber | 11mg cholesterol | 254mg sodium | 79mg potassium | 47RE vitamin A | 1mg iron | 75mg calcium | 77mg phosphorus

Scones

Sweeter and more varied in their incarnations than biscuits, scones have struck the American fancy and are showing up everywhere. What we think of as scones here in America, and see labeled as such in bakeries and stores, probably bear little resemblance to the original, but they surely are good. Scones can be embellished with just about any flavor, from fruit to chocolate, cinnamon, coffee, coconut or ginger, from nuts and seeds to savory cheese and vegetable versions.

Basic Scones and Variations

16 SCONES

The following is a basic scone recipe that's easily enhanced by the addition of different dried fruits and spices.

3 cups (12¾ ounces) unbleached all-purpose flour, or 3¼ cups (13 ounces) unbleached pastry flour

⅓ cup (2⅜ ounces) sugar

¼ cup (1½ ounces) buttermilk powder or nonfat dry milk

¾ teaspoon salt

1 tablespoon baking powder

¾ cup (3 to 4 ounces) currants, raisins, apricots, or other dried fruit

2 large eggs

2 teaspoons vanilla extract

½ cup (4 ounces) milk, buttermilk, or water

8 tablespoons (1 stick, 4 ounces) cold butter, or a combination of shortening and butter

1 egg beaten with 1 teaspoon water, for topping

Coarse sugar or cinnamon-sugar, for topping (optional, but good)

Preheat the oven to 450°F.

In a medium-sized mixing bowl, whisk together all the dry ingredients, including the fruit. In a separate bowl, whisk together the eggs, the vanilla, and the milk. (Milk will give you a richer scone than water; buttermilk, because of its acidic interaction with the baking powder, will give you a tender, slightly higher-rising scone with a touch of tang.)

The next step, cutting in the fat, is important because this largely determines the texture of the scones. Use cold butter, shortening, or a mixture of both. (Liquid vegetable oil isn't a good choice because scones get their flaky texture from small bits of fat that separate thin layers of a flour-and-water matrix.) As the biscuit or scone bakes, the fat holds these dough layers apart. Finally the fat reaches its melting point and disappears into the dough—but by that time, the biscuit's structure has set into many thin layers of dough, which in the finished product create tenderness and flakiness. (And, in the case of butter, wonderful flavor. Since butter's melting point is lower than shortening's, we like to use a combination of the two: butter for its flavor, shortening for its superior ability to create the flaky effect.)

Begin with cold fat, as cold fat retains its integrity in the dough better than warm. It helps to have the fat cut into marble-sized pieces before adding it to the flour. One of our favorite methods is to freeze a half-stick of butter, then grate it coarsely into the dry ingredients, while adding ¼ cup of cold shortening that we've broken into marble-sized pieces (messy, but that's what paper towels are for). Be sure there are pieces of fat that remain the size of baby peas. If you cut the shortening in until the flour is evenly crumbly (like coarse sand), you'll have mealy rather that flaky scones.

Next, add the liquid ingredients to the flour-fat mixture. Be careful: too much mixing or kneading at this point will result in tough, heavy scones. Gently fold everything together until the mixture is mostly moistened; a bit of the flour may remain dry.

Turn out the dough onto a lightly floured surface and fold and gather it together until it's cohesive. Divide the dough in half and place both halves on a lightly greased or parchment-lined baking sheet. Pat each half into a 7-inch circle approximately ½ inch thick, then cut each circle into 8 wedges. Separate the wedges slightly, leaving about a half inch between each at the outer edge; at the center, they'll be about ¼ inch apart. Alternatively, you can pat the entire piece of dough into a rectangle and cut it into 1½- to 2-inch rounds, using a biscuit cutter; or into 1½- to 2-inch squares.

Brush the scones with the beaten egg, then sprinkle with coarse sugar or cinnamon sugar, if desired. Bake them for 7 minutes, then turn the oven off and, without opening the door, let the scones remain in the oven for an additional 8 to 10 minutes, or until they're golden brown. (It's important to bake scones on your oven's middle rack.) Remove the scones from the oven, and let them cool minimally on a wire rack.

Serve the scones immediately or within a few hours, for best flavor. Conveniently enough, scone dough lends itself to being made ahead, shaped, and either frozen or refrigerated overnight before baking. For scones refrigerated overnight, bake for the same amount of time; for frozen, add 2 minutes to the baking time before you turn the oven off.

nutrition information per serving   **1 basic scone, fruit added, 50g**

170 cal | 6g fat | 3g protein | 26g complex carbohydrates | 4g sugar | 1g dietary fiber | 17mg cholesterol | 131mg sodium | 98mg potassium | 56RE vitamin A | 1mg iron | 1mg calcium | 121mg phosphorus

Variations CRANBERRY-ORANGE: Use cranberries as the added fruit, add 2 tablespoons grated orange zest or ½ teaspoon orange oil to the dough, and use orange juice for the liquid.

LEMON–POPPY SEED: Add 3 tablespoons poppy seeds and ¼ to ½ teaspoon lemon oil, or 2 tablespoons grated lemon zest, to the dough.

CHERRY-ALMOND: Substitute 2 teaspoons almond extract or ¼ teaspoon bitter almond oil for the vanilla, and add ½ cup dried sweet or sour cherries to the dough.

GINGER-CHOCOLATE CHIP: Add ¼ cup finely diced crystallized ginger and 1 teaspoon ground ginger or 1 teaspoon fresh crushed ginger to the dough, along with ½ cup chocolate chips.

CINNAMON-PECAN: Add ¾ cup chopped, toasted pecans to the dough, and substitute 2 teaspoons ground cinnamon for the vanilla.

Apricot Cream Cheese Scones

ABOUT 18 MEDIUM-SIZED SCONES

We love the bright flavor and color of apricots in scones; cream cheese lends added richness. If you have access to unbleached pastry flour, it will give you a final product that's more tender and delicate than that produced by a higher-protein flour. If you don't have unbleached pastry flour, substituting some cornstarch for the all-purpose flour will serve to make your scones more tender, as well.

3¼ cups (13 ounces) unbleached pastry flour, or 3 cups (12¾ ounces) unbleached all-purpose flour plus ¼ cup (1 ounce) cornstarch

½ cup (3½ ounces) granulated sugar

2½ teaspoons baking powder

½ teaspoon salt

8 ounces cream cheese (cold)

8 tablespoons (1 stick, 4 ounces) cold butter

1 cup (4½ ounces) diced or slivered apricots

1 large egg

2 teaspoons vanilla extract

¼ cup (2 ounces) milk

TOPPING

Milk

Sparkling white sugar or pearl sugar

Preheat the oven to 425°F.

In a medium-sized mixing bowl, whisk together the flour, sugar, baking powder, and salt. Cut in the cream cheese and butter, using your fingers, a pastry blender, fork, or a mixer, until the mixture resembles coarse cornmeal, then stir in the apricots. In a separate bowl, whisk together the egg, vanilla, and milk.

Combine the liquid and dry ingredients and stir until the dough becomes cohesive. Don't mix and mix and mix; the more you work with the dough, the tougher it will get.

Turn out the dough onto a floured work surface and fold it over several times, until it holds together. Pat the dough into a ¾-inch-thick rectangle.

Cut scones with a round cutter, gathering the scraps and re-rolling the dough. Or simply cut the dough into squares or diamonds. Brush the tops lightly with milk and sprinkle with sparkling white or pearl sugar.

Place scones about 2 inches apart on an ungreased or parchment-lined baking sheet. Bake them for 8 minutes. Turn the oven off, leave the door closed, and continue to bake for 8 more minutes, until the scones are a light golden brown. Serve hot, with clotted cream and jam or raspberry curd.

nutrition information per serving | 1 scone, 60g

207 cal | 10g fat | 4g protein | 21g complex carbohydrates | 5g sugar | 1g dietary fiber | 40mg cholesterol | 171mg sodium | 160mg potassium | 167RE vitamin A | 2mg iron | 58mg calcium | 65mg phosphorus

Christmas Scones

16 SCONES

Here's a relative of the Scottish bannock, perfect for a leisurely holiday breakfast. Using whole oats gives these scones a marvelous texture.

2 cups (8½ ounces) unbleached all-purpose flour

1 cup (3½ ounces) rolled oats or oat flour

1 tablespoon baking powder

½ teaspoon baking soda

½ to 1 teaspoon salt, to taste

½ cup (4 ounces) brown sugar, packed

8 tablespoons (1 stick, 4 ounces) butter, at room temperature

1½ cups (7½ ounces) cranberries cut in half, or 1 cup (4½ ounces) dried

1½ cups (5⅜ ounces) pecans, halved

1 cup (8 ounces) buttermilk

Preheat the oven to 500°F.

Mix the dry ingredients, including the brown sugar, together in a large mixing bowl. With a pastry cutter or your fingertips, gently cut or rub the butter into the dry ingredients until it looks like cornmeal. Mix in the fruit and nuts until they're fairly evenly distributed.

Stir in the buttermilk, taking only 20 seconds to do it. Turn out the dough onto a well-floured board and, with floured hands, knead gently 8 to 10 times, just enough to bring it together.

Cut the dough into two pieces. (Keep sprinkling on flour if you need to.) Form each into a disk and, with a floured rolling pin, gently coax each disk into a round about 7 inches in diameter. With a bench knife or sharp knife, cut the round into 8 wedges. Do this by cutting straight down through the dough so you shear the edges. If you saw the dough, you tend to press the edges together, which keeps the scones from rising as they bake.

Place the wedges on a lightly floured baking sheet (two pizza pans are perfect for this), turn down the oven to 450°F, and bake for 15 to 20 minutes, or until they just begin to brown. Remove from the oven and serve warm with butter or double cream.

nutrition information per serving   1 scone, 72g

231 cal | 13g fat | 4g protein | 19g complex carbohydrates | 7g sugar | 2g dietary fiber | 17mg cholesterol | 250mg sodium | 131mg potassium | 60RE vitamin A | 1mg vitamin C | 1mg iron | 83mg calcium | 106mg phosphorus

The Cream Tea Scone

18 SCONES

Beginning as oat farls, or Scottish griddle cakes, the scone has traveled beyond Scottish borders and been taken to heart by the English. Here's the prototypical cream tea scone that we've come to associate with that very British of rites, afternoon tea. This institution developed in the nineteenth century, as the time period between luncheon and dinner lengthened to eight or nine hours. Few people's digestive systems could survive that long untended, so this "meal" evolved to bridge the gap. (Afternoon tea is not the same as high tea, which is served later in the evening and is what most of us on this side of the Atlantic call supper.)

Taking tea, unlike drinking coffee, is a sane and restorative interlude, one that can give you the energy to finish the day with some enthusiasm. It was this rite that propelled the scone into an arena that would make it known to the rest of the tea-drinking world.

3 cups (12¾ ounces) unbleached all-purpose flour (or half all-purpose and half unbleached pastry flour)

2 teaspoons baking powder

½ teaspoon baking soda

2 tablespoons (⅞ ounce) granulated sugar

1 teaspoon salt

8 tablespoons (1 stick, 4 ounces) butter, at room temperature

1 cup (4½ ounces) currants (optional)

1 large egg

1 cup (8 ounces) buttermilk (a bit more during the winter when the flour is dry)

Preheat the oven to 450°F.

Blend the dry ingredients in a mixing bowl and rub in the butter. Stir in the currants if you opt to use them.

In a small bowl, beat together the egg and buttermilk. Make a well in the flour/butter mixture and pour in the liquid. Mix together for about 20 seconds.

Turn out this dough onto a well-floured surface and dust the top of the dough with flour. Using a bench knife or bowl scraper, knead together gently about 10 times. With a well-floured rolling pin, roll or pat the dough until it's just over ½ inch in thickness. (Some scone aficionados feel the dough should not be rolled any thinner than ¾ inch.)

Cut out circles with a 2¼-inch biscuit cutter, pressing down firmly. Don't twist the cutter to free the dough, as that will compress the sides of the scones and keep them from rising to their fullest. After you cut out as many as you can, gently re-roll the remainder of the dough and continue cutting. You should be able to get 12 perfect scones in the first rolling, and 5 not-so-perfect ones the second time around. Take the remaining dough and press it gently together to make a slightly peculiar, but perfect-for-testing final scone.

Place the scones gently on a lightly floured baking sheet and bake for 12 to 15 minutes. Cool slightly and place in a cloth-lined basket. Serve with a bowl of strawberry jam, double or clotted cream, and cups of Earl Grey tea.

nutrition information per serving   **1 scone, 44g**

124 cal | 6g fat | 3g protein | 14g complex carbohydrates | 1g sugar | 1g dietary fiber | 30mg cholesterol | 217mg sodium | 47g potassium | 56RE vitamin A | 1mg iron | 77mg calcium | 43mg phosphorus

Curried Ginger Scones

25 SCONES

These simple scones mirror their main flavor element, ginger: sweet and spicy-hot.

3 cups (12¾ ounces) unbleached all-purpose flour

1 tablespoon baking powder

½ teaspoon baking soda

1 teaspoon salt

½ cup (2½ ounces) chopped crystallized ginger

½ teaspoon curry powder

5 tablespoons (2⅛ ounces) sugar

8 tablespoons (1 stick, 4 ounces) butter, cut into pieces

1 cup (8 ounces) buttermilk, yogurt, or sour cream (low-fat is fine)

Preheat the oven to 425°F.

In a medium-sized mixing bowl, combine the flour, baking powder, baking soda, and salt. Add the ginger, mixing to distribute, then the curry and sugar. Cut in the butter until the mixture is crumbly.

Add the buttermilk, stirring until the dough just holds together. Transfer the dough to a lightly floured work surface, and pat it into a 10-inch square, about ½ inch thick. Cut the dough into 25 small squares and transfer them to a lightly greased baking sheet. Bake the scones for 20 minutes, or until they're golden.

Remove the scones from the oven and paint them with ginger syrup (p. 342) while still warm, if desired.

nutrition information per serving   **1 scone, with ginger syrup, 35g**

106 cal | 4g fat | 2g protein | 11g complex carbohydrates | 5g sugar | 1g dietary fiber | 11mg cholesterol | 182mg sodium | 37mg potassium | 37RE vitamin A | 1mg vitamin C | 1mg iron | 47mg calcium | 35mg phosphorus

New Hampshire Maple-Walnut Scones

16 LARGE SCONES

New Hampshire maple syrup is every bit as tasty—and its creation every bit as magical—as Vermont maple syrup, though it's never enjoyed the same fame (or acclaim). If you're ever visiting northern New England in the early spring—late February through March—try to stop at a sugar house. The hot, rich maple steam billowing from the flat sugar pans, as the maple sap slowly boils down to golden syrup, is a smell you'll never forget. To northern New Englanders (Maine included, even though it's the Pine Tree State), it's the very first smell of spring.

This recipe comes to us courtesy of Barbara Lauterbach, cooking teacher, author, and a longtime King Arthur Flour spokesperson and, more important, friend.

3½ cups (14¾ ounces) unbleached all-purpose flour

4 teaspoons baking powder

1 teaspoon salt

⅔ cup (4¼ ounces) vegetable shortening (or unsalted butter, or a combination)

1 cup (4 ounces) finely chopped walnuts*

1 cup (8 ounces) milk

½ cup (6 ounces) maple syrup

½ teaspoon maple flavoring (optional, but really good)

Preheat the oven to 425°F.

In a large bowl, combine the flour, baking powder, and salt. Cut in the shortening and/or butter until the mixture resembles coarse crumbs. Stir in the walnuts.

In a separate bowl, combine the milk, ⅓ cup of the maple syrup, and the maple flavoring. (You can leave out the maple flavoring if you wish, but it really adds a nice touch.) Add the wet ingredients to the dry ingredients and mix until you've formed a very soft dough.

Flour your work surface generously and scrape the dough out of the mixing bowl onto the floured surface. Divide the dough in half.

Working with one half at a time, gently pat the dough into a 7-inch circle about ⅞ inch thick. Transfer the circle to a parchment-lined or lightly greased cookie sheet or other flat pan; it'll be very soft, and if you have a giant spatula, it's the tool of choice here. Repeat with the remaining half of the dough, placing it on a separate pan.

Using a sharp bench knife or rolling pizza wheel, divide each dough circle into eight wedges. Gently separate the wedges so that they're almost touching in the center, but are spaced about an inch apart at the edges. Pierce the tops of the scones with the tines of a fork and brush them with some of the remaining maple syrup.

Bake the scones for 15 to 18 minutes, or until they're golden brown. Remove them from the oven and brush them with any remaining maple syrup. Wait a couple of minutes, then gently separate the scones with a knife (they'll be very fragile), and carefully transfer them to a cooling rack. Serve warm or at room temperature, with jam or maple butter (or even better, maple cream, an amber-colored, spreadable version of maple syrup, available at just about any New England shop selling native maple syrup).

*The walnuts are tastier if you toast them before chopping. Place walnut pieces in a single layer in a flat pan and toast them in a preheated 350°F oven for 7 to 9 minutes, or until they smell toasty and are beginning to brown.

nutrition information per serving | **1 scone, made with half unsalted butter/half shortening, and 1 percent milk, 66g**

224 cal | 12g fat | 4g protein | 19g complex carbohydrates | 6g sugar | 1g dietary fiber | 12mg cholesterol | 250mg sodium | 101mg potassium | 48RE vitamin A | 1mg iron | 136mg calcium | 77mg phosphorus

Peach Nutmeg Scones

12 SCONES

The flavors of almond and nutmeg are the perfect supporting cast for one of summer's star flavors: ripe, fresh peaches. Frozen sliced peaches will do in a pinch, if you're looking for an antidote to winter blahs.

2 cups (8½ ounces) unbleached all-purpose flour, or unbleached pastry flour (8 ounces)

½ teaspoon salt

¼ cup (1¾ ounces) granulated sugar

1 teaspoon nutmeg

1 tablespoon baking powder

6 tablespoons (¾ stick, 3 ounces) cold butter, cut into pieces

2 large eggs, beaten

⅓ cup (2¾ ounces) vanilla yogurt

½ teaspoon almond extract

1 cup diced peaches (about 1 good-sized peach)

2 tablespoons (1 ounce) butter, melted

2 tablespoons (1 ounce) granulated sugar

Preheat the oven to 375°F.

In a large bowl, sift the flour, salt, sugar, nutmeg, and baking powder together. Work the butter into the dry ingredients, using your fingertips or a fork or pastry blender.

In another bowl, mix the eggs, yogurt, and almond extract. Stir this into the dry ingredients. Add the peaches and stir just until mixed. This is a very sticky dough.

Liberally flour the counter and your hands. Put the dough on the counter and pat it into a 6 x 9-inch rectangle about 1 inch thick. Cut the rectangle into 6 pieces and cut each small rectangle in half, forming two triangles. You'll have 12 triangles.

Place scones on a well-greased cookie sheet. Brush with the melted butter and sprinkle with the sugar. Bake for 20 minutes, or until nicely browned and a cake tester inserted into a scone comes out dry.

1 scone, 57g

179 cal | 9g fat | 3g protein | 16g complex carbohydrates | 5g sugar | 1g dietary fiber | 58mg cholesterol | 226mg sodium | 65mg potassium | 96RE vitamin A | 1mg vitamin C | 1mg iron | 85mg calcium | 69mg phosphorus

Scallion Cheddar Scones

12 SCONES

These savory wedges pair nicely with baked ham or tomato soup, or with a summer salad to round out the meal. Cut smaller, they are a quick and easy way to serve a bite-sized savory appetizer.

2 cups (8½ ounces) unbleached all-purpose flour, or unbleached pastry flour (8 ounces)

½ teaspoon salt

1 tablespoon sugar

1 tablespoon baking powder

6 tablespoons (¾ stick, 3 ounces) cold butter, cut into pieces

2 large eggs, beaten

⅓ cup (2¾ ounces) cream or sour cream

1 tablespoon Dijon mustard

1 cup (4 ounces) grated sharp cheddar cheese

3 to 5 scallions (1 cup, 2 ounces) chopped

Preheat the oven to 375°F.

Sift together the flour, salt, sugar, and baking powder. Rub in the butter with your fingers.

Mix together the eggs, cream, and mustard. Add this to the dry ingredients. Stir in the grated cheese and the scallions. Mix just until combined. This is the consistency of drop-cookie dough.

Liberally flour the counter and your hands. Pat the dough into a 6 x 9-inch rectangle, about 1 inch thick. Cut the rectangle into 6 smaller rectangles, and cut each smaller rectangle into two triangles, forming 12 triangular scones. Place on a well-greased cookie sheet.

Bake for 20 minutes, or until nicely browned and a cake tester inserted into a scone comes out dry.

1 scone, 57g

189 cal | 11g fat | 6g protein | 15g complex carbohydrates | 1g sugar | 1g dietary fiber | 64mg cholesterol | 316mg sodium | 64mg potassium | 112RE vitamin A | 1mg vitamin C | 1mg iron | 150mg calcium | 114mg phosphorus

Soda Breads

Irish soda bread is a term that encompasses everything from the simplest flour-buttermilk-salt-baking soda bread to those featuring sugar, eggs, butter, raisins, and caraway seeds. The latter are more to our American taste, as they make a lighter, softer, sweeter bread—more cake than bread, actually.

The original Irish soda bread, known as dairy bread, was basically flour, salt and buttermilk, with just a bit of leavening, baked into a round loaf in a pot hung over a peat fire. It was very straightforward and eaten with many an Irish stew, or with just potatoes. What we now think of as Irish soda bread contains additional ingredients that would have made a native Irishman scratch his head in puzzlement, but it is the additions that combine to give this bread the flavor that we recognize as "Irish."

Irish Dairy Bread

ONE 9-INCH ROUND LOAF

The advantage of a "quick" white bread is that it's just that, reasonably quick to make. When white flour became readily available in Ireland, this was the bread first made with it, and it has graced the Irish table ever since. This original is hearty and delicious and perfect with soup, or toasted the next day to be eaten with butter, jam, and tea.

This bread used to be baked in a "bastable" oven, an iron pot with a lid, very much like a Dutch oven, that was placed over a turf fire. A good substitute is a large, lidded cast iron casserole that can be placed in a moderately hot oven. Short of this, a baking sheet will do nicely.

4 cups (17 ounces) unbleached all-purpose flour	¾ teaspoon baking soda
1 teaspoon salt	1 tablespoon (½ ounce) butter
	1½ cups (12 ounces) buttermilk*

Preheat the oven to 375°F.

Place the dry ingredients in a large mixing bowl, making sure you press out any lumps in the baking soda. Blend thoroughly. With your fingers, rub in the butter until it's evenly distributed. Make a well in the center and pour in the buttermilk. Taking about 20 seconds, gently stir it in.

Turn out the dough onto a lightly floured surface and knead several times until the dough comes together. Shape it into a ball, press it down until it's 1½ to 2 inches thick, cut a cross in the top, and place in a floured cast-iron pot or on a floured baking sheet. Place the lid on the pot, if you are using one, and put the dough in the oven. Bake for about 40 minutes. If you're using a baking sheet, 35 minutes may do it. Cool on a rack pretty thoroughly before you try to cut into it, as the structure of the loaf needs to set so it won't compact and become gummy.

*If your flour is very dry, you may need 2 or 3 more tablespoons of buttermilk. In summer, you may need a bit less. You want a dough that is kneadable but not overly stiff.

nutrition information per serving   **1 slice, 64g**

133 cal | 1g fat | 4g protein | 26g complex carbohydrates | 1g dietary fiber | 3mg cholesterol | 233mg sodium |
80mg potassium | 10RE vitamin A | 1mg iron | 89mg calcium | 53mg phosphorus

Irish Freckle Bread

16 PIECES

This recipe is one of our favorites. It's a moist, close-grained, packed-with-fruit breakfast bread, in which the flavor of the whole grain is clearly discernible, yet not overpowering because it's complemented by just the right degree of sweetness. Substantial and satisfying, it keeps extremely well, too. Beyond breakfast and snacking, though, this sturdy quick bread, served with a dollop of hard sauce, makes a heavenly old-fashioned dessert.

1 cup (8 ounces) hot strong plain tea

1 cup (6 ounces) raisins

½ cup (2 ounces) currants

1 cup (5 ounces) pitted prunes snipped into small pieces

1 cup (5 ounces) pitted dates snipped into small pieces

1 cup (8 ounces) brown sugar, firmly packed

2 cups (10½ ounces) graham flour or Irish-style flour, or 1 cup (5 ounces) white whole wheat flour plus 1 cup (4 ounces) whole wheat pastry flour

1 tablespoon baking powder

½ teaspoon salt

1 large egg

1 tablespoon granulated sugar

Pour the tea over the raisins, currants, prunes, and dates in a medium-sized mixing bowl, stirring occasionally until the mixture is completely cool. Preheat the oven to 325°F.

In a medium-sized mixing bowl, combine the brown sugar, flour, baking powder, and salt, then add to the fruit mixture. The batter will be stiff. Beat in the egg and mix well.

Spread the mixture into a greased 8-inch round pan, sprinkle the top evenly with the granulated sugar, and bake for approximately 1 hour and 10 minutes, or until a cake tester inserted in the center of the bread comes out clean.

nutrition information per serving   **1 slice, 84g**

208 cal | 1g fat | 3g protein | 34g complex carbohydrates | 14g sugar | 5g dietary fiber | 17mg cholesterol | 80mg sodium |
545mg potassium | 26RE vitamin A | 1mg vitamin C | 2mg iron | 77mg calcium | 152mg phosphorus

Irish Soda Bread, American Style

ONE SWEET, MOIST, CRUMBLY TEXTURED LOAF, 24 SERVINGS

Sweeter and more tender than traditional Irish soda bread, this Americanized version is sure to please anyone who appreciates this genre.

4½ cups (19 ounces) unbleached all-purpose flour

5 teaspoons baking powder

1½ teaspoons salt

1 teaspoon baking soda

1 cup (2 sticks, 8 ounces) butter or margarine

2 large eggs

1 cup (7 ounces) sugar

2 cups (16 ounces) milk

1 tablespoon caraway seeds

1½ cups (9 ounces) raisins

Preheat the oven to 325°F.

In a large bowl, sift together the flour, baking powder, salt, and baking soda; set aside. In another bowl, cream together the butter, eggs, and sugar until light and fluffy.

Fold the dry ingredients into the wet ingredients alternately with the milk. Stir in the caraway seeds and raisins.

Spoon the batter into a greased, deep (9 x 4-inch round) cake pan or springform pan, or a deep angel food or tube pan. Bake the bread for about 1½ hours (less in a tube or angel food pan), or until a cake tester inserted in the center comes out clean. Remove the bread from the oven and cool on a wire rack.

nutrition information per serving   1 slice, 76g

221 cal | 8g fat | 4g protein | 25g complex carbohydrates | 8g sugar | 1g dietary fiber | 39mg cholesterol | 305mg sodium | 147mg potassium | 91RE vitamin A | 1mg vitamin C | 2mg iron | 93mg calcium | 81 mg phosphorus

Simply Wonderful Stollen

TWO 1-POUND LOAVES, 10 SLICES EACH

Laura Lane of Jefferson City, Tennessee, was nice enough to send us one of her favorite recipes, this easy-to-make stollen, perfect for the busy December holidays. Unlike traditional stollen, this one is leavened with baking powder, not yeast, and moistened with ricotta cheese. Rather than the typical yeast-bread texture, it's more like a rich biscuit.

DOUGH

2¼ cups (9½ ounces) unbleached all-purpose flour

½ cup (3½ ounces) sugar

1½ teaspoons baking powder

¼ teaspoon salt

6 tablespoons (3 ounces) cold butter

1 cup (8 ounces) ricotta cheese

1 large egg, plus 1 egg yolk from a large egg

1 teaspoon vanilla extract

½ teaspoon lemon zest

½ cup (2⅝ ounces) diced candied lemon peel (or mixed dried fruit)

½ cup (3 ounces) raisins (dark or golden)

⅓ cup (1½ ounces) slivered almonds, toasted and cooled

GLAZE

1 cup (4 ounces) confectioners' or glazing sugar

⅛ teaspoon almond extract (optional)

2 to 3 tablespoons cream or evaporated milk, or 1 to 2 tablespoons water

Preheat the oven to 325°F.

FOR THE DOUGH In a large bowl, whisk together the flour, sugar, baking powder, and salt. Cut the cold butter into small chunks, then cut it into the flour mixture.

In a separate bowl, mix together the ricotta cheese, egg, egg yolk, vanilla, and lemon zest.

Toss the lemon peel, raisins, and toasted almonds into the flour mixture and stir until evenly distributed. Then combine the contents of the two bowls, mixing until most of the flour is moistened. Turn out the dough onto a lightly floured work surface and knead it two or three times, until it holds together. Divide it in half and pat each half into a circle.

Roll each piece of dough into an 8 x 7-inch oval about ½ inch thick. Place the ovals on a lightly greased or parchment-lined baking sheet and fold each one roughly in half, leaving the edge of the top half about ½ inch short of the edge of the bottom half. Press with the edge of your hand about 1 inch in back of the open edge, forcing the dough edges to come apart just slightly; this will make the traditional stollen shape.

Bake the stollen for 40 to 45 minutes, until they're very lightly browned around the edges. A cake tester inserted into the center should come out clean. Transfer the stollen to a wire rack to cool.

FOR THE GLAZE In a small bowl, mix together the sugar, flavoring, and cream. Use cream or evaporated milk for a creamy glaze, water for a harder glaze. Brush the stollen with the glaze while they're still slightly warm. Let them cool for several hours for easier slicing.

nutrition information per serving   1 slice, 54g

175 cal | 6g fat | 4g protein | 14g complex carbohydrates | 12g sugar | 1g fiber | 37mg cholesterol | 113mg sodium | 84mg potassium | 62RE vitamin A | 1mg iron | 64mg calcium | 79mg phosphorus

Buckles, Cobblers, and Crisps

There's a time in late summer when the days, almost overnight, seem to change. Like climbing up one side of a mountain, reaching the peak, then starting down the other, the view is different. Goldenrod and marigolds replace the dandelions and daisies of early summer. The sun starts to slant low in the late afternoon, not after dinner. Fields that were dewy and fresh at summer's beginning hold a permanent patina of pollen and dust from a long, dry summer. Fall is coming, and our part of the earth is once again turning toward winter.

The growing season draws to a close in August and September, and it does so in a spectacular burst of color and flavor. Carpe diem. Summer is the time for peach cobbler, blueberry buckle, and cherry crisp, while these fruits are at their freshest and best. Red plums, black plums, and purple plums; sour pie cherries and Bing cherries; peaches, nectarines, and apricots;

raspberries, blueberries, strawberries, and blackberries: all can be tucked into a pie shell, sliced onto shortcake, wrapped in a turnover, baked into a crisp—the possibilities are endless.

Living in New England, we sometimes forget that bakers in other parts of the country aren't necessarily familiar with the complete range of baked desserts native to this region. Things like blueberry slump. And blackberry grunt. And apple pandowdy. Cobbler is probably a familiar term in most regions, but how about buckle? Or crumble, or crisp? All are made with fruit, sugar, flour, and butter, in different proportions and configurations. And all are good to keep in mind when it's apple-picking time, or the strawberries are ripe, or crates of low-bush blueberries, hand-raked from Maine's windswept coastal fields, are being sold alongside the road.

Easy, fast, and delicious, these fruit-based desserts were a godsend to the harried New England farmwife who had fruit (but not time) on her hands, and needed to serve her family something sweet before they headed back out into the fields after their midday dinner. Like that farmwife, you can treat your family to something fresh, sweet, and tasty—even if they're only heading to the field for baseball or soccer, rather than to cut hay.

Not So Fast!

Most fruit desserts—especially crisps, cobblers, and other juicy sweets—are best eaten warm, after about 30 minutes of resting on a cooling rack. This cooling-off time gives the juices a chance to set, and will also prevent you from burning your mouth on the scalding combination of bubbling fruit juice and sugar.

Crisps and Crumbles

A crisp and a crumble are not the same: crumble toppings contain oatmeal, crisps do not. That makes sense; a topping made of just sugar, butter, and flour is more likely to be crisp, while one that adds oatmeal will be crumbly.

Blueberry Crisp

10 SERVINGS

We love our northern New England blueberries, but this recipe can easily be tailored to just about any kind of seasonal fruit or berry. Just adjust the sugar and thickening as needed. It's the easy concept we're sharing here, not really the specific recipe.

FILLING

2 pints (4 generous cups, about 24 ounces) blueberries, cleaned and stemmed*

½ cup (3½ ounces) sugar

¼ cup (1 ounce) unbleached all-purpose flour

¼ teaspoon salt

2 teaspoons lemon juice, or 2 drops lemon oil

TOPPING

1½ cups (6¼ ounces) unbleached all-purpose flour

¼ teaspoon salt

½ cup (3½ ounces) sugar

10 tablespoons (1¼ sticks, 5 ounces) butter, melted

1 cup (3½ to 4 ounces) walnuts or pecans, chopped

Grease and flour a 9-inch pie pan. Preheat the oven to 350°F.

FILLING Put the berries in the pan. Mix the sugar, flour, salt, and lemon together, and sprinkle this mixture over the berries.

TOPPING In a medium-sized mixing bowl, stir together the flour, salt, sugar, melted butter, and nuts. Sprinkle the topping over the fruit.

Bake the crisp for 45 to 50 minutes, until the top is golden and the filling is bubbly. Cool slightly, then serve warm, with vanilla ice cream or whipped cream.

NOTE To cut the amount of fat in this recipe to 12g per serving and the calories to 292, leave out the nuts.

*Or use any mixture of fruit; peach slices combined with blueberries are wonderful.

nutrition information per serving ¹⁄₁₀ **of crisp, 140g**

364 cal | 20g fat | 4g protein | 27g complex carbohydrates | 19g sugar | 3g fiber | 33mg cholesterol | 235mg sodium | 140mg potassium | 122 RE vitamin A | 10mg vitamin C | 1mg iron | 12mg calcium | 62mg phosphorus

Apple Crumble

16 SERVINGS

The warm, cinnamon-sweet apples in this dish are a perfect base for vanilla ice cream, which gradually sends vanilla-scented rivulets through the crisp, buttery streusel topping, and into the apples.

FILLING

2 pounds Granny Smith apples (about 5 medium to large)

1 pound McIntosh or Cortland apples (about 2 large)

¼ cup (2 ounces) rum or apple cider

2 tablespoons (1 ounce) butter, melted

2 tablespoons (1 ounce) boiled cider (optional, but good)

¾ cup (6 ounces) brown sugar

1 teaspoon cinnamon

¼ teaspoon nutmeg

¼ teaspoon ground ginger

3 tablespoons (2 ounces) tapioca flour or unbleached all-purpose flour*

¼ teaspoon salt

STREUSEL TOPPING

½ cup (2 ounces) unbleached all-purpose flour

½ cup (1¾ ounces) thick oat flakes (old-fashioned rolled oats)

⅛ teaspoon salt

½ cup (4 ounces) brown sugar

½ teaspoon cinnamon

¾ teaspoon baking powder

8 tablespoons (1 stick, 4 ounces) butter

Preheat the oven to 350°F.

FILLING Peel, core, and slice the apples into ¼-inch-thick pieces. Place them in a bowl with the remainder of the filling ingredients and stir vigorously to combine. In the process the apple pieces will break into smaller bits; this is fine. Spoon the apple mixture into a lightly greased 9 x 9-inch cake pan, or a ceramic pan of similar capacity and surface area.

TOPPING In a medium-sized mixing bowl, stir together the flour, oats, salt, brown sugar, cinnamon, and baking powder. Add the butter, cutting it in with a mixer, your fingers, or a pastry blender as you would when making piecrust. Mix until crumbly; if you work it too much the mixture will clump together, so use a light touch but be thorough. Sprinkle the topping over the filling.

Bake the crumble for 1½ hours, or until it's bubbly and a deep, golden brown. Remove it from the oven and let it cool to lukewarm before serving.

*Tapioca flour will make the sauce in the filling clearer looking; flour will make it opaque. They will do their job as thickener equally well.

nutrition information per serving   2¼-inch square, 122g

208 cal | 7g fat | 1g protein | 17g complex carbohydrates | 14g sugar | 3g dietary fiber | 1g alcohol | 20mg cholesterol | 109mg sodium | 169mg potassium | 93RE vitamin A | 3mg vitamin C | 2mg iron | 52mg calcium | 34mg phosphorus

Pear Crumble

10 GENEROUS SERVINGS

Everyone loves apple crisp, and this variation with pears is sure to become a family favorite as well. It's warm, comforting, and just the right way to end dinner on a chilly fall evening. There's a high ratio of "crumble" to fruit here; if you prefer more fruit, simply double the amount of filling.

TOPPING

1 cup (3¾ ounces) pecan pieces

¾ cup (3 ounces) unbleached all-purpose flour

1 teaspoon cinnamon

¼ cup (2 ounces) light brown sugar, packed

½ cup (1¾ ounces) thick oat flakes (old-fashioned rolled oats)

¼ cup (½ stick, 2 ounces) unsalted butter

FILLING

8 Bartlett or Anjou pears, peeled, cored, and sliced (8 cups, 2¼ pounds fruit)

½ cup (4 ounces) light brown sugar, packed

1 tablespoon fresh lemon juice, or ¼ teaspoon lemon oil

¼ cup (1 ounce) unbleached all-purpose flour

½ teaspoon cinnamon

Preheat the oven to 400°F. Grease a 9 x 13-inch baking pan.

TOPPING Toast the pecan pieces in the oven for 5 to 10 minutes, or until lightly browned and aromatic. Let the pecans cool, then combine them with the flour, cinnamon, brown sugar, and oats. Cut in the butter until the mixture forms coarse crumbs, about the size of peas.

FILLING Mix the pears with the sugar, lemon juice, flour, and cinnamon. Pour the filling into the prepared baking pan and sprinkle the topping over it.

Bake the crumble for 30 to 40 minutes, or until the topping has become golden brown and crunchy and the fruit is bubbly.

nutrition information per serving   ¹/₁₀ **of recipe, 184g**

315 cal | 4g fat | 3g protein | 33g complex carbohydrates | 16g sugar | 5g dietary fiber | 13mg cholesterol | 7mg sodium | 301mg potassium | 50RE vitamin A | 6mg vitamin C | 2mg iron | 41mg calcium | 80 mg phosphorus

Buckles

A buckle is a streusel- and fruit-topped coffeecake, plain and simple. Tradition has it that the name comes from the way the cake "buckles" as it bakes, rising around its fruit topping (which is also sinking), so that the cake finishes with a craggy top surface.

Blueberry Buckle

ONE 9-INCH SQUARE COFFEECAKE, ABOUT 16 SERVINGS

August is a luxuriant time of year, when all growing things are yielding the results of long days and warm nights. Flowers burst into frenetic bloom, the berries are in, and we're able to indulge in the bounty of the garden just by strolling out the door with a basket and a pair of scissors.

This rich, moist coffeecake is one of our favorite summer morning treats, when the blueberries are ripe and abundant. It's rarely around for more than an hour out of the oven, but should you have admirable restraint, it will still be just as delicious for dessert.

BATTER
¾ cup (5½ ounces) sugar
4 tablespoons (½ stick, 2 ounces) butter
1 large egg
½ cup (4 ounces) milk
2 cups (8½ ounces) unbleached all-purpose flour
2 teaspoons baking powder
½ teaspoon salt
¼ teaspoon ground cardamom (optional)
1 teaspoon vanilla extract (optional)

2 cups (11 ounces) blueberries (fresh or, if frozen, unthawed)

STREUSEL
¾ cup (5½ ounces) sugar
¾ cup (3 ounces) unbleached all-purpose flour
1 teaspoon cinnamon
2 to 3 teaspoons lemon zest, or ⅛ teaspoon lemon oil
½ teaspoon salt
5⅓ tablespoons (⅔ stick, 2⅔ ounces) soft butter

Grease and flour a 9-inch square or 9-inch round pan and preheat the oven to 375°F.

BATTER Cream together the sugar and butter, then add the egg and mix at medium speed for 1 minute. Whisk together the dry ingredients. Stir in the milk alternately with the dry ingredients and vanilla, scraping down the sides of the bowl. Gently fold in the blueberries. Spread the batter in the prepared pan.

STREUSEL In a medium-sized bowl, whisk together the sugar, flour, cinnamon, lemon, and salt. Add the butter, mixing to make medium-sized crumbs. Sprinkle the streusel evenly over the batter.

Bake the buckle for 45 to 50 minutes, or until a cake tester inserted into the center comes out clean. Remove from the oven, and cool it (in the pan) on a rack. Serve the buckle with coffee in the morning, or with whipped cream for dessert.

one 2¼-inch square, 72g

226 cal | 7g fat | 3g protein | 18g complex carbohydrates | 19g sugar | 1g dietary fiber | 32mg cholesterol | 204mg sodium | 62mg potassium | 77RE vitamin A | 3mg vitamin C | 1mg iron | 50mg calcium | 48mg phosphorus

Variation   BLUEBERRY-PEACH BUCKLE: This variation on the preceding recipe features one of our favorite fruit combinations, blueberries and peaches. If you are using fruits other than blueberries (which are small and tend to stay put in the batter, rather than sinking to the bottom as the buckle bakes), put half the batter in the pan first, add the fruit, then top with the remaining batter.

Prepare the batter from the preceding recipe, substituting ¼ teaspoon nutmeg for the ¼ teaspoon cardamom.

Prepare the topping from the preceding recipe, substituting ½ teaspoon almond extract for the lemon.

Spread half the batter (about 18 ounces) in the greased pan. Layer with the peach slices. Fold the blueberries into the remaining batter and dollop it on top; a cookie scoop works well here. Sprinkle the streusel over the batter. Bake as for blueberry buckle.

Grunts and Slumps

These are desserts whose name alone will bring a smile to the face of anyone familiar with traditional New England desserts—and a quizzical look from those unfamiliar with them. To understand the provenance of the terms *grunt* and *slump*, you need to picture how they're put together and cooked.

To make slump or grunt—the two terms are interchangeable—take a quart of berries or diced fruit, stir in some sugar and water, and put the mixture in an iron spider (a cast iron skillet) or casserole dish that can sit on a burner. (Grunts used to be cooked in an open cast iron Dutch oven over the coals of a fire.) Then top the berries with spoonfuls of biscuit dough and let the mixture cook very slowly.

As the concoction begins to heat, bubbles slowly work their way up from the bottom of the pot to break through the biscuit dough topping. The wet snufflings you hear bear some resemblance to an animal's grunt. Once served, the dessert slumps on the plate in a sweet, juicy, hot-biscuit heap. (Really, this is much more appetizing than it sounds.)

Maine Blueberry Grunt

10 TO 12 SERVINGS

A blueberry is a blueberry until you've tried fresh-picked low-bush blueberries, which grow in profusion on low, scrubby bushes scattered over rather barren land in Maine and all over the Northeast; the tiny tart ones from Maine are by far the most famous. In August, school-age kids all over the state put aside whatever other summer activities they were pursuing and take up their blueberry rakes and buckets, intent on earning a "stash" to buy new school clothes (or new computer games); the kids vie with each other (and the adults alongside them) to see who can rake the most berries in a day. Often those days stretch from predawn to dark, particularly for the teenage boys who, like their counterparts all over the world, are both full of energy, and ultra-competitive.

FRUIT

1 cup (8 ounces) water

1 cup (7 ounces) sugar

1 teaspoon lemon juice (if the berries aren't tart)

½ teaspoon ground cinnamon (optional)

1 quart blueberries, cleaned

DOUGH

2 cups (8½ ounces) unbleached all-purpose flour

2 teaspoons baking powder

½ teaspoon baking soda

½ teaspoon salt

4 tablespoons (½ stick, 2 ounces) butter

1 cup (8 ounces) buttermilk

A grunt is made by dropping a moist biscuit-style dough onto simmering fruit.

Blend the water, sugar, lemon juice, and cinnamon in a skillet and stir in the blueberries. Bring to a gentle boil over low heat.

While the blueberries are heating, blend the dry dough ingredients together in a mixing bowl. Rub in the butter with your fingertips. Quickly stir in the buttermilk.

Drop the dough in blobs over the blueberry mixture. Cover and cook over low heat until the biscuit dough is done, about 15 minutes. To serve, scoop up the berries and a biscuit and invert on a plate, so that the berries fall over the biscuit. Spoon extra berry mixture over the biscuit.

nutrition information per serving ¹⁄₁₁ **of recipe, 142g**

218 cal | 5g fat | 3g protein | 24g complex carbohydrates | 17g sugar | 2g dietary fiber | 13mg cholesterol | 271mg sodium | 109mg potassium | 48RE vitamin A | 7mg vitamin C | 1mg iron | 80mg calcium | 64mg phosphorus

Blueberry Slump

12 TO 15 SERVINGS

Louisa May Alcott named her home in Concord, Massachusetts, "Apple Slump," perhaps because it evoked for her the same thing that her apple slump did: something warm and comforting, with a hint of spice. Her apple slump consisted of 6 sliced apples simmered in half a cup of water to which had been added 1 cup of sugar and a teaspoon of cinnamon. She topped this mixture with pieces of "lean" (low-fat) biscuit dough, covered the pot, and let the dumplings steam over low heat for about half an hour. The apples with dumplings were served with syrup on top, and a little cream for richness.

This blueberry version of slump is an offspring of Apple Dumpling Slices (p. 146). By adding some fat to the dumpling dough, you change its nature enough so you can bake it, rather than steam it, and produce something tender and crisp rather than tough and rubbery (which a "lean" dumpling would translate to if baked). The dumplings will continue to absorb the syrup and will taste even better the second day. This version is rich enough that it can be served without cream (unless the occasion demands).

SYRUP

4 tablespoons (½ stick, 2 ounces) butter

1 cup (8 ounces) water

1 cup (8 ounces) brown sugar

⅛ teaspoon allspice

⅛ teaspoon nutmeg

1 tablespoon lemon juice

DUMPLINGS

2 cups (8½ ounces) unbleached all-purpose flour

1 tablespoon baking powder

½ teaspoon salt

6 tablespoons (¾ stick, 3 ounces) butter

¾ cup (6 ounces) milk

FILLING

1 quart blueberries

FOR THE SYRUP Melt the butter in a 9 x 13-inch baking dish. In a small saucepan, warm the water, brown sugar, spices and lemon juice over low heat until the sugar dissolves.

FOR THE DUMPLINGS Put the flour, baking powder, and salt in a medium-sized mixing bowl and rub in the butter with your fingertips, a pastry blender, or two knives. Pour in the milk and stir together until you have a shaggy dough.

TO ASSEMBLE Pour the blueberries into the prepared baking dish. Place blobs of dumpling dough on top of the blueberries and pour the syrup over the top. Bake the slump for 40 minutes, or until the biscuits are golden and the mixture is bubbly. Serve the slump warm.

nutrition information per serving   1 serving, 127g

241 cal | 8g fat | 2g protein | 115g complex carbohydrates | 25g sugar | 1g dietary fiber | 22mg cholesterol | 176mg sodium | 148mg potassium | 83RE vitamin A | 5mg vitamin C | 1mg iron | 59mg calcium | 79mg phosphorus

Cobblers

Cobbler, featuring fruit baked under (or in) a blanket of crust or cake, is a distinctly American dish. Its name is said to come from the phrase "to cobble," meaning to patch something together roughly; to "cobble up," put something together in a hurry; or perhaps from the fact that the combination of fruit and dough on top of the dish looks like cobblestones.

Three very different types of crust are what differentiate cobblers from one another. Originally, a cobbler's top crust was thick spoonfuls of biscuit dough, dumplings that cooked on top of the hot fruit layer (similar to slumps or grunts.) Later, that dough was rolled and fitted atop the fruit; still later, pastry (piecrust) dough was rolled and fitted over the fruit, making cobbler akin to a deep-dish fruit pie without the bottom crust. The most recent variation finds a cakelike batter being poured atop the fruit, or fruit being placed atop the batter; the fruit and batter create a "marbled" effect, each remaining distinct though effectively melded. Any way you put together a cobbler, the fruit and crust end up mixing and mingling, the fruit softening some of the crust, the crust absorbing the fruit juices.

Use your imagination to pair various fruits with different flavors in the crust. There are very few desserts as flexible as this one.

For cake-style cobbler, pour the batter over the fruit in a prepared pan.

Basic Fruit Cobbler
(fruit atop a cake crust)

NINE 2-INCH SQUARES OR 8 TO 10 WEDGES

Cobbler can be made with many different fruits, alone or in combination. First a few words about measuring. This is not an exact science, because fruit is an inexact ingredient. It can vary in size, water content, sugar or acid content, and pectin; all of those have an impact on the other ingredients with which it may be combined. When we give fruit measurements, they are meant to be general guidelines. Your experience and common sense may cause you to vary both the type of fruit and the amounts, and when the result is a success, you've become a real baker.

Basically, any fruit you'd use to make a pie is appropriate for cobbler. Berries of all sorts; stone fruits (cherries, peaches, plums, and nectarines); rhubarb; and apples and pears are all good candidates. Whatever fruit you use, it should be peeled and cored (if necessary), and cut into small bite-sized pieces; berries should be hulled, but unless they're mammoth strawberries, can remain whole.

1 cup (4¼ ounces) unbleached all-purpose flour

1 teaspoon baking powder

½ teaspoon salt

2 large eggs

1½ cups (10½ ounces) sugar

2 tablespoons (1 ounce) butter, softened

2 tablespoons (1 ounce) milk

½ cup (4 ounces) sherry, brandy or bourbon*

3 to 4 cups fresh fruit (large fruits sliced; berries left whole)

Whipped cream or ice cream

Preheat the oven to 375°F. Grease a 9 x 9-inch square pan (or similar-size casserole dish) or an 11-inch round quiche dish.

Mix the flour, baking powder, and salt and set aside. Beat together the eggs and 1 cup of the sugar. Add butter and milk. Add the flour mixture, stirring just to combine. Pour the batter into the greased pan.

In a medium-sized saucepan, simmer together the sherry and the remaining ½ cup of sugar for 3 to 4 minutes. Add the fruit and stir to coat with the syrup. Pour this hot fruit mixture over the batter in the pan.

Bake for 30 minutes. Serve warm with whipped cream or ice cream.

*If you prefer not to use any liquor, increase the milk in the recipe to ¼ cup and use a mixture of 1 tablespoon lemon juice, 1 teaspoon vanilla extract, ½ teaspoon almond extract, and ¼ cup of water in place of the liquor.

nutrition information per serving   using cherries as fruit, 1 square, 171g

273 cal | 4g fat | 4g protein | 18g complex carbohydrates | 32g sugar | 1g dietary fiber | 55mg cholesterol | 196mg sodium | 130mg potassium | 120RE vitamin A | 2mg vitamin C | 2mg iron | 51mg calcium | 56mg phosphorus

Apple and Maple-Walnut Cobbler
(fruit under a cake crust)

ABOUT 12 SERVINGS

There no longer seems to be any season for apples, coming as they do to our American groceries from all over the world. Our favorite baking apple is the bright green Granny Smith; it's available year-round and strikes the perfect note of tart-sweetness and tender-crispness when baked.

4 medium-to-large Granny Smith apples, peeled, cored, and sliced ¼ inch thick (5 to 6 cups)

8 tablespoons (1 stick, 4 ounces) butter

½ cup (3½ ounces) sugar

½ cup (4 ounces) buttermilk or plain yogurt

1 cup (4¼ ounces) unbleached all-purpose flour

1 teaspoon baking soda

1 teaspoon baking powder

¼ teaspoon salt

1 teaspoon vanilla extract

¾ cup (8¼ ounces) maple syrup

1 cup (4 ounces) chopped walnuts

Lightly grease an 8- or 9-inch square pan and place the apple slices in it. Set the pan aside. Preheat the oven to 350°F.

In a medium-sized mixing bowl, beat together the butter and sugar until smooth. Add the buttermilk, flour, baking soda, baking powder, salt, and vanilla and beat again until smooth. Spoon the batter—it should be rather stiff—over the apples in the pan, using a spatula or your fingers (it helps to wet the spatula or your fingers with a little water first).

Pour the maple syrup over the batter, then sprinkle the nuts over all. Bake the cobbler for 55 to 60 minutes, covering with a piece of aluminum foil, shiny side up, after the first half-hour of baking (or when your cobbler has become a deep golden brown). Remove the cobbler from the oven and let it cool for at least 20 minutes before serving. Serve it warm, or at room temperature, plain or with ice cream or very lightly sweetened whipped cream.

nutrition information per serving   **1 serving, 124g**

281 cal | 13g fat | 3g protein | 17g complex carbohydrates | 20g sugar | 2g dietary fiber | 251mg cholesterol | 178mg potassium | 2mg vitamin C

Peach and Raspberry Cobbler
(fruit under a piecrust)

There's something seductive in the classic peach-raspberry combination; surely the great chef Georges Escoffier must have thought so when he created the classic Peach Melba for one of his favorite customers, Australian opera singer Nellie Melba. Peach Melba's got nothing on this cobbler.

CRUST

1 cup (4¼ ounces) unbleached all-purpose flour

¼ teaspoon salt

4 tablespoons (½ stick, 2 ounces) cold unsalted butter

¼ cup (1⅝ ounces) cold vegetable shortening

2 to 4 tablespoons (1 to 2 ounces) ice water

FILLING

5 cups peeled, sliced peaches (12 to 13 peaches, 4 to 4½ pounds)

1 cup (5 ounces) raspberries

1 teaspoon lemon juice

¾ to 1 cup (5¾ to 7 ounces) sugar (to taste)

1 tablespoon cornstarch*

¼ teaspoon salt

¼ teaspoon nutmeg

2 tablespoons coarse white sugar (optional)

Preheat the oven to 425°F.

CRUST Butter a 9-inch round cake pan or pie dish. Whisk together the flour and salt in a medium-sized mixing bowl, or use a food processor, then cut or pulse in the butter and shortening until the mixture is coarse and crumbly. Add just enough water to form a cohesive dough (bring the dough together with your hands, or if using a food processor, pulse just enough times for the dough to form a ball in the bowl). Wrap the dough and refrigerate for 30 minutes.

FILLING Combine the peaches, raspberries, and lemon juice in a large bowl. Mix together the sugar, cornstarch, salt, and nutmeg and stir into the fruit. Spoon the filling into the prepared pan.

Roll out the crust to a 9-inch circle and place on top of the fruit. Sprinkle with sugar. Cut several vents in the top and bake the cobbler for 15 minutes. Reduce the oven heat to 350°F and bake for an additional 40 to 45 minutes, until the crust is golden and the juices are bubbling. Remove the cobbler from the oven and cool it on a wire rack.

*Use an extra tablespoon of cornstarch if the peaches are very juicy.

nutrition information per serving   ¹⁄₁₀ **of cobbler, 139g**

203 cal | 5g fat | 2g protein | 20g complex carbohydrates | 18g sugar | 3g dietary fiber | 107mg sodium | 202mg potassium | 48RE vitamin A | 9mg vitamin C | 1mg iron | 7mg calcium | 23mg phosphorus

Bumbleberry Cobbler
(fruit under a biscuit crust)

10 SERVINGS

You've never heard of a bumbleberry? Sure you have—you just don't recognize the name. Bumbleberry is an idiomatic term for a mixture of blackberries, blueberries, and raspberries; it makes a delicious pie, emblematic of high summer and, in this case, an equally good cobbler.

2 pounds (about 8 cups) fresh or frozen berries, a mixture of blackberries, blueberries, and raspberries

1 tablespoon cornstarch

1 cup (7 ounces) granulated or brown sugar

1½ cups (6¼ ounces) unbleached all-purpose flour*

1 cup (4 ounces) unbleached pastry flour*

1 tablespoon sugar

1 tablespoon baking powder

¼ teaspoon salt

4 tablespoons (½ stick, 2 ounces) butter

¾ cup (6 ounces) buttermilk

1 large egg

Preheat the oven to 350°F. Grease a 9-inch round cake pan, preferably one with 3-inch sides. Or use a 9 x 9-inch pan or 2-quart casserole, or something that's approximately the same size. The cobbler will bubble up and spill over if you try to bake it in something smaller or less deep.

Place the berries in the greased pan or casserole. Mix the cornstarch into the sugar and sprinkle over the fruit. While the sugar begins to draw the juice out of the fruit, make the dough.

Put the flours in a mixing bowl and blend in the remaining dry ingredients. With your fingertips, mix in the butter until the blend looks like coarse cornmeal. In a smaller bowl, beat together the buttermilk and egg. Make a well in the dry ingredients and pour in the buttermilk-egg mixture. Quickly mix these together with a spoon, taking about 20 seconds. The dough will be quite wet and sticky, but you can keep it under control if you keep everything that comes in contact with it well-floured.

Turn the dough out onto a well-floured surface and knead or fold over gently until it's reasonably cohesive. A bowl scraper or bench knife, also well-floured, will facilitate this. When you've shaped the dough into a nice ball, gently roll it out until you have a circle that will roughly cover the berries. It can be a bit smaller in diameter than the pan because it will expand as it bakes. Place over the fruit and bake for about 45 minutes.

The cobbler is done when the top is lightly browned and the fruit is soft and bubbling. Remove it from the oven and let it sit for a few minutes. You can leave it as is and serve it "right-side-up" with lightly sweetened whipped cream, or you can take a serving dish, upend it over the cobbler, and flip it over quickly so the crust will be on the bottom. There will be a lot of quite hot juice in the bottom of the pan so this must be done very fast, with great care, and preferably over a sink. Serve warm with whipped cream or ice cream.

*Or substitute 2⅓ cups unbleached all-purpose flour for the all-purpose and pastry flour.

nutrition information per serving   ¹⁄₁₀ of recipe, 201g

315 cal | 6g fat | 5g protein | 42g complex carbohydrates | 20g sugar | 7g dietary fiber | 35mg cholesterol | 238mg sodium | 238mg potassium | 67mg vitamin A | 4mg vitamin C | 3mg iron | 143mg calcium | 118mg phosphorus

Apple Pandowdy

ABOUT 12 SERVINGS

Apple pandowdy is a traditional American dish dating to the early 1800s. A combination pie and pudding, the name may come from the method in which the recipe is completed: after an apple-based filling is baked in a crust-topped casserole, the baker takes a fork and "dowdies" the crust, breaking it into pieces that manage to remain crisp despite being partly immersed in the filling. (Some have the origin of the word stemming from the dish's humble, "dowdy" appearance).

The filling is juicy; don't be surprised when you cut into the crust and find a sea of liquid. As the dish cools, the "dowdied" crust absorbs a lot of the liquid, leaving you with an almost puddinglike confection. This dish is best served right from its baking pan.

1 recipe piecrust for double-crust 9-inch pie (see p. 408 for medium-flake piecrust)

7 or 8 large apples

½ cup (3½ ounces) granulated sugar

¼ teaspoon salt

¼ teaspoon cinnamon

¼ teaspoon nutmeg

¼ cup (2 ounces) water

½ cup (6 ounces) molasses or maple syrup (5½ ounces)

3 tablespoons (1½ ounces) butter, cut into bits

Put the oven rack on its lowest rung and preheat the oven to 425°F.

Divide the pie dough into two pieces, one slightly larger than the other. Roll out the larger piece to fit into the bottom and up the sides of a casserole dish (a 9 x 9-inch pan, or equivalent, is the right size). Peel, core, and cut the apples into ¼-inch slices. You should have abut 9 cups. Toss the slices with the sugar, salt, cinnamon, and nutmeg. Spoon apples into piecrust.

Mix water and molasses and pour over apples. Dot with butter.

Roll out second piece of dough and fit it over apple mixture. Brush the edge of the bottom crust with milk and squeeze together the edges of the bottom and top crust, sealing them; the protein in the milk will act as glue, keeping a tight seal while the pandowdy bakes. Brush top crust with milk and sprinkle with granulated sugar, if desired (this will make a brown, sugary crust).

Bake for 45 minutes, then decrease heat to 325°F and continue to bake until crust is well browned (the initial 45 minutes may be enough for the browning, each oven is a bit different).

Remove from the oven and cool on a wire rack for 5 minutes. After 5 minutes, take a knife and slash, in a random pattern, all the way through the pan dowdy. With a fork and spoon, gently lift pieces of crust from the bottom and submerge pieces of the top crust; in effect, you're really messing this whole thing up. Don't get carried away; crust pieces should remain in fairly large (2-inch-square) chunks. Let the dish cool to warm before serving; if you serve it too hot, it will be very runny.

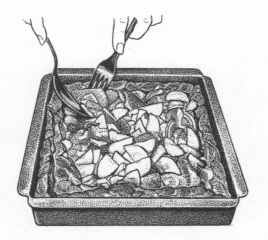

Use a fork and spoon to "dowdy" the crust for apple pandowdy.

nutrition information per serving	1 square, 149g

280 cal | 12g fat | 2g protein | 26g complex carbohydrates | 17g sugar | 2g dietary fiber | 19mg cholesterol | 225mg sodium | 147mg potassium | 69RE Vitamin A | 3mg vitamin C | 1mg iron | 15mg calcium | 25mg phosphorus

Dumplings

Dumplings come in both sweet and savory versions, and the two resemble one another in shape only. The sweet dumpling category can be broken in half as well: fruit that's surrounded with a pastry crust and baked (as in traditional apple dumplings); and baking powder biscuit–like dough that's simmered in a sweet sauce and served with cream. Savory dumplings roam the landscape from biscuit dumplings simmered in soup or stew (probably what most people think of when they think about dumplings), to quenelles (ground meat or seafood mixed with egg, and poached in salted water), to gnocchi (small rolled shapes of flour and potato, usually simmered in a savory sauce), to stuffed wontons and some types of dim sum.

The dumplings we'll concentrate on are the sweet, fruit-filled ones and the ones based on biscuit dough that simmer in another medium, be it sweet or savory.

Apple Dumplings

8 DUMPLINGS

The marriage of apples and pastry is a familiar, comforting one. And dumplings seem both homier and dressier at the same time than the ubiquitous apple pie or tart.

If you're new to making dumplings, rest assured they aren't difficult. We give two different dough recipes here: one is more like pastry, flaky and tender. The other is more like a biscuit in texture. Each version has its fans, so you can choose which type of dough you'd like to use. Either of these would make a yummy breakfast. You could fancy up the center with some dried cherries or raisins, if you like. As a dessert, they should be served warm with whipped cream or ice cream. Or, if you're a New Englander, a big fat slice of sharp cheddar cheese on top would be just right.

This recipe is made with large, tart, crisp baking apples, such as Granny Smith, Rome, or Empire. Other eating apple varieties won't stand up to the baking time before turning into applesauce.

PASTRY-STYLE DUMPLING DOUGH

2 cups (8½ ounces) unbleached all-purpose flour

2 teaspoons baking powder

½ teaspoon salt

⅔ cup (4¼ ounces) vegetable shortening

½ cup (4 ounces) milk

In a medium-sized bowl, whisk together the flour, baking powder, and salt. Using a pastry blender or pastry fork, your fingers, or a mixer, blend in the shortening until the mixture is crumbly, then stir in the milk until a soft dough forms. Divide the dough in half, wrap each half in plastic, and refrigerate it while you're preparing the syrup and apples.

BISCUIT-STYLE DUMPLING DOUGH

3 cups (12¾ ounces) unbleached all-purpose flour

4 teaspoons baking powder

¾ teaspoon salt

¼ cup (1 ounce) confectioners' or glazing sugar

8 tablespoons (1 stick, 4 ounces) cold butter

¾ to 1 cup (6 to 8 ounces) milk

In a medium-sized bowl, whisk together the flour, baking powder, salt, and sugar. Cut in the butter until the mixture is crumbly, using your fingers, a pastry fork or blender, or a mixer, leaving some pea-sized pieces. Sprinkle in the milk (starting with the lesser amount) and stir just until the dough comes together. Divide the dough in half, wrap each half in plastic, and refrigerate while preparing the syrup and apples.

SYRUP

1½ cups (10¾ ounces) sugar

1½ cups (12 ounces) water

½ teaspoon cinnamon

¼ teaspoon nutmeg

1 tablespoon (½ ounce) lemon juice

8 tablespoons (1 stick, 4 ounces) butter

APPLES

4 medium tart, crisp baking apples, peeled and cored, sliced in half across the equator

½ cup (3½ ounces) sugar mixed with ¾ teaspoon cinnamon

Raisins or other dried fruit (optional)

FOR THE SYRUP Combine the sugar, water, spices, lemon juice, and butter in a small saucepan or in a microwave-safe cup. Heat to boiling, remove from the heat, and set aside, stirring occasionally to melt the butter.

TO ASSEMBLE THE DUMPLINGS Preheat the oven to 375°F. Lightly grease a 13 x 9 x 2-inch pan.

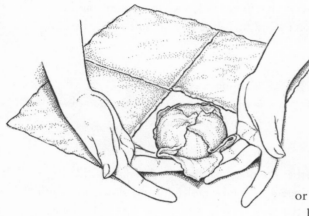

Wrap the dough for apple dumplings up around the sides, and tuck in at the top.

Take half the dough from the refrigerator (keep the other half chilled until you are ready to roll it; it will be less likely to stick if kept cold). On a floured surface, roll it from its center outward until it's ⅛ inch thick, about a 16-inch square. Cut the dough into four squares. Repeat with the remaining half of dough. Place half an apple in the center of each piece of dough. Sprinkle apples with the cinnamon-sugar and fill the centers with raisins or dried fruit. Paint the edges of the dough with a little water and wrap the dough around each apple half. A baker's bench knife or thin spatula is helpful with this, to scoop up the dough and gently bring it up and around. Tuck the edges of the dough down into the center of the apple.

Place the apples in the pan and pour the prepared syrup over all. Sprinkle the tops with additional sugar, if you like. Bake the dumplings for 45 to 50 minutes, until they're golden brown. Remove them from the oven and let them sit for 5 to 10 minutes, to allow the dough to set up, then use a spoon and a spatula to transfer each dumpling to a plate or shallow bowl. Serve warm with whipped cream or ice cream.

nutrition information per serving   biscuit dough, 1 dumpling, 253g

625 cal | 24g fat | 6g protein | 45g complex carbohydrates | 56g sugar | 3g dietary fiber | 63mg cholesterol | 460mg sodium | 180mg potassium | 231RE vitamin A | 4mg vitamin C | 3mg iron | 181mg calcium | 127mg phosphorus

nutrition information per serving   pastry dough, 1 dumpling, 229g

621 cal | 31g fat | 4g protein | 33g complex carbohydrates | 52g sugar | 2g dietary fiber | 32mg cholesterol | 266mg sodium | 144mg potassium | 119RE vitamin A | 4mg vitamin C | 2mg iron | 99mg calcium | 76mg phosphorus

Berry Dumplings

26 TO 28 DUMPLINGS

These dumplings are cooked in a delicious bath of simmering fruit, then finished with a dusting of cinnamon or confectioners' sugar. The liquid from the fruit will thicken slightly as they cook. Resist the temptation to peek under the lid: it will keep the dumplings from being as light as they should. We think these would make a very comforting breakfast on a snowy morning.

1 quart (20 ounces) fresh or frozen raspberries or other berries

1 cup (7 ounces) sugar

1 cup (8 ounces) water

2 tablespoons (1 ounce) lemon juice

1 cinnamon stick, or ½ teaspoon cinnamon

DOUGH

2 cups (8½ ounces) unbleached all-purpose flour

1 teaspoon salt

¼ cup (1¾ ounces) sugar

2½ teaspoons baking powder

4 tablespoons (½ stick, 2 ounces) cold butter

¼ cup (1¾ ounces) cold shortening

½ cup (4 ounces) milk, cream, or half-and-half*

1 large egg

½ teaspoon vanilla or almond extract (optional)

Put the fruit, sugar, water, lemon juice, and cinnamon in a large skillet for which you have a lid, or a large heatproof casserole. Set aside.

In a medium-sized mixing bowl, whisk together the flour, salt, sugar, and baking powder. Cut the butter into pats and work the butter and shortening into the flour, using a pastry blender, mixer, or your fingers (you can also use a food processor up to this point). When thoroughly combined, the mixture should resemble uneven, coarse crumbs; don't keep working it until it's perfectly homogeneous. The tender texture of the dumplings comes from pockets of cold fat in the dough, which in the cooking process don't melt until after the dough is set, leaving butter-catching fissures in the finished dumpling.

Put the fruit over medium heat to start simmering while you mix the dough.

Measure the milk into a liquid measuring cup, add the egg and vanilla, and whisk until smooth. Add this to the flour-fat mixture, and stir just until the dough is evenly mixed; it will be stiff. Drop the dough by tablespoons into the simmering fruit. Once all the dough is scooped out, put a lid on the pan and reduce the heat to low. Let the dumplings simmer for 10 to 12 minutes, until cooked all the way through. Remove from the heat immediately and spoon into bowls to serve warm. Sprinkle with cinnamon-sugar or confectioners' sugar, or serve with a scoop of ice cream if you prefer.

*You can use any kind of milk, from skim right up through whipping cream. The higher-in-fat the milk, the richer and more tender your dumpling will be.

`nutrition information per serving`   **3 dumplings, with fruit, 225g**

361 cal | 12g fat | 4g protein | 33g complex carbohydrates | 27g sugar | 6g dietary fiber | 39mg cholesterol | 252mg sodium | 219mg potassium | 83RE vitamin A | 21mg vitamin C | 2mg iron | 47mg calcium | 61mg phosphorus

Apple Dumpling Slices

ABOUT 16 SMALL BUT DELICIOUS SERVINGS

This dish hovers somewhere between dumplings and sticky buns and pie and cobbler, combining the best aspects of each. Tangy-sweet, soft, and buttery, it's true comfort food.

10 tablespoons (1¼ sticks, 5 ounces) butter

2 cups (16 ounces) water*

2 cups (14 ounces) sugar*

2 cups (8½ ounces) unbleached all-purpose flour

1 tablespoon baking powder

½ teaspoon salt

⅓ cup (2⅝ ounces) milk, at room temperature

1 teaspoon cinnamon

2 cups (8 to 9 ounces) peeled, diced apple

Preheat the oven to 350°F. Melt 4 tablespoons (2 ounces) of the butter in a 9 x 13-inch baking dish; glass or ceramic is preferable. Set the dish aside.

In a medium-sized saucepan, heat the water and sugar until the sugar melts. Meanwhile, combine the flour, baking powder, and salt with the remaining 6 tablespoons butter in a medium-sized mixing bowl. Rub the butter into the flour with the tips of your fingers, a pastry blender, or two knives until the mixture is crumbly. Stir in the milk and mix until the dough just comes together and leaves the sides of the bowl. Chill the dough while preparing the apples.

Turn the dough out onto a floured surface and knead it gently, until it's somewhat cohesive. Roll it gently into a 10 x 15-inch rectangle. Mix together the cinnamon and apples and spread them over the dough. Carefully roll the dough into a log sticky-bun style, pinching the edges together to seal. It may tear, but don't worry; mend it as best you can. (It's actually better if it comes apart a bit as it bakes.)

With a bench knife or serrated knife, cut the log into 16 slices, starting in the middle and moving out toward the ends. Arrange the slices over the butter in the baking dish as artfully as possible. The slices may want to fall apart, but again, not to worry. The finished product will look fine.

Pour the sugar syrup over the apple dumpling slices and place this quite-liquid conglomeration in the oven. Bake for 40 to 45 minutes. When you take the baking dish out of the oven, the biscuits will be lightly browned and on top of a still-very-liquid syrup. The whole thing can surge from one end to the other very easily if you're not extremely careful as you're moving it.

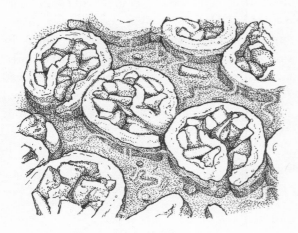

Apple dumpling slices look very wet before baking; the dough will expand to fill the spaces between them as they bake.

Let the slices cool a bit, then serve them with syrup poured over the top. We found that by leaving this uncovered at room temperature overnight (we actually did have some left over), the texture of the biscuits remained crisp and it was just as good the next day.

*This is a great place to use boiled cider, a tart-sweet syrup made by simply boiling apple cider until it's thickened. Decrease the sugar and water to 1½ cups each, prepare the sugar syrup, then add ½ cup boiled cider.

Basic Savory Dumplings

10 TO 12 DUMPLINGS

Dumplings are a wonderful addition to simmering soup; not only do they add body in the form of a delicious, tender piece of bread, but some of their starch leaches out into the soup as they cook, thickening it nicely.

1 cup (4¼ ounces) unbleached all-purpose flour	2 tablespoons (1 ounce) butter or vegetable shortening
¾ teaspoon salt	½ cup (4 ounces) milk
1½ teaspoons baking powder	

Mix the flour, salt, and baking powder together in a bowl. Cut in the cold butter until the mixture is the texture of coarse sand. Add the milk all at once, stirring quickly and as little as possible, just until everything is moistened. Drop the dough by rounded spoonfuls into a simmering soup or stew. Cook, uncovered, for 10 minutes, then cover and simmer for 10 minutes more, or until the dumplings are cooked through. Depending on how your soup or stew is seasoned, 1 tablespoon chopped parsley or chives, black pepper, or a pinch of thyme is a flavorful addition to your dumplings.

nutrition information per serving   **1 large dumpling, 36g**

106 cal | 4g fat | 2g protein | 15g complex carbohydrates | 1g dietary fiber | 11mg cholesterol | 378mg sodium | 39mg potassium | 41RE vitamin A | 1mg iron | 108mg calcium | 48mg phosphorus

Herbed Dumplings

12 TO 14 DUMPLINGS

These are made with essentially the same recipe as biscuits, but with an increased amount of liquid. To make them a bit more tender (dumplings can go from light to soggy/heavy fairly quickly), use half all-purpose flour and half pastry flour.

The herbs are appropriate to go in a chicken or turkey soup. You can leave the herbs out or add whatever seems appropriate to whatever soup you're making (such as basil and rosemary for minestrone). Have your soup ready and simmering, as dumplings are the finale to this dish. It's best to have the soup in a pan that will provide a lot of surface area, as dumplings swell to about twice their size as they cook.

Dumplings are best made small so they're well flavored with the broth. This recipe will make about a dozen scant tablespoon-sized dumplings.

2 cups (8½ ounces) unbleached all-purpose or unbleached pastry flour

1 tablespoon baking powder

½ teaspoon salt

¼ teaspoon dry mustard

1 teaspoon dry, crumbled sage

1 teaspoon celery seed

2 to 4 tablespoons (1 to 2 ounces) butter (this can be omitted if you eat the dumplings quickly)

2 large eggs

½ cup (4 ounces) milk or water.

In a mixing bowl, blend together the dry ingredients and the herbs. Rub in the butter with your fingers. Beat together the eggs and milk or water (water will make lighter dumplings) and stir quickly (20 seconds) into the dry ingredients.

To cook, dip a tablespoon into the soup and then into the dumpling batter. Drop it gently into the soup and continue until the surface is covered, keeping in mind how much they'll swell. Don't let the soup rise above a simmer, as too high a heat will toughen the protein in the egg, which translates into tough, rubbery dumplings.

Cover the pot and cook for about 5 minutes with the temperature very low. Flip the dumplings over and cook for a further 5 minutes. Serve them quickly, as they don't improve with age.

`nutrition information per serving`   **1 dumpling, made with 3 tablespoons butter, 38g**

91 cal | 2g fat | 3g protein | 14g complex carbohydrates | 1g dietary fiber | 6mg cholesterol | 231mg sodium | 70mg potassium | 1mg iron | 82mg calcium | 73mg phosphorus

Italian Dumplings

12 DUMPLINGS

These bread dumplings, redolent of Parmesan, are a wonderful addition to any broth-based soup. They are also an excellent use for that last bit of tasty bread that needs to be used up.

2 large eggs

⅓ cup (1¼ ounces) grated Parmesan cheese

1 cup (3 ounces) soft bread crumbs

3 tablespoons (1½ ounces) unsalted

butter, melted

1 teaspoon dried basil

1 teaspoon lemon peel, grated (or a couple of drops of lemon oil)

1 tablespoon chopped parsley

Combine all the ingredients in a bowl. With lightly greased hands, shape the mixture into 1-inch balls (or use a teaspoon cookie scoop for this step). Drop about ten dumplings at a time into the simmering broth and cook them for about 8 minutes. Remove from the broth and keep them warm while cooking the rest. Place the dumplings in soup bowls and ladle the soup over them. Serve with additional grated Parmesan, if desired.

nutrition information per serving   **2 dumplings, 24g**

75 cal | 5g fat | 3g protein | 3g complex carbohydrates | 15mg cholesterol | 108mg sodium | 28mg potassium | 50RE vitamin A | 60mg calcium | 37mg phosphorus

Potato Puff Dumplings

48 DUMPLINGS

A vague takeoff on cream puffs (baked, they're a cross between cream puffs and biscuits), these taste like a soft potato biscuit when added to soup. (Then again, if you want a special treat, throwing these in the deep fryer will make wonderful, golden, potato fritterlike creations.)

5 tablespoons (2½ ounces) butter

½ cup (4 ounces) milk

1 teaspoon salt

1 cup (4¼ ounces) unbleached all-purpose flour

3 large eggs

1 cup (5 ounces) mashed potato, lightly packed (2 to 3 medium potatoes, cooked and riced)

2 tablespoons chopped fresh parsley or chives

In a medium-sized saucepan, melt the butter in the milk and add the salt. Bring the mixture to a boil, add the flour all at once, and stir until it forms a ball. Remove the pan from the heat and beat to remove some of the steam. Add the eggs one at a time, beating well after each addition, then beat in the mashed potato and parsley or chives.

Drop the dough by teaspoonfuls into boiling salted water or soup, about 15 at a time. Boil them for 5 to 6 minutes, then remove from the broth and keep them warm in the oven while cooking the remaining dumplings. Or drop them by the teaspoonful into hot, deep fat, cook until golden brown (3 to 4 minutes), and place on a rack to drain. Finally, you may drop by the tablespoonful onto baking sheets and bake in a preheated 400°F oven for 12 to 15 minutes, or until they're a light golden brown. Each method of cooking makes a very different product—soft white boiled dumplings, crunchy fritters, or golden puffs.

nutrition information per serving | **2 puffs, boiled or baked, 52g**

128 cal | 7g fat | 3g protein | 12g complex carbohydrates | 20mg cholesterol | 374mg sodium | 58mg potassium | 75RE vitamin A | 92mg calcium | 45mg phosphorus

Raspberry Roly-Poly

TWELVE 1-INCH SLICES

This is an old-fashioned English dessert that defies classification. Is it a cobbler? A giant dumpling? With its multitude of versions—cooked in or over a boiling water bath or baked in an oven; made with a suet pastry crust or with baking powder biscuit dough—it just can't be pinned down. But, like all things raspberry, it's delicious. Choose one of the casings below and give it a go.

PASTRY CASING

2 cups (8½ ounces) unbleached all-purpose flour

2 teaspoons baking powder

1 teaspoon salt

½ cup (3 ounces) lard, butter, or shortening*

4 to 6 tablespoons cold water

In a mixing bowl, combine the flour, baking powder, and salt. (You can see that this is a cross between a pie dough and a biscuit dough with the merits of both.) Cut the fat in pieces and, with your fingertips, quickly rub it into the flour mixture until it looks like coarse cornmeal. Sprinkle the water over the mixture and gently mix it in. Turn the dough out onto a floured board and knead it gently, like a biscuit dough, until it is fairly smooth and cohesive.

BISCUIT CASING

2 cups (8½ ounces) unbleached all-purpose flour

1 teaspoon baking powder

½ teaspoon baking soda

2 tablespoons (⅞ ounce) sugar

½ to 1 teaspoon salt

⅓ to ½ cup (2¾ to 4 ounces) butter or shortening

½ cup (4 ounces) buttermilk

In a mixing bowl, mix the flour, baking powder, baking soda, sugar, and salt. Cut the butter into pieces and, with your fingertips, quickly rub it into the flour mixture until it looks like rough cornmeal. Pour in the buttermilk and stir until the mixture is moistened. Turn the dough out onto a floured board and knead it gently, like a biscuit dough, until it's fairly smooth and cohesive.

FILLING

2 tablespoons butter (optional)

2 cups (10 ounces) raspberries, black raspberries, blackberries, blueberries

¼ cup (2 ounces) brown sugar, packed

¼ teaspoon ground cinnamon (or nutmeg is nice with blueberries)

With a rolling pin, roll out whichever dough you've chosen to a 9 x 12-inch rectangle about ¼ inch thick. Spread the surface with the butter, leaving 1 inch around the outside edge clear. Spread the berries down the middle and sprinkle on the sugar and spice.

Roll up the dough lengthwise like a jelly roll, moisten the edges, and seal them tight. Loosely wrap the roly-poly in a piece of aluminum foil, giving it enough room to expand as it cooks. Fold the top edge of the foil over twice and fold the ends up rather than down to contain any filling that may escape from the roll as it cooks.

Here are two cooking options: steaming or baking.

STEAMING The easiest way to do this is with a canner that has a rack that holds at least seven 1-quart jars. Place a pie plate (preferably perforated) or a 12-inch pizza pan on the jar rack in the pan. This is what you'll put the roly-poly on. The plate or pan needs to be small enough so the steam can move up and around the roll.

Pour in boiling water to just below the top of the jar rack. You don't want it coming over the top of the pan your roll is on. Place the roll on the plate, cover the canner, bring the water back to a boil, and turn the heat down low so the water is just simmering. Cook the roll for 1½ hours. You'll need to add water about halfway through the steaming process. When the roly-poly is done, carefully remove it from the steamer—steam is very hot.

BAKING While you are preparing the roll, preheat the oven to 350°F. Don't wrap the roll in aluminum foil this time. With a large spatula, lift and place it on a well-greased or parchment-covered baking sheet and bake for about 30 minutes.

SERVING Either version tastes wonderful hot from the oven or steamer, but a bit of chilled cream over the top is ambrosial. Here's another option to prepare ahead: Heat ¼ cup fruit jelly, any kind, until it's liquid; blend it into 1 cup of cream, chill, and serve in place of plain cream.

*Lard, because of its large crystalline structure, makes an incredibly light and tender crust.

nutrition information per serving   pastry style, 1 slice, 95g

182 cal | 3g fat | 2g protein | 19g complex carbohydrates | 4g sugar | 3g dietary fiber | 8mg cholesterol | 261mg sodium | 97mg potassium | 5RE vitamin A | 7mg vitamin C | 1mg iron | 59mg calcium | 40mg phosphorus

nutrition information per serving   biscuit style, 1 slice, 86g

167 cal | 6g fat | 2g protein | 19g complex carbohydrates | 6g sugar | 3g dietary fiber | 16mg cholesterol | 239mg sodium | 114mg potassium | 59RE vitamin A | 7mg vitamin C | 1mg iron | 49mg calcium | 42mg phosphorus

Clafouti

And now, to conclude this chapter of baked goods with bizarre names, we have clafouti, a native of France. Clafouti begins with fresh fruit placed in a shallow layer in a wide pan, often a large pie pan or cake pan. An eggy, cakelike sweetened batter is poured over the fruit, where it sinks to the bottom of the pan, then the whole is baked until the crust has risen over the fruit and becomes brown. Typically, more sugar is sprinkled on top just before serving.

The best-known clafouti is made with dark sweet cherries. Peaches, apples, pears, and plums also make good clafouti. The more delicate berries, like raspberries, aren't good clafouti candidates; they turn to mush before the clafouti finishes baking. But blueberries or strawberries are good choices.

Peach or Apricot Clafouti

8 SLICES

Clafouti originally used cherries or plums from the Limousin region of France as the fruit, but we decided to give peaches a go and were very happy with the results. They fan nicely in the bottom of the pan and the brown sugar gives a slightly taffy-like crust to the dish as it bakes. You could put a few raspberries in the pan for an extra visual kick if you're lucky enough to have them around.

3 cups (2 pounds) sliced peaches or quartered fresh apricots

⅓ cup (2⅜ ounces) packed brown sugar

¾ cup (3 ounces) unbleached all-purpose flour

⅓ cup (2⅜ ounces) sugar

½ teaspoon salt

3 large eggs

1¼ cups (10 ounces) milk

¾ teaspoon almond or vanilla extract

Preheat the oven to 375°F. Thoroughly butter a 10-inch round pan or ovenproof skillet. Arrange the peach slices or apricot quarters on the bottom of the pan and sprinkle with the brown sugar.

In a mixing bowl, whisk together the flour, sugar, and salt. In a separate small bowl or large mixing cup, combine the eggs, milk, and vanilla. Beat until thoroughly combined, then gradually whisk into the flour mixture, smoothing out the lumps. Pour the batter over the fruit in the prepared baking pan and bake for 35 to 40 minutes. A cake tester inserted into the center should come out clean. Serve warm or at room temperature.

nutrition information per serving   1 slice, 148g

168 cal | 2g fat | 5g protein | 17g complex carbohydrates | 15g sugar | g dietary fiber | 81mg cholesterol | 179mg sodium | 250mg potassium | 93RE vitamin A | 5mg vitamin C | 1mg iron | 66mg calcium | 89mg phosphorus

Pear-Ginger Clafouti

8 TO 10 SLICES

When summer's fruits have faded, pears come into the produce aisles to cheer us up. This recipe works exceedingly well with Anjou pears, red or green. They will hold their shape a little better while baking if they aren't completely ripe. The snap of grated fresh ginger in this recipe highlights the silky flavor of the pears, and the sprinkling of dried cranberries adds a jewel-like effect. To complete this elegant presentation, brush the top of the clafouti after baking with ginger syrup, page 342.

3 large pears (1½ to 2 pounds), slightly underripe

1 tablespoon fresh lemon juice

2 teaspoons fresh ginger, peeled and grated

½ cup (2 ounces) dried cranberries

¾ cup (3 ounces) unbleached all-purpose flour

⅔ cup (4¾ ounces) sugar

½ teaspoon salt

3 large eggs

1 cup (8 ounces) milk

2 teaspoons vanilla extract

3 tablespoons (1½ ounces) butter, melted

Butter a 10-inch pie or tart pan and preheat the oven to 375°F.

Peel and quarter the pears, then trim out the core and seeds. Slice each section into a medium-sized bowl in ¼-inch pieces. Sprinkle the lemon juice over the slices, then add the grated ginger and cranberries and stir everything together to coat it. Pour the fruit into the prepared pan.

Whisk together the flour, sugar, and salt and gradually beat in the vanilla, eggs, milk, and melted butter. Pour this mixture over the fruit and bake for 35 to 40 minutes, until golden brown and crust is set.

Remove from the oven, brush with ginger syrup if desired, and serve warm.

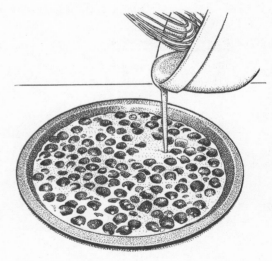

Pour the batter over the fruit before baking a clafouti.

nutrition information per serving   1 slice, 135g

194 cal | 3g fat | 4g protein | 15g complex carbohydrates | 17g sugar | 2g dietary fiber | 83mg cholesterol | 158mg sodium | mg potassium | 87RE vitamin A | 3mg vitamin C | 1mg iron | 49mg calcium | 70mg phosphorus

Cherry Clafouti

8 SLICES

This relatively quick and oh-so-simple summer dessert mirrors France's best-known clafouti.

¾ cup (3 ounces) unbleached all-purpose flour

⅔ cup (4¾ ounces) granulated sugar

3 large eggs

1¼ cups (10 ounces) milk

1 teaspoon almond or vanilla extract

3 cups (about 2 pounds) pitted sweet cherries

Preheat the oven to 375°F. Thoroughly grease a 10-inch round pan or ovenproof skillet.

In a mixing bowl, whisk together the flour and sugar. In a separate bowl or large measuring cup, beat the eggs until foamy. Beat in the milk and the vanilla. Gradually whisk the egg mixture into the flour and sugar, stirring to smooth out any lumps.

Place the fruit in the prepared dish and pour the batter over it. Bake for 35 to 40 minutes. A cake tester inserted in the center should come out clean. Serve warm or at room temperature.

Note: For a more custard-like clafouti, bake in a 9-inch pan at 350°F for 40 to 45 minutes.

nutrition information per serving   **1 slice, 133g**

162 cal | 1g fat | 5g protein | 18g complex carbohydrates | 15g sugar | 1g dietary fiber | 3mg cholesterol | 38mg sodium | 211mg potassium | 1g iron | 75mg calcium | 58mg phosphorus

Crackers and Flatbreads

If you have any affinity at all for a rolling pin, you can
make all kinds of flatbreads, including crackers, tortillas, Indian breads
like naan, Armenian lavash (crackerbread), and all the variations on
flatbread, crispbread, and parchment bread that have made their way
to America from various cultures around the world.
Don't let the word *bread* scare you away; when people say they can't make bread,
they usually mean they're afraid to deal with yeast. We'll allay all those fears
farther along in this book, but for now, fear not: most of the following recipes
don't use yeast. Just flour, a rolling pin, and a do-it-yourself attitude.

Crackers

Crackers and milk. Crackers and soup. Cheese and crackers. Crackers and peanut butter. Crackers are light on the appetite, a wonderful prelude to a more substantial meal. They're also a great "go-with": with dips, with spreads, with wine and cheese. They're exceedingly simple to make and they make an unusual and thoughtful gift.

The following cracker recipes range from very plain (water biscuits) to exotic (curry and ginger), but they all have one thing in common: they begin with a simple combination of flour, fat, and liquid. In fact, crackers are a lot like piecrust and exhibit the same changes when the formula is varied: the more fat and less water, the flakier and more tender the cracker; the less fat and more water, the crisper and harder the cracker. The following recipe will familiarize you with the basics of the cracker-making process.

Basic Crackers

ABOUT 8 DOZEN 2½-INCH CRACKERS

2 cups flour (all-purpose, pastry, whole wheat, rye, barley, or semolina)

Flavorings (spices, herbs, extracts, seeds, minced vegetables) optional

2 to 8 tablespoons fat (butter, margarine, shortening, or oil)

2 to 8 tablespoons liquid (water, milk, beer, wine, yogurt, buttermilk, or sour cream)

Preheat the oven to 350°F.

Place flour in mixing bowl. Add flavorings, if any. Cut in fat as if you were making piecrust. Work the fat together until the mixture forms small, even crumbs. Then quickly stir in liquid. Use only enough liquid to hold the dough together. Too much liquid will toughen the crackers and make them hard to roll out. Remember, the more fat you use, the less liquid you'll need.

Transfer dough to a lightly floured work surface or to a pastry cloth or board. Using a heavy rolling pin and a firm hand, use a minimal number of strokes to roll the dough very thin—1/16 to 1/8 inch is the norm. The fewer strokes it takes you to roll out the dough, the more tender your crackers will be. Prick the dough all over with a fork.

Cut the dough into squares, rounds, triangles, or even into holiday shapes.

Transfer the crackers to a parchment-lined or lightly greased baking sheet and bake for 20 to 25 minutes, until the crackers just begin to brown.

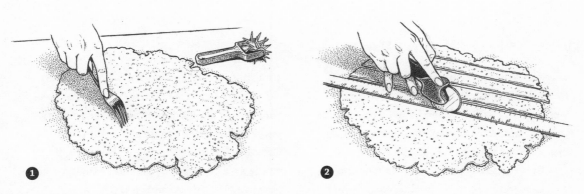

1. Roll out cracker dough to ⅛" thick. Brush with water and sprinkle with salt, if desired, then prick holes all over the dough with a fork or dough docker (pictured). **2.** Use a ruler and a pizza wheel to cut the dough into strips, then cut again into cracker shapes.

Remove the crackers from the oven and transfer them to a rack to cool. They'll become crisp as they cool. Store in an airtight container.

NOTE Due to the variability in the ingredients called for in this recipe, we are unable to provide a nutritional analysis.

Cracker-Making Tools

As we made batch after batch of crackers, we discovered a couple of tools that make the whole job incredibly easy. One is a giant spatula (see Tools, p. 605), with a 10 x 10-inch blade, perfect for lifting the dough as you roll (to sprinkle more flour underneath to prevent sticking), and also ideal for transferring the unbaked crackers to the baking sheets and the baked crackers to the cooling rack. The other tool we just couldn't have done without is a rolling pizza cutter (or, for a more festive look, a crimped pastry wheel). Using the cutter, we were able to cut 95 to 100 crackers out of a piece of rolled dough in less than 10 seconds. And we discovered a 1-liter clamp-top Mason jar is just about the perfect size to hold most batches of crackers; the rubber gasket keeps crackers nice and fresh, and a red ribbon tied around the top is all you need in the way of wrapping or decoration if you're giving the crackers as a present.

Which Flour Should I Use?

Crackers are one of the baking world's most flexible inhabitants. Hard flour, soft flour, whole grain or white, even bean flour, you can make a successful cracker from just about any type of flour you choose.

Bakers usually prefer to use a medium-soft to medium-hard flour, thus combining in their crackers the best attributes of each: a tender bite, with sufficient body to avoid crumbling. We like a medium-protein (about 11.7 percent) all-purpose flour, one that nicely treads the tightrope between the extremes of pastry flour (9.2 percent protein) and high-gluten flour (14.0 percent protein). We find all-purpose flour makes a dough extensible enough to roll out very nicely without fighting back, yet strong enough to hold together while you're rolling and cutting; the resulting cracker is crisp/hard. For a cracker that's crisp but more tender, try blending one part cake or pastry flour with three parts all-purpose; the price you'll pay is a bit more difficulty handling the dough. However, if you're an accomplished piecrust baker, we suggest you give this formula a try.

To make whole-grain crackers, substitute a whole-grain flour—rye, whole wheat, or white whole wheat (see pp. 517–520)—for one fourth to just about one third of the all-purpose flour in the recipe. You won't experience any noticeable problems in handling the dough at this level of substitution, but any greater percentage of nonwhite flour will produce a crumbly or sticky dough; the gluten that makes dough hang together simply won't have a large enough presence.

Rich Crackers

ABOUT 8 DOZEN 2½-INCH ROUND CRACKERS.

We don't call these rich for nothing. Butter, egg, and cream enrich the dough, which is made just like piecrust.

2 cups (8½ ounces) unbleached all-purpose flour

1 teaspoon salt

1 teaspoon baking powder

2½ tablespoons sugar

4 tablespoons (½ stick, 2 ounces) cold butter

1 large egg

6 tablespoons (⅜ cup) cream (half-and-half, light, whipping, or heavy)

2 to 3 tablespoons butter, melted

In a large bowl, mix together flour, salt, baking powder, and sugar. Cut in the butter. In a separate bowl, use a fork to stir egg and cream together until smooth. Add to flour-butter mixture and stir until mixture forms a loose ball. Gather in your hands and squeeze together. Pat into an oval about 1 inch thick, wrap in waxed paper, and chill for 1 hour.

Preheat the oven to 425°F.

On a lightly floured surface, roll dough into a circle between 1/16 and 1/8 inch in thickness. Cut dough into rounds with a 3-inch or smaller cutter. Repeat with remaining dough scraps. Unlike piecrust, this repeated rolling doesn't seem to toughen the final product. Transfer rounds to lightly greased or parchment-lined baking sheets and prick each round several times with a fork.

Bake crackers for 6 minutes. Remove pan from oven, turn crackers over, and bake an additional 5 minutes, or until crackers are lightly browned. Remove crackers from oven and brush with melted butter. Transfer to a rack to cool completely.

nutrition information per serving   **2 crackers, 11g**

42 cal | 2g fat | 1g protein | 4g complex carbohydrates | 1g sugar | 12mg cholesterol | 57mg sodium | 9mg potassium | 25RE vitamin A | 8mg calcium | 10mg phosphorus

Cheese Pennies

ABOUT EIGHTY 1½-INCH PENNIES

The following recipe is a throwback to one of our favorite fifties snacks: cheese pennies, a high-fat concoction of cheese and butter held together with a bit of flour and baked until golden brown. We never had the spicy variety as kids; but our well-worn taste buds welcome a hit of cayenne these days. These are good served with drinks—nonalcoholic or otherwise.

8 ounces (2 cups) finely grated sharp cheddar or grated fresh Asiago cheese

8 tablespoons (1 stick, 4 ounces) butter

1½ cups (6¼ ounces) unbleached all-purpose flour

¾ teaspoon salt

½ teaspoon dry mustard

⅛ to ¼ teaspoon cayenne*

Paprika (optional)

In a medium-sized mixing bowl, combine all the ingredients except paprika to make a cohesive dough, sprinkling in a tablespoon or so of water if the dough doesn't seem to come together. As soon as it does, turn off the mixer and gather it into a rough ball. Transfer it to a lightly floured work surface and roll it into a 16-inch log about 1½ inches in diameter.

Wrap the log in waxed paper or plastic wrap and chill it in the freezer for 30 minutes. (If you want to freeze it longer, make sure to remove it from the freezer about 30 minutes before you want to slice it into pennies.)

Preheat the oven to 400°F.

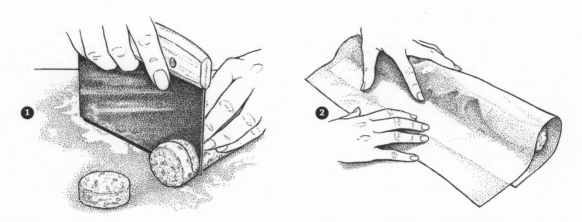

1. Chilled dough can be cut into uniform disks with the help of a bench knife. **2.** To roll dough into a log, put it on a sheet of parchment or waxed paper. Fold the paper over, and press on the top sheet. Pull the bottom sheet toward you to tighten the dough into a log shape before refrigerating.

Remove the plastic wrap or waxed paper, and, using a bench or serrated knife, slice the log crosswise into ⅛-inch rounds. Place them on an ungreased or parchment-lined baking sheet, leaving only about ½ inch between; they won't spread much as they bake. Sprinkle them with a bit of paprika, if desired.

Bake the cheese pennies for 12 to 14 minutes, or until they're just beginning to brown. Remove them from the oven and let cool on the pan for several minutes before transferring them to racks to cool completely.

*⅛ teaspoon is discernible, while ¼ teaspoon packs a moderate punch. Use more if you want a truly eye-watering experience.

nutrition information per serving   **5 pennies, 34g**

150 cal | 10.2g fat | 5g protein | 8g complex carbohydrates | 32mg cholesterol | 189mg sodium | 31mg potassium | 101RE vitamin A | 1mg iron | 124mg calcium | 86mg phosphorus

Benne Wafers

3 DOZEN 3-INCH WAFERS

These ethereally light, snapping-crisp, sweet sesame crackers are native to the "low country" of South Carolina. Sesame, a plant with a long history of cultivation, was probably first grown in Africa: West Africans, brought to this country as slaves in the seventeenth and eighteenth centuries, called sesame "benne," and legend had it that eating sesame seeds brought good luck. Middle Easterners also called sesame seeds "benne"; there must have been trade routes that brought together buyers from the Middle East with African sellers. Food, as usual, seems to have been a key component in bringing cultures together.

These rich brown crackers, sweet and nutty, have an interesting texture: solid and crisp on the bottom, crunchy-light on top. They are awfully close to being a cookie.

8 tablespoons (1 stick, 4 ounces) unsalted butter

1 cup (8 ounces) light brown sugar, firmly packed

¼ teaspoon salt

¼ teaspoon baking soda

1 teaspoon vanilla extract

1 large egg

1 cup (4¼ ounces) unbleached all-purpose flour

1 cup (5 ounces) toasted sesame seeds

Preheat the oven to 350°F.

In a large mixing bowl, cream together the butter, sugar, salt, baking soda, vanilla, and egg. Add the flour and mix until smooth. Stir in the sesame seeds.

Drop the dough by tablespoonfuls (a tablespoon cookie scoop works well here) onto parchment-lined or lightly greased baking sheets. Bake the wafers for 8 to 9 minutes, until they're golden brown. Remove them from the oven, let cool for 1 minute on the pan, then transfer the wafers to a wire rack to cool completely.

nutrition information per serving   1 wafer, 18g

84cal | 5g fat | 1g protein | 3g complex carbohydrates | 6g sugar | 1g dietary fiber | 13mg cholesterol | 30mg sodium | 45mg potassium | 28RE vitamin A | 1mg iron | 12mg calcium | 40mg phosphorus

Rye Crisps

5 DOZEN 2-INCH CRACKERS

This is a deep-dark-brown substantial rye cracker whose flavors are a worthy base for smoked Gouda cheese and the best German wurst you can find.

CRACKERS

1½ cups (6¼ ounces) unbleached all-purpose flour

1½ cups (6 ounces) medium rye flour or pumpernickel

3 tablespoons (¾ ounce) nonfat dry milk

2 teaspoons baking powder

2 teaspoons instant yeast

2 teaspoons caramel color (optional, for color)

2 teaspoons cider vinegar

2 teaspoons salt

1 tablespoon caraway seeds, or 2 teaspoons ground caraway

½ cup (2¾ ounces) vegetable oil

¾ cup (6 ounces) lukewarm milk

1 egg, separated (use the white for the dough, the yolk for the glaze)

GLAZE

1 egg yolk (reserved from above)

1 tablespoon milk or water

In a medium-sized bowl, whisk together the flours, dry milk, baking powder, and yeast. Add the caramel color, vinegar, salt, caraway, and oil. The mixture will be crumbly because you're coating some of the flour with oil; this prevents some gluten from developing that would otherwise toughen the cracker unpleasantly.

In a small bowl, whisk the warmed milk and egg white together, then add this to the flour mixture. Mix, then knead the dough by hand or by mixer to form a smooth ball.

(You can also mix this dough in a bread machine. Program the machine for Dough or Manual and press Start. Cancel the machine after the dough has become a cohesive, semi-firm ball, 5 to 8 minutes into the first kneading cycle.)

Place the dough into a greased bowl, turn it to coat, and cover the bowl with plastic wrap. Let the dough rise for 1 hour, then refrigerate it for several hours, or for up to 24 hours. Don't expect a big, breadlike rise; it will just become a bit puffy, but the flavor will be improving as it rests.

Turn out the dough onto a lightly greased or floured work surface. Roll it into a 14 x 17-inch rectangle, slightly less than ⅛ inch thick. If the dough starts to shrink or tear, cover it and let it rest for a few minutes before continuing. Before cutting it, transfer the dough onto a piece of parchment paper or a lightly greased sheet pan. Remember, though, you'll be cutting the crackers on the pan, so place the dough only onto a pan that may be cut on, or line a nonstick pan with parchment.

Prick the dough all over with a fork; or, to make fast work of this project and give the crackers a professional look, use a dough docker (see Tools section, p. 604) to roll perforations into the dough.

Cut the dough into sticks or triangles using a pizza wheel, pastry cutter, or bench knife. Don't worry about separating them; they'll break apart easily along the scored lines when cool.

FOR THE GLAZE Mix the reserved egg yolk with the tablespoon of milk or water. Brush the top of the crackers with this mixture and let them rest, covered, for 1 hour.

Preheat the oven to 375°F.

Bake the crackers for 10 minutes, then reduce the oven heat to 325°F and continue to bake for 30 to 40 minutes. If you've used the optional caramel color, the dough itself is already brown, so it's hard to judge doneness by color. However, you can judge by smell and touch: you'll suddenly catch the aroma of caraway when the crackers are done, and they'll feel firm when pressed.

Remove the crackers from the oven and transfer them to a rack to cool completely. Store them in airtight containers for 4 to 5 days.

`nutrition information per serving` **5 crackers, 62g**

208 cal | 11g fat | 4g protein | 24g complex carbohydrates | 3g dietary fiber | 20mg cholesterol | 450mg sodium | 117mg potassium | 13RE vitamin A | 2mg iron | 73mg calcium | 94mg phosphorus

Curry and Ginger Crackers

9 TO 10 DOZEN 1½-INCH CRACKERS

These crackers are one of our favorites. A beautiful golden-yellow in color, they're spicy and slightly sweet, with a finishing zing of ginger. Serve them with pumpkin or squash soup; chutney and cream cheese, or just on their own, with drinks.

2 cups (8 ounces) unbleached pastry flour
or unbleached all-purpose flour

½ cup (about 2 ounces) candied
(crystallized) ginger

1 teaspoon salt

1 tablespoon curry powder

½ teaspoon turmeric

1 tablespoon granulated sugar

¼ to ½ teaspoon cayenne (optional)

4 tablespoons (½ stick, 2 ounces) butter

About 6 tablespoons (3 ounces) cold water

Bake crackers until they're golden brown at the edges. They will continue to get crisp as they cool.

Preheat the oven to 325°F.

In a blender or food processor, combine 1 cup of the flour and the candied ginger. Process until the ginger is very finely diced.

In a large mixing bowl, combine flour and ginger, the remaining flour, salt, curry powder, turmeric, sugar, and cayenne pepper. Cut in the butter, working it into the flour until the mixture forms small, even crumbs. Add enough water to form a workable dough.

Divide the dough into two pieces and roll it out, one piece at a time, to a thickness of ⅛ to 1/16 inch. Cut the dough into 1½-inch squares and transfer to lightly greased or parchment-lined baking sheets.

Bake the crackers for 20 to 25 minutes, until they're a very light golden brown around the edges; don't let these crackers become dark as they'll get bitter. Remove the crackers from the oven and transfer them to a wire rack to cool completely.

nutrition information per serving   **10 crackers, 40g**

112 cal | 4g fat | 2g protein | 15g complex carbohydrates | 1g sugar | 11mg cholesterol | 220mg sodium | 55mg potassium | 1 mg iron | 1mg vitamin C | 39mg calcium | 21mg phosphorus

Putting Them Through the Wringer

If you have a pasta machine, many cracker doughs can be rolled out, from fairly thick to ultra-thin. Those made with more fat/less liquid, and/or with a lower-protein flour, may be too fragile to put through the machine's rollers; you'll need to be the judge of whether the dough you're working with is strong enough to take it. But if it is, once the pasta machine spits out the dough in a long strip, it's very simple to cut it into square or rectangular crackers with a rolling pizza wheel.

Potato, Dill, and Onion Crackers

ABOUT 8 DOZEN CRACKERS

This cracker will give you the chance to make something truly memorable out of the leftover mashed potatoes from your Sunday or holiday feast. There are a lot of ball games to get through on any given weekend, which means that handy grazing foods are a good thing to have around. These have a hearty potato flavor and are a nice match with any number of cheeses or dips. If you don't have any leftover mashed potatoes, these crackers are worth the effort of peeling, grating, and roasting one (see instructions below). The resulting cracker is a little more crunchy, with a hint of potato chip flavor.

2 cups (8½ ounces) unbleached all-purpose flour

½ teaspoon baking powder

½ teaspoon salt

3 tablespooons dried dill weed

1 tablespoon onion powder

4 tablespoons (½ stick, 2 ounces) butter

1 cup (10 ounces) mashed potatoes, or 1 medium russet potato (about 8 ounces) plus 3 tablespoons (1½ ounces) salad oil and 1 teaspoon salt*

¼ cup (2 ounces) water

In a large bowl, whisk together the flour, baking powder, salt, dill, and onion powder. Cut in the butter with a pastry blender or a fork until the mixture looks like small crumbs. Add the mashed or roasted potatoes, mixing to combine everything evenly. Sprinkle the water over the mixture a tablespoon at a time, mixing with a fork to distribute it evenly. Continue adding water until the dough just comes together. Wrap the dough in plastic wrap and chill for at least 1 hour before rolling out.

Preheat the oven to 375°F.

To make the crackers, roll out the dough as thin as possible (about ⅛ inch thick) on a lightly floured surface or on a sheet of parchment paper. Prick the dough all over with a fork, brush with water, then sprinkle with coarse salt. Cut the dough into strips with a ruler and a pizza cutter or fluted pastry wheel. You can make whatever shape and size you like: small squares, diamonds, or rectangles. Any scraps or odd shapes can be squeezed together, then rolled again.

Transfer the dough to a lightly greased baking sheet, or slide the parchment with the cut crackers on it onto your baking pan. Bake the crackers for 18 to 22 minutes, until they begin to take on a light golden brown color. Remove the pan from the oven and put it on a rack to cool the crackers. They will finish crisping as they cool.

*If you're not using mashed potatoes, peel and grate the russet potato on a box grater. Sprinkle potato with salt and toss with the vegetable oil. Put the grated potato on a parchment-lined cookie sheet that has been sprayed with nonstick spray and bake at 350°F, stirring occasionally, until the potatoes are golden brown. Cool, then use these potatoes in the recipe where the mashed potatoes are called for.

nutrition information per serving   **3 crackers, 15g**

46 cal | 2g fat | 1g protein | 6g complex carbohydrates | 4mg cholesterol | 112mg sodium | 32mg potassium | 13RE vitamin A | 1mg vitamin C | 11mg calcium | 12mg phosphorus

Sesame Thins

ABOUT 6 DOZEN CRACKERS

Sesame oil gives these crackers a strong, nutty taste; if you want a milder cracker, substitute shortening for some or all of the oil. These are a marvelous accompaniment to hummus.

½ cup (2½ ounces) sesame seeds, toasted in a 350°F oven for 10 to 15 minutes, until they're golden brown

1 cup (5 ounces) unbleached pastry flour

1 cup (5¼ ounces) whole wheat flour or white whole wheat flour

1 teaspoon salt

¼ cup (1¾ ounces) sesame oil

½ cup to ¾ cup (4 to 6 ounces) cold water

Preheat the oven to 325°F.

In a large bowl, combine the seeds, flours, and salt. Add the oil, stirring until the mixture forms even crumbs. Add just enough water to form a workable dough.

Divide the dough into three pieces and roll it, one piece at a time, until it's about $\frac{1}{16}$ inch thick. Cut the dough into squares, rectangles, triangles, or whatever you like, and transfer the crackers to lightly greased or parchment-lined baking sheets.

Bake the crackers for 25 to 30 minutes, or until they're beginning to brown around the edges. Remove the crackers from the oven and transfer them to a rack to cool completely.

nutrition information per serving   **10 crackers, 55g**

184 cal | 7g fat | 3g protein | 24g complex carbohydrates | 2g sugar | 3g dietary fiber | 299mg sodium | 128mg potassium | 1mg iron | 51mg calcium | 59mg phosphorus

Smoky Chili Crackers

ABOUT 6 DOZEN CRACKERS

These crackers smell deliciously of cumin as they bake, and they turn a very attractive deep golden orange. Serve them with guacamole, or salsa, or chile con queso. Chipotle powder (available in some of the more imaginative grocery stores) gives the crackers a pleasing, smoky flavor; use Tabasco if you can't find chipotle powder.

1½ cups (6¼ ounces) unbleached all-purpose flour

½ cup (2⅜ ounces) yellow or white cornmeal

2 tablespoons tomato powder, or 1 tablespoon tomato paste

1 tablespoon nonfat dry milk

1 teaspoon ground cumin

½ teaspoon baking soda

¾ teaspoon salt

2 teaspoons sugar

½ teaspoon chipotle powder, or ¼ to ½ teaspoon Tabasco sauce

¼ cup (1⅝ ounces) shortening

Scant ½ cup (about 7½ tablespoons, 3¾ ounces) water

Preheat the oven to 350°F.

In a large bowl, whisk together the flour, cornmeal, tomato powder (if you're using tomato paste don't add it just yet), dry milk, cumin, baking soda, salt, sugar, and chipotle powder or Tabasco sauce. Cut in the shortening (and tomato paste, if you're using it), then add enough water to make a workable dough. Gather the dough into a ball and divide it into two pieces.

Working with one piece at a time, roll the dough on a lightly floured surface to ⅛ inch thickness. Cut it into 1½-inch squares and bake the crackers for 20 minutes. Remove them from the oven and cool on the pan. Store in an airtight container.

nutrition information per serving   **3 crackers, 10g**

52 cal | 2g fat | 1g protein | 7g complex carbohydrates | 96mg sodium | 23mg potassium | 3RE vitamin A | 1mg iron | 1mg calcium | 12mg phosphorus

Crisp Crackers

Crackers may be made totally without leavening, in which case their texture comes solely from the inner steam created as they bake (as with a flaky piecrust). Unleavened crackers are generally tender and flaky (rather than crisp) if they're fairly thick; or quite hard (think hardtack) if they're rolled thin. Adding a leavening agent, either yeast or chemical (baking soda, baking powder, baker's ammonia, or cream of tartar), will produce a crisper, lighter cracker. These leaveners contribute to the mouth-feel we recognize as "crisp" by producing carbon dioxide gas, which is trapped within the cracker dough as it bakes. The mixture of air and baked dough is what transforms "tough" or "hard" into "crisp."

To produce crisp crackers, moisture that begins in the dough needs to leave the cracker as it bakes. This is why crackers are often "docked"—that is, pricked with a fork, in the case of the home baker. Not only do these holes allow steam to escape, they prevent the cracker from blowing up like a balloon. A typical cracker dough may contain 45 percent liquid; by the time the cracker is baked, that number should be down to 5 percent to 6 percent. Thus crackers need a thorough baking, either at a high temperature for a short amount of time, or at a lower temperature for a correspondingly longer length of time. Very thin cracker doughs (1/16 inch) seem to do better with a short, hot bake (though you need to watch them very carefully, as the thinner the cracker, the more quickly it goes from baked to burned). Thicker cracker doughs (up to 1/4 inch) do better with a longer, slower bake, in order to completely dry out the interior of the cracker without burning the exterior.

Thin Wheat Crackers

ABOUT 8 DOZEN CRACKERS

These snappy-crisp, golden brown wheat crackers are much better than the ones you buy in the store.

1 cup (4¼ ounces) unbleached pastry flour or unbleached all-purpose flour

1 cup (5 ounces) whole wheat flour or white whole wheat flour

¼ cup (1¼ ounces) sesame seeds

¼ cup (1¾ ounces) granulated sugar

½ teaspoon salt

4 tablespoons (½ stick, 2 ounces) butter

Scant ½ cup (3¾ ounces) milk

Coarse salt (optional)

Preheat oven to 325°F.

In a large bowl, combine the flours, sesame seeds, sugar, and salt. Cut in the butter, then stir in the milk, adding just enough milk to form a workable dough.

Divide the dough into three pieces and roll it out ultra-thin, one piece at a time—$\frac{1}{16}$ inch, if you can manage it. Sprinkle with a bit of coarse salt, if desired, and use the rolling pin to press the salt into the dough.

Cut the dough into 1 x 2-inch rectangles. Transfer the crackers to baking sheets and bake for 20 to 25 minutes, until they begin to brown. Cool on a rack.

nutrition information per serving   **9 crackers, 50g**

140 cal | 2g fat | 4g protein | 21g complex carbohydrates | 5g sugar | 3g dietary fiber | 1mg cholesterol | 127mg sodium | 108mg potassium | 2mg iron | 27mg calcium | 103mg phosphorus

Wine Biscuits

ABOUT 32 BISCUITS

These sweet, peppery-hot biscuits are a variation on a traditional Italian favorite, biscotti di vino, hard, semisweet biscuits served with an after-dinner cheese, or as a pre-dinner aperitif. Sangria, the Spanish concoction of mild wine and fruit, is a perfect accompaniment. But they're fine with a grape juice spritzer, too, or lemon-scented club soda. By the way, the term *biscuit,* as it's used here, refers to a hard, fairly dense cracker-type of bread, rather than the biscuit Americans know.

2½ cups (10½ ounces) unbleached all-purpose flour

2 teaspoons coarsely ground black pepper

4 to 6 tablespoons (1¾ to 2½ ounces) sugar, to taste*

1 teaspoon salt

2 teaspoons baking powder

½ cup plus 2 tablespoons (5 ounces) dry red wine, such as Cabernet Sauvignon (nonalcoholic red wine is fine)

¼ cup (1¾ ounces) vegetable oil

In a medium-sized mixing bowl, combine the flour, pepper, sugar, salt, and baking powder. In a separate bowl, whisk together the wine and vegetable oil. Add the liquid ingredients to the dry ingredients and beat vigorously until the mixture is smooth, about 1 minute. Cover the bowl and refrigerate the dough for at least 1 hour, or overnight.

Preheat the oven to 350°F.

These biscuits are traditionally shaped into a round, mini-bagel shape, but we found that they were more appealing when cut into shapes with a cutter. Stars and half-moons were our favorites; we cut them out of dough that was rolled ½ inch thick. If you want to make the more traditional shape, break off a piece of dough about the size of a walnut (about ¾ ounce) and roll it into a ball. Poke a hole in the middle of the ball to make a small bagel-shaped biscuit. Place it on a lightly greased or parchment-lined baking sheet. Repeat with the remaining dough.

Bake the biscuits for 35 to 40 minutes, or until they're golden brown (they'll actually look kind of purple from the red wine). Remove them from the oven and cool completely on a wire rack.

*The greater amount of sugar will make a biscuit that is just about as sweet as a cookie; the lesser amount will yield a more savory type of biscuit.

nutrition information per serving | **1 biscuit, 20g**

72 cal | 3.3g fat | 1g protein | 7g complex carbohydrates | 2g sugar | 94mg sodium | 18mg potassium | 32mg calcium | 14mg phosphorus

Crisp Seeded Mega-Crackers

8 MEGA-CRACKERS

We truly believe that if the four food groups consisted of chips, dips, crackers, and cheese, most Americans could die happy. From good old sour cream onion dip and rippled chips to an ultra-creamy St. André spread on a light, crisp crostini, America happily munches on these salty/savory/creamy/crisp treats from sea to shining sea.

The following recipe makes snapping-crisp, saucer-sized crackers that look lovely presented in a bread basket. Serve them with hummus or baba ghanoush for a really-not-so-bad-for-you snack. We thank author Lora Brody, a fellow nosher, for the inspiration behind these crackers.

3 cups (12¾ ounces) unbleached all-purpose flour

1¼ teaspoons salt

½ teaspoon baking powder

⅔ cup (3⅜ ounces) toasted sesame seeds, or a blend of your favorite small seeds

1 teaspoon freshly ground black pepper

2 tablespoons (¾ ounce) olive oil

1 cup (8 ounces) cool water

In a medium-sized bowl, whisk together the flour, salt, baking powder, seeds, and pepper. Stir in the olive oil, mixing thoroughly, then add the water, tossing with a fork until the dough becomes cohesive. Turn out the dough onto a lightly floured surface and knead and turn it over a few times to smooth it out. Divide the dough into eight pieces and allow them to rest, covered, for 15 minutes.

Preheat the oven to 450°F. If you have a baking stone, be sure to use it; it will make the crispest crackers.

Roll one or two pieces of dough (as many as will fit on your baking stone at once) as thin as possible; you'll make rounds 8 to 9 inches across. Using a peel or giant spatula, transfer the rounds to the stone and bake them for about 4 minutes, then flip them over and bake about 2 minutes on the second side, until they're golden brown on both sides.

If you don't have a baking stone, bake these on a lightly greased or parchment-lined baking sheet set on the middle rack of your oven; they'll take about 6 minutes on the first side, 4 minutes on the second. Remove the crackers from the oven as soon as they're brown and transfer them to a rack to cool. Repeat with the remaining dough rounds. Store crackers airtight.

nutrition information per serving   **1 cracker, 77g**

254 cal | 9g fat | 7g protein | 36g complex carbohydrates | 3g dietary fiber | 365mg sodium | 115mg potassium | 4mg iron | 134mg calcium | 121mg phosphorus

Flatbreads

When you think flatbread, think big. And round (usually); and thin, sometimes soft and flexible (tortillas), sometimes crackly-crisp (crackerbread or crispbread), sometimes sturdy enough (knäckebröd) to support a large helping of pickled herring in sour cream. We've included only those breads that are unleavened; leavened with a chemical leavener, like baking powder; or leavened with yeast, but just barely, so that they remain flat.

Flatbreads, being much quicker and easier to make than yeast breads, are represented in most ethnic cuisines, from Ethiopia's injera (a soft, naturally leavened bread based on teff flour) to Norway's flatbrod (a hard and crisp whole-grain round) to China's moo shu pancakes. If you're interested in delving deeply into flatbreads, we recommend *Flatbreads and Flavors: A Baker's Atlas,* by Jeffrey Alford and Naomi Duguid. We'll just dip our toe into the water here, examining some of the flatbreads that have become a part of the American culinary landscape.

Carta di Musica
(Sardinian parchment bread)

12 FLATBREADS

This bread's colorful name comes from the dough, which is supposed to be rolled so thin that you can read sheet music through it. It is best baked on a stone, where it crisps up beautifully. Carta di musica is the perfect vehicle for anything from roasted garlic to spoonfuls of caponata.

2 cups (8½ ounces) unbleached all-purpose flour

1 cup (5¾ ounces) semolina

1½ teaspoons salt

1¼ cups (10 ounces) water

Olive oil for brushing on after baking

2 teaspoons fresh rosemary (optional)

Preheat the oven for at least 40 minutes at 450°F; if you have a baking stone, put it in the oven before preheating. If working without a baking stone, preheat a baking sheet by putting it in the oven for 10 minutes so the breads are placed on a hot surface.

In a large bowl, whisk together the flours and the salt. Slowly add the water, stirring with a wooden spoon or dough whisk until the mixture forms a soft dough—all of the water may not be necessary. Knead the dough with your hands to form a ball. Place on a lightly floured work surface and knead until the dough is firm and smooth, but not sticky. Divide the dough evenly into twelve balls. Place the balls on a lightly floured surface. Flatten each ball into a 4-inch round. Cover and let rest for 15 minutes. After dough has rested, generously flour the work surface and roll each portion of the dough as thin as possible into an 8- or 9-inch round.

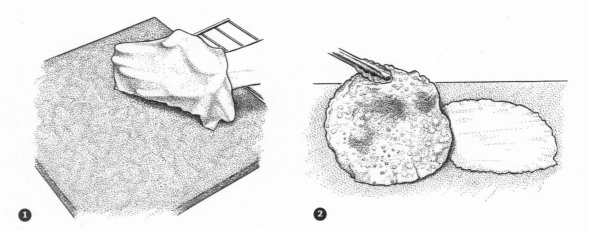

1. Carefully drape the rolled carta di musica over your hand, and place on the baking stone. **2.** The cooked, crisp carta di musica, left, and an unbaked piece on the right.

Place several rounds of dough on an ungreased baking sheet and place in the oven, or transfer to a baking stone using a baker's peel. Bake until the top of the bread is firm and lightly browned, 3 to 4 minutes. Turn the rounds over and bake until the other side is slightly browned. Transfer the bread to a wire rack to cool. Brush with olive oil and sprinkle with salt and rosemary.

nutrition information per serving   **1 bread, no toppings, 59g**

117 cal | 4g protein | 24g complex carbohydrates | 1g dietary fiber | 267mg sodium | 50mg potassium | 2mg iron | 3mg calcium | 36mg phosphorus

Lavash

4 SHEETS, ABOUT 8 SERVINGS PER SHEET

This easy-to-make unleavened bread breaks with a satisfying snap, and often towers over the dinner rolls in the bread basket. It is the ideal complement to any kind of spread, from soft butter to smoked salmon and cream cheese.

3½ cups (14¾ ounces) unbleached all-purpose flour

1½ teaspoons salt

¾ teaspoon sugar

¼ cup (1¾ ounces) shortening

1 large egg

1 cup (8 ounces) milk

½ cup (2½ ounces) sesame seeds, toasted, or a combination of any small seeds you like

The dough can most easily be rolled thin on the back of a greased baking sheet. Brush with water, then sprinkle the top with seeds.

In a large bowl, whisk together the flour, salt, and sugar. Cut in shortening. Beat the egg and milk together and stir into flour mixture, mixing well. The dough will be firm. Cover and let it rest for 30 minutes.

Preheat the oven to 375°F.

Divide dough into four pieces and roll each to ¹⁄₁₆-inch thickness on the back of a lightly greased sheet pan or on a piece of parchment paper. Brush the lavash with water and sprinkle the tops with seeds. Go over the dough once more, lightly, to press the seeds into the surface. Bake for 12 to 15 minutes, until browned and crisp. Break into pieces and serve with butter or your favorite spread.

Rich Potato Flatbread

8 FLATBREADS

This soft, moist, white-flour bread, an Americanized version of Norway's traditional potato flatbread, lefse, is true comfort food. Made with heavy cream and fresh potatoes, it's almost like a very rich gnocchi dough, shaped into patties and fried, rather than into small curls and boiled. If you love mashed potatoes—or gnocchi—you'll adore this bread, which is wonderful served warm, spread with butter (and sprinkled with cinnamon-sugar, if desired), or with a bit of sour cream. Soup or stew are good main-dish accompaniments. And spread with jam or preserves, or drizzled with maple syrup and rolled up, this bread is a delicious anytime snack.

2 pounds potatoes (Idaho or other dry, mealy potatoes work best)

5⅓ tablespoons (⅔ stick, 2⅝ ounces) butter, softened

½ cup (4 ounces) heavy cream

1½ teaspoons salt

2 cups (8½ ounces) unbleached all-purpose flour

Cook the potatoes until soft, then put them through a ricer. Make sure there are no lumps. Put the riced potatoes in a medium-sized mixing bowl.

Stir in the butter, cream, and salt and blend well. Add the flour and mix until well combined. Shape the dough into a ball, cover it, and refrigerate overnight.

Divide the dough into eight balls. Working with one ball at a time, roll it out until it's ⅛ inch thick. Fry the bread in a heavy ungreased skillet set over medium heat; there's no need to grease the pan as the bread won't stick due to its butter and cream content. Continue with the remaining dough. Store lefse in the refrigerator.

Seeded Crackerbread

3 PANS OF CRACKER BREAD, ABOUT 12 PORTIONS PER PAN

Crackerbread, an extra-thin focaccia type of loaf, is quick and easy to make, bakes fast, and can be broken into serving-sized pieces at the table. Eat it with a meal, spread it with dip or a soft spread, use it to scoop up caponata or another cold vegetable salad, or just munch it with a drink; this is an all-purpose bread.

2½ teaspoons instant yeast

1½ cups (12 ounces) lukewarm (110°F) water

5 cups (approximately 21¼ ounces) unbleached all-purpose flour

1 tablespoon sugar

1 tablespoon salt

1 tablespoon olive oil

¼ to ⅓ cup (1¼ to 1⅝ ounces) sesame or poppy seeds

Coarsely ground pepper and salt, for sprinkling

Stir together yeast, water, flour, sugar, and salt. Knead them to form a smooth dough and place in a large greased bowl, turning to coat all over with oil. Cover it and let rise for 1 hour, or until nicely puffed.

Punch down the dough, shape into a ball, and let rest for 10 minutes. In the meantime, lightly oil the bottom of three half-sheet pans (13 x 18 inches).

Divide dough into thirds. Take one third, place it on the bottom of a half-sheet pan, and roll it out as thin as you can; it should be ¹⁄₁₆ inch thick or less. If dough resists rolling and keeps springing back, let it rest for 5 or 10 minutes, then start again. Dough should cover entire bottom of pan.

Preheat the oven to 450°F.

Lightly brush dough with oil and sprinkle with sesame or poppy seeds, and coarsely ground pepper and salt, if desired. Bake for 7 to 10 minutes, until bread is very brown. Remove it from the oven and let cool; bread will become crisp as it cools, and is actually better 24 hours after you bake it.

NOTE Any type of large flat pan will work here. You want a large enough pan—or enough smaller pans—to be able to roll the dough very thin. Since this bread bakes so quickly, you can do the whole thing using only one pan; it will simply take longer.

nutrition information per serving   **1 serving, 28g**

66 cal │ 1g fat │ 2g protein │ 12g complex carbohydrates │ 1g dietary fiber │ 178mg sodium │ 29mg potassium │ 1mg iron │ 10mg calcium │ 23mg phosphorus

Sesame Crisps

8 CRISPS

Crisp and crunchy, nutty with the taste of sesame, these saucer-sized ultra-thin crackers are a snap to make, and teamed with hummus or baba ghanoush make a wonderful hors d'oeuvre. Try them with tabbouleh or another summer salad, or just enjoy as is with a cool twilight drink.

1½ cups (6 ounces) Italian 00 flour or pastry flour	⅓ cup (2¾ ounces) water
¾ teaspoon salt	2 tablespoons (⅞ ounce) olive oil
	½ cup (2½ ounces) sesame seeds, toasted

Combine all the ingredients to make a stiff dough. You can do this by hand, with the help of an electric mixer, or in a bread machine set on the manual cycle. Knead the dough for a minute or less; you don't need to develop the gluten, just make sure all of the ingredients are thoroughly combined. Shape the dough into a flattened ball, cover it with plastic wrap, and set it aside to rest and relax at room temperature for 15 minutes.

Divide the dough into eight equal pieces, each about the size of a golf ball (1¼ to 1 ½ ounces each). Roll each piece into a ball, then flatten the balls. Cover them and let rest for 15 minutes.

Preheat the oven to 425°F. If you have a baking stone, place it on the floor of your gas oven, or on the lowest rack of your electric oven. If you don't have a baking stone, place a cookie sheet on the lowest rack of the oven.

Transfer the dough to a lightly greased work surface. Working with one piece at a time, roll the dough into a thin, 6-inch-wide circle. Set the circle aside and continue rolling the dough until you've got eight thin rounds.

Working quickly, pick up two pieces of dough and gently toss them onto the baking stone or baking sheet, making sure they lie flat. Close the oven door and bake for 3 minutes. Using a spatula or tongs, turn the rounds over and bake for 3 minutes on the other side, until the rounds are a light golden brown around the edges. (Check them after 2 to 2½ minutes to be sure they're not too brown; they can burn quickly.) Remove the crisps from the oven and quickly spray or brush them with garlic or sesame oil. Place on a rack to cool. Repeat with the remaining rounds. Eat immediately, or store in an airtight container.

nutrition information per serving　1 crisp, 44g

145 cal | 6.6g fat | 3g protein | 18g complex carbohydrates | 1g dietary fiber | 201mg sodium | 60mg potassium | 2mg iron | 109mg calcium | 64mg phosphorus

Swedish Knäckebröd

4 DOZEN FLATBREADS

Contrary to many versions of knäckebröd ("break bread"), this one contains no rye flour. Instead, it's an earthy wheat-based formula, combining a few basic elements—wheat flour, butter, milk, sugar, salt—with two kinds of leavening to create a flatbread that is crisp yet strong, perfect for spreading with sweet butter, layering with cheese and meat, or using as a scoop for herring salad. Though not at all traditional, a layer of sesame seeds pressed into the flatbread before baking gives it a pleasingly nutty taste and a bit of extra crunch.

8 tablespoons (½ stick, 4 ounces) butter, melted

¾ cup (6 ounces) milk

2½ teaspoons active dry yeast or instant yeast

¼ cup (2 ounces) lukewarm water

1 teaspoon sugar

1 teaspoon salt

½ teaspoon baking soda

1 cup (5¼ ounces) whole wheat flour

2 cups (8½ ounces) unbleached all-purpose flour

Sesame seeds (optional)

In a small mixing bowl, combine the melted butter and milk. In a separate bowl, dissolve the yeast in the warm water with the sugar. Let the mixture sit for 5 minutes, then add it to the milk mixture.

In a separate bowl, stir together the salt, baking soda, and flours. Add them to the milk mixture, stirring to combine. Knead the dough for about 5 minutes, by hand or machine, then let it rest, covered, for 5 minutes.

(If you have a bread machine, place all the ingredients in the pan of your machine in the order recommended by the manufacturer, usually liquids first. Program the machine for Manual or Dough and let it knead for 10 minutes, or until it's very smooth. Cancel the machine and remove the dough.)

Preheat the oven to 350°F.

Grease the outside bottom of a 13 x 18-inch half-sheet pan or similar-sized pan; try not to use a pan too much smaller, as your crackers will be too thick. Divide the dough into two pieces. Working with one piece at a time, roll it onto the outside bottom of the baking pan, going all the way to the edges and trying to make the dough an even thickness all over the pan. Sprinkle the dough with sesame seeds, giving the dough one more pass with the rolling pin to press them in. Prick the dough all over with a fork and cut it into 4 x 2-inch pieces (a practical size for holding substantial cheese or meat slices). Don't try to spread the pieces apart; they're fine as is. Repeat with the remaining piece of dough.

Bake the flatbread for 25 minutes, until it's a deep golden brown. Make sure you don't underbake this bread or it will be soggy and pliable, rather than crisp. (If you do underbake it by mistake and it's a bit soft once it's cooled, just leave it out, uncovered, overnight; it will get crisp.) Remove the pans from the oven and transfer the flatbread to a wire rack to cool completely, breaking it apart if necessary.

nutrition information per serving **1 flatbread, with sesame seeds, 17g**

55 cal | 3g fat | 1g protein | 6g complex carbohydrates | 1g dietary fiber | 6mg cholesterol | 76mg sodium | 31mg potassium | 21RE vitamin A | 1mg iron | 30mg calcium | 29mg phosphorus

Wraps and Tortillas

The wrap is nothing more than a variation on the traditional flour tortilla. Spinach powder or tomato powder add brilliant color and great flavor to wraps; and, leaving no possibility unthought of, you may also choose to turn a plain wrap (or tortilla) into one flavored with cheese, or herbs and spices, or garlic.

Wraps can be filled with any number of imaginative sandwich fillings, from a simple chicken salad to Thai-spiced grilled beef. Just pile the filling onto the wrap, tuck in the ends, and roll it up. Flour tortillas can become burritos, and corn tortillas tacos, using the same technique.

Picnic Wraps

8 WRAPS

This thin, flexible bread is ideal for stuffing with fresh tomatoes, kalamata olives, lettuce, red peppers, cheese—any of your favorite sandwich fillings. By folding over the ends before rolling, the wrap is sealed to ensure safe transport to the sylvan picnic spot of your choice.

WRAPS
2 cups (8½ ounces) unbleached bread flour
3 tablespoons (1 ounce) vegetable oil

½ to ¾ cups (4 to 6 ounces) water
½ teaspoon salt

In a medium-sized bowl, mix together the flour and oil. Gradually mix in the water and salt. Knead briefly, just until the dough is smooth.

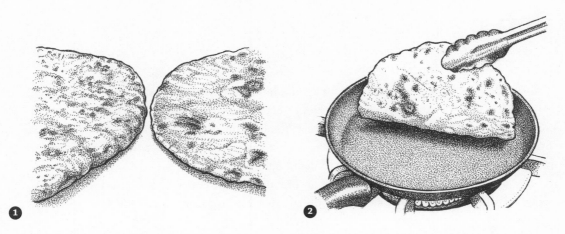

1. Picnic wraps are pictured on the right; on the left is Soft Wrap Bread, p. 184. **2.** Dry-frying the wrap will give it a freckled appearance. It should be ready to turn after 45 seconds of cooking on the first side.

Divide the dough into eight pieces. Round them into balls, flatten slightly, and let them rest, covered, for at least 30 minutes.

Preheat an ungreased heavy frying pan over medium heat. Working with one piece of dough at a time, roll it out until it's about 8 inches in diameter. Fry the wrap for about 45 seconds on each side until it's a mottled brown. Cool and store in an airtight container.

nutrition information per serving   **1 wrap, 59g**

170cal │ 6g fat │ 4g protein │ 25g complex carbohydrates │ 1g dietary fiber │ 134mg sodium │ 35mg potassium │ 2mg iron │ 6mg calcium │ 33mg phosphorus

Filling

ENOUGH FILLING FOR 8 WRAPS

8 ounces goat cheese, at room temperature

¼ cup (2 ounces) cream cheese

1 cup (7 ounces) puréed pitted kalamata olives, or olive tapenade

4 tomatoes, thinly sliced

Sliced red peppers

Lettuce leaves

In a small bowl, mash together the cheeses until smooth. Spread a thin layer of the cheese on one side of a wrap, add a thin layer of olive purée, then top with thinly sliced tomatoes, red peppers, and lettuce. Roll the wrap so that all the ingredients are contained within. Repeat with the remaining wraps.

Roti

8 ROTI

The world of Indian flatbreads is huge and varied, representing as it does its host of cultures. Rather than go into a definitive examination of even part of this subject, we chose one bread that's fairly typical of the genre. Roti can refer to all of India's griddle-baked flatbreads collectively; to an unleavened, whole wheat bread within that category; or to a white flour, leavened, fat-enriched bread. We chose the latter to detail here.

Roti can be served as part of an Indian meal, of course, but it also is excellent wrapped around your favorite sandwich filling, especially hot from the griddle.

3 cups (12¾ ounces) unbleached all-purpose flour

1½ teaspoons baking powder

1 teaspoon salt

2 tablespoons (⅞ ounce) vegetable oil

¾ to 1 cup (6 to 8 ounces) water

In a large mixing bowl, whisk together the flour, baking powder, and salt. Add oil and enough water to form a dough that is soft but not sticky. Let rest for 30 minutes, then cut the dough into 8 equal pieces. Roll the dough into balls, then cover and let rest for 5 minutes. Roll out each piece on a floured board to make a 6- to 8-inch disk.

Heat a griddle over medium heat. Brush the griddle with oil, then brush the roti disks with oil on both sides. Place the roti on the griddle and cook until the top starts to blister. Flip roti and cook for 1 minute more. Serve warm, or cool completely and use to wrap around your favorite filling for sandwiches.

nutrition information per serving 1 roti, 75g

180 cal | 4g fat | 4g protein | 32g complex carbohydrates | 1g dietary fiber | 461mg sodium | 54mg potassium | 2mg iron | 35mg calcium | 51mg phosphorus

Soft Cornmeal Wraps

TEN 8-INCH WRAPS

Just as tortillas come in plain flour and cornmeal versions, so do our favorite wraps. Cornmeal adds golden color and an elusive hint of sweetness to these soft, pliable rounds.

2 cups (8½ ounces) unbleached all-purpose flour

1 cup (4⅞ ounces) yellow cornmeal

1 teaspoon baking powder

1 teaspoon salt

¼ teaspoon yeast, instant or active dry

2 tablespoons (⅜ ounce) nonfat dry milk

2 tablespoons (¾ ounce) vegetable shortening or lard

1 cup (8 ounces) water

In a medium-sized bowl, mix together all the dry ingredients, then cut in the shortening. Gradually mix in the water. Knead briefly, just until the dough is smooth.

(If you have a bread machine place all the ingredients in the pan of your machine, program for Manual or Dough, and press Start. Cancel the machine and remove the dough when it's smooth, after about 5 minutes of kneading.)

Divide the dough into ten pieces, weighing about 2 ounces each. Round them into balls, flatten slightly, and let them rest, covered, for at least 30 minutes. This resting period improves the texture of the dough by giving the flour time to absorb the water, and it also gives the gluten time to relax, making the wraps easier to roll out.

Preheat an ungreased cast iron griddle or heavy frying pan over medium heat. Working with one piece of dough at a time (keep the remaining dough balls covered), roll out the balls until they're about 8 inches in diameter. Fry the wraps in the ungreased pan for about 45 seconds on each side. (Or use a tortilla baker.) Stack wraps on top of one another as you fry them to keep them soft and pliable. Serve warm or at room temperature. Store, tightly wrapped, in a plastic bag at room temperature. To store wraps longer than a couple of days, freeze them.

nutrition information per serving   1 wrap, 55g

151 cal | 3g fat | 4g protein | 27g complex carbohydrates | 2g dietary fiber | 275mg sodium | 92mg potassium | 13RE vitamin A | 2mg iron | 47mg calcium | 75mg phosphorus

Soft Wrap Bread

8 BREADS

We use a rather unusual method to make this bread: boiling water is added to the flour, "cooking" the starch and making the resultant dough soft and easy to roll out. In addition, precooking the starch this way eliminates any possibility of a starchy taste in the final bread; all in all, we find these wraplike rounds better tasting than conventional flour tortillas or other wraps. In texture, they're more like a Taco Bell gordita or a pita bread than a tortilla, so if you like the bread in your sandwich to be a substantial part of the whole, this is a good recipe for your files.

3 to 3¼ cups (12¾ to 13¾ ounces) unbleached all-purpose flour

1½ cups (12 ounces) boiling water

¼ cup (1½ ounces) potato flour, or ½ cup (⅝ ounce) potato flakes

1¼ teaspoons salt

2 tablespoons (⅞ ounce) vegetable oil

1 teaspoon instant yeast*

Place 2 cups of the flour in a bowl. Pour the boiling water over the flour and stir until smooth. Cover the bowl and set aside to cool the mixture for 30 minutes.

In a separate bowl, whisk together the potato flour and 1 cup of the remaining flour with the salt, oil, and yeast. Add this to the cooled flour-water mixture, stir, then knead for several minutes (by hand or mixer) to form a soft dough. The dough should form a ball, but will remain somewhat sticky. Add additional flour only if necessary; if kneading by hand, keep your hands and work surface lightly oiled. Place the dough in a greased bowl and let it rise, covered, for 1 hour.

Divide the dough into eight pieces (each about the size of a handball, about 3 ounces), cover, and let rest for 15 to 30 minutes. Roll each piece into a 7- to 8-inch circle and dry-fry them (fry without oil) over medium-high heat for 1 to 2 minutes per side, until they're puffed and flecked with brown spots. Adjust the heat if they seem to be cooking either too quickly or too slowly; cooking too quickly means they may be raw in the center, while too slowly will dry them out. Transfer the cooked breads to a wire rack, stacking them to keep them soft. Serve immediately, or cool slightly before storing in a plastic bag.

*This recipe works best with instant yeast because it dissolves during the kneading process, so you don't have to knead liquid into the dough. If you prefer to use active dry yeast, use only 1 cup boiling water for the initial dough, dissolve the yeast in ¼ cup warm water, and add this mixture to the dough along with the potato flour mixture. It'll be somewhat slippery at first, but will knead in and eventually become smooth.

nutrition information per serving   1 bread, 98g

202 cal | 4g fat | 5g protein | 36g complex carbohydrates | 2g dietary fiber | 336mg sodium | 150mg potassium | 1mg vitamin C | 3mg iron | 3mg calcium | 55mg phosphorus

Thin Cornmeal Tortilla

10 TORTILLAS

The following is classically tortilla in texture, wafer-thin and pliable. However, it includes both flour and cornmeal, something a real tortilla would never do. We just happen to love the faint sweetness of cornmeal paired with flour's soft texture.

1⅓ cups (5½ ounces) unbleached all-purpose flour

⅔ cup (3¼ ounces) yellow cornmeal

¼ cup (1¾ ounces) corn oil or vegetable oil

½ cup plus 1 tablespoon (4½ ounces) water

½ teaspoon salt

In a medium-sized bowl, mix together the flour, cornmeal, and oil. Gradually mix in the water and salt. Knead briefly, just until the dough is smooth.

(If using a bread machine place all the ingredients in the pan of your machine, program for manual or dough, and press Start. Cancel the machine and remove the dough when it's smooth, after about 5 minutes of kneading.)

Divide the dough into ten pieces, weighing about 1⅜ ounces each. Round the pieces into balls, flatten them slightly, and let them rest, covered, for at least 30 minutes. This resting period improves the texture of the dough by giving the flour time to absorb the water, and it also gives the gluten time to relax, making the tortillas easier to roll out.

Preheat an ungreased cast iron griddle or heavy frying pan over medium heat. Working with one piece of dough at a time (keep the remaining dough balls covered), roll out each ball until about 8 inches in diameter. Fry the tortillas in the ungreased pan for about 45 seconds on each side. (Or use a tortilla baker.) Stack tortillas on top of one another as you remove them from the pan, to keep them soft and pliable. Serve warm or at room temperature. Store, tightly wrapped, in a plastic bag at room temperature. To store tortillas longer than a couple of days, freeze them.

nutrition information per serving   1 tortilla, 36g

130 cal | 6g fat | 2g protein | 17g complex carbohydrates | 1g dietary fiber | 110mg sodium | 42mg potassium | 4RE vitamin A | 1mg iron | 1mg calcium | 33mg phosphorus

Yeast Breads

Bread was one of the first foods prepared by humans, one of the first of which we have a written record. It appears in the Bible, in the Koran, in the Talmud. The rallying cry of the Russian Revolution was "Bread, peace, and land." More recently, anti-capitalist demonstrators in Istanbul held loaves of bread as they shouted "No bread, no peace." Pundits speak of bread and circuses, or bread and roses; our mothers tell us "half a loaf is better than none." Bread fills the stomach and tastes wonderful. Our earliest food memories probably include bread in some comforting incarnation; it follows us through life like a constant friend, happy to stay in the background, but always present. Is there a better example of comfort food than warm bread and butter?

In years gone by, Americans universally baked bread at home. These days it's much more rare, as cookies, muffins, and other sweet treats have taken center stage in the kitchen of the modern American baker.

But the plain truth is, here at King Arthur we find yeast bread easier to make than cake or biscuits or pie. Yes, it takes longer, but unlike other baked goods, its schedule is flexible. Start it in the morning, finish it at night; speed it up in a warm oven, slow it down in the refrigerator. It will happily bend itself to your agenda. And with the easy access most of us have to time-saving appliances—electric mixers, food processors, bread machines—even the vigorous ten minutes or so of required kneading can be taken out of your hands, quite literally. Good homemade bread is a goal any baker can easily achieve.

And what a broad landscape lies before us! Yeast bread is open to all kinds of variations. If you think of white, whole wheat, rye, and whole-grain as the four main

Fitting Bread into Your Schedule

The amount of yeast you use in your bread dough has a significant bearing on how quickly it will rise, and thus on your own schedule. By reducing the yeast, you ensure a long, slow rise rather than a series of quick rises and resultant falls.

You can reduce the yeast in most types of bread recipes (sweet breads being the exception) to produce a dough that will rise slowly over a long period of time, rather than one that rises for an hour in the bowl and half an hour in the pan before baking. This long rise is often much more convenient than the regular, short-rise method. In recipes calling for a packet of yeast (2¼ teaspoons), we recommend cutting the amount back to ½ to 1 teaspoon of instant yeast, depending on how long you want to let the dough ferment before the final shape-rise-bake process; ½ teaspoon would give you lots of flexibility, such as letting the dough rest for 16 to 20 hours; 1 teaspoon would be a good amount for an all-

day or overnight rise (10 hours or so, at cool room temperature). If you're using active dry yeast, which isn't as vigorous as instant yeast, we'd up the range to ¾ to 1½ teaspoons.

The easiest, safest dough to subject to a long, slow rise is one containing only a small amount of sugar, if any, and no dairy products (eggs, milk, butter, etc.). Sweet doughs are notoriously slow risers, anyway; by cutting back on the yeast, you're just slowing them down even more. Sweet doughs are best slowed down by refrigeration, rather than reducing the amount of yeast. Also, doughs that contain dairy products (and shouldn't, for food safety reasons, be left at room temperature all day) should also be refrigerated if you want to slow them down.

Whole grain doughs are naturally slow rising, due to the bran in the grain, which interferes with gluten development. If you'd like to slow down a familiar whole grain recipe, then do cut back on the yeast; but if you're making a types of yeast breads, just think how many variations there are on each of those themes, ranging from white sandwich bread to crusty baguettes, light sandwich rye to raisin-pecan pumpernickel, and honey oatmeal bread to a ten-grain loaf. And what's fascinating is, even when you've drilled right down to, say, rye bread, there's still not just one "right" recipe. You can use white, cream, medium, or dark rye flour, or pumpernickel; add caraway, mustard, fennel or anise seeds; begin with a starter, or add pickle juice or sauerkraut; shape it into a sandwich loaf, or a buxom round.

So come with us as we explore the wonderful world of bread. You'll be helping to carry on a piece of the world's culture that's as ancient as the first tilled fields—and as welcoming as a peanut butter and jelly sandwich.

particular whole-grain recipe for the first time, we recommend using the amount of yeast indicated and seeing just how long it takes the dough to rise fully. Often it takes longer than the directions say, and there's probably no need to slow things down even more.

Basic flour-water-yeast-salt doughs (which may also contain a bit of oil and/or sugar), such as those for baguettes, focaccia and pizza, are the best candidates for an all-day countertop rise. Keep in mind, however, the vagaries of your own kitchen. If you bake bread all the time, your kitchen is full of wild yeast and any dough you make there will rise vigorously. If you seldom bake bread, or are just beginning, your kitchen will be quite "sterile"; your dough won't be aided by wild yeast and will rise more slowly than it would in a more "active" kitchen. We've found that here in our King Arthur kitchen, where we bake bread every day, we can cut the yeast back to ⅛ teaspoon in a 3-cup-of-flour recipe and get a good overnight rise. In a kitchen where bread is seldom baked, we needed ½ teaspoon of yeast to get the same effect. Use your judgment in rating your own kitchen as to "yeast friendliness."

Keep in mind, also, that this slow rise usually extends to the shaped loaf, as well as dough in the bowl. Once you've shaped your loaf, covered it, and set it aside to rise again, it may take 2 hours or more, rather than the usual 1 to 1½, to rise fully and be ready for the oven.

There is no hard and fast rule for the amount of yeast you should use in any particular recipe. It depends on how slow (or fast) you want the dough to rise; the composition of the dough itself (whole grain, sweet/dairy, or "straight"); and your kitchen. Be flexible and experiment; you'll soon discover the formula that will work just right for you, producing a ready-to-shape dough when you're ready to shape it.

How Does Yeast Work?

First, what is it? Yeast is a "thallophyte," a complete, smaller-than-we-can-see one-celled plant. Each cell is the same, that is, as they grow, they don't become differentiated to form more complex organisms like the plants that we can see. The name for all strains of bakers' yeast (with the exception of sourdough or wild yeast) is *Saccharomyces cerevisiae.*

The tiny pellets you see in a container of dried yeast are not single yeast cells, but agglomerations of many cells. It takes about 25 billion of them to make a gram ($\frac{1}{28}$ of an ounce). One yeast cell may be tiny, but in huge numbers they can certainly make their presence known—primarily by their waste products, which are very valuable to the baker. The most important ones are carbon dioxide, which leavens bread; alcohol, which contributes to the bread's aroma; and organic acids, which give it flavor.

A mixture of flour and water creates one of the most favorable growing conditions for yeast. It provides a good source of the carbohydrates and other minerals that yeast needs to grow. But beyond this, yeast also needs proper hydration, the right temperature, and an appropriate pH.

What are the optimum living conditions for yeast? The temperature should be in the range of 75°F to 90°F, although a dough can stray somewhat above or below these temperatures without undue effect.

If actively fermenting yeast is too cold for too long, the yeast cells slowly die. Thus, if you freeze a dough, it will remain viable only for a couple of months. On the other hand, yeast that is dormant, or not actively fermenting, can remain in the freezer (above 0°F, and not self-defrosting) for years at a time.

Yeast also needs access to the sugars and minerals in dough, and while it ultimately has the ability to break these down itself, bakers sometimes add a small amount of sugar to start the process. In addition, the pH of the liquid plays an important role. Soft (alkaline) water is relatively free of minerals. Because yeast has its own characteristic mineral content, it wants a growing medium that's similar. So it doesn't like soft water. Hard (acidic) water, on the other hand, contains lots of minerals and yeast will grow very quickly when it has access to such abundance. A small amount of ascorbic acid (vitamin C) can help correct water that is too soft. Slightly more yeast can help overcome water that is too hard.

Primer: How to Make a Loaf of Bread

In simplest terms, bread is a combination of flour, yeast, and water. Most bakers add salt, and from there the list of ingredients can grow in direct proportion to the baker's imagination. It's the basic ingredients you use, however, and how you treat them that makes or breaks your loaf of bread.

Start with the Flour

Flour is the dominant ingredient in bread, and thus carries much of the responsibility for its success or failure. While bread can be made from most any flour, the majority of yeast-leavened breads are most successfully made with a medium-to-high protein wheat-based flour. That means all-purpose or bread flour; the protein level on the side of the bag should read 3g to 4g per ¼-cup serving.

Flour can vary from region to region and season to season; just as a particular type of grape doesn't always produce the exact same kind of wine, the particular wheats used to make all-purpose and bread flour may produce a slightly different

Yeast: Active Dry vs. Instant

You may substitute active dry yeast for the instant yeast called for in our recipes without making any changes in the amount; if the recipe calls for 2 teaspoons of instant yeast, use 2 teaspoons of active dry yeast.

To proof active dry yeast, dissolve it in a few tablespoons of the liquid in your recipe, along with a half teaspoon or so of sugar, or a tablespoon of flour. Wait 10 to 15 minutes; if you don't see any activity (small bubbles forming), try some newer yeast. If the yeast is active and producing bubbles, add the liquid mixture along with the other liquid ingredients.

Active dry yeast is a little bit slower off the mark than instant, as far as dough rising goes; but in a long (2- to 3-hour) rise, the active dry yeast catches up. If a recipe using in-stant yeast calls for the dough to "double in size, about 1 hour," you may want to mentally add 15 to 20 minutes on to this time if you're using active dry yeast. When dough is rising, you need to judge it by how much it's risen, not how long it takes; cold weather, low barometric pressure, how often you bake, and a host of other factors affect dough rising times, so use them as a guide, not an unbreakable rule. Remember, bread-baking involves living things (yeast), your own personal touch in kneading technique, and the atmosphere of your kitchen; there are so many variables that it's impossible to say that "Dough X will double in size in 60 minutes." Baking with yeast is a combination of art, science, and a bit of magic; stay flexible, and your bread will be just fine.

product from one growing season to the next. It's up to the flour manufacturer to ensure that the flour remains as consistent as possible; here at King Arthur flour we have very high specification standards. It's up to you to discover which brand of flour works best for you.

Bread bakers rely on wheat flour because of its ability to form gluten. (For more information on wheat, flour, and gluten, see pages 510 to 529).The protein in wheat flour, when combined with a liquid, forms long strands called gluten. These strands become elastic when you knead the dough; they're responsible for the final high-rising shape your bread assumes as it bakes. Other flours—rye, oat, corn—contain minimal amounts, if any, of this gluten; thus breads made with them alone won't be able to rise very high.

Combine It with Yeast, Any Other Dry Ingredients, and Liquid

Mix the yeast, salt, and sugar (if you're using it) into the flour. If you're using active dry yeast rather than instant, dissolve it in a couple of tablespoons of water, then add it to the flour with the remainder of the liquid called for in the recipe. Once you combine the flour in your recipe with liquid, gluten starts to form. You'll notice that the dough starts to become cohesive very quickly; before you know it, it's following your spoon around the bowl (or the flat paddle around the mixer). At this point—just as the dough has barely come together and is still extremely rough-looking—one option you have is to give the dough a twenty-minute rest. This rest (called the autolyse by French bread bakers) allows the flour to absorb the liquid fully, making it easier to knead, and less likely that you'll make the mistake of adding too much flour as you go along. This step isn't crucial, and can be skipped if you're in a hurry.

When to Add the Salt

There's much disagreement among professional bread bakers (and among ourselves—see p. 278) about when to add salt to the dough, with the discussion centering on the preferred order of certain chemical reactions. Our preference is to combine all the basic dry ingredients with the flour—salt, sugar, instant yeast—and then to add the liquid. We don't feel it makes a discernible difference to hold the salt out until after the autolyse; and frankly, if we don't add it right at the beginning, we sometimes forget to add it at all—not a good thing!

Add the Remaining Ingredients

Now it's time to add any other ingredients you're using: butter or oil, eggs, whole grains, flavors, whatever your recipe calls for. The only ingredient you don't want to add at this point would be dried fruit or any other sweet add-in; sugar may leach from these ingredients into the surrounding dough, upsetting the sugar balance and slowing down the yeast. Combine thoroughly, using a mixer, bread machine, or your hands.

Time to Knead

Sprinkle your work surface with flour or spray with vegetable oil spray. Knead the dough until it's smooth and supple. It will become more and more elastic as you develop the gluten, until eventually it should feel like a baby's bottom—soft but springy. Take a break at about the five-minute mark; giving the dough a five-minute rest at this point allows the gluten to relax, making the remaining kneading a lot easier.

A Little Sweet, A Little Salt

Can you make bread without sugar or salt? Sure. But keep the following points in mind.

• It won't taste very good. Both sugar and salt are flavor enhancers. Without salt in particular, your bread will taste flat. Cardboard is the best descriptor for saltless bread.

• It will rise very quickly. Both salt and sugar tend to temper the yeast's growth, allowing it to occur in a calm, regular manner.

Without this tempering, the yeast grows very quickly and the dough rises too fast, without the chance to develop flavor.

• It may collapse. Both salt and organic acids, developed over a long. slow fermentation (rise), help strengthen the gluten in your loaf, allowing it to hold its shape until the hot oven does its job. Without them, your loaf is likely to rise and then collapse.

Too Much Sweet, Too Much Salt

If a little salt is good for your bread dough, is a lot even better? No. Too much salt attracts water in the dough, robbing the yeast of the liquid it needs to do its job. Sugar acts similarly; an "overdose" of sugar also coaxes your yeast to "overeat," resulting in yeast that acts like you do after Thanksgiving dinner: tired and lethargic.

We find that for a typical 3-cup-flour recipe, 1½ teaspoons of salt and up to ¼ cup of sugar won't result in any slowdown. More than that, you're tempting fate. To add more sugar for a sweeter bread, you may choose yeast that's designed specifically for sweet breads; or you may choose to increase the amount of yeast, and give the dough a much longer window in which to rise.

The Most Effective Kneading

We've been wrestling with different methods of kneading bread for years and have come to some conclusions. Of bread dough kneaded by hand, by electric stand mixer, or by bread machine, the bread machine dough is noticeably better kneaded than either the hand or electric mixer dough. In tests we conducted, dough from the bread machine was more extensible—the gluten stretched farther before breaking—than dough made by hand or mixer. Breads made with bread machine-kneaded dough rose higher in the pan, higher in the oven, and displayed a better crumb.

If you just love to knead bread dough by hand, go for it—but remember, your rising times may be longer than what we give in these recipes, and your final loaf probably won't rise as high. If you want a good all-around baking tool—something to whip up cake batter, mix cookie dough, knead bread, or cut butter into flour for a piecrust—a stand mixer is the right choice. If you're interested strictly in the best bread dough possible, and expending the least amount of time and effort, use a bread machine set on the dough cycle.

The First Rise

Put the kneaded dough into a lightly greased bowl or dough-rising bucket (see Tools, p. 592) with a capacity two to three times the size of the dough. Cover the bowl with plastic wrap and let the dough rise, at warm room temperature (70°F to 80°F), until it's doubled in bulk or until it looks like the recipe tells you it should; not all doughs will double in bulk during this first rise.

Shaping

Pick the dough up out of the bowl and squeeze it gently to deflate it. Forget all that stuff you might have heard about punching down the dough or slamming it onto the counter. All this rough treatment does is (a) excite the gluten so that it becomes tough and resistant to shaping, and (b) drive the air out of the dough, those same gases you're counting on to make a tall, light loaf. So treat it gently.

Now it's up to you (and the recipe) to decide what shape your bread will take. A sandwich loaf? Baguette? Cloverleaf rolls? Pizza? Work on a lightly greased work surface to divide and/or shape the dough as the recipe directs.

Rise and Shine

If you live in snow country, it's fairly certain your house will be a bit cool for optimum dough rising during the winter. There are a number of things you can do to help yeast remain warm and happily multiplying. First, seek out the naturally warm areas of your house, which may include the top of the water heater or the top of the refrigerator. Cover the top of your bowl of dough with lightly greased plastic wrap, wrap the bowl in a large dish towel or not-too-thick bath towel, and set it in this warm place. If you have a wood stove, any area near and above the stove (heat rises), such as a bookshelf, will be ideal. Ditto a radiator or hot air vent.

Second, for a more reliable, controllable source of heat, set a heating pad on low, swaddle it in a towel, and set your covered bowl on top. We've known a lot of bakers who've had great luck with this method. Or try this: Preheat the oven on "warm," for 1 minute, turn the oven off, then set the bowl of dough inside. Turn your oven on to warm for 1 minute every 45 minutes or so, until the dough has risen sufficiently. We've also heard of bakers setting their covered bowl of rising dough in a dishwasher that's just completed its cycle.

You can also make a temporary proof box (a box for raising bread dough) out of a chest-type cooler. Put a cooling rack in the bottom of the cooler, then preheat the cooler by pouring a couple of cups of boiling water into it and shutting the lid. When your dough is ready, quickly open the top of the cooler, put in the bowl of dough, and shut the lid; the dough stays warm and moist and rises very nicely. If you're looking for a long rise, add another cup of boiling water every hour or so.

The Second Rise

Most breads rise again once they're shaped. An exception would be ultra-flat breads, like a thin-crust pizza or very thin flatbreads. Cover the shaped dough with thoroughly greased plastic wrap or a proof cover, which is a plastic box designed to shelter your rising loaf from drafts and keep it moist (see Tools, p. 592).

Again, your recipe will tell you how the dough should look at the end of its second rise. Sometimes dough needs to double; sometimes, for extra-light breads (like ciabatta), it should at least triple. Sometimes it needs to rise just a bit before going into the oven to complete its rise. Follow your recipe.

Baking

In general, crusty hearth breads bake for a short amount of time at a high (425°F to 450°F or hotter) temperature. Soft sandwich loaves or sweet breads bake at a lower temperature (350°F to 375°F) for a longer amount of time. A hot, fast bake produces a crisp crust; a slower, cooler bake yields a more tender crust. An exception to this is large breads without much fat or sugar, such as round country loaves. These breads need a lower temperature and longer time in the oven in order to bake all the way through; in the process, their crust tends to become thick and chewy rather than tender.

What should you do if your bread appears to be perfectly browned, but it's not ready to come out of the oven according to the times given in the recipe? This sometimes happens with breads that are high in sugar (especially honey) or fat. If your bread appears to be browning too quickly, lightly tent a sheet of aluminum foil over it; this should slow down the browning enough that the center has a chance to finish before the outside burns.

The Perfect Loaf

You can tell if your bread is done if an instant-read thermometer whose tip has been pushed into the center of the loaf reads 190°F. Dense, whole-grain hearth loaves should be baked to about 200°F or 210°F. We've come to rely entirely on our instant-read thermometer, and no longer use the traditional tapping method.

However, if you don't have a thermometer and want to check your bread the classic way, by sound, here's what to do: When you feel the bread is done, remove it from the oven, take it out of the pan and, holding it in one hand, give it a few quick, hard taps on the bottom with your index or middle finger. A loaf that's done will sound hollow, like a drum. Tapping that sounds muffled or dull means the loaf needs a bit more baking time. If that's the case, there's no need to put it back into the pan; simply place it right on the rack of the oven.

If you have tough hands (baker's hands!), you can do this quickly and quite easily without the aid of a potholder or mitt. If your hands are too sensitive to use the "macho method," use a mitt or potholder to hold the loaf while you tap it with your bare finger.

Storing Yeast

A vacuum-sealed bag of yeast stored at room temperature will remain fresh indefinitely. Once the seal is broken, it should go into the freezer for optimum shelf life. A vacuum-sealed bag of yeast stored at high temperatures, however—for example, in a hot kitchen over the summer, or in a hot warehouse before delivery—will fairly quickly lose its effectiveness. After a while, if stored improperly, yeast cells will slowly become inactive (die). If you aren't using your yeast fairly quickly (or even if you are), it's a good idea to keep it in an airtight container in the freezer. It will keep for quite long periods of time that way (years in the freezer, if your freezer isn't self-defrosting). If you think you got some bum yeast, take it back to the store and ask for a new batch. Any business worth its salt will certainly replace it.

The bread is done when its interior temperature registers between 190°F (for most loaves) and 210°F (for heavier, denser country-type loaves). Remove it from the oven and transfer it from its pan to a cooling rack as soon as possible. Cooling bread left in a pan will steam, making the crust rubbery. For extra-crisp bread, turn off the oven, remove the bread from the pan, and set it on the oven rack. Prop the door open a couple of inches and allow the bread to cool in the oven. This prevents steam from migrating from the bread's center and condensing on its crust, which would tend to soften the crust.

Enjoy!

Warning! Tempting though it may be, it's better to wait ten to fifteen minutes before cutting into your bread. Until it has a chance to set as it cools a bit, it's very tender. Cutting into bread at this point tends to mar its shape, as well as allow too much moisture to escape, which can result in it becoming stale more quickly.

What Size Pan?

The most common cause of poorly shaped pan loaves is using the wrong size pan. A good rule of thumb is as follows: A recipe using 2¾ to 3 cups flour and about 1 cup liquid will make a loaf of approximately 1 pound, which will rise to a nice shape in an 8½ x 4½-inch bread pan. Such a recipe will also work in a 9 x 5-inch pan, but will make a somewhat flatter loaf; the optimal amount of flour for a 9 x 5-inch pan is 3½ to 4 cups. To make a 1½-pound loaf, which will rise nicely in a 10 x 5-inch pan, use approximately 4½ cups flour and 1½ cups liquid.

If you're using the correct amount of flour and right size pan, and you think your bread is too flat, try letting it rise twice in the bowl before shaping and baking. This second rise not only gives the yeast more of a chance to do its work, but also improves your bread's texture and flavor. Flat-topped bread may also indicate your dough needs more flour, due to summer humidity; a slack dough tends to be flatter on top.

Sandwich and Pan Loaves

Pan bread—the soft, rectangular sandwich loaf we grew up with—has gotten a bad rap as the popularity of crusty artisan-style loaves has increased. Well, this is a big world; there's room for more than one type of bread. For toast and French toast, sandwiches and grilled cheese, stuffing or bread pudding or croutons, nothing beats a good loaf of close-grained, tender white bread. Or its siblings—oatmeal, whole wheat, and rye.

But this familiar bread doesn't stand alone. The same type of dough can be rolled into balls, built into a loaf, and called Monkey Bread; it can be spread with filling and rolled, to make a swirl loaf; it can even be enriched with eggs and butter to become an alluring brioche. The thread that joins all these loaves is texture; soft and light, they're ideal for youngsters, as well as any of us who feel that nostalgic pull toward an egg salad sandwich.

White Bread 101

1 LOAF, 16 SLICES

The name of this bread refers to its basic nature—making it is child's play and the result is a delicious, fine-textured loaf, perfect for toast or sandwiches (especially peanut butter and jelly).

3 cups (12¾ ounces) unbleached all-purpose flour

2 teaspoons instant yeast

1¼ teaspoons salt

3 tablespoons (1¼ ounces) sugar

4 tablespoons (2 ounces) butter

¼ cup (1¼ ounces) nonfat dry milk

¼ cup (1½ ounces) potato flour, or ⅓ cup (¾ ounce) potato flakes

1⅛ cups (9 ounces) lukewarm water

Combine all the ingredients and mix and knead them together—by hand, mixer, or bread machine—until you've made a soft, smooth dough. Adjust the dough's consistency with additional flour or water as needed; but remember, the more flour you add while you're kneading, the heavier and drier your final loaf will be. Cover and let the dough rise for 1 hour, until it's puffy (though not necessarily doubled in bulk).

Transfer the dough to a lightly greased work surface and shape it into an 8-inch log. Transfer the log to a lightly greased 8½ x 4½-inch loaf pan, cover the pan (a proof cover works well here), and let the bread rise until the outer edge has risen about 1 inch over the rim of the pan, about 1 hour.

Preheat the oven to 350°F.

Uncover the pan and bake the bread for 35 to 40 minutes, tenting it lightly with aluminum foil for the final 10 to 15 minutes if it appears to be browning too quickly.

Remove the bread from the oven, take it out of the pan, and place it on a wire rack to cool completely. After 15 minutes, brush it with butter, if desired; this will give it a soft crust.

nutrition information per serving   **1 slice, 55g**

129 cal | 3g fat | 3g protein | 19g complex carbohydrates | 2g sugar | 1g dietary fiber | 9mg cholesterol | 179mg sodium | 116mg potassium | 38RE vitamin A | 1mg vitamin C | 2mg iron | 26mg calcium | 50mg phosphorus

Herbed Monkey Bread

10 SMALL SERVINGS

This soft, pull-apart bread is a fun company loaf. Serve it with a mild-flavored creamy soup, such as cream of mushroom, onion, or tomato.

1 recipe White Bread 101

HERB COATING
3 to 5 tablespoons (1¼ to 2⅜ ounces) olive oil*

1 tablespoon fresh stemmed thyme, or 1½ teaspoons dried

2 tablespoons chopped fresh parsley, or 1 tablespoon dried

1 teaspoon dried oregano

1 garlic clove, minced

Combine the oil, herbs, and garlic. Set the mixture aside.

Prepare White Bread 101 up through its first rise. Grease the bottom and sides of a small (8-inch) tube or bundt-style pan, or a deep (2 inches or deeper) 8-inch cake pan or soufflé dish. Turn out the risen dough onto a lightly floured work surface and divide it into 32 small pieces, each about the size of a chestnut and weighing approximately ¾ ounce. Place about a third of them in the bottom of the pan if you're using a small bundt-style pan. If you're using a cake pan, put about two-thirds of the pieces into it. Brush the dough in the pan with the herb coating. Continue to layer with the remaining balls, brushing the top layer with the remaining herb oil. (If you've used the greater amount of olive oil, dip each piece of dough into the oil to coat it completely before layering it into the pan.) Let the bread rise, covered, for 1 hour.

Preheat the oven to 375°F. Bake the bread for 30 to 35 minutes, until it's golden. Remove it from the oven and invert it onto a serving platter; the crispy bottom crust should be on top. Serve warm.

*Use 3 tablespoons of oil if you simply want to drizzle the herb coating over the dough balls once they're in the pan. To thoroughly coat each dough ball before putting them in the pan, use 5 tablespoons olive oil. This extra oil will give the bread a delicious crisp crust.

nutrition information per serving   **4 small pieces, 87g**

235 cal | 7g fat | 6g protein | 33g complex carbohydrates | 2g sugar | 1g fiber | 7mg cholesterol | 322mg sodium | 113mg potassium | 34RE vitamin A | 3mg iron | 39mg calcium | 70mg phosphorus

Help! My Bread ...

... is coarse, dry, and crumbly

There are several causes for dry bread—bread that won't hold together in a sandwich—but the No. 1 culprit is usually too much flour.

When you're kneading bread, and it's sticking to your hands, it's always a temptation to add more flour. But an overdose of flour will cause the resulting bread to be coarse-grained, crumbly, and dry. There are several solutions. First, use a dough scraper when you first start to knead, scooping underneath the dough and flopping it over on itself as you gradually sprinkle flour onto the dough. This is easier than constantly scraping the dough off your fingers. Second, once dough gets to the point where it's fairly kneadable by hand—though still sticky—try spraying your work surface and hands with non-stick vegetable oil spray. This will help you handle the dough without adding more flour. Third, let the dough remain a bit sticky. Yes, it's harder to work with, but the resultant loaf will have a much nicer texture.

A coarse grain in bread can also occur when bread is baked at too low a temperature. We like to bake loaf bread at 350°F or 375°F, while baguettes and other free-form loaves are usually baked at 425°F or 450°F. Another way to ensure your bread will have a fine grain is to let it rise twice in the bowl, rather than just once; this will also give better flavor, as the longer the dough rises, the more flavorful the bread will be.

Another cause of coarse-grained or dry bread is a lack of sufficient mixing or kneading. When making your dough, try adding only about ⅓ the flour to the liquid ingredients at first, then beat well, for about 2 minutes, with a spoon or mixer; this insures everything is well-mixed. Mix in the remaining flour, then knead. Dough should be kneaded a good 8 to 10 minutes, at least. If you get tired, give the dough a rest after 5 minutes; this rest not only benefits you, it helps the dough as well, as the developing gluten has a chance to relax, making any further kneading that much easier and more effective.

Finally, crumbly bread may be caused by too much fat in the dough. The right amount of fat in a recipe will prevent moisture loss and staling. Too much fat, however, will prevent the gluten strands in the flour from bonding properly—thus the crumbling..

... has a wrinkled top crust

Wrinkling occurs for several reasons. First, if bread rises too much it will develop a thin layer of air under the crust. If, at the same time, the crust dries out as it rises—if the dough is covered with a dry cloth or insufficiently covered—when you put the bread in the oven to bake, the crust doesn't allow steam from the interior of the bread to escape as readily as it would if it were more moist and porous. Instead, the crust absorbs the moisture. Add to that the fact that, once you take the bread out of the oven, the interior continues to cook, sending off steam, while the outer crust rapidly cools and contracts, causing moisture to condense on its surface, and you have the perfect recipe for wrinkling.

There are two things you can try to avoid this. First, let the bread rise only three-quarters of the way to full, then put it in a cold oven, set the temperature, and go from there. Your bread will require an additional 10 minutes or so baking time, but its gradual rising as the oven heats will help prevent the top crust from separating from the interior.

Second, when your bread is done, turn off the oven, crack open the door, and leave the loaf in the oven for an additional 10 minutes. Steam from the interior will have an easier time evaporating through the crust into the hot oven air; because the crust remains hot, the steam won't condense on it.

One more hint: If you want to brush your finished loaf with butter, wait until it's cool; fat forms a seal when applied to a hot loaf, preventing steam from escaping.

. . . gets stale too quickly

Storing bread is a many-faceted challenge. If you can eat it quickly enough, wrap the bread in plastic and keep it on the kitchen counter or in a bread box. Bread will keep well for several days up to maybe a week, depending on the weather (in extremely hot, humid weather, bread will mold quickly at room temperature; you'll have to freeze it).

Staling happens most quickly at refrigerator temperature—about five times faster than at room temperature. So don't store bread or other baked goods in the refrigerator; they're much better off at room temperature or in the freezer.

By the way, the best way to store crunchy-crusted, country-type loaves—typically sourdough-based—is neither in the freezer nor wrapped at room temperature. Instead, store the bread, cut side down, on the counter. This keeps the outer crust crunchy and the inner bread soft.

Interestingly, you can reverse the staling process by reheating, which sends all the molecules spinning back into their just-out-of-the-oven physical alignment. Reheating stale bread (stale bread, not rock-hard, days-old bread) to 140°F, the temperature at which starch gelatinizes, will make stale bread soft again for a short period of time.

Dividing dough

When you're making monkey bread (or rolls or breadsticks), you need to divide the dough evenly into smaller pieces. The best way to do this is with a bench knife and a scale (see Tools, pp. 591 and 601). Weigh the dough (using the metric option, if your scale has one; it's much easier to do math with grams than ounces and pounds). Divide it in half, weighing each half to make sure they're the same size. Then, depending on how many pieces you want to end up with, keep dividing the halves in half, continuing to use the scale to make sure the pieces are all the same size. (Once you get used to using a scale, this process goes fairly quickly, particularly if you're adept at doing simple division in your head.)

An exception to this process is if you want to end up with a number of dough pieces that's not divisible by 4—say, 15 or 18 pieces of dough. In that case, you'll need to divide the dough into three pieces at some point, rather than two. It's up to you to figure out when that point is, depending on how many rolls or breadsticks you're making. And you thought those division problems back in elementary school were a waste of time!

Up-sizing

Unlike many baking recipes, you can increase the size of most bread recipes simply by doubling, or tripling all the ingredients. The exception is the yeast; if you increase the amount of yeast at the same rate you increase everything else, you may find yourself with a lot of dough on your hands and not enough time to deal with it. For example, by the time you've shaped the eighth loaf, the first may be well on its way to doubled in size.

Most home bread bakers prefer to stick with 1 tablespoon of yeast for up to eight loaves, and giving the bread a longer, slower rise. Not only does this improve the flavor, it slows down the rising dough so that you can work with the dough more effectively.

Vermont Oatmeal Maple-Honey Bread

2 SANDWICH LOAVES, 16 SLICES PER LOAF

Maple sugar and honey augment the very slightly sweet taste of the oats in this moist sandwich loaf. Try this toasted and spread with peanut butter, or use it for all manner of sandwiches.

2¼ to 2½ cups (18 to 20 ounces) boiling water

1 cup (3½ ounces) thick oat flakes (rolled oats)

½ cup (2¾ ounces) maple sugar or brown sugar (4 ounces)

½ teaspoon maple flavor (optional)

1 tablespoon honey

4 tablespoons (½ stick, 2 ounces) butter

1 tablespoon salt

1 teaspoon cinnamon

1 tablespoon instant yeast

1½ cups (7¾ ounces) whole wheat flour

4 cups (17 ounces) unbleached all-purpose flour

In a large mixing bowl, combine the water, oats, maple sugar, maple flavor, honey, butter, salt, and cinnamon. Let cool to lukewarm.

Add the yeast and flours, stirring to form a rough dough. Knead (about 10 minutes by hand, 5 to 7 minutes by machine) until the dough is smooth and satiny. Transfer the dough to a lightly greased bowl, cover the bowl with lightly greased plastic wrap, and let the dough rise for 1 hour; it should double in bulk.

Divide the dough in half and shape each half into a loaf. Place the loaves in two greased 8½ x 4½-inch bread pans. Cover the pans with lightly greased plastic wrap (or a proof cover) and allow the loaves to rise until they've crowned about 1 inch over the rim of the pan, about 1 hour.

Preheat the oven to 350°F. Bake the loaves for 35 to 40 minutes. Remove them from the oven when they're golden brown and the interior registers 190°F on an instant-read thermometer.

nutrition information per serving   1 slice, 39g

105 cal | 2g fat | 3g protein | 17g complex carbohydrates | 3g sugar | 2g dietary fiber | 4mg cholesterol | 69mg sodium | 68mg potassium | 15RE vitamin A | 1mg iron | 9mg calcium | 51mg phosphorus

Sandwich Rye Bread

1 LOAF, 16 SLICES

To us, a darned good loaf of sandwich rye bread should be dark on the outside and light brown, a kind of putty-beige color, on the inside. It should taste strongly of caraway and should have that distinctive rye bread flavor—a combination of caraway, the rye flour itself, with perhaps a hint of sour pickle. It should be shaped like sandwich bread and should have a slightly chewy crust and a tender crumb. Finally, it should be moist enough to hold together when piled with pastrami or layered with ham and cheese and mustard.

This bread is all of that. Each of the four flours adds its own special characteristic: height and structure from the bread flour, taste from the rye, texture from the pumpernickel, and added moistness from the potato flour. Pickle juice adds just the right amount of tang.

2 cups (8½ ounces) unbleached bread flour	1 tablespoon sugar
1 cup (4 ounces) rye flour	2 teaspoons instant yeast
⅓ cup (1⅜ ounces) pumpernickel	¼ cup (1¾ ounces) vegetable oil
¼ cup (1½ ounces) potato flour, or ⅓ cup (¾ ounce) potato flakes	¼ cup (2 ounces) dill pickle juice or sour pickle juice
1 tablespoon (¼ ounce) caraway seeds	1 cup (8 ounces) water
1½ teaspoons salt	

Mix all the dry ingredients in a large bowl. Add the vegetable oil, pickle juice, and water and mix until a shaggy mass forms. Let the dough rest for 30 minutes; this resting period allows the flour to absorb the liquid fully, making it easier to knead.

Knead the dough for about 10 minutes; it should feel firm and smooth. though somewhat sticky. Put it into a greased bowl, turning to coat, then cover the bowl and let the dough rise until it's almost doubled in bulk. (The amount of time this takes will depend on the temperature of your kitchen, as well as how often you make bread—the more often you make bread, the more wild yeast is living in your kitchen and the more quickly the dough will rise.)

Turn out the dough onto a lightly oiled or lightly floured surface and shape it into an 8-inch log. Place the log in a lightly greased 8½ x 4½-inch loaf pan, cover the pan with greased plastic wrap or a proof cover, and let the loaf rise until it's just about crowned over the edge of the pan. This will take about 1 hour if you've kneaded the dough with a mixer or bread machine, or up to 90 minutes if you've kneaded it by hand.

Preheat the oven to 350°F. Bake the bread for about 35 minutes, until it's a deep golden brown and its internal temperature registers 190°F on an instant-read thermometer. (If the bread appears to be browning too quickly, tent it with aluminum foil, shiny side up, for the final 10 minutes of baking.) Remove the bread from the oven, take it out of the pan, and cool it on a wire rack.

1 slice, 51g

126 cal | 3.5g fat | 3g protein | 20g complex carbohydrates | 2g dietary fiber | 202mg sodium | 103mg potassium | 1mg vitamin C | 1mg iron | 33mg calcium | 50mg phosphorus

Variation SAUERKRAUT RYE LOAF: Use this bread to make a Reuben Melt: corned beef and Swiss cheese layered on two slices of bread, cooked on the griddle like grilled cheese. Coleslaw and Dr. Brown's Cel-Ray Tonic on the side, of course.

Prepare the sandwich rye dough, adding ¾ cup (4 to 5 ounces) very well drained, chopped sauerkraut, and reducing the water to ¾ cup. Another nice addition is up to 4 teaspoons mustard seeds (yellow, brown, or a mix). Shape and bake the bread as directed above; it may take a bit longer to rise.

One Potato . . .

Many traditional American bread recipes call for cooked potato or potato water as one of the ingredients. In the days before yeast was readily available, bakers had to rely on wild yeasts, present in the air, to leaven their breads. Yeast is attracted to starch, and the starch-filled water in which potatoes have been boiled is a good medium for capturing and propagating wild yeast.

It's this same starch that accounts for the crisp brown crust, moist airy interior, and wonderful keeping qualities of potato bread. The starch in potatoes (or in potato water)

absorbs liquid as bread dough is kneaded, and holds onto that liquid as the bread bakes.

If you want or need potato water for your recipe, peel potatoes, leave them whole, and boil in water to cover until tender, 25 to 30 minutes. The resulting water will be cloudy and full of starch, ideal for using in yeasted breads. (Yeast happily converts starch to sugar, so starch is an excellent food for yeast.)

Potato flour—dried, ground potatoes—or potato starch are good stand-ins for potato water. Use 3 to 4 tablespoons potato flour or starch in a 3-cup-flour (1 pound) bread recipe.

Cinnamon Swirl Bread

1 LOAF, 16 SLICES

This tender white bread, with its swirl of cinnamon in the center, fairly cries out for toasting and buttering (or peanut-buttering). The streusel topping adds a just-right final touch.

The following recipe incorporates a couple of tips for successful cinnamon swirl bread that we've discovered over the years. First, for a deep-dark, moist cinnamon swirl inside the bread, whirl sugar, cinnamon, and raisins or currants together in a blender or food processor until smooth. The fruit adds moistness as well as subtle flavor to the filling. And second, rather than brush the dough with butter before sprinkling on the filling, brush it with beaten egg. Butter acts as a barrier between the pieces of rolled-up dough, preventing them from cohering and giving you bread that "unravels" when you cut it. On the other hand, the protein in egg acts like glue, cementing the bread and filling together, and allowing much less (though still a bit) unraveling.

DOUGH

3 cups (12¾ ounces) unbleached all-purpose flour

¼ cup (1½ ounces) potato flour, or ⅓ cup (¾ ounce) potato flakes

¼ cup (1¼ ounces) nonfat dry milk

1¼ teaspoons salt

½ teaspoon cinnamon

3 tablespoons (1¼ ounces) sugar

2½ teaspoons instant yeast

4 tablespoons (½ stick, 2 ounces) butter

1 cup (8 ounces) water

FILLING

¼ cup (1¾ ounces) sugar

1½ teaspoons cinnamon

¼ cup (1½ ounces) raisins or currants

2 teaspoons unbleached all-purpose flour

Egg wash, made from 1 large egg beaten with 1 tablespoon water

TOPPING

2 tablespoons (1 ounce) butter

2 tablespoons (⅞ ounce) sugar

¼ teaspoon cinnamon

¼ cup (1 ounce) unbleached all-purpose flour

FOR THE DOUGH In a large mixing bowl, combine all the dough ingredients, mixing until the dough begins to come away from the sides of the bowl. Knead (about 10 minutes by hand, 5 to 7 minutes by machine) until the dough is smooth and satiny. Transfer the dough to a lightly oiled bowl, cover the bowl with plastic wrap, and set it aside to rise for 1 to 1½ hours; it will be puffy, if not doubled in bulk.

FOR THE FILLING Pulse filling ingredients except the egg wash in a food processor.

TO ASSEMBLE Transfer the dough to a lightly oiled work surface and shape it into a long, narrow rectangle, about 16 x 8 inches. Brush the dough with some of the egg wash (set the remainder aside) and pat the filling gently onto the dough. Beginning with a short edge, roll the dough into a log. Pinch the side seam and ends closed (to keep the filling from bubbling out) and place the log in a lightly greased 8½ x 4½-inch loaf pan.

Cover the pan with lightly greased plastic wrap or a proof cover and let the bread rise for about 1 hour at room temperature, or until it's crowned about 1 inch over the rim of the pan.

FOR THE TOPPING In a small bowl or mini processor, combine the butter, sugar, cinnamon, and flour until the mixture is crumbly. If you're using a mini processor, watch carefully; topping will go from crumbly to a cohesive mass in just a second or so.

Brush the top of the loaf with some (or all) of the reserved egg wash and gently press on the topping.

Preheat the oven to 350°F. Bake the bread for about 45 minutes, tenting it lightly with aluminum foil for the final 15 minutes or so if it appears to be browning too quickly. Remove the loaf from the oven, and after about 5 minutes, gently remove it from the pan. Some of the streusel will fall off, but you can alleviate this by first loosening all around the edges of the loaf with a knife, then turning the pan on its side and gently pulling it away from the loaf. Topping will continue to fall off as you maneuver the bread—we've never figured out how they make that stuff adhere so nicely on the store-bought loaves—but you'll still be left with a lot of nice sweet topping.

Coming Undone?

Does your cinnamon-swirl bread unravel when you cut it? Don't spread the dough with butter before you add the cinnamon and sugar, as the fat will keep the dough from bonding as it bakes. After rolling out the dough, brush it with an egg wash made by beating one egg until the yolk and white are combined. Then sprinkle on the cinnamon and sugar, and raisins if you're using them, and roll. The protein in the egg white will form a bond between the dough surfaces as the bread bakes.

By the way, if you do use raisins along with the cinnamon and sugar, try chopping the raisins (in a blender or food processor), or use currants, which are smaller. The bread will be easier to slice cleanly if the raisins are in small pieces.

| nutrition information per serving | 1 slice, 62g |

171 cal | 5g fat | 4g protein | 22g complex carbohydrates | 6g sugar | 1g dietary fiber | 25mg cholesterol | 183mg sodium | 145mg potassium | 56RE vitamin A | 1mg vitamin C | 2mg iron | 33mg calcium | 61mg phosphorus

Easy Cinnamon Bread

1 LOAF, 16 SLICES

This bread is a cross between a typical baking powder–leavened quick bread and a yeast bread. The result: a loaf that tastes like cinnamon coffeecake, wonderful served plain and incredible toasted.

3 cups (12¾ ounces) unbleached all-purpose flour

½ cup (3½ ounces) sugar

2 teaspoons instant yeast

1 teaspoon cinnamon

1 teaspoon salt

1 cup (8 ounces) warm milk

¼ cup (2 ounces) butter, melted

1 large egg

1 teaspoon baking powder

1 cup (6 ounces) cinnamon chips

Cinnamon-sugar, for topping

In a large bowl, mix together the flour, sugar, yeast, cinnamon and salt. In a separate bowl, whisk together the milk, butter, and egg. Combine the wet and dry ingredients, beating until smooth. Cover and let the batter rest at room temperature for 1 hour, then stir in the baking powder and cinnamon chips.

Preheat the oven to 350°F.

Spoon the batter into a greased 8½ x 4½-inch loaf pan. Sprinkle the top with the cinnamon sugar.

Bake the bread for 35 to 40 minutes, until a cake tester inserted into the center comes out clean. Remove the bread from the oven, let it rest in the pan for 5 minutes, then transfer it from the pan to a rack to cool completely. Don't slice the bread while it's hot; it will slice much better when it's completely cool.

nutrition information per serving   **1 slice, 66g**

223 cal | 9g fat | 4g protein | 20g complex carbohydrates | 12g sugar | 1g dietary fiber | 23mg cholesterol | 193mg sodium | 134mg potassium | 43RE vitamin A | 1mg vitamin C | 2mg iron | 66mg calcium | 70mg phosphorus

Adding Whole-Grain Goodness

When making breads that use whole, flaked, or cracked grain berries, it's a good idea to soak these grains first, before adding them to your dough. This accomplishes a number of things. First, it makes the grain kernels themselves softer and easier to chew. Second, it prevents them from drawing moisture from the dough, which can cause dry dough and heavy, dry bread. Third, they'll assist in the gluten formation in the dough.

There are two ways to soak grains. If you're not in a hurry to make your bread, put the grain and an equal amount of cold water in a nonreactive bowl and soak overnight. By morning, the water should be totally absorbed. If it's not, drain off any excess.

If time is a factor, combine equal parts grain and water in a saucepan, bring to a boil, and simmer for 5 minutes. Remove from the heat and cool to lukewarm before using.

Remember, the water you've added to the grain should be taken into account when you're making your bread dough. About half the soaking water you used will remain in the grain, while half will leave the grain and join the dough. So if you use ½ cup of water to soak your grain, reduce the amount of liquid in your dough recipe by ¼ cup. (This isn't a hard-and-fast rule, as the moisture in your flour will vary from season to season; just use it as a jumping-off place.)

100 Percent Whole Wheat Loaf

1 LOAF, 16 SLICES

Most whole wheat bread you buy at the supermarket is in fact white bread with just a smidgen of whole wheat flour and a lot of added color and chemicals. Thus, many folks try to bake their own whole wheat bread at home—often with limited success. If your experience with home-made 100 percent whole wheat bread is a loaf that's heavy and dry, with a slightly bitter undertone, this recipe will change your mind.

1½ cups (12 ounces) water

3 tablespoons (1¼ ounces) olive oil

5 tablespoons (3¾ ounces) honey, molasses, or maple syrup

3½ cups (18⅜ ounces) whole wheat flour

1 tablespoon bread dough enhancer (optional)

¼ cup (1¼ ounces) sunflower seeds, chopped*

¼ cup (1⅛ ounce) walnuts, chopped*

1½ teaspoons salt

1½ teaspoons instant yeast

In a large mixing bowl, or in the bowl of an electric mixer, combine all the ingredients, mixing to form a shaggy dough. Let the dough rest for 20 minutes, which gives the flour a chance to absorb the liquids, then knead it for about 10 minutes, until it's smooth and supple. The dough will seem very wet and slack at first; just keep mixing and eventually it will come together, though it will remain sticky. Note: For the optimal rise, we recommend using either a bread machine (set on the dough setting) or electric mixer to mix and knead this dough, with the bread machine being the first choice; kneading by hand will result in a smaller, denser loaf.

Let the dough rise, in a greased, covered bowl, for 1 hour. Shape it into a log and place it in a lightly greased 8½ x 4½-inch bread pan. Cover the pan (with a proof cover or lightly greased plastic wrap) and let it rise for about 1 hour, until it has crowned about 2 inches over the rim of the pan.

Preheat the oven to 350°F. Bake the bread for 45 minutes, tenting it lightly with aluminum foil for the final 20 minutes of baking. Remove from the oven, turn it out of the pan, and cool it on a rack.

*This is most easily accomplished with the aid of a mini (or regular) food processor.

nutrition information per serving | 1 slice, 59g

156 cal | 6g fat | 5g protein | 20g complex carbohydrates | 4g dietary fiber | 203mg sodium | 143mg potassium | 3RE vitamin A | 2mg iron | 10mg calcium | 144mg phosphorus

Seasons of Change

Flour is porous, like a sponge. When the air around it is dry, flour will be dry. When the air is humid, flour will absorb the moisture in it. Just as a dry sponge can soak up more water than a wet sponge, so can dry flour. You'll find that during cold, dry months you'll often need less flour when making a dough, and in hot, humid months, a bit more. Find a dough consistency that works well for you, then snap a mental picture of it; that's the consistency you're after all year long, no matter how the balance of ingredients may change.

You'll also find that, on rainy or stormy days (great days for baking anyway), when the barometric pressure is low, your bread will rise more quickly than it does ordinarily. This is because the dough doesn't have as much air to push against it; the air is not as dense or heavy as it is on clear days.

Cheese Bread

1 LOAF, 16 SLICES

This golden loaf, soft and high-rising, has a nicely assertive sharp cheese flavor and aroma. Use it for the ultimate grilled cheese sandwich, or a BLT. Cut any stale bread into cubes, drizzle with olive oil, and toast them in the oven for cheese croutons.

2¼ teaspoons instant yeast

¼ cup (2 ounces) water

1 cup (8 ounces) milk

1¼ teaspoons salt

1 tablespoon sugar

3½ cups (14¾ ounces) unbleached all-purpose flour

1 cup (4 ounces) finely grated cheddar cheese

½ cup (2 ounces) finely grated Parmesan

2 tablespoons butter or vegetable oil

2 teaspoons tomato powder or tomato paste (optional, for color)

Combine all the ingredients and mix and knead them together—by hand, mixer, or bread machine—until you've made a soft, smooth dough. Adjust the dough's consistency with additional flour or water as needed; this dough should be soft but not sticky. Cover and let the dough rise for 1 hour, or until it's puffy (though not necessarily doubled in bulk).

Transfer the dough to a lightly greased work surface and pat it into an 8-inch log. Transfer the log to a lightly greased 8½ x 4½-inch loaf pan, cover the pan (a proof cover works well here), and let the bread rise until the outer edge has just barely risen over the rim of the pan, about 45 minutes.

Preheat the oven to 350°F. Bake the bread for 35 to 40 minutes, tenting it lightly with aluminum foil for the final 10 to 15 minutes if it appears to be browning too quickly. Remove the bread from the oven, take it out of the pan, and place it on a wire rack to cool completely.

nutrition information per serving   1 slice, 57g

150 cal | 5g fat | 6g protein | 19g complex carbohydrates | 1g sugar | 1g dietary fiber | 14mg cholesterol | 261mg sodium | 74mg potassium | 49RE vitamin A | 1mg iron | 102mg calcium | 98mg phosphorus

Stuffing Bread

ONE LOAF, 16 SLICES

This moist, whole-grain bread tastes like stuffing in loaf form; use it as the base for your Thanksgiving turkey's dressing, or to make wonderful turkey sandwiches the next day.

3 cups (12¾ ounces) unbleached all-purpose flour

1½ teaspoons salt

2 teaspoons sugar

3 tablespoons (1¼ ounces) vegetable oil

¼ cup (1¼ ounces) yellow cornmeal

¼ cup (1½ ounces) potato flour, or ⅓ cup (¾ ounce) potato flakes

2 tablespoons (⅝ ounce) nonfat dry milk

2 teaspoons instant yeast

¼ cup (1¼ ounces) sunflower seeds ("midget," if you can get them)

¼ cup toasted (1¼ ounces) sesame seeds

2 teaspoons poultry seasoning, or 2 teaspoons ground sage

1 tablespoon bread dough enhancer (optional)

1¼ cups (10 ounces) water

Combine all the ingredients and mix and knead (by hand or electric mixer) until the dough is smooth and supple, adding additional liquid or all-purpose flour as needed. This should take about 5 minutes in a mixer, 8 minutes by hand. Let the dough rise in a covered bowl for 1 hour.

Shape the dough into an 8-inch log and place it in a lightly greased 8½ x 4½-inch loaf pan. Set the loaf aside to rise, covered, for about 45 minutes, or until it's crowned about 1 inch over the rim of the pan.

Preheat the oven to 350°F. Bake the bread for about 35 minutes, until it's golden brown and the interior of the loaf registers 190°F on an instant-read thermometer. Remove it from the oven, turn it out of the pan, and cool on a wire rack.

nutrition information per serving | 1 slice, 51g

125 cal | 4g fat | 3g protein | 18g complex carbohydrates | 1g sugar | 1g dietary fiber | 10mg cholesterol | 204mg sodium | 49mg potassium | 35RE vitamin A | 1 mg iron | 5mg calcium | 31mg phosphorus

Brioche

1 ROUND LOAF, 12 SLICES

Brioche is a yeast bread that's so rich it can be eaten pleasurably with absolutely no adornment at all. Which isn't to say that a tart-sweet raspberry preserve, or orange marmalade, or peach jam, Devon cream, or butter aren't all welcome additions.

Brioche can be shaped in the traditional tête shape, a fluted round with a jaunty top-knot; but it can also be made into sandwich loaves or shaped into balls, the balls laid side by side to make a ring. You can even pile it into a loaf pan to make a kind of French monkey bread. However you shape it, brioche is a versatile loaf that can move easily from plain sliced, to toasted with jam, to French toast, to slices of savory (rather than sweet) brioche serving as the base for smoked salmon, caviar, or roasted asparagus and hollandaise—now that's gilding the lily!

With all its butter, this is a difficult dough to develop by hand and we don't suggest trying it. An electric mixer or bread machine is ideal for the task; if you have access to either of these helpers, don't hesitate to tackle this recipe. It's only a tad more challenging than any other yeast bread recipe, and the results are out of this world.

2½ cups (10½ ounces) unbleached all-purpose flour	4 large eggs, plus 1 yolk for glaze
1½ teaspoons instant yeast	2 tablespoons (⅞ ounce) sugar
¼ cup (2 ounces) cool water (about 70°F)	¾ teaspoon salt
	1 cup (8 ounces) cold unsalted butter

Place 1½ cups (6¼ ounces) of the flour, the yeast, water, and whole eggs in a mixer bowl. Beat at medium speed, using the flat beater paddle, until smooth. Cover the mixture and let it sit for 45 minutes. It will develop some bubbles, but not change very much due to the thinness of the batter. The yeast, however, is getting a jump-start.

Add the remaining 1 cup (4¼ ounces) of flour, the sugar, and salt, and beat for 8 to 10 minutes, until the dough cleans the sides of the bowl and is shiny and elastic.

Sprinkle a work surface with 2 tablespoons of flour. Place the butter on the flour. Pound the butter with the side of a rolling pin until it has become a cohesive rectangle about ¼ inch thick. Fold it over several times as you pound; it will become pliable without getting too warm or soft. Add the butter to the dough and beat until it's fully incorporated.

Cover the dough and let it rise for 1 hour. It'll be very soft at this point and should have grown by about one third. Turn out the dough onto a lightly floured surface and fold it over several times. (Use a bench knife to scrape up any bits that stick to the table.) Place the dough in a greased bowl, cover the bowl, and refrigerate it for a minimum of 4 hours and up to about 16 hours. The dough will firm up considerably.

Remove the dough from the refrigerator and form it into a round loaf. Work quickly, because as the dough warms it becomes very sticky. Place it in a 9-inch brioche pan. (We've chosen not to make the top-knotted brioche here; it's a fair trick to get the knob on top to stay centered throughout the rising and baking process, and as we don't like the look of tipsy brioches, we usually just form it into a plain round.) Cover the dough lightly and let it rise for 2½ to 3 hours, until it's doubled and is crowned well over the top of the pan.

Preheat the oven to 375°F. Beat the egg yolk with 1 tablespoon of water and brush all exposed surfaces with the egg wash. (Try not to let any egg wash drip onto the edge of the pan, as the bread will stick there.) Cut four slashes into the top of the loaf (see instructions, p. 240). Bake the brioche for 45 to 50 minutes, until its internal temperature reads 190°F on an instant-read thermometer and is golden brown. For brioche with lighter crust, tent it with aluminum foil after 20 minutes of baking.

Remove the brioche from the oven and cool it in the pan for 10 minutes. Turn it out of the pan and cool it completely on a rack. Serve the brioche when it's completely cool.

nutrition information per serving   **1 slice, 68g**

268 cal | 18g fat | 5g protein | 19g complex carbohydrates | 2g sugar | 1g dietary fiber | 116mg cholesterol | 320mg sodium | 69mg potassium | 183RE vitamin A | 1mg vitamin C | 2mg iron | 13mg calcium | 65 mg

Juicing Up Your Bread

Adding a tablespoon of orange juice concentrate or vinegar or a pinch of ascorbic acid to bread dough will aid in its rising. Yeast loves to grow in an acidic environment. Basically, yeast requires only a bit of food, and a bit of warmth, to multiply. But like any living organism, it will grow slowly if given a minimal amount of food and comfort. Increase the food (sugar, diastatic malt powder), give it a comfortable (acidic) home, and watch the yeast and your bread dough take off.

A little extra acid works particularly well in rich sweet doughs, which often rise very, very slowly. In a side-by-side test we did with kuchen, a plain sweet dough, the kuchen with ascorbic acid rose 50 percent higher than the plain kuchen, in the same amount of time.

Sweet Breads

Soft like pan breads, sweet breads add sugar (and often additional fat) to that formula to become even more tender and rich. Sweet bread dough is often braided, or braided and shaped into a wreath, fashioned into rolls and stuffed with filling, or spread with filling, rolled, and sliced. These breads may take a bit longer to make, due to their increased sugar content, so be sure to read the recipe all the way through before beginning, and allow yourself plenty of time from start to finish.

Raspberry Cream Cheese Braid

2 BRAIDS, ABOUT 16 SERVINGS EACH

This tasty braid is impressive looking, but easy to make. The dough, soft and pliable, is a joy to work with, and the braiding, which looks challenging, is anything but. Serve as the centerpiece of a Sunday brunch. This dough is ideal for all manner of soft sweet breads—monkey bread, sweet glazed braids, hot cross buns, and the like.

DOUGH

2 teaspoons instant yeast

¼ cup (2 ounces) warm water

¼ cup (1¾ ounces) sugar

3 cups (12¾ ounces) unbleached pastry flour or all-purpose flour*

6 tablespoons (3 ounces) sour cream or yogurt

6 tablespoons (3 ounces) butter, soft

1¼ teaspoons salt

1 large egg

¼ teaspoon lemon oil, or 1 teaspoon grated lemon peel

FILLING

1 package (8 ounces) cream cheese, softened

2 tablespoons (1 ounce) soft butter

¼ cup (1¾ ounces) sugar

⅛ teaspoon salt

1 teaspoon vanilla extract

2 tablespoons (¾ ounce) Instant ClearJel, or 3 tablespoons (1¾ ounces) unbleached all-purpose flour

1 large egg

½ cup (6 ounces) raspberry jam mixed with 2 tablespoons ClearJel or flour

¼ cup (1¾ ounces) coarse white sugar (optional)

TO MAKE THE DOUGH In a large bowl, combine the yeast, warm water, 1 teaspoon of the sugar, and ½ cup of the flour. Cover with plastic wrap and set aside until bubbly and very active, 10 to 15 minutes.

Stir in the remaining dough ingredients and knead the dough—by hand or mixer—until it's soft and pliable but not sticky. (The secret to a soft, tender bread is a soft dough.)

Place the dough in a lightly greased bowl, cover with plastic wrap, and let sit in a warm place for about 45 minutes, or until doubled.

TO MAKE THE FILLING In a medium-sized bowl, beat together the cream cheese, butter, sugar, salt and vanilla. Mix in the ClearJel or flour and the egg, scraping the bottom and sides of the bowl thoroughly.

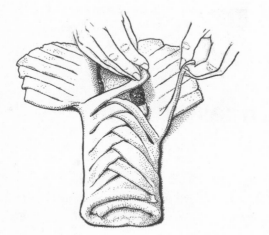

Make parallel cuts about 2½ inches long at a 45-degree angle down each side of the braid, ¾ inch apart. Take one strip at a time from alternate sides and bring them to the center. Let the ends overlap on top of the filling, continuing until the whole loaf is braided. Tuck in the ends. Brush with an egg beaten with a tablespoon of milk or water before baking.

Gently deflate the risen dough and divide it in half. Roll each half into a 15 x 10-inch rectangle and place each onto lightly greased or parchment-lined baking sheets. Spread half of the jam in a 2½-inch-wide swath, lengthwise, down the center of each dough rectangle, leaving a 1-inch border at the top and bottom.

Top the jam with half of the filling. Make 2½-inch cuts every ¾ inch down both long sides of the dough. Fold the ends over the filling, then pull the cut strips up and over, alternating sides. Repeat with the remaining piece of dough.

Cover the braids and let them rise for 30 to 45 minutes, until they're puffy looking.

Preheat the oven to 350°F.

If desired, brush the braids with an egg mixed with 1 tablespoon water (this will make a darker, shinier crust), or spritz with water, then sprinkle with coarse sugar. Bake the braids for 32 to 36 minutes, until they're golden brown. Remove from the oven and let them cool for 15 minutes before slicing.

*If you use all-purpose rather than pastry flour, expect a loaf that's a bit chewy (rather than totally tender). You'll need to increase the water by a couple of tablespoons, as well.

nutrition information per serving 1 slice, 33g

98 cal | 3g fat | 2g protein | 9g complex carbohydrates | 6g sugar | 21mg cholesterol | 110mg sodium | 32mg potassium | 37RE vitamin A | mg vitamin C | 1mg iron | 8mg calcium | 25mg phosphorus

Cinnamon Buns

12 BUNS

These are quintessential cinnamon buns, stuffed with rich filling and smeared with thick white icing.

DOUGH

3½ cups (14¾ ounces) unbleached all-purpose flour

2 teaspoons instant yeast

3 tablespoons (1¼ ounces) sugar

1 tablespoon granular lecithin (optional, but helpful)

2 tablespoons (⅝ ounce) nonfat dry milk

1¼ teaspoons salt

1 large egg plus enough water to make 1 cup

1 teaspoon vanilla extract

2 tablespoons (1 ounce) soft butter

FILLING

¼ cup (2 ounces) soft butter

¾ cup (5¼ ounces) sugar mixed with 1 tablespoon cinnamon

½ cup nuts, raisins, or chocolate chips

ICING

3 tablespoons (1½ ounces) heavy cream, or 2 tablespoons water

1 cup (4 ounces) confectioners' sugar

FOR THE DOUGH Mix and knead together all the dough ingredients—by hand or mixer—to form a soft, smooth dough. Place it in a greased bowl, cover, and let it rise in a warm place for 1 to 1½ hours; it should almost double in size.

TO ASSEMBLE Turn out the dough onto a lightly greased work surface and roll it into a rectangle measuring about 11 x 20 inches. Spread a thin layer of soft butter over the dough, leaving about 1 inch uncovered on the short side nearest you. Sprinkle with the cinnamon sugar and nuts, raisins, or chips of your choice. Starting with the short edge covered with filling, roll the dough (see illustration) into a log. Use a serrated knife to gently saw the log in half, then cut each side of the log into six equal pieces (see illustration). Place the buns in a lightly greased 9 x 13-inch pan, pressing down slightly. Cover the buns and let them rise in a warm place for 45 minutes to 1¼ hours, until they're quite puffy.

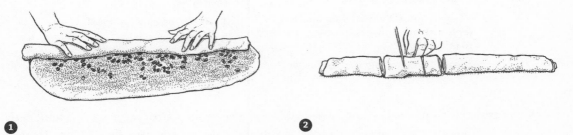

1. After sprinkling the dough with filling, roll into a log, starting with the long end. Try not to stretch or pull the dough, or roll it too tightly, as this will make the centers pop up when baking. **2.** Gently slice through the center of the rolled dough, then cut each half in half. Slice each of these pieces in thirds to make 12 equal pieces.

Preheat the oven to 350°F. Bake the buns for 20 to 25 minutes, until they're golden brown. Remove from the oven and let them cool in the pan for 10 minutes, then turn them out of the pan and let them cool to just slightly warm before frosting.

TO MAKE THE ICING Mix the heavy cream and confectioners' sugar to make a creamy glaze; use water for a thinner glaze. Spread the icing on the buns.

`nutrition information per serving`   **1 bun, with frosting, 93g**

302 cal | 10g fat | 5g protein | 26g complex carbohydrates | 23g sugar | 2g dietary fiber | 34mg cholesterol | 237mg sodium | 156mg potassium | 71 RE vitamin A | 1mg vitamin C | 2mg iron | 24mg calcium | 77mg phosphorus

Favorite Sticky Buns

1 DOZEN BUNS

These gooey dark-gold buns feature a thick cinnamon filling and a topping of rich brown sugar sauce sprinkled liberally with pecans. We guarantee these will rival or surpass any bakery sticky buns you've ever enjoyed.

STARTER

2 cups (8 ounces) unbleached pastry flour*

1 cup (8 ounces) water

1/16 teaspoon instant yeast

DOUGH

1½ cups (6¼ ounces) unbleached all-purpose flour

¼ cup (1¼ ounces) nonfat dry milk

2 tablespoons (¾ ounce) potato flour, or ¼ cup dried potato flakes (optional, but makes a more tender roll)

3 tablespoons (1 ounce) dough relaxer (optional, but it makes the dough easier to roll out)

¼ cup (1¾ ounces) granulated sugar

2 teaspoons vanilla extract

1¼ teaspoons salt

2¼ teaspoons instant yeast

6 tablespoons (3 ounces) butter

FILLING

1 cup (7 ounces) granulated sugar

1½ tablespoons cinnamon

GLAZE

½ cup (5½ ounces) golden syrup or light corn syrup

1 tablespoon rum (optional)

3 tablespoons (1½ ounces) butter, melted

1 cup (8 ounces) brown sugar

1 cup (3¾ ounces) diced pecans

FOR THE STARTER Combine the flour, water, and yeast in a medium-sized bowl, stirring until fairly smooth. Cover the bowl and let the mixture rest, at room temperature (cooler than 75°F), overnight, or for 12 to 16 hours.

FOR THE DOUGH Combine the overnight starter with all of the dough ingredients and mix and knead them together—by hand or mixer—until you have a soft, smooth dough. Cover and let the dough rise for about 1 hour; it will become slightly puffy but won't double in bulk.

While the dough is rising, prepare the pans—two 9-inch round cake pans, a 9 x 13-inch pan, a 12 x 12-inch square pan, or a 12-inch round pan. Spray with nonstick pan spray or lightly grease with vegetable shortening or butter.

FOR THE FILLING Combine the sugar and cinnamon. Set aside.

FOR THE GLAZE In a small bowl, whisk together the golden syrup, rum, and melted butter. Pour the glaze into the pan, or divide it evenly between the pans if you're using two pans. Sprinkle the brown sugar and pecans on top of the glaze.

TO ASSEMBLE Transfer the dough to a lightly greased work surface and roll it into a rectangle approximately 14 x 20 inches. Spread it with the prepared cinnamon-sugar filling, leaving an uncovered strip about 1 inch wide along one short end of the dough. Starting with the short end without the filling, roll the dough into a log and slice it into 12 slices, each about 1 to 1¼ inches wide. (See instructions on page 217 on slicing.) Place the buns in the prepared pan(s), leaving about ½ inch between them. Cover the pan(s), and let the buns rise for 90 minutes; again, they won't rise much, they'll just seem to spread a bit.

Preheat the oven to 350°F. Bake the buns for about 30 minutes, tenting them lightly with aluminum foil for the final 5 minutes if they appear to be browning too quickly. The finished buns will be golden brown. Loosen the edges of the buns with a knife, then carefully (the sugar is hot!) turn them out onto a rack or parchment-covered sheet pan to cool, scraping any glaze that may have stuck to the pan onto the warm buns. Serve warm or at room temperature.

*Using a combination of pastry flour and all-purpose flour, as we do here (with pastry flour in the starter, all-purpose in the dough) will give you a delightfully tender roll. However, if you don't have pastry flour, use all-purpose, increasing the amount of water to 1 cup plus 2 tablespoons.

nutrition information per serving   **1 bun, 136g**

473 cal | 15g fat | 6g protein | 31g complex carbohydrates | 48g sugar | 2g dietary fiber | 25mg cholesterol | 262mg sodium | 240mg potassium | 99RE vitamin A | 1mg vitamin C | 3mg iron | 62mg calcium | 103mg phosphorus

Portuguese Sweet Rolls

16 ROLLS

This takeoff on Portuguese sweet bread is simply that big round loaf broken down into smaller puffs, ideal for carrying in a lunchbox (or brown bag). Serve these soft, almost-sweet rolls with jam and double Devon cream for a light, simple addition to afternoon tea.

1 tablespoon instant yeast	¼ cup (1½ ounces) potato flour
½ cup (4 ounces) milk	2 large eggs
6 tablespoons (3 ounces) butter	⅓ cup (2⅜ ounces) sugar
¼ cup (2 ounces) water	2 teaspoons vanilla extract
1 teaspoon salt	¼ teaspoon lemon oil, or 1½ teaspoons grated lemon peel
3 cups (12¾ ounces) unbleached all-purpose flour	

Mix and knead together all the ingredients—by hand or mixer—to form a soft, smooth dough. Transfer the dough to a lightly greased bowl, cover the bowl, and let the dough rise until puffy but not necessarily doubled in bulk, about 90 minutes, depending on the warmth of your kitchen.

Transfer the dough to a lightly greased work surface and divide it into 16 pieces. Round each piece into a smooth ball. Place the balls in a lightly greased 12 x 12-inch square pan, or equivalent (two 9-inch round pans, a 9 x 13-inch pan, or a 14-inch round pan). Cover the pan and let the rolls rise for about 1 hour; they should double in bulk.

Preheat the oven to 325°F. Bake the rolls for 30 minutes, tenting lightly with aluminum foil after the first 20 minutes. Remove them from the oven when they're golden brown and transfer them to a rack to cool.

nutrition information per serving 1 roll, 62g

191 cal | 6g fat | 5g protein | 25g complex carbohydrates | 4g sugar | 1g dietary fiber | 40mg cholesterol | 193mg sodium | 105mg potassium | 57RE vitamin A | 1mg vitamin C | 2mg iron | 20mg calcium | 60mg phosphorus

Small Breads

Buns and bagels, rolls and breadsticks—these small, single-serve breads are self-contained, each one an entity unto itself. All of them are easily obtainable at the supermarket, but if you love to bake, you'll want to try making them at home. Even the very freshest store-bought roll can't compare with a crusty homemade hard roll, or a soft, tender crescent or cloverleaf, hot from the oven.

Soft Rolls

16 DINNER ROLLS

With the focus these days on crusty, crisp, and crunchy artisan-style bread and rolls, it's comforting at times to drift back into childhood and the soft, squishy white rolls that graced so many of our tables, particularly at the holidays. Cloverleafs, crescents, fantans, knots—any baker worth her salt can put together a festive-looking bread basket with just one simple dough and a few different shaping techniques.

The following rolls all begin with the dough for White Bread 101, page 198. For ease of rolling, you might want to add 3 tablespoons of dough relaxer to the dough along with the rest of the dry ingredients; while not critical, it does make rolls easier to shape.

Choose the shapes you want to create, and divide the dough into 16 pieces, or roll out as required. Shape according to the illustrations on pages 222.

After shaping, let the rolls rise until puffy and almost double in size. Preheat the oven to 350 degrees. Bake for 15 to 18 minutes, until golden brown with an internal temperature of 190°F.

Finished rolls can be brushed with butter for a delicious soft crust; a double coating of butter for a soft, satiny crust; or lightly dusted with flour, if you prefer.

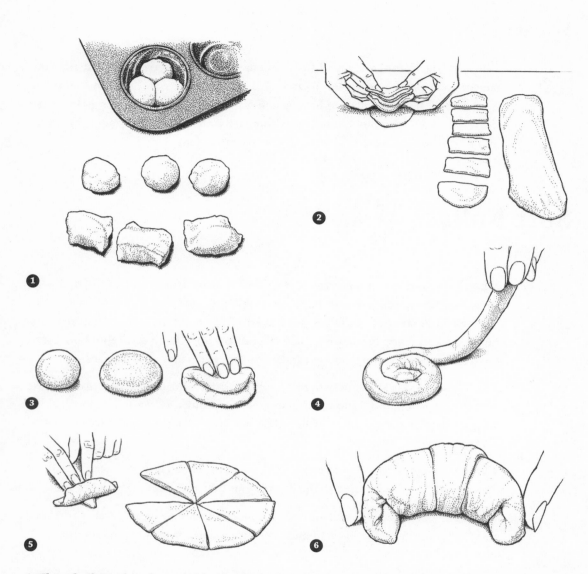

1. Cloverleaf: Divide each piece of dough into thirds. Roll each of the three pieces into a small ball. Place the three balls in the well of a greased muffin tin. **2. Fantans:** Roll the dough into a 16-inch square. Cut the square in half, and cut each piece crosswise into 2-inch strips. Butter each strip, then cut into four 2-inch squares. Stack four squares on top of each other, and put them on edge in a greased muffin tin. **3. Parker House:** Roll each piece of dough into a ball, then flatten the ball with the heel of your hand or a rolling pin. Fold the circle just short of in half and press together. Place the roll, seam side up, on a greased baking sheet. **4. Snail:** Roll each piece of dough into a log, hold one end down, then wind the other around it to form a spiral or snail shape. Place into a greased muffin tin or on a baking sheet. **5-6. Crescent:** Divide the dough in half, and roll each half into a ¼ inch–thick circle. Cut each circle into 8 wedges. Roll each wedge into a compact log, starting with the wider side and rolling toward the tip. Pinch the tip to seal the roll, then push the sides of the roll toward the center to form a crescent shape. Transfer the rolls to a lightly greased baking sheet, making sure to keep the tips on the bottom.

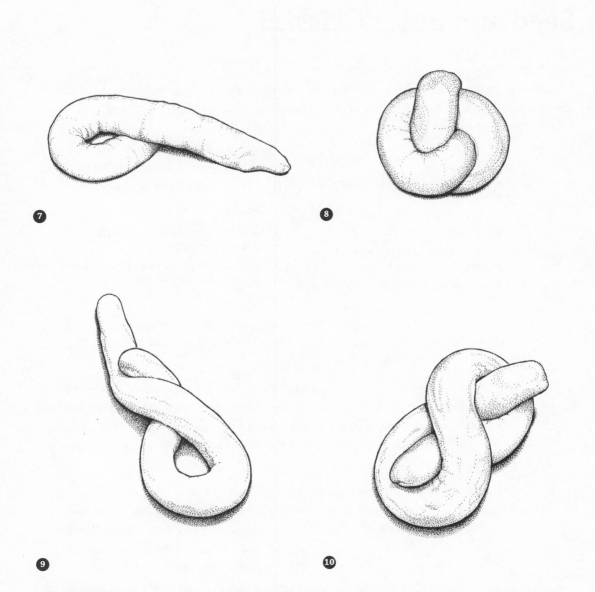

7-8. Single Knot: Roll each piece of dough into a log roughly four inches long. Tie the dough in a simple knot, leaving one end in the center of the top and tucking the other underneath. Place on a lightly greased or parchment-lined baking sheet. **9-10. Double Knot:** Roll each piece of dough into a rope 8 inches long. Make a loop with the top half of the dough, giving the closed end a half-inch overlap of dough. Turn this loop over so the long piece is on top. Wind the long piece behind the overlap, and bring the end back up through the loop to make a figure 8.

Seed and Spice Grissini

3 TO 6 DOZEN GRISSINI

Whenever we crave a savory snack, we whip up a bunch of these thin, crunchy breadsticks (grissini, in Italian). Extremely light and crisp as a bright fall day, they're a great complement to a bowl of soup or chowder.

DOUGH

2½ cups (10½ ounces) unbleached all-purpose flour

1½ teaspoons instant yeast

1 teaspoon salt

2 rounded tablespoons dough relaxer (optional, but helpful)

3 tablespoons (1 ounce) nonfat dry milk

3 tablespoons (1¼ ounces) olive oil

⅞ to 1⅛ cups (7 to 9 ounces) water*

TOPPING

1 large egg white whisked with 1 tablespoon water

1 to 2 tablespoons seeds or seed mixture of your choice, for topping

Combine all the dough ingredients and mix and knead them together—by hand or mixer—until you have a soft, smooth dough. Cover and let the dough rise for 1 to 1½ hours; it should double in bulk.

Transfer the dough to a lightly greased work surface and roll it into a roughly 10 x 20-inch rectangle. Brush the dough lightly with the egg white mixture and sprinkle it with the seeds. Roll the dough lightly with a rolling pin to press the seeds in. If you prefer your grissini without seeds, brush the dough with 1 tablespoon olive oil instead of the egg white.

Use a pizza wheel or sharp knife to cut the dough (the short way) into ¼- to ½-inch-wide strips. Twist the ends of each strip in opposite directions (see illustration) and place them on lightly greased or parchment-lined baking sheets. Cover and let the grissini rest for 30 minutes.

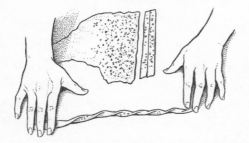

After cutting the dough into ¼-inch strips, twist the ends of each strip in opposite directions to form a spiral. Transfer the twisted dough to a baking sheet.

Preheat the oven to 425°F. Put the grissini in the oven and bake for 12 to 14 minutes, until they're golden brown. Note that these go from golden brown to burned very quickly, so start keeping a close eye on them at about the 10-minute mark.

*You'll use the greater amount of water in winter, the lesser amount in summer.

nutrition information per serving   3 grissini, cut in ¼-inch strips, with sesame seeds, 27g

66 cal | 2g fat | 2g protein | 10g complex carbohydrates | 1g dietary fiber | 97mg sodium | 42mg potassium | 5RE vitamin A | 1mg iron | 20mg calcium | 28mg phosphorus

Bagels

8 BAGELS

These days, every corner luncheonette seems to have a ready supply of top-flight bagels, as do shops that are devoted exclusively to bagels and their accompanying spreads. With all kinds of good bagels available just about wherever you turn, why make your own? First, so you know what's in them; who wants azodicarbonmide in their pumpernickel bagel? Second, so you can customize them to taste, as in pesto bagels with sun-dried tomatoes and pine nuts. And third, it's fairly easy and fun! If you can make bread dough, you can easily make bagels.

If you're a seasoned bread baker, you may notice that the dough for these bagels is quite a bit stiffer than that for most breads. This is to ensure that the bagels attain their typically dense, close-grained, chewy texture; you don't want them rising very much, and a dry (stiff) dough naturally rises much less than a wetter dough.

DOUGH

1 tablespoon instant yeast

4 cups (17 ounces) unbleached bread flour

2 teaspoons salt

1 tablespoon non-diastatic malt powder, brown sugar, or barley malt syrup

1½ cups (12 ounces) lukewarm water

WATER BATH

2 quarts (64 ounces) water

2 tablespoons (1 ounce) non-diastatic malt powder, brown sugar, or barley malt syrup

1 tablespoon granulated sugar

Combine all the dough ingredients in a mixing bowl and knead vigorously, by hand for 10 to 15 minutes, or by machine on medium-low speed for about 10 minutes. Since you're using a high-protein bread flour, it takes a bit more effort and time to develop the gluten. The dough will be quite stiff; if you're using an electric mixer it will "thwap" the sides of the bowl and hold its shape (without spreading at all) when you stop the mixer. Place the dough in a lightly greased bowl and set it aside to rise until noticeably puffy though not necessarily doubled in bulk, 1 to 1½ hours.

Transfer the dough to a work surface and divide it into eight pieces. Working with one piece at a time, roll it into a smooth, round ball. Cover the balls with plastic wrap and let them rest for 30 minutes. They'll puff up very slightly.

While the dough is resting, prepare the water bath by heating the water, malt powder, and sugar to a very gentle boil in a large, wide-diameter pan. Preheat the oven to 425°F.

Use a bagel cutter, or use your index finger to poke a hole through the center of each ball (see illustration on next page), then twirl the dough on your finger to stretch the hole until it's about 2 inches in diameter (the entire bagel will be about 4 inches across). Place each bagel on a lightly greased or parchment-lined baking sheet and repeat with the remaining pieces of dough.

Transfer the bagels, four at a time if possible, to the simmering water. Increase the heat under the pan to bring the water back up to a gently simmering boil, if necessary. Cook the bagels for 2 minutes, gently flip them over, and cook 1 minute more. Using a skimmer or strainer, remove the bagels from the water and place them back on the baking sheet. Repeat with the remaining bagels.

Bake the bagels for 20 to 25 minutes, until they're as deep a brown as you like, turning them over after about 15 minutes, which will help them remain tall and round. Remove the bagels from the oven and cool completely on a wire rack.

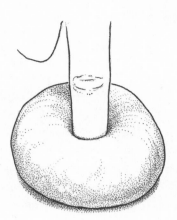

After forming the dough into a ball, poke a hole through the center with your finger. Stretch this opening (twirling the dough around your finger works well) until you have a hole that is 2 inches across.

nutrition information per serving   **1 plain bagel, 111g**

211 cal | 1g fat | 7g protein | 43g complex carbohydrates | 2g sugar | 2g dietary fiber | 536mg sodium | 101mg potassium | 3mg iron | 106mg calcium | 67mg phosphorus

Variations   SESAME SEED BAGELS: Brush each bagel, just before baking, with a glaze made of 1 egg white beaten until frothy with 1 tablespoon of water. Glaze each bagel and sprinkle heavily with seeds.

ONION BAGELS: Bake bagels for 20 to 22 minutes (or until they're almost as brown as you like) and remove the pan from the oven, keeping the oven turned on. Working with one bagel at a time, glaze as instructed above and sprinkle with minced, dried onion. Return the bagels to the oven for no more than 2 minutes (the onions will burn if the bagels are left in longer than that).

CINNAMON-RAISIN BAGELS: Knead about ⅔ cup of raisins into the dough toward the end of the kneading process. Just before you're done kneading, sprinkle your work surface heavily with cinnamon-sugar and give the dough a few more turns; it will pick up the cinnamon-sugar in irregular swirls. Divide the dough into eight pieces, form each piece into a ball, and roll each ball in additional cinnamon-sugar. Let rest and shape as directed above.

CLASSIC PRETZELS: The traditional street vendor pretzel, with its characteristic dark brown, highly glazed appearance, is difficult to make at home; professional bakers often use food-safe lye to give pretzels their characteristic sheen. You can use bagel dough to make a dense, chewy, Philadelphia-style pretzel; it will lack only in appearance.

Prepare bagel dough up through its first rise. Divide the dough into 12 pieces and roll each piece into a 25- to 30-inch rope. Shape ropes into pretzels (see illustrations) and simmer and bake as directed in the bagel recipe, understanding that the pretzels are larger and will be a bit more challenging to deal with as you move them from counter to water bath to baking sheet.

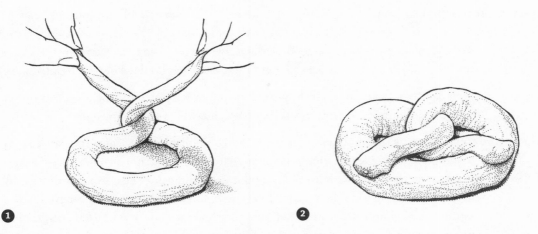

1-2. Form the rope of dough into a circle, leaving 4 inches free on each end of the rope. Twist these ends around each other, and fold the twist down the middle of the circle. Press the ends of the dough to the outside of the ring to make the pretzel shape.

English Muffins

10 TO 12 MUFFINS

Sure, you can buy excellent English muffins at the store, but for those of you who always like the challenge of making your own, this is a fun recipe.

We find these muffins are best made the day before you want to serve them. You may certainly sample them straight off the griddle, but we find them a bit gummy at that point; they definitely benefit by drying out.

STARTER

1½ cups (6¼ ounces) unbleached all-purpose flour

¾ cup (6 ounces) water

⅛ teaspoon instant yeast

DOUGH

1¾ cups (7¼ ounces) unbleached all-purpose flour

2 tablespoons (½ ounce) cornstarch

1 teaspoon instant yeast

1 teaspoon salt

2 tablespoons (⅞ ounce) sugar or non-diastatic malt powder

2 teaspoons baking powder

2 tablespoons (1 ounce) butter, melted

¾ cup (6 ounces) milk, warm

1 to 2 tablespoons cornmeal, for sprinkling on the pan (if you're baking the muffins)

TO MAKE THE STARTER Mix the flour, water, and yeast in a medium-sized bowl to form a smooth batter. Cover and leave at room temperature for at least 4 hours, or up to 16 hours. The starter should be puffy and full of holes when it's ready to use.

TO MAKE THE DOUGH In a large mixing bowl, beat together the starter and all the dough ingredients to form a smooth batter. The batter needs to be beaten for 5 to 8 minutes, so unless you feel like giving your biceps a good workout, we suggest using an electric mixer. Cover the bowl and place it in a warm spot until the batter has doubled in size, about 1 hour.

Now you can bake the English muffins in the oven or dry-fry them on top of the stove. Read both sets of directions first to decide which you want to do.

TO PREPARE MUFFINS FOR BAKING Lightly grease 10 to 12 English muffin rings (nonstick spray works well) and place the rings on a lightly greased or parchment-lined baking sheet that's been sprinkled with a small amount of cornmeal. (The cornmeal isn't really necessary, but it makes the muffins look more authentic.) If you don't have English muffin rings, simply drop the batter onto the pan and shape it with your fingers. The muffins won't be as symmetrical, but their taste will be just fine.

Stir the dough, then drop a scant ¼ cup of dough into each ring. Sprinkle lightly with cornmeal. Smooth the dough, if desired, with your fingers, dipped in water first. Cover the pan and place in a warm place to rise for 1 hour, or until the muffins have grown by at least a third.

BAKING Preheat the oven to 350°F. If you've used muffin rings, place a clean baking sheet atop the muffins, which keeps them flat on both sides (rather than crowned on the top) so they'll fit better in the toaster slot. (If you're not using muffin rings, don't put a pan on top of them—they'll squish.) Bake the muffins for 25 minutes, until they're lightly browned on both sides. (The bottoms will be more brown than the tops, just like the ones you buy at the store.) The muffins may be fork-split and eaten immediately (they'll be soft) or, for crunchier muffins, cool them completely, split them, and toast.

TO DRY-FRY ENGLISH MUFFINS Let the batter rise for 1½ hours, until it's very puffy looking. Preheat a griddle to 325°F. Lightly grease English muffin rings. Place the rings on the griddle. Lightly stir the batter, then use a ¼-cup measure or muffin scoop to fill each ring about a third full. If you're not using muffin rings, simply drop the batter by ¼ cupfuls onto the griddle. Dry-fry the muffins (frying without grease) for 10 to 12 minutes on the first side before turning them over to cook on the other side. You'll know the muffins are ready to turn when the top side has formed a dry skin. Cook the muffins for about half the time you cooked them on the first side, remove them from the griddle, carefully remove the rings, and allow them to cool.

nutrition information per serving **1 muffin, 82g**

179 cal | 3g fat | 5g protein | 30g complex carbohydrates | 2g sugar | 1g dietary fiber | 8mg cholesterol | 108mg sodium | 90mg potassium | 33RE vitamin A | 2mg iron | 91mg calcium | 152mg phosphorus

Hot Buttered Pretzels

8 PRETZELS

Pretzels are available crisp and hard from your grocery; bagel-like and chewy from a street vendor; or, if you're lucky and in the right place, soft, buttery, and tender, usually at the mall or airport. This recipe is for mall-type pretzels.

DOUGH

2½ cups (10½ ounces) unbleached all-purpose flour

½ teaspoon salt

1 teaspoon sugar

2¼ teaspoons instant yeast

⅞ to 1 cup (7 to 8 ounces) warm water*

TOPPING

½ cup (4 ounces) warm water

1 teaspoon sugar

Coarse, kosher, or pretzel salt (optional)

3 tablespoons (1½ ounces) salted butter, melted

Place all the dough ingredients in a bowl and beat until well combined. Knead the dough, by hand or mixer, for about 5 minutes, until it's soft, smooth, and quite slack. Dust the dough with flour (to keep it from sticking) and place it in a plastic bag; close the bag, leaving room for the dough to expand, and let it rest for 30 minutes.

Preheat the oven to 500°F. Prepare two baking sheets by spraying them with vegetable oil spray or lining them with parchment paper.

Transfer the dough to a lightly greased work surface and divide it into eight equal pieces (about 2¼ ounces each). Let the pieces rest, uncovered, for 5 minutes.

Roll each piece of dough into a long thin rope (around 28 inches) and twist each rope into a pretzel (see illustration. p. 227). Dip the pretzels in the warm water mixed with 1 teaspoon sugar, and place them on the baking sheets. Sprinkle them lightly with the salt. Let them rest, uncovered, for 10 minutes.

Bake the pretzels for 8 to 9 minutes, until they're golden brown, reversing the baking sheets halfway through.

Remove the pretzels from the oven and brush them thoroughly with the melted butter. Keep brushing the butter on until you've used it all; it may seem like a lot, but that's what gives these pretzels their ethereal taste. Eat the pretzels warm, or reheat them in an oven or microwave.

*Use the greater amount in the winter, the lesser amount in the summer, and somewhere in between in the spring and fall. Your goal is a soft dough.

---

nutrition information per serving   **1 pretzel, 85g**

171 cal | 4.7g fat | 4g protein | 27g complex carbohydrates | 1g sugar | 1g dietary fiber | 12mg cholesterol | 444mg sodium | 63mg potassium | 43RE vitamin A | 2mg iron | 66mg calcium | 44mg phosphorus

Variation   SOFT BREADSTICKS: For soft, fat, chewy breadsticks, prepare the pretzel dough up through its first rest. Divide it into 24 pieces and shape each piece into an 8- to 10-inch log. Transfer the breadsticks to a lightly greased or parchment-lined baking sheet, brush with warm water, and sprinkle with salt (for salt sticks) or seeds. Let rest and bake as directed in the preceding pretzel recipe.

Freeze!

Most yeast doughs respond very well to being refrigerated or frozen for a while. The exceptions are doughs very high in milk, eggs, and/or sugar, which tend to start fermenting after several days in the refrigerator (they do better in the freezer); or doughs with a lot of added fresh ingredients, such as cheese, fruit, or vegetables. These doughs tend to become watery when frozen, then thawed.

Interestingly, it's not advisable to freeze bread dough at temperatures under 20°F. Dough contains yeast, and once it's been activated by liquid, yeast is a living, breathing, feeding entity. Low temperatures, below 0°F, tend to kill yeast quickly. On the other hand, a temperature of 20°F (thankfully, that found in the freezer portion of a typical home refrigerator/freezer) puts yeast into hibernation without killing it. Dough may be stored at around 20°F for 4 to 5 weeks for optimum results.

We've discovered the best way to produce freezer dough is to prepare your dough, let it rise once, deflate it, and freeze it before it can rise again. With loaf bread dough, we shape the dough, place it in a greased loaf pan, place the pan inside a plastic bag, seal it, and freeze for 24 hours; then remove it from the pan, wrap it tightly in plastic, then in aluminum foil, and return to the freezer. When you want to bake bread, unwrap the dough, place it in a greased loaf pan, cover it with lightly greased plastic wrap, and let it thaw and rise at room temperature. Typically, it will take about 4 hours for the dough to thaw and begin to rise, and another hour or so for it to rise fully; these times, of course, depend on the temperature of your kitchen. You also may thaw the dough by placing it in its greased pan in the refrigerator overnight, then removing it for its final rise next morning.

Crusty Hard Rolls

12 ROLLS

These feathery light hard rolls have a delicious shiny, crunchy crust, partly the result of allowing them to proof overnight in the refrigerator, partly from an egg-white wash applied just prior to baking. This recipe starts with a poolish (pool-EESH), a premixed starter of flour, water, and a touch of yeast. Stirred together 12 to 16 hours before the remainder of the dough, the organic acids and alcohol produced by the growing yeast do wonders for both the bread's taste and its texture. Poolish is an idiomatic French word for Polish, as in Poland, which is where the French believe this type of starter originated.

POOLISH
1 cup (4¼ ounces) unbleached all-purpose flour
½ cup (4 ounces) water
⅛ teaspoon instant yeast

DOUGH
3½ cups (14¾ ounces) unbleached all-purpose flour

1 cup (8 ounces) water
1½ teaspoons salt
½ teaspoon instant yeast

WASH
1 large egg white
½ cup (4 ounces) water

FOR THE POOLISH Mix together the ingredients until smooth, cover, and let rest at room temperature overnight.

FOR THE DOUGH Combine the polish and all the dough ingredients and mix and knead them together—by hand or mixer—until you've made a soft, somewhat smooth dough. It should be cohesive but the surface should still be a bit rough; don't knead it until completely smooth. Cover and let the dough rise for 3 hours, gently deflating it and turning it over after 1 hour, and again after 2 hours.

TO ASSEMBLE Turn out the dough onto a lightly greased or floured work surface. Divide it into 12 pieces, about 2 ounces each. Shape the pieces into balls and firm them up by rolling them under your lightly cupped fingers on an unfloured work surface (see illustrations). Place the rolls on a parchment-lined baking sheet, cover them, and let them rise for 1½ to 2 hours, until they've doubled in size. Refrigerate them for several hours, or overnight.

Preheat the oven to 425°F.

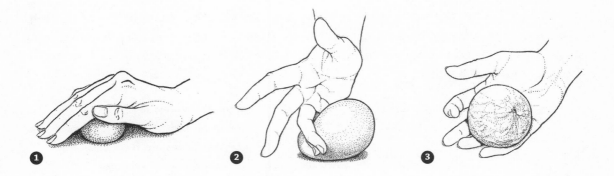

To roll a piece of dough into a round ball, place it on an unfloured, ungreased work surface. Cup your fingers lightly over the dough, and roll it quickly and gently in a circular motion, using the very top of your palm (at the base of your fingers) and applying the barest amount of downward pressure. Rolling the dough this way gives a tight, smooth top with a small "belly button" on the bottom.

④

The ball on the left still has a shaggy, rough surface. Continue rolling under your cupped hands to get a smooth, round ball, right.

Remove the rolls from the refrigerator. Whisk together the egg white and water and brush this wash on the rolls (you won't use it all). Slash a ¼-inch-deep cut across the top of each roll and bake for 30 to 35 minutes, until they're a deep golden brown. Remove them from the oven and cool on a rack. For an extra-crisp crust, let them cool in the oven with the door propped open after you've turned it off.

nutrition information per serving | 1 roll, 82g

152 cal | 5g protein | 32g complex carbohydrates | 1g dietary fiber | 272mg sodium | 63mg potassium | 2mg iron | 1mg calcium | 42mg phosphorus

Rolling Rolls

When the recipe directs you to shape pieces of dough into smooth balls, the process involves rounding the pieces on an unfloured, ungreased work surface. This is important; if you try to roll the balls of dough on a work surface covered with flour or coated with oil, you'll lack the dynamic tension between dough and rolling surface necessary for the rolls to become round. If the dough is very sticky, use a very light coating of oil on your work surface; never use flour.

Beautiful Burger Buns

8 LARGE BUNS

Soft, vaguely sweet, and golden yellow from the butter and egg, these simple buns are perfect for burgers, but also fine for any kind of sandwich. Or shape them into round balls and crowd them close together in a pan to make dinner rolls. This recipe first appeared on bakingcircle.com, where it was posted by Ellen Dill, and quickly adopted as everyone's favorite soft bun.

1 cup (8 ounces) water

2 tablespoons (1 ounce) butter

1 large egg

3¼ cups (13¾ ounces) unbleached all-purpose flour

¼ cup (1¾ ounces) sugar

1 teaspoon salt

1 tablespoon instant yeast

1 teaspoon onion powder (optional)

½ teaspoon dried minced onion (optional)

Combine all the ingredients and mix and knead them together—by hand or mixer—until you've made a soft, smooth dough. Place the dough in a lightly greased bowl, cover it, and let it rise for 1 hour.

Divide the dough into 8 pieces and shape each piece into a flattened ball. Place the buns on greased baking sheets, cover, and let rise 30 to 40 minutes, until they're quite puffy.

Preheat the oven to 375°F. Bake the buns for 12 to 15 minutes, until they're golden brown. Remove them from the oven and cool them on a rack. Split and use for burgers or sandwiches. For burgers, butter the split sides and fry them, buttered side down, until they're golden brown and warmed through.

nutrition information per serving | **1 bun, 90g**

211 cal | 4g fat | 6g protein | 32g complex carbohydrates | 6g sugar | 1g dietary fiber | 35mg cholesterol | 276mg sodium | 72mg potassium | 40RE vitamin A | 2mg iron | 5mg calcium | 57mg phosphorus

Cheese Rolls

16 LARGE DINNER ROLLS

These rolls are rich and fragrant. Use sharp cheddar cheese, or spice them up with some pepper-jack. The key to success with dinner rolls is to remember that a soft roll requires a soft dough; try not to add much additional flour if you're kneading by hand (if you're kneading by machine, you won't find additional flour necessary).

Don't be afraid to double this simple recipe; everything can be increased by the same proportion except the yeast, which should remain the same.

DOUGH

4½ teaspoons instant yeast

½ cup (4 ounces) warm water (95°F to 105°F)

1 teaspoon sugar

½ cup (2 ounces) unbleached all-purpose flour

1 cup (8 ounces) lukewarm milk

¼ cup (2 ounces) butter

1 teaspoon salt

⅓ cup (2⅜ ounces) sugar

1 large egg, lightly beaten

4 to 5 cups (17 to 21¼ ounces) unbleached all-purpose flour

FILLING

8 ounces cheddar or pepperjack cheese, cut into 16 cubes

TOPPING

2 tablespoons (1 ounce) butter

¼ cup (1 ounce) Italian-flavored bread crumbs

¼ cup (1 ounce) grated Parmesan cheese

1 egg yolk beaten with 1 tablespoon water

FOR THE DOUGH Combine all the dough ingredients and mix and knead—by hand or mixer—until you have a soft, elastic dough. Place the dough in a lightly greased bowl, cover, and let rise in a warm place for about 20 minutes.

TO ASSEMBLE Prepare a 9 x 13-inch pan by lightly greasing the bottom and sides with butter. Gently deflate the dough and divide into 16 pieces (about 2½ ounces each). Shape the pieces of dough into rounds and punch a cube of cheese from the bottom up into the center of each piece. Pinch the dough tightly together to close the bottom. Place the rolls, pinched side down, in the prepared baking pan about 1 inch apart. Cover and let rise again for another 15 to 20 minutes, or until doubled.

While the rolls are rising, heat the butter over low heat in a small saucepan. Remove from heat and stir in the flavored bread crumbs and grated cheese. Set aside.

Preheat the oven to 375°F. When the rolls have risen, brush the tops with the egg yolk beaten with water. Sprinkle the tops of the rolls liberally with the bread crumb mixture. Bake for 15 to 18 minutes, until the tops of the rolls are nicely browned. Remove from the pan immediately and cool on a rack. Serve warm.

nutrition information per serving 1 roll, 74g

222 cal | 7g fat | 9g protein | 26g complex carbohydrates | 4g sugar | 1g dietary fiber | 34mg cholesterol | 367mg sodium | 95mg potassium | 75RE vitamin A | 2mg iron | 141mg calcium | 139mg phosphorus

Starter, Sponge, Poolish, Biga . . . I'm Confused!

A wide array of methods to help jump-start your bread's rising (fermentation) process fall under the heading of preferments—as in preferments, something that happens before the first major fermenting (rising) of your bread dough. All the terms below refer to a type of starter, a combination of flour, water, and yeast that's prepared prior to the main body of the dough when making bread.

How do you know which, if any, of these preferments to use? When you're just getting started, rely on your recipe; if it calls for a particular preferment, use it. Once you've become acquainted with the various types, use the one that fits your schedule, and that you feel produces the best flavor and texture in your bread.

- The term *starter*, often used as a generic substitute for the word *preferments*, can also refer specifically to sourdough starter, a mixture of flour, water, and wild yeast used to provide the leavening (and wonderful flavor) in bread.

- A sponge is typically made by using all of the liquid, half of the flour, and half of the yeast in a bread recipe. These three elements are mixed together, placed in a cool spot, and left to bubble for 3 to 10 hours or so. The remaining dough ingredients are added, and the bread is kneaded, shaped, raised, and baked as directed. This method is a good way to start your bread in the morning, then finish it relatively quickly just before dinner; you'll still need to let the shaped dough rise before baking, but you can skip the usual initial rise because the sponge has been bubbling all day.

- Poolish and biga are overnight starters, both utilizing domestic yeast (as well as wild). Poolish is a wet starter (the consistency of thick pancake batter), made from flour, water, and a touch of yeast (about ⅛ teaspoon).

Hearth or Country Breads

When you hear the phrase "artisan bread," what do you imagine? A crisp-chewy crusted loaf, dense and moist, perhaps loaded with pecans and dried cherries, or scented with fresh herbs. Or maybe a big round of sourdough with a shower of seeds on top. Or perhaps just the ultimate, perfect baguette.

What distinguishes artisan breads is the time that goes into them; most are made with an overnight (or longer) starter. As opposed to true sourdough, leavened by wild yeast, these loaves are often prepared using commercial yeast; but the flavor that develops from a series of long, slow rises is what sets these breads apart.

Most artisan-style hearth breads rely on just four ingredients: flour, water, yeast and salt. Some include olive oil or other fat, but most are fairly simple breads. How, then, can there be such an incredible variety of breads made from these four basic ingredients? The methods used to make the dough, the time the dough is given to develop flavor, and the way the loaves are shaped and baked have an enormous effect

A biga—the Italian name for a starter—can be either wet (batterlike consistency) or dry (stiff dough consistency). Like the poolish, it begins with flour, water, and a tiny bit of yeast. It can develop overnight, or for up to three days. As it develops, it will become more acidic and more complex in flavor. The longer you let the biga develop, the more sour it will become.

Why are some bigas wet, and some dry? This has to do with how much time you want to spend developing them, and how sour you want your bread to be. A wet biga will produce acetic acid, the acid that makes bread taste sour, more quickly than a dry biga. Most often, use a wet biga if you want to make dough within 10 to 12 hours; a dry one if you'd like to wait longer. For sourdoughs, use either, but just be sure to give them enough time to develop the degree of sourness you like.

- Levain is the French incarnation of what we know as sourdough starter. But, rather than taking the form of a slurry, a fairly liquid combination of flour and water, a levain is in the form of a dough, and the bread it leavens is not particularly sour. Because of the diet it has during its initial days, it develops a high enough concentration of wild yeast that it can leaven bread without the addition of commercial yeast. The slight acidity imparted by the levain allows the flavor of breads made with it to improve over time.

- A chef or mère (they're the same thing) is actually just part of a levain. In order to make bread, you break off part of the levain (it's stiff and doughlike); this piece is called a chef or mère. The chef or mère is fed with additional flour or water and allowed to ferment; this process can be followed up to three times, each time the chef's flavor becoming more complex, before finally it's used as the leavening agent in a bread recipe.

on the final product. The following are some hints that we've come up with over the years that will help you successfully make artisan-style breads at home.

Choosing your ingredients: Use unbleached, unbromated flour with a protein level between 10.5 and 12 percent. If your water has a strong chlorine taste/smell or other off-flavors, use bottled water. To eliminate chlorine from tap water, let the water sit in an open container for a few hours. There are many different yeasts on the market, each with its own following. We recommend instant yeast because it's so easy to use, easy to store, and can withstand some mishandling.

Time: Flavor comes from long, slow fermentation (rising) at relatively low temperatures. An ambient rising temperature of 70°F to 80°F results in the best-flavored bread. Using a preferment (a sponge, poolish, biga, or levain) helps develop even more flavor.

Use less yeast: If you plan to use a preferment and to allow time for a long first rise, you can use less yeast. Using less yeast allows the dough to develop slowly, leaving time for all the enzymatic and chemical changes that lead to flavorful bread.

Use more water: Wetter is usually better. A slack dough allows for a more active fermentation and complete development of the gluten structure. A hydration of 65 percent or more based on total flour weight is a good place to start. (Consider the weight of the flour is 100 percent, then divide the weight of the water by the weight of the flour to find the hydration level. For example, if your flour weighs 12 ounces, using 6 ounces of water would give you 50 percent hydration.)

Mix (knead) less: Mix and knead your dough less than to full development. The gluten continues to develop during fermentation, so if you knead the dough fully it will be hard to handle after fermentation; it will be too strong to shape properly and won't rise to its full volume in the oven. Full development is reached when your dough

Adding Dried Fruit

When making a yeast bread with fruit, be aware that the fruit will inevitably release some of its sugar into the dough, which will change the sugar ratio and may slow your bread's rise. To impact rising time as little as possible, do the following:

• If you're using raisins or other fruits that can remain whole (currants, dried cranberries, etc.), don't soak them first; it isn't necessary and it allows their sugar to begin leaching out.

• When adding fruits that need to be chopped (dried apricots, large pieces of dried pineapple, etc.), leave the fruit pieces as large as possible; the finer you chop the fruit, the more sugar it will release into the dough.

• Don't add fruit to your initial dough; let it go through its first rise, then briefly knead the fruit in before shaping. This gives the yeast a good strong start before you add the fruit.

is very smooth, cleans the sides and bottom of the bowl, and will stretch, without tearing, to make a transparent "window," that is, you can see light through it. Dough at less than full development will be slightly sticky to the touch, won't be totally smooth, and will tear after stretching a small amount.

Handle with care: Handle dough gently during shaping. When you're deflating dough at any point during its fermentation process, simply fold it over gently onto itself. And when you're shaping, you don't want to expel all the air; just make the dough smooth, without huge air pockets.

Baking with steam: Bake breads directly on a baking stone with steam in the oven for the first 10 minutes. It's nearly impossible to get the amount of steam in a home oven that a professional steam-injected oven has. That said, a good home approximation is putting a cast iron skillet into the bottom of the oven, preheating the oven for at least 30 minutes on the highest heat possible, and pouring boiling water (3 to 4 ounces) into the hot pan just after the bread is put in. This method should allow you to keep the outside surface of the dough moist enough to let the loaf expand. Spritzing the loaves with water just before baking also helps.

Thorough baking: Bake the loaves until they've reached an internal temperature of 190° to 210°F and the crust is medium to dark brown. Much of the flavor of bread is concentrated in the crust, and the darker the crust (within reason, of course; don't let it blacken), the more flavorful the bread.

Raisin Pecan Rye Bread

1 LOAF, ABOUT 16 SERVINGS

There's something very right about the combination of rye flour, raisins, and pecans. The subtle earthy flavor of rye, the nuttiness of the pecans, and the offsetting sweetness of raisins combine to make a bread whose flavor seems to hit all parts of your tongue and taste buds at once. This dense, moist bread is delicious spread with butter (toasted or not); or serve it with Roquefort or another assertive cheese.

BIGA

⅛ teaspoon instant yeast

1 cup (4¼ ounces) unbleached all-purpose flour

⅓ cup (2⅞ ounces) water

DOUGH

1½ teaspoons salt

3 tablespoons (1½ ounces) brown sugar

½ cup (2 ounces) rye flour

½ cup (2 ounces) pumpernickel

1 cup (4¼ ounces) unbleached all-purpose flour

¾ cup (6 ounces) water

2 teaspoons instant yeast

2 tablespoons (1 ounce) butter

½ cup (1⅞ ounces) chopped pecans

1 cup (5¼ ounces) currants or raisins

Make the biga by stirring together the yeast, flour, and water. The dough will be quite stiff. Place it in a lightly greased bowl, cover it, and let it rest at room temperature overnight.

Next day, combine the biga with the remaining ingredients (except the pecans and fruit) in a large mixing bowl, or in the bowl of an electric mixer, mixing to form a shaggy dough. Knead the dough until smooth, then place it in a lightly greased bowl and let it rest for 1 hour; it will become quite puffy, though it may not double in bulk.

Transfer the dough to a lightly greased work surface, gently deflate it, and knead in the nuts and fruit. Shape the dough into a slightly flattened ball and place it on a lightly greased sheet pan. Cover the pan with a proof cover or some lightly greased plastic wrap. Let the loaf rise for 45 minutes to 1 hour, until it's puffy.

Preheat the oven to 350°F. Bake the bread for about 40 minutes (tenting it lightly with aluminum foil for the final 15 minutes) until its interior registers 190°F on an instant-red thermometer. Remove the bread from the oven and cool it on a rack.

nutrition information per serving   **1 slice, 79g**

236 cal | 6g fat | 6g protein | 38g complex carbohydrates | 3g sugar | 2g dietary fiber | 9mg cholesterol | 214mg sodium | 189mg potassium | 38RE vitamin A | 1mg vitamin C | 2mg iron | 40mg calcium | 88mg phosphorus

Variation   RAISIN-RYE CRISPS: The preceding recipe makes a very nice sandwich or toasting bread. But, to make rye crisps—delightfully crunchy slices of oven-toasted bread—we use more rye and less wheat flour. This makes a denser bread, more easily sliced to make crisps. In addition, we shape the breads differently: The bread for crisps is formed into two baguettes, to be sliced crosswise. These small, oval slices show less tendency to crumble, and also toast more evenly than would a large sandwich slice.

Prepare the biga as directed above. Next day, when making the dough, change the flour amounts to ⅔ cup each rye and pumpernickel flours, and ⅔ cup unbleached bread flour. Reduce the amount of yeast from 2 teaspoons to 1½ teaspoons. Prepare dough as directed up to the point when it's ready to shape.

Currants vs. Raisins

We like to use currants in place of raisins in bread that's served in medium-to-thin slices; the smaller currants are more likely to remain embedded in the bread, rather than being ripped out by the knife as it cuts.

Transfer the dough to a lightly oiled work surface and divide it in half. Shape each half into a thin baguette about 15 inches long. Place the baguettes on a baking sheet and cover them with a dough cover or lightly greased plastic wrap. Let the baguettes rest for 1 hour. They won't appear to rise very much; that's okay.

Preheat the oven to 350°F. Bake the loaves for about 30 minutes, or until they're brown and their interior registers 190°F on an instant-read thermometer. Remove them from the oven and place on a wire rack to cool. When the bread is cool, wrap each loaf loosely in a clean dish towel and let them rest overnight.

Next day, cut the bread, making slightly diagonal cuts (as if you're making biscotti) into ¼-inch slices. Place the slices in a single layer on ungreased cookie sheets.

Preheat the oven to 275°F. Bake the slices for 25 to 30 minutes, until they're a light golden brown and very crisp. Remove from the oven and let them cool on the cookie sheets. When the crisps are completely cool, store them in an airtight container. Serve them plain, or with cheese.

Baguettes

3 BAGUETTES, 13 TO 14 SLICES EACH

The first goal of every budding artisan-bread baker is a crusty, flavorful baguette. Let this recipe be the starting point on a journey that may last for quite a long time—the "perfect" baguette is a serious challenge for the home baker.

This recipe makes use of a poolish (see description, p. 234) to enhance the baguettes' flavor. Notice the symmetry of the ingredient amounts: equal amounts of flour and water (by weight) in the poolish; in the dough, the same amount of water again and double the amount of flour. These are the classic French proportions for a baguette.

POOLISH (STARTER)	DOUGH
1¼ cups (5¼ ounces) unbleached all-purpose flour	Generous 2½ cups (10½ ounces) unbleached all-purpose flour
⅔ cup (5¼ ounces) cool (approximately 60°F) water	1½ teaspoons instant yeast
⅛ teaspoon instant yeast	2 teaspoons salt
	⅔ cup (5¼ ounces) cool (approximately 60°F) water

TO MAKE THE POOLISH Combine the flour, water, and yeast in a medium-sized mixing bowl and mix just until blended. Let the poolish rise for 12 hours or so (overnight is usually just fine). It should dome slightly on top and look aerated and spongy. Try to catch it before it starts to fall, as it will be at its optimum flavor and vigor when it's at its highest point. On the other hand, don't make yourself crazy about this; we've used plenty of starters that are either pre- or post-prime and they work fine.

FOR THE DOUGH Place the flour, yeast, and salt in a mixing bowl, the bucket of your bread machine, the work bowl of a food processor, or the bowl of an electric mixer. Add the poolish and water and mix the dough until it just becomes cohesive, about 30 seconds (it's okay if there's still flour in the bottom of the bowl). Cover and let the dough rest for 20 minutes. This resting period allows the flour to absorb the liquid, which will make kneading much easier. (If you're using a bread machine, simply program it for dough, then cancel it once the ingredients are fairly mixed.)

Knead the dough, using your hands or a mixer, until it's cohesive and elastic but not perfectly smooth; the surface should still exhibit some roughness. You'll want to knead this dough less than you think you should; while it will shape itself into a ball, it won't have the characteristic "baby's bottom" smoothness of fully kneaded dough. You aren't kneading this dough all the way because you'll give it a nice long rise, and during that rising time the gluten continues to develop. If you kneaded the dough fully before rising, the gluten would become unpleasantly stiff during the long rise.

Transfer the dough to a lightly oiled bowl (or oil your mixer bowl and leave it in there). Cover and let it rise for 2 hours, folding it over after the first hour (or more frequently if the dough is very slack or wet; folding helps strengthen the gluten). To fold the dough, lift it out of the bowl, gently deflate it, fold it in half, and place it back in the bowl; this expels excess carbon dioxide and redistributes the yeast's food.

Divide the dough into three pieces and gently form them into rough logs. Let them rest for 20 minutes, then shape into long (13- to 14-inch) thin baguettes. Proof the baguettes, covered, in the folds of a linen or cotton couche (see Tools, p. 591) until they've become noticeably puffy, 30 to 40 minutes. If you don't have a couche, place them in a perforated triple baguette pan, or on a lightly greased or parchment-lined baking sheet, and cover them lightly with a proof cover or greased plastic wrap.

Preheat the oven and baking stone to 500°F. (Baguettes baked on a stone will have a crispier crust, but those baked on a pan will be just as tasty, if not equally crunchy.) Just before putting the loaves into the oven, use a lame (see Tools, p. 592) or sharp serrated knife to gently make four diagonal cuts in each loaf. These cuts should angle into the dough at about 45 degrees (in other words, don't cut straight down) and should be a good ¼ inch deep. Be gentle but quick; if you hesitate and drag your lame or knife through the dough, it will stick rather than cut.

Spray the loaves heavily with warm water; this will somewhat replicate a steam oven. (For other ways to create steam, see p. 277.) Put the loaves in the oven. Reduce the oven heat to 475°F and bake the loaves for 20 minutes or so. Remove the loaves from the oven when they're a deep golden brown and transfer them to a wire rack to cool. Listen closely just as you take the loaves out of the oven; you'll hear them "sing," crackling as they hit the cool air of your kitchen. Let the loaves cool completely before slicing; if you can't wait, understand that the texture of the loaves where you cut them may be gummy as they still contain moisture, which will migrate out as they cool.

nutrition information per serving   two 1-inch slices, 39g

76 cal | 2g protein | 16g complex carbohydrates | 16g dietary fiber | 214mg sodium | 35mg potassium | 1mg iron | 1mg calcium | 24mg phosphorus

Crostini with Basil, Garlic, Goat Cheese, and Sun-Dried Tomato Topping

ABOUT 9 DOZEN CROSTINI

A coarse-grained bread with lots of large uneven holes—typical of Italian ciabatta or some French baguettes—often comes from dough that is very slack, or wet. It's simple to make a slack dough in a mixer or bread machine, and virtually impossible to make one by hand; you'll find the dough is so sticky that it can't be kneaded by hand without adding additional flour, which would change the bread's texture. This dough should never form a ball that cleans the sides of the pan; instead, it should remain sticky. It will mound up as if trying to form a ball, but it never will.

The best way to make bread for crostini is in French baguette pans. The resulting loaves, long and skinny, make bite-sized crostini when sliced into thin rounds, ideal for appetizers. Simply grease the pans and scoop the dough into them, stretching and patting it to fit with lightly greased fingers. There's no need to try to roll the dough into a log and transfer it to the pan; though the stretching and patting method makes a messy looking loaf at first, once it's risen and baked it will be as smooth as any shaped loaf.

CROSTINI LOAVES	TOPPING
2 teaspoons instant yeast	16 ounces goat cheese (plain or herbed)
3 cups (12¾ ounces) unbleached all-purpose flour	3 cups loosely packed fresh basil leaves
1½ teaspoons salt	1 to 1½ heads fresh garlic, cloves separated, peeled, and sliced thin
2 teaspoons granulated sugar	2 to 3 cups (9 to 14 ounces) sun-dried tomato slices packed in oil, drained (snipped in half if large)
1¼ cups (10 ounces) lukewarm water	
¼ cup (1¾ ounces) olive oil	
Coarse semolina or cornmeal for the pan	

TO MAKE THE LOAVES In the bowl of an electric mixer or the bucket of a bread machine, combine all the ingredients, mixing until a rough dough forms. If using a mixer, knead the dough with the flat beater for about 7 minutes; it will become smooth but won't form a ball or clean the sides of the bowl. Transfer the dough to a lightly greased bowl, cover the bowl with lightly greased plastic wrap, and let the dough rise for 1 hour.

Transfer the dough to a lightly oiled work surface. Divide it into three pieces. If you're using a baguette pan, grease the molds of the pan and sprinkle them with coarse semolina or yellow cornmeal. Working with one piece at a time, lay the dough in the pan and stretch and pat it to within 1 inch of each end. Repeat with the remaining pieces of dough. If you're not using a baguette pan, pat the dough as best you can into three 16-inch logs and place them on a two lightly oiled baking sheets. Cover the dough with lightly oiled plastic wrap or a proof cover and set aside to rise until it's very puffy, 1 to 1½ hours.

When the bread has risen, preheat the oven to 425°F. Bake the loaves for 20 to 25 minutes, until they're golden brown. Remove the loaves from the oven and transfer them to a wire rack to cool completely. When the bread is cool, drape it with a cloth towel and let it rest overnight; it needs to be a bit stale before you cut it.

Preheat the oven to 275°F. Slice the bread crosswise into ⅓-inch rounds. Pour a generous coating of olive oil (about ⅛ inch) into a couple of half-sheet pans or two large cookie sheets with sides; use your fingers to spread the oil completely over the bottom of the pans. Put the bread slices in the pans in one layer, as close together as you can get them. Drizzle the slices lightly with olive oil (or spray them with olive oil spray) and bake them for 45 minutes, or until they're very dry and are just beginning to brown. Remove the crostini from the oven and let them cool. If not serving them the same day, store the crostini in an airtight container.

TO MAKE THE TOPPING Note that all of the amounts are approximate. You'll use more or less depending on a variety of factors, including the size of the basil leaves and tomatoes, how thin you slice the garlic, and how generous you are with the cheese. To say nothing of how many crostini you've sampled before even getting to the topping. If you find yourself with leftover topping ingredients, make salad.

Gently crumble the goat cheese into a small bowl. Spread each crostini with 1 teaspoon of cheese, then top with a basil leaf, a slice or slices of garlic, and a sun-dried tomato slice, snipped in half if overly large. Serve immediately; the crostini will get soggy if they wait more than about half an hour. Serve as an appetizer or as part of a large antipasto.

nutrition information per serving   **1 serving, 5 pieces, without the topping, 72g**

185 cal | 10g fat | 7g protein | 16g complex carbohydrates | 1g dietary fiber | 16mg cholesterol | 286mg sodium | 271mg potassium | 360RE vitamin A | 14mg vitamin C | 2mg iron | 75mg calcium | 118mg phosphorus

Crusty Italian Bread

1 BRAIDED LOAF, 16 GENEROUS SLICES

The term "Italian bread" is as uninformative a term as, say, "American soup"—there are as many types of Italian bread as there are regions in Italy, and bakers within those regions. The following recipe will make what Americans would consider a typical Italian loaf: a golden brown, buxom braid, sprinkled with sesame seeds, with a crisp-crunchy crust.

BIGA (STARTER)

1 cup (8 ounces) cool water, about 65°F

2 cups (8½ ounces) unbleached all-purpose flour

¼ teaspoon instant yeast

DOUGH

½ cup (4 ounces) cool water, about 65°F

2 to 2½ cups (8½ to 10½ ounces) unbleached all-purpose flour

2 teaspoons instant yeast

1½ teaspoons salt

TOPPING

1 egg white lightly beaten with 1 tablespoon water

Sesame seeds

FOR THE BIGA Combine all biga ingredients, mixing just until a cohesive dough forms. Cover and let the starter rest for 12 to 16 hours at room temperature. When the biga is ready, it will be filled with craters and large bubbles.

FOR THE DOUGH Add the water to the biga and mix until smooth. Add the flour, yeast, and salt and knead the dough until it's fairly smooth but not necessarily elastic, about 3 minutes by electric mixer, or 5 minutes by hand. (The gluten will continue to develop as the dough rises, so you don't want to develop it fully during the kneading process.)

Place the dough in a lightly greased bowl, cover, and let the dough rise at room temperature for 1½ hours. To help develop the gluten and distribute the yeast's food, gently deflate the dough and turn it over every 30 minutes during the rising time (see illustration, p. 245).

Preheat the oven to 425°F. Divide the dough in thirds and roll each third into a 20-inch-long rope. Braid the ropes. Set the braid on a lightly greased baking sheet, cover, and let rise for 1 to 1½ hours, until just puffy. Gently brush the braid with beaten egg white and sprinkle with sesame seeds. Put the bread in the oven and bake for 25 to 35 minutes. Take the bread out of the oven when its internal temperature reaches 190°F and cool on a rack.

nutrition information per serving   1 slice, 56g

102 cal | 4g protein | 23g complex carbohydrates | 1g dietary fiber | 204mg sodium | 52mg potassium | 2mg iron | 1mg calcium | 35mg phosphorus

Ciabatta

2 LOAVES, 8 SERVINGS EACH

Ciabatta, an airy, white hearth bread from Italy's Lake Como region, receives its name from its appearance: the finished loaf, a fat oval, looks like a homely, comfortably broken-in slipper. Ciabatta embodies the maxim, It takes a slack dough to make light bread: this dough is so slack (wet) that it must be kneaded by machine, not hand.

The texture of this bread is what sets it apart. The interior is soft and porous, with large irregular holes, while the crust is crunchy and crisp, rather than chewy. Serve ciabatta with pasta, where it's a great sauce-mopper. Or use it to make pan bagna ("bathed bread"), Italy's famous stuffed sandwich. To make pan bagna, cut the ciabatta in half to make a top and bottom crust. Brush the cut sides with olive oil, layer on meats, cheeses, and vegetables, then wrap the sandwich and weigh it down for several hours before serving.

BIGA (STARTER)

¼ teaspoon instant yeast

½ cup (4 ounces) water

1½ cups (6¼ ounces) unbleached all-purpose flour

DOUGH

1 teaspoon (a very scant ⅛ ounce) instant yeast

2 teaspoons (⅛ ounce) nonfat dry milk

1½ teaspoons (¼ ounce) salt

¾ cup plus 3 tablespoons (7¾ ounces) water*

1 tablespoon (⅜ ounce) olive oil

2 cups (8½ ounces) unbleached all-purpose flour

TO MAKE THE BIGA Mix all the ingredients in a medium-sized bowl, cover the bowl, and let it rest for about 12 hours, or overnight.

FOR THE DOUGH Use your fingers to pull the biga into walnut-sized pieces, and place the pieces into the bowl of an electric mixer. Add the yeast, dry milk, salt, and water and beat slowly with a flat beater paddle or beaters for about 3 minutes. Replace the beater paddle with the dough hook(s), increase the speed to medium, and knead for 10 minutes. The dough should be very sticky and slack. Transfer the dough to a lightly greased bowl or dough-rising bucket, cover the bowl or bucket, and let the dough rise for 2 to 3 hours, gently deflating it and turning it over every 45 minutes or so.

TO SHAPE THE LOAVES Transfer the dough to a lightly greased work surface and use a bench knife or dough scraper to divide it in half. Working with one half at a time, shape the dough into a rough log. Transfer the log to a parchment-lined baking sheet, or one sprinkled with cornmeal or semolina, and flatten it into an irregular 10 x 4-inch oval. Use your fingers—your entire finger, not just the tip—to indent the surface of the dough vigorously and thoroughly. Repeat with the remaining piece of dough. Cover the loaves with heavily greased plastic wrap or a proof cover, and set them aside to rise until very puffy, 2 to 3 hours, depending on the warmth of your kitchen.

1. The dough will be wet and sticky. **2–3.** Gently deflating the dough and turning it over will help to develop its gluten. **4.** Pat the dough into a rough oval about 10 inches long and 4 inches wide. Press into the dough with your fingers to dimple it, as shown.

BAKING THE BREAD Half an hour before you want to bake the bread, preheat the oven to 425°F. Spritz water into the oven with a clean plant mister for about 5 seconds. Place the bread in the oven and spritz water into the oven three more times during the first 10 minutes of baking. Bake the loaves for a total of about 25 minutes, or until they're a deep golden brown and their interior temperature measures 210°F. Remove the loaves from the pan and return them to the oven. Turn off the oven, crack the door open a couple of inches, and let the loaves cool completely in the oven. Dust the loaves generously with flour.

*Use an additional 2 to 3 tablespoons of water in the winter, or in very dry weather conditions.

nutrition information per serving   **1 slice, 51g**

103 cal | 1g fat | 3g protein | 20g complex carbohydrates | 1g dietary fiber | 269 mg sodium | 45mg potassium | 2RE vitamin A | 1mg iron | 5mg calcium | 31mg phosphorus

Swedish Limpa

1 LARGE ROUND LOAF

This orange- and spice-scented Swedish rye is a favorite at the smorgasbord table. It's especially delightful toasted and spread with sweet butter.

2 cups (8½ ounces) unbleached bread flour

½ cup (2½ ounces) whole wheat flour

½ cup (2 ounces) pumpernickel

¼ cup (2¾ ounces) dark corn syrup

2½ teaspoons instant yeast

1½ teaspoons each: caraway, fennel, and aniseed

¼ teaspoon orange oil, or 1 tablespoon orange zest

1½ teaspoons salt

¼ cup (1¼ ounces) nonfat dry milk

1 to 1¼ cups (8 to 10 ounces) water

4 tablespoons (2 ounces) butter or vegetable oil

In a large bowl, combine all the ingredients until a rough dough forms, then knead (about 10 minutes by hand, 5 to 7 minutes by machine) until the dough is smooth and satiny. Transfer the dough to a lightly greased bowl, cover the bowl with lightly greased plastic wrap, and let the dough rise for 1 hour. It will become somewhat puffy, but probably won't double in bulk.

Shape the dough into a slightly flattened ball and place it on a lightly greased or parchment-lined baking sheet. Cover with a proof cover or lightly greased plastic wrap and let it rise for 1¼ to 1½ hours, until it's puffed up noticeably.

Preheat the oven to 350°F. Place the bread in the oven and bake for 35 minutes, tenting it with aluminum foil for the final 10 minutes if it appears to be browning too fast. When the internal temperature reaches 190°F, remove it from the oven and cool on a rack.

nutrition information per serving   1 slice, 54g

139 cal | 4g fat | 4g protein | 20g complex carbohydrates | 4g sugar | 2g dietary fiber | 9mg cholesterol | 220mg sodium | 120mg potassium | 38RE vitamin A | 1mg vitamin C | 1mg iron | 38mg calcium | 86mg phosphorus

Yeasted Flatbreads

Yeasted flatbreads are familiar to cultures all over the world. From Middle Eastern pita, to French fougassse, to that most familiar and beloved flatbread of all—pizza— these loaves are short in stature but broad in their appeal. Flatbreads come in two types: those that are given yeast and encouraged to rise, and those that aren't. These flatbreads have the unmistakable flavor and texture that comes from yeast (for other flatbreads, see "Crackers and Flatbreads" chapter).

The majority of flatbreads are topped with seeds, herbs, and spices, or any of a wide array of vegetables, cheeses, even fruit. Or they're designed, like pita, to be split and filled once they're out of the oven. One thing all these breads have in common is their suggestion of community; when you serve a big, table-dominating flatbread, it demands a crowd, pulling off pieces, reaching across one another, talking and laughing and enjoying the meal, and one another.

Now or Later Pizza

TWO 10- TO 13-INCH PIZZAS, 8 SLICES EACH

Of all the pizzas we've made over the years, this recipe is our favorite. An overnight rest for the dough in the refrigerator gives the crust superb flavor and a delightfully crisp-chewy texture.

DOUGH

1¾ cups (7⅞ ounces) unbleached all-purpose flour*

1¼ cups (7⅛ ounces) semolina*

2 tablespoons dough relaxer (optional, but helpful)

1 teaspoon instant yeast

1½ teaspoons salt

2 tablespoons (¾ ounce) olive oil

1¼ to 1½ cups (10 to 12 ounces) water

TOPPINGS

Tomato sauce, cooked meats, vegetables, and cheeses of your choice

Mix and knead together all the dough ingredients—by hand or mixer—until you've created a smooth, soft dough. Don't overknead the dough; it should hold together but look fairly rough on the surface.

Cover and let the dough rise for 45 minutes, then refrigerate it for 4 hours (or up to 36 hours); this step will develop the crust's flavor.

Divide the dough in half. Shape each half into a 9- to 12-inch round (thicker or thinner crust) and place each on a piece of parchment paper cut to fit. Cover the dough and let it rest while you heat the oven (and baking stone) to 500°F.

After about 30 minutes, use a giant spatula or pizza peel to transfer the pizzas and parchment to your hot oven stone; or place the pizzas and parchment on a pan and place the pan on the middle rack of the oven. Bake for 4 minutes, then remove from the oven.

TO MAKE YOUR PIZZA NOW Top the pizza with your favorite toppings, return to the lowest rack of the oven (not to the stone), and bake for an additional 8 minutes, or until the crust is golden brown and the filling bubbly.

TO MAKE YOUR PIZZA LATER Remove the parchment, cool the un-topped crusts, wrap them well in plastic wrap, and refrigerate (for up to 5 days) or freeze (for up to 4 weeks). When you're ready to serve remove the crusts from the refrigerator or freezer and heat the oven to 450°F. Top them with your favorite toppings and place them on a parchment-lined or greased baking sheet, then into the oven. Bake the pizzas on the lowest rack of the oven (not on a stone) for 8 minutes, or until the crust is golden brown and the filling bubbly.

*Use a total of 3 cups all-purpose flour if you don't have semolina.

nutrition information per serving   **1 slice without toppings, 51g**

110 cal | 2g fat | 3g protein | 19g complex carbohydrates | 1g dietary fiber | 272mg sodium | 62mg potassium | 5RE vitamin A | 1mg iron,15mg calcium | 41mg phosphorus

No-Knead Deep-Dish Pizza

1 THICK-CRUST PIZZA, 6 SERVINGS

High-rising and soft (rather than chewy/crusty), this pizza is a favorite of kids.

DOUGH

1¼ cups (10 ounces) lukewarm water

2¾ cups (11⅝ ounces) unbleached all-purpose flour*

½ cup (2⅞ ounces) semolina flour*

2 tablespoons (¾ ounce) olive oil

2 teaspoons instant yeast

1½ teaspoons salt

TOPPINGS

1 cup (8 ounces) of your favorite pizza sauce

2 teaspoons mixed dried Italian herbs

1½ cups (6 ounces) grated cheese of your choice

additional toppings of your choice

Grease (or oil with olive oil) a 9 x 13-inch or 12 x 12-inch pan. In a medium-sized bowl, stir together the dough ingredients to form a slightly sticky soft dough. Cover and let the dough rise for 30 minutes, then place it in the pan. Let it rest for 10 to 15 minutes, then pat and stretch it to cover the bottom of the pan. Let it rest, covered, for 30 minutes.

Preheat the oven to 425°F. Spread the sauce on the pizza and bake it for 15 minutes. Remove from the oven and add the seasoning, cheese, and toppings. Return it to the oven and bake for an additional 10 to 15 minutes, until the cheese is bubbly and the edges are golden brown. Remove from the oven and serve warm.

*Use a total of 3¼ cups all-purpose flour if you don't have semolina.

nutrition information per serving   **1 slice with sauce and cheese, 152g**

204 cal | 12g fat | 9g protein | 16g total carbohydrate | 1g sugar | 2g dietary fiber | 22mg cholesterol | 909mg sodium | 261mg potassium | 123RE vitamin A | 3 mg vitamin C | 1mg iron | 155 mg calcium | 171 mg phosphorus

Portable Pizza

1 PIZZA, 8 SLICES

Pizza comes under the heading of Things We Never Get Tired Of, like chocolate cake and Chinese food and ice cream. But how can you enjoy pizza at a picnic? By making it portable. This pizza has a top crust to keep the filling soft, delicious, and contained.

This double-crust pizza is spectacular right out of the oven, the bubbly filling nesting inside a crisp, chewy crust. Later, it becomes more like a sandwich—less crisp, but still chewy and delicious.

POOLISH (STARTER)	DOUGH
1 cup (4¼ ounces) unbleached all-purpose flour	2¼ cups (9½ ounces) unbleached all-purpose flour
½ cup (4 ounces) water	¾ cup (6 ounces) water
⅛ teaspoon instant yeast	1 teaspoon instant yeast
	1 teaspoon sugar
	1¼ teaspoons salt
	1 tablespoon olive oil

FOR THE POOLISH In a mixing bowl, stir together the flour, ½ cup water, and ⅛ teaspoon yeast. Set aside, covered, to rest at room temperature for 6 to 12 hours (overnight is fine).

FOR THE DOUGH Add the flour and water to the poolish, mix well, and let it rest for 20 minutes. Add the remaining dough ingredients, mixing and kneading briefly to form a semi-smooth dough. The dough should be slightly sticky and soft feeling and may still have a rough surface. We recommend kneading about 5 minutes in an electric mixer, 6 or 7 minutes by hand. Cover and let the dough rise for 45 minutes; gently fold the edges to the middle, turn it over, and let it rise an additional 45 minutes. Prepare your choice of fillings while the dough is rising for the second time.

TO ASSEMBLE THE PIZZA Divide the dough in half. Roll one half into a 14-inch circle. Place it in a lightly greased round pizza pan, or on a lightly greased or parchment-lined pan big enough to hold it. Top with the filling of your choice, leaving a ½-inch margin around the edge of the dough. Roll the second piece of dough into a 14-inch circle. Place it over the top of the filling, pressing down all over. Pull the edges of the bottom dough up and over the edges of the top dough and press together to seal. Cut several small holes in the top to allow steam to escape while baking. Let the pizza rest and rise for 20 minutes.

Preheat the oven to 500°F. Bake the pizza for 30 to 35 minutes, until it's golden brown all over. Let it cool for about 5 minutes before cutting so the filling has time to settle.

Spinach and Cheese Filling

10 ounces fresh spinach (about 8 cups, cleaned and torn), or two 10-ounce packages frozen chopped spinach, thawed and thoroughly squeezed dry

3 tablespoons (1¼ ounces) olive oil

2 garlic cloves, peeled and minced

4 cups (11 ounces) mushrooms, washed and sliced

½ teaspoon salt

1 teaspoon coarsely ground black pepper

1 cup (4 ounces) crumbled feta cheese

½ cup (2½ ounces) kalamata olives, pitted and sliced (optional)

Clean and remove the stems from the spinach. Heat a large skillet until hot, add the oil and garlic, then immediately add the mushrooms. Stir with a heatproof spatula; the mushrooms will begin to give off their juice. After about 2 minutes, add the spinach, salt, and pepper. Cook just enough to wilt the spinach. Add the feta and olives. Remove the pan from the stove and set aside until you're ready to use the filling.

nutrition information per serving spinach filling, 1 slice, 215g

356 cal | 15g fat | 12g protein | 44g complex carbohydrates | 1g sugar | 4g dietary fiber | 25mg cholesterol | 991mg sodium | 419mg potassium | 318RE vitamin A | 7mg vitamin C | 5mg iron | 207mg calcium | 210mg phosphorus

Ricotta and Basil Filling

1½ cups (12 ounces) ricotta cheese (part skim is fine)

1 lightly packed cup fresh basil, shredded

1 large (about 8 ounces) green or red pepper, seeded and chopped

½ teaspoon salt

1 teaspoon black pepper

2 garlic cloves, peeled and crushed

¾ cup (3 ounces) shredded Parmesan cheese

1 cup (4 ounces) shredded cheddar cheese

1 cup (2¾ ounces) golden baking onions or French fried onions (optional)

Mix the ricotta with the cleaned and shredded fresh basil. Add the diced peppers, salt, black pepper, garlic, cheeses, and onions. Set aside.

nutrition information per serving ricotta filling, 1 large slice, 187g

359 cal | 12g fat | 17g protein | 43g complex carbohydrates | 2g dietary fiber | 35mg cholesterol | 743mg sodium | 278mg potassium | 123RE vitamin A | 15mg vitamin C | 4mg iron | 331mg calcium | 277mg phosphorus

Pita Bread

8 PITAS

Pita bread is one of those things (like English muffins and soft pretzels) that most people simply don't think of making. "It's too hard. It won't work. They won't puff up." Baloney. This is just a simple white bread recipe cooked in an unusual way. They will puff up, and fresh, golden pita bread, hot from the oven, is a revelation. It makes those packaged pitas pale (literally) by comparison.

3 cups (12¾ ounces) unbleached all-purpose flour

2 teaspoons instant yeast

2 teaspoons dough relaxer*

2 teaspoons sugar

1½ teaspoons salt

1 cup (8 ounces) water

2 tablespoons (⅞ ounce) vegetable oil

In a large mixing bowl, or in the bowl of an electric mixer, combine all the ingredients, mixing to form a shaggy dough. Knead the dough by hand (10 minutes) or by machine (5 minutes) until it's smooth. Place the dough in a lightly greased bowl and let it rest for 1 hour. It will become quite puffy, though it may not double in bulk.

Turn the dough onto a lightly oiled work surface and divide it into eight pieces. Roll two to four of the pieces into 6-inch circles (the number of pieces depends on how many rolled-out pieces at a time can fit on your baking sheet). Place the circles on a lightly greased baking sheet and let them rest, uncovered, for 15 minutes.

Preheat the oven to 500°F. (Keep the unrolled pieces of dough covered. Roll out the next batch while the first batch bakes.) Place the baking sheet on the lowest rack in the oven and bake the pitas for 5 minutes; they should puff up. (If they haven't puffed up, wait a minute or so longer. If they still haven't puffed, your oven isn't hot enough; raise the heat for the next batch.) Transfer the baking sheet to the oven's middle-to-top rack and bake for an additional 2 minutes, or until the pitas have browned. Remove the pitas from the oven, wrap them in a clean dish towel (this keeps them soft), and repeat with the remaining dough. Store cooled pitas in an airtight container or plastic bag.

*Optional, but it relaxes the dough's gluten, allowing you to roll it into pita shapes much more easily. Also, the bit of baking powder in the relaxer helps puff up the pitas.

nutrition information per serving   1 pita bread, 83g

187 cal | 4g fat | 5g protein | 33g complex carbohydrates | 1g sugar | 1g dietary fiber | 401mg sodium | 2mg iron | 79mg calcium | 49mg phosphorus

Tender Focaccia

TWO 8-INCH ROUND OR ONE 12- TO 14-INCH ROUND FOCACCIA, 12 SERVINGS

This focaccia, whose crumb is softened by the addition of both potato flour and dry milk, is ideal for slicing and turning into stuffed sandwiches. For a chewier, flatter focaccia, simply use the dough for the Now or Later Pizza (p. 247), substituting a drizzle of olive oil for the pizza toppings; sprinkle with coarse salt and fresh or dried rosemary once it's out of the oven, if desired.

2 cups (16 ounces) boiling water

3¾ cups (16 ounces) unbleached all-purpose flour

¼ cup (1½ ounces) potato flour, or ⅓ cup (¾ ounce) potato flakes

¼ cup (1¼ ounces) nonfat dry milk

2½ teaspoons instant yeast

1½ teaspoons salt

2 tablespoons (⅞ ounce) olive oil, plus 2 to 3 tablespoons to grease the pan and the surface of the dough

¼ to ½ teaspoon kosher salt, sea salt, or Fleur de Sel, for topping

Put the hot water and 2 cups of the flour in a large bowl and beat for several minutes to develop a smooth batter. If you have the time, add ⅛ teaspoon yeast once the batter has cooled to lukewarm, and set the sponge aside for several hours or overnight; this helps develop flavor in the finished loaf, as well as the soft interior texture.

Whisk the potato flour with the remaining flour, dry milk, yeast, and salt. Add this to the batter a little at a time, while continuing to beat. Add 2 tablespoons of olive oil. Beat, by hand with a large spoon or with the paddle attachment of a mixer set at medium speed, for 8 to 10 minutes, changing to a dough hook when the dough begins to hold together.

After the dough has become smooth and shiny, put it in an oiled bowl, cover it with a damp towel or plastic wrap, and let it rise for 30 minutes. The dough should have increased by about one third and be puffy-looking. Don't punch down the dough, but pull the sides of the dough up and over in a folding motion. Do this several times to release some of the gas, then let the dough rise for another 30 minutes.

Drizzle 2 tablespoons of olive oil into a 12- or 14-inch round pan, or 1 tablespoon olive oil into each of two 8-inch round pans. Place the dough in the oiled pan(s), gently stretching it to fit. Let the dough rest for 30 minutes, then stretch it out a little more. At this point you may refrigerate the dough in the pan(s), tightly covered, for up to 24 hours.

Preheat the oven to 400°F.

Just before baking the focaccia, dimple it with your fingers, brush it with a little olive oil, and sprinkle it with coarse salt or a few sprigs of fresh herb. Bake the focaccia for 25 to 30 minutes, until it's deep brown all over. Remove it from the pan(s) and cool it for 15 minutes before eating. Serve with flavored olive oil, or split for sandwiches.

180 cal | 5g fat | 5g protein | 31g complex carbohydrates | 1g dietary fiber | 1mg cholesterol | 283 mg sodium |
161mg potassium | 12RE vitamin A | 1mg vitamin C | 3mg iron | 34mg calcium | 70mg phosphorus

Dimpling Dough

What does it mean to dimple dough? It's simply using your fingertips to poke fairly deep indentations in the dough; it's a technique used on both ciabatta and focaccia, to give them their distinctive craggy appearance (see illustration, p. 245).

The trick is to be firm, yet gentle. You'll be poking risen dough; you don't want to deflate it. Don't punch the dough with your fingers; rather, lay a fingertip against the dough and press down until it's about half to two-thirds of the way to the bottom of the dough. Repeat until the dough is marked all over with indentations (not holes) at about 1½-inch intervals. Don't worry if the dough loses a bit of its loft during this process; it's almost inevitable. What you don't want is total deflation.

Blue Cheese and Walnut Fougasse

1 LOAF, 16 SERVINGS

Fougasse, (pronounced foo-GOSS) a specialty of Provence, France, is made from a pain ordinaire dough—a basic flour/water/yeast/salt dough—into which is incorporated fresh herbs, nuts, cheese, anchovies, raisins, or any other combination of like ingredients that sounds enticing. The dough is shaped into an oval and allowed to rise partway, at which point it receives three to four diagonal slashes, completely through the dough, and is pulled apart at the slashes, forming a rough ladder shape. After completing its rise it's baked in a hot oven until golden brown. The finished loaf is delicious as is, with no need for butter or other toppings. The special shaping method results in a loaf with more brown crunchy crust than an ordinary loaf, so fougasse is a special treat for those of us who love crust.

The following recipe is for our favorite pain ordinaire dough, and an assertive blue cheese filling. We add sugar, which helps the yeast grow and promotes a golden crust, and olive oil, which makes the dough a bit more supple and easier to work with, and also keeps the loaf fresh.

Fougasse can feature any variety of delightful fillings, which can be kneaded directly into the dough, as we've done here, or spread onto half the surface of the rolled-out dough, then covered with the remaining half and reshaped. We feel the direct-add method is easier but, for very messy or wet fillings, you may want to try the spreading version.

This dense, chewy, highly flavored bread is wonderful as is, but serve it with fresh, crunchy apple slices for a special treat.

POOLISH (STARTER)

1 cup (4¼ ounces) unbleached all-purpose flour

½ cup (4 ounces) water

⅛ teaspoon instant yeast

DOUGH

½ cup (4 ounces) water

1½ cups (6¼ ounces) unbleached all-purpose flour

½ cup (2⅝ ounces) whole wheat flour

2 teaspoons instant yeast

1¼ teaspoons salt

2 tablespoons (⅞ ounce) olive oil

FILLING

1 cup (4 ounces) coarsely chopped toasted walnuts

½ cup (about 2½ ounces) crumbled blue cheese

FOR THE POOLISH Combine the flour, water, and yeast, stirring until well combined, and set aside to rest at room temperature, covered, overnight.

FOR THE DOUGH Add the water and flours to the poolish and mix until just combined. Cover the bowl and let the mixture rest for 20 minutes. Add the yeast, salt, and olive oil and knead the dough until it's fairly smooth but not necessarily elastic, about 3 minutes by machine, or 5 minutes by hand. Place the dough in a lightly greased bowl, cover the bowl, and let the dough rise at room temperature for 1½ hours, gently deflating it and turning it over after 45 minutes.

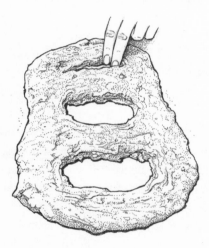

Cut three parallel slashes all the way through the partially risen dough. Stretch open these slashes to form a ladder shape.

Knead in the walnuts and cheese; this will be a messy process, but just stick with it (literally!), and it'll get done. Shape the dough into a 6 x 12-inch oval, place it on a lightly greased baking sheet, and let it rise for about 30 minutes. Cut three deep diagonal slashes (see illustration) all the way through the dough, in the center of the loaf, and pull it apart to form a ladder shape. Let it rise for another 30 to 45 minutes.

Preheat the oven to 400°F. Bake the fougasse for 25 minutes, or until it's light golden brown. Transfer it to a rack to cool.

nutrition information per serving   **1 slice, 51g**

152 cal | 7g fat | 4g protein | 18g complex carbohydrates | 1g dietary fiber | 3mg cholesterol | 303mg sodium | 93mg potassium | 10RE vitamin A | 1 mg iron | 73mg calcium | 89mg phosphorus

Celebration Breads

When you think of Christmas, do you also immediately think of cookies? At Easter, is it homemade chocolates you dream about? In many of the world's cultures, the signature holiday baked good is a traditional yeast bread. In Sweden, for instance, "dipping bread" is a centerpiece at the Christmas Eve smorgasbord. In a ritual called *doppa i grytan*, a piece of rye bread is dipped into a pot of stock in which a variety of meats has been simmered; the bread is then eaten as a reminder to savor the blessings of the land while they're available, for hard times may come. In Italy, the day before Easter is celebrated with Easter Pie, a yeast dough wrapped around all manner of rich meats, eggs, and cheeses, a celebration of the end of Lent (and its culinary deprivations). And what would Christmas in Germany be without a fruit-studded butter-and sugar-gilded stollen?

The following signature celebration breads represent a small sampling of the many ways the world's cultures combine bread and religion. As we said before, bread is at the center of countless food cultures worldwide; at no time is this more evident than at the holidays.

Challah

1 LOAF, ABOUT 16 SLICES

Challah must be one of the world's most revered breads. Rich with eggs and butter (or oil, to keep it kosher with a meat-based meal), shaped in various braids and coils and often gilded with a sprinkle of poppy seeds, this bread is a Sabbath staple. Though not quite as rich, it's similar to French brioche, and like brioche, it makes wonderful toast and French toast.

Challah is usually braided; a three-strand braid is common, but beautiful four- or six-strand braids are almost as popular. It's prepared for the Jewish New Year, Rosh Hashanah; for that occasion, challah is formed into a round coil, symbolizing the continuity of life.

This recipe begins with making a sponge, a quick starter used in recipes that are high in sugar, in order to let the yeast get a head start.

SPONGE

1 cup (4¼ ounces) unbleached all-purpose flour

1 cup (8 ounces) water

2 teaspoons instant yeast

DOUGH

3½ cups (14¾ ounces) unbleached all-purpose flour

1¾ teaspoons salt

⅓ cup (2⅜ ounces) sugar

¼ cup (1¾ ounces) vegetable oil

2 large eggs plus 1 yolk (save 1 egg white for the wash, below)

WASH

1 egg white

1 teaspoon sugar

1 tablespoon water

Poppy seeds (optional)

TO MAKE THE SPONGE   Mix the flour, water, and yeast together in a large bowl and let it sit for about 45 minutes.

TO MAKE THE DOUGH   Add the dough ingredients to the starter and mix and knead together—by hand, mixer, or bread machine—until a smooth, supple dough is formed. This dough is a pleasure to work with—smooth and silky, it almost feels as if you're rubbing your hands with lotion. Place the dough in a greased bowl, turning it over once to coat it lightly with oil. Cover and let rise for 1½ hours, or until it has doubled in size.

TO SHAPE THE DOUGH   Turn the dough out onto a lightly floured surface and fold it over once or twice to gently deflate it. Divide the dough into three or four pieces, depending on what kind of braid you want to make. Roll each into a log; if you've got three pieces, roll each to about 24 inches; for four pieces, roll to about 18 inches each. On a lightly greased or parchment-lined baking sheet, braid a four-strand braid (see illustration).

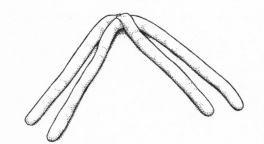

❶

TO MAKE THE WASH   In a small bowl, mix together the reserved egg white, sugar, and water. Brush the loaf with this mixture, reserving some for a second wash. Cover the loaf with lightly greased plastic wrap and let it rise for 45 minutes to 1 hour, until it's almost doubled in size.

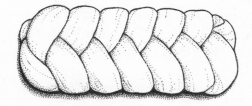

❷   **❸**

1. Pinch the four ropes of dough together at one end, and lay out as shown. **2.** Take the left outside rope and lay it at the inside of the right two strands. Next take the right outside rope and move it to the inside left. Repeat the process, moving the outside piece of dough to the inside of the opposite side, until all the dough has been used. **3.** Pinch the ends together to seal.

Preheat the oven to 375°F. Brush the loaf with the remaining egg wash (this will give the finished loaf a beautiful shiny crust, as well as provide "glue" for the seeds), sprinkle with poppy seeds, if desired, and bake for 35 to 40 minutes, until the challah is lightly browned. Remove it from the oven and cool completely before slicing.

nutrition information per serving   one 1-inch slice, 63g

177 cal | 4g fat | 5g protein | 25g complex carbohydrates | 4g sugar | 1g dietary fiber | 40mg cholesterol | 246mg sodium |
64mg potassium | 18RE vitamin A | 2mg iron | 5mg calcium | 53mg phosphorus

Panettone

1 PANETTONE, ABOUT 24 SLICES

This ubiquitous (at Christmas) sweet bread of Milan is golden, high-rising, and traditionally studded with citron and citrus peel. A sweet bread made with a starter is unusual. The use of a biga—a flour, water and yeast starter, the consistency of a firm bread dough—gives bread added flavor and keeping qualities. We often use a biga when making ciabatta or other Italian loaves; we feel it helps bring out the wheat flavor in breads that might otherwise seem a bit plain. But in a sweet bread—loaded with sugar, butter, and fruit—who needs a biga?

Well, we both do. Panettone made with a biga has a moist fine texture and rises better than anything with that amount of sugar and fat has a right to. Though the dough still needs a big kick of instant yeast, the biga gives it the strength to take off and rise, despite the sugar and fat doing their best to retard the whole process.

The use of a biga makes this panettone traditional. What separates it from the norm is the fruits we use to flavor the bread, and the pan we bake it in. For those of you who turn up your nose at the traditional candied fruits of Christmas—citron, lemon peel, orange peel—we offer this version using dried pineapple, apricots, and golden raisins. And for those who don't have a traditional panettone pan—a tall, round loaf pan—or who've encountered difficulties using such a pan (raw center, burned crust), we suggest the use of a tube or angel food pan.

BIGA (STARTER)

1½ cups (6¼ ounces) unbleached all-purpose flour

½ cup (4 ounces) water

½ teaspoon instant yeast*

DOUGH

3 large eggs

½ cup (1 stick, 4 ounces) unsalted butter, cut into about 10 chunks

2½ cups (10½ ounces) unbleached all-purpose flour

⅓ cup (2½ ounces) granulated sugar

5 teaspoons instant yeast*

1½ teaspoons salt

2 teaspoons vanilla extract

⅛ teaspoon lemon oil

1½ cups (about 9 ounces) dried fruit**

FOR THE BIGA Combine the flour, water and yeast, kneading briefly to make a stiff dough. Place the dough in a lightly greased bowl and let it rise overnight at room temperature, about 12 hours.

FOR THE DOUGH In the bowl of an electric mixer, combine the biga with all the ingredients except the dried fruit. (This dough is very difficult to make by hand; we suggest the use of a machine of some sort.) Knead the dough until it's smooth and supple; it will seem very gummy at first but will come together nicely at the end. Place the dough in a lightly greased bowl and let it rest for 1 hour.

Knead the fruit into the dough, by hand or machine; knead only until the dough accepts the fruit, as overhandling will cause the fruit to release too much sugar into the dough, slowing the rise. Let the dough rest for 10 minutes, then shape it into a log about 24 inches long. Place this log in the bottom of a lightly greased 9- to 10-inch tube pan or angel food pan, cover the pan, and set the dough aside to rise for 2 hours or so. It probably won't double in size but will puff up a bit.

Preheat the oven to 350°F. Bake the panettone for 45 minutes, tenting it with aluminum foil for the final 15 minutes of baking if it appears to be browning too quickly. The internal temperature of the dough should register 190°F to 205°F when it's done. Remove the panettone from the oven, turn it out of the pan, and let cool on a rack.

*Instant yeast formulated for sweet doughs (e.g, SAF Gold Label) is a good selection here. If you use regular instant yeast, you may need to increase the rising times a bit.

**We use a mixture of dried apricots, pineapple, and golden raisins; chopped dates, dark raisins, and toasted walnuts would also seem appropriate, as would dried cranberries and cherries.

nutrition information per serving   one ³/₄-inch slice, 52g

151 cal | 5g fat | 3g protein | 21g complex carbohydrates | 3g sugar | 2g dietary fiber | 45mg cholesterol | 145mg sodium | 192mg potassium | 216RE vitamin A | 2mg iron | 43mg calcium | 49mg phosphorus

Poticza

2 LOAVES, 16 SERVINGS EACH

This traditional Slovakian bread (pronounced po-TEET-sah) features many thin, alternating layers of bread and sugar-nut filling. Each crosswise slice is an intricate combination of light and dark, kind of like the sinuous swirls made by gasoline when a drop falls into a bucket of water. Poticza is served at holidays, particularly Christmas and Easter, and on other "fancy" occasions; while it's a bit time-consuming to make, it keeps well and makes an impressive presentation.

Thankfully, this is a great, easy-to-roll-out dough. Use it as a base for any filling; lekvar and poppy seed are both good choices. And if you don't want to do the folding and rolling required for the traditional loaf, make a simple wreath; we've included instructions for both shapes.

DOUGH

¾ cup (6 ounces) milk

4 tablespoons (½ stick, 2 ounces) butter

¼ cup (1¾ ounces) sugar

1 teaspoon salt

3 cups (12¾ ounces) unbleached all-purpose flour

¼ cup (1½ ounces) potato flour, or ⅓ cup (¾ ounce) potato flakes (optional)

2½ teaspoons instant yeast

2 teaspoons vanilla extract

2 large eggs

FILLING

2 cups (8 ounces) chopped nuts*

3 cups (10½ ounces) pecan meal (finely ground pecans)

1 cup (7 ounces) sugar

3 tablespoons Instant ClearJel, or ⅓ cup (1⅜ ounces) unbleached all-purpose flour

Pinch of salt

½ teaspoon cardamom (optional)

1 teaspoon ground cinnamon

3 large eggs

FOR THE DOUGH Heat the milk in a small saucepan set over medium heat or in a microwave until small bubbles form around the edge and it starts to steam; this is "scalding" the milk. Add the butter and stir until it melts. Set the mixture aside to cool to lukewarm.

In a large bowl, whisk together the sugar, salt, flours, and yeast. Add the cooled milk, vanilla, and eggs. Mix and knead (by hand or electric mixer) until the dough is smooth and supple, adding additional liquid or flour as needed. The dough may be quite sticky at first; resist the urge to add more flour until you've kneaded for a while. When the dough forms a smooth ball, put it in a greased bowl, turn to coat all sides, then cover with a damp cloth. Set the dough aside to rest in a warm place for about 1 hour. The dough does not need to double but should seem puffy. If it hasn't showed any signs of rising, give it another hour. Make the filling while the dough is rising.

TO MAKE THE FILLING Preheat the oven to 350°F. Lightly toast the nuts by spreading them on an ungreased baking sheet and baking them for 6 to 8 minutes, until they smell toasty and are starting to brown. Set them aside to cool.

Finely chop the nuts (about ⅛-inch dice; a food processor works well here). Mix the nuts with the pecan meal, sugar, ClearJel, salt, and spices; whisk until well blended. Add the eggs, then stir well. The mixture will now be a stiff paste. Cover and refrigerate until you're ready to use it.

ASSEMBLY AND BAKING Lightly grease or flour your work surface. Roll the dough into a 14 x 28-inch rectangle about ⅛ inch thick. Cut the dough into two pieces, each 14 x 14 inches in size. Spread each piece with half the nut mixture. Working with one piece at a time, use a piece of parchment paper or waxed paper to cover the nut mixture and press it down with a rolling pin until it's evenly spread across the dough. Remove the paper and fold two opposite sides in 1 inch toward the center. Fold each side over two more times, then once again; they should meet in the middle. Fold the ends over onto themselves so that they also meet in the center. You should now have a loaf. Repeat with the remaining piece of dough.

Grease two 8½ x 4½-inch loaf pans. Turn the loaves seam side down (smooth side up) and place them in the greased pans, tucking the ends under. Cover the loaves and let them rise for 1½ to 2 hours; the dough should look puffy and should have crowned to the top of the pan.

Preheat the oven to 350°F.

Bake the poticza for 40 to 50 minutes. After the bread has baked for 15 minutes, brush or spritz it lightly with water, then sprinkle it with granulated or coarse sugar. Tent the bread with aluminum foil after 30 minutes if it's browning too fast. Remove the bread from the oven when its internal temperature registers 195°F on an instant-read thermometer. Let the loaves cool in the pan for about 10 minutes, then loosen the edges (if necessary) and turn them out onto a rack to cool completely. After the loaves have cooled and you've cut them, you'll see the unique pattern of the filling.

*A combination of walnuts, pecans, and hazelnuts is good, but choose whichever nuts you prefer.

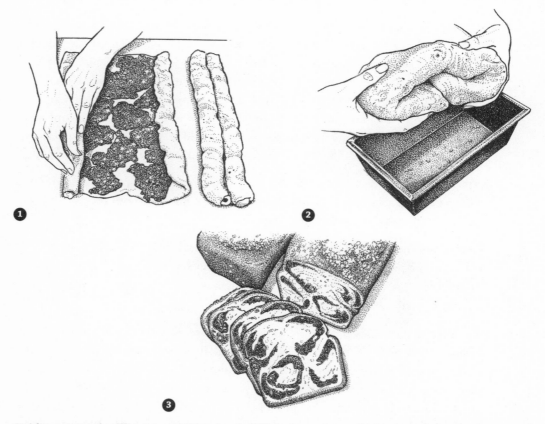

1. After putting the filling on top of the dough, fold the long edges an inch toward the center. Repeat this twice more. **2.** Turn the ends of the folded rectangle under to meet in the center; this will form a loaf shape. **3.** Folding the dough in this manner gives a distinct pattern to the finished loaf.

one ½-inch slice, 109g

213 cal | 13g fat | 4g protein | 13g complex carbohydrates | 8g sugar | 2g dietary fiber | 37mg cholesterol | 81mg sodium | 132mg potassium | 33RE vitamin A | 1mg vitamin C | 1mg iron | 23mg calcium | 86mg phosphorus

Wreath variation Roll the dough into a 16 x 28-inch rectangle and cut it into two 16 x 14-inch pieces. Follow the directions above for spreading the filling then, starting with a long edge, roll each piece into a log. Place the logs on parchment-lined or lightly greased baking sheets and shape each into a circle (wreath), pinching the ends together. Cover and let them rise for 1½ hours, or until they've grown by at least one-third.

Preheat the oven to 350°F. Just before placing the wreaths in the oven, use scissors or sharp knife to cut V shapes into them at about 3-inch intervals. (Hold the scissors vertically above the loaf with the blades open about ½ inch. Stab down into the loaf about 1 inch, then bring the scissor blades together.)

Bake the wreaths for 30 to 40 minutes, until they're golden brown and an instant-read thermometer inserted in the center reads 195°F. Remove them from the oven and drizzle with the sugar glaze or icing of your choice, or brush with melted butter and sprinkle with sugar.

Almond Stollen

THREE LOAVES, 10 SERVINGS EACH

You may, at some holiday season in your life, have encountered a tough, ultra-dry little nugget of bread stuffed with noxious-colored and horrid-tasting bits of candied fruit. Ah, stollen, poor misunderstood child of the American Christmas scene! This German yeasted coffee bread, when made the right way, is a delightful mixture of dense, flavorful bread and bits of tasty dried fruit wrapped in a butter-brushed, sugar-dusted coat. What's not to like? Well, if it's been made with cheap ingredients; or not made well; or made well but allowed to go stale, it's not going to present a very good face to the public. But catch a good stollen when it's fresh and you'll understand why this bread has been a staple of German Christmases for centuries.

We especially like this recipe because it includes a luscious almond paste filling. If you're not a fan of almond paste or marzipan, just leave it out.

DOUGH

1 cup (6 ounces) golden raisins

1 cup (5 to 6 ounces) chopped dried fruits of your choice

2 tablespoons brandy or dark rum, or apple or cranberry juice

¾ cup (6 ounces) milk

2 cups (8 ounces) unbleached pastry flour

2 teaspoons instant yeast

3 large eggs

3 cups (12¾ ounces) unbleached all-purpose flour

⅓ cup (2⅜ ounces) sugar

1 teaspoon salt

1 tablespoon lemon zest

¼ teaspoon lemon oil

1 teaspoon ground cinnamon

1 teaspoon vanilla extract

6 tablespoons (3 ounces) butter, softened

½ cup (2 ounces) slivered almonds, lightly toasted

ALMOND FILLING

1 cup (8 ounces) almond paste*

½ cup (2 ounces) confectioners' sugar*

1 cup (3½ ounces) fresh bread crumbs

2 tablespoons (1 ounce) butter

⅛ teaspoon bitter almond oil or extract, or 1 teaspoon almond extract (optional)

3 tablespoons (1½ ounces) butter, melted

1 cup (4 ounces) confectioners' sugar

In a small bowl, toss together the golden raisins and mixed fruit with the brandy. Set the fruits aside for several hours. In a saucepan set over medium heat or in a microwave, scald the milk (see instructions on p. 259), then cool it to lukewarm.

In a medium-sized mixing bowl, stir together the milk, pastry flour, and yeast. Cover the wet, sticky dough with a damp cloth or plastic wrap. Set it aside in a warm place to triple in size, about 2 hours. The dough will become puffy, but also will look as if it's slightly curdled, which is okay.

Put the eggs, all-purpose flour, sugar, salt, lemon zest and oil, cinnamon, and vanilla in a large bowl, or the bowl of a stand mixer. Add the first dough mixture and begin to mix on slow speed. The dough will seem dry at first, but will start to come together after several minutes of mixing. Add the softened butter and continue mixing until the dough becomes shiny and elastic. This will take 6 to 8 minutes using a dough hook on a stand mixer, or 10 to 12 minutes of kneading by hand. Add the fruits and nuts and knead until they're evenly distributed. Place the kneaded dough into a well-greased bowl, cover the bowl, and let the dough rise for 45 minutes; it won't look much different that when it started its rise.

Remove the dough from the bowl and divide it into three pieces. Round each piece into a rough ball and let the dough rest, covered, for 15 minutes or so.

TO MAKE THE FILLING In a medium-sized mixing bowl, mix together the almond paste, confectioners' sugar, bread crumbs, butter, and almond extract. Divide the filling into three pieces and roll each piece into a log about 6 inches in length and ¾ inch in diameter. Note: It helps to use confectioners' sugar to dust the mixture to keep it from sticking to your fingers or the work surface.

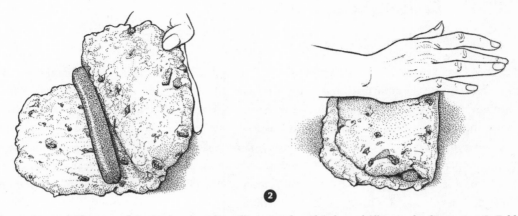

1. After making a shallow trough in the dough with a rolling pin, place the almond filling in the depression. **2.** Fold the dough over the filling, and press with the heel of your hand to seal it to make the traditional stolen shape.

Lightly dust your work surface with flour. Pat each ball of dough into a 7 x 8-inch oval. Use a rolling pin to make the crosswise center of the oval thinner than the edges. Place a log of filling about a third of the way from one short side of the dough (at the edge between where the dough is still fat and where you've rolled it thinner; see illustration. Grasping the short edge of the stollen farthest away from the filling, bring it across the filling to meet the other short edge. Just behind where the two edges come together, press firmly with the heel of your hand to seal (see illustration); this will allow the front of the stollen to open up somewhat, giving it its traditional shape. Repeat with the remaining pieces of dough.

Set the stollen on a lightly greased or parchment-lined baking sheet. Cover them lightly with a damp cloth or with a proof cover. Let them rise for 45 minutes; they won't seem to do much, but this rising period is important for the slightly lighter texture it lends, as well as added tenderness.

Preheat the oven to 350°F. Bake the stollen for 25 to 30 minutes, until they're very lightly browned. An instant-read thermometer inserted into the center of the dough (not the filling) should read 195°F, and the stollen should feel firm. Remove the stollen from the oven and transfer them carefully (they're very tender when hot) to a wire rack to cool for 10 minutes. Brush the stollen with melted butter and sprinkle them with confectioners' sugar. Let them cool, then dust them with sugar again. Wrap them well, first in plastic wrap then in aluminum foil. Stollen improves with mellowing for a few days in a cool, dry place.

*You may substitute marzipan. If you do, omit the sugar.

nutrition information per serving   **1 slice, ¹⁄₁₀ of loaf, 65g**

224 cal | 8g fat | 5g protein | 24g complex carbohydrates | 9g sugar | 1g dietary fiber | 34mg cholesterol | 135mg sodium | 214 potassium | 121RE vitamin A | 1mg vitamin C | 2mg iron | 45mg calcium | 95mg phosphorus

Italian Easter Pie

TWO 10- TO 12-INCH PIES, 8 SLICES EACH

Easter pie (as in "pizza pie," rather than, say, "cherry pie")—both its preparation and its consumption—is a venerable tradition in most Italian, and many American-Italian homes. Served through the three-day Easter holiday (Holy Saturday, Easter Sunday, Easter Monday), Easter pie is the antidote to a long Lenten season of fasting. A wonderful combination of eggs, meat, and cheese stuffed between a couple of thin layers of yeast dough, this pie is good hot, cold, or at room temperature; as a main course, an appetizer, or snack. The following recipe makes a pie that's comforting in its simplicity; the mild ricotta, sharp Parmesan, smoky ham, and the textural element of hard-boiled eggs strike just the right balance.

The glaze is interesting; it's very sweet, but it's applied in such a thin layer that the end result is each bite of pie having just a touch of sweetness, which very nicely complements the saltiness of the ham.

CRUST

4¾ cups (20 ounces) unbleached all-purpose flour, or 2½ cups (10½ ounces) unbleached all-purpose flour plus 2½ cups (10 ounces) unbleached pastry flour

2 teaspoons salt

2 teaspoons instant yeast

2 tablespoons (⅞ ounce) sugar

¼ cup (1¼ ounces) dough relaxer (optional)

¼ cup (1¾ ounces) olive oil

1½ cups (12 ounces) warm water

FILLING

1 dozen large eggs

1 pound good-quality, full-flavored ham*

1 cup (about 8 ounces) ricotta cheese

⅓ cup (1¼ ounces) grated Parmesan

Salt, pepper, and chopped fresh parsley, to taste

GLAZE

1 large egg yolk

3 tablespoons (1¼ ounces) sugar

FOR THE CRUST Knead together all the ingredients until you've made a soft, smooth dough. Place the dough in a lightly greased bowl, cover with plastic wrap, and let it rise at room temperature (65°F to 75°F) for 1 to 2 hours, until it's doubled in bulk. While the dough is rising, prepare the filling.

FOR THE FILLING Hard-boil and then peel 6 of the eggs. Finely chop and combine the boiled eggs and ham; an old-fashioned meat grinder or food processor works well here. The ham and eggs should be very finely chopped, though you don't want them turned to mush.

Combine the ham and eggs with the remaining 6 raw eggs, ricotta, and Parmesan. (You may be tempted to just go ahead and use the entire container of ricotta, but don't; you'll end up with a filling that's bland and too copious for the crust.) Add as much parsley as you want (3 to 4 tablespoons is a good amount), and season to taste with salt and coarsely ground black pepper. Go easy on the salt if the ham you've used is quite salty; in fact, if it's very salty, you probably won't need any additional salt at all, so taste first.

ASSEMBLY AND BAKING Gently deflate the dough, transfer it to a lightly greased work surface, and cut it into four pieces. If you haven't used dough relaxer, cover the dough and let it rest for 10 minutes, to relax the gluten.

Roll two of the dough pieces into rounds about 12 inches in diameter and place them on lightly greased 12-inch pizza pans, or onto cookie sheets. Spread the filling evenly onto the two bottom crusts, covering the crusts to within an inch of their edges. Roll out the other two pieces of dough and place them over the filled crusts, gently stretching them, if necessary, until the filling is completely covered. Seal the crust edges together, first by pressing the top crust onto the bottom crust all around the edge, then by folding the bottom crust up and over; you want to create a pretty good seal so the filling doesn't leak out.

Using a sharp knife or pair of scissors, cut a 1-inch round hole in the very center of the top crust; simply pinch up a bit of the crust and cut or snip it off. Make the glaze by whisking together the egg yolk and sugar until the sugar has dissolved. Paint each crust with some of the glaze, using a pastry brush or your fingers to spread it around as evenly as possible. Let the pies rest while you preheat the oven to 350°F, about 15 minutes.

Bake the pies for about 25 minutes, until they're a deep, golden brown. Remove them from the oven and place them on a rack. You'll probably see some liquid bubbling in the hole in the crust; siphon off as much of this liquid as you can with a bulb baster, as this step will help keep the pie from getting soggy. Let the pies cool, then serve warm or at room temperature. Refrigerate any leftovers.

*It's worthwhile to branch out beyond domestic boiled ham here. Most of the flavor of the pie will come from the ham, so choose one that's full-flavored. Usually, the darker the ham, the stronger its flavor, so keep that in mind when you're standing in line at the deli case.

nutrition information per serving   **1 slice, 154g**

252 cal | 7g fat | 16g protein | 28g complex carbohydrates | 3g sugar | 2g dietary fiber | 179mg cholesterol | 790mg sodium | 246mg potassium | 187RE vitamin A | 2mg vitamin C | 3mg iron | 89mg calcium | 143mg phosphorus

Leftovers

When life hands you stale bread—make salad, or croutons, a big bread pudding, a strata. The following recipes represent the merest hint of the wonderful dishes you can make from your day- or week-old bread.

Down-Home Bread Pudding

ONE 9-INCH SQUARE BREAD PUDDING, ABOUT 16 SQUARES

Bread pudding is one of the most welcome and versatile desserts you can create. Warm, slightly sweet, and flecked with bits of your favorite dried fruits, it's quintessential comfort food. We like combinations like apples with dried cranberries, maple syrup and walnuts, even bananas and chocolate chips.

1 quart (32 ounces) milk

½ cup (1 stick, 4 ounces) butter

9 to 10 cups (9 to 10 ounces) cubed stale bread*

1 cup honey, sugar, brown sugar, molasses, golden or maple syrup

1 cup (6 ounces) raisins, dates, dried cranberries, or cherries**

¾ cup (3 ounces) chopped walnuts or pecans

4 large eggs

½ teaspoon salt

¾ teaspoon nutmeg

2 teaspoons cinnamon

1 teaspoon vanilla extract

Preheat the oven to 350°F.

In a medium-sized saucepan, heat the milk and butter together until the butter has melted. Place the bread cubes, honey, and your choice of fruit and nuts in a large mixing bowl. In a separate bowl, beat together the eggs, salt, spices, and vanilla. Mix in the milk and butter mixture and pour everything over the bread cubes. Stir to distribute the liquid evenly, then pour the mixture into a buttered 9-inch square pan.

Bake for 40 to 45 minutes, until a knife inserted into the center comes out clean. Remove from the oven and let set for 5 minutes. Serve warm, with whipped cream or ice cream.

*The richer the bread, the richer the dessert. White bread, brioche, raisin bread, croissants, dinner rolls, any or all of them will work.

**Feel free to add any other fruit, chocolate chips, or flavored chips you like.

nutrition information per serving | one 2½-inch square, made with brown and white sugars, raisins, and walnuts, 134g

297 cal | 9g fat | 6g protein | 16g complex carbohydrates | 14g sugar | 1g dietary fiber | 88mg cholesterol | 230mg sodium | 211mg potassium | 171RE vitamin A | 1mg vitamin C | 1mg iron | 123mg calcium | 125mg phosphorus

Plain-but-Good Thanksgiving Stuffing

ABOUT 8 CUPS OF STUFFING (ENOUGH TO FILL A 10- TO 12-POUND TURKEY)

There are as many variations on stuffing as there are imaginative cooks. The bread element can be plain white bread, cornbread, whole wheat, herb bread, or even a cranberry loaf; moisteners range from water to butter to spirits; and additions include anything from fruits and nuts to meat and shellfish, with a wide range of vegetables, herbs and spices enlivening the whole affair.

This is one of our favorite stuffing recipes. It's not heavily seasoned; the main tastes are of plain white bread and butter, with onions and celery adding some texture and tang, and the poultry seasoning some traditional taste. For larger turkeys, this recipe can be increased by half, or doubled.

8 cups (12 ounces) bread cubes, made from about 12 slices firm white bread (such as White Bread 101, p. 198)*

1 cup (2 sticks, 8 ounces) butter

4 large onions (12 ounces), finely chopped (about 3 cups)

1 cup (4 ounces) finely chopped celery stalks (including tops)

¼ cup chopped dried parsley (or ½ cup fresh)

2 teaspoons poultry seasoning

2 teaspoons salt

1 teaspoon pepper (less for a milder stuffing)

Preheat the oven to 350°F. Place bread cubes on a cookie sheet or other wide flat pan and bake for 10 minutes. Remove from oven and set aside.

Melt the butter in a large frying pan and sauté the onions and celery until soft, about 5 minutes. Remove from heat.

Place bread cubes in a large bowl. Spoon onion-celery mixture over bread. Add parsley, poultry seasoning, salt, and pepper and toss mixture until it's thoroughly combined (the best way to do this is to roll up your sleeves, wash your hands, and dig in). Spoon stuffing loosely (it needs some room to expand) into both the body and neck cavities of the turkey, and roast.

NOTE If you have more stuffing than your bird can hold, add ½ cup chicken or turkey stock to each 1½ cups of stuffing mixture and bake in a buttered, covered casserole dish at 350°F for 30 minutes. Uncover for the last 10 minutes of baking if you like the top to be crisp.

*Alternatively, use Stuffing Bread, page 212. Leave the poultry seasoning out of this stuffing recipe, or if you're really fond of the taste, cut it back to 1 teaspoon.

nutrition information per serving   ½ cup, 72g

171 cal | 8g fat | 2g protein | 11g complex carbohydrates | 1g sugar | 1g dietary fiber | 33mg cholesterol | 110mg sodium | 98mg potassium | 115RE vitamin A | 2mg vitamin C | 1mg iron | 35mg calcium | 33mg phosphorus

Fattoush
(pita bread salad)

Italy's panzanella, that inspired marriage of vegetables, chopped basil, olive oil, and chunks of day-old Italian bread, has a cousin in the Mideast: Fattoush. This pita bread salad is right up there with tabbouleh in popularity as far as everyday salads go; it'll turn up at lunch, alongside a pita-bread sandwich, or as a first course later in the day. You might say fattoush is the Lebanese equivalent of America's iceberg-lettuce-and-tomato.

This salad goes through several transformations on its journey from full bowl to gone. At first the pita chips are very crunchy, almost jarringly so; but after 10 minutes they begin to soften and absorb the other flavors in the salad.

The salad is at its peak up to about 40 minutes after preparation; at that point the bread begins to become soggy. However, the only way you'll discover this is if there's any left after 40 minutes—unlikely!

3 small-to-medium pita breads

3 tomatoes, 1¼ to 1½ pounds total

¼ head romaine lettuce (about 3 ounces), chopped

1 medium cucumber (9 to 10 ounces), peeled, seeded, and cubed

6 scallions, including about half the green part, chopped

½ cup (⅞ ounce) fresh parsley

⅓ cup (2⅜ ounces) olive oil

¼ cup (2 ounces) lemon juice

1½ to 2 tablespoons dried mint, or 4 to 6 tablespoons fresh mint, snipped

Salt and pepper to taste

Preheat the oven to 375°F.

Split the pita breads into rounds and cut each round into 1½-inch wedges. Place the bread on a baking sheet and spray it with garlic-flavored olive oil spray (or drizzle with olive oil and sprinkle lightly with garlic powder). Bake the bread for 12 minutes or so, turning once, until it's completely dry and crisp. Set it aside to cool.

About 10 minutes before you're ready to serve the salad, place the bread in a large bowl and add the remaining ingredients. Toss to combine (your well-washed bare hands are the best tools here) and serve within 30 minutes or so.

nutrition information per serving **1 side serving, about 1¼ cups, 160g**

175 cal | 10g fat | 2g protein | 16g complex carbohydrates | 3g dietary fiber | 403mg sodium | 300mg potassium | 189RE vitamin A | 29mg vitamin C | 2mg iron | 49mg calcium | 51mg phosphorus

Panzanella
(Mediterranean bread salad)

ABOUT 3 QUARTS, 12 SERVINGS

This is one of our favorite side dishes (or dinners) in the summer. If you're lucky enough to live near a farmers' market, the ultra-fresh produce you'll find there will take this dish over the top. You can also make this salad without adding the bread cubes, serving it with slices of baguette or toasted sourdough as an appetizer.

Most bread salads call for the bread to be soaked in water, but we skip this in favor of letting the bread soak up the juice from the tomatoes and dressing, and still keep a slight crunch in the center.

DRESSING

½ cup (3½ ounces) extra virgin olive oil

¼ cup (2 ounces) red wine vinegar

2 tablespoons (1 ounce) water

2 shallots (½ ounce), peeled and minced or crushed

1 garlic clove (¼ to ½ ounce), peeled and minced or crushed

¼ teaspoon salt

½ teaspoon freshly ground black pepper

SALAD

4 cups (1½ to 2 pounds) diced zucchini or summer squash

1 tablespoon vegetable oil

4 large ripe tomatoes (1½ pounds, about 4 cups chopped)

1 large red or sweet onion (8 ounces, about 2 cups chopped)

¼ cup (1¼ ounces) black olives, chopped

¼ cup (1¼ ounces) green olives, chopped

2 large red or green bell peppers (1 pound), roasted, peeled, and chopped (optional)

1 cup (1¾ ounces) flat-leaf parsley, chopped

1 cup (2 ounces) fresh basil, chopped

1 pound bread, sourdough or a chewy country bread (like a baguette), not a soft white pan bread

TO MAKE THE DRESSING Mix all the ingredients together and let sit for an hour or so or up to several days in the refrigerator.

TO MAKE THE SALAD Put the dressing in a large bowl. Sauté the zucchini in the oil; use high heat and work quickly so the squash will brown but stay somewhat firm. Remove the squash from the pan and let it cool. Clean and chop the tomatoes, reserving as much of the juice as possible; it adds flavor to the salad. Put the tomatoes in the bowl with the dressing, add the remaining chopped vegetables (including the squash), parsley, and basil and mix well. Let the salad sit in the refrigerator for several hours. Note: This is a good place to use up any leftover grilled vegetables.

TO PREPARE THE BREAD Preheat the oven to 350°F. Trim the tough bottom and end crusts from the bread. Cut the loaf into ½- to ¾-inch cubes. Spread it on an ungreased baking sheet and toast it in the oven for 15 minutes, checking the cubes after 8 to 10 minutes and moving them around with a spatula so they dry evenly. (The bread doesn't need to toast, just dry out and get crunchy.) Remove the bread cubes from the oven, cool them, then store in an airtight container.

TO ASSEMBLE THE PANZANELLA About 30 minutes before you want to serve the salad, add the bread cubes and toss; if you prefer a softer salad, add the bread cubes earlier.

nutrition information per serving about 1 cup, 194g

215 cal | 10g fat | 5g protein | 23g complex carbohydrates | 3g sugar | 3g dietary fiber | 471mg sodium | 369mg potassium | 113RE vitamin A | 23mg vitamin C | 2mg iron | 67mg calcium | 83mg phosphorus

Sourdough

Flour and water, mixed together and left alone,
come to life and become something truly amazing: sourdough. Faster,
more reliable, and more convenient leaveners exist today, yet none of them
has the allure of sourdough. Perhaps it's because sourdough starters, for
ages the only means of leavening bread, have been treasured and passed down
among bakers for generations.

What a treasure they are, and what wonderful breads they make.
Breads leavened with sourdough and given the time they need to develop have
wonderful, complex flavors that cannot be attained by any other method. Time
for the dough to rest and rise, and plenty of it, is perhaps the most critical
ingredient for crafting delicious sourdough breads.

There are many distinct varieties of sourdough throughout the world; we've chosen to present a typical American-style sourdough starter here, because we find it easy to work with and it's familiar to many of us. It's a batter rather than a stiff dough, and is made mostly with white rather than whole grain flour.

How does a simple slurry of flour and water become a powerful leavener, strong enough to raise a dough much larger than itself? Wild yeast and friendly bacteria called lactobacilli settle and grow in the warm mass, and the leavening capability of a sourdough starter is a result of the by-products of these tiny living creatures, which are collectively called the sourdough's microflora.

Wild yeast is a tiny fungi—it's the white, dusty film you see on grapes and on grains, and it exists all around us in varying degrees, in the air and settling on surfaces. The friendly bacteria, lactobacilli, busy themselves breaking down flour's complex carbohydrates into simple sugars—exactly what wild yeast needs for food. Wild yeast, feeding on the simple sugars, produces carbon dioxide bubbles that raise the dough when trapped in the gluten webbing. As by-products, the lactobacilli produce flavorful organic acids: lactic acid, which adds a rich, mellow flavor to bread; and to a lesser degree and over a longer time, acetic acid, which gives sourdough bread its mouth-puckering tang.

Why is time important? The amount of wild yeast in a sourdough starter isn't nearly the multitudes we employ when we use domestic yeast. The less yeast, the slower carbon dioxide bubbles accumulate in the dough. The wild yeast organisms in a sourdough starter are reproducing rapidly as they feed, but it still takes time for them to produce the amount of carbon dioxide necessary to achieve the rise.

Time is also necessary to develop flavor. The sour flavor in sourdough bread comes from the acids produced as the lactobacilli work. As the acid accumulates, the flavor increases. Since they accumulate slowly, the baker who wants those flavors must allow the fermentation to stretch out over time. By understanding the roles of wild yeast and lactobacilli, and learning what does and does not spur these creatures to action, an attentive baker is able to adjust timing and temperature for the desired flavor characteristics.

One more note about flavor: There are many different strains of wild yeast and lactobacilli that grow and thrive all over the world, and the flavors they produce vary accordingly. Sourdough starters adopt the flavor profile of the microflora wherever they exist. The sourdough microflora in San Francisco starter is famed for producing a very sharp sour flavor, while the microflora in Vermont produce a much milder flavor. If you receive a starter from someone who lives in a different locale, it will soon become populated with your own unique local microflora. After a several-week metamorphosis, the culture will stabilize and exhibit the flavor of your locale. In this regard, sourdough bread is truly a local food.

Creating Your Own Sourdough Starter

While there's something very special about inheriting a sourdough starter with a history, starting your own from scratch is deeply gratifying. Although you may have a nostalgic attachment to your starter, especially if it has a long history, a new one in the same environment will contain the same resident microflora. The confidence of knowing you can start again will bring a certain freedom to your endeavors.

While there are many extravagant methods for starting a new starter, a simple, reliable method, and the one we teach at our King Arthur Flour Baking Education Center in Vermont, uses nothing more than whole rye flour, water, and a touch of molasses. We depart from the common practice of leaving the starter uncovered, or covered only with a loose cloth. While it's true that an uncovered or loosely covered starter will be visited by the wild yeasts in the air of your kitchen (especially if you bake bread often and thus have a healthy population of wild yeast living in your kitchen), the uncovered starter will also develop a dry skin on top, from the exposure to air. We have success starting new starters in covered containers because there's enough wild yeast present on the whole rye flour to get the system going. Here's how to proceed:

Day 1

In a nonreactive container, combine the following:

½ cup (4 ounces) 80°F water

Generous ¾ cup (3½ ounces) whole rye (pumpernickel) flour

⅛ teaspoon molasses

Mix all the ingredients thoroughly, cover, and allow the mixture to rest (ferment) for 24 hours at 80°F. A gas oven with a pilot light is just about the right temperature, or perhaps a heating pad, set on very low and set beneath your towel-wrapped bowl, will provide the right environment.

Day 2

Discard half the starter, and to the remainder add:

½ cup (4 ounces) 80°F water

¾ cup (3½ ounces) whole rye (pumpernickel) flour

Mix thoroughly, cover, and allow the mixture to ferment for 24 hours at 80°F. This is known as feeding the starter.

Day 3, Day 4, Day 5, and Day 6

By day three some tiny bubbles will appear. If you're using a clear container, you can see these bubbles throughout the mixture. This activity will increase day by day. From now on you'll need to feed the starter with unbleached all-purpose flour instead of the whole rye flour you used initially. You're literally giving the bacteria food to live on. Feed the starter twice a day on these days, with at least 8 hours between feedings.

To feed, remove and discard half the starter, and to the remainder add:

½ cup (4 ounces) 80°F water

1 cup (4¼ ounces) unbleached all-purpose flour

Mix thoroughly, cover, and allow the mixture to ferment for at least 8 hours at 80°F before the next feeding. If you miss a feeding, don't fret, just pick up the schedule and continue as if nothing happened.

After a week the starter should taste and smell sour. It will be bubbly and active and strong enough to leaven bread. The volume of the starter will have increased by at least half and it will taste sharply sour. Now that your starter is established, you need to increase its quantity so you'll have enough to use and some to keep.

Day 7, or as soon as your starter is established

Stir the mixture well. Pour off and discard all but 4 ounces (about ½ cup) of your starter, place it in a 2- to 4-quart nonreactive, wide-mouthed container, and add:

1 cup (8 ounces) 80°F water

Scant 2 cups (8 ounces) unbleached all-purpose flour

Be Patient!

If your young starter still doesn't appear active after the first week, don't be discouraged. Simply continue the twice daily feeding schedule. It's not uncommon for sourdough starter to require more than a week to become established. Cool winter temperatures and the absence of wild yeast in your kitchen are factors that extend the time needed for a starter to become mature and ripe. The value of a long, slow process is a central theme in the world of sourdough, and while this may be your first encounter with this theme, it will certainly not be your last. Again and again we are reminded that *time* is a critical ingredient, with no substitute.

Stir until the mixture is free of lumps. Scrape the walls of the container clean (so that you can see how high the starter rises), cover, and allow the starter to ferment for 6 to 8 hours.

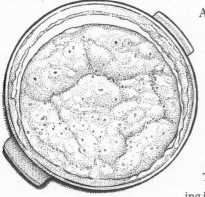

At this point the starter should be active, with bubbles breaking on the surface. Touch it, and you will find that gluten has developed; it should feel somewhat elastic. It is ready to be used, or placed on one of the two maintenance schedules that follow.

RIPE STARTER. Sourdough starter that's ripe and ready to use has bubbles that break the surface and are visible throughout the starter. The creases are a sign that the starter has recently fallen after achieving its greatest volume.

Care and Feeding of an Established Starter: Two Methods

ON THE COUNTERTOP (MAINTAINING YOUR STARTER AT ROOM TEMPERATURE) As far as the sourdough bacteria are concerned, room temperature is the preferable environment for your starter. Maintenance is a daily task, but a simple one (you can do it in the time it takes to wait for toast). You can always stash it in the refrigerator when you need to, but do follow this schedule for a while. You will learn a lot about your starter by observing it under these optimum conditions.

Feed the starter once a day as follows: Stir the starter well and pour off all but 4 ounces (about ½ cup). Add 8 ounces of water and 8 ounces of flour, mix until smooth, and cover.

If you plan to use the starter the next day, feed it twice, with a minimum of 6 hours between feedings. The last feeding should be 6 to 8 hours before you want to use it.

IN THE REFRIGERATOR If daily sourdough feeding is too much trouble, you can store your starter in the refrigerator and feed it once a week instead. Take the starter out of the fridge, stir well, and pour off all but ½ cup (4 ounces). Add 8 ounces of water and 8 ounces of unbleached all-purpose flour, mix until smooth, and cover. Allow the starter to work at room temperature for at least 2 hours before putting it back in the refrigerator.

Three days before you're planning to bake you'll need to raise the activity of your starter. Take the starter out of the refrigerator in the morning, feed it as usual, and let it ferment for 24 hours at room temperature. The next day feed it twice, once in the morning, then again about 12 hours later. On the third morning, feed the starter early and allow it to ferment until it's ripe, about 6 hours. It should then be ready to use in your recipe. Pour off what you will need for the recipe and feed the remaining starter with 8 ounces of flour and 8 ounces of water. Mix until smooth, and allow the starter to work for at least 2 hours at room temperature before putting it back in the refrigerator. Note: You should keep your starter in the refrigerator if your kitchen is very warm, over 85°F. In a hot summer kitchen, a starter left on the counter will ferment like crazy and you'd have to feed it very frequently to prevent it from becoming overripe.

Baking Sourdough Bread

As you bake with sourdough, pay close attention to your results. Get into the habit of really looking at the bread closely, of inhaling the aroma deeply; this is how your skill increases.

Essential Tool: An Instant-Read Thermometer

If we could choose only one tool to recommend for bread bakers, we'd have to settle on our trusty instant-read thermometer. Crafting great bread depends largely on working with ingredients at the proper temperatures, and this simple, inexpensive tool will increase your precision, and therefore your success, enormously.

The dough of naturally leavened breads should be quite wet. Resist the temptation to add flour as you work. Even though the moisture makes the dough a bit more difficult to handle, the high percentage of water helps create beautifully open interiors and nice volume, and increases the shelf life of the baked loaf substantially.

You'll make better bread if you closely monitor the temperature of the dough throughout the process. Optimum temperature for fermenting dough is 78°F to 80°F. Dough that's too cold will not ferment adequately and will be dense, unless it is given a very long fermentation time. Dough that's too warm will ferment very quickly, and the resulting loaf will rise excessively, tend to have thick, pale crust and an off-flavor, and will go stale more quickly than it should.

Slowing Down Your Dough

How can we increase dough's fermentation time, and build up its sour taste, without overfermenting? A technique called "retarding" enables you to slow down the fermentation by decreasing the temperature. This is one way to retard your bread: Once it has been shaped, allow it to rise for an hour or two. When you see it beginning to rise and get puffy, cover it well with plastic wrap and place it in your refrigerator. The bread will be ready to bake 12 to 24 hours later.

Professional bakers retard their dough in special coolers that maintain a temperature of about 50° F, but the refrigerator is a practical alternative for home bakers. Refrigerator temperatures are a bit low and can seriously slow down the action of the dough, so place your dough on the top shelf if possible (it's usually slightly warmer near the top of the refrigerator). The dough may need some time at room temperature for the last bit of rising, but if the bread looks ready to go the minute you pull it from the fridge, it is fine to put it directly in the oven. Cold dough going into the oven will, however, reduce initial baking temperature in the oven, so compensate by preheating the oven 50°F higher than the recipe calls for. Once the bread is in the oven, reduce the heat to the recommended temperature and bake as usual.

Creating a Steamy Hearth in the Home Oven

When you put a loaf of risen dough onto a hot oven stone (see Tools, p. 592), the heat from the stone immediately flows into the dough. This intense heat stimulates the yeast into a feeding frenzy. The carbon dioxide produced by the yeast builds up in the dough and the loaf rises dramatically, which bakers describe as "oven spring." This increase in volume is facilitated by a steamy environment, because steam slows the formation of a rigid crust, allowing the dough to keep expanding. In a dry oven, the crust forms and hardens much more quickly than in a steamy oven, resulting in a baked loaf with low volume and a dense interior. Steam also produces a nicely caramelized crust: glossy, deep brown, and delicious.

The best way to create a hearth oven at home is to use a baking stone, stone oven insert, or common firebrick. They all provide the thermal mass from which the loaf gets its dramatic oven spring. When we bake at home, we place a baking stone in the oven and preheat both for 45 minutes to an hour before it's time to bake. This gives the baking stone time to absorb and store heat, which is then transferred to the loaf when it's placed directly on the stone.

To create a steamy oven at home, here's the method we recommend: Place an empty cast iron pan in the bottom of a preheating oven, on the rack beneath the baking stone. Put a kettle of water on the stove and bring it to a boil just before it's time to put the bread in the oven. Before opening the oven door, take time to arrange everything you'll need—the risen loaf on the baker's peel (see Tools, p. 592), the kettle of boiling water, and a spray bottle filled with hot water. When you're all set, proceed swiftly: Open the oven door, slide the loaf onto the baking stone, pour about ½ cup boiling water into the cast iron pan, spray a mist of water into the oven chamber, and close the oven door. (If possible, ask a helper to operate the spray bottle while you are loading the oven.) Be careful: Once the water gets poured into the pan, steam rises immediately and a steam burn can happen quickly.

Once the oven door is closed, resist the temptation to check on the bread for the first 20 minutes. The temperature must remain high for the crust to caramelize. Open the oven door after 20 minutes to allow the steam to escape and remove the pan of water, because hearth breads should finish baking in a dry oven. A very steamy environment for more than 25 minutes will result in a tough crust.

The Autolyse

Most of the recipes in this chapter include a step called an autolyse (pronounced ahh-toe-lease), in which the flour, starter, and water are combined and allowed to rest for 20 to 30 minutes before the remaining ingredients are added and the dough is mixed. This simple step prepares the dough for the mixing or kneading that follows. When flour and water are first brought together, the gluten is disorganized and tangled, and it must be mechanically pulled apart by kneading before it can reassemble into organized long strands. An autolyse gives naturally occurring enzymes the chance to untangle the gluten, so less mixing is necessary to develop the dough. Salt and additional yeast, if used, are not added until after the autolyse, because they tighten the gluten—just the opposite of what an autolyse accomplishes. An autolyse also increases the dough's extensibility, which is its abiity to stretch without pulling back like a rubber band. This makes the dough easier to shape and increases its ability to rise in the oven.

Sourdough Breads

Pain au Levain

ONE 3-POUND LOAF OR TWO 1½-POUND LOAVES (24 SLICES)

This is a traditional French-style sourdough with a mildly sour flavor. It's an everyday bread, delicious but uncomplicated, and we enjoy mixing it by hand. You can make a single large loaf with this recipe, or divide the dough and make two smaller ones. Large round loaves of pain au levain are reminiscent of the loaves peasants baked for centuries in the communal ovens of Europe. Large loaves have a longer shelf life than smaller ones.

5 cups (1 pound, 5 ounces) unbleached all-purpose flour

⅔ cup (3 ounces) whole wheat flour

1¾ cups (14 ounces) water

2½ cups (1 pound) ripe starter (best measured by weight; volume varies with ripeness)

2½ teaspoons salt

Combine the flours in a large bowl. Add the water to the starter and stir into the flours. Mix by hand for 2 minutes, until the flour is thoroughly incorporated but not yet smooth. Cover the bowl loosely with plastic and let the dough rest for 20 to 30 minutes.

Add the salt and knead the dough until it becomes smooth, supple, and slightly tacky. Avoid adding flour; the dough should be soft. The dough temperature should be 78°F to 80°F. Return the dough to the bowl, cover, and let rise for 1 hour. Turn out the dough onto a lightly floured surface and fold it. Folding is a gentler and preferred alternative to "punching down" this bread dough. The object is to develop the gluten while not degassing the dough. Lightly dust the dough (still in the bowl) and your work surface with flour. Turn the dough out of the bowl onto the work surface—a flexible dough scraper works perfectly for this step. Gently pull and pat the dough flat, without deflating all of the bubbles, then fold the bottom third up and the top third down, as you would a letter. Turn the dough 90 degrees on your work surface and repeat the folds (top down, bottom up), so that now all four sides have been folded into the center. Pick up this folded package and deposit it gently, folded side down, back into the bowl. The dough will be noticeably tighter after the fold. Let it rise, covered, for another hour.

Divide the dough into two pieces, or keep it as one if you wish to make a single large round loaf. Preshape each piece into a loose ball by drawing the edges together, so that one side becomes the outer surface, with all the corners coming together at the bottom of the ball. Place the dough smooth side up on a lightly floured surface. Cover and let it rest for about 20 minutes.

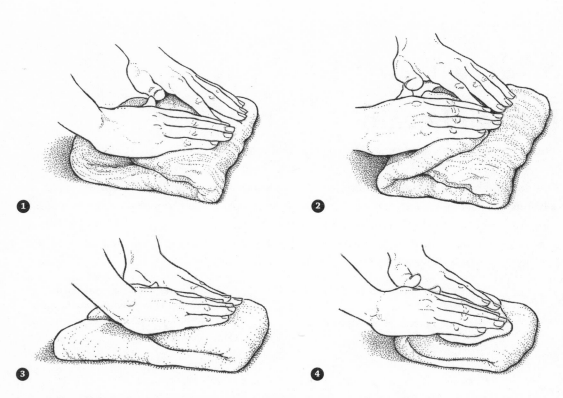

FOLDING SEQUENCE **1.** Gently pat out the dough and fold the top edge two-thirds of the way toward the bottom edge. **2.** Bring the bottom edge halfway over the dough and pat lightly to seal. **3.** Turn the dough 90 degrees and fold the top edge two-thirds of the way toward the bottom edge. **4.** Bring the bottom edge halfway over the dough and pat lightly to seal. This four-step series is considered one fold, and the dough is now ready to be placed back in the bowl to rise again.

Shape the loaves into tight round boules—"boule" is French for "ball" and is often used to describe a round loaf of artisan bread—and place them, smooth side down and covered, in well-floured proofing baskets for 2 hours. An hour before baking, preheat the oven and baking stone to 450°F. When ready to bake, turn the loaves onto parchment paper set on a baker's peel, or a semolina-dusted peel, and score the loaves (most easily done with sharp single edged razor blade or a baker's lame, pronounced lahm). Slide the loaves onto the baking stone and fill the oven with steam as directed on page 277, or spritz with water. Bake for 45 to 50 minutes for a large loaf (about 40 minutes for two loaves), until the crust is richly colored and the internal temperature of the loaf is about 200°F.

nutrition information per serving   one 2-ounce slice, 56g

105 cal | 3g protein | 22g complex carbohydrates | 2g dietary fiber | 223mg sodium | 60mg potassium | 2mg iron | 3mg calcium | 46mg phosphorus

Variations Nuts (especially lightly toasted pecans, coarsely chopped) or whole, pitted dark olives are wonderful additions to this bread. Add about 6 ounces of either ingredient to the dough when the mixing is nearly finished. Nuts will tend to make the dough a bit drier, so add a

Shaping Boules

It takes practice to properly shape dough into perfectly round balls. You want to achieve a tight skin, and the tension should be evenly distributed across the ball's surface. For this step you don't want too much flour on you work surface. Cup both hands around the boule and drag it toward you, letting the skin of the boule get pulled tighter by the friction against the work surface. Rotate the boule in your hands as you drag it, so that the entire surface is tightened evenly and the resulting boule will not be lopsided. As the surface draws tighter, seal the edges together at the base of the boule with the side of your hand.

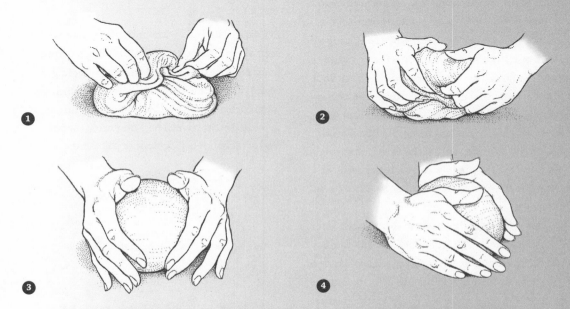

1. Gather the edges of the dough together. The point where all the edges come together will be the bottom seam of the shaped loaf. **2.** Turn the dough over and begin tightening the surface by pulling the loaf toward you repeatedly on an unfloured work surface. Continue to tuck the loose edges into the bottom of the ball. Roll the loaf sideways as you work to create an evenly round boule. The goal is equal tension over the loaf's surface. **3.** To further tighten and round the loaf, drag it across the unfloured work surface with cupped hands. Repeat this step several times, until you're satisfied that the boule is sufficiently tight. **4.** Once the boule is tight and round, seal the bottom seam. Turn the boule on its side, and press the seam together with the side of your hand as you roll the boule away from you.

touch more water when mixing. The opposite is true of olives. Also, if you plan to add olives, reduce the salt in the recipe to 2 teaspoons. In addition, try to enclose the nuts or olives in the dough as much as possible, poking in any that stick out, as they're likely to burn.

Proofing Baskets

It's ideal to provide a cradle for your shaped loaf as it rises, especially for the wet doughs we recommend for artisan breads. A proofing basket serves as an effective cradle, preventing the loaf from spreading and flattening excessively as it rises, as it would if left to rise (or "proof") on a flat surface. There are several beautiful and effective proofing baskets on the market, from linen-lined French *bannetons* to German coiled wooden *brotforms,* and while they each lend a unique appearance to the finished loaf, they all serve as a supportive cradle in which to raise your dough. These are deluxe additions to your bread baking tool kit—authentic proofing baskets can be pricey—but they will last and last. An economical option is to simply line a bowl, basket, or colander with a tea towel, or if you are handy with a needle and thread, sew a cotton or linen liner to fit a bowl or basket of your choosing.

Dust the proofing basket with enough flour to prevent the dough from sticking, but don't use too much. An excessive layer of flour stuck to the surface of the loaf will inhibit the development of the good crust color, and lends a taste of dry flour to the finished bread. Place the shaped loaf into the floured basket smooth side down, let it rise, and then turn it out onto an oven peel directly from the basket. The floured coils of the German brotform give the finished loaf a beautiful spiral pattern.

PROOFING BASKETS Examples of proofing baskets: a French linen-lined *banneton* (top), a German coiled *brotform* (left), and a homemade proofing basket, easily made by lining a bowl with a linen tea towel (right). The shaped loaf is placed bottom up in the basket for its final rise, then turned out of the basket onto a baking stone or pan to bake.

The rings of flour on this sourdough boule are characteristic markings of the coiled *brotform*. This loaf was scored in a circular pattern to enhance the appearance of the rings.

Scoring the Loaf

Scoring, or "slashing," aids the loaf's expansion in the oven and prevents asymmetrical ruptures in the crust. To properly score a loaf, first mentally rehearse the cuts you will make, and then swiftly draw the blade through the dough, making cuts about ¼ inch deep.

Whole Wheat Sourdough

TWO 1½-POUND LOAVES OR ONE 3-POUND LOAF, 24 SLICES

This is a hearty whole wheat sourdough with a dark crust and interior, and a flavor that suggests the ancient tradition of bread baking. The whole grain flour and honey will create an active fermentation, so follow the timing of the recipe closely. This bread makes a stunning presentation when baked as one large loaf, but the smaller loaves have a charm of their own.

1 cup (4¼ ounces) unbleached all-purpose flour

2½ cups (14 ounces) whole wheat flour

1¼ cups (10 ounces) water

2 tablespoons (1½ ounces) honey

2 cups (14 ounces) ripe starter (best measured by weight; volume varies with ripeness)

2 teaspoons salt

Whole-Grain Flours

The additional nutrients present in whole-grain flours provide extra food for the sourdough microflora, and therefore increase fermentation and acid production. Whole rye flour (pumpernickel), in particular, is recognized as adding more sour flavor to sourdough breads.

Combine the flours in a large bowl. Add the water and honey to the starter and stir into the flours. Mix by hand for 2 minutes, until the flour is thoroughly incorporated but not yet smooth. Cover the dough and allow it to rest for 20 to 30 minutes.

Add the salt and knead the dough until it becomes smooth, supple, and slightly tacky. Avoid adding flour. The dough should be soft but strong and be 78°F to 80°F. Return the dough to the bowl and allow it to ferment, covered, for 1½ hours, folding (see instructions on p. 280) once after 45 minutes.

Divide the dough into two pieces, or keep it as one if you wish to make a single large round loaf. Shape each piece into a loose ball and place seam side up on a lightly floured surface. Cover loosely with a tea towel so air does not dry the skin of the dough, and let it rest for about 15 minutes.

Shape the loaf or loaves into round boules (see p. 281) and place them seam side up in a well-floured linen basket, covered, for 2 to 2½ hours. The loaves will be very soft when they are ready to be baked.

One hour before baking, preheat the oven and baking stone to 450°F. When ready to bake, turn over the loaves onto parchment paper set on a baker's peel, or a semolina-dusted peel—now the loaves are right side up and the seams are on the bottom. Score the loaves with swift strokes of a baker's lame. Take care that this sticky dough doesn't snag the blade as the surface is cut; slash quickly and confidently. Slide the loaves onto the baking stone and fill the oven with steam (see p. 277). After 15 minutes, lower the oven temperature to 400°F and open the oven door for a few seconds to let the steam escape. Bake for another 35 minutes for a large loaf, 25 minutes for two smaller loaves. Turn off the heat, open the door, and leave the bread in the oven for another 10 minutes. This will ensure that this bread will be completely baked without becoming too dark, as can happen with bread containing honey or other sugars. The internal temperature of the loaf should be about 200°F.

nutrition information per serving   **one 2-ounce slice, 53g**

94 cal | 3g protein | 19g complex carbohydrates | 1g sugar | 2g dietary fiber | 224mg sodium | 88mg potassium | 1mg iron | 7mg calcium | 72mg phosphorus

Variation   This dough is well suited for the inclusion of cracked or rolled grains. Cover 4½ ounces of your favorite whole grains or combination of grains with cool water and soak overnight. The next day, drain and squeeze the water from the grains and use it as part of the water in the dough. Add the grains toward the end of mixing, just before the dough is fully developed.

Rosemary Olive Oil Sourdough

TWO 1½-POUND LOAVES, 24 SLICES

Fresh rosemary and extra virgin olive oil infuse this white sourdough with a Mediterranean fragrance and flavor. While it's wonderful baked in the round loaves as directed, this dough lends itself well to fougasse (see p. 253), brushed with olive oil and sprinkled with coarse salt and pepper before baking. We also use this dough to make individual rolls, and dress them up by firmly pushing a peeled clove of garlic into the center of each one. The baking time for the fougasse and rolls will be significantly less than that for the loaves, 20 to 25 minutes.

5¼ cups (22¼ ounces) unbleached all-purpose flour	2 cups (14 ounces) ripe starter (best measured by weight; volume varies with ripeness)
1½ cups (12 ounces) water	
¼ cup (1¾ ounces) extra virgin olive oil	2½ teaspoons salt
	3 tablespoons fresh rosemary, chopped

Put the flour in a large bowl. Add the water and olive oil to the starter and stir into the flour. Mix by hand for 2 minutes, until the flour is thoroughly incorporated but not yet smooth. Cover the dough and let it rest for 20 to 30 minutes.

Add the salt and knead the dough until it becomes smooth, supple, and slightly tacky. Gently knead in the rosemary until it is evenly distributed. Avoid adding flour;

When You Want a Really Sour Sourdough

Although you can't change the characteristics of your local wild yeast and lactobacilli, some conditions and ingredients can be manipulated to increase the sour taste of your sourdough bread.

Be careful, though; it's possible to over-acidify dough, and the result is the infamous, inedible "hockey puck." While acetic acid is great for achieving a sour flavor, too much acetic acid will break down the gluten, resulting in a flat dense loaf. If you prefer your bread very sour, you'll need to balance the factors of sour taste and good volume.

the dough should be soft. The dough temperature should be 78°F to 80°F. Return the dough to the bowl, cover, and let it ferment for 2 hours, folding once (see folding instructions, p. 280) after 1 hour.

Divide the dough into two pieces, shape each piece into a loose ball and place seam side up on a lightly floured surface. Cover the loaves loosely with a tea towel and let them rest for about 20 minutes.

Shape the loaves into tight round boules and place them seam side up in well-floured, floured, proofing baskets for 2 hours.

One hour before baking, preheat the oven and baking stone to 450°F. When ready to bake, turn the loaves onto parchment paper set on a baker's peel, or a semolina-dusted peel, and score the loaves with a razor or lame. Slide the loaves onto the baking stone and fill the oven with steam (see instructions, p. 277). Bake at 450°F for about 40 minutes, opening the oven door to let out the steam after 20 minutes. When the bread is ready, the crust will be richly colored. The internal temperature of the loaf should be about 200°F.

nutrition information per serving   one 2-ounce slice, 60g

130 cal | 2g fat | 3g protein | 23g complex carbohydrates | 1g dietary fiber | 223mg sodium | 56mg potassium | 1RE vitamin A 2mg iron | 7mg calcium | 38mg phosphorus.

Variation   The local San Francisco sourdough microflora won't inhabit your starter unless you happen to live there, so there's no way to bake real San Francisco sourdough bread anywhere else. But for a good approximation, try this: Omit the rosemary and olive oil, and increase the water by 3 tablespoons to make up for the olive oil. Replace ½ cup of the all-purpose flour with ½ cup rye flour. Retard the bread overnight (see instructions, p. 276) and bake it the next day.

Breads with Levain de Pâte: Sourdough Starter and Domestic Yeast

Breads that contain both wild (sourdough) and domestic yeast have the attributes of both: the complex flavor and extended keeping quality of sourdough and the greater volume, softer crumb, and speedier production of domestic yeast. A small amount of yeast is added to the dough at the final stage of mixing. This method, although not a "pure" sourdough, is widely used in the bakeries of Europe (in France it's known as the *levain de pâte* method). We've grown to love the variety of breads this method enables us to bake.

Golden Sesame Bread

TWO 1¼-POUND LOAVES, 20 SLICES

This beautiful loaf has sesame seeds in the dough as well as covering the outside of the loaf. The bread's golden color comes from durum flour, which is the high-protein wheat used to make pasta. (Semolina also comes from durum wheat. The flavor is similar but the texture is distinct: semolina is coarser than durum flour.) Fermentation and proofing times are slightly shorter in breads with a high percentage of durum flour.

1 cup (4¼ ounces) unbleached all-purpose flour	½ teaspoon instant yeast
3½ cups (16 ounces) durum flour	2 teaspoons salt
2 cups (16 ounces) water	¼ cup (1¼ ounces) sesame seeds for the dough
2 cups (14 ounces) ripe starter (best measured by weight; volume varies with ripeness)	1 cup (5 ounces) sesame seeds for the exterior

Combine the flours in a large bowl. Add the water to the starter and stir into the flours. Mix by hand for 2 minutes, until the flour is thoroughly incorporated but not yet smooth. Cover the dough and let it rest for 20 to 30 minutes.

Add the yeast and salt and knead the dough until it becomes smooth, supple, and slightly tacky. Gently knead in the 1½ ounces sesame seeds. Avoid adding flour; the dough should be soft. The dough temperature should be 75°F. (You can adjust dough temperature by using cooler or warmer water when mixing.) Return the dough to the bowl, cover and let it ferment for 1½ hours, folding (see folding instructions, p. 280) once after 45 minutes.

Divide the dough into two pieces, shape each piece into a loose ball, and place seam side up on a lightly floured surface. Cover the loaves and let them rest for about 15 minutes.

Preheat the oven and baking stone to 450°F.

Shape each loaf into a boule (see shaping instructions, p. 281). Put about a cup of seeds in a dish or platter large enough to hold one boule. Moisten each boule by laying it on a damp tea towel, then place it in the platter containing the seeds. Coat the boule with seeds, then place it, bottom up, on an unfloured cloth. Cover the loaves loosely with a tea towel and let them proof for about 1 hour. Turn the loaves onto a piece of parchment set on a baker's peel, or a semolina-dusted peel (now they'll be right side up), and score the loaves, using a razor blade or baker's lame. Slide the loaves onto the baking stone and fill the oven with steam (see instructions, p. 277). Bake at 450°F for about 20 minutes. Reduce the temperature to 400°F, open the oven door briefly to let any remaining steam escape, and bake for another 20 minutes, until the crust is richly colored and the internal temperature of the loaf is about 200°F.

nutrition information per serving   1 slice, 88g

203 cal | 5g fat | 7g protein | 33g complex carbohydrates | 3g dietary fiber | 269mg sodium | 128mg potassium | 3mg iron | 95mg calcium | 120mg phosphorus

Extended Care

If you decide that you want to take a vacation from sourdough baking, you can freeze your starter. Transfer it to an airtight container with enough room for it to expand as it freezes. To use it again, let it thaw, and feed it as you would a dormant or neglected starter.

Black Bread

ONE 13-INCH PULLMAN LOAF, 26 SLICES

This recipe makes a dense rye bread. It's baked in a rectangular lidded pan called a pain de mie or pullman pan, so named for its shape, which is reminiscent of a Pullman railcar (see Tools, p. 585). Black bread is traditionally sliced thin, and is delicious with a wide array of toppings.

Almost everything about this rye bread is different from the wheat breads in this chapter. Rye flour contains less gluten than wheat flour, so the dough is much less cohesive when mixed and is very sticky. Due to these unique characteristics, there is no autolyse and no primary fermentation punctuated by a fold. The dough will go directly from the mixing bowl into the pullman pan.

Cracked rye can be purchased in health food stores, or you can pulse whole rye berries very briefly in a food processor—each whole rye berry need only be broken into about five pieces.

SOAKER
½ cup (2¼ ounces) cracked rye

½ cup (4 ounces) cool water

RYE SOUR
2¼ cups (9 ounces) whole rye (pumpernickel) flour

1 cup (8 ounces) water

1 tablespoon (½ ounce) ripe starter

FOR THE RYE SOAKER Combine the cracked rye and water in a covered container and let soak overnight.

FOR THE RYE SOUR Combine the rye flour, water, and starter and mix until smooth. Dust the surface with rye flour, cover, and let stand for 12 to 15 hours. The sour will have risen noticeably and it will taste and smell very sour.

DOUGH
¾ cup (6 ounces) water

All of the soaker

All of the rye sour

1 cup (7½ ounces) ripe sourdough starter (best measured by weight; volume varies with ripeness)

1½ teaspoons blackstrap molasses

1 cup plus 2 tablespoons (4½ ounces) high-gluten flour (14 percent protein)

2 cups (8 ounces) whole rye flour, preferably organic

1 teaspoon whole fennel seed, coarsely ground

2 teaspoons instant yeast

2 teaspoons salt

Preheat the oven to 500°F. Lightly grease and flour (using rye flour) a 13-inch lidded Pullman pan.

Combine all the ingredients in your mixer bowl, using the flat beater paddle. (Add the wet ingredients first, so they'll be at the bottom of the bowl.) Switch to the dough hook and mix on low speed for about 4 minutes, scraping the dough hook and bowl several times, as necessary. Increase the speed to medium and mix for an additional 4 minutes. The dough should be sticky and shiny, with visible gluten strands. Its temperature should be 80°F to 85°F.

The tight-fitting lid of the Pullman pan protects this black bread from getting too dark during its long bake. While this bread doesn't quite reach the top of the pan, lidded Pullman pans are wonderful for creating loaves that make perfectly square slices, such as the classic white sandwich bread called *pain de mie*.

Using a spatula or flexible dough scraper, scoop the dough into the prepared pan. Make sure the dough is evenly distributed in the pan and smooth the top. Dust the surface of the loaf with a generous coating of rye flour, slide the lid onto the pan, and let the dough rise for 45 to 50 minutes. The loaf will be puffy and will have risen to within an inch of the top of the pan; gently pull back the lid an inch or so to check.

Place the pan in the oven and bake at 500°F for 15 minutes, then reduce the temperature to 400°F and bake for another 15 minutes. Remove the lid, reduce the temperature to 325°F, and bake until done, about 45 minutes more. The crust will be quite dark and the side walls of the loaf will be glazed and rigid. Remove the bread from the oven, turn it out of the pan, and cool it on a rack.

In order to avoid a gummy interior, rye breads of this type must sit for 24 hours before being sliced.

NOTE This black bread freezes very well, and since this recipe makes a large loaf we often freeze half of it after 24 hours for later use.

nutrition information per serving   **one ½-inch slice, 42g**

87 cal | 1g fat | 3g protein | 18g complex carbohydrates | 4g dietary fiber | 165mg sodium | 131mg potassium | 2mg iron | 14mg calcium | 103mg phosphorus

What to Do with Your Excess Starter

One of the unsung pleasures of maintaining a sourdough starter is the gift of excess starter that you will pour off at each feeding. Don't throw it away. It is a flavorful leavening ingredient, ready to be used in a variety of delicious ways. In other sections of this book you will find simple delicious recipes for pancakes and waffles, and we encourage you to try them. Who knows, sourdough pancakes may become a weekly treat as you establish a regular weekly feeding schedule for your precious starter.

Choosing a Container for Your Starter

Ceramic sourdough crocks are a beautiful and traditional choice, but any nonreactive 2- to 4-quart lidded container will do. Clear plastic or glass containers are convenient because you can see the activity beneath the surface, and you can easily monitor the progress of your starter as it matures. We find a clear, hard plastic container convenient, too, when we want to track the growth of the starter over time—using erasable markers, we simply mark the level and note the time on the outside of the container. Whatever container you choose, make sure the mouth is wide, to facilitate the feeding and removal of ripe starter.

Established Starters Don't Need a Sugar Fix

Although we recommend that you use a bit of molasses when creating a starter from scratch, you should avoid feeding an established starter with sugar of any kind. When sugar is added to a starter, the sourdough microflora go on a feeding frenzy. This increased metabolism speeds up the fermentation, and if you're not careful, your starter will be overfermented, or exhausted, by the time you mix your dough. While this does lead to a sour taste, it is a compromised, sharp sour, not the desirable sour taste that comes from the buildup of acetic acid during a long, slow fermentation. Remember that slower is usually better in the world of natural leavens, and in general resist the temptation to speed things up.

Increasing the Quantity of Your Starter

To increase the quantity of your starter for a large recipe, or for use in more than one recipe at once, simply feed the starter as usual without discarding any. You may also increase volume by increasing the amount of flour and water you add at each feeding; just remember to follow the one-to-one ratio of equal parts (by weight) flour and water.

Cookies and Bars

Think back—way, way back, to your earliest memories of food. We guarantee that if you're an American, somewhere in the mists of time lurks a childhood experience including cookies. Maybe it was a classic: the aroma of baking chocolate chip cookies filling Grandma's kitchen. Perhaps it was more contemporary: licking the filling out of Oreos, or being taken to Mrs. Fields' at the mall. But whatever time frame your personal era encompasses, cookies have managed to span it.

Cookies are the number-one home-prepared baked good in this country; more bakers bake more cookies, more often, than they do anything else. And cookies—like bread, like pie, like any number of baked goods—are at their ravishing best when served fresh and warm from the oven. Cookie manufacturers know this; why else would they bother to manufacture frozen cookie dough that's already shaped, portioned, and put on a pan, so that all we have to do is pop them into the oven?

Cookie recipes come in a variety of options, categorized both by technique (e.g., drop, roll-out) and flavor (chocolate, molasses, sugar). The following cookie survey represents just a sampling of the vast number of cookie recipes out there.

To Spread or Not to Spread?

Why do some cookies flatten out as they bake (indeed, turn to molten puddles on the cookie sheet), while others stand firm and leave the oven looking exactly as they did going in? In large part, it's the liquid in cookies that makes them flatten out. Liquid in the dough ingredients—the egg, the butter, the milk, or any other liquid—is "freed" by the oven's heat and causes cookies to "flow"—that is, flatten. In addition, some dry ingredients (such as sugar) become liquid at high heat, adding to the spread. Cookies made with a liquid sweetener, such as corn syrup, honey, maple syrup, or molasses, tend to spread more than cookies made with a dry sweetener.

The rate at which cookies flatten out has to do with the rate at which the various ingredients become liquid. Thus a cookie made with shortening and granulated sugar will flatten more slowly than one made with butter (whose melting point is lower than shortening's) and a liquid sweetener. When cookies flatten very little it's because their ingredients "liquefy" so slowly that the dough structure actually sets up and hardens first.

There are a number of other reasons why cookies may flatten more than you like as they bake. Here are a few tips for avoiding this.

First, be sure to use shortening in recipes that call for it. Substituting butter, margarine, or oil will result in cookies that spread because these fats have a lower melting point than shortening's; where shortening will allow the rest of the cookie's structure (eggs, flour, etc.) to "set up" before it melts, using another fat means, when it reaches its melting point, the cookie won't be solid enough to hold its own and will spread. If a recipe calls for butter, and the spreading is excessive, try using shortening instead; butter-flavored shortening is a good substitute.

Other reasons cookies may spread:

Drop Cookies

These are by far the simplest cookies to make. Drop cookie dough is mixed up, then dropped—from a spoon or cookie scoop—onto a sheet to bake. Drop cookie dough is the "wettest" of all the cookie doughs; therefore, it's also the most likely to spread too much as it bakes. To prevent this, and to make the dough easier to handle, drop cookie dough is often refrigerated for up to 24 hours before being baked. This is a good cookie to start the kids off with; the steps are few, but the rewards (including sticky, lickable fingers) are many.

- **A cool oven. Baking cookies in a too-cool oven allows the fat to melt before the rest of the cookie "sets up." When preheating, be sure to allow the oven to get to the proper temperature before putting in the cookies.**

- **An overgreased cookie sheet. Most cookies need only a touch of oil to keep them from sticking; don't overdo it.**

- **A hot cookie sheet. This allows the shortening to melt before the cookies are even in the oven.**

- **Too much sugar. Sugar is hygroscopic, which means it attracts water. Water molecules in your cookie dough, rather than be absorbed by the flour, are attracted by the sugar (which doesn't absorb the water, but simply attracts it). The dough remains soft and "liquid" and spreads as it bakes. By cutting back on the sugar,** you're increasing the amount of water that will be absorbed by the flour, thus stiffening the dough and preventing spread. Try cutting back the sugar in your recipe by a quarter and see what happens.

Finally, if all else fails, try substituting bleached cake flour for the flour you've been using. Due to a number of factors—including the particle size of the flour itself, as well as the effect of the bleach—cookies baked with cake flour will set up and bake faster, and thus spread less.

On the other hand, if you *want* your cookies to spread and flatten more than they're doing, try baking soda. Add up to ¾ teaspoon baking soda to a 3-cup-of-flour cookie recipe. Cookies that use baking powder as their leavening may be slightly acidic, which means they'll bake faster and so spread less. Baking soda reduces the acidity to the point that the cookie will spread a bit more and brown faster.

Simple Sugar Cookies

ABOUT 1½ DOZEN 3-INCH COOKIES

Like many old-time New England favorites, these cookies are plain and simple. We theorize that frugal Yankee housewives saw no sense in using more sugar than was absolutely necessary, to say nothing of adding "fancy" ingredients, like butter, when lard would do. However, being New Englanders but not old-time New Englanders, we fancied these up just a bit with the addition of vanilla and nutmeg, a combination that simply sings "sugar cookie." And lard isn't in our cookie repertoire; vegetable shortening has taken its place.

You could probably pat these out and cut them with a cutter. We found it ever so much easier to simply plop them onto a cookie sheet with a cookie scoop, then flatten them with the bottom of a drinking glass dipped in sugar (or not, as you please).

½ cup (3¼ ounces) vegetable shortening

⅔ cup (4¾ ounces) sugar

¼ cup (2 ounces) buttermilk or sour milk*

1 tablespoon vanilla extract

⅛ to ¼ teaspoon nutmeg, to taste

2 cups (8½ ounces) unbleached all-purpose flour

½ teaspoon baking soda

¼ teaspoon salt

Preheat the oven to 350°F.

In a large mixing bowl, beat together the shortening and sugar until smooth. Add the buttermilk and vanilla, again beating until well combined. The mixture may look a bit curdled, which is okay.

Add the nutmeg, flour, baking soda, and salt to the wet ingredients and beat until the mixture forms a cohesive dough.

Drop the dough in round blobs onto a parchment-lined or greased baking sheet. They should be a bit bigger than a Ping-Pong ball, a bit smaller than a golf ball. Using a cookie scoop (or a small ice cream scoop that holds about 2 level tablespoons of liquid) makes this task extremely simple. Leave about 2 inches between the dough balls, as they'll spread as they bake. If you want a crisp cookie, flatten the cookies as described above. If you like a chewier center, leave them as is.

Bake the cookies for 16 to 18 minutes, until they're just beginning to brown around the bottom edges. Remove them from the oven and cool on a wire rack. As they cool, they'll become crisp. If you want them to remain crisp, store them in an airtight container when they're totally cool. If you want them to get a bit chewy, store them in a bag with a slice of apple or a sugar softener (p. 608).

*Add ¾ teaspoon lemon juice to ¼ cup milk to make it sour.

NOTE To make 4-inch cookies, make balls of dough about the size of a hand ball (about 2 inches in diameter). Flatten them and bake as directed above. Yield: about ten 4-inch cookies.

nutrition information per serving   1 sugar cookie, 30g

124 cal | 5g fat | 1g protein | 17g complex carbohydrates | 8g sugar | 68mg sodium | 21mg potassium | 1mg iron | 4mg calcium | 15mg phosphorus

Variation   SNICKERDOODLES: Preheat the oven to 400°F. Place about ½ cup cinnamon-sugar in a shallow bowl or in a large plastic bag. (Mix cinnamon and sugar until you've got just the flavor and color you want; if you have no idea where to begin, try 1 teaspoon cinnamon mixed with ½ cup sugar.)

Using a cookie scoop, a spoon, or your fingers, dip out 1 level tablespoon of dough and roll it into a ball. Place the ball in the bowl or bag of cinnamon sugar. When you've got five or six dough balls in the sugar, gently shake them until they're completely coated. Place them on a lightly greased or parchment-lined cookie sheet, leaving about 1½ inches between them. Using the bottom of a glass, flatten each cookie until it's about ½ inch thick.

Bake the snickerdoodles for 12 minutes, reversing the position of the pans (top to bottom, and back to front) midway through. Remove the cookies from the oven and cool them on a wire rack.

How to Change Your Cookie's Personality

- For a light whole wheat flavor, and added fiber and nutrition, try whole wheat flour in combination with unbleached all-purpose flour. The percentage you use is up to you; many cookies can be made with 100 percent whole wheat flour, though their taste and character will change noticeably. Start by substituting whole wheat for a quarter of the all-purpose flour and go from there. In addition, white whole wheat flour has a much milder (more acceptable to kids) flavor than traditional red whole wheat flour.

- If the recipe calls for vanilla extract, and most do, add another flavoring as well, such as almond, lemon, or peppermint.

- Cookies made completely with butter have the best flavor, but because butter contains some milk solids, it tends to produce cookies with a firmer "bite." It also makes cookies spread more than cookies made with vegetable shortening. In cookies where the butter's flavor will be overwhelmed by other ingredients, use a vegetable shortening.

- Add a teaspoon of espresso powder to a typical-size chocolate or chocolate chip cookie recipe; it will make the chocolate sing!

- Replace ¼ cup of the sugar in your sugar cookie recipe with a small box of instant pudding mix, your choice of flavor; pistachio makes a lovely light green cookie, perfect for St. Patrick's Day.

Chewy Chocolate Chip Cookies

3 DOZEN 2½-INCH COOKIES

Invented at the Toll House Restaurant (thus the cookie's alternate name, Toll House), in Whitman, Massachusetts, back in the 1930s, the chocolate chip cookie has become an American icon, right up there with apple pie and birthday cake. Everyone has a favorite recipe, from back-of-the-Nestlé's-bag to Mom's to the supposed Neiman Marcus recipe that made the rounds years ago.

The following recipe yields a soft and chewy cookie: get ready to pour a big, frosty glass of milk.

12 tablespoons (1½ sticks, 6 ounces butter)

1¼ cups (10 ounces) light brown sugar, firmly packed

¼ cup (2½ ounces) light corn syrup

2 teaspoons vanilla extract

¾ teaspoon baking powder

¾ teaspoon salt

¼ teaspoon baking soda

1 large egg

2¼ cups (9½ ounces) unbleached all-purpose flour

1 cup (4 ounces) chopped nuts (toasted, optional)

2 cups (12 ounces) semisweet or bittersweet chocolate chips

Preheat the oven to 375°F.

Beat the butter, light brown sugar, and corn syrup together until fluffy. Beat in the vanilla, baking powder, salt, and baking soda, and then mix in the egg. Beat well. Beat in the flour, then stir in the nuts and chocolate chips. Drop cookie dough by the rounded tablespoon onto lightly greased or parchment-lined sheet pans. Bake for 12 to 14 minutes, just until lightly browned at the edges. For the chewiest cookies, do not overbake. The cookies will look slightly underdone in the middle, but will set up as they cool. Cool on the baking sheet for 5 minutes, and then remove to a wire rack to cool completely. To maintain the chewiest texture, store in an airtight container with a slice of apple or a sugar softener (see Tools, p. 608).

To be sure you have the amount of spread you like in a cookie, we recommend baking one cookie to test it. Then if it does not spread enough, simply flatten the cookie before baking. If it spreads more than you would like, mix in an extra ¼ cup of flour.

nutrition information per serving   1 cookie, without nuts, 32g

143 cal | 7g fat | 1g protein | 6g complex carbohydrates | 14g sugar | 10mg cholesterol | 69mg sodium | 65mg potassium | 36RE vitamin A | 1mg iron | 16mg calcium | 21mg phosphorus | 7mg caffeine

Crisp Chocolate Chip Cookies

3½ DOZEN 2½-INCH COOKIES

Crunchy yet tender, packed with chocolate and nuts, these cookies are the favorite of everyone who opts for a crisp (rather than chewy) chocolate chip cookie.

8 tablespoons (1 stick, 4 ounces) butter

½ cup (3¼ ounces) shortening

1 cup (8 ounces) dark brown sugar

½ cup (3½ ounces) granulated sugar

2 teaspoons vanilla extract

¼ teaspoon almond extract

1 large egg

¾ teaspoon salt

1 teaspoon baking soda

2 cups (8½ ounces) unbleached all-purpose flour

1 cup (4 ounces) chopped toasted nuts (optional)

2–2½ cups (12 to 15 ounces) semisweet chocolate chips

Preheat the oven to 375°F.

In a large mixing bowl, beat together the butter, shortening, sugars, vanilla and almond extracts, egg, salt, and baking soda. Beat until the mixture is smooth and light in color. Add the flour, nuts, and chocolate chips, mixing on slow speed until thoroughly combined.

Scoop by tablespoons onto lightly greased or parchment-lined cookie sheets, spacing them 1½ to 2 inches apart. Bake the cookies for 12 to 14 minutes. To check, put a spatula under one side of the cookie, and lift it off the sheet at a 45-degree angle. If the bottom stays together, the cookies are ready to come out of the oven. Transfer the cookies to a rack to cool.

nutrition information per serving 1 cookie, 36g

156 cal | 3g fat | 2g protein | 5g complex carbohydrates | 18g sugar | 16mg cholesterol | 56mg sodium | 88mg potassium | 25RE vitamin A | 1mg iron | 23mg calcium | 33mg phosphorus | 7mg caffeine

Lace Cookies

FIFTY-FOUR 3-INCH COOKIES

These gossamer cookies have just enough flour in them to keep them from flowing off the cookie sheet. They spread enormously to become "cookies made of lace." Like snowflakes, they should be a winter phenomenon, as they will become totally limp in any but the driest weather.

3 tablespoons (¾ ounce) unbleached all-purpose flour	1 teaspoon salt
2¼ cups (7¾ ounces) rolled oats	1 cup (2 sticks, 8 ounces) butter
2¼ cups (18 ounces) light brown sugar	1 large egg
	1 teaspoon vanilla extract

Preheat the oven to 375°F.

In a large mixing bowl, mix together the flour, oats, sugar, and salt. In a small saucepan, warm the butter until it's just melted. Mix this into the dry ingredients. In a small bowl, beat the egg with the vanilla and blend it into the rest of the ingredients.

Drop this dough in small spoonfuls onto a parchment-covered cookie sheet, allowing plenty of room for cookies to spread. Bake for 5 to 7 minutes, depending on the size of your cookies.

Let the cookies cool just enough on the parchment so you can get a spatula under without tearing them. If you wait any longer, they will stick tenaciously. Cool them thoroughly on a rack and store in a cool, dry, airtight container.

nutrition information per serving   1 cookie, 19g

82 cal | 4g fat | 1g protein | 3g complex carbohydrates | 9g sugar | 14mg cholesterol | 45mg sodium | 46mg potassium | 36RE vitamin A | 11mg calcium | 21mg phosphorus

Variation   MOLDED LACE COOKIES: If you leave out the oats from the above recipe and increase the flour to ¼ cup (1 ounce), you can mold these cookies in a number of ways while they are still warm. They can be placed in the lightly greased wells of a muffin tin, to make pretty, edible "bowls" for ice cream or mousse; or they can be rolled around the handle of a wooden spoon, a cannoli mold, or cream horn mold. Once shaped, these can be dipped in chocolate and filled with sweetened mascarpone or ricotta cheese, whipped cream, mousse, or diced fresh fruits or berries.

Meringues

ABOUT 36 MERINGUES

Making egg whites into meringue is something we've always loved to do. How can a yellowish, gluey blob suddenly turn into a lighter-than-air pure white puff, a delicate, melt-in-your-mouth sweet? Well, it's the oxygen, which, when beaten into egg whites with a bit of acid to stabilize everything, creates both light color and airy texture. Add sugar and you've got meringue.

The following recipe makes three dozen delightful puffs. They're cholesterol-free and very low in fat (2 egg whites contain just a trace of fat). Meringues are innately versatile and can be flavored with your favorite extract or flavoring.

2 large egg whites	**½ cup (3½ ounces) sugar**
¼ teaspoon cream of tartar	**½ teaspoon vanilla extract**
Dash of salt	**Extra sugar, for sprinkling**

Preheat the oven to 200°F.

In a large bowl, combine the egg whites, cream of tartar, and salt. Beat until soft peaks form, then gradually add the sugar, continuing to beat until the mixture is stiff and glossy. Add the vanilla extract at the end.

Line a cookie sheet with parchment paper or aluminum foil, shiny side up. Drop the meringue by large teaspoonfuls onto the paper and sprinkle each meringue with a bit of sugar. Bake for 1½ hours. Turn off the heat and leave the meringues in the oven until they're completely cool, 3 hours or more. These are good to make in the evening; they can be left in the oven, with the heat turned off, overnight. Store them in an airtight container to keep them crisp.

nutrition information per serving   3 meringues, 5g

31 cal | 8g sugar | 31mg sodium | 8mg potassium

Variations COCOA MERINGUES: Sift together ¼ cup (1 ounce) confectioners' sugar and 2 tablespoons (⅜ ounce) unsweetened cocoa. Use ¼ cup (1¾ ounces) of granulated sugar while beating the egg whites and fold in the cocoa mixture and vanilla extract before baking.

CHOCOLATE CHIP MERINGUES: Fold in ½ cup (3 ounces) of mini chocolate chips (or any other flavored chips you like) or shaved chocolate before baking.

VERMONT MAPLE MERINGUES: Substitute the following for the sugar in the above recipe:
½ cup plus 1 tablespoon (3 ounces) granulated maple sugar
½ to 1 teaspoon maple flavor (to taste)
Additional maple sugar, for topping

COCONUT MACAROONS: Preheat the oven to 325°F. Fold 3 cups (about 12 ounces) shredded, sweetened coconut into the meringue, then scoop onto greased parchment-lined cookie sheets in 1½-inch mounds. Bake for 18 to 22 minutes, until coconut is toasted golden brown and centers of the cookies are set. (They should still be moist inside.) Take out of the oven and let cookies cool on the pan for 5 to 10 minutes before transferring to a rack to finish cooling completely. Store in an airtight container.

Fudge Drops

ABOUT 2 DOZEN 2-INCH COOKIES

These cookies develop an attractive shiny, cracked top surface as they bake. Be sure to let them cool for 5 minutes before moving them off the baking sheet, as they're very delicate while hot. They're very good with a chocolate nonpareil placed in the center before baking, or with 1 cup chopped toasted nuts added to the batter.

12 ounces (about 2 cups) bittersweet or semisweet chocolate chips

2 tablespoons (1 ounce) butter

¾ cup (5¼ ounces) sugar

3 large eggs

2 teaspoon espresso powder (optional)

1 teaspoon vanilla extract

¼ teaspoon baking powder

¼ teaspoon salt

¾ cup (3 ounces) unbleached all-purpose flour

Preheat the oven to 325°F.

In a double boiler or in the microwave, gently melt together the chocolate and butter. To avoid heating the chocolate too much and possibly burning it, the best method is to heat until the butter has melted and the chocolate has partially melted, then remove from the heat. Stir until all the chocolate melts.

In a separate bowl, beat together the sugar and eggs until they're thoroughly combined. Add the espresso powder, vanilla, baking powder, and salt, then stir this mixture into the melted chocolate, mixing until well blended. Stir in the flour. Let the batter sit for 5 minutes to thicken; it should be the consistency of thick cake batter.

Drop the cookie dough in round blobs onto a parchment-lined or greased baking sheet. They should be a bit smaller than a Ping-Pong ball. Using a cookie scoop (or a small ice cream scoop that holds about 2 level tablespoons of liquid) makes this task extremely simple. Leave about 2 inches between the dough balls, as they'll spread as they bake. Place a nonpareil or chocolate kiss in the middle of each, if desired.

Apple Crumble (top, page 130),
Peach and Raspberry Cobbler
(center, page 139), and Blueberry
Buckle with Lemon-Scented
Streusel (bottom, page 132) are
distinguished by their different
toppings.

The sponge cake used in a Jelly Roll (right, page 362) shows a very different texture than the finer-grained Chocolate Mint Cake (center, page 345) or Elegant White Cake (left, page 353). Cake textures vary depending on their leavening (eggs versus baking powder or baking soda); mixing method (creamed or stirred); and flour (cake or all-purpose).

Popovers (page 56). The protein in milk, eggs, and flour combines with the flour's starch to form a crust that contains the steam generated by baking. Steam makes the popovers "pop."

The quintessential scone is tender and pleasingly crumbly, like this Cranberry Orange Scone (page 114).

Strawberry Shortcake made with the Biscuits for Breakfast recipe (page 108). Scones and biscuits share a similar craggy, flaky texture.

These Lemon-Ricotta Puff-Pancakes (page 6) are light, airy, and spongy from the beaten egg whites folded into the batter.

The Chewy Chocolate Chip Cookie (below, page 296) gets its texture from an all-butter base, corn syrup, and two eggs. The Crisp Chocolate Chip Cookie (right, page 297) omits one egg and the corn syrup, and substitutes vegetable shortening for part of the butter.

The fine crumb, thinness, and crisp
texture of Simple Sugar Cookies
(page 294) contrasts with the
coarser-crumbed, thicker, and
chewier Peanut Butter Crisscrosses
(page 303).

Traditional Italian Biscotti, apricot–almond and hazelnut–white chocolate variations shown here (page 320). The distinctive texture of biscotti results from baking powder leavening and two stints in the oven.

The light, airy interior of these pastries comes from the beaten eggs in a choux paste dough in the Almond Puff Loaf (foreground, page 99), and from a combination of yeast and laminated dough in Croissants de Boulanger (rear, page 494).

Clockwise from lower right: Ricotta Pie (page 460) is made with a Cookie Crumb Crust (page 418); a long-flake Basic Piecrust (page 415) holds Mr. Washington's Cherry Pie (page 429); while Strawberry–Lemon Chess Pie (page 441) is made with a medium-flake Basic Piecrust (page 408).

Clockwise from top right: White Bread 101 (page 198), Raisin Pecan Rye Bread (page 237), Soft Dinner Rolls (page 221), and Ciabatta (page 244).

Clockwise from far right: French Baguettes (page 239); Golden Sesame Bread (page 286); Rosemary Olive Oil Sourdough boule (page 284); and Whole Wheat Sourdough (page 283).

Tender Focaccia (bottom and center, page 252); Crisp Seeded Mega-Crackers (third from top, page 172); Pizza (thin, page 247, or deep-dish, page 248) and parchment-thin Carta di Musica (below left, page 174). Yeast quantity, liquid-to-flour ratio, and rising time all account for the varying interior textures of these wonderful flatbreads.

Bake the cookies for 10 to 12 minutes, until their tops are shiny and cracked. You want these baked all the way through, but just barely; additional baking will make them cakey rather than fudgy. To make sure they're baked, take the pan out of the oven and use a spoon or fork to gently cut into a cookie; it shouldn't have any raw-appearing or liquidlike batter remaining in the center, but should still be moist.

Remove the cookies from the oven, wait 5 minutes, and transfer them to a wire rack to cool.

nutrition information per serving   **1 cookie, made with espresso powder, 32g**

131 cal | 6g fat | 2g protein | 4g complex carbohydrates | 13g sugar | 1g dietary fiber | 29mg cholesterol | 37mg sodium | 64mg potassium | 21RE vitamin A | 1mg iron | 9mg calcium | 39mg 39phosphorus | 14mg caffeine

Keeping Cookies Soft

To keep chewy cookies soft, cover the cookie pan loosely with a clean dish towel as soon as you take them out of the oven. Once they've cooled to just warm, wrap them in plastic wrap. The breathable dish towel allows cookies to release some of their moisture without trapping it all, which would make them rubbery; wrapping them in plastic helps contain what moisture is left.

Another way to ensure cookies' continued softness is to wrap them airtight with a cookie softener, also known as a sugar softener. This small piece of porous ceramic (see p. 608) is soaked in water, then gradually lets out its moisture over time, keeping the cookies soft.

Speaking of soft cookies, here's a neat trick. When you take your baked cookies out of the oven, drop the pan from about thigh height onto the floor (right side up, of course). Any air in the cookies is driven out, and they flatten and stay moist and chewy. Crazy? It works.

Chewy Oatmeal Raisin Cookies

ABOUT 5 DOZEN 3-INCH COOKIES

Remember the cookie dough that came in a refrigerated plastic-wrap tube and you simply peeled off the plastic, sliced the dough, put the slices on a cookie sheet, and baked them? No muss; no fuss. As kids, we used to think those cookies were pretty neat, and tasty, too; not for us the tastes of the highly developed palate.

The following cookies are evocative, in flavor and texture, of those long-ago slice-and-bake treats. Strangely pallid-looking—they certainly won't win any beauty contest—if you wrap them well, they'll remain soft and chewy until they're all gone (which won't take long, if our experience is any indication).

2¼ cups (9½ ounces) unbleached all-purpose flour

1 teaspoon baking soda

¾ teaspoon salt

1½ teaspoons cinnamon

½ teaspoon nutmeg

½ cup (3¼ ounces) vegetable shortening

4 tablespoons (½ stick, 2 ounces) butter

2 tablespoons (⅞ ounce) vegetable oil

2¼ cups (18 ounces) brown sugar

2 large eggs

½ cup (4 ounces) yogurt, plain or vanilla, regular, low-fat or nonfat

2 teaspoons vanilla extract

3 cups (10½ ounces) rolled oats

1½ cups (9 ounces) raisins

Preheat the oven to 350°F.

Sift together the flour, baking soda, salt, cinnamon, and nutmeg. Set aside.

In a large bowl, cream together the shortening, butter, oil, and brown sugar. Add the eggs, one at a time, beating well after each addition. Beat in the yogurt and vanilla.

Stir in the oats and raisins, then add the flour mixture, in three additions, beating well after each addition.

Drop the batter from a tablespoon-size cookie scoop (or from a tablespoon) onto parchment-lined baking sheets. Bake the cookies for 14 minutes. They'll still be light tan; don't let them brown, or they'll be crisp instead of chewy. Let them cool on the parchment until lukewarm, then carefully transfer them to a wire rack; they'll be delicate when warm, then chewy as they cool. Store the cookies in a tightly closed container or plastic bag.

nutrition information per serving   **1 cookie, 26g**

96 cal | 3g fat | 2g protein | 8g complex carbohydrates | 7g sugar | 1g dietary fiber | 11mg cholesterol | 45mg sodium | 81mg potassium | 10RE vitamin A | 1mg iron | 22mg calcium | 32mg phosphorus

HARVEST OATMEAL COOKIES: For a fruit-packed treat, try this variation on the preceding recipe: Use 1½ cups (5¼ ounces) rolled oats. Substitute 1½ cups (4½ ounces) dried apple pieces for all or part of the raisins. Add ½ cup (2 ounces) dried cranberries.

Peanut Butter Crisscrosses

FOUR DOZEN 2½-INCH COOKIES

An all-time favorite, perfect after school with a glass of cold milk.

1 cup (6½ ounces) vegetable shortening

1 cup (7 ounces) granulated sugar

1 cup (8 ounces) brown sugar, packed

2 large eggs

1 teaspoon vanilla extract

1 cup (9½ ounces) peanut butter

3 cups (12¾ ounces) unbleached all-purpose flour

2 teaspoons baking soda

½ teaspoon salt

Preheat the oven to 350°F.

In a large bowl, cream together the shortening, sugars, eggs, vanilla, and peanut butter. Sift together flour, baking soda, and salt and add to the peanut butter mixture, stirring to combine.

Drop cookies by spoonfuls onto a greased cookie sheet and press down with a fork (or small potato masher), making a crisscross design. Bake cookies for 10 minutes, or until lightly browned. Remove from the oven and cool on a wire rack.

nutrition information per serving   1 cookie, 28g

129 cal | 7g fat | 3g protein | 6g complex carbohydrates | 9g sugar | 1g dietary fiber | 11mg cholesterol | 86mg sodium | 62mg potassium | 3RE vitamin A | 1mg iron | 19mg calcium | 31mg phosphorus

Half-and-Half Cookies

TWENTY 5-INCH COOKIES

These jumbo-sized cookies, a New York City bakery staple, are soft and spongy and would be quite plain save for the hint of lemon in the cookie and the assertive vanilla and chocolate frosting on top. Their distinctive taste (and look) seems to be a great attraction to many kids, the ones who also like vanilla ice cream and plain sugar cookies. Though we provide a recipe for icing, feel free to use your own favorite chocolate and vanilla icings. If pressed for time, you may also use icing out of a can (it's okay; we won't tell).

COOKIES

8 tablespoons (1 stick, 4 ounces) unsalted butter

½ cup (3¼ ounces) shortening

1 teaspoon grated lemon zest

1½ teaspoons salt

2 teaspoons vanilla extract

1½ cups (10½ ounces) sugar

2 large eggs

4½ cups (19 ounces) unbleached all-purpose flour

1 teaspoon baking soda

1 teaspoon baking powder

1 cup (8 ounces) sour cream or plain or vanilla yogurt*

ICING

8 tablespoons (1 stick, 4 ounces) butter

½ cup (4 ounces) yogurt

1 teaspoon clear vanilla** (optional)

4½ cups (17 ounces) confectioners' sugar plus ¼ cup

⅓ cup (2 ounces) chopped unsweetened chocolate

Preheat the oven to 400°F.

In a large mixing bowl, cream together the butter, shortening, zest, salt, and vanilla. Beat in the sugar, then the eggs, one at a time, beating well after each addition.

Whisk together the flour, baking soda, and baking powder. Add the flour mixture to the wet ingredients alternately with the sour cream or yogurt, beginning and ending with the flour and adding the sour cream or yogurt in three additions.

Using a muffin scoop, a ¼-cup measure, or ice cream scoop, drop the dough onto parchment-lined or lightly greased baking sheets in nice round balls. Flatten each ball to a circle ¼ to ⅜ inch thick, about 4½ inches across. Leave 2 to 2½ inches between each cookie.

Bake for 10 to 11 minutes, until there's a hint of brown at the edges. Cool for 5 minutes on a wire rack. Cover them with a dish towel while they finish cooling to keep them soft. When the cookies are completely cool, seal them in a plastic bag so they stay soft. Let the cookies rest for at least an hour before frosting them.

To make the icing, melt the butter in a large saucepan, over low heat. Remove from the heat, then stir in the yogurt, vanilla, and 4 cups of the confectioners' sugar. The icing will be soft and runny. Immediately separate it into two halves, 1 cup each. Add the remaining ¼ cup confectioners' sugar to the one-half of the white icing, and the chopped unsweetened chocolate to the other half. Stir to melt the chocolate. Set the chocolate icing in a pan of hot water, or in a saucepan over very low heat, to keep it spreadable.

Dip one side of the top half of each cookie into the white frosting and put on a rack to drip and dry. As soon as you can handle the cookies without leaving fingerprints in the frosting, dip the other front half of each cookie in the chocolate frosting.

*You may use low-fat sour cream or low-fat or nonfat yogurt.

**If you use regular vanilla extract, your white icing will be tan-colored. You may do this if you don't mind compromising the cookie's look.

nutrition information per serving | 1 cookie, 100g

364 cal | 13g fat | 4g protein | 20g complex carbohydrates | 39g sugar | 1g dietary fiber | 52mg cholesterol | 266mg sodium | 82mg potassium | 119RE vitamin A | 2mg iron | 41mg calcium | 62mg phosphorus | 2mg caffeine

Hot Cookies, and What to Do with Them

Though it's tempting to just stand and eat cookies as they come hot from the oven, there comes a point when you need to cool the cookies, then store them. Remove the pan of cookies from the oven and set it on a heatproof spot for about 5 minutes; this gives the cookies a chance to set so that they'll be easier to move. Working with one cookie at a time, slide a turner underneath it, supporting it on all sides. Transfer the cookie to a rack to cool. Repeat with remaining cookies.

Using a rack allows escaping heat from the cookies to dissipate; if you left them on the pan, their bottoms would steam and become soggy.

If the cookies are large and your turner fairly small—small enough so that it doesn't support the cookie—you'll have to work fast enough that the cookie doesn't have a chance to bend and break. Holding the cookie sheet in one hand, position it above and close to the rack. Use your turner to gently flip the cookie from sheet to rack.

If you've used a nonstick cookie sheet without sides (and/or ends), and the cookies seem fairly sturdy, you can carefully slide them, en masse, from the sheet to the cooling rack.

Soft Molasses Cookies

FORTY 3-INCH COOKIES

These generously spiced cookies will stay soft, chewy, and pliable for days if you store them in a bag or cookie jar with a couple of pieces of cut apple. They may not be a favorite of kids—too many strong-tasting spices—but adults love them, and older folks especially seem to be transported back to their childhood when they take that first bite.

8 tablespoons (1 stick, 4 ounces) butter, softened

½ cup (3¼ ounces) shortening

1½ cups (10½ ounces) sugar

½ cup (6 ounces) unsulfured molasses

2 large eggs, lightly beaten

4 cups (17 ounces) unbleached all-purpose flour

1 teaspoon salt

2¼ teaspoons baking soda

2¼ teaspoons ground ginger

1½ teaspoons ground cloves

1½ teaspoons ground cinnamon

Granulated sugar, to coat cookies

In a large mixing bowl, cream together the butter, shortening, and sugar. Beat in the molasses and eggs.

In a separate bowl, whisk together flour, salt, baking soda, and spices. Stir the dry ingredients into the wet ingredients and blend until smooth. Refrigerate for 1 hour, or until the dough has stiffened sufficiently to handle easily.

Preheat the oven to 350°F.

Roll the dough into balls about the size of a golf ball—about 2 tablespoons (1 ounce) of dough. Roll each ball in a sugar-filled shallow bowl to coat it. Place the cookies 2 inches apart on lightly greased or parchment-lined cookie sheets.

Bake for 13 minutes. They will have flattened, but won't have browned significantly. If you let them get brown around the edges, they'll be less chewy and moist. When you take them out of the oven they should still feel soft on top and be just barely colored.

Cool the cookies completely on a wire rack and store them in a plastic bag with a slice of apple to keep them soft.

nutrition information per serving   1 cookie, 33g

130 cal | 5g fat | 2g protein | 9g complex carbohydrates | 10g sugar | 20mg cholesterol | 107mg sodium | 93mg potassium | 27RE vitamin A | 1mg iron | 32mg calcium | 19mg phosphorus

Gingersnaps

SIX DOZEN 1½-INCH COOKIES

These crisp, spicy rounds with their crackled, sugary tops are equally at home dunked in tea, coffee, or milk, and frequently enjoyed during the November/December holiday season. But we prefer to accompany them with a mellow, golden, late September afternoon, a comfortable lounge chair, and a very large glass of fresh-squeezed lemonade.

2⅓ cups (9¾ ounces) unbleached all-purpose flour

1 teaspoon ginger

1 teaspoon cinnamon

½ teaspoon cloves

½ teaspoon salt

2 teaspoons baking soda

¾ cup (4⅞ ounces) shortening

1 cup (7 ounces) sugar

1 large egg

⅓ cup (4 ounces) molasses

½ cup (3½ ounces) cinnamon-sugar (2 teaspoons cinnamon mixed into ½ cup granulated sugar)

Preheat the oven to 375°F.

Sift together the flour, spices, salt, and baking soda in a small bowl. In a large mixing bowl, beat the shortening, sugar, and egg together until light and fluffy. Beat in the molasses. Stir in the dry ingredients to make a soft, smooth dough.

Measure out slightly rounded teaspoonfuls of dough, shape into balls, and roll each in cinnamon-sugar. Place the cookies 2 inches apart on lightly greased or parchment-lined cookie sheets. Bake for 10 minutes, until they're golden brown. These are snaps; they're supposed to be crisp. Cool on wire racks and store in a tightly closed container.

nutrition information per serving   1 cookie, 12g

50 cal | 2g fat | 3g complex carbohydrates | 5g sugar | 40mg sodium | 22mg potassium | 12mg calcium | 4mg phosphorus

Keeping Cookies Crisp

To keep cookies crisp, try cooling them in the turned-off oven, with the oven door ajar. In cool, dry weather, crisp cookies will stay crisp for several days in a cookie jar or crock. Hot and humid weather will make crisp cookies wilt, so if you're not going to eat them immediately, put them in an airtight plastic bag after they've cooled. You can even store them in the freezer. Just make sure to remove them from the bag while they're thawing so moisture won't condense on them as they come back to room temperature.

Rolled Cookies

Generally drier than drop cookie dough, rolled cookie dough is almost identical to piecrust in texture and consistency. And you can roll it out the same way: gently, using a sufficient amount of flour and sliding a spatula underneath frequently to ensure the dough is not sticking to the work surface. Once rolled cookie dough is rolled out to sufficient thinness (ranging from ⅛ to ¼ inch), it's cut with a shaped cutter, baked, and (often) decorated. Or decorations, such as colored sugar, can be pressed into the cookies before they're baked. Gingerbread men and cookies cut into shapes (e.g., Christmas cookies) are good examples of this genre.

Gingerbread Roll-Out Cookies

3½ DOZEN 4½-INCH GINGERBREAD MEN

This is a good dough for cut-out cookies because it holds a shape with very little distortion. The result: a very crisp, medium-spicy cookie that looks the way you want it to.

COOKIES

1 cup (2 sticks, 8 ounces) butter

1 cup (8 ounces) packed brown sugar

1½ teaspoons salt

1½ teaspoons allspice

2 teaspoons ginger

1 teaspoon cloves

2 teaspoons cinnamon

1 cup (12 ounces) molasses

1 large egg

5½ cups (23¼ ounces) unbleached all-purpose flour

1½ teaspoons baking soda dissolved in ¼ cup water

SHINY COOKIE GLAZE

3½ cups (14 ounces) confectioners' sugar, sifted

6 tablespoons (3 ounces) milk

3 tablespoons pasteurized egg white*

1 teaspoon vanilla, almond or other extract of your choice

Food coloring (optional)

Cream the butter, brown sugar, salt, and spices together. Add the molasses and egg and mix well. Stir in half of the flour and the soda dissolved in water, mixing until well combined. Add the remaining flour. Depending on the power of your mixer, you may need to add the last bit of flour by hand and knead it in. Divide the dough in half and wrap well. Refrigerate for several hours or overnight. The dough changes over the resting period, making it easier to work with and adding flavor to the cookies.

Preheat the oven to 350°F.

Work with half the dough at a time on a well-floured surface. Roll the dough to ¼ inch thick. Use cookie cutters to cut the cookies into shapes. Transfer the cookies to ungreased baking sheets, leaving about ½ inch between them. Bake for 8 to 10 minutes, being careful not to overbake. The cookies will still be soft when done. Let them rest on the baking sheet to firm before transferring to a rack to cool.

To make the glaze: Place the sifted confectioners' sugar in a medium-sized bowl. Stir together the milk and egg white and add to the sugar. Mix by hand or at the mixer's lowest speed until the glaze is the consistency of molasses. Adjust the consistency with a tablespoon of water if necessary. Mix in the extract and food coloring. Keep the glaze covered while working with it, to keep it from forming a skin.

Dip the cooled cookies in the glaze, then sweep a spatula over the top of each cookie to remove the excess. Place on a wire rack for several hours or overnight to let the glaze harden and dry.

*You can also use ¼ cup meringue powder, if you prefer. Mix it in with the confectioners' sugar before adding the liquids, and mix for 4 to 5 minutes to allow the mixture to become smooth.

nutrition information per serving | 1 glazed 3-inch cookie, 33g

120 cal | 3g fat | 1g protein | 7g complex carbohydrates | 14g sugar | 12mg cholesterol | 58mg potassium | 1mg iron | 14mg calcium | 17mg phosphorus

Rolling? Not a Necessity

- Sliced cookies: Roll the dough into a log about 1½ to 2 inches in diameter. Before chilling the log, roll it in chopped nuts, seeds, or shaved chocolate for some extra texture and flavor, if desired. If it doesn't roll easily into a log right after you've made the dough, chill it for awhile until it becomes more cooperative. You can also press it into a clean, lightly greased juice can to give it the appropriate shape. Or slit the cardboard tube from a roll of paper towels lengthwise; wrap the cookie roll in plastic and press it into the tube. The tube will help it keep its shape as it chills.

  Let the dough chill until it's quite hard, or freeze it. To bake, slice it into ⅛ to ¼-inch-thick rounds.

- Hand-rolled cookies: An easy way to handle roll-out dough after it's been chilled is to roll balls of dough between your hands (a great technique for children). Then put the balls of dough on a lightly greased baking sheet and press them flat with a fork or the bottom of a glass that's been dipped in flour, sugar, or cocoa.

All-Purpose Cutout Cookies

ABOUT 3½ DOZEN COOKIES

Cutout cookies should be thin, light, and crisp, sturdy enough to decorate, yet tender rather than hard. This is one of our favorite cutout cookie recipes; it plays a starring role in our Christmas preparations.

½ cup (3¼ ounces) vegetable shortening

8 tablespoons (1 stick, 4 ounces) butter

½ cup (4 ounces) brown sugar, firmly packed

½ cup (3½ ounces) granulated sugar

½ teaspoon salt

1 teaspoon baking powder

2 teaspoons vanilla extract

1 large egg

2½ cups (10½ ounces) unbleached all-purpose flour

½ cup (2 ounces) white rice flour or cornstarch

In a large bowl, beat together the shortening, butter, sugars, salt, baking powder, and vanilla. When well blended, add the egg, beating until fluffy. Whisk the flours and/or cornstarch together and stir in. Divide the dough in half, form into disks, wrap well, and refrigerate for 30 minutes.

Preheat the oven to 350°F.

Remove the chilled dough from the refrigerator and roll it ⅛ inch thick on a lightly floured surface. Cut with cookie or biscuit cutters, place the cookies on lightly greased or parchment-lined baking sheets, and bake them for 8 to 10 minutes, until they're very lightly browned on the edges. Remove them from the oven and cool on racks.

nutrition information per serving one 2½-inch cookie, unfrosted, 20g

93 cal | 5g fat | 1g protein | 6g complex carbohydrates | 5g sugar | 11mg cholesterol | 40mg sodium | 20mg potassium | 24RE vitamin A | 10mg calcium | 12mg phosphorus

Linzer Cookies

3½ TO 4 DOZEN COOKIES

Linzer cookies are a traditional Christmas cookie from Austria, and have been lovingly adopted in this country, appearing in many a Christmas cookie gift box. Traditionally made with nut flour, these cookies are sandwiched around jam or preserves—with one cookie featuring a decorative cutout, so the filling peeks through. Americans usually make these from a crisp sugar cookie dough.

COOKIES

½ cup (3¼ ounces) vegetable shortening

¼ cup (½ stick, 2 ounces) butter

¼ cup (2 ounces) sour cream

½ cup (3½ ounces) granulated sugar

½ cup (4 ounces) brown sugar

½ teaspoon salt

1 teaspoon baking powder

1 teaspoon vanilla extract

1 large egg

2½ cups (10½ ounces) unbleached all-purpose flour

½ cup (2 ounces) cornstarch

FILLING

¾ cup (9 ounces) seedless raspberry jam

FROSTING

2 tablespoons (1 ounce) butter, melted

2 cups (8 ounces) confectioners' sugar

½ teaspoon almond extract

3 to 4 tablespoons (1½ to 2 ounces) milk or cream

TO MAKE THE COOKIES In a large bowl, beat together the shortening, butter, sour cream, sugars, salt, baking powder, and vanilla. Add the egg, beating until fluffy. Whisk the flour and cornstarch together and stir in. Divide the dough in half, form into disks, wrap well, and refrigerate for 30 minutes.

Preheat the oven to 350°F.

Remove the chilled dough from the refrigerator and roll it ⅛ inch thick on a lightly floured surface. Cut into 2½- to 3-inch rounds. Cut a smaller shape (circle, diamond, heart, or other shape, depending on the cutters you have) in the center of half of the rounds to make the tops of the cookies. (You can buy special Linzer cookie cutters made just for cutting out these cookies.) Place the cookies on lightly greased or parchment-lined baking sheets and bake them for 8 to 10 minutes, until they're very lightly browned on the edges. Remove from the oven and cool on racks.

FOR THE FROSTING Combine the frosting ingredients and put a thin layer of frosting on the cookies with cutouts. Place them on a rack to drain and dry.

TO ASSEMBLE Place a half teaspoon of jam on the unfrosted cookie circles, then place the frosted cutouts on top.

Freezing Cookies

If you want to bake Christmas cookies and freeze them until you're ready to make up your gift bags, put each batch first in a heavy-duty plastic freezer bag. Close the bag partway, use a drinking straw to suck out any excess air, and finish sealing the bag. Wrap the entire bag in heavy-duty aluminum foil.

`nutrition information per serving`   **1 cookie, 42g**

123 cal | 4g fat | 1g protein | 8g complex carbohydrates | 13g sugar | 10mg cholesterol | 43mg sodium | 24mg potassium | 19RE vitamin A | 11mg calcium | 14mg phosphorus

Variation For a more traditional Linzer dough, replace ½ cup of the flour with ½ cup ground almonds or hazelnuts.

Christmas Cookie History

The American name "cookie" probably comes from the Dutch word *koeckje,* which means "little cake." Many of our original colonists, having been driven out of England for religious reasons, took refuge in Holland before coming to America, which exposed them to Dutch ways and words. The Dutch came themselves and peppered New York State, and all the way south to Virginia, with their wonderful Dutch names. However it happened, the "koeckje" seed found fertile ground in America. As our country has grown and developed its many-faceted personality, so has the cookie.

Cookies have long been a holiday favorite, whether for eating or giving. The history of the cookie, however, casts a slight shadow on the happy associations we have with them: the first "cookies" were made by the Egyptians who, when unable to find live sacrifices, brought small cakes to the altar, cut with designs to represent an oxen's cloven hoof.

Like many other baked goods, cookies have cast their dark past aside and come to be synonymous with caring. Countries around the world have developed their own cookie customs during the holiday season. Many of the customs are ancient, and have been carried out for thousands of years.

Danish cooks bake small cookies called peppernuts *(pfefferneusse)* in quantities to last through the holiday season. If a visitor leaves the house without sampling a cookie, it's considered bad luck. In Switzerland, honey pastries resembling angels, animals, and birds are hung on holiday trees and eaten when the tree is taken down. The Scots make a traditional cookie of whole wheat flour, brown sugar, and dates, which is shared with the hungry at Christmastime. Germany is famous for its holiday lebkuchen ("darling cook"). The cookies are cakelike with a spicy molasses base. They're often dipped in dark or white chocolate and studded with currants and blanched almonds. Germans also enjoy intricately molded, anise-flavored *springerle.*

When the first star appears in the sky on Christmas Eve, many in Poland eat *oplatki,* cookies stamped with figures of the Nativity scene. While in Belgium, small "angel's cakes" are found under the pillows of good children on Christmas Day.

And then, of course, there are the cookies some American children leave, with a glass of milk, for Santa and Rudolph. And the venerable cookie gift-giving tradition that sees bakers all over the country baking, decorating, wrapping, and giving one another boxes and bags and tins of cookies.

Shaped, Stamped, and Filled Cookies

As cookie dough goes from drop (wet) to rolled (drier), it becomes easier to handle. Rather than rolling out cookies, the same type of dough can be shaped in a number of alternate ways. It can be rolled into individual balls by hand and stamped with a cookie stamp or flattened with the bottom of a drinking glass (to ensure it bakes to the desired thickness); rolled into a rectangle, spread with filling, and folded or rolled up so the filling is enclosed; pressed into a cookie mold and unmolded onto a sheet to bake; baked in a decorative shortbread pan; or baked in a log, sliced, and baked again (e.g., biscotti and mandelbrot). British shortbread, various German Christmas cookies (lebkuchen, springerle), and Italian biscotti are prime examples of this type of cookie.

Shortbread

32 COOKIES

These cookies are a perfect example of how beautiful a simple combination can be. Butter, sugar, and flour are all it takes to make a complex, crispy cookie that takes on more personality if aged for a time in an airtight container.

1 cup (2 sticks, 8 ounces) unsalted butter

1 teaspoon salt

¾ cup (5¼ ounces) sugar

2 cups (8½ ounces) unbleached all-purpose flour

In a medium-sized bowl, cream the butter, salt and sugar together with a mixer or by hand. Add the flour and blend until the mixture resembles fine cornmeal. To shape, roll the dough into 1½-inch balls, press with a cookie stamp (or the bottom of a glass, dipped in sugar, to prevent it from sticking) and chill in the freezer for 30 minutes before baking. Or form the dough into a long roll, 1½ to 2 inches in diameter, cover with parchment paper, and freeze until very firm. When ready to bake, preheat the oven to 300°F. If you've made a roll of dough, slice the roll into cookies no thinner than ¼ inch and prick

Do You Have Designs on Your Cookies?

Many bakers use any old cookie dough with their cookie stamps or shortbread molds, and then are disappointed when the design disappears during baking. It's important you use a dough recipe that's designed to be stamped (or molded); such a recipe won't include any leavening (as this would erase the design), and the type of fat or combination of fats used will be carefully paired to the liquid in the recipe to ensure the design stays its best and sharpest.

each cookie twice with a fork (or stamp with a stamp). You can also press the dough into a shortbread mold; no need to freeze it. Bake on ungreased baking sheets for about 20 minutes. Watch the cookies carefully—when the bottoms are a light sand color, remove them from the oven and transfer to a rack to cool completely.

Store the cookies in tins lined with waxed or parchment paper. You'll find that shortbread improves with a little age.

nutrition information per serving 1 cookie, 26g

123 cal | 8g fat | 1g protein | 7g complex carbohydrates | 6g sugar | 23mg cholesterol | 46mg sodium | 15mg potassium | 75RE vitamin A | 1mg iron | 2mg calcium | 11mg phosphorus

Variations ALMOND OR PECAN SHORTBREAD: Add ¾ teaspoon almond extract to the dough and roll the balls of dough in finely chopped almonds or pecans before pressing flat to bake.

CINNAMON-CHOCOLATE-CAPPUCCINO SHORTBREAD: Replace ¼ cup of the flour with ¼ cup (1 ounce) unsweetened cocoa and add 1 teaspoon of espresso powder and 1 large egg to the dough. Roll the balls of dough in cinnamon-sugar before pressing flat to bake.

LEMON SHORTBREAD: Add 1 tablespoon of finely grated lemon zest (or ½ teaspoon lemon extract or ¼ teaspoon lemon oil) and 1 teaspoon of lemon juice to the dough; roll the balls in granulated sugar before pressing flat to bake.

MAPLE SHORTBREAD: In place of ¾ cup sugar, use:
¼ cup (1¾ ounces) granulated sugar
¼ cup plus 1 tablespoon (1½ ounces) pure granulated maple sugar, or ½ cup maple-flavored sugar
½ to 1 teaspoon maple flavor powder or maple extract (optional, for increased maple flavor)

Peppermint Candy Canes

ABOUT 36 CANDY CANE COOKIES

These festive holiday cookies are fun to bake with the kids around—you roll brightly colored dough into long strips, a perfect job for small hands. The result is a treat for the eyes and the taste buds.

5⅓ tablespoons (2⅝ ounces) butter

⅓ cup (2⅛ ounces) vegetable shortening

¾ cup (5¼ ounces) sugar

1 teaspoon baking powder

¼ teaspoon salt

1 large egg

1 tablespoon milk

½ teaspoon vanilla extract

½ teaspoon peppermint extract

2 cups (8½ ounces) unbleached all-purpose flour

⅛ to ¼ teaspoon red paste food coloring or 1 to 2 teaspoons liquid red food coloring

Sugar, for sprinkling

In a large bowl, beat the butter and shortening together with an electric mixer on medium to high speed for 30 seconds. Add the sugar, baking powder, and salt; beat until combined, scraping the sides of the bowl occasionally. Beat in the egg, milk, and extracts until combined. Beat in as much of the flour as you can with the mixer. Stir in the remaining flour with a wooden spoon.

Remove one fourth of the dough; color it red with food coloring. Divide the remaining dough in half; color one portion pink and leave the last portion plain. If the dough is too soft to handle easily, chill it for 30 to 60 minutes before continuing to shape it.

Preheat the oven to 375°F.

Divide each dough portion into six pieces. Roll each piece into a 12-inch long rope. (The red rope will be smaller in diameter.) Lay the ropes side by side on a lightly floured surface, alternating colors. Roll the ropes with a rolling pin into a single 14 x 9-inch rectangle about ¼ inch thick. Using a pizza wheel, pastry cutter, or long sharp knife, cut the rectangle diagonally into ½-inch-wide strips (see illustration 1). Cut the strips into pieces 5 to 7 inches long. Press the ends of the shorter strips together to make a strip of the desired length. Place on an ungreased cookie sheet. Curve one end of each piece to form a candy cane (see illustration 2), then sprinkle each candy cane with sugar.

Bake for 7 to 8 minutes, until edges are firm and bottoms are very lightly browned. Transfer to racks to cool.

nutrition information per serving   **1 cookie, 15g**

71 cal | 4g fat | 1g protein | 5g complex carbohydrates | 4g sugar | 5mg cholesterol | 15mg sodium | 9mg potassium | 17RE vitamin A | 1mg calcium | 7mg phosphorus

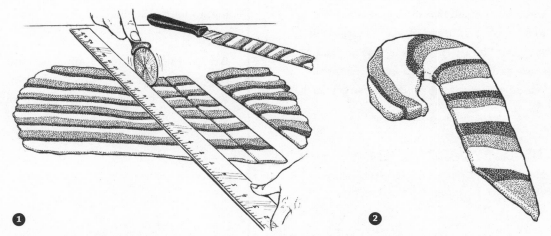

1. After rolling dough into a rectangle, use a pizza wheel or sharp knife and a ruler to cut strips ½ inch thick. A frosting spatula is helpful to transfer the dough to the cookie sheet. **2.** Bend one end of the dough to make the candy cane shape.

Vanilla Dreams

ABOUT THIRTY 2½-INCH COOKIES

The ultra-tender, light, melt-in-your-mouth texture of these cookies is unlike anything you can get using baking powder or baking soda. The secret ingredient? Baker's ammonia (ammonium bicarbonate), an old-fashioned, inexpensive chemical leavener that may be available in your local pharmacy, and is certainly available from *The Baker's Catalogue* (see "Where to Find It," p. 609).

1¼ cups (8¾ ounces) sugar

1 cup (2 sticks, 8 ounces) unsalted butter

1 teaspoon salt

1½ teaspoons vanilla extract

2 cups (8½ ounces) unbleached all-purpose flour

¼ teaspoon baker's ammonia

Preheat the oven to 300°F.

In a medium-sized bowl, beat together the sugar, butter, salt, and vanilla. Add the flour and baker's ammonia and beat until the dough almost comes together; it will seem quite dry at first, but keep beating, eventually it will become chunky and cohesive. Squeeze the dough together, gather it into a ball, and break off in small pieces. Roll the pieces into ¾-inch balls, and roll them in coarse sugar (or granulated sugar) if desired. Put them on parchment-lined or lightly greased baking sheets, and use the bottom of a glass, dipped in sugar to prevent sticking, to flatten the balls to about ¼ to ⅜ inch thick.

Bake the cookies for 30 minutes, until they're a very light golden brown. Remove them from the oven, and cool on a rack.

Baker's Ammonia

Baker's ammonia (ammonium bicarbonate) is an old-fashioned type of leavening, used mainly in cookies and crackers, and sometimes in cream puffs and éclairs. It reacts with both heat and moisture and, while the products are baking, produces a noxious smell of ammonia, a smell that disappears once the cookies are fully baked. Baker's ammonia is wonderful for extra-thin crisp cookies and crackers. It leaves no trace—smell or taste—behind, as long as the product is fairly thin.

nutrition information per serving   1 cookie, 23g

108 cal | 6g fat | 1g protein | 5g complex carbohydrates | 8g sugar | 16mg cholesterol | 67mg sodium | 11mg potassium | 57RE vitamin A | 2mg calcium | 8mg phosphorus

Fig Bars

56 COOKIES

These resemble supermarket fig cookies, but are so much fresher. We recommend that you tote a bunch of these soft, nutritious bars (figs are a good source of iron, phosphorus, and calcium) along on your next autumn outing, be it a brisk afternoon of touch football or a weekend-long hiking expedition.

COOKIE DOUGH

⅓ cup (2 ounces) shortening

1 cup (8 ounces) brown sugar, firmly packed

2 large eggs

1 teaspoon vanilla extract

1½ cups (6¼ ounces) unbleached all-purpose flour

1 cup (5 ounces) whole wheat flour

¼ teaspoon baking soda

¼ teaspoon salt

2 teaspoons baking powder

FILLING

1 pound dried figs

¼ cup (1¾ ounces) granulated sugar

1 cup (8 ounces) water

1 tablespoon lemon juice

1 tablespoon orange juice

TO MAKE THE COOKIE DOUGH In a large mixing bowl, beat together the shortening, sugar, eggs, and vanilla until creamy. In a separate bowl, whisk together the flours, baking soda, salt, and baking powder. Add this mixture to the wet ingredients gradually, beating until blended thoroughly. Refrigerate the dough for 2 hours. Meanwhile, prepare the filling

TO MAKE THE FILLING Grind the figs in a food processor or blender until a sticky, cohesive mass forms (or you can snip them with scissors into extremely fine pieces, but you'll need a bit of patience). Combine the figs, sugar, water, and juices in a medium saucepan, stir well to distribute the ingredients evenly, and cook over medium heat, stirring constantly, until the mixture becomes very thick, 3 to 5 minutes. Set aside to cool.

Lift the dough over the filling and press it together to seal it. Working on parchment paper will make transferring the cookies to the baking pan easier.

When you're ready to bake the cookies, preheat the oven to 375°F. Remove the dough from the refrigerator and roll it on a lightly floured surface into a 14 x 16-inch rectangle. Cut the dough into 4 strips, each measuring 4 x 14 inches. Spoon fig filling evenly down the center of each strip. Lift the sides of each strip up over the filling and press the edges together to seal. Cut each strip in half crosswise, making a total of eight 7-inch strips.

Place the strips seam side down, leaving 3 inches between them, on lightly greased or parchment-covered baking sheets. Cut each strip into seven 1-inch pieces, but don't separate them (yet).

Bake the cookies for 13 to 15 minutes, until they're puffed and firm to the touch. Cool for several minutes on the baking sheet before separating and cooling completely on racks.

nutrition information per serving   **1 cookie, 37g**

109 cal | 2g fat | 2g protein | 13g complex carbohydrates | 7g sugar | 2g dietary fiber | 15mg cholesterol | 54mg sodium | 138mg potassium | 6RE vitamin A | 1mg iron | 49mg calcium | 37mg phosphorus

Faux-Reos

ABOUT 50 SANDWICH COOKIES

Very thin and crunchy, with an intensely chocolate, not-too-sweet taste, these dark, almost black cookies look nice when pressed with a cookie stamp. Though you'll never duplicate exactly the look of an Oreo, this homemade version comes close to matching the taste and texture of those wonderful cookies.

COOKIES

1 cup plus 2 tablespoons (7⅞ ounces) granulated sugar

¾ cup (1½ sticks, 6 ounces) unsalted butter

½ teaspoon salt

1 large egg

1 tablespoon water

1 teaspoon vanilla extract

1½ cups (6¼ ounces) unbleached all-purpose flour

¾ cup (2¼ ounces) Dutch-process cocoa powder*

FILLING

½ envelope (1 teaspoon plus heaping ¼ teaspoon) unflavored gelatin

2 tablespoons (1 ounce) cold water

½ cup (3¼ ounces) shortening

1 teaspoon vanilla extract

2½ cups (10 ounces) confectioners' sugar

In a medium-sized mixing bowl, cream together the sugar and butter. Add the salt, egg, water, and vanilla and beat until smooth. Beat in the flour and cocoa until well combined; the dough will be very stiff.

Roll the dough into balls about the size of a shelled chestnut, or a "shooter" marble—the big marble you use to shoot at the little ones. (For those unfamiliar with either chestnuts or marbles, this is about 2 level teaspoons of dough.) Place the balls on parchment-lined or lightly greased cookie sheets and flatten each ball until it's ⅛ inch thick, using the bottom of a glass dipped in cocoa powder. You may also use a cookie stamp, for a more realistic faux-reo effect. To get a nice crisp cookie, it's important to press them thin; use a ruler on the first one so you can see just how thin ⅛ inch is. (If you press them thinner than ⅛ inch, you run the risk of having them burn.) Place the baking sheets in the refrigerator to chill the dough for 30 minutes.

Preheat the oven to 325°F. Bake the cookies for 18 minutes. It's important to bake them just the right amount of time: too little and they won't crisp properly; too much and they'll scorch. Watch them closely at the end of the baking time, and at the first sign of darkening edges or first whiff of scorching chocolate, remove them from the oven immediately. Remove the cookies from the baking pans and cool them completely on a wire rack.

To make the filling, soften the gelatin in a cup containing the 2 tablespoons of cold water, then place the cup in a larger dish of hot water and leave it there until the gelatin is completely dissolved and the liquid is transparent. Remove the gelatin from the hot water and let it cool until it's room temperature but hasn't begun to set.

In a medium-sized mixing bowl, cream the shortening, then beat in the vanilla and the confectioners' sugar, a little at a time, beating until the mixture is light and creamy. Beat in the gelatin.

Sandwich the cookies, using about 1½ teaspoons for regular faux-reos, more for double-stuffed. (You'll have some filling left over if you fill the cookies moderately.)

*You may use regular cocoa, but Dutch-process will give you a darker, more "chocolaty" cookie.

nutrition information per serving   **1 filled sandwich cookie, 23g**

102 cal | 5.1g fat | 1g protein | 3g complex carbohydrates | 10g sugar | 1g dietary fiber | 13mg cholesterol | 24mg sodium | 28mg potassium | 29RE vitamin A | 9mg calcium | 16mg phosphorus

Filling Variations CAPPUCCINO FILLING: Substitute 1 teaspoon espresso powder and ¼ cup (¾ ounces) sifted unsweetened cocoa for ¼ cup of the confectioners' sugar.

MINT FILLING: Add 1 teaspoon mint extract to filling.

PEANUT BUTTER FILLING: Cut the shortening amount to ¼ cup and add ¾ cup (7 ounces) smooth peanut butter to the remaining shortening when it is whipped.

A Decadent Dip

What's the best way to gild a cookie with chocolate? Start by slowly melting the chocolate of your choice; the easiest way is in a microwave. Heat the chocolate, stirring occasionally, until it's very soft and partially melted but some chunks still remain. Remove the chocolate from the heat and stir until smooth; melting chocolate this way, so that it never gets overly warm, helps it stay smooth and shiny.

If the chocolate is the consistency you like, go ahead and start spreading. For a more liquid chocolate, for drizzling or smooth dipping, stir in solid vegetable shortening about a teaspoon at a time (up to a maximum of 1 tablespoon shortening per 1 cup melted chocolate), until the chocolate is the proper consistency. Why solid vegetable shortening instead of vegetable oil? Because once the chocolate cools, the vegetable shortening will become solid again, helping the chocolate to set up.

Traditional Italian Biscotti

ABOUT 60 BISCOTTI

The Italian biscotti has its etymological origin in the Middle French bescuit, which referred to a type of hard seamen's bread, and literally means "twice cooked." The German zwieback means the same thing. So, zwieback, the current French biscotte, biscotti, and rusk all refer to variations on a theme: a bread that is baked once, sliced, then baked again until it's very dry. From its original consumption as a bread suitable for long ocean voyages, it's evolved into a snack bread ideal for dipping into coffee or tea, as well as a type of teething biscuit beloved by gap-toothed 1-year-olds and their parents. This recipe uses the traditional flavors of anise and lemon to produce a taste that's evocatively Italian.

4 tablespoons (½ stick, 2 ounces) unsalted butter

¼ cup (1⅝ ounces) vegetable shortening

¾ cup (5¼ ounces) sugar

3 large eggs

1 teaspoon vanilla extract

1 teaspoon anise extract, or 1 tablespoon aniseed

⅛ teaspoon lemon oil, or 1 teaspoon lemon extract

1 teaspoon baking powder

¾ teaspoon salt

3 cups (12¾ ounces) unbleached all-purpose flour

1½ cups (6 ounces) whole blanched almonds or whole blanched hazelnuts (filberts), toasted*

Preheat the oven to 375°F.

In a large mixing bowl, cream together the butter, shortening, and sugar, then add the eggs one at a time, beating well after each addition and scraping down the bowl midway through. Beat in the vanilla, anise, lemon oil, baking powder, and salt. Mix in the flour, 1 cup at a time, until you have a cohesive, well-mixed dough. Add the nuts, mixing until they're distributed throughout the dough.

Transfer the dough to a work surface (we don't bother to flour the surface; the dough is sticky, but is easily scraped up with a bench knife or dough scraper). Divide it into three fairly equal pieces and shape each piece into a rough 12-inch log. Transfer each log to a parchment-lined or lightly greased baking sheet, leaving about 3 inches between them; you may need to use two baking sheets. Wet your fingers and pat the logs into smooth-topped rectangles 12 inches long x 2½ inches wide x ⅞ inch thick.

Bake the logs for 20 to 25 minutes, until they're beginning to brown around the edges. Remove them from the oven and let rest for 20 minutes. Lower the oven temperature to 300°F.

Gently transfer the logs to a cutting surface and use a serrated knife to cut them on the diagonal into ½-inch-wide slices. Because of the nuts and the nature of the dough, the biscotti at this point are prone to crumbling; just be sure to use a slow, gentle sawing motion and accept the fact that some bits and pieces will break off. Carefully transfer the slices, cut sides up, to a parchment-lined or ungreased baking sheet. You can crowd them together, as they won't expand further; about ¼-inch breathing space is all that's required.

Return the biscotti to the oven and bake them for 20 minutes. Remove from the oven, quickly turn them over, and bake for an additional 20 minutes, or until they're very dry and beginning to brown. Remove them from the oven, cool completely, and store in an airtight container.

*Toast almonds or hazelnuts by placing them in a single layer on an ungreased pan and baking them in a preheated 350°F oven for 7 to 9 minutes, until they smell "toasty" and are beginning to brown.

nutrition information per serving   **1 biscotti made with almonds, 16g**

63 cal | 3g fat | 1g protein | 5g complex carbohydrates | 2g sugar | 1g dietary fiber | 16mg cholesterol | 38mg sodium | 31mg potassium | 12RE vitamin A | 22mg calcium | 26mg phosphorus

Variations ALMOND-APRICOT: Use 1 teaspoon almond extract and omit the anise and lemon extracts. Substitute 1 cup (4 ounces) lightly toasted, coarsely chopped almonds and ¾ cup (3 ounces) dried or glazed apricots for the nuts.

HAZELNUT–WHITE CHOCOLATE: In place of the anise and lemon extracts, use 1 teaspoon hazelnut flavoring (2 to 3 drops if it's extra-strong), or increase the vanilla extract to 2 teaspoons. Substitute 1 cup (4 ounces) lightly toasted blanched whole hazelnuts and ¾ cup (4½ ounces) white chocolate chips or chunks for the nuts.

CRANBERRY-ORANGE: In place of the anise and lemon extract, use 1 tablespoon orange zest and/or ¼ teaspoon orange oil. Substitute 1 cup (4 ounces) dried cranberries for the nuts.

Bars and Squares

If you've ever been a parent, or been at all involved in your community, you've no doubt experienced the potluck supper/fundraising culture that's so much a part of life in most areas of this country. For newcomers, the terminology involved can be somewhat mystifying. Sure, the directive from the PTO president that "A to H bring casseroles, I to P bring salads" is pretty straightforward. But when it comes to Q to Z bringing bars and squares, you may be lost. Bars and squares of what?

The term encompasses everything from brownies to lemon squares to date-nut bars—in other words, any pan dessert that can be easily cut and eaten out of hand. A quick and easy substitute for the cookie-baking process, bars and squares often involve the same dough you'd use for cookies, but spread in a pan instead of shaped into individual portions. Being flat and straight-edged, bars and squares are simple to pack and carry along to bake sales, community dinners, or Scout meetings, whatever occasion demands dessert for a crowd.

Bars and squares come in two basic types, which we'll categorize as one-step and two-step. The one-step bar, the most familiar of which is the brownie, involves mixing dough, spreading it into a pan, and baking. The two-step bar, like some types of pie, includes an initial bake of its crust, then the addition of filling and additional baking, if necessary. The lemon square is a good example of this type of bar.

Brownies

2 DOZEN 2-INCH SQUARE BROWNIES

Cakey/fudgy, chewy/tender, light/dark, with nuts/without—the Great Brownie Debate has been raging for years. If the chocolate chip cookie is the most written about, talked about, baked, and consumed cookie, then the brownie holds the same distinction in the bar category.

And for good reason. You want chocolate? A brownie is simply chocolate held together with some sugar, flour, and eggs. But, as in so many instances, the whole is greater than the sum of its parts. A plain chocolate candy bar is satisfying, but oh, what bliss derives from an inch-thick slab of moist, dense chocolate, slightly crackly on the top but smooth within. A cup of coffee or a glass of milk is the perfect accompaniment.

There must be hundreds of recipes for brownies out there, and we made quite a few of them before we decided that these were the best. We finally decided that our perfect brownie should be fudgy but not gooey. Rich enough to satisfy on its own, it should also be chocolaty enough to stand up to hot fudge sauce and vanilla ice cream. This final version is based on Maida Heatter's Palm Beach Brownies, in her *Maida Heatter's Best Chocolate Desserts*.

6 ounces unsweetened baking chocolate

12 tablespoons (1½ sticks, 6 ounces) unsalted butter

5 large eggs

2 teaspoons vanilla extract

½ teaspoon salt

2½ cups (17½ ounces) sugar

⅓ cup (3⅜ ounces) light corn syrup (optional)*

1⅓ cups (5¾ ounces) unbleached all-purpose flour

optional add-ins: 1½ cups chopped walnuts or pecans, 1½ cups mini marshmallows, 1 cup melted caramel, 1 cup chocolate chips

In a medium-sized saucepan, melt the chocolate and butter together over low heat. Set aside to cool slightly.

In a large mixing bowl, beat the eggs, vanilla, salt, sugar, and corn syrup together until light and fluffy, which takes a few minutes.

Preheat the oven to 375°F and lightly grease a 9 x 13-inch pan.

Stir the flour into the chocolate and butter mixture. Fold the chocolate batter into the egg mixture, stirring to combine. Stir in optional ingredients, if using.

Spread the batter in the pan. For an extra-glossy top, brush with 1 tablespoon milk. Bake the brownies for 35 minutes; the top should be crisp, but a toothpick inserted in the center will come out coated with chocolate. Remove the brownies from the oven, and let them cool for several hours before cutting into squares.

IN A HURRY METHOD Following the procedure above will yield a brownie that's crisp on top with a dense, intensely chocolate middle. If you're in a hurry, or want an even darker colored brownie, leave out the corn syrup and don't beat the sugar and eggs until light and fluffy. Just melt the butter and baking chocolate, mix in the sugar, vanilla, salt and flour, then beat in the eggs one by one. While we didn't like these brownies quite as much as the version above, they're just as fast as brownies from a box, and much better.

*Corn syrup will keep the brownies fresh longer and will make them denser—almost-but-not-quite gooey. However, if you choose to do the "in a hurry" method, it will give the brownies a sticky bottom crust; thus we suggest leaving it out.

NOTE When you cut these brownies (or any sticky dessert), spray your knife with a lecithin-based vegetable-oil spray; the knife will glide right through. You can also use a plastic knife to cut brownies; it works better than a metal one.

nutrition information per serving one 2-inch square, made with corn syrup, without additions, 56g

226 cal | 6g fat | 3g protein | 7g complex carbohydrates | 1g dietary fiber | 60mg | cholesterol | 65mg sodium | 80mg potassium | 73RE vitamin A | 1mg iron | 12mg calcium | 58mg phosphorus | 12mg caffeine

Ultra-Butterscotch Brownies

2 DOZEN 2 X 2-INCH BROWNIES

We use both butter-rum flavor and butterscotch chips to deepen the flavor of these rich, chewy bars.

8 tablespoons (1 stick, 4 ounces) soft butter

2 cups (16 ounces) brown sugar

½ teaspoon salt

1 teaspoon baking powder

¼ teaspoon butter-rum flavor, or 2 teaspoons vanilla extract

1½ cups (6¼ ounces) unbleached all-purpose flour

3 large eggs

1½ cups (9 ounces) butterscotch chips

1½ cups (6 ounces) diced pecans or walnuts

Preheat the oven to 350°F oven.

Melt the butter in a medium-sized mixing bowl in the microwave, and mix in the sugar, salt, baking powder, and flavoring. Stir in the flour, then the eggs, one at a time. Stir in 1 cup of the chips and 1 cup of the nuts. Scoop the batter into a lightly greased 9 x 13-inch pan. Sprinkle the remaining chips and nuts over the top of the batter.

Does the Pan Make a Difference?

Absolutely, for cookies and bars both—though for different reasons.

When a bar recipe calls for a certain size pan, it is because the recipe has been developed and tested using that size pan with the indicated baking temperature and time. Use a pan that's larger, the dough will be thinner and will bake more quickly; a smaller pan will make the bar thicker and require longer baking. You may certainly choose a different size pan than what the recipe recommends (for example, switching from a 9 x 13-inch pan to a 9 x 9-inch pan, to make thicker brownies), but be aware of the ramifications such a switch will trigger. Also, when going from a larger to a smaller pan, never fill the smaller pan more than two thirds full—it might bubble over.

The size of pan you use for your cookies has more to do with the size of your oven than anything else. For best baking, top and bottom, cookies should be baked on a pan that, when it's set on the oven rack, has at least 2 inches of clearance on all sides, for best heat circulation. A pan that covers the entire oven rack may cause cookies to burn on the bottom.

In addition, bright, shiny cookie sheets are more likely to produce a cookie that's golden brown on the bottom, rather than burned. A dark, thin cookie sheet—typical of those many of us have used for years, especially if they've been handed down through the generations—heats faster and hotter than a shiny sheet, meaning your cookie's bottoms will brown much faster than their tops. Put the cookie sheets in the middle or lower third of the oven. If all you have is dark, thin pans, try nesting them one within the other; the thin layer of air between the pans will act as insulation, helping to prevent cookies from burning.

Bake the brownies for 30 to 35 minutes, until the top is shiny but the middle is still gooey (though not liquid). Just like a fudge brownie, you don't want to overbake these; underbake a bit for chewiest texture. Remove them from the oven and cool completely before slicing.

`nutrition information per serving`   **1 brownie, 76g**

321 cal | 12g fat | 3g protein | 7g complex carbohydrates | 45g sugar | 1g dietary fiber | 37mg cholesterol | 91mg sodium | 139mg potassium | 48RE vitamin A | 1mg iron | 38mg calcium | 58mg phosphorus

Variations   BLONDIES: Use vanilla instead of butter-rum flavor and omit butterscotch chips.

CONGO BARS: Substitute vanilla for the butter-rum flavoring. Add 1½ cups semisweet chocolate chips. You also could change all or part of the butterscotch chips to another flavor, if you like, such as macadamia, cappuccino, peanut butter, or cinnamon.

Raspberry Truffle Brownie Bars

ABOUT 2 DOZEN 2 X 2-INCH BARS

These are very dark and fudgy, with a nice hint of raspberry.

BROWNIES
1 cup (2 sticks, 8 ounces) butter, melted
¾ cup (2¼ ounces) Dutch-process cocoa
1¾ cups (12¼ ounces) sugar
½ teaspoon salt
⅔ cup (8 ounces) raspberry jam
1 teaspoon raspberry flavor (optional)
1 cup (4¼ ounces) unbleached all-purpose flour
4 large eggs

1 cup (6 ounces) semisweet or bittersweet chocolate chips (optional)

RASPBERRY FUDGE GLAZE
¼ cup (3 ounces) raspberry jam
¾ cup (4½ ounces) chopped semisweet or bittersweet chocolate
2 tablespoons (1¼ ounces) light corn syrup
2 tablespoons (1 ounce) butter
½ teaspoon raspberry flavor (optional)

Preheat the oven to 325°F.

In a medium-sized bowl, whisk together the melted butter, cocoa, sugar, salt, jam, and flavor. Stir in the flour, eggs, and chips. Pour the batter into a lightly greased 9 x 13-inch pan, spreading until it's level.

Bake the brownies for 28 to 32 minutes, until a cake tester inserted into the center comes out clean; the brownies will look slightly wobbly in the middle. Cool them for 1 hour before glazing.

To make the glaze, combine all the ingredients and cook over low heat, or in the microwave, until the chocolate and butter are melted. Stir until smooth and spread over the cooled bars. Cool for several hours before cutting the brownies with a knife that you've run under hot water.

nutrition information per serving   1 bar, 60g

234 cal | 11g fat | 2g protein | 6g complex carbohydrates | 25g sugar | 1g dietary fiber | 60mg cholesterol | 66mg sodium | 182mg potassium | 96RE vitamin A | 1mg iron | 11mg calcium | 50mg phosphorus | 10mg caffeine

S'more Granola Bars

SIXTEEN 2¼-INCH SQUARES

S'mores. If you can read that word without immediately conjuring up memories of smoky campfires were ten years old—then you were never a Scout. Granola Bars. If you can read those words without immediately thinking of a green, leafy canopy overhead; the good feeling of a heavy pack resting on your hips, the cool mountain air—then you've never been hiking.

Even if you weren't a Scout and have never been hiking, don't let that stop you from enjoying these delicious, simple-to-make snack bars.

6 tablespoons (¾ stick, 3 ounces) unsalted butter

¼ cup (2 ounces) firmly packed light brown sugar

6 tablespoons (4 ounces) golden syrup, maple syrup, or dark corn syrup

2¼ cups (7¾ ounces) rolled oats

½ cup (2 ounces) unbleached all-purpose flour

½ teaspoon salt

1 cup (3½ ounces) graham cracker crumbs

1 cup (6 ounces) semisweet or bittersweet chocolate chips

1¼ cups (5½ ounces) mini marshmallows, or 1 cup (6 ounces) marshmallow creme

In a medium-sized saucepan set over medium heat, melt and stir together the butter, sugar, and syrup, cooking until the sugar has dissolved. Stir in oats, flour, salt, and graham cracker crumbs.

Press slightly more than half of the mixture into a lightly greased 9 x 9-inch pan. Let cool completely. Preheat the oven to 350°F. Sprinkle the chocolate chips evenly over the top, then the marshmallows. If using marshmallow creme, oil your fingers and a spoon and drop by teaspoonfuls evenly over the chocolate chips. Top with remaining crust mixture. Bake the bars for 15 to 20 minutes. Remove from the oven and let them rest for 20 minutes, then cut into squares while still slightly warm.

nutrition information per serving   1 square, 54g

228 cal | 9g fat | 3g protein | 15g complex carbohydrates | 20g sugar | 2g dietary fiber | 12mg cholesterol | 125mg sodium | 108mg potassium | 44RE vitamin A | 1mg iron | 16mg calcium | 76mg phosphorus | 8mg caffeine

Yuletide Toffee Squares

96 SMALL PIECES

When it's that gift-giving time of year, what better way to show you're thinking of someone than to present him or her with a beautiful gift-wrapped box of homemade candy? If the mere thought, however, of bringing a mysterious potion to the hard-ball stage (or of even owning a candy thermometer) stops you in your tracks, we offer here a short-cut solution. A meltingly buttery yet crisp base, slathered with a just-thick-enough layer of chocolate and dusted with finely chopped nuts, make these faux candy bars a pressed-for-time baker's newfound friend.

4½ cups (15½ ounces) rolled oats

1 cup (8 ounces) brown sugar, firmly packed

12 tablespoons (1½ sticks, 6 ounces) butter, melted

¾ cup (8¼ ounces) light corn syrup

1 tablespoon vanilla extract

½ teaspoon salt

2 cups (12 ounces) semisweet chocolate chips

2 tablespoons (¾ ounce) vegetable shortening

⅔ cup (about 3 ounces) chopped nuts

Preheat the oven to 450°F. Lightly grease a 15 x 10-inch pan.

Combine the oats, sugar, butter, corn syrup, vanilla, and salt and mix well. Press the mixture into the pan, using lightly greased hands to help the process along.

Bake the squares for 12 to 15 minutes, or until they're a light golden brown. Remove the pan from the oven and cool completely on a wire rack.

In a medium saucepan set over very low heat, melt the chocolate and shortening together, stirring constantly until smooth. Spread the mixture evenly over the oat base and sprinkle on the chopped nuts.

Cover very loosely and chill the squares in the pan until the chocolate is firm. Remove from the refrigerator and cut into squares. The easiest way to do this is to use a chef's knife to cut the bars into long strips while they're still in the pan, and then transfer each long strip to a cutting board to cut into bite-sized pieces.

nutrition information per serving   2 pieces using walnuts, 33g

147 cal | 7g fat | 2g protein | 6g complex carbohydrates | 14g sugar | 1g dietary fiber | 9mg cholesterol | 31mg sodium | 77mg potassium | 27mg vitamin A | 1mg iron | 14mg calcium | 52mg phosphorus | 2mg caffeine

Chocolate Mint Squares

ABOUT 36 SMALL 1 X 1-INCH SQUARES

Peppermint is a flavor that seems to appear during the holidays and disappear just as quickly once the New Year's arrived. This recipe combines mint and chocolate in a dense, rich bar, made festive by a layer of white icing offset by a final drizzle of bitter chocolate. If you like Thin Mint Girl Scout cookies, you'll love these.

DOUGH

2 squares (2 ounces) unsweetened (baking) chocolate

8 tablespoons (1 stick, 4 ounces) butter or margarine

1 cup (7 ounces) sugar

¼ teaspoon salt

2 large eggs

½ cup (2 ounces) unbleached all-purpose flour

½ cup (2 ounces) chopped walnuts or pecans

½ teaspoon peppermint extract or peppermint oil*

FROSTING

1 cup (4 ounces) confectioners' sugar

2 tablespoons (1 ounce) butter or margarine, melted

¾ teaspoon peppermint extract or peppermint oil*

1 tablespoon (½ ounce) milk

GLAZE

1 square (1 ounce) bitter chocolate

1 tablespoon (½ ounce) butter or margarine

Preheat the oven to 350°F.

TO MAKE THE DOUGH In a double boiler, or in a microwave, melt together the chocolate and butter. In a medium-sized mixing bowl, beat together the sugar, salt, and eggs. Add the chocolate mixture, stirring to combine, then the flour, nuts, and peppermint, mixing until well blended.

Pour the batter into a lightly greased 9 x 9-inch pan. Bake the squares for 25 minutes. Remove them from the oven and cool to room temperature.

To frost the squares, whisk together the sugar, melted butter, peppermint, and milk in a small bowl. Spread the frosting over the cooled squares in a thin layer.

FOR THE GLAZE: In a double boiler or in a microwave, melt together the chocolate and butter. Drizzle this over the frosted squares. Refrigerate the squares until they're well chilled. To serve, cut into 1½-inch squares.

*Peppermint oils vary in strength; add them judiciously, tasting as you go.

nutrition information per serving **1 square made with walnuts, 22g**

99 cal | 6g fat | 1g protein | 2g complex carbohydrates | 8g sugar | 25mg cholesterol | 20mg sodium | 35mg potassium | 40RE vitamin A | 9mg calcium | 22mg phosphorus | 2mg caffeine

Hermit Bars

ABOUT 8½ DOZEN 1-INCH SQUARE COOKIES

Everyone thinks there's ginger in these soft, moist, chewy bars, but the true hero of the recipe is allspice. Among the many virtues of this confection is that it keeps for weeks in an airtight container. It also ships very, very well. You can cut these into bite-sized pieces, about 1-inch square, which can be put in individual mini paper cups for giving as gifts. When you bake these bars, they'll puff up in the oven and the top will get shiny. As soon as you see this, pull the pan from the oven. The top will fall back down and the interior of the cookies will have an almost fudgy consistency. If you leave them in the oven longer, they'll be more cakelike and won't be as moist and irresistible.

BARS

1⅓ cups (10 ounces) sugar

½ cup plus 2 tablespoons (4 ounces) vegetable shortening

4 tablespoons (½ stick, 2 ounces) butter

¼ cup (3 ounces) molasses

¾ teaspoon salt

¾ teaspoon allspice

¾ teaspoon cinnamon

1¾ teaspoons baking soda

2 large eggs

5 cups (20 ounces) sifted cake flour

⅓ cup (2⅝ ounces) water

2 cups (12 ounces) raisins

GLAZE

1 cup (4 ounces) sifted confectioners' sugar

3 tablespoons (1½ ounces) milk

Preheated the oven to 350°F.

To make the bars: In a large mixing bowl, cream together the sugar, shortening, and butter, beating at medium speed until fluffy. Add the molasses, salt, spices, and baking soda. Mix for 1 minute, then stop the mixer and scrape down the sides. Add the eggs one at a time, beating well after each addition. Add half the flour. Once it's mixed in, add the water, then the other half of the flour. When the batter is mixed completely, add the raisins and stir until combined.

Spread the batter in a lightly greased 10 x 15-inch jelly roll pan (or into two pans: a 9 x 9-inch square pan and a 9-inch round cake pan to approximate the size of the jelly roll pan). Bake the hermits for 18 to 20 minutes, until their edges are light brown and the top is shiny. Remove from the oven and cool them in the pan on a rack before glazing.

To glaze the bars, stir together the glaze ingredients until they're smooth—it will be quite thin. Use a pastry brush to brush it on top of the hermits.

nutrition information per serving   1-inch square hermit, 13g

47 cal | 1g fat | 1g protein | 5g complex carbohydrates | 4g sugar | 5mg cholesterol | 37mg sodium | 26mg potassium | 6RE vitamin A | 4mg calcium | 8mg phosphorus

Ginger Squares

ABOUT 54 SQUARES

English bakers have long been famous for their gingerbread and the numerous forms it can take, from sticky toffee pudding to gingerbread men (supposedly "invented" by Queen Elizabeth I). The following recipe for thin, chewy gingerbread topped with streusel and crystallized ginger was inspired by a sample from Cornwall, England, where a locally famous bakery sells it, wrapped in foil.

BATTER

1¼ cups (5 ounces) unbleached all-purpose flour

2 teaspoons ground ginger

1 teaspoon ground allspice

¾ teaspoon salt

¼ teaspoon baking soda

½ cup (2¾ ounces) diced crystallized ginger

¼ cup (3 ounces) molasses

2 large eggs

1⅓ cups (11 ounces) dark brown sugar, firmly packed

4 tablespoons (½ stick, 2 ounces) butter, melted

STREUSEL TOPPING

1⅓ cups (5¼ ounces) unbleached all-purpose flour

8 tablespoons (1 stick, 4 ounces) butter

Pinch of salt

¾ cup (6 ounces) dark brown sugar, firmly packed

½ cup (2¾ ounces) diced crystallized ginger

Preheat the oven to 350°F.

To make the batter: In a medium-sized mixing bowl, whisk together the flour, ground ginger, allspice, salt, baking soda, and crystallized ginger.

In a separate bowl, stir together the molasses, eggs, brown sugar, and butter. Combine the wet and dry ingredients, beating until smooth. Spread the batter in a lightly greased 13 x 9-inch pan.

To make the topping: Using a pastry blender, electric mixer, or your fingers, mix together the flour, butter, salt, and brown sugar until it's fairly well blended; some chunks of butter can remain. Mix in the crystallized ginger. Bake the bars for 20 minutes. Sprinkle on the streusel and bake an additional 25 minutes, until the streusel is a deep golden brown.

Remove the squares from the oven and run a knife around the edges of the pan to loosen them. Allow them to cool, then cut into 1½-inch squares.

nutrition information per serving | **1 square, 24g**

90 cal | 3g fat | 1g protein | 5g complex carbohydrates | 10g sugar | 18mg cholesterol | 53mg sodium | 63mg potassium | 28RE vitamin A | 1mg iron | 24mg calcium | 13mg phosphorus

Lemon Squares

THIRTY-FIVE 2-INCH SQUARES

We always feel that spring has truly arrived when we smell the lilacs and see rhubarb for sale at the farmers' market. These lemon squares have their own clean sunny taste and look wonderful with just a dusting of powdered sugar to set them off. If you are one of those who anticipate spring in part because it means that you may now indulge in rhubarb, they can be gilded with a bright red topping of sweetened strawberry-rhubarb purée for an incredible sweet/tart taste.

CRUST

8 tablespoons (1 stick, 4 ounces) butter

¼ cup (1¾ ounces) granulated sugar

½ teaspoon salt

2 teaspoons vanilla extract

2½ cups (10½ ounces) unbleached all-purpose flour or unbleached pastry flour

2 large eggs

FILLING

8 tablespoons (1 stick, 4 ounces) butter, melted

1¼ cups (8¾ ounces) sugar

2 tablespoons (⅝ ounce) cornmeal

2 tablespoons (½ ounce) cornstarch

½ teaspoon salt

4 large eggs

½ cup (4 ounces) fresh lemon juice (2 to 3 large lemons)

TOPPING

For lemon squares: confectioners' sugar for dusting

FOR STRAWBERRY-RHUBARB SQUARES

2 pints (12 to 16 ounces) strawberries

2 cups (8 to 9 ounces) diced rhubarb (4 to 5 medium stalks)

Pinch of salt

1 cup (7 ounces) sugar

3 tablespoons (¾ ounce) cornstarch dissolved in ¼ cup (2 ounces) water

Few drops of red food coloring

Preheat the oven to 350°F.

TO MAKE THE CRUST In a medium-sized mixing bowl, cream the butter until fluffy. Add the sugar, salt, and vanilla and beat well. Stir in the flour and eggs, mixing until well blended. Note: If you're using a hand mixer, you'll need to finish kneading in the flour by hand, as this dough is quite stiff.

Lightly grease a 10 x 15-inch jelly roll pan. Press the dough into the pan, being sure to press it up to the top edge of the pan. An easy way to level the dough is to cover it with plastic wrap, then use a small rolling pin or a can on its side to flatten it. Prick the dough all over with a fork. Bake the crust for 8 minutes; it won't brown much, just become set. Leave the oven on.

To make the lemon filling: In a medium-sized mixing bowl, whisk together the melted butter, sugar, cornmeal, cornstarch, salt, eggs, and lemon juice. Top the baked crust with the lemon filling. Return it to the oven and bake for an additional 25 to 28 minutes, until the top is lightly browned on the top and edges.

If you're making lemon bars, cool them completely at this point, then dust with confectioners' sugar before cutting into squares.

Variation   STRAWBERRY-RHUBARB SQUARES: For strawberry-rhubarb squares, finish with this topping. To make the glaze, rinse the strawberries and rhubarb. Place the strawberries on a towel or a rack to dry, then dice about 1 cup of them.

Place the rhubarb, diced strawberries, salt, and ½ cup of the sugar in a small saucepan. Over low heat, stirring constantly, bring the mixture to a boil. Add the remaining sugar and the cornstarch dissolved in the water, return the mixture to a boil, then remove it from the heat. Let the mixture cool slightly. Add a few drops of red food coloring, if desired. To finish, either dice the remaining berries and mix with the glaze, then spread over the filling; or spread the glaze over the filling, then arrange sliced fresh berries over the top. If you're serving the bars within a few hours, arrange the berries on top as it looks a little more festive; but mixing the berries completely into the glaze keeps them looking fresh longer.

nutrition information per serving   **1 lemon square, 37g**

116 cal │ 5g fat │ 2g protein │ 8g complex carbohydrates │ 8g sugar │ 48mg cholesterol │ 73mg sodium │ 26mg potassium │ 55RE vitamin A │ 1mg vitamin C │ 1mg iron │ 7mg calcium │ 25mg phosphorus

nutrition information per serving   **1 strawberry-rhubarb square, 62g**

153 cal │ 7g fat │ 2g protein │ 8g complex carbohydrates │ 14g sugar │ 1g dietary fiber │ 51mg cholesterol │ 73mg sodium │ 69mg potassium │ 69RE vitamin A │ 9mg vitamin C │ 1mg iron │ 14mg calcium │ 29mg phosphorus

Peanut Butter Fudge Bars

36 BARS

Chocolate (cake, cookies, bars) and peanut butter (sandwiches, crackers) are certainly two of the flavors most of us learn about quite early in life; it's inevitable that at some point they'd come together.

Bars are quick and (usually) easy to make and, being flat and straight-edged, are also simple to pack and carry along to a picnic. These bars are "rich and delicious, possibly illegal, certainly immoral," according to one taster.

CRUST

4 tablespoons (½ stick, 2 ounces) butter

⅓ cup (3⅛ ounces) peanut butter

¾ cup (5¼ ounces) sugar

¼ teaspoon salt

1 teaspoon vanilla extract

¼ teaspoon baker's ammonia (optional)

1¼ cups (5¼ ounces) unbleached all-purpose flour

FILLING

¾ cup (4½ ounces) chopped unsweetened baking chocolate

8 tablespoons (1 stick, 4 ounces) butter

½ teaspoon salt

¼ cup (2¾ ounces) light corn syrup

1 cup plus 2 tablespoons (7½ ounces) sugar

1 cup (4¼ ounces) unbleached all-purpose flour

2 large eggs

½ cup (3 ounces) chocolate chips, peanut butter chips, or peanut butter candy pieces (optional)

FROSTING

¾ cup (4½ ounces) butterscotch chips, white chocolate chips, white confectionery coating disks, or a combination

¼ cup (2⅜ ounces) peanut butter

Preheat the oven to 350°F.

TO MAKE THE CRUST In a medium-sized bowl, beat the butter and peanut butter until soft and well blended. Stir in the sugar, salt, vanilla, and baker's ammonia. Mix in the flour; the mixture will feel dry and be crumbly. Press the dough into a lightly greased 9 x 13-inch pan; using a small pastry rolling pin (or a can on its side) helps, as does covering the crumbs with a piece of plastic wrap. Bake the crust for 8 to 10 minutes, until it's lightly browned around the edges. Remove the pan from the oven and leave the oven turned on.

FOR THE FILLING In a medium-sized pan (or microwave-safe bowl), melt and stir together the chocolate, butter, salt, and corn syrup. Remove the pan from the heat and blend in the sugar and flour. Beat in the eggs until well blended, then mix in the chips, or whatever embellishment you've decided to use (if any).

Pour the filling onto the crust and bake the bars for 22 to 24 minutes. The top should be shiny and look set. For the fudgiest texture, don't overbake; a tester inserted into the center won't come out clean, but with sticky crumbs clinging to it.

TO MAKE THE FROSTING Melt the chips over low heat (or in a microwave), stirring often. Stir in the peanut butter and spread the mixture over the warm bars. Cool completely before cutting. You can definitely cut these bars on the small side (1½ x 2 inches); they're sinfully rich. Use a knife sprayed with nonstick vegetable oil spray or warmed in hot water, and wipe it often.

nutrition information per serving　1 bar, 38g

169 cal | 9g fat | 3g protein | 7g complex carbohydrates | 14g sugar | 1g dietary fiber | 22mg cholesterol | 75mg sodium | 74mg potassium | 41RE vitamin A | 1mg iron | 5mg calcium | 42mg phosphorus | 6mg caffeine

Almond Toffee Bars

ABOUT 48 SQUARES

This recipe makes a rich, buttery bar gilded with a sweet, dark-caramel-like topping.

COOKIE BASE

1 cup (2 sticks, 8 ounces) butter

1 teaspoon almond extract

½ cup (2 ounces) confectioners' sugar

2 cups (8½ ounces) unbleached all-purpose flour

½ teaspoon baking powder

½ teaspoon salt

TOPPING

1 cup (8 ounces) brown sugar, packed

5⅓ tablespoons (⅔ stick, 1⅞ ounces) butter

¼ cup (2 ounces) milk

1 cup (3 ounces) sliced unblanched almonds

Preheat the oven to 350°F.

TO MAKE THE BASE In a medium-sized mixing bowl, cream the butter, then add the almond extract and the confectioners' sugar, beating all the while. Sift together the flour, baking powder, and salt and stir the dry ingredients into the wet ingredients. Press the dough into an ungreased 15 x 10 x 1-inch baking sheet, coming up the sides just a little. Bake the crust 15 to 20 minutes, until it's golden brown. Set it aside.

TOPPING Combine the brown sugar, butter, and milk in a saucepan, stirring over low heat just until the brown sugar is dissolved and the butter has melted. Spread this mixture over the cookie base. Sprinkle with the sliced almonds.

Put the pastry under the broiler until the top bubbles, 3 minutes at the most. After 2 minutes, open the oven door and watch the bubbling action. As soon as the nuts are golden brown, remove the bars from the oven. (It's easy to burn this if you're not careful.) When cool, cut into small squares, about 1½ inches.

nutrition information per serving | **1 square, 21g**

98 cal | 6g fat | 1g protein | 4g complex carbohydrates | 5g sugar | 15mg cholesterol | 86mg sodium | 40mg potassium | 51RE vitamin A | 23mg calcium | 19mg phosphorus

Dream Bars

ABOUT 2 DOZEN 2¼-INCH BARS

These bars won't pass muster on their looks alone; indeed, they're as plain-looking as a date square. But just take that first bite and you'll forget the visual impression. Coconut, nuts, and sugar combine to form a gooey, rich topping on a buttery cookie base. Sprinkle these with a shower of snowy confectioners' sugar and you've got bars whose looks begin to live up to their taste.

COOKIE LAYER
8 tablespoons (1 stick, 4 ounces) butter
½ cup (4 ounces) dark brown sugar
1 cup (4¼ ounces) unbleached all-purpose flour
¼ teaspoon salt

TOPPING
2 cups (16 ounces) dark brown sugar

1 tablespoon unbleached all-purpose flour
¼ teaspoon baking powder
2 large eggs, well beaten
1 cup (3½ ounces) shredded (or shaved) coconut, sweetened or unsweetened, toasted or not
1 cup (4 ounces) diced nuts: walnuts, pecans, hazelnuts, or your favorite nut

Preheat the oven to 300°F.

TO MAKE THE COOKIE LAYER In a large mixing bowl, cream together the butter and brown sugar until smooth. Stir in the flour and salt; the mixture will be crumbly. Pat the crumbs into a lightly greased 9 x 13-inch pan. Bake the cookie layer for 10 minutes, while you prepare the topping. Turn the oven up to 325°F.

TO MAKE THE TOPPING In a medium-sized mixing bowl, combine the brown sugar, flour, and baking powder. Stir in the eggs, mixing until smooth, then add the coconut and nuts, again mixing until well combined. Dollop the topping onto the crust in the pan, spreading it out; wet your fingers and spread it around as evenly as possible.

Bake the bars for 30 minutes, until they're golden brown. Remove from the oven and let them cool. Sprinkle them with confectioners' sugar, if desired, and cut them when they're completely cool.

nutrition information per serving | **1 bar, 45g**

192 cal | 8g fat | 2g protein | 6g complex carbohydrates | 22g sugar | 1g dietary fiber | 34mg cholesterol | 69mg sodium | 120mg potassium | 1mg iron | 36mg calcium | 37mg phosphorus

Date Squares

THIRTY-SIX 1½-INCH SQUARES

We remember date squares from our Sunday-morning-after-church-at-the-bakery days—two layers of crumbly, crunchy, sweet oatmeal crust sandwiching a gooey layer of smooth date filling. It was best to eat the squares over a plate or napkin, as much of the crust inevitably crumbled away as you took each bite.

You may think date square recipes are a dime a dozen; open any cookbook and you'll find date bars listed in the index. The problem is, those are date *bars*—a homogeneous, rather than layered, mixture of dates and oatmeal, not at all what we remember. In desperation, we finally went ahead and made up our own recipe and have been enjoying it ever since.

FILLING

15 to 16 ounces (3 cups) chopped dates

1 cup (8 ounces) water

Heaping ¼ teaspoon salt

1 tablespoon plus 1 teaspoon lemon juice

2 teaspoons vanilla extract

CRUST

1½ cups (5¼ ounces) rolled oats

1½ cups (6¼ ounces) unbleached all-purpose flour*

1 cup (8 ounces) brown sugar, light or dark, packed

¾ teaspoon baking soda

¾ teaspoon salt

12 tablespoons (1½ sticks, 6 ounces) butter or margarine, melted

½ cup (2 ounces) chopped walnuts or pecans

Preheat the oven to 350°F.

TO MAKE THE FILLING In a small saucepan, combine the dates, water, salt, and lemon juice. Bring the mixture to a boil, reduce the heat to low, and simmer for 3 to 4 minutes, until the water is absorbed and mixture has thickened somewhat. Remove the pan from the heat, stir in the vanilla, and set aside to cool while you prepare the crust.

TO MAKE THE CRUST In a medium-sized mixing bowl, whisk together the oats, flour, sugar, baking soda, and salt. Stir in the melted butter.

TO ASSEMBLE Press 2½ cups of the crust mixture into a lightly greased 9 x 9-inch pan, smoothing it out to completely cover the bottom of the pan with no gaps. Top the crust with the date filling. Add the walnuts to the remaining crust mixture and sprinkle it over the filling.

Bake the squares for 30 minutes, or until the crust is golden brown. Remove the squares from the oven and allow them to cool before cutting.

*You may use a half-and-half combination of unbleached all-purpose and whole wheat flours, if you like.

nutrition information per serving   **1 square, 41g**

134 cal | 5g fat | 2g protein | 14g complex carbohydrates | 6g sugar | 2g dietary fiber | 11mg cholesterol | 90mg sodium | 130mg potassium | 39RE vitamin A | 1mg iron | 23mg calcium | 33mg phosphorus

Cakes

Have you ever noticed that all of life's happy milestones—
birthdays, graduations, weddings, anniversaries—are marked by cake? Every
time the occasion turns festive, there's a cake, right at its center. From early
Greek nut and honey cakes, right on up through today's intricately crafted
wedding cakes, cake has been a constant player.

What makes cake different from other baked goods? Cake (cupcakes)
and muffins are actually quite similar, but on the whole cake, especially
in its layered form, is a much grander, more festive offering than the comfortable
old muffin. And cake, though perceived by some as a more formal dessert, is
also the essence of comfort food—sweet, soft, and often chocolate, it's
a throwback to most any American's childhood.

Cakes, like most baked goods, come in a wide variety of types. Think dense, dark Christmas fruitcake, a fudge-frosted yellow cupcake, angel food, New York cheese-cake, a raspberry-jam-filled jelly roll, flourless chocolate cake; all are cake, but how different, in flavor, texture and form. You could bake a cake every day of the year and not come close to girdling their wide world. And, if you're a passionate baker, the wideness of that universe is somehow comforting; no matter what, you'll never run out of new cake recipes to try.

Easy or One-Bowl Cakes

When you think of comfort cakes, what comes to mind? A warm, raisin-studded apple cake, drizzled with caramel icing? Gingerbread with a topknot of whipped cream? How about everyone's favorite, carrot cake with cream cheese icing? These cakes, often containing a wide array of ingredients, and usually dense rather than light, are called one-bowl cakes because you need only one bowl to prepare them. The simplest of all the cakes, they're stirred together like muffins, though usually this stirring comes closer to beating. Because of the tenderizing properties of their high amounts of both sugar and fat (compared to most muffins), these cakes are able to withstand a fairly heavy workout without becoming tough.

The leavening in this type of cake comes almost entirely from chemicals, either baking powder, baking soda, or a combination. A small amount of air is created through beating, but nothing like what occurs in butter or foam cakes, which rely much more heavily for their leavening on the way in which they're prepared, rather than simply the baking powder or baking soda in the list of ingredients.

Apple Cake

ONE 9 X 13-INCH CAKE, 16 SERVINGS

Apples and ginger have a natural affinity for each other, as shown in this moist, tasty cake.

1 cup (5¼ ounces) whole wheat flour

1⅓ cups (5½ ounces) unbleached all-purpose flour

1 cup (7 ounces) sugar

1 cup (8 ounces) firmly packed brown sugar

2 teaspoons baking soda

¾ teaspoon salt

2 teaspoons apple pie spice or 1 teaspoon cinnamon plus ½ teaspoon each allspice and nutmeg

8 tablespoons (1 stick, 4 ounces) soft butter

3 tablespoons (1½ ounces) minced crystallized ginger (optional)

4 cups (28 ounces) cored, chopped, unpeeled apples

½ cup (2 ounces) diced pecans or walnuts

½ cup (3 ounces) raisins, golden raisins, or currants

2 large eggs

Preheat the oven to 325°F.

In a large mixing bowl, whisk together the flours, sugars, baking soda, salt, and spice(s). Cut the softened butter into chunks and add it along with the ginger, apples, nuts, raisins, and eggs. Beat at medium speed until well blended.

Turn the batter into a greased and floured 9 x 13-inch pan and smooth the top. Bake the cake for 45 minutes, or until it springs back when lightly touched in the center. Remove it from the oven and cool completely on a wire rack. Leave the cake in the pan and spread with caramel frosting, page 396.

nutrition information per serving   one 2½-inch square, unfrosted, 96g

279 cal | 4g fat | 9g protein | 22g complex carbohydrates | 27g sugar | 3g dietary fiber | 42mg cholesterol | 274mg sodium | 191mg potassium | 67RE vitamin A | 2mg vitamin C | 2mg iron | 31mg calcium | 69mg phosphorus

Carrot Cake

ONE 9 X 13-INCH CAKE, OR ONE THREE-LAYERED 8-INCH CAKE

Carrot cake is a touchstone dessert. We know lots of folks for whom nothing else will do on their birthdays. But if someone asks you for carrot cake, make sure to ask which kind they're thinking about, since there are really two distinct styles. One camp garnishes with raisins and nuts, while the other heads for crushed pineapple and/or coconut; the recipe below will work perfectly well either way. Or, if you're the sort for whom too much is just enough, put all of them in.

This is a good-sized recipe; it will generously fill a 9 x 13-inch pan or three 8-inch round pans, if you want to make it as a layer cake. It's moist and flavorful enough to stand on its own with just a dusting of confectioners' sugar, but we know of no better way to enjoy cream cheese frosting than with carrot cake!

4 large eggs

1½ cups (10½ ounces) vegetable oil

2 teaspoons vanilla extract

1¾ cups (12¼ ounces) sugar

2 cups (8½ ounces) unbleached all-purpose flour

1½ teaspoons baking powder

2 teaspoons baking soda

1 teaspoon salt

1 tablespoon cinnamon

½ teaspoon nutmeg

2½ cups (8¾ ounces) finely grated carrots

1 cup (4 ounces) chopped pecans or walnuts

1 cup (3 ounces) shredded or flaked coconut*

1 can (8 ounces) crushed pineapple, drained*

Preheat the oven to 350°F.

In large mixing bowl, beat the eggs and add oil while mixer is running. Add vanilla, then gradually add the sugar. You'll have a thick, foamy, lemon-colored mixture. In a separate medium-sized bowl, whisk together the flour, baking powder, baking soda, salt, and spices. Add these dry ingredients to the wet mixture, stirring to make a smooth batter. Add the carrots and nuts, then additional garnishes of your choice (coconut, pineapple, and/or raisins).

Pour the batter into a greased 9 x 13-inch sheet pan or three 8-inch round pans and bake for 45 to 50 minutes (sheet) or 35 minutes (rounds). Cake is done when tester inserted in the center comes out clean. Cool in the pan 10 minutes, then turn out to cool completely. Dust with confectioners' sugar or frost with cream cheese frosting (p. 397), or the icing of your choice.

*Or substitute 2 cups (12 ounces) raisins for the coconut and pineapple.

nutrition information per serving   one 2-inch square, unfrosted, 77g

280 cal | 19g fat | 3g protein | 11g complex carbohydrates | 15g sugar | 1g dietary fiber | 36mg cholesterol | 257mg sodium | 108mg potassium | 339RE vitamin A | 2 mg vitamin C | 1mg iron | 33mg calcium | 55mg phosphorus

Gingerbread Plus

ONE 9 X 13-INCH CAKE, ABOUT 18 SERVINGS

Gingerbread, a cake with a long international history, has become an American classic. Known in northern Europe since the eleventh century, gingerbread arrived on these shores along with the settlers; each wave of new Americans carried with them a number of variations particular to their own region and country. All of those types of gingerbread eventually metamorphosed into the gingerbread we know today.

Moist, gingery, and dense (but not heavy), this single-layer cake has a way of transporting you right back to your childhood, sitting at the kitchen table after school eating a square of warm gingerbread adorned with whipped cream. Our thanks to Karyl Bannister of Southport, Maine, for the original recipe that inspired this one.

¾ cup (6 ounces) light brown sugar

¼ cup (3 ounces) molasses

½ cup (5 ounces) ginger syrup (see following recipe), golden syrup, or light corn syrup

8 tablespoons (1 stick, 4 ounces) butter, melted

¼ cup (1¾ ounces) vegetable oil

2 large eggs

2½ cups (10½ ounces) unbleached all-purpose flour

2 teaspoons baking soda

1 tablespoon ground ginger

1 teaspoon cinnamon

½ teaspoon nutmeg

½ teaspoon salt

⅔ cup (4½ ounces) minced crystallized ginger (optional)

1 cup (8 ounces) boiling water

Preheat the oven to 350°F.

In a medium-sized bowl, mix together the sugar, molasses, syrup, melted butter, oil, and eggs, beating until smooth. Stir in the flour, baking soda, spices, salt, and crystallized ginger. Then carefully stir in the water; go slowly, as it will want to splash up. Scrape the sides and bottom of the bowl and stir in any of the pasty patches that have gathered there.

Pour the batter into a lightly greased 9 x 13-inch pan or tube pan. Bake for 30 to 40 minutes, until it tests done. Brush with additional ginger syrup (see recipe on next page), if desired.

nutrition information per serving   one 2 x 3-inch piece, 70g

215 cal | 9g fat | 2g protein | 12g complex carbohydrates | 20g sugar | 1g dietary fiber | 38mg cholesterol | 228mg sodium | 88mg potassium | 61RE vitamin A | 1mg iron | 20mg calcium | 31mg phosphorus

Ginger Syrup

2 ¼ CUPS

Bitingly hot and sweet, this ginger syrup is a snap to make. Drizzle it over ginger-bread, biscuits or scones, pancakes, or oatmeal. It's a wonderful addition to tea, too.

4 cups (about 13 ounces) fresh gingerroot, unpeeled, cut into ⅛- to ¼-inch-thick slices (a food processor makes short work of this task)

3½ cups (24½ ounces) sugar

3½ cups (28 ounces) water

In a large heavy saucepan, bring the ginger, sugar, and water to a boil. Boil the mixture for 45 minutes to 1 hour, until it registers 216°F to 220°F on an instant-read thermometer. The lower temperature will give you a thinner syrup, one that's easy to stir into drinks; the higher temperature will yield a thicker syrup, more the consistency of corn syrup. (You can't tell how thick the syrup will be while it's still hot; you have to go by its temperature, as it'll thicken as it cools.)

Remove the pan from the burner and carefully strain the syrup into a nonreactive container. Store in the refrigerator.

nutrition information per serving   **1 tablespoon, 34g**

9 cal | 2g complex carbohydrates | 2mg sodium | 42mg potassium | 1mg vitamin C | 2mg calcium | 3mg phosphorus

A Very Light Fruitcake

THREE 8½ X 4½-INCH FRUITCAKES

Fruitcake seems to elicit either groans of dismay or timid—very timid—admissions of pleasure. While for some folks fruitcake is simply fodder for culinary jokes, for others it's a time-honored Christmas tradition.

The year's production of fruitcake usually begins at Thanksgiving; over the course of a couple of days, fruit is soaked in brandy, all of the various components are assembled, combined, and baked, and finally fruitcakes line the kitchen counter. Most of them are given as gifts, but one or two are always stashed in a cool place to wait for Christmas, when the fruitcake lovers in the family will be in their element.

We like the following recipe because it omits the usual citron and peel, a plus if you're not a fan of those somewhat bitter fruits. With its light-colored, mild-flavored cake cradling a variety of tasty dried fruits, this is a fruitcake even non-fruitcake-lovers will embrace.

FRUIT

2¼ pounds (6 cups) of your favorite dried fruits

1 cup (6 ounces) candied red cherries

¼ cup (2 ounces) brandy, rum, or whiskey, or apple juice or water

CAKE

1 cup (2 sticks, 8 ounces) butter

1 cup (7 ounces) granulated sugar

½ cup (4 ounces) brown sugar

2 teaspoons baking powder

½ teaspoon salt

½ teaspoon ground ginger

1 teaspoon cinnamon

½ teaspoon nutmeg

4 large eggs

¼ cup (2¾ ounces) light corn syrup

3 cups (12¾ ounces) unbleached all-purpose flour

¾ cup (6 ounces) milk

2 cups (8 ounces) diced pecans or walnuts (optional)

TO PREPARE THE FRUIT Combine the dried fruit and the liquor, water, or juice in a nonreactive bowl, cover, and allow to macerate overnight.

Preheat the oven to 300°F.

TO PREPARE THE CAKE Beat together the butter, sugars, baking powder, salt, and spices until well blended. Beat in the eggs and corn syrup, beating until fluffy. Add the flour and beat until smooth. Beat in the milk, then mix in the fruit (don't drain it), and the nuts. Spoon the batter into three lightly greased 8½ x 4½-inch loaf pans, or into smaller pans of your choice. Fill them about three-quarters full.

Bake the cakes for 40 to 70 minutes, depending on the size of the pans; the full-sized cakes will take the longer amount of time. When the cake is done, it will be a light golden brown all over and a cake tester inserted into the center will come out clean.

Remove the fruitcakes from the oven, allow them to cool for 10 minutes, then turn them out of the pans. Brush them with brandy or the liquor of your choice (or apple juice) while they're still warm. When they're completely cool, wrap them well and let rest at least 24 hours before serving.

This cake can be made several weeks ahead; just brush it with brandy, rum, whiskey, or simple syrup (p. 390) and wrap it tightly in plastic wrap. For long-term storage (up to two months), brush with the liquor of your choice once a week, keeping the cake tightly wrapped between times. If you don't choose to brush the cake with liquor, freeze it for up to two months before serving.

nutrition information per serving   ½-inch slice, 51g

162 cal | 5g fat | 2g protein | 20g complex carbohydrates | 9g sugar | 2g dietary fiber | 29mg cholesterol | 55mg sodium | 195mg potassium | 133RE vitamin A | 1mg iron | 33mg calcium | 38mg phosphorus

Traditional Fruitcake

If your idea of fruitcake is dark and lustrous, try the following variations on the preceding recipe:

- Use a total of 1½ cups (12 ounces) brown sugar, omitting the white sugar
- Substitute dark corn syrup for the light corn syrup
- Substitute the fruits of your choice, including mixed dried peel and citron
- Add 2 tablespoons unsweetened cocoa or 1 teaspoon caramel color, for color.

Chocolate Mint Cake

ONE 2-LAYER, 9-INCH ROUND CAKE, 16 SERVINGS

Deep, dark chocolate cake, layered around a rich, creamy filling, and glazed with sumptuous fudge glaze—what's not to love? The hint of mint in the garnish reminds us of our favorite Girl Scout cookies, but leave it out if you like; or substitute a chocolate-covered espresso-bean garnish, to put it in mocha mode. The cake for this confection is made in a similar fashion to gingerbread, with hot water the final ingredient. We recommend filling this cake with the marshmallow filling on page 401 and icing it with the chocolate glaze on page 396.

CAKE

1¾ cups (12¼ ounces) sugar

2¼ cups (9½ ounces) unbleached all-purpose flour

2 tablespoons (½ ounce) cornstarch

¾ cup (2¼ ounces) Dutch-process cocoa

¼ cup (1¼ ounces) buttermilk powder*

1 teaspoon baking powder

1 teaspoon baking soda

1 teaspoon salt

2 large eggs

¾ cup (6 ounces) water*

½ cup (3½ ounces) vegetable oil

2 teaspoons vanilla extract

1 cup (8 ounces) hot water

Preheat the oven to 350°F. Lightly grease and flour two 9-inch round cake pans.

TO MAKE THE CAKE In a large bowl, stir together the sugar, flour, cornstarch, cocoa, buttermilk powder, baking powder, baking soda, and salt. Add the eggs, ¾ cup water, oil, and vanilla; beat on medium speed for 2 minutes. Stir in the hot water; the batter will be thin. Pour the batter into the pans.

Bake the cakes for 30 to 35 minutes, or until a cake tester inserted into the center of one comes out clean. Cool for 10 minutes in the pans, then turn them out to cool completely on a rack.

TO ASSEMBLE THE CAKE Place one layer of cake, top side down, on a serving platter. Spread with the filling. Top with the remaining cake layer, also putting it top side down. Pour the glaze very slowly over the top of the cake. If the mixture is too thin and runs off, let it cool longer. For garnish, use four to five striped peppermint candies or two small peppermint candy canes, crushed, or 10 chocolate-mint cookies, crushed. Sprinkle the top with the crushed candy or cookies.

*If desired, substitute ¾ cup (6 ounces) fresh buttermilk for the buttermilk powder and ¾ cup water.

`nutrition information per serving`   **1 serving, 105g**

330 cal | 16g fat | 4g protein | 45 g carbohydrates | 27g sugar | 1g dietary fiber | 45 mg cholesterol | 310 mg sodium
191mg potassium | 55RE vitamin A | 2mg iron | 33mg calcium | 96mg phosphorus | 11mg caffeine

A Butter Cake Primer

Butter cakes are a bit more involved than one-bowl cakes. Their preparation is lengthier, both before going into the oven and afterward; they're nearly always iced, and often stacked in layers and decorated as well. Devil's food cake, yellow cake, a white wedding cake, pound cake, all of these are familiar examples of butter cake. Aside from pound cake, which in the old days was leavened by nonchemical means (and sometimes still is), all of these cakes get their light texture from both a chemical leavener and the air beaten into the batter before it's spooned into the pan.

Making a butter cake (or creamed cake; they're the same thing), the most common of all American cakes, takes a bit more skill and attention to detail than making a one-bowl cake. But it's easy to make if you follow the recipe instructions carefully. A butter cake's texture depends on the ingredients you use, how you mix them, and how you bake the cake. Here's the process, one step at a time.

Flour

The role of flour in a butter cake is to provide just enough framework to support the cake as it rises in the oven. Because the cake has other supports as well, such as protein from dairy products and eggs, the cake isn't relying solely on the protein in the flour to enclose the air pockets and support the cake. In yeast bread, there's often no other framework to trap the air bubbles, so a high-gluten flour is necessary. But if cake is made with high-gluten flour, and the butter is beaten (to trap air), the final product will be tough.

We've experimented with baking cakes with all-purpose flour, with a protein content of 11.7 percent; pastry flour, with a protein content of about 9 percent; and bleached cake flour, whose protein is 8 percent. We found that while the cakes with the pastry flour had a more tender crumb, they also were more crumbly. The cakes made from cake flour were also tender, fine-grained, and high-rising, but again, their texture was crumbly. The cakes made with the all-purpose flour were a shade denser and held together well. If you don't have pastry or cake flour and want to lighten your all-purpose flour, substitute 1 tablespoon of cornstarch for 1 tablespoon of flour in each cup of flour in the recipe. The key is to handle the batter lightly when you're incorporating the flour so that you don't activate the gluten too much.

Butter

The most important thing to remember about butter is that it needs to be at room temperature. Creaming the butter with the leavener, flavors, and sugar is usually the first step. Creaming butter means to whip it, incorporating as much air as you can. If the butter is at room temperature, the fat cells are able to expand and encapsulate millions of minuscule air bubbles.

The best way to bring butter to room temperature is to let it sit out on the counter. We're often in a rush and tempted to microwave butter to get it to room temperature. However, microwaved butter isn't uniformly softened; it comes out with a few melted spots, more or less soft with some still-cold zones. This isn't a positive scenario for cake; a liquid fat has nowhere near the capacity to contain air that a solid, room-temperature fat does. And neither does a cold one. Once butter has been melted, you need to use it for something other than a butter cake. And don't think that by refrigerating melted butter you can bring it back to its original state. The cellular structure has been broken down in the heating process, and a once-melted fat cannot hold air the way a room-temperature fat can.

Because the butter is creamed until it has trapped a lot of air (i.e., it's become light and fluffy), it becomes one of the cake's chief leaveners. Fat also permeates the batter and serves to soften it, contributing to the tender texture of the cake. If you refrigerate a butter cake, the fat hardens and the cake will be quite stiff; this type of cake is best stored at room temperature or, if it absolutely needs to be refrigerated (e.g., it has a whipped cream or other perishable filling or frosting), it should be brought to room temperature before serving.

Sugar

Sugar serves five purposes in a cake. When it's creamed with butter, it helps increase butter's ability to hold air; as you add sugar to the creamed butter and continue to whip, you'll notice an increase in volume. The second purpose is flavoring. The third is to help absorb moisture, which prevents the cake from drying out. The fourth is to help in the browning of the cake. Both the starch content of the flour and the browning of sugar that occurs as it's exposed to heat contribute to a lightly browned cake. The final purpose is to enhance tenderness; sugar binds with the proteins in the flour, preventing them from forming the long, elastic (tough) protein chains known as gluten.

Eggs

The eggs used in cake, like the butter, need to be at room temperature. If you add cold eggs to room-temperature butter, the butter cells will turn solid and actually break, releasing all of the air that you've just beaten into them. If the recipe calls for separated eggs, separate the yolks and whites as soon as you take the eggs out of the refrigerator. If you try to separate a room-temperature egg, you're likely to end up with egg yolk in the whites.

If the recipe calls for beating the yolks and whites separately, the whites must be beaten in a bowl that has no trace of fat, or they won't expand to their full capacity.

The addition of cream of tartar (an acid) stabilizes the alkaline egg whites and they'll hold their beaten volume while you incorporate them into the cake batter.

Eggs are able to expand to many times their original volume when they're whipped. The air that's beaten into them is also a primary leavener in cakes. In the oven, the proteins in the egg white set first and help maintain the structure of the cake. The egg yolks contain lecithin, a type of fat, which helps to soften the texture of the cake.

Baking Powder and Baking Soda

Double-acting baking powder is a combination of two acids, sodium acid pyrophosphate and tartaric acid; an alkaline, sodium bicarbonate, a.k.a. baking soda; and cornstarch. Some baking powder contains aluminum, some does not. When baking powder is beaten with butter and sugar at the beginning of the cake preparation process, it begins to react with the moisture in the butter, giving off tiny bubbles of carbon dioxide that will eventually help to leaven the cake. In the oven, the heat causes a second round of leavening ("double-acting") to occur, hence cakes continue to rise in the oven.

Baking soda is an alkali and needs an acid in the batter to react to it. Usually buttermilk, yogurt, natural cocoa (not Dutch-process), or a citrus fruit juice will do the job. To make your own baking powder, mix ½ teaspoon cream of tartar with ¼ teaspoon baking soda. This is equivalent to 1 teaspoon of baking powder.

Liquids

Liquids moisten the baking powder and baking soda (if they're used), which starts them reacting and leavening the batter. They also are absorbed by the flour, activating its gluten, which helps to build the cake's structure. In addition, if the liquids are dairy based (such as milk or buttermilk), their protein gives additional help to the structure of the cake, and their fat added tenderness.

Cocoa Powder

Natural cocoa powder is an acid ingredient. When added to a mix that contains baking soda (an alkali), it reacts to produce carbon dioxide, which leavens baked goods.

Dutch-process cocoa powder has been treated to reduce its acidity and needs to be used in combination with baking powder. If it's used with baking soda alone, the pH is too alkaline and the resulting cake will be dense, heavy, and soapy tasting.

If your recipe specifies Dutch or natural cocoa, use the one that it specifies. If you're not sure which to use, remember the following: If the recipe calls for baking soda alone, or for baking soda and baking powder and the amount of baking soda is more than the amount of the baking powder, use natural cocoa powder.

If the recipe calls for baking powder, or for both baking powder and baking soda but the amount of the baking soda is less than the baking powder, use Dutch-process cocoa powder.

If the recipe doesn't call for leavening, you may use either kind of cocoa. Dutch-process cocoa has a smoother, mellower flavor and a darker, redder color.

Making the Cake

The first step is to cream or whip the butter, to incorporate air. The fat needs to be solid (you can't substitute oil), and it needs to be at room temperature. Beat until the butter lightens in color and starts to become fluffy.

Next, add the leavener, salt, flavors, and sugar to the beaten butter; as you beat, the mixture will again increase in volume. This second step of creaming separates the encapsulated air bubbles and evenly incorporates them into the mixture. You need to beat this mixture until it's very light and fluffy, which may take up to 5 minutes in a stand mixer, longer in a hand-held one.

Next come the eggs, which need to be at room temperature, and added one at a time. If they're cold, or are poured in all at once, they'll cause the butter and sugar mixture to deflate and curdle or separate. Any cold ingredients will cause the butter to harden, seize up, and collapse, thus releasing the air bubbles. Again, adding the eggs should take up to 5 minutes or so, depending on how many eggs you're adding (typically, four). Be sure to scrape down the sides and across the bottom of the mixing bowl at least twice during this process. The mixture should be extremely light in color and fluffy. In fact, it should look almost like whipped cream cheese.

What's the Temperature of a Fully Baked Cake?

How do you know when a cake is done? Almost every recipe you read gives a similar set of descriptions for what the cake should look like before taking it out of the oven: springs back in the center when touched gently, beginning to pull from the side of the pan, even hearing the slightest crackling noise from bubbles in the batter popping. We decided to put more concrete standards to use and measure the internal temperatures of different types of cakes when they exhibited the characteristics described above. Here is what we found for the types of cakes in this chapter:

TYPE OF CAKE	SIZE OF PAN	INTERNAL TEMPERATURE
CHOCOLATE BUTTER CAKE	9-inch round	209°F
JELLY ROLL SPONGE	10 x 15-inch	191°F to 194°F
CHIFFON	9-inch round	210°F
POUND	9 x 5-inch	209°F

The next step is to add the flour and liquid(s) alternately to the creamed butter mixture. By adding these heavy ingredients gradually, they can be mixed in fully with the least deflation of the batter.

A light hand is also needed at this stage so that you don't release all of the air that's held in fragile suspension. First fold in a third of the flour, then gently stir in liquid, then fold in more flour, stir in more liquid, and end with flour, which binds everything together. As soon as the last bit of flour is fully incorporated, stop mixing; your batter is ready.

Lightly grease and flour your cake pan(s). A typical layer cake can be baked in three 8-inch round pans; two 9-inch round pans; a 9 x 13-inch sheet cake pan, or 2 dozen cupcake molds. If you use a vegetable oil pan spray and your cakes always stick in the pans, try using vegetable shortening, carefully applying a light coating to every nook of the pan. Sprinkle 2 tablespoons of all-purpose flour into the greased pan and shake and rotate it until every surface is covered with a light dusting. Shake the pan over the trash bin to get out any extra flour before spooning in the batter.

Alternatively, you can add a layer of parchment to the bottom of the pan. Grease the pan, add the parchment, and grease and flour the parchment. This provides extra insurance that your cake will come out of the pan easily.

Next pour or spoon the batter into the prepared cake pan. Smooth the top with a spatula, making the sides slightly higher than the center, which keeps the cake from "doming" too much. Fill the pan no more than three quarters full. For a flat, even, easier-to-ice top, fasten a Magi-Cake Strip (see Tools, p. 605) around the side of the pan. This water-soaked piece of cloth will emulate baking in a water bath, which evens out the heat reaching the batter, so that the sides don't set and stop rising before the cooler center. Place the pans in a preheated oven. If you're baking in a dark pan, be sure to reduce the oven heat by 25°F; you'll probably need to reduce the baking time by 10 percent as well.

You know the cake is done when a cake tester (a broom straw, in our grandmothers' day) inserted into the center of the cake comes out clean, or with just the hint of a moist crumb. In addition, a cake that's done will spring back when pressed lightly in the center, and should have begun to barely pull away from the sides of the pan. And, if the cake is chocolate, its aroma should have begun to fill the kitchen. A tried-and-true way to know is to insert an instant-read thermometer into the center of the cake; see page 349.

After baking, remove the cake from the oven and let it cool for 10 to 15 minutes with the pan upright. Then loosen the sides with a table knife, if necessary, and carefully turn it out of the pan onto a cooling rack. With this method, we make perfect cakes without torn or gouged crusts—most of the time!

Devil's Food Cake

TWO 9-INCH ROUNDS, THREE 8-INCH ROUNDS, OR A 9 X 13-INCH SHEET CAKE

This cake is a moist, deep dark chocolate treat that can happily wear any number of frostings. Since chocolate is such a versatile partner, there's no end of possibilities for what you can create. Cherry filling (p. 400) for a Black Forest Cake, peanut butter frosting (p. 397) for a candy bar-style classic, German chocolate frosting (p. 398) for coconut lovers . . . no wonder this cake is associated with being sinfully delicious! And speaking of sin, whence the name devil's food? The combination of natural cocoa powder and baking soda produces a cake with a very slight reddish (devilish) tint.

12 tablespoons (1½ sticks, 6 ounces) butter

1¾ cups (12¼ ounces) superfine or granulated sugar

½ teaspoon salt

1½ teaspoons baking soda

2 teaspoons vanilla extract

2 cups (8½ ounces) unbleached all-purpose flour

¾ cup (2¼ ounces) natural cocoa powder

4 large eggs

1½ cups (12 ounces) milk or water

Preheat the oven to 350°F.

In a large mixing bowl, cream together the butter, sugar, salt, baking soda, and vanilla until fluffy and light, at least 5 minutes. In a separate bowl, whisk together the flour and cocoa. If lumps remain, sift the mixture.

Add the eggs to the butter mixture one at a time, beating well after each addition. Slowly blend one third of the flour mixture into the creamed mixture, then half the milk, another third of the flour, the remaining milk, and the remaining flour. Be sure to scrape the sides and bottom of the bowl occasionally throughout this process.

Grease and flour two 9-inch round cake pans, two or three 8-inch round pans, or a 9 x 13-inch sheet cake pan. Divide the batter evenly between the pans. Wrap the pans with Magi-Cake Strips (to prevent doming), if desired. Bake the cakes for 30 to 35 minutes (a bit longer for the sheet cake, shorter if you've used three 8-inch pans), until a cake tester inserted into the center comes out clean, and the sides of the cake begin to pull away from the pan. Remove the cakes from the oven, cool them for 5 to 10 minutes, then remove them from the pan.

nutrition information per serving   ¹⁄₁₆ of 2-layer cake, without frosting, 87g

252 cal | 11g fat | 5g protein | 13g complex carbohydrates | 21g sugar | 2g dietary fiber | 77mg cholesterol | 217mg sodium | 140mg potassium | 118RE vitamin A | 1mg iron | 43mg calcium | 92mg phosphorus | 10mg caffeine

Classic Yellow Cake

TWO 9-INCH ROUNDS, TWO OR THREE 8-INCH ROUNDS, OR A 9 X 13-INCH SHEET CAKE

If devil's food cake is the yin of the cake world, yellow cake is the yang—together they form the cornerstone of the genre.

12 tablespoons (1½ sticks, 6 ounces) butter	4 large eggs, plus 2 yolks
1¾ cups (12¼ ounces) sugar	2¾ cups (11½ ounces) unbleached all-purpose flour
¾ teaspoon salt	
2½ teaspoons baking powder	1½ cups (12 ounces) milk, buttermilk, or yogurt
2 teaspoons vanilla extract	

Preheat the oven to 350°F.

In a large mixing bowl, cream together the butter, sugar, salt, baking powder, and vanilla until fluffy and light, at least 5 minutes.

Add the eggs to the butter mixture one at a time, beating well after each addition. Slowly blend one-third of the flour into the creamed mixture, then half the milk, another third of the flour, the remaining milk, and the remaining flour. Be sure to scrape the sides and bottom of the bowl occasionally throughout this process.

Pour the batter into greased and floured or parchment-lined 8- or 9-inch round pans, or a 9 x 13-inch pan. Bake for 23 to 26 minutes (for 8-inch pans), 25 to 30 minutes (for 9-inch pans), or about 35 minutes for the 9 x 13-inch pan. Remove the cakes from the oven, cool for 10 minutes in the pan, then turn out on a rack to cool completely before frosting.

nutrition information per serving ¹⁄₁₂ **of one layer, 61g**

179 cal | 8g fat | 3g protein | 11g complex carbohydrates | 14g sugar | 71mg cholesterol | 137mg sodium | 54mg potassium | 90RE vitamin A | 1mg iron | 55mg calcium | 61mg phosphorus

Elegant White Cake

TWO OR THREE 8-INCH ROUNDS, TWO 9-INCH ROUNDS, OR ONE 9 X 13-INCH CAKE

This is a very fine-grained, very white (rather than yellow) cake. It's our favorite base for a trifle, petits fours, or a fancy layered cake, such as wedding cake.

8 tablespoons (1 stick, 4 ounces) butter, softened

½ cup (3¼ ounces) vegetable shortening

1 tablespoon (½ ounce) baking powder

1¾ cups (12¼ ounces) superfine or granulated sugar

¾ teaspoon salt

2 teaspoons vanilla extract

1 teaspoon almond extract

5 large egg whites (6 to 7 ounces)

2¾ cups (11 ounces) cake flour

1 cup (8 ounces) milk

Preheat the oven to 350°F.

In a large mixing bowl, cream together the butter, shortening, baking powder, sugar, salt, and extracts until fluffy and light, at least 5 minutes. Add the egg whites to the butter mixture one at a time, beating well after each addition.

Stir one-third of the flour into the creamed mixture, then half the milk, another third of the flour, the remaining milk, and the remaining flour. Be sure to scrape the sides and bottom of the bowl occasionally throughout this process.

Pour the batter into two greased and floured or parchment-lined 8- or 9-inch round pans, three 8-inch round pans, or a 9 x 13-inch pan. Bake the cakes for 23 to 26 minutes (for 8-inch pans), 25 to 30 minutes (for 9-inch pans), or about 35 minutes (for the 9 x 13-inch pan). Remove the cakes from the oven, and cool them on a rack.

nutrition information per serving ¹/₁₂ **of one layer, 51g**

186 cal | 8g fat | 2g protein | 12g complex carbohydrates | 14g sugar | 11mg cholesterol | 145mg sodium | 42mg potassium | 44RE vitamin A | 1mg iron | 50mg calcium | 36mg phosphorus

Variation   COCONUT CAKE: To make coconut cake, make the following adjustments to Elegant White Cake: substitute 2 to 3 drops coconut flavor or 1 teaspoon coconut extract for the almond extract and fold 1 cup toasted coconut into the batter. Finish with Silky Buttercream (p. 392), substituting 2 to 3 drops coconut flavor (or 1 teaspoon coconut extract) for half of the vanilla. Decorate the frosted cake with grated, sweetened coconut.

Boston Cream Pie

ONE 9-INCH ROUND CAKE, 16 SERVINGS

We know many people who ask for this misnamed pie—it's really a cake—on special occasions. A specialty of Boston's Parker House hotel dating back to 1855, it's been a part of the American cake scene for decades; in fact, Boston Cream Pie is the official state dessert of Massachusetts. The combination of comforting custard filling, light butter cake, and deep chocolate frosting makes this dessert an enduring classic. The frosting recipe below makes just enough to cover the top of the cake and drip seductively down the sides. You can use another frosting from the frosting section, but this one is traditional.

CAKE

1 cup (7 ounces) superfine or granulated sugar

4 tablespoons (½ stick, 2 ounces) butter

¼ teaspoon salt

1 teaspoon almond extract, or a few drops of bitter almond oil

1 teaspoon vanilla extract

3 tablespoons (1¼ ounces) vegetable oil

3 large eggs

1¼ cups (5¼ ounces) unbleached all-purpose flour

¼ cup (1 ounce) cornstarch

2 teaspoons baking powder

½ cup (4 ounces) milk

FILLING

1 recipe chilled pastry cream (see p. 398)

CHOCOLATE GLAZE

½ cup (4 ounces) whipping or heavy cream

1 tablespoon light corn syrup

¾ cup (4½ ounces) chopped semisweet or bittersweet chocolate or chocolate chips

Pinch of salt

½ teaspoon vanilla extract

Preheat the oven to 350°F.

FOR THE CAKE In a large mixing bowl, beat together the sugar, butter, salt, and flavorings until fluffy. Beat in the oil, then the eggs, one at a time, beating until the mixture is very fluffy. In a separate bowl, whisk together the flour, cornstarch, and baking powder. Add the dry ingredients to the butter and egg mixture alternately with the milk, beating until well combined, about 2 minutes.

Lightly grease and flour a 9-inch round cake pan that is at least 2 inches deep, or an 8 x 8 x 3-inch square pan. Spoon the batter into the pan. Bake the cake for 38 to 45 minutes, until the edges have started to pull away from the sides of the pan. Cool the cake for 15 minutes before removing it from the pan.

FOR THE GLAZE Bring the cream and corn syrup to a boil. Remove the cream mixture from the heat and stir in the chocolate and salt. Continue stirring until the chocolate has melted and the glaze is smooth. Stir in the vanilla and set the glaze aside, but don't refrigerate it.

ASSEMBLY Slice the cake in half horizontally. Place one layer, cut side up, on a plate. Spoon the pastry cream onto the cake, spreading it almost to the edges. Top with the remaining cake layer, cut side down. Pour the glaze onto the top of the cake, spreading it toward the edges and letting some of it drip over the sides. Refrigerate until ready to serve.

nutrition information per serving   **1 slice, 92g**

313 cal | 10g fat | 4g protein | 12g complex carbohydrates | 23g sugar | 1g dietary fiber | 87mg cholesterol | 207mg sodium | 96mg potassium | 143RE vitamin A | 1mg iron | 85mg calcium | 86mg phosphorus | 2mg caffeine

Boston Latin Cream Pie

For a contemporary version of the above classic that has a Latin American flair, try the following dulce de leche–laced substitutions for the filling and frosting.

FILLING

1 can (14 ounces, 1¼ cups) prepared dulce de leche*

2 teaspoons dark rum (optional)

1¼ cups (10 ounces) milk or cream

1 package (3.4 ounces) instant vanilla pudding mix

GLAZE

3 tablespoons (1½ ounces) cream or milk

½ cup caramel (5 ounces, 14 to 16 individual caramels, unwrapped)

½ cup (3 ounces) semisweet or bittersweet chocolate (chips or chopped)

TO MAKE THE FILLING Place the dulce de leche in a medium-sized bowl. Stir in the rum and the milk, a bit at a time, whisking until the mixture is smooth before adding more milk. When all is added, mix in the instant pudding mix, beating well.

TO MAKE THE GLAZE Heat the cream, caramel, and chocolate together over medium-low heat or in the microwave, stirring until melted and smooth. Pour the glaze over the cake, letting some run over the edge.

*Or ¾ cup (7½ ounces) caramel, melted (21 to 23 individual caramels, unwrapped)

Pound Cakes

A subset of butter cakes, pound cakes were originally made from a pound each of flour, sugar, butter, and eggs. Over the years the proportions have changed somewhat and flavors have been added; but the result is still a very fine-textured, moderately heavy moist cake, perfect for slicing and serving as a base for fruit or ice cream.

One of our very favorite ways to serve pound cake is to brush both sides of a slice with butter, then sauté it, as you would a grilled cheese sandwich. When it's golden brown, remove it from the heat and top with ice cream, choosing a flavor that's complementary to the cake. Add fudge sauce and whipped cream and you've reached cake nirvana.

Vanilla Pound Cake

ONE CAKE, ABOUT 16 SERVINGS

Pound cake is the perfect vehicle for vanilla; the butter-sugar-eggs-flour combination is a rich-but-plain base on which to overlay other flavors. While the recipe calls for a large amount of vanilla extract (1 tablespoon), we know vanilla has a tendency to fade in the heat of the oven, so we decided to add a clear vanilla glaze, poking holes in the warm cake so that the strong flavor of vanilla would permeate it both inside and out. The result: a dense, moist vanilla cake, perfect to serve as is, or adorned with berries or sliced peaches.

CAKE

1 cup (2 sticks, 8 ounces) butter

1 cup (7 ounces) granulated sugar

3 tablespoons (1½ ounces) light brown sugar, packed

½ teaspoon salt

1 tablespoon vanilla extract

1 teaspoon baking powder

1¾ cups (7⅛ ounces) unbleached all-purpose flour or cake flour

4 large eggs

GLAZE

½ cup (3½ ounces) granulated sugar

¼ cup (2 ounces) water

Pinch of salt

1 tablespoon vanilla extract

Preheat the oven to 350°F.

FOR THE CAKE In a large mixing bowl, beat together the butter, sugars, salt, vanilla, and baking powder until smooth and fluffy. Add the flour and mix well; the batter will be almost like paste. Beat in the eggs one at a time, beating well and scraping the bottom and sides of the bowl after each addition; the batter will be quite fluffy.

Spoon the batter into a lightly greased 9- to 10-inch tube pan, 9- to 10-cup bundt-style pan, or 9 x 5-inch loaf pan. Bake the cake for about 45 minutes, or until a cake tester inserted into the center comes out clean. Remove the cake from the oven and let it cool in the pan for 10 minutes, while you're making the glaze.

FOR THE GLAZE Bring the sugar, water, and salt to a boil in a small saucepan and boil for 1 minute. Remove the pan from the heat and stir in the vanilla.

Turn the warm cake out onto a rack. Poke the cake all over with something long and thin, like a cake tester or ice pick. Slowly drizzle or brush the glaze over the cake, continuing to brush until all the glaze is used. Let the cake cool fully before slicing. Serve with sliced fresh fruit, if desired.

`nutrition information per serving`   **1 slice, 65g**

246 cal | 13g fat | 3g protein | 8g complex carbohydrates | 21g sugar | 86mg cholesterol | 116mg sodium | 42mg potassium | 137RE vitamin A | 1mg iron | 29mg calcium | 42mg phosphorus

Lemon-Glazed Pound Cake

ONE CAKE, ABOUT 16 SERVINGS

The sunny taste of citrus highlights this buttery pound cake.

CAKE

14 tablespoons (1¾ sticks, 7 ounces) butter

1 package (3 ounces) cream cheese

½ teaspoon salt

1½ cups (10½ ounces) sugar

1 teaspoon baking powder

2 teaspoons vanilla extract

½ teaspoon lemon oil, or 1 tablespoon lemon zest

1¾ cups (7¼ ounces) unbleached all-purpose flour

5 large eggs

GLAZE

¼ cup (2 ounces) fresh lemon juice

½ cup (3½ ounces) sugar

Preheat the oven to 350°F and grease two 8½ x 4½-inch loaf pans or a 9- to 10-cup tube or bundt-style pan.

FOR THE CAKE In a medium-sized mixing bowl, beat together the butter and cream cheese until soft and fluffy. Add the salt, sugar, baking powder, vanilla, lemon, and flour and beat for 5 minutes; the batter will be stiff.

Add 1 egg, beating until well combined. Continue to add the eggs, one at a time, beating well and scraping the sides and bottom of the bowl after each addition.

When done, the batter will be very fluffy. Spoon the batter into the prepared pan(s).

Bake the cake for 55 to 60 minutes (for the tube or bundt-style pans) or 35 to 40 minutes (for the two loaf pans), or until a cake tester inserted into the center comes out clean.

FOR THE GLAZE Just before the cake is done, combine the lemon juice and sugar and heat over low heat (or in the microwave) until the sugar has dissolved; don't let the mixture boil.

Remove the cake from the oven and let it cool for 10 minutes in the pan. Turn it out onto a wire rack or serving platter. Poke the top all over with a cake tester or toothpick and gradually drizzle the glaze over it, pausing occasionally to let it sink in. Let the cake cool for several hours before slicing.

nutrition information per serving   1 slice, 74g

268 cal | 14g fat | 4g protein | 9g complex carbohydrates | 24g sugar | 101mg cholesterol | 134mg sodium | 48mg potassium | 152RE vitamin A | 2mg vitamin C | 1mg iron | 33mg calcium | 53mg phosphorus

Cream Cheese Pound Cake

ONE CAKE, ABOUT 12 SERVINGS

Grilled pound cake is a delightful, summery treat. When you want to grill a piece of cake, it's clear you need cake with some body, a slice that won't crumble or disintegrate on the griddle or grill. Pound cake is the ideal solution; it's close-grained and moist and responds nicely to the heat of the grill: the outside browns while the inside stays soft.

This recipe is fun to play around with. Add different flavorings, or coconut, dried fruit, or nuts. It makes a tender cake with just the slightest tang from the cream cheese.

8 tablespoons (1 stick, 4 ounces) butter, at room temperature

6 ounces (two 3-ounce packages) cream cheese (not low-fat)

½ teaspoon salt

1 cup (7 ounces) sugar

2 teaspoons vanilla extract*

½ teaspoon baking powder

1¾ cups (7¼ ounces) unbleached all-purpose flour

4 large eggs, at room temperature

Preheat the oven to 350°F.

In a medium-sized mixing bowl, beat together the butter and cream cheese until soft and fluffy. Add the salt, sugar, flavor, and baking powder and beat for 5 minutes. Add the flour, beating well and scraping the bottom and sides of the bowl occasionally. The batter will be stiff.

Add the eggs one at a time, beating well and scraping the sides and bottom of the bowl after each addition. When done, the batter will be very fluffy. Fold in up to 1 cup of dried flaked coconut or dried fruit or nuts, if desired.

Spoon the batter into a greased 9 x 5-inch loaf pan, or 9-cup tube or bundt-style pan. Bake the cake for 55 to 60 minutes for the 9 x 5-inch loaf pan, or 50 to 55 minutes for the tube or bundt-style pans. A cake tester inserted into the center of the loaf should come out clean.

Remove the cake from the oven and let it cool for 15 minutes in the pan. Turn the cake out onto a rack or serving platter. Let the cake cool for several hours for best slicing. The cake will be dark brown on the edges and golden on top, with a fine crumb inside. Serve the cake at room temperature; store it well wrapped at room temperature.

*Flavor variations: In addition to the vanilla, add 1 teaspoon almond extract, or ¼ teaspoon coconut flavoring. Or skip the vanilla and use ½ teaspoon lemon oil plus 1 tablespoon lemon zest; or butterscotch, hazelnut, raspberry, or the flavor of your choice.

nutrition information per serving ¹⁄₁₂ **of cake, 76g**

268 cal | 15g fat | 5g protein | 30g complex carbohydrates | 16g sugar | 1g dietary fiber | 107mg cholesterol | 174mg sodium | 57mg potassium | 136RE vitamin A | 1mg iron | 22mg calcium | 62mg phosphorus

Chocolate Pound Cake

ONE CAKE, 16 SERVINGS

Moist, light, and with just the right degree of richness, this versatile cake is an ideal candidate for a dessert buffet or dinner party. Complement it with whipped cream, frozen yogurt, fresh fruit or raspberry sauce; glaze it, or simply dust it with confectioners' sugar. Swirling a cup of chocolate chips, chopped nuts, coconut, or dried fruit into the batter only widens the horizon.

1 cup (2 sticks, 8 ounces) unsalted butter

2½ cups (17½ ounces) sugar

2 teaspoons vanilla extract

½ teaspoon baking powder

½ teaspoon baking soda

1 teaspoon salt

5 large eggs

3 tablespoons (½ ounce) espresso powder or instant coffee powder

¼ cup (2 ounces) warm water

¾ cup (6 ounces) buttermilk

1 cup (3 ounces) Dutch-process cocoa powder

2 cups (8½ ounces) unbleached all-purpose flour

Preheat the oven to 325°F. Lightly grease a 10-inch (12-cup) tube pan or 12-cup bundt-style pan.

Cream the butter in a medium-sized bowl until light and fluffy, and continue to beat while gradually adding the sugar, then the vanilla, baking powder, baking soda, and salt. Beat the mixture at high speed for 2 to 3 minutes. Add the eggs one at a time, beating well after each addition and scraping the sides of the bowl occasionally.

Dissolve the espresso in the warm water and combine this with the buttermilk. Sift or whisk together the cocoa and flour. Beat the dry ingredients into the egg mixture alternately with the liquid. (This part can be pretty messy, so try adding the dry ingredients just by the spoonful at first.) Blend well and pour into the prepared pan.

Bake the cake for about 1 hour and 20 minutes, or until a cake tester inserted into the center comes out clean. Remove the cake from the oven and place it (in its pan) on a rack to cool for at least 15 minutes. Turn out the cake onto the rack and let it cool completely.

nutrition information per serving   ¹⁄₁₆ of cake, 99g

325 cal | 15g fat | 5g protein | 14g complex carbohydrates | 28g sugar | 3g dietary fiber | 119mg cholesterol | 198mg sodium | 201mg potassium | 139RE vitamin A | 2mg iron | 66mg calcium | 108mg phosphorus | 14mg caffeine

Scandinavian Gold Cake

ONE CAKE, 20 TO 22 SLICES

This vanilla- and almond-scented cake adds almond flour for extra flavor and a lightly flecked appearance.

CAKE

1 cup (2 sticks, 8 ounces) butter

1⅓ cups (9¼ ounces) sugar

½ teaspoon salt

1½ teaspoons baking powder

½ teaspoon almond extract, or 3 drops bitter almond oil

1 teaspoon vanilla extract

1 cup (3½ ounces) toasted almond flour*

1¾ cups (7¼ ounces) unbleached all-purpose flour

6 large eggs, at room temperature

GLAZE

2 cups (8 ounces) confectioners' sugar

¼ cup (2 ounces) heavy cream or evaporated milk

1 teaspoon vanilla extract

¼ teaspoon almond extract, or 1 drop bitter almond oil

Preheat the oven to 325°F. Grease and flour a 10-inch tube pan or a 12-cup bundt-style pan.

In a large mixing bowl, beat the butter until it's soft. Add the sugar, salt, baking powder and flavorings. Beat them together until well blended.

Add the flours and mix; it will be crumbly. Beat in the eggs one at a time, scraping the bottom and sides of the bowl after each addition. The batter will become fluffy after the third or fourth egg has been added.

Scrape the batter into the pan and level it with a spatula. Bake the cake for about 1 hour, until a tester inserted in the center comes out clean and the edges pull away from the pan.

Remove the cake from the oven and place it on a rack to cool. Turn it out of the pan after about 10 minutes to cool completely.

Mix all the glaze ingredients together, adding a bit of water if needed to make it spreadable. Use a spatula to spread it over the top of the cake. Let the glaze set for a few minutes before serving. (If you want to skip the glaze, though we don't recommend it, simply sift confectioners' sugar over the cake.)

*We prefer the nutty taste of toasted almond flour, but use regular almond flour if you prefer.

nutrition information per serving ¹⁄₂₀ **of cake, 100g**

392 cal | 21g fat | 6g protein | 11g complex carbohydrates | 37g sugar | 1g dietary fiber | 132mg cholesterol | 160mg sodium | 102mg potassium | 180RE vitamin A | 1mg iron | 65mg calcium | 104mg phosphorus

Foam Cakes

The broad category of foam cakes encompasses everything from sponge cake and hot milk cake to genoise and angel food; the common denominator for these cakes is their very light airy texture, derived mainly from beating air into eggs. Most are significantly lower in fat than butter cakes; when they do contain fat, it's in the form of vegetable oil or the fat in egg yolks. For that reason, these cakes are often layered with a rich filling, fruit, or some other element to complement their simplicity.

Foam cakes are one of the very earliest genre of cake. Taking over from yeast-risen cakes in the mid-1700s, they quickly became a favorite of the rich, who had both the white flour and the access to sweeteners (to say nothing of the servants to beat the eggs) necessary for foam cakes. The cakes were baked in a variety of sizes and shapes, fancifully decorated, and otherwise honored as the centerpiece of the banquet table.

Nowadays, foam cakes appear regularly in most folks' homes, in one guise or another. Two of Italy's most familiar cake-based creations, tiramisù and cassata, are based on foam cakes. Mexico's famous celebration cake, tres leches, starts with a foam cake. Many French desserts are based on a classic genoise. And, closer to home, pineapple upside-down cake relies on a light-textured foam cake to hold its heavy crown of pineapples and sugar in place.

Jelly Roll

ONE 9- TO 9½-INCH CAKE, ABOUT 9 SERVINGS

The basis for a jelly roll, sponge cake, is made with more eggs, less fat, and less flour than typical cakes. Leavened mainly by air, which is beaten into and held by whole eggs, sponge cake may also be boosted with a chemical leavener, either baking soda or baking powder.

A light and airy cake, sponge cake is similar to angel food but, because of the addition of egg yolks and a minimal amount of fat in the form of unsalted butter, it's a more tender, less springy cake. Typical sponge cake applications include not only jelly rolls, but trifles, "maryann" cakes (the yellow, spongy cake that forms the base of some kinds of berry shortcakes), and petits fours. With the addition of boiling milk and a pat of butter, sponge cake becomes a traditional American favorite, hot milk cake.

SPONGE CAKE

¾ cup (3 ounces) unbleached all-purpose flour

¾ teaspoon baking powder

¼ teaspoon salt

4 large eggs, at room temperature

¾ cup (5¼ ounces) sugar

1 teaspoon vanilla extract

FILLING

1 heaping cup (12 ounces) jam, preserve, or any thick fruit purée*

Preheat the oven to 400°F. Line the bottom of a 10 x 15-inch jelly roll pan with waxed paper or parchment.

In a small bowl, sift together the flour, baking powder, and salt. Set aside.

In a large bowl, beat the eggs until foamy. Sprinkle in the sugar gradually, beating all the while, and continue beating until the batter is very thick and light lemon in color, 3 to 8 minutes. The batter will have doubled in volume. When the batter is sufficiently aerated it should fall from the beaters in a thick ribbon and mound on top of the remaining batter in the bowl temporarily, before being reabsorbed. Just before you stop beating the batter, add the vanilla.

Gently fold in the flour mixture, using a rubber spatula or whisk. Spread the batter evenly into the prepared pan.

Bake the cake for 12 to 14 minutes, until it's golden brown and springy to the touch. Remove the cake from the oven and invert it onto a (non-terry) dish towel that's been lightly sprinkled with confectioners' sugar. Peel off the paper and, using scissors, a sharp knife, or a rolling pizza wheel, trim the crusty edges of the cake, if necessary. Starting with a short end, roll the cake and towel together into a log, and cool completely on a wire rack.

Just before serving, unroll the cake, spread it with the jam, preserves, or fruit purée, and re-roll it. Place the jelly roll on a plate, seam side down, and dust it with confectioners' sugar.

*Despite its being called a jelly roll, we find jelly too thin to hold up in a jelly roll; jam or preserves are preferred.

Jelly Roll Tips

For easiest handling, we strongly suggest using parchment if you're baking sponge cake in a jelly roll pan. Another hint: When a sponge type of cake is done, you should be able to hear a very faint crackling noise, as some of the air pockets rupture.

nutrition information per serving | one 1-inch slice, 86g

225 cal | 3g fat | 4g protein | 12g complex carbohydrates | 35g sugar | 1g dietary fiber | 122mg cholesterol | 125mg sodium | 73mg potassium | 35RE vitamin A | 1mg iron | 48mg calcium | 57mg phosphorus

Variations • A wonderful, creamy dessert can be made by substituting pudding for the jam or fruit purée. While we don't generally advocate the use of "box mixes," instant pudding is a snap to make and comes in a range of yummy flavors. For filling that ranges from plain to super-rich, climb the ladder of which milk product you use, from skim milk to whipping cream.

• Flavor the sponge cake batter with lemon oil or orange oil, maple flavoring, or the extract of your choice. Or brush it with a bit of liqueur before filling with jam.

Red, White, and Blue Trifle

16 SERVINGS

Trifle is an English concoction whose roots go back two or three hundred years, not quite to the time of King Arthur, but long enough to make it a venerable presentation. A trifle is an elegant way to capture the flavors of summer and, in this particular one, the colors of the Fourth of July.

1 recipe sponge cake baked in a jelly roll pan (p. 362), slightly stale

½ cup (4 ounces) sherry or rum, or simple syrup (optional)

1 to 1½ cups (6 to 8 ounces) strawberries, cut into pieces and sprinkled with ¼ cup (1¾ ounces) sugar (save some perfect berries for decoration)

1 recipe pastry cream (p. 398), prepared and cooled

1 cup (3 ounces) sliced almonds, toasted

1 to 1½ cups (6 to 8 ounces) blueberries, cooked gently in a saucepan with ¼ cup (1¾ ounces) sugar until the sugar has melted and the juices have begun to run (save some perfect berries for decoration)

Cut the sponge cake into 2-inch squares and use it to line the bottom of a trifle or other medium-sized glass bowl. Sprinkle 3 or 4 tablespoons of sherry over the cake and spoon on the strawberries. Spread half the pastry cream over the berries and half the sliced almonds over the custard.

Add another layer of cake and repeat the process with the sherry, blueberries, and custard.

To decorate the top, first sprinkle on the remainder of the almonds. Then pipe some whipped cream around the outside edge of the trifle; slice the reserved strawberries in half and lay them in a ring inside the whipped cream. Sprinkle the reserved blueberries in the center. Cover with plastic wrap and chill for several hours or overnight.

nutrition information per serving　　**1 serving, 159g**

350 cal | 8g fat | 8g protein | 18g complex carbohydrates | 23g sugar | 2g dietary fiber | 170mg cholesterol | 174mg sodium | 250mg potassium | 168RE vitamin A | 1mg vitamin C | 1mg iron | 116mg calcium | 169mg phosphorus

Tiramisù

ONE CAKE, 16 SERVINGS

This would have to be the quintessential Italian dessert. Tiramisù (pronounced teer-ah-me-sue) is the Italian equivalent of the English trifle. It's rich and delicious, loaded as it is with mascarpone (Italian cream cheese), coffee liqueur, and espresso.

Tiramisù means "pick me up" in Italian. Not only will it pick you up; it will carry you away. Best of all, it's easy, and can be made early in the day for an important dinner. While it will keep overnight, the layers become less distinct.

1 recipe sponge cake baked in a jelly roll pan (p. 362)

½ cup (4 ounces) espresso or coffee-flavored liqueur (or a mixture of ¼ cup of each)

1 tablespoon cocoa (preferably Dutch-process, for its darker color and flavor)

½ cup (3 ounces) grated or curled semisweet or milk chocolate

MASCARPONE FILLING

1 pound mascarpone cheese or cream cheese*

2 cups (16 ounces) heavy or whipping cream

1½ cups (6 ounces) confectioners' sugar

2 teaspoons vanilla extract

FOR THE FILLING In a food processor or medium-sized mixing bowl, beat the cheese until soft. Add the cream, sugar, and vanilla and beat or process until smooth. Refrigerate the filling until you're ready to assemble the cake.

TO ASSEMBLE THE DESSERT Cut the cake into three 5 x 10-inch slices. Brush each slice with the espresso or coffee-flavored liqueur. Let the cake sit for a few minutes to absorb the liquid, then brush it again. Place one slice on a serving platter and top it with one-third of the filling, top it with a second layer and another third of the filling, then place the third layer of cake on top. Cover the top and sides with the remaining filling, dust with cocoa, and top with chocolate curls for garnish. Wrap the cake well and refrigerate it for several hours (or overnight) before serving.

*If you're using cream cheese, combine it with 2 tablespoons sour cream.

nutrition information per serving   **¹⁄₁₆ of cake, 102g**

323 cal | 18g fat | 6g protein | 32g complex carbohydrates | 20g sugar | 133mg cholesterol | 204mg sodium | 135mg potassium | 161RE vitamin A | 1mg iron | 34mg calcium | 85mg phosphorus | 4mg caffeine

Cassata

Pan di Spagna (literally, "bread from Spain") is a classic European-style sponge cake, enriched with butter and leavened only by the air beaten into the eggs. It may be used as the base for many different Italian desserts, including tiramisú and cassata, a rich, layered cake often filled with ricotta cheese and served at weddings. There's a lot of room to customize the filling for cassata to your taste; the background of ricotta cheese can be garnished with candied fruits, nuts, chocolate, or any combination of these that appeals to you.

SPONGE CAKE

6 large eggs

1 cup (7 ounces) sugar

¼ teaspoon salt

1 cup (4¼ ounces) unbleached all-purpose flour

¼ teaspoon vanilla extract

¼ cup (½ stick, 2 ounces) butter, melted and cooled to lukewarm

FILLING

3 cups (1½ pounds) ricotta cheese*

2 tablespoons heavy cream

¾ cup (3 ounces) confectioners' sugar

2 tablespoons grated orange rind, or ¼ teaspoon orange oil or flavoring of your choice, such as vanilla or almond extract, rum, or orange liqueur

½ cup (2¾ ounces) candied orange peel, citron, and/or candied cherries (optional)

½ cup (2 ounces) toasted chopped almonds or chopped pistachios (optional)

½ cup (3 ounces) chopped chocolate (optional)

BRUSHING LIQUID

¼ to ½ cup (2 to 4 ounces) rum, brandy, Grand Marnier, or Simple Syrup (see p. 390) mixed with ½ teaspoon vanilla extract

CHOCOLATE GLAZE

1⅓ cups (8 ounces) chopped semisweet or bittersweet chocolate, or chocolate chips

1 cup (8 ounces) whipping or heavy cream

2 tablespoons (1⅜ ounces) light corn syrup

⅛ teaspoon salt

1 teaspoon vanilla extract

Preheat the oven to 350°F.

FOR THE CAKE Place the eggs (make sure they are at room temperature) in a large bowl and, starting on low to medium speed and increasing to high speed as the volume of the eggs increases, beat them until they're pale yellow and thick. Gradually add the sugar and salt while continuing to beat on high speed. When the mixture is a very pale yellow and very light and fluffy, it's beaten enough. (If you're using a handheld mixer, this could take 10 minutes or longer.)

Sift the flour, then sprinkle it one third at a time over the egg mixture, gently folding it in. If done by hand, use a large balloon whisk; if done in a mixer, use the whisk attachment. A few strokes in a down-and-around motion is all that's needed. Add the vanilla to the melted and slightly cooled butter, then add the butter to the batter in two additions, using the same folding motion.

Gently spoon the batter into lightly greased and floured or parchment-lined pans (either two 8 x 2-inch round or 9 x 2-inch round cake pans, or one 10 x 15-inch jelly roll pan). Level the batter with a spatula. Bake the cake for 25 to 30 minutes for the round pans, or 18 to 20 minutes for the jelly roll pan, or until the cake springs back when touched lightly in the center. Let the cakes cool in the pan for 20 minutes, then loosen the edges with a flexible spatula and turn the cakes out onto a wire rack to finish cooling. While the cakes are cooling, make the filling.

FOR THE FILLING In a medium-sized mixing bowl, blend together the ricotta cheese, cream, confectioners' sugar, and flavorings until smooth. (For an extra-smooth filling, blend in a blender or food processor.) Fold in the garnishes of your choice (fruit, nuts, or chocolate). Refrigerate the filling until the cakes are cool enough to assemble.

FOR THE GLAZE Chop the chocolate into ¼-inch pieces. Bring the cream and corn syrup to a boil. Remove the cream mixture from the heat and stir in the chocolate and salt. Continue stirring until the chocolate has melted. Add the vanilla and stir to blend. Set the glaze aside, but don't refrigerate it.

ASSEMBLY USING A ROUND CAKE Using a long serrated knife, cut each cake layer in half horizontally to make two rounds out of each layer. Brush the cut side of each round with approximately 2 tablespoons liquor or syrup, or a mixture of both. Place one layer on a cake plate, cut side up, and spread with one-third of the ricotta filling. Top the second and third layers with the remaining filling. The cake layers are fragile, so using an extra-large spatula to lift them will help minimize cracking. Top with the final layer, cut side down. Pour the chocolate glaze over the cake and smooth it down and over the sides with a spatula. (You may omit the chocolate glaze if you wish, simply brushing the top of the cake with liquor or syrup and dusting it with confectioners' sugar.) Refrigerate the cake for several hours (or overnight) before serving to allow the flavors to meld, and the filling to firm.

ASSEMBLY USING JELLY ROLL CAKE Follow the directions above, but instead of cutting the cake through its center, cut it into three strips, each about 5 x 10 inches in size. Stack the strips with the filling; glaze and finish as directed above.

*If the ricotta cheese is at all watery—it may be, especially if you use whole-milk ricotta—place it in a cheesecloth-lined colander and drain it for 1 hour or more.

nutrition information per serving   **cassata made with orange filling, ¹/₂₀ of cake, 121g**

323 cal | 12g fat | 9g protein | 13g complex carbohydrates | 29g sugar | 1g dietary fiber | 89mg cholesterol | 177mg sodium | 181mg potassium | 101RE vitamin A | 1mg vitamin C | 1mg iron | 161mg calcium | 156mg phosphorus | 9mg caffeine

Harvest Spice Roll

ONE CAKE, 15 SERVINGS

This twist on the familiar chocolate-and-cream roll or jelly roll is particularly apropos at Thanksgiving, when pumpkin plays a starring role at the table.

CAKE

¾ cup (3 ounces) unbleached all-purpose flour

1 teaspoon baking powder

2 teaspoons cinnamon

1 teaspoon pumpkin pie spice or a mixture of cloves, ginger, and allspice

½ teaspoon nutmeg

½ teaspoon salt

3 large eggs, lightly beaten

1 cup (7 ounces) sugar

⅔ cup (5¼ ounces) pumpkin purée (not pumpkin pie filling)

1 teaspoon lemon juice

1 cup (4 ounces) chopped walnuts (optional)

FILLING

1 cup (4 ounces) confectioners' sugar

6 tablespoons (¾ stick, 3 ounces) butter, softened

1 teaspoon vanilla extract

1 package (8 ounces) cream cheese, softened

¼ cup (1⅝ ounces) finely chopped crystallized ginger (optional)

Preheat the oven to 375°F. Grease a jelly roll pan. Line it with waxed paper or parchment, then grease and flour the paper.

FOR THE CAKE In a small bowl, sift together the flour, baking powder, spices, and salt; set aside. In a large bowl, beat together the eggs and sugar until thick, fluffy, and light in color. Beat in the pumpkin and lemon juice.

Invert the warm cake onto a clean kitchen towel that has been liberally dusted with confectioners' sugar. Trim the crusty edges with a sharp knife or scissors, then use the towel to roll the cake into a spiral. Let the rolled cake rest, seam side down, to finish cooling.

Add the dry ingredients to the wet ingredients and mix well. Pour the batter into the prepared pan and spread it out evenly with a rubber spatula. Sprinkle the batter with the nuts.

Bake the cake for about 15 minutes, or until it's lightly browned and springs back when touched lightly. Remove the cake from the oven and loosen it around the edges with a knife. Invert it onto a clean kitchen towel dusted very heavily with confectioners' sugar and peel off the paper. Trim the hard, crusty edge (about ¼ inch) from all sides of the cake.

Roll up the cake and towel together, starting with a long side. Place the roll, seam side down, on a wire rack to cool completely.

FOR THE FILLING Sift the sugar into a medium-sized bowl and beat it with the butter until smooth. Mix in the vanilla. Add the cream cheese in chunks, beating well after each addition; the mixture should be completely smooth. Stir in the ginger.

When the cake is completely cooled, gently unroll it and spread the cake with the filling, then reroll, without the towel, to place the seam side down. Refrigerate until ready to serve, then dust with confectioners' sugar.

nutrition information per serving   1-inch slice, 83g

264 cal | 16g fat | 4g protein | 6g complex carbohydrates | 20g sugar | 1g dietary fiber | 89mg cholesterol | 175mg sodium | 82mg potassium | 433RE vitamin A | 1mg vitamin C | 1mg iron | 38mg calcium | 60mg phosphorus

Genoise

ONE CAKE, ABOUT 16 SERVINGS

Genoise is a type of sponge cake enriched with butter and egg yolk. With its mild flavor, it's used as a base for a wide range of European-style tortes and cream-filled cakes. To that end, it's nearly always brushed with a flavored syrup, which helps keep it moist as well as adding a complementary flavor to the finished cake.

While genoise isn't hard to make, it takes careful attention to detail as well as a light touch: fold the flour into the batter gently or you'll end up with a dense cake.

6 large eggs

1 egg yolk

¾ cup (5¼ ounces) superfine or granulated sugar (superfine is best)

⅛ teaspoon salt

¾ cup (3¼ ounces) unbleached all-purpose flour

1 tablespoon cornstarch

4 tablespoons (½ stick, 2 ounces) butter, melted and slightly cooled

2 teaspoons vanilla or almond extract (or one of each)

Preheat the oven to 350°F.

Grease and flour (or line with parchment) two 9-inch round pans; three 8-inch round pans; a 10 x 15-inch jelly roll pan, or a 9 x 3-inch springform pan.

Place the room-temperature eggs and egg yolk, ½ cup of the sugar, and the salt in a heatproof bowl and immerse the bottom of the bowl in warm water. Whisk over the warm water until the sugar dissolves; you'll be able to feel if the sugar has dissolved by rubbing a small amount of the batter between your fingers—it shouldn't feel gritty. Check the temperature of the batter occasionally; don't let it go over 110°F, as the eggs may begin to cook. You're after batter that's just warm to the touch. Once

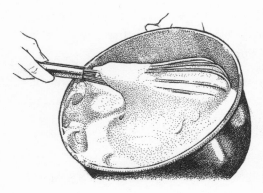

The eggs should be very light and fluffy when they are properly beaten. Use a hand whisk to gently fold the flour mixture into the beaten eggs without deflating them.

the sugar has dissolved, remove the bowl from the hot water. Using an electric mixer, beat the egg mixture on high speed until it becomes very light and fluffy. This will take up to 10 minutes. It should double (or more) in volume and be very thick.

Whisk together the flour, cornstarch, and remaining ¼ cup sugar to eliminate any lumps and aerate the mixture. Using very low speed on an electric mixer, or a hand whisk, gently fold the flour mixture into the eggs, about a third at a time. Stir together the butter and extract; mix about a third of the flour-and-egg mixture into the butter, then fold that back into the remaining batter. Spoon or pour the batter into the prepared pans, smoothing the surface.

Bake the 8- or 9-inch round layers for 20 to 25 minutes, the jelly roll for 14 to 18 minutes, or the springform for 30 to 35 minutes. All should be light golden in color and spring back when touched lightly in the center. Allow to cool in the pans for 15 minutes.

nutrition information per serving ¹⁄₁₆ **of recipe, 30g**

80 cal | 5g fat | 3g protein | 5g complex carbohydrates | 5g sugar | 102mg cholesterol | 41mg sodium | 31mg potassium | 70RE vitamin A | 1mg iron | 12mg calcium | 44mg phosphorus

Variation   CHOCOLATE GENOISE: To make a chocolate genoise, cut the amount of flour to ½ cup and whisk it together with ¼ cup (¾ ounce) Dutch-process cocoa before folding it into the egg-and-sugar mixture.

Hot Milk Cake

ONE CAKE, 16 SERVINGS.

This golden, fine-grained, single-layer cake, an American classic, can be eaten as is; frosted; or sliced, split, and filled and topped with fruit, or a whipped cream or pastry cream filling (p. 398). It's prepared very much like a sponge cake, though the addition of heated milk helps to set the protein in the eggs, meaning they're more easily able to hold onto the air you've beaten into them.

3 large eggs

1½ cups (10½ ounces) sugar

1 teaspoon vanilla extract

¾ cup (6 ounces) milk

1 tablespoon butter

1½ cups (6¼ ounces) unbleached all-purpose flour or cake flour

1½ teaspoons baking powder

½ teaspoon salt

Preheat the oven to 325°F.

In a large bowl, beat together the eggs and sugar until very thick; the batter should fall from the beaters in a thick ribbon. Beat in the vanilla.

While you're beating the eggs and sugar, heat the milk and butter in a small saucepan to just simmering. Add the hot milk to the egg mixture in a slow, steady stream as you continue beating.

In a separate bowl, whisk together the flour, baking powder, and salt. Fold the dry ingredients into the wet ingredients, stirring until they're just combined.

Pour the batter into a lightly greased 9 x 9-inch cake pan. Bake for 55 minutes to 1 hour, until the cake is a deep golden brown and starting to pull away from the sides of the pan. Remove the cake from the oven and cool it in the pan for 10 to 15 minutes. Run a knife around the sides of the pan, if necessary, and invert the cake onto a serving plate.

nutrition information per serving   2¼ x 2¼-inch piece, 52g

132 cal | 12g fat | 3g protein | 9g complex carbohydrates | 17g sugar | 54mg cholesterol | 126mg sodium | 45mg potassium | 29RE vitamin A | 1mg iron | 61mg calcium | 46mg phosphorus

Chiffon Cake

Chiffon cakes were a significant phenomenon of the fifties—touted in some cookbooks as the first new cake in one hundred years. Light as air but with the richness of a butter cake, chiffon cakes were "invented" by a Los Angeles insurance salesman, Harry Baker, who kept the formula secret for many years, baking and selling cakes to movie stars and some of the area's finest restaurants. In 1947 he sold his secret recipe to General Mills. And the secret is? Vegetable oil. The process used to refine vegetable oil was invented in 1870, but not until much later did neutral-flavored, good-quality vegetable oil become readily available to home cooks. Until the fifties, most cake recipes called for butter or lard as the fat of choice.

Chiffon cake was made plain and fancy in just about any flavor you could think of: lemon, orange, chocolate, peppermint, banana, or with bits of chocolate or nuts. It was often served with just a dusting of confectioners' sugar; with whipped cream and fresh fruit; or frosted with a fluffy boiled icing. (Skip the buttercream icing, it's too heavy for this light-textured cake.) The cake also was often hollowed out and filled with chiffon filling for a truly elegant dessert. (Cookbooks of the fifties seemed to use the word *elegant* quite often. We assume that after the ration-ticket war years, being able to be elegant once again was every housewife's dream.)

Chiffon cakes may be baked either in tube (angel food) pans, or in 9-inch round cake pans. Like angel food cakes, they must be cooled upside down to maintain their full height. This recipe makes a large cake, enough for 16 to 20 slices. It freezes well and is a good base for Baked Alaska or filled cakes that need to be served cold, because unlike butter- or shortening-based cakes it retains its soft texture in the refrigerator.

7 eggs, separated	¾ teaspoon salt
½ teaspoon cream of tartar, or 1 teaspoon lemon juice	½ cup (3½ ounces) vegetable oil
1½ cups (10½ ounces) sugar	¾ cup (6 ounces) milk (whole or skim, or buttermilk for chocolate cake)
2 cups (8½ ounces) unbleached all-purpose flour	2 teaspoons vanilla
2½ teaspoons baking powder	1 teaspoon almond extract

Preheat the oven to 325°F.

In a large mixing bowl, beat the egg whites with the cream of tartar until foamy. Gradually add ½ cup of the sugar and continue beating until stiff and glossy. Set aside.

Whisk together the remaining 1 cup sugar with the flour, baking powder, and salt. In a separate bowl, beat the oil, milk, egg yolks, and flavorings until pale yellow. Add the dry ingredients and beat until well blended, about 2 minutes at medium speed using a stand mixer, or longer with a hand mixer.

Gently fold in the whipped egg whites, using a wire whisk or cake whisk. Be sure to scrape the bottom of the bowl so the batter is well blended. Pour the batter into an ungreased 10-inch tube pan or angel food pan, or two 9-inch round ungreased cake pans. If it's in a tube or angel food pan, bake it for 1 hour. If you're using two 9-inch cake pans, bake for about 50 minutes. Don't open the oven during the first 45 minutes of baking; the cake will rise high above the pan, then settle back almost even. It's done when a finger gently pressed in the center doesn't leave a print; you'll be able to hear a crackling sound if you listen carefully.

Remove the cake from the oven and cool it upside down for 30 minutes before removing it from the pan. If you've used a tube pan, set it atop a thin-necked bottle, threading the bottle neck through the hole in the tube. When the cake is completely cool, run a knife around the outside edge and around the tube. Turn the pan upside down and tap it to remove the cake. Frost the cake and cut it just before serving. Dip a serrated knife in hot water between each slice if you want smooth, even pieces.

nutrition information per serving   **an unfilled, unfrosted 2½-inch slice of cake, ¹⁄₁₈ of cake**

165 cal | 7g fat | 4g protein | 10g complex carbohydrates | 10g sugar | 79mg cholesterol | 168mg sodium | 47mg potassium | 51RE vitamin A | 75mg calcium | 58mg phosphorus

Variations   LEMON OR ORANGE CHIFFON: Replace the cream of tartar with 1 tablespoon of lemon or orange juice; eliminate the almond extract and 1 teaspoon of the vanilla extract. Fold in 1 tablespoon lemon or orange zest, or add ½ teaspoon lemon or orange oil at the same time you add the vanilla.

CHOCOLATE CHIFFON: Decrease the amount of flour to 1½ cups and sift ½ cup natural cocoa into the flour–baking powder mixture.

COCONUT CHIFFON: Substitute coconut flavor for the almond extract using 1 teaspoon if it's a mild-strength flavor, or a few drops if it's a very strong flavoring oil. Beat 1 cup shredded sweetened coconut into the batter along with the flour.

VANILLA CHIFFON: Increase vanilla extract to 1 tablespoon and omit the almond extract.

Tres Leches Cake

ONE CAKE, ABOUT 20 SERVINGS

This golden sponge cake, a native of Latin America, is liberally soaked with *tres leches* (three milks: condensed, evaporated, and heavy cream) and seems, at first read-through of the recipe, to be unbearably sweet. But the cake itself is actually only mildly sweet, allowing the sugar in the milks and frosting to contribute their share of sweetness without overwhelming the whole. For a delightful dessert, serve this with tropical fruit: mango slices, or a compote of bananas and pineapple.

CAKE

1½ cups (6¼ ounces) unbleached all-purpose flour

2 teaspoons baking powder

½ teaspoon salt

6 large eggs, separated

½ teaspoon cream of tartar, or ¼ teaspoon lemon juice

1½ cups (10½ ounces) sugar

⅓ cup (2⅝ ounces) cold water

2 teaspoons vanilla extract

1 teaspoon almond flavoring

TRES LECHES

1 cup (8 ounces) heavy cream

1 can (14 ounces) sweetened condensed milk

1 small can (5 ounces) evaporated milk

1 tablespoon brandy or light rum, or 2 teaspoons vanilla extract

FROSTING

4 egg whites, or ¼ cup (1½ ounces) meringue powder dissolved in ½ cup (4 ounces) cool water

⅛ teaspoon salt

¼ teaspoon cream of tartar (omit if using meringue powder)

1¼ cups (8¾ ounces) sugar

3 tablespoons (2¼ ounces) light corn syrup

½ cup (4 ounces) water

1 teaspoon vanilla extract

Preheat the oven to 350°F.

FOR THE CAKE In a medium-sized mixing bowl, whisk together the flour, baking powder, and salt; set aside. In a large mixing bowl, beat the egg whites with the cream of tartar until soft peaks form. Set aside. In a separate bowl, beat the egg yolks until they're pale yellow and fluffy. Add the sugar and continue to beat until the mixture is very thick and falls from the beaters in ribbons.

Add the ⅓ cup cold water, vanilla, and almond to the egg yolk mixture, then stir in the dry ingredients. Gently whisk in the beaten egg whites.

Grease and flour a 9 x 13-inch pan. Spoon the batter into the pan and level it with a spatula. Bake the cake for 28 to 30 minutes, until a cake tester inserted in the center comes out clean. Let the cake cool in the pan for 20 minutes.

Loosen the sides of the cake with a knife, place a serving platter upside down over the pan and gently turn the cake out onto the platter. Using a fork, poke holes all over the cake and let it cool for an additional 30 minutes.

FOR THE TRES LECHES While the cake is cooling, combine the heavy cream, condensed milk, evaporated milk, and brandy in a small bowl or measuring cup with a spout. When the cake has cooled to room temperature, pour the milk mixture over it slowly, pausing occasionally to allow it to soak in. Refrigerate the cake for several hours before frosting; this allows the cake to absorb the milk.

FOR THE FROSTING In a large mixing bowl, beat together the egg whites (or meringue powder and water), salt, and cream of tartar until soft peaks form.

In a medium saucepan set over medium heat, bring the sugar, corn syrup, and water to a boil. Cover the pan and let the mixture boil for several minutes. Uncover the pan and boil the mixture until the temperature reaches 240°F (soft-ball stage) on an instant-read or candy thermometer. Immediately remove the pan from the heat and pour the sugar syrup slowly over the egg whites, beating them on slow speed all the while. After all the sugar is mixed in, beat the frosting on high speed for several minutes, until it's thick and glossy. Stir in the vanilla.

ASSEMBLY AND SERVING Spread the frosting over the cake. Serve with fresh fruit, if desired.

---

nutrition information per serving   1 square, 2¼ x 2½ inches, ¹⁄₂₀ of cake, 107g

286 cal | 7g fat | 6g protein | 11g complex carbohydrates | 41g sugar | 83mg cholesterol | 168mg sodium | 165mg potassium | 80RE vitamin A | 1mg vitamin C | 1mg iron | 142mg calcium | 169mg phosphorus

Pineapple Upside-Down Cake

ONE CAKE, 10 SLICES

Some may think this cake is old-hat, but it's one of those surefire simple recipes that delivers a whole lot of oomph for a minimum of effort on your part. It's also a very versatile recipe. You can turn any fruit you want upside down: apples, peaches, pears, or any dried fruit you like. Warm, with whipped cream or ice cream, it's truly a classic.

5 tablespoons (2½ ounces) butter	½ teaspoon baking powder
½ cup (4 ounces) packed dark brown sugar	½ teaspoon salt
1 can (16 ounces) pineapple rings, drained, juice reserved	⅓ cup (2¾ ounces) reserved pineapple juice
12 to 16 maraschino cherries	1½ teaspoons vanilla extract
16 to 20 pecan or walnut halves	2 large eggs
1 cup (4¼ ounces) unbleached all-purpose flour or cake flour (4 ounces), sifted	⅔ cup (4½ ounces) sugar

Preheat the oven to 350°F.

Melt the butter in a 10-inch skillet or heavy 10-inch round cake pan. A 9 x 2-inch cake pan will also work, but the cake will be a bit thicker. Sprinkle brown sugar evenly over the butter and place the pineapple rings on top. Arrange the cherries in the center of rings and nuts in spaces between.

Sift the flour, baking powder, and salt together; set the mixture aside. Combine the juice and vanilla and set aside.

In a large mixing bowl, beat the eggs until they're thick and lemon-colored and the whisk leaves tracks as it travels through them. With the mixer still running, gradually sprinkle in the sugar. Add the juice, then slow down the mixer. Add sifted dry ingredients all at once and beat on medium speed for 1 minute.

Pour the batter over the prepared fruit in the cake pan. Bake the cake for 45 minutes, until its center springs back when touched lightly and it's just barely starting to pull away from the edge of the pan. Remove it from the oven and place a serving plate over the cake pan. While keeping a firm grip on both, flip the pan over and place plate and cake on a rack. Leave the pan on top for 5 minutes while the hot topping drips back down over the cake. After 5 minutes, remove the pan and rearrange any fruit that's shifted.

nutrition information per serving   1 slice, 114g

247 cal | 8g fat | 2g protein | 16g complex carbohydrates | 26g sugar | 1g dietary fiber | 59mg cholesterol | 106mg sodium | 132mg potassium | 76RE vitamin A | 7mg vitamin C | 1mg iron | 34mg calcium | 45mg phosphorous

Variations   APPLE, DATE, AND GINGER UPSIDE-DOWN CAKE: Use two peeled and cored apples, sliced into rings, in place of the pineapple, and apple cider or juice in place of the pineapple juice. Stir ⅓ cup of chopped crystallized ginger into the cake batter and use dates to decorate between the apple rings.

PEACH OR APRICOT UPSIDE-DOWN CAKE: Substitute fresh or canned (in water) peach or apricot slices for the pineapple, and use peach nectar or orange juice in place of the pineapple. Use pecan halves and dried cherries or cranberries to decorate.

Cheesecake

For something that's really so simple to make, and that produces such a rich, soul-satisfying dessert, it's amazing that the average home baker doesn't make cheesecake more frequently. This is another dessert with a long history, an antecedent of it being noted in print as early as the fifteenth century.

In America, there's a general perception of two kinds of cheesecake: New York cheesecake, and not New York cheesecake. New York cheesecake (embodied in the version popularized by Lindy's restaurant in New York City) is very dense and tight-textured, creamy, consisting of cream cheese, eggs, sugar, a touch of citrus, and a bit of heavy cream. Other cheesecakes, generally lighter and drier, may include beaten egg whites, Ricotta or cottage cheese, and/or sour cream, or even gelatin. To those of you who grew up on New York cheesecake, anything else will seem wan and insubstantial; to those in the other camp, New York cheesecake is distastefully rich and heavy.

Cheesecakes are most often made by pouring the sweetened egg and cheese batter atop a graham cracker crust in a springform pan. However, the crust may also be made of crushed cookies, a nut-based pastry dough, or cookie dough (featured in the original Lindy's version). And the cake may be made in a regular pie pan, or even in a square or rectangular cake pan. Though the springform certainly makes the cake a lot easier to get out of the pan, it'll taste just as good baked in another form.

Classic Cheesecake

ONE 9- OR 10-INCH CHEESECAKE, ABOUT 16 SERVINGS

This cheesecake balances the tang of cream cheese and sour cream with just enough sweetness; vanilla and lemon provide a nice accent. For a slightly sweeter version, substitute a cup of heavy cream for the sour cream (making 1½ cups total heavy cream).

1 recipe pâte sucrée (p. 458)

FILLING

3 packages (8 ounces each) cream cheese, at room temperature

1¼ cups (8¾ ounces) sugar

¼ teaspoon salt

4 large eggs

3 tablespoons (1½ ounces) freshly squeezed lemon juice, or ½ teaspoon lemon oil

1 tablespoon vanilla extract

1 cup (8 ounces) sour cream

½ cup (4 ounces) heavy cream

Preheat the oven to 375°F.

FOR THE CRUST Press the pâte sucrée into the bottom and about ½ inch up the sides of a 9- or 10-inch springform pan. Use a piece of plastic wrap to cover the dough while pressing it into place. Prick the crust all over and bake it for 12 to 15 minutes, until lightly browned. Remove from the oven and set aside to cool. Reduce the oven temperature to 325°F.

FOR THE FILLING Using an electric mixer, beat the cream cheese until soft and no lumps remain, stopping to scrape down the bowl once or twice. Do this using the slow speed; you don't want to incorporate air into the mixture. Add the sugar and salt and mix until well blended. Add the eggs one at a time, beating until the mixture is smooth before adding the next egg, and scraping the bottom of the bowl after each addition. Stir in the lemon, vanilla, sour cream, and heavy cream. Stir just until the mixture is smooth.

Pour the batter into the prepared pan. Bake the cake in a 325°F oven for 45 to 50 minutes; the edges of the cake will look set and be a light golden brown and the middle should still jiggle when you nudge the pan. The internal temperature when measured an inch from the center should be 165°F or above. Turn the oven off, open the door slightly, and let the cheesecake cool slowly in the oven for 1 hour. During this time the center will finish setting. Cooling the cake slowly will keep the top from cracking and ensure an even, smooth texture inside.

After an hour, remove the cake from the oven and run a knife around the edge to allow the cake to contract as it cools. Refrigerate overnight before serving. Top with fruit or whipped cream, if desired.

nutrition information per serving   ¹⁄₁₆ **of 10-inch cheesecake, 114g**

390 cal | 17g fat | 7g protein | 9g complex carbohydrates | 17g sugar | 132mg cholesterol | 219mg sodium | 123mg potassium | 322RE vitamin A | 2mg vitamin C | 1mg iron | 64mg calcium | 102mg phosphorus

Variation   CHOCOLATE SWIRL CHEESECAKE: Start with the Classic Cheesecake recipe, but leave out the lemon juice and sour cream, using 1½ cups (total) heavy cream. Set aside ¾ cup of the batter and pour the remainder into the crust in the pan. In a heatproof bowl set over simmering water, or at low power in your microwave, melt together ¾ cup (4½ ounces) chopped semisweet or bittersweet chocolate (or chocolate chips) and ½ cup (4 ounces) heavy cream. Stir the mixture until it's smooth and let it cool to room temperature. Blend the chocolate with the reserved batter. Drop by tablespoons over the top of the plain cheesecake batter. Run a knife through the batter several times to create a swirl pattern. Bake as directed in the Classic Cheesecake recipe.

Drop the flavored batter onto the plain one, using a tablespoon. Take a knife and run it through both batters several times, to create a pattern.

Pumpkin Cheesecake

ONE 9- OR 10-INCH CHEESECAKE, 16 SERVINGS

The rich flavor of cheesecake melds beautifully with the color and sweet, hearty taste of pumpkin. To make this cake even more indulgent, we've added a spicy gingersnap crust.

CRUST

4 tablespoons (½ stick, 2 ounces) butter

1¼ cups (6¾ ounces) gingersnap crumbs

¼ to ½ teaspoon ground ginger (optional, if the snaps aren't strong-flavored)

2 tablespoons (1 ounce) brown sugar

CHEESE FILLING

3 packages (8 ounces each) cream cheese, at room temperature

1¼ cups (8¾ ounces) sugar

¼ teaspoon salt

2 tablespoons (½ ounce) cornstarch

4 large eggs

1 tablespoon vanilla extract

1 cup (8 ounces) heavy cream

½ cup (4 ounces) pumpkin purée (canned is fine)

1 large egg

½ teaspoon cinnamon

¼ teaspoon ginger

Pinch of allspice

Preheat the oven to 350°F.

FOR THE CRUST   Use a food processor or blender to blend together the butter, gingersnaps, ginger, and sugar until the mixture is evenly crumbly. Press the crumbs into the bottom and about ½ inch up the side of a 9-inch springform pan. Bake the crust for 16 to 18 minutes, just until it's set. Set aside to cool. Reduce the oven temperature to 325°F.

FOR THE FILLING Using an electric mixer set on low speed, beat the cream cheese until it's soft and no lumps remain. Add the sugar, salt, and cornstarch and mix until well blended. Beat in the 4 eggs one at a time, being sure the mixture is smooth and scraping the bottom of the bowl after each addition. Add the vanilla and the heavy cream, stirring just until the mixture is smooth.

Remove 1 cup of batter from the bowl and combine it with the pumpkin purée, 1 egg, and spices.

Pour the vanilla cheesecake batter into the cooled crust. Drop tablespoonfuls of the pumpkin batter over the vanilla batter. Use a knife to swirl the pumpkin through the batter (see illustration, p. 379).

Bake the cake at 325°F for 40 to 55 minutes. The internal temperature when measured an inch from the outside edge should be 165°F or above, and the middle should jiggle. Turn off the oven, open the door slightly and let the cheesecake cool slowly for 1 hour in the turned-off oven. Remove it from the oven, run a knife around the top edge of the pan to free the cake (so it can contract as it cools), then refrigerate overnight. Top with cinnamon-flavored whipped cream, if desired.

`nutrition information per serving`   **1 slice, 138g**

432 cal | 29g fat | 7g protein | 24g complex carbohydrates | 24g sugar | 1g dietary fiber | 147mg cholesterol | 307mg sodium | 321mg potassium | 499RE vitamin A | 2mg vitamin C | 1mg iron | 71mg calcium | 108mg phosphorus

White Chocolate Hazelnut Cheesecake

ONE 9- OR 10-INCH CHEESECAKE, 16 SERVINGS

This is rich, rich, RICH! Leave out the praline paste if you like, but it does add to the cake's flavor and appearance.

CRUST

1 cup (4¼ ounces) unbleached all-purpose flour

½ cup (2 ounces) confectioners' sugar

¼ teaspoon salt

6 tablespoons (¾ stick, 3 ounces) butter

1 cup (4 ounces) toasted, chopped hazelnuts

FILLING

3 packages (8 ounces each) cream cheese, softened

1 cup (7 ounces) sugar

¼ teaspoon salt

1 tablespoon vanilla extract

3 large eggs

1 cup (8 ounces) heavy cream

1 cup (6 ounces) chopped white chocolate, melted

½ cup (5½ ounces) praline paste (optional)

Preheat the oven to 350°F.

FOR THE CRUST Use a food processor to whisk the flour, sugar, salt, and butter together until it forms very fine crumbs. Add the nuts and pulse once or twice to distribute. If you don't have a food processor, beat the butter until soft, then mix in the remaining ingredients; the mixture will be crumbly. Press the crust into the bottom and up the sides of a 9- to 10-inch springform pan. Bake for 10 to 12 minutes, until lightly browned. Reduce the oven temperature to 325°F.

FOR THE FILLING In a medium-sized mixing bowl, beat the cream cheese until soft, then blend in the sugar, salt, and vanilla. Beat in the eggs one at a time, mixing just until blended, and scraping the bottom and sides of the bowl after each addition. Stir in the heavy cream and melted white chocolate. Reserve about ½ cup of the batter (if you're using the praline paste) and pour the remaining batter into the cooled crust.

Mix the reserved batter with the praline paste; the mixture will be thick. Drop dollops over the top of the batter in the pan. Use a knife to swirl the praline into the cheesecake batter (see illustration, p. 379),

Bake the cake at 325°F for 45 to 55 minutes, just until it's set around the edges but wobbly in the middle. An instant-read thermometer should register 165°F when inserted 1 inch in from the edge. Turn off the oven and let the cake rest in the oven with the door open slightly for an hour to cool slowly and finish setting in the center. Remove it from the oven and run a knife around the edge of the pan to loosen the sides, so the cake can contract as it cools. Refrigerate overnight before serving. Decorate with whipped cream and chocolate-covered hazelnuts, if desired. Serve in small wedges.

nutrition information per serving   1 slice, made without praline paste, 132g

490 cal | 38g fat | 8g protein | 9g complex carbohydrates | 22g sugar | 1g dietary fiber | 125mg cholesterol | 227mg sodium | 179mg potassium | 333RE vitamin A | 2mg vitamin C | 1mg iron | mg calcium | 119mg phosphorus

Special Cakes

Some cakes just don't categorize well. These include flourless cakes, whose structure is based entirely on eggs, and mousse cakes, where the cake plays almost a secondary role to the whipped cream and filling. These cakes are more pure confection than cake, delighting us with their rich ingredients and sometimes whimsical presentation.

Three-Layer Chocolate Mousse Cake

ONE CAKE, AT LEAST 16 SERVINGS

This deep, dark chocolate cake, which features milk chocolate mousse topped by raspberry white chocolate mousse, is a risk to your waistline—but it's worth every bite! While the directions may seem a bit long, the only really hard part is forcing yourself to take the time to be sure the ingredients are at the proper temperature. Don't try to rush the melting of the chocolate by microwaving it on high power; don't forget to let the chocolate mixtures cool to lukewarm before adding the whipped cream; and don't try to rush the cooling by putting the chocolate in the refrigerator. Also, don't skip warming the eggs. These are all seemingly little steps that can make a big difference in how the finished product turns out. This cake serves 16 people, but after a rich dinner the slices could be made thinner to serve even more.

CAKE

10 ounces (about 1⅔ cups chopped) bittersweet or semisweet chocolate*

4 large eggs (at room temperature), separated

⅓ cup (2¼ ounces) sugar

⅛ teaspoon salt

1 teaspoon vanilla extract

8 tablespoons (1 stick, 4 ounces) soft butter**

MILK CHOCOLATE MOUSSE

10 ounces (about 1⅔ cups chopped) milk chocolate

1½ cups (12 ounces) heavy cream (not whipping cream, and preferably not ultra-pasteurized)

1 teaspoon unflavored gelatin softened in 2 tablespoons cool water, or 2 sheets gelatin soaked in cool water

RASPBERRY WHITE CHOCOLATE MOUSSE

5 ounces (about 1 scant cup, chopped) white chocolate

½ cup (4 ounces) raspberry purée (about 1 cup fresh or frozen berries, mashed or blended, seeds left in)

1 teaspoon unflavored gelatin softened in 2 tablespoons cool water, or 2 sheets gelatin soaked in cool water

1 cup (8 ounces) heavy cream

GARNISH

Fresh raspberries and mint leaves

Preheat the oven to 350°F. Prepare a 9- or 10-inch springform pan by lightly greasing the bottom. Cut a circle of waxed paper or parchment to fit the bottom of the pan and place it in the pan. If you have Magi-Cake Strips, wet them and wrap them around the pan. If you don't have Magi-Cake Strips, the cake should be baked in a water bath (pan of hot water) so the edges don't dry out. If you're using a water bath, wrap the pan in two layers of aluminum foil so no water will seep in while the cake is baking.

FOR THE CAKE Chop the chocolate into small chunks. Melt it slowly over very low heat—in the top of a double boiler or, the easiest method, in a microwave. If you use the microwave, start with 1 minute at medium power, let the chocolate sit for several minutes, stir, then continue microwaving in increments of 15 to 20 seconds on medium to low power, stirring often. (Chocolate will burn fairly easily, and since it's an expensive ingredient, taking a few extra minutes to melt the chocolate slowly is worth it.) When most of the chocolate is fluid, set the bowl aside or remove the pan from the heat, and stir occasionally; the residual heat will finish the job for you.

While the chocolate finishes melting, place the room-temperature egg whites (if eggs are cold, warm them in a bath of hot water from your tap for 5 minutes) in a large mixing bowl and add about a third of the sugar. Using an electric mixer, start beating on slow speed, gradually increasing the speed. Beat until the whites are beginning to look fluffy. Add the remaining sugar, salt, and vanilla and continue to beat until the sugar has dissolved and the meringue is shiny.

Next, using a whisk, stir the soft butter into the melted chocolate. If the butter is too cold, it will cause the chocolate to lump; if this happens, heat the mixture very briefly. When the butter is totally incorporated into the chocolate, whisk in the egg yolks.

Using a wire whisk, fold half of the meringue into the chocolate mixture. Fold in the remaining meringue with a rubber spatula, being sure to mix in the heavier batter at the bottom of the bowl.

Pour the batter into the prepared pan. Place the cake in the oven. Note: If you're using a water bath, the water should be hot when the pan is placed in it, and it should come about 1½ inches up the side of the pan. Bake the cake for 26 to 28 minutes. The top will be shiny, and a cake tester inserted into the center will come out clean; however, the cake won't spring back when touched in the center.

Remove the cake from the oven and let it cool for 1 hour; as it cools, it will sink and lose about a quarter of its volume; that's okay. Refrigerate the cake for another hour, then run a knife around the edge of the pan and invert the cake onto a plate. Remove the bottom of the pan and the waxed paper, place the cake on a serving plate, and replace the ring from the springform around the cake; it will be the mold for the two mousses.

FOR THE MILK CHOCOLATE MOUSSE Chop the milk chocolate, and place it in a microwave-safe bowl or the top of double boiler. Bring ½ cup of the heavy cream to a boil and pour it over the chopped chocolate. Stir the chocolate and cream mixture until smooth; if the chocolate doesn't melt completely, heat it briefly in the microwave, or over very low heat in a double boiler.

While the chocolate is melting, soften the gelatin. Once the gelatin has softened, heat it over low heat or in the microwave, stirring to dissolve. When the gelatin mixture is completely free of lumps, stir it into the melted chocolate. In a medium-sized mixing bowl, whip the remaining 1 cup of heavy cream, being very careful not to overwhip it. It should just hold a soft peak. Check the chocolate mixture. It must be free of lumps and the temperature should be about 80°F—warm enough to keep the chocolate from setting up, but not so hot the whipped cream melts when it's whisked in. Add about half of the whipped cream to the chocolate and whisk and fold as you did while making the cake, folding in the remaining whipped cream once the first half is whisked in. When the chocolate and cream are evenly blended, pour the mousse over the top of the cooled cake in the ring. Use an offset spatula to smooth the top. Return the cake to the refrigerator.

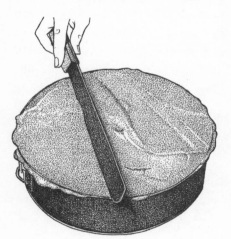

After pouring the second layer of mousse on top of the cake, use a long knife or icing spatula to smooth off the top, even with the rim of the springform pan.

FOR THE RASPBERRY WHITE CHOCOLATE MOUSSE
While the chocolate mousse is setting up, prepare the raspberry mousse. Melt the white chocolate very slowly, in a microwave or double boiler set over low heat. Heat the raspberry purée to warm and mix it into the white chocolate. It may look curdled as you first begin to stir, but will smooth out as you add more purée.

Soften the gelatin as directed for chocolate mousse, then add it to the raspberry–white chocolate mixture. Whip the cream as directed previously, being careful not to overwhip it. Check that the white chocolate–raspberry mixture is warm to the touch but not hot. Whisk it briefly, then fold it into the whipped cream. Pour the raspberry mousse over the milk chocolate mousse, smoothing the top. Refrigerate for several hours before serving.

TO SERVE   Remove the ring by running a thin knife around the edge of the pan, then open the lock and lift it off. Hold an icing spatula or dinner knife perpendicular to your work surface and run it around the edge of the cake, smoothing it and removing any excess mousse that may have oozed out and smeared the layers. Slice the cake with a wet knife, wiping it off between slices; this will ensure a pretty presentation. Place the cake slices on plates garnished with a few fresh raspberries and a mint leaf.

This dessert may be made ahead and frozen for up to several weeks. Or you can prepare just the cake layer and freeze it, filling it the day you're going to serve it.

NOTE Either of these mousses makes very good filling for cream puffs or a sponge cake.

*We don't recommend using inexpensive store-bought chocolate chips, as many have a stabilizer that may give the cake a slightly grainy mouth-feel. We suggest you use a strongly flavored, high-quality couverture chocolate.

**The butter should be at warm room temperature, looking as if it's almost (but not quite) ready to melt.

nutrition information per serving   **1 slice, ¹⁄₁₆ of cake, 103g**

399 cal | 28g fat | 5g protein | 6g complex carbohydrates | 27g sugar | 2g dietary fiber | 99mg cholesterol | 150mg sodium | 183mg potassium | 161RE vitamin A | 3mg vitamin C | 1mg iron | 67mg calcium | 105mg phosphorus | 11mg caffeine

Raspberry Mousse Cake

ONE 8- OR 9-INCH CAKE, 12 SERVINGS

This cake, which is inspired by one of our King Arthur Bakery showstoppers, includes a genoise that's paired with a rich, light raspberry mousse and a covering of whipped cream. Fresh raspberries on top are the perfect garnish.

CAKE

One 8- or 9-inch round layer genoise (p. 369)

FILLING

3 cups (one 12-ounce bag) unsweetened frozen raspberries

1 cup (7 ounces) sugar

1 tablespoon lemon juice

1½ teaspoons unflavored powdered gelatin

¼ cup (2 ounces) cold water

1 cup (8 ounces) heavy cream

SYRUP

1 cup (11 ounces) simple syrup (p. 390), flavored with framboise or kirsch (flavoring optional)

FROSTING

1½ cups (12 ounces) heavy cream

1 teaspoon vanilla extract

¼ cup (1 ounce) confectioners' sugar

½ pint (4 ounces) fresh raspberries, for garnish (optional)

FOR THE FILLING Bring the frozen raspberries, sugar, and lemon juice to a simmer in a medium-sized saucepan set over medium heat. Remove from the heat and press the fruit through a fine strainer; discard the seeds and any solids, reserving the purée. Set it aside to cool to room temperature. You should have at least 1½ cups.

In a small heatproof bowl or measuring cup, combine the gelatin and cold water. Let the mixture sit until all of the water has been absorbed (this only takes a minute or so). Whip the cream until soft peaks form; set it aside. Heat the gelatin-water mixture over low heat until it becomes a clear liquid. Stir this into the raspberry purée, then fold in the whipped cream. Refrigerate the mousse for about 90 minutes, to let it begin to set up.

TO ASSEMBLE THE CAKE Slice the cake layer horizontally into three even rounds. Place one of the rounds on a serving plate, cut side up, and brush with the simple syrup. Spread half the raspberry mousse on this layer, then place the second round, cut side up, on top. Don't worry if the mousse seems a little soft; once the cake is assembled it will continue to firm up in the refrigerator. Brush with syrup, then top it with the remaining mousse. Place the last cake layer on top, cut side down, and brush with any remaining syrup. Refrigerate the cake for 1 hour before finishing.

FOR THE FROSTING Whip the heavy cream, vanilla, and confectioners' sugar until soft peaks form (overwhipping will create grainy lumps). Cover the sides and top of the cake with whipped cream, decorating the top with fresh raspberries. Refrigerate for another hour before serving.

nutrition information per serving   **1 slice, 167g**

310 cal | 19g fat | 2g protein | 9g complex carbohydrates | 26g sugar | 3g dietary fiber | 73mg cholesterol | 22mg sodium | 127mg potassium | 221RE vitamin A | 12mg vitamin C | 47mg calcium | 41mg phosphorus

Chocolate Lava Cake

ONE 9-INCH CAKE, 12 SERVINGS, OR 16 SMALL CAKES

This cake, which is free of flour or leavening, can be made as a single 9-inch round, or as individual cakes. Either way, the airy, chocolaty cake holds a pool of milk chocolate truffle that oozes beautifully when pierced with a fork. The trick is to mix up the milk chocolate "lava," chill it, then bury it in the cake batter halfway through the baking process. By the time the cake is done, the lava will have melted.

MILK CHOCOLATE LAVA TRUFFLE

4 ounces (⅔ cup) milk chocolate, finely chopped

2 tablespoons (1 ounce) heavy cream

1½ teaspoons softened butter

1½ teaspoons rum or other liqueur of your choice (optional), or ½ teaspoon flavoring or extract of your choice

CAKE

4 ounces (⅔ cup) semisweet chocolate, chopped

8 tablespoons (1 stick, 4 ounces) butter

4 large eggs, separated

⅔ cup (4½ ounces) sugar

¼ cup (¾ ounce) natural cocoa, sifted

½ teaspoon vanilla extract

¼ teaspoon salt

Sifted confectioners' sugar for dusting

FOR THE TRUFFLE FILLING In a heatproof bowl, combine the milk chocolate, cream, butter, and flavoring. Place over an inch of simmering water and melt, stirring, until the mixture is smooth (or melt slowly, stirring regularly, in the microwave). Remove the bowl from the heat and set aside.

If you're making the 9-inch cake, take a 7-inch plate (salad or dessert size) and spray it with nonstick pan spray. Pour the melted chocolate onto the plate and refrigerate it for at least 30 minutes.

If you're making small cakes, put the bowl in the refrigerator and stir every 5 minutes until the mixture becomes thick. Scoop individual truffles out of the bowl (you'll need 16) with a teaspoon, cookie scoop, or melon baller. Put the scooped truffles on a plate and refrigerate.

Preheat the oven to 325°F.

FOR THE CAKE Melt the chocolate and butter together in a heatproof bowl over simmering water, or in the microwave. Stir until the chocolate has completely melted, then remove from heat and set aside.

In a large mixing bowl, beat the egg yolks with ⅓ cup of the sugar until they're thick, lemon-colored, and fall in a ribbon from the beater. Add the sifted cocoa, vanilla, and salt to the egg mixture, stirring until combined. Fold the melted chocolate into the egg mixture. In a separate bowl, beat the egg whites with the remaining ⅓ cup sugar to soft peaks. Fold these gently into the chocolate mixture, one third at a time, taking care not to deflate the whites. It's okay if some streaks of white remain when the batter is poured into the pan. Set aside 1½ cups of the batter.

FOR THE 9-INCH CAKE Pour the rest of the batter into a greased 9-inch cake pan. Bake for 15 minutes. After 15 minutes, remove the pan from the oven. Peel the hardened chocolate truffle mixture from the plate and place it in the center of the cake, pressing very gently. Cover the truffle completely, sealing it inside the cake, with the 1½ cups of reserved batter. Return the pan to the oven and bake for another 25 minutes, until the cake pulls from the edge of the pan and the top looks set. Remove from the oven and cool on a rack for 20 minutes.

Put a plate on top of the cake pan, then flip everything over to invert the cake. Dust the top with some confectioners' sugar and serve warm.

FOR SMALL CAKES Pour the batter into 16 greased wells in 2 muffin pans, filling the wells to ½ inch below the top. Bake the cakes in a preheated 300°F oven for 15 minutes; remove from the oven and place one truffle in each cup, pushing them down until they're flush with the top of the cake. Cover the holes with a heaping tablespoon of the reserved batter. Return to the oven and bake for an additional 20 minutes, until the cakes have risen and fallen back down again. Remove from the oven and let cool on a rack for 20 minutes to set up before taking the cakes out of the pans. You can serve the cakes, with raspberry sauce or whipped cream, at this point. Or cool the cakes completely, wrap them well, and reheat them before serving, in a microwave on medium power for 45 seconds, or in a 300°F oven for 3 minutes.

nutrition information per serving   **1 slice, ¹⁄₁₂ of cake, 45g**

212 cal | 12g fat | 2g protein | 3g complex carbohydrates | 21g sugar | 1g dietary fiber | 39mg cholesterol | 69mg sodium | 106mg potassium | 68RE vitamin A | 1mg iron | 29mg calcium | 78mg phosphorus | 17mg caffeine

nutrition information per serving   **1 individual cake 34g**

159 cal | 9g fat | 2g protein | 2g complex carbohydrates | 15g sugar | 1g dietary fiber | 29mg cholesterol | 52mg sodium | 80mg potassium | 51RE vitamin A | 1mg iron | 22mg calcium | 59mg phosphorus | 12mg caffeine

Whoopie Pies

9 LARGE WHOOPIE PIES

Whoopie Pies, a venerable habitué of the bake sale table, are a specialty of both northern New England and Amish country in Pennsylvania. They're not fancy, not elegant—just down-home good.

CAKES

½ cup (3¼ ounces) shortening

1 cup (8 ounces) brown sugar, packed

1 large egg

1 teaspoon baking powder

1 teaspoon baking soda

1 teaspoon salt

1 teaspoon vanilla extract

¼ cup plus 2 tablespoons (1⅛ ounces) natural cocoa

2 cups (8½ ounces) unbleached all-purpose flour

1 cup (8 ounces) milk

FILLING

1 cup (6½ ounces) shortening

1 cup (4 ounces) confectioners' sugar

1⅓ cups (4 ounces) marshmallow creme

Heaping ¼ teaspoon salt dissolved in 1 tablespoon water

1½ teaspoons vanilla extract

Preheat the oven to 350°F.

FOR THE CAKES In a large mixing bowl, cream together the shortening, sugar, egg, baking powder, baking soda, salt, and vanilla. In a separate bowl, whisk together the cocoa and flour. Add the dry ingredients to the shortening mixture alternately with the milk, beating until smooth.

Drop the dough by the ¼-cupful onto parchment-lined or lightly greased baking sheets, leaving about 2 inches between each cake. Bake the cakes for about 15 minutes, or until they're firm to the touch. Remove them from the oven and cool completely on a wire rack.

FOR THE FILLING Beat together the shortening, sugar, and marshmallow, then stir in the salt and vanilla. Spread half of the cakes with the filling; top with the remaining cakes.

nutrition information per serving   1 whoopie pie, 196g

768 cal | 53g fat | 7g protein | 23g complex carbohydrates | 45g sugar | 2g dietary fiber | 89mg cholesterol | 441mg sodium | 266mg potassium | 223RE vitamin A | 1mg vitamin C | 2mg iron | 122mg calcium | 133mg phosphorus | 9mg caffeine

Frostings, Glazes, and Fillings

Here's the icing on the cake—and the filling inside. Some of the cakes in this chapter call for specific icings or fillings; the following recipes can be paired with any cake as you see fit.

Simple Syrup

1 CUP, ENOUGH FOR 4 CAKE LAYERS

Brushing your cake with simple syrup will ensure it stays moist.

1 cup (7 ounces) sugar

1 cup (8 ounces) water

Bring the mixture to a boil, stirring until the sugar dissolves. Remove from the heat, allow to cool, then store in the refrigerator until you're ready to use.

Flavor syrup however you like by starting with a combination of water and liquor, liqueur, or juice, then adding a vanilla bean, whole spices, citrus rind, or sliced, peeled gingerroot.

nutrition information per serving   made with water, 1 teaspoon, 9g

16 cal | 4g sugar

Easy Buttercream

SUFFICIENT FROSTING TO FROST AN 8- OR 9- INCH LAYER CAKE, 9 X 13-INCH CAKE, OR 24 CUPCAKES

This buttercream frosting, a standby in professional bakeries, goes together in a snap. It's deliciously smooth and creamy.

5⅓ tablespoons (⅔ stick, 2⅝ ounces) butter

⅓ cup (2 ounces) vegetable shortening

⅛ teaspoon salt

4 to 5 cups (1 to 1¼ pounds) confectioners' sugar, sifted

2 teaspoons vanilla extract

¼ to ⅓ cup (2 to 2¾ ounces) milk or cream

In a large mixing bowl, beat together the butter, shortening, and salt until fluffy. Add about half the confectioners' sugar and beat slowly until well blended. Add the vanilla and half the milk and beat until fluffy.

Continue mixing in sugar and milk alternately until they've been completely incorporated, and beat until the frosting is light and fluffy. To increase the yield, if you want some frosting left over to use in decorating, change the ingredient amounts as follows: ½ cup butter, ½ cup vegetable shortening, approximately 6 cups sugar, and up to ½ cup milk or cream.

Easy Chocolate Buttercream

2 TO 3 CUPS, ENOUGH TO FROST AN 8- OR 9- INCH LAYER CAKE, 9 X 13-INCH CAKE, OR 24 CUPCAKES

This is a simple chocolate frosting that's deliciously smooth and creamy. You can customize it for your particular taste by using unsweetened, bittersweet, or semi-sweet chocolate.

½ cup (3 ounces) unsweetened, bittersweet, or semisweet chocolate, chopped

4 tablespoons (½ stick, 2 ounces) butter

⅛ teaspoon salt

4 to 5 cups (1 to 1¼ pounds) confectioners' sugar, sifted

2 teaspoons vanilla extract

6 tablespoons (3 ounces) milk or cream

Place the chocolate in a heatproof bowl or measuring cup. Using the medium power setting on your microwave, or over simmering water, melt the chocolate about three quarters of the way. Remove from the heat or microwave and stir the chocolate until it's completely smooth. Set aside to cool at room temperature.

In a large mixing bowl, beat together the butter and salt until fluffy. Add about half of the confectioners' sugar and beat slowly until well blended. Add the vanilla and half the milk and beat until fluffy. Add the melted chocolate and mix until thoroughly blended. Scrape down the sides of the bowl and add the remaining sugar and milk alternately until they've been completely incorporated. Beat until the frosting is light and fluffy, adjusting the consistency with more milk or confectioners' sugar as needed. If you want some frosting left over to use in decorating, change the ingredient amounts as follows: ½ cup butter, ⅔ cup chocolate, approximately 6 cups sugar, and up to ½ cup milk or cream.

Silky Buttercream

4½ TO 5 CUPS FROSTING, ENOUGH TO FROST, FILL, AND DECORATE AN 8- OR 9- INCH LAYER CAKE, 9 X 13-INCH CAKE, OR 24 CUPCAKES

Our favorite traditional buttercream, ultrarich and smooth, is based on cooked meringue. This recipe takes a bit of time to put together, but the results are worth it. If you are lucky enough to have two bowls for your mixer, the job is easier.

½ cup (4 ounces) egg whites (the whites from 2 to 3 large eggs), or ¼ cup (1¼ ounces) meringue powder dissolved in ½ cup (4 ounces) cool water

¼ cup (2¾ ounces) light corn syrup

1 cup (7 ounces) sugar

⅓ cup (2⅝ ounces) water

½ teaspoon cream of tartar

½ teaspoon salt

1 cup (2 sticks, 8 ounces) butter

½ cup (3¼ ounces) vegetable shortening (you may use all butter, but the frosting will be more stable with the vegetable shortening)

2 teaspoons vanilla extract

½ teaspoon almond extract (optional)

Place the egg whites or meringue powder and water in the bowl of your mixer.

Place the corn syrup, sugar, and water in a medium-sized saucepan. Stir over heat until combined and the sugar has dissolved. Cover the pan, bring to a boil, and boil for 3 minutes without stirring. Remove the cover and cook to the soft ball stage, 240°F.

Meanwhile, begin to beat the egg whites on slow speed. When they are foamy, add the cream of tartar and salt. (If using the meringue powder, you will not need the cream of tartar, but still add the salt.) Gradually increase the speed of the mixer, continuing to beat until soft peaks form.

As soon as the sugar syrup reaches the soft ball stage, remove it from the heat. Turn off the mixer. Very carefully pour about a quarter of the syrup down the inside of the mixing bowl. Turn the mixer on and beat well. Add the syrup in two more additions, working as quickly as possible. If the sugar is slightly overcooked and begins to harden, return it to the heat for a moment to re-melt it. Don't pour the sugar syrup into the bowl while the mixer is on or you may splash yourself with hot sugar syrup, or the sugar syrup will end up on the sides of the bowl.

Continue to beat the meringue until it cools to room temperature. This takes about 20 minutes. If you need to hurry it along, place the bowl of your mixer in an ice bath. If you attempt to add the butter before the meringue is cool, the butter will melt.

When the meringue is cool, beat in the room-temperature butter a bit at a time. If the frosting starts to separate, continue beating without adding any more butter until the frosting looks fluffy again. Beat in the vegetable shortening. Beat in your choice of flavoring.

If the frosting is very soft, refrigerate before using, or beat in extra vegetable shortening. Beating the butter and vegetable shortening together first, before beating them into the meringue, will ensure you end up with the lightest, fluffiest frosting.

nutrition information per serving   **3 tablespoons, 31g**

145 cal | 12g fat | 10g sugar | 21mg cholesterol | 53mg sodium | 16mg potassium | 72RE vitamin A | 3mg calcium | 3mg phosphorus

Flavoring options:

- ½ cup (6 ounces) lemon curd plus ⅛ teaspoon lemon oil

- ¼ cup (3 ounces) strained raspberry purée

- ¼ cup (2¾) hazelnut paste plus 2 tablespoons (1 ounce) hazelnut liqueur

- 2 ounces unsweetened chocolate, melted and cooled slightly

Marshmallow Icing

ENOUGH ICING TO FROST A 10-INCH TUBE CAKE, OR FILL AND FROST A 9-INCH LAYER CAKE, A 9 X 13-INCH CAKE, OR 24 CUPCAKES

What could be better to top a light, airy chiffon cake than a light, fluffy icing? A close cousin to traditional 7-Minute Icing, we like this recipe better; while 7-Minute Icing develops a hard, crackly crust overnight, the crust that develops on this icing is softer than normal and doesn't shatter.

You'll need to use three different bowls or pans in preparing this recipe. But we think the resulting frosting—soft, smooth, with a real marshmallow flavor and not too much fat—is worth the cleanup. You may choose not to add the butter, but the result is very different with it (and, we feel, much improved). Taste before adding and then compare it after; it's amazing how much flavor the butter adds.

2 teaspoons vanilla extract	**¼ cup (1½ ounces) powdered egg whites or meringue powder, or ½ cup fresh egg whites (from about 3 large eggs)***
¼ cup (2 ounces) water	
1 packet (2 teaspoons, ¼ ounce) unflavored gelatin	**½ cup (4 ounces) cold water***
1 cup (7 ounces) sugar	**½ teaspoon cream of tartar (if using powdered egg whites)**
½ cup (5½ ounces) light corn syrup	
¼ cup (2 ounces) water	**4 tablespoons (½ stick, 2 ounces) butter, softened**

Combine the vanilla and ¼ cup water, then sprinkle in the gelatin. Set the mixture aside to let the gelatin soften.

In a saucepan set over low heat, stir together the sugar, corn syrup, and ¼ cup water, cooking and stirring until all the sugar has dissolved. Bring the mixture to a boil, cover the pan, and cook for 3 minutes, washing down any sugar crystals that cling to the sides of the pan. Remove the pan from the heat.

While the sugar syrup is cooking, whisk the powdered egg whites or meringue powder with ½ cup cold water, then add the cream of tartar (if you've used egg whites, either fresh or powdered). Beat until soft peaks form. Carefully add the hot sugar syrup to the beaten egg whites, continuing to beat until the mixture is stiff and glossy.

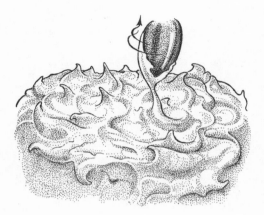

Fill the cake layers with frosting, then completely cover the top and sides of the cake with frosting to seal it. Use the back of a spoon or the tip of your icing spatula to make a swirl pattern in the frosting.

Melt the softened gelatin in a saucepan set over low heat, or in a microwave oven. Add it to the beaten egg whites and beat until the icing feels cool, about 10 minutes. Beat in the soft butter quickly. Don't overbeat at this point; if the mixture is too warm or you beat it too much, you'll lose volume (though the icing will still taste good). It will be soft, but should hold a peak.

The icing is easy to spread when warm, and will yield a smooth appearance. If you wait too long, the icing will be thick and hard to spread. Ice the cake, then set it aside for an hour or more to give the icing a chance to set. If you've made a cake with perishable filling, be sure to refrigerate it while this is taking place. As it sets it will develop the texture of soft marshmallows.

*If you use fresh egg whites, omit the ½ cup water.

nutrition information per serving the amount of icing covering a slice of chiffon cake, 38g

95 cal | 2g fat | 1g protein | 17g sugar | 7mg cholesterol | 37mg sodium | 11mg potassium | 24RE vitamin A | 2mg calcium | 2mg phosphorus

Thick Fudge Frosting

ENOUGH TO FROST AN 8- OR 9-INCH LAYER CAKE, 9 X 13-INCH CAKE, OR 24 CUPCAKES

This thick, deep-chocolate frosting is poured, rather than spread over the cake. As it cools it becomes glossy and smooth, very much like fudge.

8 tablespoons (1 stick, 4 ounces) butter

¼ cup (¾ ounce) cocoa powder, natural or Dutch-process

⅛ teaspoon salt

½ cup (4 ounces) yogurt or sour cream*

4 cups (1 pound) sifted confectioners' sugar

1 teaspoon vanilla extract

In a medium-sized saucepan, melt the butter over medium heat. When it has melted, stir in the cocoa, salt, and yogurt, then bring the mixture to a boil. Place the confectioners' sugar and vanilla in a mixing bowl, pour the hot cocoa mixture over it, and beat until smooth.

Working quickly, pour about half the frosting over one cake layer, spreading it around the sides. Center the second layer over the first and pour on the remaining frosting, spreading it evenly to the edge and along the sides of the cake. (If you're making a three-layer cake, use one third of the frosting for each layer; for a sheet cake, just pour it all on top of the cake.) Don't scrape the very bottom of the pan, as the frosting stuck there won't have a nice gloss and may be grainy.

*Use regular, low-fat, or nonfat yogurt or sour cream and, in the case of yogurt, plain, vanilla, or coffee-flavored.

nutrition information per serving   1 slice, ¹⁄₁₂ of cake, 161g

546 cal | 20g fat | 5g protein | 22g complex carbohydrates | 66g sugar | 1g dietary fiber | 55mg cholesterol | 438mg sodium | 136mg potassium | 186RE vitamin A | 2mg iron | 138mg calcium | 189mg phosphorus | 4mg caffeine

Chocolate Glaze

1½ CUPS

½ cup (4 ounces) heavy cream

2 tablespoons (1½ ounces) corn syrup, light or dark

Pinch of salt

1 heaping cup (6 ounces) semisweet or bittersweet chocolate, chopped into ¼-inch pieces; or chocolate chips

Place the ingredients in a small saucepan and warm over low heat, or put the ingredients in a microwave-safe bowl and microwave at low power. Heat, stirring often, until the chocolate has melted and the mixture is smooth. Cool, stirring occasionally, for 10 to 15 minutes, so that the glaze thickens slightly but is still pourable.

nutrition information per serving   **2 tablespoons, 33g**

147 cal | 10g fat | 2g protein | 1g complex carbohydrates | 12g sugar | 21mg cholesterol | 47mg sodium | 79mg potassium | 51RE vitamin A | 50mg calcium | 60mg phosphorus

Caramel Frosting

3 CUPS, ENOUGH TO FROST AN 8- OR 9-INCH LAYER CAKE, 9 X 13-INCH CAKE, OR 24 CUPCAKES

This is an easy frosting to put together. When matched with chocolate cake and some crushed peanuts, you can create your favorite candy-bar flavored creation.

8 tablespoons (1 stick, 4 ounces) butter

¼ teaspoon salt

1 cup (8 ounces) packed brown sugar

¼ cup (2 ounces) milk

1 teaspoon vanilla extract

4 cups (1 pound) confectioners' sugar

Melt the butter in a heavy 2-quart saucepan. Stir in the salt and brown sugar and heat the mixture to boiling, stirring constantly. Cook over low heat for 2 minutes, until the sugar is totally dissolved. Stir in the milk and return to a boil. Remove the pan from the heat and cool to lukewarm. Stir in the vanilla, then gradually stir in the powdered sugar. Adjust consistency with a little more milk, if necessary.

nutrition information per serving   **3 tablespoons, 45g**

170 cal | 5g fat | 31g sugar | 14mg cholesterol | 39mg sodium | 55mg potassium | 52RE vitamin A | 20mg calcium | 11mg phosphorus

Peanut Butter Frosting

3 CUPS FROSTING, ENOUGH TO FROST AN 8- OR 9-INCH LAYER CAKE, 9 X 13-INCH CAKE, OR 24 CUPCAKES

Who can resist peanut butter frosting with chocolate cake, or banana cake, or any cake?

¾ cup (7 ounces) creamy peanut butter

1½ teaspoons vanilla extract

4 cups (1 pound) confectioners' sugar

½ cup to 10 tablespoons (4 to 5 ounces) milk

In a large mixing bowl, combine the peanut butter and vanilla. Add the confectioners' sugar in three parts, alternating with the milk, stirring until you have a smooth, spreadable frosting.

nutrition information per serving 3 tablespoons, 42g

160 cal | 6g fat | 3g protein | 1g complex carbohydrates | 23g sugar | 1g dietary fiber | 60mg sodium | 90mg potassium | 4RE vitamin A | 10mg calcium | 46mg phosphorus

Cream Cheese Frosting

3 CUPS, ENOUGH TO FROST AN 8- OR 9-INCH LAYER CAKE, 9 X 13-INCH CAKE, OR 24 CUPCAKES

This frosting is rich but not overly sweet, and spreads beautifully. It's the perfect complement for carrot cake (p. 340), of course, but also very nice on Apple Cake (p. 339).

6 tablespoons (¾ stick, 3 ounces) butter, at room temperature

1 package (8 ounces) cream cheese, softened

1 teaspoon vanilla extract

4 cups (1 pound) confectioners' sugar

1 cup (4 ounces) chopped nuts (optional)

½ cup (3¼ ounces) minced crystallized ginger (optional)

2 to 4 tablespoons (1 to 2 ounces) milk, to make frosting spreadable

Combine the butter, cream cheese, and vanilla in a medium-sized bowl and beat them together until they're light and fluffy. Add the sugar gradually, beating well. Stir in the nuts and/or ginger, then beat in the milk a little at a time, until the frosting is spreadable.

nutrition information per serving 2 tablespoons, 40g

169 cal | 9g fat | 1g protein | 1g complex carbohydrates | 20g sugar | 18mg cholesterol | 32mg sodium | 37mg potassium | 49RE vitamin A | 1mg vitamin C | 9mg calcium | 24mg phosphorus

German Chocolate Frosting

5 TO 6 CUPS, ENOUGH TO FILL AND FROST TWO 8- OR 9-INCH LAYER CAKES, A 9 X 13-INCH SHEET CAKE, OR 24 CUPCAKES

German chocolate cake, that wonderful combination of chocolate, caramel, and coconut, gets most of its pizazz from this frosting.

1 cup (8 ounces) heavy cream or evaporated milk

2 cups (20 ounces) caramel, or 1½ (14-ounce) bags individual caramel candies, unwrapped

2½ cups (10 ounces) chopped toasted pecans

2½ cups (7½ ounces) sweetened shredded coconut

Heat the cream in a medium-sized saucepan over medium heat until it simmers; add the caramel and stir until it melts. Bring the mixture to a boil and remove it from the heat. Stir in the pecans and coconut.

nutrition information per serving ¼ cup, 60g

275 cal | 8g fat | 3g protein | 7g complex carbohydrates | 21g sugar | 2g dietary fiber | 17mg cholesterol | 95mg sodium | 150mg potassium | 50RE vitamin A | 1mg vitamin C | 1mg iron | 49mg calcium | 85mg phosphorus

Pastry Cream

5 CUPS

This is the delicious custard filling you'll find in éclairs, napoleons, or Boston Cream Pie.

3 cups (24 ounces) whole milk

½ cup (3½ ounces) sugar*

¼ teaspoon salt

2 teaspoons vanilla extract, or ⅓ vanilla bean, split lengthwise

¼ cup (1¼ ounces) cornstarch

1 tablespoon (¼ ounce) unbleached all-purpose flour

4 large egg yolks

4 tablespoons (½ stick, 2 ounces) butter

1 cup (8 ounces) heavy cream, whipped to soft peaks

In a medium-sized saucepan, stir together 2½ cups of the milk, the sugar, salt, and the vanilla bean. (If you're using vanilla extract, add it at the end.) Bring the mixture to a boil over medium heat.

Meanwhile, whisk the cornstarch, flour, and egg yolks with the remaining ½ cup milk.

Whisk some of the boiling milk mixture with the egg yolks, then pour back into the hot milk mixture and return to the heat. Bring to a boil, stirring constantly, and boil for 30 seconds. Remove from the heat, strain through a fine sieve, and stir in the butter and vanilla extract (if you're using it). Rub a piece of butter over the surface of the cream, top with a piece of plastic wrap, then refrigerate until cool.

To complete, fold the cooled cream into the whipped cream.

*This amount of sugar makes a pastry cream that is just barely sweet, perfect for profiteroles, as a base for the following flavor combinations, or for pastries that include a sweet sauce. If you're planning to use the pastry cream for a pie filling, you'll want it to be a bit sweeter; increase the sugar to ¾ cup.

nutrition information per serving   about 6 tablespoons, 94g

173 cal | 12g fat | 3g protein | 6g complex carbohydrates | 8g sugar | 106mg cholesterol | 81mg sodium | 107mg potassium | 132RE vitamin A | 1mg vitamin C | 88mg calcium | 93mg phosphorus

Flavoring Options Pastry cream can be flavored in an infinite variety of ways. Here are some of our favorites:

BUTTERSCOTCH: Add ¼ teaspoon butter-rum flavor and/or 1 cup (6 ounces) butterscotch chips to the pastry cream while it is still hot, stirring until the chips have melted.

CARAMEL: Add ¾ cup (7½ ounces) chopped caramel (21 to 23 individual caramels, unwrapped) to the hot pastry cream, stirring until melted and the mixture is smooth.

CHOCOLATE: Add 1 cup (6 ounces) chopped chocolate to the hot pastry cream, stirring until melted and the mixture is smooth.

HAZELNUT: Omit the butter and increase the sugar to ¾ cup (5¼ ounces). Add ¾ cup (8¼ ounces) praline paste to the hot pastry cream, stirring until well combined.

ORANGE: Increase the sugar to ¾ cup (5¼ ounces). Add 1 teaspoon orange extract, ¼ teaspoon orange oil, or 3 tablespoons orange zest to the hot pastry cream.

PEANUT BUTTER: Add ¾ cup (7¼ ounces) peanut butter to the hot pastry cream, stirring until melted and the mixture is smooth.

PISTACHIO: Omit the butter and increase the sugar to ¾ cup (5¼ ounces). Add ¾ cup pistachio paste (8¼ ounces) or blanched, puréed pistachio meats.

Cherry Filling

ABOUT 3 CUPS

This is the filling of choice for traditional Black Forest Cake, which features a combination of cherries and chocolate.

¼ cup (1¾ ounces) sugar

2 tablespoons (½ ounce) cornstarch

¼ cup (2 ounces) water

¼ cup (2 ounces) cherry brandy, white wine, or water

3 to 4 cups (10 to 14 ounces) pitted fresh or frozen cherries (about 2 pounds unpitted)

1 cup (6 ounces) dried sour cherries

Mix all the ingredients together in a medium-sized saucepan, bring to a boil over medium-high heat, and cook until thickened, adding additional sugar to taste.

nutrition information per serving about ¼ cup, 65g

97 cal | 1g protein | 18g complex carbohydrates | 4g sugar | 2g dietary fiber | 2mg sodium | 184mg potassium | 9RE vitamin A | 3mg vitamin C | 12mg calcium | 20mg phosphorus

Lemon Curd

1½ CUPS

This smooth, tangy custard is perfect when layered with fruit and cake in a trifle, or as a filling for a tart or cake.

4 large egg yolks

½ cup (4 ounces) juice and zest of 3 to 4 lemons*

⅛ teaspoon salt

1½ cups (10¾ ounces) sugar

6 tablespoons (¾ stick, 3 ounces) butter

Stir all the ingredients together in the top of a double boiler set over medium heat. Whisk or stir constantly, being sure that nothing is sticking to the bottom. Continue to cook for 15 to 20 minutes, until the mixture starts to thicken; it should coat a spoon. The curd will thicken more as it cools. Remove it from the heat and spoon into a small bowl. Rub a piece of butter over the top, then place plastic wrap on the surface to prevent a skin from forming. Refrigerate until ready to use. The curd will keep, refrigerated, for five days.

*Zest the lemons first, then heat them in a microwave for 15 to 18 seconds; this will allow them to yield more juice.

nutrition information per serving 2 tablespoons, 57g

203 cal | 5g fat | 1g protein | 1g complex carbohydrates | 29g sugar | 107mg cholesterol | 26mg sodium | 24mg potassium | 108RE vitamin A | 6mg vitamin C | 13mg calcium | 37mg phosphorus

Variations LIME CURD: Substitute fresh lime juice for the lemon juice. Since limes are generally more tart than lemons, add an additional ¼ cup sugar and an additional 2 tablespoons butter to smooth the flavor.

RASPBERRY-LEMON CURD: Reduce the sugar to 1 cup and substitute ½ cup raspberry-lemon juice for the lemon juice: mash 1 heaping cup (5 ounces) raspberries with 2 tablespoons (1 ounce) fresh lemon juice, then push through a fine sieve.

Lemon Curd Whipped Cream

4½ CUPS

This is a sinfully rich combination of whipped cream and lemon curd, its sweetness tempered by the refreshing taste of citrus.

1½ cups (12 ounces) heavy cream

1½ cups (19 ounces) lemon curd, home-made (see preceding recipe) or bottled

Whip the cream just until thick—it shouldn't even hold a peak. Add the lemon curd and whip until the mixture holds a soft peak.

nutrition information per serving   6 tablespoons, 59g

221 cal | 13g fat | 1g protein | 1g complex carbohydrates | 24g sugar | 110mg cholesterol | 31mg sodium | 32mg potassium | 153RE vitamin A | 5mg vitamin C | 20mg calcium | 40mg phosphorus

Marshmallow Filling

ABOUT 2 CUPS

¼ cup (1⅝ ounces) vegetable shortening
¼ cup (½ stick, 2 ounces) butter
Pinch of salt (extra-fine, if you have it)
1 teaspoon vanilla extract

1 cup (4 ounces) confectioners' sugar
¼ cup (2¾ ounces) corn syrup
¾ cup (4½ ounces) marshmallow creme (optional, for extra-fluffy filling)

Beat together the shortening, butter, salt, vanilla extract, and confectioners' sugar until fluffy. Beat in the corn syrup, a bit at a time, until well blended. Beat in the marshmallow creme, just until blended.

Pies, Tarts, and Quiches

Ah! On Thanksgiving Day, when from East and from West

From North and from South come pilgrim and guest,

When the gray-haired New Englander sees round his board

The old broken links of affection restored,

When the care-wearied man seeks his mother once more,

And the worn matron smiles where the girl smiled before,

What moistens the lip and what brightens the eye?

What calls back the past, like the rich pumpkin pie?

—John Greenleaf Whittier, "The Pumpkin," 1844

Pie, defined as a sweet or savory filling encased in a pastry crust, has been a part of the world's culinary landscape for centuries. The first written formula for pie was published in Roman times (it was a goat cheese and honey pie in a rye crust, for the record). By the fourteenth century, pie was well known in Europe. It had a tough pastry crust used primarily as a baking container for savory, meat-based fillings. Pies remained strictly savory until the eighteenth century, when America's Pennsylvania Dutch became the first to enclose sweetened fruit fillings in a crisp crust. Since then, pie has remained a steady companion of America's home bakers.

Making pie pastry is an acquired skill, and we believe it's one well worth learning. You can't just stir the ingredients together willy-nilly and expect to get great results. The proportions of flour to fat to liquid have to be just right, and the technique for rolling it must be correct. What's more, the baking time and temperature, as well as the pan you use, combine to produce a crisp, golden crust.

A Pie Primer

Recipes for basic piecrust call for flour, fat, salt, and water; some add eggs, sugar, flavoring, vinegar, lemon juice, or buttermilk. The basic ratio (according to our grandmothers and the Culinary Institute of America) is 3:2:1—3 parts flour, 2 parts fat, and 1 part water. That ratio makes a very rich, tender crust.

Looking at the ingredients, and how they react in crust, will help you decide which ingredients and method to use for the type of crust you prefer.

Flour

The best piecrust is made with a flour whose protein level is medium to low, 11 percent or lower. For pie-making purposes, the protein level equals the amount of gluten, and in piecrust, the more gluten, the tougher the piecrust. (You do need some gluten, in order for the crust to hold together.) Our favorite flour for piecrust is a mixture of equal parts unbleached all-purpose and pastry flours. A crust made with only pastry flour will be very delicate and quite challenging to roll out, tending to crumble when you transfer it to the pie pan. A crust made with only all-purpose flour has to be handled very gently, so as not to develop the gluten. We recommend using equal parts of each for dough that's tender but still easy to handle.

Salt

Salt plays two roles in piecrust. First, and most important, it adds flavor. Like bread made without salt, piecrust made without salt will be flat-tasting. Second, it toughens the gluten in the crust ever so slightly, making the dough easier to handle.

Because the salt-to-flour ratio in piecrust must be fairly exact (for best flavor), we stick with table salt, rather than kosher or other granulations that won't measure the same.

Sugar

Sugar may be added to piecrust dough for flavor and browning. The amount is usually about 1 tablespoon for 3 cups of flour. Some sources recommend never using sugar in piecrust dough, as it's hygroscopic (water-attracting) and will cause the crust to become soggy. Other sources recommend adding sugar, as it attracts the water that would otherwise go toward developing gluten, resulting in a more tender crust. We've made two piecrusts, side by side, and used 1 tablespoon of sugar in one and none in the other. Truthfully, there was very little difference in browning, tenderness, crispness, or flavor. In our opinion, the amount of sugar used in most piecrust recipes is so small that it doesn't have a significant impact on texture, so use it if you like.

Buttermilk, Vinegar, or Lemon Juice

These liquids are often added to piecrusts because acids break down protein in the flour, so they'll help keep the crust tender, even if it's overworked a bit. In addition, adding dried buttermilk powder to a crust enhances its flavor.

Eggs or Egg Yolks

Whole eggs add protein, water, and fat to piecrust dough, along with color and flavor. Adding a lightly beaten egg should enhance browning and texture. Adding just the yolk adds mostly fat, which will enhance tenderness and color.

Fat

In our opinion, fat has the biggest influence on a piecrust. The role of fat is to coat the flour—thereby inhibiting the gluten development. Where we want gluten development in making bread, we *don't* want it in making a piecrust. Gluten binds the molecules into long strings. Here, we want the molecules kept separated. That's what makes for a flaky consistency. The fat melts as the crust bakes. But the flour will have formed layers or flakes before that fat disappears. Those spaces where the fat was are what separates those flakes.

Lard yields the flakiest crust because of its large crystals and its consistency. It's somewhat soft even when cold and is therefore easier to work with. Lard stays in larger flakes and melts at a slightly higher temperature than butter—keeping the layers of flour and water separate for a longer time than butter or shortening. This allows what little water is in the dough to turn to steam and separate the layers, which is where flakiness comes from. Lard does develop an off-flavor fairly quickly, so try to buy it fresh and use it soon.

Vegetable shortening is similar to lard in that its consistency stays the same over a wide temperature range. This makes it easy to work with. It also makes a flaky crust, as long as the dough isn't overworked. Vegetable shortening is bland-flavored and stable, and can remain on your shelf for quite some time without going rancid. The downside of vegetable shortening is its lack of flavor, and the fact that it's full of trans-fatty acids, a current nutritional no-no.

Butter is a more brittle fat than lard or vegetable shortening. It's harder when cold and becomes softer when warmed to room temperature, so everything must be kept cool when working with butter. If the butter is overworked and warm, too much will melt into the flour, resulting in a sandy-textured crust. Butter is also only about 81 percent fat, so you may need to use more butter and less water if substituting butter for lard or vegetable shortening in a recipe. Butter has the most pleasing flavor and contributes to the color and browning of the crust.

Chill the Dough

Why does every pastry recipe tell you to chill the dough, find a cool surface on which to roll it, use a rolling pin that's been placed in the freezer?

Because fat doesn't like heat; it melts and loses one of its main attributes, a just-right melting point in the oven. When you combine fat, flour, and a little water, the gluten in the flour is activated and strands start to form. If you don't handle the dough too much, the gluten will form only weak, short strands— flakes—perfect for pastry. Minute chunks of butter separate these strands, preventing them from joining together. Once put into a hot oven, these strands quickly cook and retain their shape—with the fat holding them in place just until they're sturdy enough, at which time the fat melts, lending its flavor and tenderness to the dough. The result? Flaky pastry.

By the way, it never hurts to place your rolled-out crust, in the pan, into the freezer while you're preparing the filling. Any fat that's beginning to get too warm and soft will firm right up again.

Salted vs. Unsalted Butter

All our pie recipes, as well as the other recipes in this book, assume the baker will use unsalted butter. Because salt can mask "off" flavors in butter, grocers like to fill their dairy case with salted butter, as it will seem fresh longer. If you buy unsalted butter, you'll have a better chance of getting a fresher product. In addition, we prefer to balance the salt/flour ratio in piecrust ourselves, rather than have to deal with the additional salt (¼ teaspoon salt per 4 ounces butter) in salted butter.

We prefer, for reasons of taste, texture, and health, to make piecrust with half butter and half vegetable shortening or lard. However, each to his own (diet); a crust made with 100 percent vegetable shortening (or butter, or lard), is perfectly acceptable.

Water

Water binds the piecrust dough, activating its gluten so it holds together. In order to keep the fat as cold and solid as possible (for the best flaky crust), we recommend using ice water (water in which you've floated a couple of ice cubes). Water is another element that needs to be precisely balanced in piecrust dough: too much, and you have a sticky, unrollable mess; too little, and the crust won't hold together or will crack around the edges as you roll it. Time is the great teacher here; the more frequently you make crust, the better you'll be at recognizing exactly what it should look like before rolling.

There are a number of different types of crust within reach of the home baker. The three major types of basic piecrust—medium-flake, long-flake, and short-flake—all contain the same ingredients. The way the shortening and flour are combined gives each crust its name and its characteristics. When you break a medium-flake piecrust with your fingers, it separates into flakes rather than breaking "clean." A long-flake crust breaks into larger flakes. A crust that breaks clean is called a short-flake crust or "short crust;" it's crisp rather than flaky. A French crust made this way is called pâte brisée; when it's sweetened, it becomes pâte sablée. We'll examine the most popular of all, medium-flake crust, and will then go on to show variations for short-flake and long-flake crusts.

Basic Piecrust

ONE 9-INCH DOUBLE PIECRUST

2½ cups (10½ ounces) unbleached all-purpose flour, pastry flour, or a combination of both

1 teaspoon salt

1 cup cold shortening (6½ ounces), or lard (8 ounces), or butter (2 sticks, 8 ounces)*

¼ to ½ cup (2 to 4 ounces) ice water

Medium-Flake Method

MIX DRY INGREDIENTS. Whisk together the flour and salt in a bowl large enough that you'll be able to plunge both hands in to work with the dough.

CUT IN HALF OF THE FAT, COMBINING THOROUGHLY. The mixture should form very small, very even crumbs. If using a single type of fat, cut half the fat into the flour. If using our recommended combination of shortening and butter, cut all the shortening into the flour and reserve the butter.

"Cutting the fat into the flour" simply means combining them. The degree to which you combine them defines the final texture of the crust. Barely combining will yield a flaky crust, thoroughly combining, a crisp, nonflaky crust. This can be done by plunging your hands into the bowl and working the pieces of fat with the flour. Or you can use a pastry fork or pastry blender. Combining flour with half the fat thoroughly, then combining with the remaining fat and leaving large chunks (pea-sized, or even larger) will yield a medium-flake crust.

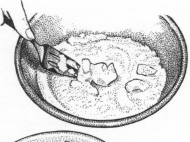

Use a fork or pastry cutter to cut the fat into the flour and salt.

CUT IN REMAINING FAT. Cut or pinch the remaining fat into small bits. If using butter, cut the stick into 4 lengthwise slices one way, flip it on its side, cut 4 slices the other way, then cut across the strips into ¼ inch pats (see p. 417). Toss the tiny bits of fat (butter or shortening) into the flour mixture, mixing just enough to coat them with flour.

ADD WATER. Add the water, a tablespoon at a time, and toss with a fork to moisten the dough evenly. To test for the right amount of liquid, use your hands to squeeze a

*We like a combination of ½ (3¼ ounces) cup of shortening (for the texture it lends), and 1 stick (4 ounces) of butter (for its flavor).

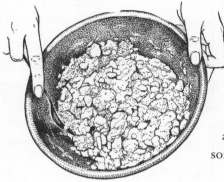

Add water gradually, stirring with a fork. The dough will look shaggy at first.

chunk of it together. If it sticks together easily, it's moist enough. If it falls apart, add a bit more water. When you're sprinkling water on the flour and fat mixture and tossing it around, keep grabbing small handfuls; when the dough barely sticks together, add 1 more tablespoon of water. This should be just the right amount to yield a dough that's soft enough to roll nicely, but not so soft that it sticks to the counter and rolling pin.

TURN OUT DOUGH AND REFRIGER-ATE. Turn out the dough onto a lightly floured surface. Divide the ball of dough in half, pat into flat disks about an inch thick, wrap both halves in plastic wrap, and refrigerate for at least 30 minutes. This lets the flour's gluten relax before rolling it out, meaning it will roll more easily and not "fight back" when you're trying to make a circle with it.

ROLL OUT THE DOUGH. Flour your work surface—counter, tabletop, pastry board, or marble slab. Unwrap one piece of dough and put it on the floured surface. Whatever size pie you're making, you'll want to roll the crust to a diameter that's about 3 to 4 inches greater than the inside diameter of the pan, for example, for a 9-inch pie pan, roll the crust to a 12 to 13-inch diameter. When rolling piecrust, be forceful but make it brief; the best piecrust is rolled from the center outward (to make an evenly round crust), with as few strokes as possible being used to stretch the crust to its necessary size. Don't roll back and forth over the dough endlessly. Roll in one

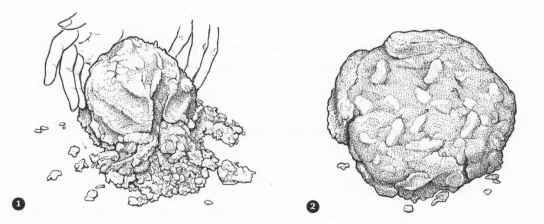

1. When the dough is moistened properly, it can be gathered together. Squeeze gently without overworking the dough. **2.** Chilling allows the gluten in the flour to relax, making the crust more tender. The chunks of butter flecked throughout the dough will help to make a flakier crust.

direction only (so as not to "confuse" the developing gluten). Don't whack the dough with the rolling pin, but be assertive enough to flatten it quickly. A crust that's fussed over too long develops a toughness that is none too appealing.

Use a spatula (a giant spatula is a big help) to lift the crust from the well-floured work surface every few strokes, adding more flour to the work surface if the crust starts to stick. If the bottom crust cracks around the edges, it can be patched and will be hidden by the filling. If it's the top crust, just roll it large enough so the cracks extend to the edge, where they will disappear when you seal the top and bottom crusts.

Some recipes diverge from the typical 9-inch pan to ones that are slightly larger or smaller. If you're making an 8-inch pie, assume you'll have some dough left over; cut it in squares or other shapes, sprinkle it with cinnamon-sugar, and bake it along with the pie (watching carefully, as it'll only need a few minutes to brown). If you're making a 10-inch pie, this amount of dough will be scanty, but sufficient. Roll thinly, and be aware you may need to do some patching here and there when you're pressing your crust into the dish, in order to make total use of the crust you have.

TRANSFER DOUGH TO PIE PAN. Next, transfer the rolled-out crust to a pie pan. It's important to use a pie pan that conducts heat well. We prefer a dark metal pan, followed (in preference) by a ceramic or clear glass pan. We don't recommend light-colored metal pans as they don't produce as brown a crust as darker metal. The pan will also affect the baking time considerably. A dark metal pan will bake in the shortest time, followed by glass or ceramic. Shiny metal pans will take the longest (see Tools section, p. 590) Hint: If using a thin, shiny, disposable pie pan, place the pie pan in a cast iron skillet, a good heat conductor, to be sure the pie is nicely browned on the bottom.

Using a spatula (or, if the crust isn't too thin and/or delicate, your fingers), fold the dough in half, then in half again the other way, so you've got a piece of dough that's just a quarter of what it was originally and should be much easier to handle. Pick up the dough, center the square center corner in the center of the pie pan, and unfold it (see illustrations on next page). Or carefully and gently roll the crust onto your well-floured rolling pin. Unroll it into your pie pan. Or use a giant spatula or small baker's peel to lift the crust and slide it into the pan.

COAT CRUST AND ADD FILLING. Brush the inside of the crust with lightly beaten egg white or milk. This very thin coating of protein will form a protective layer between crust and filling, helping to keep the crust from becoming soggy. Add the pie filling (or proceed to "Baking" on p. 413 if baking an empty crust).

ROLL OUT AND ADD TOP CRUST (IF MAKING A TWO-CRUST PIE). Roll out the top crust, just as you did the bottom crust, making it about an inch less in diameter (If you've added so much filling that it's heaped high in the pie shell, roll the top crust to the same size as the bottom crust). Center the top crust over the filling.

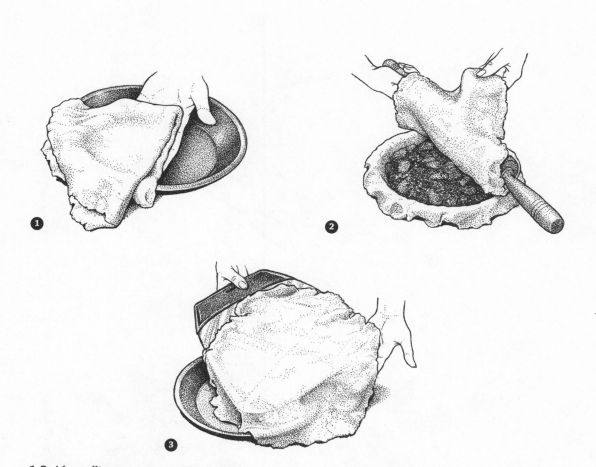

1-3. After rolling out, you can fold the bottom crust into quarters, roll the dough around a rolling pin or use a giant spatula to put it into your pie pan.

Wet the edges to be sealed with a bit of milk or beaten egg white. The protein in either, when cooked, will bond with the starch in the flour and act as "glue" between the two crusts.

Making sure your crust is well-sealed is key to avoiding the problem of having hot, bubbling fruit juice erupt from it. There are a number of decorative ways to seal a crust. If the filling is heaped high in the pan, a tall, finger-fluted seal is preferable to a thin, fork-tine seal; the taller seal gives the dough a better chance of containing the juices from the filling. For illustrations of the finger-flute, fork-tine, and other ways to shape the edge of a crust, see page 412.

The steam that tries to force those juices out has to go somewhere, so it's a good precaution to make a few slits in the top crust of a pie. Using a "pie bird" (a ceramic or stainless steel "chimney," often shaped like a bird), set in the center of your pie, is an additional help, though you'll still need to cut a couple of additional slits. Once you've made sure there's a place for steam to escape, do your best to seal any other openings.

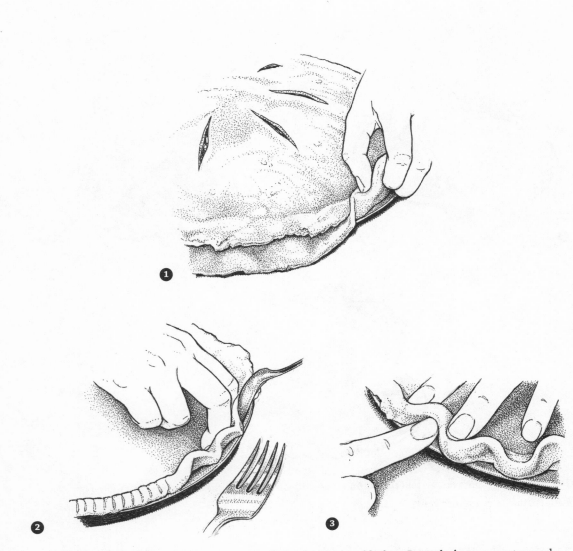

1. Roll the top crust slightly smaller than the bottom, and trim any odd edges. Bring the bottom crust up and over to seal, and pinch the two crusts together when fluting the edges. Be sure to cut vents in the top crust to allow steam to escape. **2–3.** To finish the edge of your pie, fold it under to make it even with the rim of the pan. Then press it flat with the tines of a fork, press the edge against the back of a spoon, or flute it with your fingers.

ADD GLAZE (OPTIONAL). You can bake a pie as is, but in most instances a wash or glaze makes it more attractive. Plain milk or cream will make a browner, slightly shiny crust. An egg white or yolk or both, beaten with a bit of water will intensify the color and create a gloss; the egg white wash will be clear, and the whole egg or egg yolk wash will be bronze. In either case, a sprinkle of coarse sugar will add sparkle.

A pastry brush does a fairly good job of "painting" on a wash, but if you can get hold of one, a goose feather brush does the best job. It spreads the wash evenly, doesn't exert any pressure on the dough, and can be easily rinsed out and used many times.

BAKING. Preheat the oven for the pie recipe you are baking. Bake the filled crust on the oven's bottom rack, or even on the oven floor if you have a gas oven. This gives the bottom of the crust an extra dose of high heat. Some bakers swear by putting their pie plate into a cast iron pan (not preheated), then putting pan and plate into the oven together.

If the edges of the crust start to become too brown before the filling is done, a piecrust shield (see below) is the easiest solution. Another solution is to tent just the edges of the crust with a thin strip of aluminum foil. It's smart to shape the foil before you put the crust in the oven, keeping it on the counter in case you need it. Trying to apply aluminum foil to a blistering hot, half-baked crust is a challenge.

When the pie is done, remove it from the oven and put it on a rack to cool.

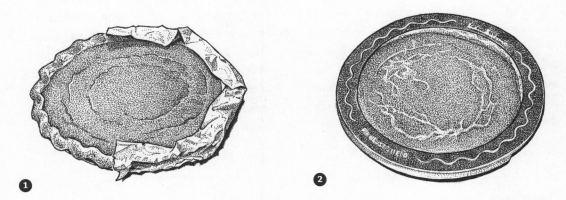

1–2. Cover the edges of the pie's crust with aluminum foil or a piecrust shield halfway through baking, to keep it from burning.

Blind Baking

Sometimes a recipe calls for you to blind-bake a piecrust—that is, bake it without filling. Some pie recipes call for fresh, uncooked fruit, and it's impossible to keep fruit uncooked if it bakes with the crust. And some recipes call for a delicate custard filling, or other egg-based filling, that could become curdled or made rubbery by the long baking needed to bake a filled pie. In addition, a crust that's blind-baked partway, then filled and finished, has a much better chance of remaining flaky and crisp.

To blind-bake a piecrust, roll it out and place it in the pan. Next, "dock" it with a pastry docker or fork—prick it all over to avoid trapping steam underneath. Then, weigh it down; otherwise steam released below the crust into the pan will cause it to expand like a blown-up balloon. In the past, bakers weighed down their piecrust with dry beans or uncooked rice; if you use this method, it's best to first line the crust with parchment paper, to make the beans or rice easier to remove. You may also choose to use pie weights, which are simply ceramic or aluminum balls, about the size of very large peas; again, lining your crust with parchment makes for easier transfer of the weights. The pie chain—choose a long, 10-foot version—is made of a series of connected stainless-steel balls; you simply coil it onto the crust. The advantage of a pie chain is its ease of removal (but watch your fingers—it gets hot!). Finally, you may use our favorite method, a set of nesting pie pans: a solid bottom one in which to put the crust, and a perforated one that nests atop that crust as it bakes, holding it down but allowing it to brown. Prior to baking, refrigerate the crust for 20 minutes; this will prevent it from shrinking in the pan, as the fat (which is providing much of the crust's structure) will have a chance to solidify.

For a fully baked crust, bake it in a preheated 375°F oven for 20 minutes with the weights; then remove the weights and bake for an additional 15 minutes or until golden brown. For a partially baked crust—one that will finish baking with its filling—bake for 15 minutes with the weights, then remove the weights, fill, and bake as directed in the recipe.

1–2. To help a blind-baked pie shell hold its shape, line it with parchment paper and weigh it down with dried beans, rice, or pie weights. Or use a pie chain, or a nesting perforated pan. After the crust is set, remove the parchment and weight to allow the center to finish cooking.

Short-Flake Method

Whisk together the flour and salt. Using a pastry fork, pastry blender, or your fingers, cut or rub the fat you are using into the flour in one stage, until the mixture looks like bread crumbs. Add the water, a tablespoon at a time. Stir with a fork to moisten the dough evenly. The dough needs to be moist enough to hold together when you're rolling it out. To test for the right amount of moistness, use your hands to squeeze a chunk of it together. If it sticks together easily, it's moist enough. If it falls apart, add a bit more water. Turn it out onto a lightly floured surface. Divide the ball of dough in half, pat each half into a flat disk about an inch thick, wrap both halves, and refrigerate for at least 30 minutes before rolling out.

Long-Flake Method

For a tender, ultra-flaky crust, use the "long-flake" method. Whisk together all the dry ingredients, reserving a few tablespoons of the flour. Cut in half of the fat, working the mixture until it's crumbly. Note: When we make a long-flake crust, we like to use half vegetable shortening, half butter or lard. We mix the shortening into the flour until it's crumbly, then add the butter or lard as directed in the next paragraph.

Place the reserved flour on your work surface and coat the remaining fat (in a single piece) with the flour. Use a rolling pin or the heel of your hand to flatten the fat until it's about ½ inch thick. Break this flour-coated fat into 1-inch pieces and mix them into the dough just until they're evenly distributed; some of the pieces of flour-coated fat should break into smaller pieces.

Sprinkle the liquid over the dough while tossing with a fork. Stop mixing as soon as you can easily squeeze the dough into a ball. Visible pieces of fat should still appear in the dough. Flatten the dough into a disk and wrap it in plastic wrap or waxed paper. Refrigerate for at least 30 minutes. This resting period allows the flour to absorb the water, making the dough easier to roll out.

Flour your work surface and roll the dough into a 12 x 9-inch (approximately) rectangle. If it isn't holding together well, sprinkle it lightly with a couple of teaspoons of water. Fold the dough into thirds (like a letter), then fold it into thirds the opposite way to form a rough square. Wrap it well and refrigerate again, for 30 minutes.

If the dough is made with all lard and/or vegetable shortening, you'll be able to work with it directly from the refrigerator. A dough made with all butter will need to warm slightly (10 to 15 minutes) before rolling, as butter becomes brittle when it's refrigerated. Dough made with a combination of butter and shortening should rest for about 5 minutes at room temperature before rolling. Roll the dough to the size needed (about 13 inches for a 9-inch pie). Fill and bake as directed.

Freezing for Extended Shelf Life

Because freezing expands and contracts the water in a piecrust, which tends to break down its structure, those that freeze most successfully are made with a significant amount of fat, which remains more stable when frozen.

Pie shells can be frozen both unbaked and baked. If you freeze them unbaked, freeze them right in a pie plate. After they're solid, remove them, stack, and seal them in an airtight plastic bag.

Baked crusts can also be frozen the same way unbaked crusts are, in the pan and then removed to an airtight plastic bag. Frozen piecrusts are great to have on hand.

To freeze a whole fruit pie (don't try this with custard or cream pies—they'll become watery), prepare it up to the point of baking, but instead of putting it in the oven, wrap it well with plastic wrap. Then add a full wrapping of foil or a zippered plastic bag, just for insurance. Put the pie in the freezer, even if it's just overnight. When you're ready to bake it, don't defrost. Preheat the oven to 425°F, unwrap the pie, and pop it in the oven. Bake it at 425°F for 15 minutes, then lower the oven temperature to 350°F and bake for another 45 to 55 minutes, until the crust is brown and the filling is bubbly. Freezing the pie, even if only overnight (rather than refrigerating it) gives you much more latitude in your choice of when to bake and serve it.

Food Processor Piecrust

ONE 9-INCH DOUBLE PIECRUST

Piecrust is an ideal vehicle to take advantage of your food processor. Your machine, when using the pulse button, will very quickly cut in the fat or shortening with the flour. Because a food processor can heat up ingredients, it works best when you freeze the butter and/or shortening before putting them into the machine's bowl, and have an ice cube or two in the water that you'll be using. The consistency of your crust will depend on how thoroughly you mix the fat with the flour. The bigger the pieces of butter and shortening, the flakier your crust. Adding a little vinegar to the liquid in the recipe will help add to the crust's flakiness, too. It's okay if you see streaks of butter or shortening when you roll it out; they create flakiness when the crust is baking. If you process the mixture further until it looks like coarse cornmeal, you'll have a shorter flake and a smaller crumb when you cut into the crust.

8 tablespoons (1 stick, 4 ounces) unsalted butter

½ cup (3¼ ounces) vegetable shortening

3 cups (12¾ ounces) unbleached all-purpose flour or a combination of all-purpose and unbleached pastry flours

1 teaspoon salt

2 teaspoons vinegar

¼ to ½ cup (2 to 4 ounces) ice water

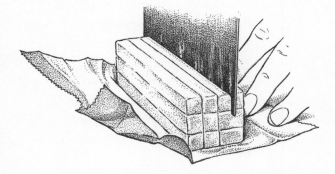

Use a bench knife to cut a stick of butter into lengthwise strips. Flip the stick of butter on its side and repeat the process, then cut across the strips to get pea-sized chunks.

Cut the stick of butter lengthwise into three slabs. Stack the slabs and cut again lengthwise twice to make nine pencil-sized strips.

With a bench scraper or knife, cut across the strips to make cubes of butter about ½ inch thick. Place the cubes in the freezer. Measure out the vegetable shortening and put it in the freezer too. Leave the fats to firm up for at least 20 minutes while you gather the other things you need for your pie.

Place flour and salt in the bowl of your food processor fitted with the chopping blade. Turn on the machine for 5 seconds to mix the dry ingredients. Add the chilled fats and pulse for two seconds at a time, four times. Sprinkle the vinegar and 4 tablespoons of water over the dough. Pulse once more for only a second.

Take the mixture out of the machine and transfer to a mixing bowl or your work surface. The dough will still look crumbly and the butter should still be visible in rounded chunks. When you gather the dough in your hands, you will find that it is almost moist enough to hold together. Sprinkle it with 1 more tablespoon of water if necessary, mixing the dough with a fork, until the dough can be gathered together into a ball. Don't work or knead the dough any more than is necessary, or it will become tough. Divide the dough into two pieces and form each of them into a disk. Wrap each disk in plastic wrap and refrigerate for at least 30 minutes before rolling out.

nutrition information per serving ⅛ of double crust recipe, 83g

368 cal | 24g fat | 5g protein | 32g complex carbohydrates | 1g dietary fiber | 83mg cholesterol | 268mg sodium | 59mg potassium | 13RE vitamin A | 2mg iron | 4mg calcium | 42mg phosphorus

Favorite Tender Crust

ONE 9-INCH SINGLE PIECRUST

The following crust, a hybrid between short-flake and medium-flake, combines the best attributes of both: short-flake's melt-in-the-mouth texture, and medium-flake's tender flakiness. Baking powder enhances the flakiness, vinegar makes it tender, and the buttermilk adds flavor.

Note that this is a single, rather than double crust, making it ideal for open-faced pies (pumpkin, pecan, custard), pies with a streusel or meringue topping, or quiches.

1½ cups (6¼ ounces) unbleached all-purpose flour or a combination of all-purpose and pastry flours

1 tablespoon (⅛ ounce) buttermilk powder (optional; it will help make the crust tender)

¼ teaspoon salt

¼ teaspoon baking powder

4 tablespoons (½ stick, 2 ounces) butter

¼ cup (1⅝ ounces) vegetable shortening

1 teaspoon white or cider vinegar

3 to 5 tablespoons (1½ to 2½ ounces) ice water

In a medium-sized mixing bowl, combine the flour, buttermilk powder, salt, and baking powder. Using a pastry fork, pastry blender, your fingers, or a mixer, cut in the butter and vegetable shortening, leaving some baby pea-sized lumps.

Mix the vinegar with 3 tablespoons of the water. Sprinkle this mixture over the flour and fat and toss with a fork. Squeeze the dough together; if it's not cohesive, add an additional 1 to 2 tablespoons water (just enough to make the dough stick together comfortably). Shape the dough into a flattened disk, wrap it in plastic wrap, and refrigerate it for 30 minutes or longer before rolling.

nutrition information per serving ⅛ **of single crust recipe, 44g**

187 cal | 12g fat | 2g protein | 16g complex carbohydrates | 1g dietary fiber | 16mg cholesterol | 88mg sodium | 29mg potassium | 57RE vitamin A | 1mg iron | 10mg calcium | 24mg phosphorus

Cookie Crumb Crusts

The easiest crusts of all to prepare are cookie crumb crusts, which are exactly what they sound like: crusts prepared from a mixture of crushed cookies, sugar, and butter. The crust is pressed into the pan rather than rolled out. Just about any crisp (as opposed to moist) cookie is a candidate for crushing and making into piecrust; we've given instructions for some of our favorites here.

Graham Cracker Crust

ONE 9-INCH SINGLE PIECRUST

You can substitute chocolate cookies, vanilla wafers, or gingersnaps here, or peruse the cookie aisle and come up with your own crumb crust. Just make sure the cookies are crisp, not moist or chewy. Try a gingersnap/vanilla wafer combo, or ginger/chocolate. These crumb crusts are the perfect foundation for creamy fillings: Key lime pie, chocolate cream pie, and cheesecakes all combine happily with cookie crumb crusts.

1¾ cups (about 5¼ ounces) graham cracker crumbs*

¼ cup (1 ounce) confectioners' sugar

6 tablespoons (¾ stick, 3 ounces) butter or margarine, melted

Use a straight-sided measuring cup to press the crumbs into palce and to smooth out the bottom and sides of your crust.

Preheat the oven to 375°F.

In a medium-sized mixing bowl, combine the crumbs, sugar, and butter. Press the mixture into the bottom and partway up the sides of a 9-inch spring-form pan, 9-inch cheesecake pan, or 9-inch deep-dish pie pan. If you're using a 9 x 1½-inch pan, you'll have ¼ to ½ cup extra crumbs. This can become a garnish for the pie, if you like.

To blind-bake the crust (cookie crumb crusts are nearly always blind-baked; no need to weigh it down), bake for 15 minutes, just until set and you smell the cookies toasting. Remove the crust from the oven, cool on a rack, and add the filling of your choice.

*One wrapped packet of graham crackers—11 whole crackers—will yield this amount of crumbs. The easiest way to obtain crumbs is to put the crackers in a plastic bag and roll them with a rolling pin until they're thoroughly and evenly crushed. Alternatively, pulse crackers in a food processor until they've become crumbs.

nutrition information per serving   ⅛ of crust, 36g

185 cal | 11g fat | 2g protein | 13g complex carbohydrates | 1g dietary fiber | 25mg cholesterol | 147mg sodium | 49mg potassium | 85RE vitamin A | 7mg calcium | 18mg phosphorus

Variations CHOCOLATE COOKIE CRUST: Replace the graham crackers with 2 cups of chocolate cookie crumbs—40 chocolate wafer cookies (one 9-ounce package) will crush down to 2 cups of crumbs.

VANILLA WAFER CRUST: Replace the graham crackers with 2 cups of vanilla wafer cookie crumbs. About 71 small cookies (8¾ ounces) will crush down to 2 cups of crumbs.

GINGERSNAP CRUST: Replace the graham crackers with 2 cups of crushed gingersnaps. About 43 gingersnaps (10¾ ounces) will crush down to 2 cups of crumbs.

Cheddar Cheese Piecrust

ONE 9-INCH DOUBLE PIECRUST

For those of us from New England who aren't totally comfortable unless there's some cheddar cheese near our apple pies, this crust gives us the chance to combine the two flavors in one neat package.

2½ cups (10½ ounces) unbleached all-purpose flour or a combination of all-purpose and unbleached pastry flours

1 teaspoon salt

½ cup (3¼ ounces) cold shortening or lard (4 ounces) or butter (1 stick, 4 ounces)

½ cup (2 ounces) grated cheddar cheese

4 to 7 tablespoons (2 to 3½ ounces) ice water

In a medium-sized bowl, combine the flour and salt.

Mix the fat into the salt-flour mixture as you would for any medium-flake piecrust. Add the cheese and toss to coat it with flour as well. Add the water, a tablespoon at a time, and stir with a fork to moisten the dough evenly. When the dough is moist enough to hold together, turn it out onto a lightly floured surface. Divide the ball of dough in half, pat each half into a flat disk about an inch thick, wrap both halves, and refrigerate for at least 30 minutes.

nutrition information per serving ⅛ **of double crust recipe, 71g**

263 cal | 14g fat | 6g protein | 26g complex carbohydrates | 7g dietary fiber | 1mg cholesterol | 332mg sodium | 52mg potassium | 21RE vitamin A | 2mg iron | 51mg calcium | 69mg phosphorus

Fruit Pie Fillings

Certainly the largest, most varied, and one of the oldest pie categories is the fruit pie. From apple to strawberry-rhubarb, fruit pies have been gracing America's tables for centuries—often à la mode, with a big scoop of ice cream on top.

There are many ways to prepare a fruit pie. The most common is to cut fruit into bite-sized pieces (coring and/or peeling it first, if necessary); mix it with sugar and a thickener (to thicken the juices exuded as it bakes); spoon it into a prepared piecrust; top with another crust, or with streusel; and bake until the crust is golden and the fruit bubbly. Another way, and one we particularly like for berries, is to prebake the crust, sweeten and cook half the berries, then mix the cooked berries with uncooked fresh berries, and spoon the resultant filling into the crust. Top with whipped cream and you've got a summertime treat folks will swoon over. A third type of fruit pie, one made less frequently, involves sweetening the fruit, then cooking it on top of the stove—with or without any thickener—until it is about three quarters of the way to the consistency you like. Spoon the cooked fruit into an unbaked crust, top with a second crust, and bake. Try this method if you consistently have problems with runny, watery fruit in your pies.

Thickeners for Pies

There's a whole range of ingredients that will help you thicken the delicious fruit juices in your pie, so you can slice your creation. Each of them behaves a little differently and has a different degree of holding power, or gel strength. The simplest way to distribute the thickener for a fruit pie evenly throughout the filling is to combine it with the sugar and spices used to flavor the pie.

All-purpose and *potato flours* have the lowest gel strength, and they will give an opaque, cloudy appearance to the fruit.

Cornstarch has the most holding power for its weight, but gives a cloudy, semitransparent look to the filling. Some people can detect its taste, as well.

Modified food starch (Instant ClearJel) has plenty of thickening power and will keep fillings thick through a greater range of temperatures. It will thicken a filling's liquid at room temperature, without cooking (this is why mixing it with sugar in advance is

very important); it will also keep a filling thick through freezing temperatures and back. It gives a hazy, semitranslucent look to liquids.

Pie Filling Enhancer is a combination of modified food starch, superfine sugar, and ascorbic acid; it will thicken fruit pie fillings the same way Instant ClearJel does. Its advantage is the added ascorbic acid (a flavor enhancer), and superfine sugar, which prevents the food starch from clumping.

Arrowroot, tapioca flour, and potato starch will give you a clear, translucent filling. Potato starch has the most holding power, followed by arrowroot, with tapioca flour third.

Quick-cooking tapioca holds better than tapioca flour by volume, but works best if combined with the filling and given time to soften and absorb its juices before baking. It will give a clear filling, but also a stippled texture. *(continued)*

Thickeners for Pies (continued)

FRUIT	THICKENER	HOW MUCH TO USE PER CUP OF FRUIT
APPLES *Need the least amount of thickener, since they are less watery. They are also high in pectin, which helps them set up as filling.*	All-purpose or potato flour	1½ teaspoons
	Arrowroot, ClearJel, or quick-cooking tapioca	½ teaspoon
	Corn or potato starch	¼ teaspoon
	Pie Filling Enhancer	1½ teaspoons
	Tapioca flour	1 teaspoon
BERRIES *Have a lot of liquid, and release even more if they've been frozen, so need more thickener. Blueberries have a lot of pectin, so will need a little less if cooked with lemon juice and sugar.*	All-purpose or potato flour	1½ tablespoons
	Arrowroot, ClearJel, or quick-cooking tapioca	2 teaspoons
	Corn or potato starch	2½ teaspoon
	Pie Filling Enhancer	2 tablespoons
	Quick-cooking tapioca	4 teaspoons
	Tapioca flour	1½ tablespoons
CHERRIES *Fresh cherries will need slightly less thickener than canned or frozen.*	All-purpose or potato flour	4 teaspoons
	Arrowroot, ClearJel, or quick-cooking tapioca	2½ teaspoons
	Corn or potato starch	2 teaspoons
	Pie Filling Enhancer	1 tablespoon
	Tapioca flour	1½ tablespoons
PEACHES, STONE FRUITS *Don't have quite as much pectin as apples, and also more liquid.*	All-purpose or potato flour	1½ tablespoons
	Arrowroot, ClearJel, or quick-cooking tapioca	1 tablespoon
	Corn or potato starch	2 teaspoons
	Pie Filling Enhancer	2½ teaspoons
	Tapioca flour	1½ tablespoons
STRAWBERRY-RHUBARB *Another juicy combination; needs as much thickener as berries do.*	All-purpose or potato flour	1½ tablespoons
	Arrowroot, ClearJel, or quick-cooking tapioca	1 tablespoon
	Corn or potato starch	2½ teaspoons
	Pie Filling Enhancer	2½ teaspoons
	Tapioca flour	1½ tablespoons

Basic Fruit Pie

ONE 8-, 9-, OR 10-INCH PIE

Once you've mastered piecrust, the filling for a fruit pie is quite simple. Fruit, sugar, thickener, a touch of spice, a splash of lemon juice, and some butter; that's all it takes. Fruit pies can be made from berries (blueberries, strawberries, raspberries, cranberries, or blackberries) or from cut-up fruits (apples, cherries, rhubarb, apricots, peaches, pears, or plums). We've also sampled grape pie, raisin pie, cantaloupe pie, and even zucchini pie and green tomato pie.

You can make a pie out of just about any fruit; the trick is finding the right combination of thickener and sugar to the amount of fruit used (see sidebar, p. 421, for helpful hints). It takes a bit of experience and experimentation, but we'll give you some guidelines that should help.

One 9-inch double piecrust

4 to 8 cups berries or cut-up fruit (most fruits and berries weigh between 4 and 5 ounces per cup; this means you will need between 1 and 2 pounds of fruit)

½ to 2 cups (3½ to 14 ounces) granulated sugar

1 tablespoon lemon juice

2 to 6 tablespoons (½ to 1½ ounces) cornstarch, potato starch, or quick-cooking tapioca, or 2 to 8 tablespoons unbleached all-purpose flour

¼ to 1½ teaspoons spices or extracts

Milk, or 1 egg white beaten with 1 tablespoon water, for glaze

2 tablespoons (1 ounce) cold butter

First, decide how much fruit you want to use. Four cups of fruit will make a fairly flat pie; 8 cups will make a high-rise pie. Then again, 4 cups of fruit in an 8-inch pie shell looks a lot different than 4 cups of fruit in a 10-inch shell; just play it by eye. Remember, also, that very juicy fruits—strawberries, raspberries, peaches—will cook down quite a bit; the filling that was heaped up when you put the pie in the oven will have settled dramatically by the time the pie is baked. Less-juicy fruits, such as apples, pears, and blueberries, will sink much less. For this reason, we recommend using a greater amount of juicy fruits and a lesser amount of "dryer" fruits (unless you want a mile-high pie, in which case use the greater amount).

After you've decided how much fruit to use, taste it and see how much sugar it will need. Very tart berries, such as early blueberries or blackberries, require more sugar; sweet ripe apples need less. If you're making a regular-sized pie (not mile-high), with what you think is very tart fruit, use about 1½ cups sugar; a regular-sized pie with sweet fruit takes only about ½ cup sugar. If you're making pie with cut-up, juicy fruit, such as strawberry or peach, combine the cut-up fruit and sugar and take a bite; your taste buds will tell you whether it's sweet enough. Pies made with 7 to 8 cups of fruit will take a bit more sugar, obviously.

Combine the fruit and sugar and stir in the lemon juice. The lemon juice acts as a flavor booster, accenting the taste of the fruit. Next comes the thickener. Again, you have a choice: flour, arrowroot, cornstarch or potato starch, potato flour, tapioca flour or quick-cooking tapioca, Instant ClearJel or Pie Filling Enhancer (see p. 421). Flour is an easy choice because you most likely have it on hand. And flour's a good choice for less-juicy fruits. But for juicy fruits and berries, we prefer one of the starches; their thickening power is greater than that of flour. Sprinkle thickener over fruit and combine well; if you're using tapioca, let it sit for 15 minutes for tapioca to soften. At the same time you add the thickener, add spices or an extract, ¼ teaspoon to 1½ teaspoons, to taste. Most fruits pair well with cinnamon and nutmeg; some, such as cherries, are good with almond extract (1 teaspoon). Or try vanilla extract for a different flavor.

Brush the inside of the piecrust with some milk, or 1 egg white beaten with 1 tablespoon water, to help keep it crisp. Spoon the fruit into the crust. Divide the cold butter into bits and spread them over the fruit filling. Cover with the top crust, sealing around the edges. Cut a few slashes or a round hole in the upper crust so steam can escape. Brush the crust with milk (for a brown crust), or an egg white mixed with 1 tablespoon water (for a brown, semi-glossy crust), and sprinkle with coarse or granulated sugar (if desired).

Place pie on a foil-covered baking sheet, to catch any spills, and bake on the bottom shelf of a preheated 425°F oven for 15 minutes. Lower heat to 350°F and continue to bake for 35 to 50 minutes, until crust is brown and fruit bubbling. Remove from oven, leaving on baking sheet; when fruit has stopped bubbling, remove pie pan from baking sheet and place on a wire rack to cool completely.

Here's an important tip: If you've baked a fruit pie and are dying to cut into it, hold your horses. You need to wait 45 minutes or so, until the pie is just barely warm. If you cut it before then, the still-liquid filling will ooze into the cut you've made, draining away from the rest of the pie and making a soupy mess.

Top Crust Tips

Just as your pie's bottom crust may be short- or long-flake, chocolate or ginger, sweet or savory, the top crust may also change its character to match the filling (or your own special taste). The simplest and most common top crust for a double-crust pie is simply a replication of the bottom crust; make a double batch of pastry and divide it in half—making one half (the bottom) just slightly larger than the other (the top). The top crust is rolled out, laid atop the filling, and sealed to the bottom crust.

Before you put the pie in the oven, cut several slits through it to allow steam to escape. This can be done as artfully as you want. Another way to be artful with your top crust is to use some of the pastry scraps to decorate it. Cut them into leaves, flowers, or something that's symbolic of what's in the pie, or the occasion the pie is for. Stick these on with a bit of water or egg beaten with a bit of water. If you paint them with a bit of the egg wash or a little milk or cream, they'll brown nicely and be more visible.

If you're making a one-crust pie, one that has only a bottom crust, make a tall fluted edge for cream or custard pies where the liquid comes right up to the rim of the pan. Clearly, it's easier to move this type of pie from counter to oven rack if there's a nice, tall dam containing the filling. By the way, if you really have trouble moving custard pies (pumpkin, etc.) into the oven, try this: place the pie pan and empty crust on the pulled-out rack of the preheated oven, fill it, gently slide the oven rack into the oven, and shut the door.

A single-crust fruit pie is often topped with streusel (which can add "crumb," "streusel," or "Dutch" to the pie's name). The same streusel that tops fruit crisps or crumbles—with oats, or without—is appropriate for fruit pies. See pages 129, 130, and 131 for a some of our favorite recipes.

Finally, the top crust of a fruit pie can be woven or cut into a lattice, an old-fashioned attractive treatment, particularly for pies with bright filling, like cherry or raspberry.

❶

❷

1–2. Cut strips of dough and weave together on a giant spatula or piece of parchment. Use the spatula or parchment to transfer the lattice to the top of the pie

The Very Freshest Fruit Pie

ONE 9-INCH PIE, 8 SERVINGS

Here's a very simple formula for fresh fruit pie that you'll find yourself making again and again. We first learned this method in East Machias, Maine, where this type of fresh blueberry pie appears each August at various restaurants and potluck suppers.

One 9-inch single piecrust, blind-baked (see p. 414)

4 cups (or a bit more) fresh whole berries (16 to 20 ounces), or other fruit, cut into pieces*

⅔ to 1½ cups (4¾ to 10½ ounces) sugar, to taste

¼ cup (1 ounce) cornstarch

1 cup (8 ounces) water

1 tablespoon lemon juice

2 tablespoons (1 ounce) butter

In a food processor or by hand, coarsely chop 1½ cups of the fruit. Put the sugar (starting with the lesser amount), cornstarch, and water in a saucepan and mix until smooth. Add the 1½ cups coarsely chopped fruit and cook over medium heat, stirring occasionally, until mixture is thick and semitransparent, 7 to 10 minutes. Stir in lemon juice.

Add the butter and remaining 2½ cups fruit. Stir well and taste; add more sugar, if necessary, until it tastes good to you. Pour into baked pie shell and chill until firm. Serve with whipped cream, lightly sweetened and flavored with vanilla, if desired.

*Berries can be left whole, unless unusually large, like strawberries; other fruit should be cut into small (½-inch) dice.

nutrition information per serving   using blueberries as the fruit, ⅛ of pie, 167g

290 cal | 7g fat | 2g protein | 32g complex carbohydrates | 24g sugar | 5g dietary fiber | 217mg sodium | 136mg potassium | 12RE vitamin A | 13mg vitamin C | 2mg iron | 17mg calcium | 32mg phosphorus

The Best Apple Pie

ONE PIE, ABOUT 10 SERVINGS

We've made many apple pies over the years, and this is our favorite—so far. One thing we consistently endorse is using more than one kind of apple in the filling.

One 9-inch double piecrust

3¼ pounds (about 9 whole apples) Cortland, Granny Smith, or other baking apples, peeled, cored, and sliced (7 to 8 cups)

¼ cup (2 ounces) apple cider

1 tablespoon rum (optional)

Juice of ½ lemon (about 2 tablespoons)

2 teaspoons vanilla extract

¾ cup (5¼ ounces) sugar

¼ cup (1 ounce) cornstarch

½ teaspoon salt

1½ teaspoons apple pie spice*

Preheat the oven to 425°F.

In a large bowl, stir together the apples, cider, rum, lemon juice, and vanilla. Whisk together the dry ingredients, mixing until well combined. Stir the dry ingredients into the apples to coat them evenly.

Roll one piece of piecrust into a 13-inch round and lay it gently in a 9-inch pie plate. Spoon in the filling. Roll out the other piece, lay it atop the filling, and seal and crimp the edges. Brush the top crust with milk and sprinkle it with coarse sugar, if desired. Or save a bit of the crust and cut decorative leaf designs, laying them in the center of the crust or around the edges. Cut a few slashes in the crust, or a round hole in the center, to vent steam.

Bake the pie for 15 minutes. Reduce the heat to 375°F, and bake for an additional 45 to 55 minutes, until the top is brown and filling is bubbly.

*If you don't have apple pie spice, use 1 teaspoon cinnamon and ¼ teaspoon each nutmeg and allspice.

nutrition information per serving   1 slice, 135g

232 cal | 10g fat | 3g protein | 32g complex carbohydrates | 1g sugar | 2g dietary fiber | 13mg cholesterol | 188mg sodium | 130mg potassium | 48RE vitamin A | 5mg vitamin C | 1mg iron | 9mg calcium | 29mg phosphorus

Variation   FRENCH APPLE PIE: To make a streusel-topped version of this pie, use 1½ cups of the streusel recipe on page 130 in place of a top pastry crust.

Favorite Apple Pie

ONE 9-INCH PIE, 8 SERVINGS

This apple pie isn't one that will make you sit up and take notice. Instead, it will invite you to snuggle into your favorite chair, heave a comfortable sigh, and enjoy bite after bite of this perfectly simple treat. The spices in the filling are understated, rather than overwhelming, and allow the flavor of vanilla to shine through. Meanwhile, the creamy vanilla-scented filling mirrors the scoop of vanilla ice cream you will probably pile on top.

One 9-inch double piecrust

2 tablespoons (⅝ ounce) unbleached all-purpose flour

¾ to 1 cup (5¼ to 7 ounces) sugar, to taste, depending on the tartness of the apples

¼ teaspoon nutmeg or ground cardamom

½ teaspoon cinnamon

¼ teaspoon salt

4 to 5 cups (1½ to 2 pounds) cored, peeled, and diced apples (Granny Smith and/or Cortland are our favorites)

1 tablespoon vanilla extract

⅔ cup (5⅜ ounces) half-and-half, light cream, or heavy cream, your choice

2 teaspoons sugar mixed with ⅛ teaspoon cinnamon, for topping

Remove the piecrust dough from the refrigerator. If it has been chilling longer than 30 minutes, let it rest for 10 to 15 minutes, until it's pliable. Roll one piece out to about 13 inches in diameter and carefully transfer it to a 9-inch pie pan (a giant spatula works well here). Using a pair of scissors, trim it to a 1-inch overhang and fold the edges under. Use the trimmed-off pieces to patch any of the rest of the crust, if necessary.

Preheat the oven to 450°F.

In a large bowl, whisk together the flour, sugar, spices, and salt. Add the apples (cut into ½-inch dice) and toss to combine thoroughly. Add the vanilla and cream and stir well. Spoon the filling into the crust. Roll the second crust to a diameter of 10 to 11 inches, lay it on top of the filling and crimp to seal. Brush the top crust with milk, then sprinkle with cinnamon sugar.

Place the pie on a foil-lined baking sheet, to catch any spills. Bake the pie for 15 minutes, then reduce the heat to 350°F and bake for an additional 40 to 50 minutes, until the top is medium-brown and the juices are clear and bubbly. If the crust appears to be browning too quickly, cover it with a piecrust shield or strips of aluminum foil.

NOTE   If you're using a light or shiny pie pan rather than a dark one, be sure to bake the pie for at least 50 minutes at 350°F to ensure that the bottom crust is done.

nutrition information per serving   1 slice, 158g

359 cal | 15g fat | 4g protein | 32g complex carbohydrates | 22g sugar | 2g dietary fiber | 23mg cholesterol | 275mg sodium | 134mg potassium | 78RE vitamin A | 3mg vitamin C | 2mg iron | 24mg calcium | 51mg phosphorus

Mr. Washington's Cherry Pie

ONE 9-INCH PIE, 8 SLICES

In honor of George, of course. The sour cherries are important—not just any canned cherry will do. When you see them at the grocery store, stock up.

One 9-inch double piecrust

5 to 6 cups (three 14½-ounce cans) sour cherries, packed in water*

¾ cup (5¼ ounces) sugar

¾ teaspoon cinnamon

¼ cup (1½ ounces) quick-cooking tapioca

1 teaspoon almond extract

½ teaspoon salt

2 tablespoons (1 ounce) butter (optional)

Line a 9-inch pie pan with one half of the rolled out pie dough. Drain the cans of cherries, reserving ⅔ cup of the water from one of them. Place the cherries and reserved liquid in a large mixing bowl. Combine the sugar, cinnamon, and tapioca. Stir into the cherries until evenly combined. Stir in the almond extract and salt. Let the filling sit for 20 minutes before filling the pie shell.

Preheat the oven to 425°F.

Spoon the filling into the pastry-lined pan and dot with butter. Roll out the second crust and place on top of the filling. Cut a design (two cherries? a hatchet?) into the top to vent steam, and seal the top and bottom crust together, fluting with your fingers or a fork.

Place the pie on a foil-lined baking sheet and bake for 15 minutes. Reduce the heat to 350°F and bake for an additional 35 to 50 minutes, until the crust is golden brown and the fruit is bubbling. Take out of the oven and cool on a rack before slicing, so the filling can set up.

*Frozen tart cherries, thawed and drained, are a great option if you can find them.

nutrition information per serving   **1 slice, 236g**

438 cal | 9g fat | 5g protein | 40g complex carbohydrates | 16g sugar | 2g dietary fiber | 29mg cholesterol | 367 mg sodium | 191mg potassium | 212RE vitamin A | 3mg vitamin C | 4mg iron | 20mg calcium | 48mg phosphorus

Blushing Peach Pie

ONE 9-INCH PIE, 8 TO 10 SERVINGS

Ever since Escoffier paired peaches and raspberries in honor of Nellie Melba, the flavor combination has been bringing down the house.

One 9-inch double piecrust

6 cups peeled, sliced peaches (12 to 14 peaches, 4 to 5 pounds), or 2 one-pound bags of individually quick frozen peach slices, thawed

½ cup (4 ounces) raspberry syrup*

¼ cup (1¼ ounces) tapioca flour or cornstarch

1 teaspoon lemon juice

¾ to 1 cup (5¼ to 7 ounces) sugar, to taste

¼ teaspoon salt

¼ teaspoon nutmeg

2 tablespoons coarse sugar

Preheat the oven to 425°F.

In a large bowl, combine the peaches, raspberry syrup, tapioca flour, lemon juice, sugar, salt, and nutmeg. Roll out half the pastry to a 13-inch circle and fit it into a 9-inch pie pan. Spoon the filling into the shell. Top with the other piece of rolled-out crust (make a lattice top, p. 425 if desired) and sprinkle with sugar. If not using a lattice top, cut several vents in the top crust and bake the pie for 15 minutes. Reduce the oven heat to 350°F and bake for an additional 35 to 50 minutes, until the crust is golden and the juices are bubbling. Remove the pie from the oven and cool it on a wire rack.

*Use prepared raspberry syrup, or make your own by simmering 1 cup raspberries, fresh or frozen, with ¾ cup of sugar until the sugar is dissolved. Strain off the syrup.

nutrition information per serving | ⅛ of pie, 204g

368 cal | 13g fat | 4g protein | 38g complex carbohydrates | 23g sugar | 4g dietary fiber | 16mg cholesterol | 268mg sodium
272mg potassium | 116RE vitamin A | 11mg vitamin C | 2mg iron | 11mg calcium | 43mg phosphorus

Bumbleberry Pie

ONE 9-INCH PIE, 8 SERVINGS

There you are, in high summer, the raspberries are at the end of their season and the blackberries are charging in. Blueberries are around also, and you have some of each but not enough of any to make a pie. That is the time for bumbleberry pie. These fruits are so used to starring roles on their own, we don't realize how delicious they can be in combination.

    In the New England tradition of "use what you have," you can take this recipe and substitute cranberries for one of the berries. If it's midwinter and you need a taste of warmer times, most stores now carry quick-frozen berries. These work just fine and are easy to measure out when frozen. We recommend you thaw them (and drain, if necessary) before proceeding with the recipe.

One 9-inch double piecrust
2 tablespoons (1 ounce) orange juice
1 teaspoon orange zest
2 cups (10 ounces) blueberries
2 cups (10 ounces) raspberries

2 cups (10 ounces) blackberries
1 cup (7 ounces) sugar
¼ cup (1 ounce) cornstarch or quick-cooking tapioca

Place all the ingredients except the dough in 2½-quart saucepan and simmer until filling is thickened. Cool to lukewarm.

Preheat the oven to 425°F.

Roll out half the pastry to a 13-inch circle and fit it into a 9-inch pie pan. Spoon the filling into the shell. Top with the other piece of rolled-out crust, and sprinkle with sugar. Cut several vents in the top. Bake for 15 minutes, then lower the heat to 350°F and bake for another 35 to 50 minutes, until the top is evenly golden brown.

nutrition information per serving   **1 slice, 243g**

447 cal | 13g fat | 5g protein | 53g complex carbohydrates | 24g sugar | 7g dietary fiber | 1mg cholesterol | 433mg sodium | 222mg potassium | 18RE vitamin A | 15mg vitamin C | 3mg iron | 29mg calcium | 64mg phosphorus

Variation   BLUEBERRY PIE: Use all blueberries (6 cups) in above recipe. Substitute lemon zest for the orange zest and add 2 tablespoons lemon juice and ½ teaspoon allspice or cinnamon to the filling.

Pineapple Chiffon Pie

ONE 9-INCH PIE, 8 SERVINGS

Chiffon pies were very popular during the fifties, coming in as many flavors as chiffon cakes (which were often filled with the same filling as chiffon pie). Just about any boxed pudding, gelatin, or custard could be prepared and then made into chiffon filling simply by folding in beaten egg whites or whipped cream. Cooks back then weren't averse to using convenience foods as ingredients; just look at all the recipes calling for a can of condensed soup. It's in this vein that we made the following chiffon filling without egg yolks (which might curdle), and using convenient powdered egg whites for the meringue.

This filling is also very good if you substitute 1 cup heavy cream, whipped, for the meringue. Just be sure to add the full cup of sugar to the custard mixture.

One 9-inch single piecrust, blind-baked
2 teaspoons gelatin (1 packet)
1¼ cups (10 ounces) pineapple juice
1 cup (7 ounces) sugar
3 tablespoons (¾ ounce) cornstarch

¼ teaspoon salt
⅔ cup (5 ounces) crushed pineapple, drained
¼ cup (1 ounce) powdered egg whites
½ cup (4 ounces) cool water

Soak the gelatin in ¼ cup (2 ounces), of the pineapple juice.

Mix ½ cup of the sugar, the cornstarch, and the salt together in a small saucepan. Add the remaining pineapple juice and bring the mixture to a boil over medium heat, stirring constantly. Remove the pan from the heat and stir in the gelatin and crushed pineapple. Set aside to cool, stirring occasionally to prevent a skin from forming.

In a large mixing bowl, beat the egg whites with the water until they're foamy. Add the remaining ½ cup sugar gradually and continue beating until stiff peaks form and the sugar is dissolved. Fold the egg white mixture into the pineapple mixture. Pour the filling into the prebaked pie shell. Refrigerate for at least 1½ hours before serving.

nutrition information per serving   **1 slice, 127g**

252 cal | 6g fat | 4g protein | 22g complex carbohydrates | 24g sugar | 8mg cholesterol | 191mg sodium | 111mg potassium | 28RE vitamin A | 6mg vitamin C | 1mg iron | 9mg calcium | 20mg phosphorus

Variations   PIÑA COLADA PIE: Add 1 teaspoon lime juice to the egg white before beating, and add ¾ cup (2¼ ounces) toasted shredded coconut to the filling before spooning it into the pie shell. Sprinkle the top with additional shredded coconut.

STRAWBERRY OR BLUEBERRY CHIFFON PIE: Substitute sliced strawberries or whole blueberries for pineapple, and use orange juice or lemonade instead of pineapple juice.

Cream or Custard Pies

Cream and custard pies encompass everything from butterscotch to pumpkin. Custard pies are prepared by pouring an uncooked milk, egg, and sugar filling into an unbaked crust, then baking. Cream pies are usually made by spooning a flavored, fully prepared pastry cream into a fully baked crust (though they're sometimes baked, like custard pies). Both are commonly topped with whipped cream or a baked meringue topping.

Fruit Cream Pie

ONE 9-INCH PIE, 8 SERVINGS

Here's an easy variation on fruit pie. Using low-fat or skim buttermilk will give you a lower-fat pie, while whole milk or cream will result in a richer pie. This type of fruit pie really doesn't need any extra embellishment, such as whipped cream or ice cream; nevertheless, we invite you to gild the lily in any way you see fit.

One 9-inch single piecrust

1½ cups (12 ounces) buttermilk, or any type of milk (low-fat, whole, or cream)

3 large eggs

3 tablespoons (¾ ounce) unbleached all-purpose flour

½ to 1 cup (3½ to 7 ounces) sugar, depending on tartness of fruit

¼ teaspoon spice of your choice (cinnamon, nutmeg, ginger, mace, or a mixture), optional

3 cups berries (15 ounces) left whole unless unusually large, or other fruit, sliced or cut into small (½-inch) dice

Roll out the piecrust and fit into a 9-inch pie pan. Trim edges and crimp or flute decoratively. Preheat the oven to 425°F.

In a mixing bowl, beat together the buttermilk and eggs. Beat in the flour, sugar, and spice. Pour the fruit into the crust. Top with the milk mixture. Bake the pie on the bottom rack of the oven for 15 minutes, then reduce heat to 350°F and bake an additional 35 to 50 minutes, until the crust is golden and the filling is set 2 inches from the edge. If the center looks wobbly, it's okay; it will finish cooking through as it sits. Remove the pie from the oven and cool completely on a wire rack. Refrigerate until ready to serve.

nutrition information per serving | **1 slice, ⅛ of pie made with buttermilk and raspberries, 159g**

254 cal | 9g fat | 6g protein | 20g complex carbohydrates | 20g sugar | 4g dietary fiber | 90mg cholesterol | 239mg sodium | 186mg potassium | 74RE vitamin A | 12mg vitamin C | 1mg iron | 74mg calcium | 96mg phosphorus

Custard Pie

ONE 9-INCH PIE, ABOUT 8 SERVINGS

Sweet, smooth, and oh-so-creamy, custard pie is just the ticket when you're tired of fruit or other more assertively flavored pies. To make a custard pie that doesn't have a soggy bottom crust, blind-bake the crust for about 15 minutes in a 425°F oven (be sure to weigh it down to keep it from puffing; see illustrations, p. 414), remove it from the oven, and brush it with beaten egg yolk. Return it to the oven and bake for 5 more minutes, to set the egg yolk. While the crust is baking, make the custard. Pour the hot custard into the hot pie shell and bake following the directions below. For best results, allow custard pie to cool and set for several hours before serving.

One 9-inch single piecrust, blind-baked as directed above*

1 egg yolk, beaten (to brush on crust)

1½ cups (12 ounces) milk

1 cup (8 ounces) cream (heavy, light, or half-and-half)

⅓ vanilla bean, split**

¼ teaspoon salt

4 large eggs

⅔ cup (4¾ ounces) sugar

¼ teaspoon nutmeg (freshly grated is best)

Preheat the oven to 425°F.

Scald the milk and cream with the piece of vanilla bean and the salt. Remove the vanilla bean. In a medium-sized mixing bowl, whisk together the eggs and sugar, then pour a quarter of the hot milk over the egg mixture and stir well. Pour the egg mixture into the remaining hot milk and stir well. Pour the custard into the hot, partially baked crust, and sprinkle it with the nutmeg. Use a crust shield or strips of aluminum foil to protect the edges of the crust from overbrowning.

Bake the pie for 10 minutes. Turn off the oven, and without opening the door, bake it for another 5 minutes. The mixture should look set around the edges but will still be wobbly in the middle. If it's not set at the edges, bake it for 5 minutes more. If you have an instant-read thermometer, remove the pie from the oven when it reaches 165°F in the center. If the mixture goes above 180°F, the custard will become watery. Cool the pie for several hours before serving.

*Bake the crust for about 15 minutes in a 425°F oven (be sure to weigh it down to keep it from puffing), remove it from the oven, and brush it with beaten egg yolk. Return it to the oven and bake it for 5 more minutes, to set the egg yolk.

**We like the sprinkle of brown flecks you get from using a vanilla bean. However, 2 teaspoons vanilla extract may be substituted for the bean. If using a bean, after scalding it, rinse it in cool water, dry it overnight, and cover it with sugar to make a lightly scented vanilla sugar.

nutrition information per serving   ⅛ of pie, 116g

274 cal | 11g fat | 7g protein | 13g complex carbohydrates | 16g added sugar | 187mg cholesterol | 226mg sodium | 120mg potassium | 224RE vitamin A | 1mg iron | 72mg calcium | 116mg phosphorus

Variation   COCONUT CUSTARD PIE: Follow the directions for custard pie, but add 1 cup sweetened shredded coconut and ¼ teaspoon coconut flavor to the custard before pouring it into the pie shell.

Caramel Custard Pie

ONE 9-INCH PIE, 8 GENEROUS SERVINGS

This dark version of classic custard pie is wonderful with a cup of strong coffee; the caramel and coffee flavors marry well, and the coffee cuts the caramel's sweetness.

One 9-inch single piecrust, partially blind-baked*

1 egg yolk, beaten (to brush on crust)

¼ cup (1¾ ounces) sugar

4 large eggs

1¾ cups (14 ounces) milk or cream

¼ teaspoon salt

1 teaspoon vanilla extract

¾ cup (4½ ounces) butterscotch chips or caramel chips

Preheat the oven to 350°F.

Mix the sugar and eggs together in a bowl until well-combined. In a small saucepan or microwave, heat the milk with the salt, vanilla, and chips. Stir until the chips have melted. Pour a little of the cream mixture into the eggs and stir well. Add the remaining cream mixture and stir to combine.

Pour the filling into the pie shell. Bake the pie for 20 minutes, until the center looks set but still wobbles and the custard's temperature reads 165°F on an instant-read thermometer. Remove the pie from the oven; don't worry, the filling will thicken as it cools. When cool, garnish with dollops of whipped cream.

nutrition information per serving   1 slice, without whipped cream, 123g

266 cal | 15g fat | 7g protein | 14g complex carbohydrates | 11g sugar | 122 mg cholesterol | 240mg sodium | 163mg potassium | 93RE vitamin A | 1mg vitamin C | 1mg iron | 77mg calcium | 120mg phosphorus

Dark Chocolate Cream Pie

ONE 9-INCH PIE, 8 GENEROUS SERVINGS

This is not your usual pallid, insipid chocolate cream pie. This is a pie with the bite and character of dark chocolate. A little goes a long way.

One 9-inch single piecrust, blind-baked*
4 large egg yolks
¾ cup (5¼ ounces) sugar
3 tablespoons cornstarch
½ teaspoon salt
2 cups (16 ounces) milk
3½ ounces (3½ squares, a generous ¾ cup

chopped) unsweetened baking chocolate
2 tablespoons (1 ounce) butter
1 teaspoon vanilla extract

TOPPING
1 cup (8 ounces) heavy or whipping cream
Chocolate shavings, jimmies, or mini chips, for garnish

In a deep mixing bowl, beat the egg yolks until light. Gradually add ¼ cup of the sugar and continue beating until the sugar has dissolved and the yolks are pale yellow.

In a saucepan, stir together the remaining ½ cup sugar and cornstarch, then whisk in the salt and milk. Once the cornstarch has dissolved, cook the mixture over medium heat, stirring constantly, until it starts to thicken. Pour about a quarter of the hot mixture into the yolks and whisk to combine. Return the milk mixture to the heat and stir in the egg mixture, cooking for 1 or 2 minutes, until it all comes to a boil. Continue cooking for 30 seconds.

Remove from the heat and stir in the chocolate, butter, and vanilla. When the chocolate has melted, pour the filling into the baked pie shell. Cover the filling with a piece of plastic wrap and refrigerate the pie for 2 hours or more. Top the chilled pie with whipped cream and chocolate curls before serving.

*The pie pan should be at least 1½ inches deep in order to hold all the filling. If, after forming the crust and pouring in the filling, you find yourself with leftover filling, simply pour it into a custard dish and refrigerate it until firm. It makes a yummy, rich pudding.

nutrition information per serving   1 slice of pie without topping, 146g

370 cal | 24g fat | 7g protein | 19g complex carbohydrates | 18g sugar | 2g dietary fiber | 102mg cholesterol | 374mg sodium | 233mg potassium | 104RE vitamin A | 1mg vitamin C | 2mg iron | 97mg calcium | 157mg phosphorus | 25mg caffeine

Variations MILK CHOCOLATE CREAM PIE: For those of you who favor dark chocolate's milder sibling, here's a pie you'll fall in love with. Follow the directions for Dark Chocolate Cream Pie, incorporating the following changes: Use only ½ cup sugar when preparing the custard. Replace the 3½ ounces baking chocolate with 6 to 8 ounces (about 1½ cups, chopped) milk chocolate and 1 ounce unsweetened chocolate. Omit the butter.

CHOCOLATE–PEANUT BUTTER PIE: Swirl 1 cup peanut butter chips into the custard just before pouring it into the pie shell.

Banana Cream Pie

ONE 9-INCH PIE, 8 SERVINGS

There's room for some creativity around this classic. Many banana cream pies are made with graham cracker crusts, while other versions of this diner staple use a pastry crust. A chocolate cookie crust with some jimmies on top is a nice variation, too.

One 9-inch single piecrust, blind-baked, or your favorite cookie crust (see p. 418), blind-baked

PASTRY CREAM FILLING

½ cup (3½ ounces) sugar

2 tablespoons (½ ounce) unbleached all-purpose flour

1 tablespoon plus 1 teaspoon cornstarch

½ teaspoon salt

2 large eggs

2 cups (16 ounces) milk

6 tablespoons (¾ stick, 3 ounces) soft butter

½ teaspoon vanilla or almond extract

PIE FILLING

2 medium-sized bananas, sliced

PIE TOPPING

1 cup (8 ounces) heavy cream

1 teaspoon vanilla extract

¼ cup (1 ounce) confectioners' sugar

Chocolate shavings, chopped nuts, or jimmies, for garnish (optional)

TO MAKE THE PASTRY CREAM Whisk the sugar, flour, cornstarch, salt, and eggs together in a medium-sized heatproof bowl. In a medium-sized saucepan, bring the milk to a boil. Add the hot milk to the egg mixture gradually, whisking continually to make everything smooth. Pour the liquid back into the saucepan and return to the heat to bring back to a boil. Stir continually with your whisk—the mixture will thicken quickly and whisking will keep it from getting lumpy. As soon as you see the pastry cream boil in the center, remove it from the heat and stir in the butter and vanilla or almond extract.

ASSEMBLY Slice the bananas into the prebaked crust. After the pastry cream is made, pour it over the bananas, smooth out the surface, and cover it with plastic wrap. Chill thoroughly in the refrigerator.

Whip the heavy cream and vanilla together until the cream begins to thicken. Sprinkle in the confectioners' sugar and whip until the cream holds its shape. Spoon or pipe the whipped cream on top of the pie and garnish however you like.

nutrition information per serving **1 slice of pie, with graham cracker crust, and whipped cream, no garnish, 139g**

396 cal | 25g fat | 4g protein | 25g complex carbohydrates | 16g sugar | 1g dietary fiber | 92mg cholesterol | 264mg sodium | 238mg potassium | 245RE vitamin A | 3mg vitamin C | 1mg iron | 62mg calcium | 78mg phosphorus

Key Lime Pie

ONE 9-INCH PIE, 8 TO 10 SERVINGS

Key lime pie is one of the most popular desserts offered in restaurants today, and for good reason: the combination of tangy-sweet smooth filling in a crisp crust is a soothing symphony of flavors and textures.

One 9-inch single vanilla cookie crust (p. 419)

8 ounces cream cheese, softened

1 (14- to 15-ounce) can sweetened condensed milk

⅓ cup (2¾ ounces) Key lime juice, fresh or bottled*

⅛ teaspoon lime oil (optional, but good)

1 cup (8 ounces) sour cream

FOR THE CRUST Combine the ingredients in the bowl of your mixer or a food processor—a few pulses will do it—then press the mixture into a 9-inch pie pan (see illustration, p. 419). Bake the crust in a preheated 350°F oven for 20 to 22 minutes, until it's golden brown. Set it aside to cool while making the filling.

FOR THE FILLING In a medium-sized bowl, beat the cream cheese until soft. Add the condensed milk and beat until well-blended. Stir in the Key lime juice and the lime oil. Add the sour cream, mixing until smooth. Pour the filling into the cooled crust and refrigerate the pie for at least 2 hours before serving. Garnish it with whipped cream and lime slices.

*Use regular fresh lime juice if you can't find Key lime.

nutrition information per serving   ⅛ of pie, without whipped cream, 181g

600 cal | 35g fat | 11g protein | 25g complex carbohydrates | 38g sugar | 97mg cholesterol | 355mg sodium | 407mg potassium | 336RE vitamin A | 7mg vitamin C | 1mg iron | 263mg calcium | 253mg phosphorus

Meringue

Here's our favorite method for making a top-shelf meringue that's light, sweet, and holds up well, with no shrinking and little weeping.

Meringues consist of whipped egg whites and sugar. To make a meringue, you need a clean, non-plastic mixing bowl with no traces of fat in it. Any fat will coat the ends of the egg white's protein and that will cut the ability of the whites to hold air by more than half. It's helpful to have your egg whites at room temperature (this gives them lower surface tension, and makes it easier to incorporate air). Many recipes for beating egg whites call for salt and/or cream of tartar; these help to increase the holding power of the whites for both water and air.

To beat, you can either use a whisk and some elbow grease, or your electric mixer. The advantage to making meringue by hand (at least once) is that you become familiar with the stages that the whites go through. At first you have a puddle of clear liquid with some large bubbles in it. Then, as you continue beating, the liquid becomes white with many more smaller bubbles. Then the whisk begins to leave tracks in the bowl. To test the character of your whites, pull your whisk or beaters straight up out of the foam. If a point forms and then falls over immediately, you're looking at a soft peak. From here, 15 to 20 more strokes will bring you to a medium peak, and another 15 to 20 to stiff peaks.

It's extremely easy to overbeat meringue. When you start to see what look like grainy white clumps, you're beyond stiff peaks, and every stroke of the whisk or beater is tearing apart the network of air, water, and protein you've worked so hard to create. You'll also see a pool of clear liquid under the foam. The good news is that the foam you have on top of the liquid will essentially still work. The bad news is that you can't really fix what has happened, other than to start over with new egg whites.

How does sugar get involved? Sugar has two properties that affect egg whites. It, too, will coat the ends of the proteins in the whites; but if it's added too soon, it will take much longer to make a meringue stiff enough to be piped or shaped. If you're beating egg whites by hand, *don't* add the sugar until you've reached the medium-peak stage. If you're using a machine, start sprinkling sugar into the meringue after it gets to soft peaks. With a machine, the sugar will help give you a little extra leeway with beating time; you can go longer without overbeating the whites. For each egg white, use 2 tablespoons of sugar to make a soft meringue. Regular granulated sugar will work, but we advise the use of superfine because it will dissolve more quickly, making the meringue less grainy. For a stiffer meringue, use more sugar; up to 4 tablespoons per white.

Add ¾ teaspoon cornstarch per white when adding the sugar to help to keep it from "weeping" (exuding liquid) after baking, though if you're serving the pie in very hot, humid conditions, weeping is inevitable. Be sure to cover your filling all the way to the crust at the outer edges of the pie, to keep it from shrinking in the refrigerator after it's cooked. Three egg whites will give you plenty of meringue to cover a 9-inch pie. If you're after a mile-high version, use 4 whites.

For finishing a pie, if your topping is between 1½ and 2 inches high, bake in a preheated oven at 350°F for 20 to 25 minutes, until the meringue is golden brown. If you're going for big height, turn your oven down to 300°F and bake for 35 to 45 minutes, to allow the meringue to cook through in the center.

Lemon Meringue Pie

ONE 9-INCH PIE, 12 SERVINGS

What would a diner pie lineup be without lemon meringue? This pie is one of those perfect combinations where opposites play off each other—tart lemon collides with sweet meringue, while flaky crust meets smooth filling.

One 9-inch single piecrust, blind-baked

LEMON FILLING
6 tablespoons (1½ ounces) cornstarch
1⅓ cups (10¾ ounces) water
1½ cups (10½ ounces) sugar
3 large egg yolks, slightly beaten
3 tablespoons (1½ ounces) unsalted butter

¼ teaspoon lemon oil, 1 tablespoon grated lemon peel
½ cup (4 ounces) fresh lemon juice (2 large lemons)

MERINGUE
3 egg whites
¼ teaspoon cream of tartar
6 tablespoons (2¾ ounces) sugar

LEMON FILLING In a medium-sized saucepan, dissolve the cornstarch in the water. Add the sugar. Cook over medium heat, stirring, until the mixture thickens and comes to a boil. Boil, stirring, for 1 minute. Remove the pan from the heat and gradually add half of the hot mixture to the slightly beaten egg yolks. Blend the hot egg yolk mixture into the remaining filling in the pan and return the pan to the stove. Simmer the mixture, stirring, for 1 minute.

Remove the pan from the heat. Stir in the butter, lemon oil, and lemon juice. Spoon the filling into the baked shell.

Preheat the oven to 400°F.

MERINGUE In a large bowl, beat together the egg whites and cream of tartar until foamy. Gradually beat in the sugar, continuing to beat until the meringue is fairly stiff and glossy, but not foamy. (If you beat meringue too long, it will become foamy and fall apart. For more on meringue, see p. 439.)

Spread the meringue atop the hot pie filling, using a knife to spread it completely over the surface of the pie. Make sure it's touching the crust all around; this will help to keep it from shrinking. (As for weeping, that's up to the weather; meringue pies almost always weep in hot, humid weather. As do we all.)

Bake the pie for 8 to 10 minutes, or until the meringue is golden brown. Remove it from the oven, and cool completely before serving.

nutrition information per serving   1 slice, 109g

264 cal | 10g fat | 3g protein | 12g complex carbohydrates | 29g sugar | 84mg cholesterol | 69mg sodium | 46mg potassium | 83RE vitamin A | 6mg vitamin C | 1mg iron | 28mg calcium | 33mg phosphorus

Strawberry–Lemon Chess Pie

ONE 9-INCH PIE, 8 TO 10 SERVINGS

This old-fashioned combination of smooth, tart-sweet lemon filling and fresh strawberries topped with a flavorful glaze is just unbeatable.

One 9-inch single piecrust

LEMON FILLING

8 tablespoons (1 stick, 4 ounces) unsalted butter

½ cup (4 ounces) fresh lemon juice (2 large lemons)

¼ teaspoon salt

1½ cups (10½ ounces) sugar

1 tablespoon cornmeal

1 tablespoon cornstarch

4 large eggs, lightly beaten

STRAWBERRY GLAZE

One 1-pound bag (3 cups) frozen strawberries, thawed, plus 1 pint fresh berries, washed and stemmed

¾ to 1 cup (5¼ to 7 ounces) sugar

3 tablespoons (1 ounce) tapioca flour

2 teaspoons lemon juice

Pinch of salt

FILLING Melt the butter and stir in the lemon juice, salt, sugar, cornmeal, and cornstarch. Add the eggs and stir until mixture is well combined. Pour into the unbaked pie shell.

Bake the pie on the bottom rack of a preheated 375°F oven for 40 to 50 minutes, or until the center is set. The top should be golden brown. Remove the pie from the oven and allow it to cool for several hours before topping.

GLAZE In a medium-sized saucepan, mix the thawed frozen berries and their juice with the sugar, tapioca flour, lemon juice, and salt. Bring to a boil, stirring constantly. When the mixture is clear and thickened, remove it from the heat and set it aside to cool to lukewarm. Add the fresh berries and mound glaze atop the pie. Cool completely before serving.

nutrition information per serving   ⅛ of pie, 216g

514 cal | 22g fat | 5g protein | 21g complex carbohydrates | 56g sugar | 3g dietary fiber | 137mg cholesterol | 254mg sodium | 201mg potassium | 158RE vitamin A | 45mg vitamin C | 2mg iron | 33mg calcium | 81mg phosphorus

Classic Pumpkin Pie

ONE 9-INCH PIE, ABOUT 8 SERVINGS

Everyone has a favorite version of this Thanksgiving classic. This is ours.

One 9-inch single piecrust*

1 can (15 ounces) pumpkin** or squash, or 1½ cups cooked pumpkin purée

3 large eggs

¾ cup (5⅔ ounces) brown sugar (light or dark)

½ teaspoon salt

1½ teaspoons cinnamon

1 teaspoon ground ginger

¼ teaspoon ground cloves or allspice

¼ teaspoon nutmeg

1½ cups (12 ounces) light cream, or 1 can (12 ounces) evaporated milk

Preheat the oven to 425°F.

In a medium-sized mixing bowl, stir together the pumpkin and the eggs until evenly combined. Whisk in the remaining ingredients. Pour the filling into the unbaked pie shell, leaving about ¼-inch of clearance between the top of the filling and the top of the crust.

Bake for 15 minutes. Reduce the oven temperature to 350°F and bake for an additional 35 to 40 minutes, until the filling is set around the edges, but still soft in the middle. The pie will firm up as it cools. Remove the pie from the oven and cool it on a rack. If desired, decorate the edges with candied nuts (see following instructions) and serve with lightly sweetened whipped cream.

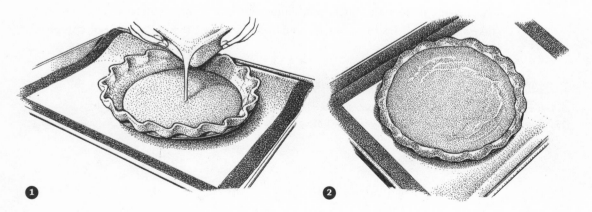

1. Line your baking sheet with a silicone mat, parchment paper, or aluminum foil to protect against spills. Pour or spoon filling into the unbaked shell. **2.** Custard-filled pies are done when the outside edges are set, but the inside is still wobbly.

*The pie pan you use should be at least 1½ inches deep in order to hold all of the filling. If, after forming the crust and pouring in the filling, you find yourself with leftover filling—simply pour it into a custard dish and bake it along with the pie.

**Be sure to use plain pumpkin or squash, not pumpkin pie filling.

nutrition information per serving ⅛ of plain pie, 163g

301 cal | 13g fat | 8g protein | 19g complex carbohydrates | 20g sugar | 2g dietary fiber | 94mg cholesterol | 355mg sodium | 363mg potassium | 1,233RE vitamin A | 3mg vitamin C | 2mg iron | 171mg calcium | 164mg phosphorus

Variation PUMPKIN PRALINE PIE: Combine ⅓ cup finely chopped, toasted pecans, ⅓ cup packed brown sugar, and 2 tablespoons soft butter. Mix until well-combined and sprinkle over the bottom of the unbaked 9-inch pie shell. Proceed with the pumpkin pie recipe above.

Candied Nuts

⅓ cup (2½ ounces) sugar

½ cup (1¾ ounces) nuts (walnuts, pecans, hazelnuts, etc.)*

½ teaspoon salt

Spread the sugar in an even layer in a small wide-bottomed pan, such as a crepe pan. Melt the sugar over low heat, stirring only if it begins to burn around the edges. When the sugar has turned to a golden syrup, add the nuts. Stir to coat all sides, sprinkle with salt, then remove the pan from the heat.

Place the nuts on a parchment-lined or lightly greased baking sheet and let them cool. Break them up if they're in large clumps. Place the nuts around the edge of the pumpkin pie after it has cooled for 1 hour. Store any additional candied nuts in an airtight container. If the day is very humid or the pie will be held for a day before serving, keep the nuts in an airtight container and place them on the pie just before serving.

*Whole pecan or walnut halves look very nice, but chopped nuts dropped in small clusters also work well.

nutrition information per serving ⅛ of candied nuts, 16g

83 cal | 5g fat | 1g protein | 1g complex carbohydrates | 8g sugar | 1g dietary fiber | 31mg potassium | 1RE vitamin A | 3mg calcium | 23mg phosphorus

Banoffee Pie

ONE 9-INCH PIE, 8 TO 10 SERVINGS

Banoffee pie is a whipped cream-topped banana/toffee pie that's been a longtime favorite in England. A specialty of The Hungry Monk restaurant in Levington, East Sussex (where it was "invented" as Banoffi Pie in 1972), the original recipe called for the toffee filling to be prepared by boiling two unopened cans of sweetened condensed milk for five hours. Now that prepared dulce de leche (a rich, sweet, thick caramelized milk that appears in everything from ice cream to cake fillings) is available, this pie is a cinch to make.

One 9-inch single piecrust, blind-baked

⅔ to 1⅓ cups (7 to 14 ounces) prepared dulce de leche*

3 medium bananas (about 1¼ pounds before peeling)

1 cup (8 ounces) heavy cream

2 tablespoons sugar (superfine preferred)

½ teaspoon espresso powder or instant coffee

Spread the dulce de leche over the bottom of the baked, cooled crust. The greater amount, which the original recipe calls for, will give you a very sweet dessert; the lesser amount (or something in between) may be more suitable to your taste. Just eyeball it while you're spooning in the dulce or caramel and quit when you think the layer is thick enough.

Peel the bananas and halve them lengthwise. Lay them atop the filling, starting in the center and working outward, cutting the bananas to fit as necessary. If you're really clever, you can pick the banana that's curved about the same as your pie plate to form the outermost layer.

Put the cream, sugar, and espresso powder in a large bowl and whip it until it's thick. Spoon it atop the bananas. Serve immediately, or refrigerate until you're ready to serve.

*For an inauthentic but still delicious substitute, use ⅔ to ¾ cup (8 to 10 ounces) caramel (from a block of caramel, or from a bag of wrapped caramels), melted with 2 tablespoons milk or cream, and 1 teaspoon vanilla extract.

nutrition information per serving   ⅛ **of pie, using the smaller amount of dulce de leche, 121g**

319 cal | 15g fat | 5g protein | 22g complex carbohydrates | 20g sugar | 1g dietary fiber | 42mg cholesterol | 106mg sodium | 340mg potassium | 126RE vitamin A | 5mg vitamin C | 1mg iron | 126mg calcium | 127mg phosphorus | 2mg caffeine

Pumpkin Cheesecake Pie

ONE 9-INCH PIE, 10 TO 12 RICH SERVINGS

With its layers of sweet/spicy pumpkin and smooth, rich cheesecake nestled in a buttery crust, this pie has won over many a traditional pumpkin pie enthusiast. We hope you can make room for it on your Thanksgiving table.

One 9-inch single piecrust or gingersnap crust (p. 419), blind baked

CHEESECAKE FILLING
8 ounces cream cheese, softened
⅓ cup (2½ ounces) sugar
1 large egg, lightly beaten
1 teaspoon vanilla extract
¼ cup (1⅝) diced crystallized ginger (optional, but good)

PUMPKIN FILLING
½ cup (3½ ounces) sugar
¼ teaspoon salt
¾ teaspoon ground ginger
¾ teaspoon ground cinnamon
¼ teaspoon ground nutmeg
¼ teaspoon ground allspice
1 cup (9½ ounces) canned pumpkin or thick pumpkin purée*
⅔ cup (5¾ ounces) light cream or evaporated milk
2 large eggs, lightly beaten

CHEESECAKE FILLING Place the cream cheese in a mixing bowl and let it warm to room temperature (this will make it easier to beat). When it has warmed, add the sugar and beat until fairly smooth. It may appear grainy, or a few lumps may remain; that's okay. Stir in the egg, vanilla, and ginger and spoon the filling into the piecrust.

PUMPKIN FILLING In a medium-sized mixing bowl, whisk together the sugar, salt and spices. Add the pumpkin, cream, and eggs and whisk gently until smooth. (You don't want to beat a lot of air into this mixture; just be sure it's thoroughly combined.) Gently spoon the pumpkin filling atop the cheesecake layer, filling to within ¼ inch of the top of the crust. Do this carefully at first, so you don't disturb the cheesecake layer; once you've covered the cheesecake, you can be less careful. Depending on the depth of your pie pan, you may have leftover filling. Simply pour it into a custard cup or other small baking dish and bake it along with the pie, removing it from the oven when it appears set and a cake tester inserted into the center comes out clean.

If you're using a pastry piecrust, place the pie in a preheated 425°F oven and bake it for 15 minutes. Reduce the oven temperature to 350°F and continue to bake for 40 to 45 minutes, covering the edges of the pie with a crust shield or aluminum foil if it seems to be browning too quickly. If you've prepared the pie with a gingersnap crust, bake it in a preheated 350°F oven for 50 to 60 minutes. The pie is done when it looks set but still wobbles a bit in the center when you jiggle it. (If you have an instant-read thermometer, the pie will register 165°F at its center when it's done.) Remove the pie from the oven, allow it to cool to room temperature, then refrigerate it until serving time. Serve with lightly sweetened whipped cream flavored with a pinch of ginger and a teaspoon of vanilla extract.

*Use plain pumpkin, not pumpkin pie filling.

nutrition information per serving   ¹⁄₁₀ **of pie, 118g**

274 cal | 15g fat | 6g protein | 13g complex carbohydrates | 16g sugar | 1g dietary fiber | 97mg cholesterol | 240mg sodium | 169mg potassium | 711RE vitamin A | 1mg vitamin C | 2mg iron | 84mg calcium | 104mg phosphorus

Chocolate Caramel Pie

ONE 9-INCH DEEP-DISH PIE, 12 SERVINGS

This pie pushes all boundaries for decadence. It's somewhere between pie and a candy bar, with its rich caramel filling. The bitterness of the chocolate and saltiness of the pecans give it balance, and of course we believe that whipped cream or ice cream can only improve the picture. This pie will do best if you have a deep-dish pie pan, which gives it plenty of room for the whipped cream.

CRUST

8 tablespoons (1 stick, 4 ounces) soft butter

¼ teaspoon salt

1 teaspoon vanilla extract

⅓ cup (1¼ ounces) confectioners' sugar

¼ cup (¾ ounce) Dutch-process cocoa

1 cup (4¼ ounces) unbleached all-purpose flour

½ cup (2 ounces) chopped pecans

CARAMEL FILLING

2 cups (12 ounces) caramel (about 35 individually wrapped caramels)

½ cup (4 ounces) heavy cream

1 cup (6 ounces) white chocolate

CHOCOLATE GLAZE

1 cup (6 ounces) bittersweet chocolate

½ cup (4 ounces) heavy cream

2 tablespoons (1½ ounces) corn syrup

½ cup (2 ounces) chopped toasted pecans*

Preheat the oven to 400°F.

CRUST Beat the butter until fluffy. Add the salt, vanilla, confectioners' sugar and cocoa. Blend until smooth. Add the flour and pecans, and stir until the flour is absorbed. The mixture should be somewhat dry. Lightly grease or spray a 9-inch deep-dish pie pan with nonstick spray. Press the crust into the pan coming up just to the bottom of the rim. Bake the crust for 15 to 18 minutes, until it has set. (The dark color makes it hard to tell if the crust is baked. You should just begin to smell the chocolate when it's done.) Set aside to cool.

FILLING Melt the caramels, heavy cream, and white chocolate together over low heat. Stir until smooth. (This may be done in the microwave, using low power and checking often.) Pour into the cooled crust and set aside to firm up while making the glaze.

GLAZE Melt the chocolate with the cream and corn syrup. Stir until smooth. Drizzle over the caramel layer. Sprinkle with the toasted pecans. Refrigerate for 1 hour or more before serving. Best served chilled but not cold; remove from the refrigerator 15 to 20 minutes before serving.

*To toast the pecans, butter a baking sheet. Place the pecans on the pan in a single layer. Sprinkle with ⅛ teaspoon salt. Toast for 7 to 8 minutes in a 350°F oven, tossing the pecans around to be sure the salt is evenly distributed. The bit of salt really sets off the very sweet nature of this pie.

nutrition information per serving   **1 slice, 112g**

515 cal | 33g fat | 6g protein | 13g complex carbohydrates | 38g sugar | 2g dietary fiber | 50mg cholesterol | 241mg sodium | 302mg potassium | 159RE vitamin A | 2mg iron | 97mg calcium | 115mg phosphorus | 15mg caffeine

Pecan Pie

ONE 9-INCH PIE, ABOUT 12 SERVINGS

Sticky, gooey, toasty-nutty, sweet and salty, flaky and smooth—what other pie combines all the "opposites attract" attributes of a pecan pie? The flaky tender crust cradles a smooth, deep brown, ultra-sweet filling tempered by the addition of toasted pecans—one small slice of this and you know you've had dessert!

One 9-inch single piecrust, partially blind-baked*

FILLING
3 large eggs
½ cup (5½ ounces) dark corn syrup
½ cup (5½ ounces) light corn syrup
¼ cup (1¾ ounces) sugar

8 tablespoons (1 stick, 4 ounces) unsalted butter, melted
¼ teaspoon salt
1 teaspoon vanilla extract
½ cup (2 ounces) chopped pecans, toasted in a 350°F oven until light brown, about 8 to 10 minutes
1 cup (4 ounces) pecan halves, not toasted

Preheat the oven to 375°F.

FILLING In a medium-sized mixing bowl, beat together the eggs, corn syrups, sugar, butter, salt, and vanilla. Stir in the chopped pecans and pour into the baked pie shell. Arrange the whole pecans on top.

Bake the pie for 45 minutes, or until it's puffed and the center seems fairly set. Remove the pie from the oven and allow it to cool on a wire rack. As it cools, the center will sink. Serve warm or at room temperature, in small slices, with vanilla ice cream or very lightly sweetened whipped cream.

*Bake the crust, with weights, in a preheated 400°F oven for 10 minutes. Remove it from the oven, remove the weights, and set aside to cool while you prepare the filling.

nutrition information per serving   **1 slice, 100g**

400 cal | 23g fat | 4g protein | 10g complex carbohydrates | 33g sugar | 1g dietary fiber | 97mg cholesterol | 220mg sodium | 88mg potassium | 130RE vitamin A | 1mg vitamin C | 1mg iron | 32mg calcium | 75mg phosphorus

Variation   YANKEE MAPLE PECAN OR MAPLE WALNUT PIE: For a Northern version of this classic, substitute 1½ cups (16½ ounces) Grade B maple syrup for the corn syrups in the recipe above and increase the eggs to 4. You can also substitute walnuts for the pecans with excellent results.

Chocolate-Pecan Pie

ONE 9-INCH PIE, 8 TO 10 SERVINGS

This gooey, chocolaty pie is traditionally served on Derby Day. The Kentucky Derby—the "run for the roses"—is an early May tradition in Kentucky, and a harbinger of spring for sports lovers all over the country.

One 9-inch single piecrust

2 large eggs, at room temperature

1 cup (7 ounces) sugar

½ teaspoon salt

½ cup (2 ounces) unbleached all-purpose flour

8 tablespoons (1 stick, 4 ounces) unsalted butter, melted and cooled

1 cup (6 ounces) semisweet chocolate chips

1 cup (4 ounces) chopped pecans, lightly toasted

1 tablespoon bourbon (optional)

1 teaspoon vanilla extract

Whipped cream, for garnish

Preheat oven to 375°F.

Beat eggs on high speed of electric mixer until light and lemon colored. Gradually beat in sugar. Reduce speed to low and add the salt, flour, and butter, beating until thoroughly combined. Stir in chocolate chips and nuts, then bourbon and vanilla.

Spoon the mixture into the unbaked pie shell. Bake until crust and top are golden brown, about 45 minutes. Serve warm, with unsweetened whipped cream if desired.

nutrition information per serving   **1 slice, 99g**

446 cal | 28g fat | 5g protein | 16g complex carbohydrates | 29g sugar | 2g dietary fiber | 75mg cholesterol | 201mg sodium | 131mg potassium | 134RE vitamin A | 2mg iron | mg calcium | 89mg phosphorus | 13mg caffeine

Tarts and Turnovers

Tarts and turnovers are offshoots of the classic fruit pie. A tart, which can range from full-sized to bite-sized, is a shallow, straight-sided pastry crust filled with cream and fruit, or fruit alone. A turnover is a half-moon or triangle of crust enclosing fruit filling. Tarts are often baked in removable-bottom pans, for ease of serving as well as a pretty presentation. Unlike pies, which often look sloppy in a comforting, overstuffed way, tarts are almost military-looking in their neatness: a straight, even crust, berries lined up in rows like soldiers. Tarts are best served in more formal circumstances (i.e., on a plate, with a fork); as opposed to turnovers, which are the perfect "grab and go" picnic or brown-bag treat.

Italian Turnovers?

An easy way to shape, cut, fill, and seal turnovers is with the aid of a calzone press, sometimes called a dumpling maker, sometimes even labeled a turnover maker. A circle of serrated plastic, hinged in the middle, is used to cut a round of rolled-out dough. The dough is set inside the circle, filling is spooned onto one side, and the handles on the press are used to turn the second side over the first, and seal it.

Berry Cream Tart

ONE TART, 9 SERVINGS

You'll want to reach around and pat yourself on the back once you've made this tart—it looks like the centerpiece of a fancy bakery window. With its alternating rows of blueberries and strawberries, it's particularly appropriate for the Fourth of July, where it can take its place of pride on the picnic table.

One 9- or 10-inch pâte sucrée crust (p. 458), blind-baked

PASTRY CREAM FILLING
¼ cup (1¾ ounces) sugar
1 tablespoon unbleached all-purpose flour
2 teaspoons cornstarch
¼ teaspoon salt
1 large egg
1 cup (8 ounces) milk

3 tablespoons (1½ ounces) soft butter
¼ teaspoon vanilla or almond extract

TOPPING
1 pint (10 ounces) strawberries, sliced
1 pint (10 ounces) blueberries

GLAZE
½ cup apricot jam, melted and strained, or ½ cup apricot juice plus 1 teaspoon unflavored gelatin

PASTRY CREAM In a medium-sized heatproof bowl, whisk together the sugar, flour, cornstarch, salt, and egg. In a small (1½-quart) saucepan, bring the milk to a boil. Add the hot milk to the egg mixture gradually, whisking continually to make everything smooth. Pour the liquid back into the saucepan and return to the heat to bring back to a boil. Stir continually with your whisk—the mixture will thicken quickly and whisking will keep it from getting lumpy. As soon as you see the pastry cream boil in the center, remove it from the heat and stir in the butter and vanilla or almond extract. Pour the pastry cream into the baked tart shell, place plastic wrap on the surface, and refrigerate. When you're ready to serve the tart, remove the wrap from the filling and top it with sliced strawberries and blueberries in alternating rows. If you're not going to serve the tart immediately, add the glaze to keep the berries looking their best.

GLAZE Melt apricot jam, thinning it with a little water if necessary. Strain or scoop out any solids, then brush the glaze over the berries to seal the top of the tart. If you're using apricot juice, soften the gelatin in the juice for 5 minutes or so, then heat the mixture in the microwave or over low heat until the gelatin dissolves. Let cool to lukewarm before brushing over the berries.

nutrition information per serving   1 slice, without glaze, 148g

286 cal | 10g fat | 4g protein | 21g complex carbohydrates | 11g sugar | 2g dietary fiber | 89mg cholesterol | 144mg sodium | 160mg potassium | 180RE vitamin A | 23mg vitamin C | 1mg iron | 50mg calcium | 74mg phosphorus

Variation   BANANA-CHOCOLATE TART: Before making the pastry cream, slice two medium bananas into the baked tart shell. Pour the pastry cream over the bananas and chill as directed. Drizzle the top of the tart with 1½ cups (9 ounces) semisweet chocolate, melted with 3 tablespoons (1½ ounces) heavy cream. Top with crushed toffee bits to garnish.

Pear and Cheese Turnovers

12 TURNOVERS

Gorgonzola cheese and pears are a traditional marriage of flavors, spelling the end of many an Italian meal. If you're not a fan of strong-flavored Gorgonzola, don't skip this recipe; just leave it out and make pear turnovers (or tone it down by using a milder-flavored cheddar or blue cheese). This looks like a long recipe, but it's really easy if you take the time to keep everything very cold. This is one recipe where once you start to assemble the turnovers or pastry, it's important to work quickly, so be sure to have everything you need ready. If the dough becomes unbearably sticky while you're working with it, just return it to the freezer or refrigerator for a few minutes; cold dough is much easier to work with.

DOUGH

2 cups (8½ ounces) unbleached all-purpose flour, for the dough

½ cup (1¾ ounces) pecan meal (finely ground pecans; optional)

1 teaspoon salt

½ teaspoon baking powder

1 cup (2 sticks, 8 ounces) butter, frozen

½ cup (2 ounces) unbleached all-purpose flour, for dusting the dough

½ cup (4 ounces) sour cream

6 to 8 tablespoons (3 to 4 ounces) cold water

FILLING

3 to 4 pears, peeled and chopped into ½-inch dice (16 to 18 ounces, about 2½ cups)

1 tablespoon lemon juice

1 teaspoon cornstarch

2 tablespoons (⅞ ounce) sugar

¼ cup (2 ounces) crumbled Gorgonzola cheese

½ cup (2 ounces) toasted pecans, chopped

2 tablespoons (1 ounce) coarse sugar

Whipped cream, for garnish

Extra toasted pecans, for garnish

DOUGH In a medium-sized bowl, whisk together the dry ingredients and place them in the freezer. Unwrap the frozen sticks of butter and press the end of each stick into some of the "dusting" flour. This will help give you a grip on the butter while you're grating it. If you have a food processor with a medium-to-large shredding disk, use it; if not, grate the butter by hand, into large flakes, on the coarse holes of a box grater. The task will seem a little messy, but isn't difficult if you dust your fingers with flour.

Remove the dry ingredients from the freezer and use your fingers to toss the cold flour and butter together until they're evenly mixed. Stir the sour cream and cold water together. Add this mixture to the flour and butter. Use a dough scraper or spatula to fold and pat the mixture until it starts to hold together. You'll be able to see individual chunks of butter, which is okay; they shouldn't mix in. Pat the dough into a rough rectangle and fold it in thirds, like a letter. Pat it down again until it's about ½-inch thick and fold in thirds a second time.

Divide the dough in half. Place each half in the center of a piece of plastic wrap and form each piece into a 6 x 6-inch square. Wrap the squares well, and refrigerate for 30 minutes.

Remove one square of dough from the refrigerator and use the dusting flour to heavily flour both sides. Quickly roll the dough into a large (10 x 12-inch) rectangle. Working with opposite shorter sides (10-inch sides), fold the dough into thirds.

Use a rolling pin to flatten and widen the dough until it's about 5 x 12 inches. Again, working with opposite shorter sides (the 5-inch sides), fold the dough into thirds to form a rectangle of about 4 x 5 inches. Return the dough to the refrigerator for 30 minutes, or until it's firm. Repeat with the remaining piece of dough. The dough may be prepared to this point up to 2 days before using, or up to 1 month before, if kept frozen.

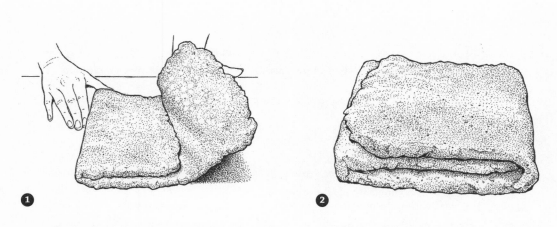

1–2. Folding the rectangle of dough in thirds will create distinct layers in the dough which will puff up during baking. The more folds, the more layers created.

FILLING   Make the filling while the dough is chilling. Place the chopped pears and lemon juice in a small saucepan or microwave-safe bowl. Combine the cornstarch and sugar, add to the pears, and cook over low heat, or in the microwave, for about 5 minutes, until the pears are tender and the liquid thickens. Set aside to cool.

ASSEMBLY   Before removing the dough from the refrigerator, preheat the oven to 425°F. Have ready the filling and a sharp knife and ruler for cutting the pastry. Line ungreased baking sheets with parchment.

Remove one piece of dough from the refrigerator. (If it's been in the freezer, let it thaw, wrapped, until it's pliable.) Heavily flour both sides and roll it into a 10 x 15-inch rectangle. Use flour to keep the dough from sticking to your work surface. Turn the dough over and flour underneath it to be sure it's not sticking.

Cut the dough into six 5-inch squares. Place 1 heaping tablespoon of pear in the center of the dough. Top with a few crumbles of Gorgonzola and pecans. Brush the edges of the pastry lightly with water. Fold one corner of the dough over the filling diagonally until it meets its opposite corner; you've now got a triangle-shaped turnover. Press the edges to seal. Repeat with the remaining dough and filling.

Place all the turnovers on the prepared baking sheets. Cut steam vents, brush with water and sprinkle with coarse sugar (Demerara, coarse white sugar, or pearl sugar are all good; if you don't have any coarse sugar, use regular granulated sugar). Bake the turnovers for 18 to 20 minutes, until they're golden brown. Remove them from the oven and serve them warm with a bit of whipped cream and toasted pecans.

nutrition information per serving   1 turnover, 106g

354 cal | 25g fat | 5g protein | 24g complex carbohydrates | 4g sugar | 2g dietary fiber | 51mg cholesterol | 270mg sodium | 131mg potassium | 179RE vitamin A | 2mg vitamin C | 2mg iron | 57mg calcium | 85mg phosphorus

Autumn Apple Turnovers

12 TURNOVERS

These lightly spiced pastry treats enliven any lunchbox. Be sure to cut the apples small to make the turnovers easier to fill.

1 recipe pastry dough from Pear and Cheese Turnovers (p. 450)

2 pounds cored, peeled, apples,* cut into ½-inch dice (4 cups)

⅓ cup (2⅜ ounces) sugar

½ teaspoon apple pie spice

1 tablespoon cornstarch

Pinch of salt

1 tablespoon boiled cider or regular cider

1 tablespoon lemon juice

1 egg white beaten with 1 tablespoon water, for glaze

Sparkling white sugar, for topping

Gently mix together the apples, sugar, spice, cornstarch, salt, cider, and lemon juice until well combined.

Preheat the oven to 400°F.

Divide the dough into two pieces; work with one piece at a time, keeping the other refrigerated. Remove one piece of dough from the refrigerator. (If it's been in the freezer, let it thaw, wrapped, until it's pliable.) Heavily flour both sides and roll it into a 10 x 15-inch rectangle.

Cut the dough into six 5-inch squares. Spoon a scant ¼ cup of filling into the center of each square, moisten the edge of the dough, and fold the other half over to make a triangle. Pinch the edges of the triangle together or crimp with a fork, and place it on an ungreased baking sheet. Repeat with the remaining pieces of dough. Brush each turnover with the egg white glaze, sprinkle with coarse sugar, prick them to make steam vents, and bake for 20 to 30 minutes, until golden brown. Remove the turnovers from the oven and cool them on a wire rack.

*Cortland or Granny Smith are good choices.

nutrition information per serving   **1 turnover, 90g**

273 cal | 18g fat | 3g protein | 20g complex carbohydrates | 6g sugar | 1g dietary fiber | 47mg cholesterol | 209mg sodium | 72mg potassium | 167RE vitamin A | 1mg vitamin C | 1mg iron | 28mg calcium | 37mg phosphorus

Variation   CHERRY OR BLUEBERRY TURNOVERS: Substitute pitted cherries or blueberries for the apples, omit the cider, and increase the cornstarch to 2 tablespoons. Cook the filling in a saucepan until it thickens, then cool and use to fill the turnovers.

Apple Pizza Pie

8 GENEROUS OR 12 AVERAGE SERVINGS

This "pizza" is simply an open-faced apple pie, combining all the ingredients of that all-American favorite. It's much thinner than a regular pie, featuring more crust and topping, per bite, than the normal pie-pan pie. Another plus: since the apples are spread over the surface in a single layer, their juices evaporate as the pie bakes, leaving the apples tender and the crust crisp, with no apple juice bubbling over onto the oven floor or soaking into the bottom crust.

For a typically New England taste treat, add about a cup of shredded cheddar cheese to the topping.

One 9-inch single piecrust

TOPPING

½ cup plus 2 tablespoons (2⅝ ounces) unbleached all-purpose flour

⅔ cup (4¾ ounces) sugar

7 tablespoons (3½ ounces) unsalted butter

1 teaspoon cinnamon

¼ teaspoon nutmeg

1 cup (4 ounces) chopped walnuts

FILLING

5 medium Cortland or Granny Smith apples (about 2 pounds), peeled, cored, and sliced ¼-inch thick

Dash of salt

2 teaspoons lemon juice

CRUST Roll the dough into a 13-inch round and transfer it to a 12-inch flat pizza pan or a cookie sheet. Crimp the edges to form a rim around the edge of the pan. Place the pan in the refrigerator while you prepare the topping. Preheat the oven to 425°F.

TOPPING In the bowl of a food processor equipped with the metal blade, combine the flour, sugar, butter, cinnamon, and nutmeg. Process until the mixture forms even crumbs. Add the walnuts and pulse a couple of times to distribute. You may also do this with an electric mixer or by hand.

ASSEMBLY Remove the crust from the refrigerator. Lay the apple slices close together in concentric rings on the crust. Sprinkle the apples with a dash of salt and the lemon juice. Distribute the topping evenly over the apples.

Bake the pizza on the bottom shelf of the oven for 15 minutes, then reduce the heat to 375°F and continue to bake until the crust and topping are golden, about 35 minutes.

nutrition information per serving   **1 slice, 115g**

325 cal | 20g fat | 3g protein | 21g complex carbohydrates | 10g sugar | 2g dietary fiber | 41mg cholesterol | 94mg sodium | 136mg potassium | 3mg vitamin C | 1mg iron | 46mg calcium | 53mg phosphorus

Open-Faced Rustic Berry Pie

6 SERVINGS

The "rustic" in the recipe title refers to the method of shaping the crust. All you have to do is roll out a big circle, pile the sugared berries in the middle, and gently fold the edges of the crust in toward the center, leaving about a 4-inch-wide circle of berries showing (that's the open-faced part). The number-one goal is to bring the crust over the berries without tearing it; a crust with holes will allow leakage of the bubbling berry syrup. You can make evenly cut, artful, overlapping folds; or if you don't have the Martha Stewart gene, just flop the dough over the berries as best you can. A turner or giant spatula definitely helps.

One 9-inch single piecrust

⅔ cup (4¾ ounces) sugar

3 tablespoons (¾ ounce) pie filling thickener of your choice (tapioca or cornstarch)

3 cups (15 ounces) berries, fresh or frozen and thawed

Preheat the oven to 425°F.

Roll the crust into a 12- to 13-inch round and transfer the round to a pizza pan or baking sheet; if you use a baking sheet, the crust may (temporarily) hang off the edges, which is okay.

In a medium-sized bowl, blend together the sugar and thickener. Add the berries, tossing to coat.

Mound the sugared berries in the center of the crust, leaving about a 3½-inch margin of bare crust all the way around; the mound of fruit will be quite high. Using a pancake turner or a giant spatula, fold the edges of the crust up over the fruit, leaving 4 to 5 inches of fruit exposed in the center.

Bake the pie for about 35 minutes, or until the filling is beginning to bubble and the edges of the crust are brown. Remove it from the oven and let it cool for 15 to 30 minutes before cutting wedges.

nutrition information per serving | 1 slice, made with raspberries, 116g

253 cal | 9g fat | 3g protein | 24g complex carbohydrates | 16g sugar | 4g dietary fiber | 41mg cholesterol | 65mg sodium | 121mg potassium | 96RE vitamin A | 11mg vitamin C | 2mg iron | 18mg calcium | 37mg phosphorus

Toaster Pastries

16 TARTS

Toaster pastries have come a long way since their invention in 1964—from the original cinnamon–brown sugar in a pastry crust, to the Frosted Screaming Strawberry and Super Fudge Earthquake varieties lining the supermarket's cereal-aisle shelves today.

If you want to get back to basics, make your own. You can use several different fillings for the amount of crust you'll have, so feel free to mix and match, and frost or not, in order to accommodate the palates around you. The tarts are best eaten within a day or two of the time they're made.

PASTRY

8 tablespoons (1 stick, 4 ounces) unsalted butter

1 cup (7 ounces) sugar

1 large egg

1 teaspoon vanilla extract

4 cups (17 ounces) unbleached all-purpose flour

2 teaspoons cream of tartar

½ teaspoon baking soda

½ teaspoon salt

½ cup (4 ounces) milk

FRUIT FILLING

1¼ cups (14½ ounces) thick raspberry, strawberry, or other flavor jam

¼ cup (1 ounce) unbleached all-purpose flour

BROWN SUGAR–CINNAMON FILLING

6 tablespoons (¾ stick, 3 ounces) soft butter

3 tablespoons (¾ ounce) unbleached all-purpose flour

¾ cup (6 ounces) light brown sugar

1½ teaspoons cinnamon

¼ teaspoon salt

FROSTING

2½ tablespoons (1¼ ounces) water or milk

1¼ cups (5⅓ ounces) confectioners' sugar

Colored sugar crystals, for decoration

PASTRY Cream the butter and sugar together in a large bowl. Add the egg and vanilla and beat well.

Blend the flour, cream of tartar, baking soda, and salt together in a small bowl. Alternately add the flour mixture and the milk to the butter mixture, beating the dough until it's well blended. Cover with plastic wrap and chill in the refrigerator for several hours, or overnight.

Just before you're ready to remove the dough from the refrigerator, prepare the filling(s). Mix the jam and flour together, or combine all of the brown sugar filling ingredients, stirring until smooth. Each filling recipe will make enough to fill all of the tarts, so make double the amount of dough if you're making both batches of filling, or cut the filling ingredients in half.

Preheat the oven to 350°F.

When the dough is well chilled, divide it into quarters and roll out each piece separately on a lightly floured work surface to a 12 x 8-inch rectangle about 1/16 inch thick. Keep the other dough pieces chilled until you roll them out. Cut each rolled-out piece of dough into eight 3 x 4-inch pieces, trimming and discarding any uneven edges as you go.

Place the 3 x 4-inch rectangles from the first two dough quarters onto lightly greased or parchment-lined baking sheets. With a pastry brush or your finger, lightly moisten the outside edge of each rectangle. Spread slightly more than 1 tablespoon of filling onto each rectangle, leaving about a 1/8-inch border all the way around.

When you've rolled and cut the remaining rectangles, place them on top of the bottom halves. Seal each tart all the way around with the flat side of a fork dipped into flour. Prick the top of each filled tart 10 to 12 times, to allow steam to escape. Bake the tarts for 18 to 20 minutes, until lightly golden brown. Remove them from the oven and transfer them to a rack to cool.

To make the frosting, simply stir the water or milk, 1/2 tablespoon at a time, into the confectioners' sugar until the mixture is of a spreadable consistency. Spread the frosting evenly onto the tarts and sprinkle each tart with a bit of colored sugar for the finishing touch.

nutrition information per serving   **1 frosted tart made with raspberry jam, 99g**

308 cal | 6.1g fat | 4g protein | 25g complex carbohydrates | 34g sugar | 1g dietary fiber | 33mg cholesterol | 64mg sodium | 90mg potassium | 63RE vitamin A | 1mg iron | 62mg calcium | 41mg phosphorus

Enriched Crusts

Pâte sucrée (in French), pasta frolla (in Italian), and sweetened, enriched short-flake crust are all the same. Richer tasting, and sandy/crumbly rather than flaky, they're often used for fruit tarts but can be used for any sweet pastry. Egg, vanilla, butter (rather than vegetable shortening), and sugar distinguish this crust from its plainer medium- and short-flake cousins.

Cream cheese crust is the approximate savory equivalent of pâte sucrée: it's an enriched basic crust, without the sugar. Because of its high fat content and lack of water, this pastry is very supple and easy to roll out without tearing or sticking. Just be sure to flour your work surface well and use a spatula (a giant spatula works well) to periodically lift the dough from the board as you roll it, adding more flour to the board as necessary.

Pâte Sucrée

ONE 9- TO 10-INCH TART SHELL

Pâte sucrée (pasta frolla in Italy) is a good choice for tarts, in which the crust usually plays a much larger role than it does in pie. Where pie is all about the filling, tarts are lower profile, with a greater percentage of crust to filling. This sweetened pastry falls midway between a classic piecrust and a cookie.

1¼ cups (5¼ ounces) pastry or unbleached all-purpose flour

1 teaspoon nonfat dry milk (optional, but helpful for browning and tenderness)

¼ cup (1¾ ounces) sugar

¼ teaspoon salt

8 tablespoons (1 stick, 4 ounces) cold butter

1 large egg yolk

1 teaspoon vanilla extract

1 tablespoon water

In a medium-sized mixing bowl, whisk together the dry ingredients, then cut in the cold butter. Whisk together the egg yolk, vanilla, and water and stir into the dry mixture; the dough should be crumbly but hold together when squeezed. Roll out the dough, or press it into the bottom and up the sides of a 9-inch square or 10-inch round (preferably removable bottom) tart pan. Prick it all over with a fork and refrigerate for 30 minutes or longer.

Preheat the oven to 375°F.

To prepare a blind-baked, ready-to-fill crust, weigh down the crust with pie weights, a nesting pie pan, or line with parchment and fill with rice or dried beans. Bake for 10 to 12 minutes, until the crust is set. Remove weights, extra pan, or parchment and return to the oven to bake for another 6 to 8 minutes, until golden brown. Remove it from the oven and cool before filling.

nutrition information per serving   ⅛ of crust, 44g

202 cal | 13g fat | 2g protein | 13g complex carbohydrates | 1g dietary fiber | 60mg cholesterol | 69mg sodium | 28mg potassium | 125RE vitamin A | 1mg iron | 7mg calcium | 30mg phosphorus

Cream Cheese Pastry Dough

ONE 9-INCH PIE OR TART SHELL, OR 36 SMALL TARTS WHEN MADE IN A MINI-MUFFIN PAN

This dough is very pliable, keeps well in the refrigerator for up to three days, and nestles nicely into a tartlet pan or mini-muffin tin, to make tiny, hors d'oeuvre–sized tarts.

½ cup (4 ounces) cream cheese
8 tablespoons (1 stick, 4 ounces) butter
1 teaspoon sugar

¼ teaspoon salt
1¼ cups (5¼ ounces) unbleached all-purpose flour

Using your favorite tool—a fork, food processor, or electric mixer—cream together the cream cheese, butter, sugar, and salt until smooth. Add the flour and mix (on low speed if you're using a mixer, or very briefly in a food processor) until the dough has formed a loose ball. Shape the dough into a flat 1-inch-thick circle, wrap it in plastic wrap or waxed paper, and refrigerate for 30 minutes. Note: If you're in a hurry, you can roll it out without any refrigeration time at all, but we find the dough rolls more easily and makes a more tender tart if it's allowed to cool for a bit.

Remove the dough from the refrigerator. If it's been chilled longer than an hour, allow it to rest at room temperature for 15 minutes; this will make it easier to roll.

If you're using the dough to make mini-tarts, roll it into a circle ⅛ inch thick, rolling from the center out to the sides and turning the dough around as you go; that's the easiest way to get a round, evenly thick circle. Use a 3-inch biscuit cutter or 3-inch round cookie cutter to cut the dough into as many rounds as you can squeeze from the rolled-out dough. Gather the remaining dough scraps into a ball, flatten the ball, wrap it in plastic or waxed paper, and refrigerate until you want to cut the next batch of rounds.

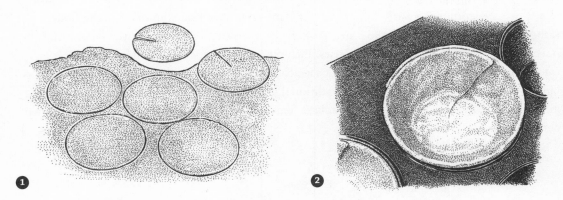

1. Cut a circle of dough that is ½-inch larger in diameter than the top of your muffin cup, then cut a radius, from the center to the outside edge. **2.** Tuck the circle of dough into the muffin cup, overlapping the edges of the cut and pressing the seam together.

Cut a radius from the center to one edge of the small rounds of dough, then place each circle into a mini-muffin cup, gently pressing it into the bottom and overlapping the edges of the cut; press together toward the sides. Remove the remaining dough from the refrigerator and roll, cut, and fit it into the pan.

Fill the tarts with 1 to 2 teaspoons filling of your choice (they make wonderful hors d'oeuvres with savory fillings) and bake them in a preheated 400°F oven for 8 to 10 minutes, or until the crust is golden brown. Remove them from the oven and use a spoon or butter knife to gently transfer the tarts to a rack to cool.

For a larger tart, roll out the dough to ⅜ inch thick, and place it into a pie or tart shell. Trim the edges, fill, and bake for 20 to 25 minutes.

nutrition information per serving   ⅛ **of single crust recipe, 48g**

221 cal | 11g fat | 3g protein | 14g complex carbohydrates | 1g dietary fiber | 48mg cholesterol | 115mg sodium | 43mg potassium | 175RE vitamin A | 1mg iron | 15mg calcium | 34mg phosphorus

Ricotta Pie

ONE 9- OR 10-INCH PIE, 12 SERVINGS

Ricotta pie is as common in Italian American communities as chocolate cake is in the Midwest. If you visit an Italian pastry bakery (as opposed to a bread bakery; the two are often separate establishments), you're almost sure to find a display of ricotta pies. We visit Boston's North End frequently and have found the ricotta pies are especially evident at Christmas and Easter, when small tables bearing the pies crowd out onto the sidewalk, and well-dressed young men are spotted carrying pies in string-bound, white cardboard boxes—probably home to a big family feast.

Ricotta pie is very similar to New York–style cheesecake, in that it has a flour- rather than graham cracker–based crust. Pasta frolla, a version of which is given here, is the all-purpose crust used in Italian sweet pastries. Including egg and sugar, as well as the more traditional elements of flour and butter, it's a rich, tender, almost cookielike crust. The filling is lighter and less sweet than cheesecake; traditionally flavored with lemon and vanilla, it can also include citron, candied peel, and/or chocolate. This is a basic version; feel free to add your own personal touches.

CRUST

1 recipe pâte sucrée (pasta frolla), page 458, made with ½ teaspoon grated lemon rind or a few drops of lemon oil

FILLING

¼ cup (1 ounce) unbleached all-purpose flour

¾ cup (5¼ ounces) granulated sugar

2 pounds (4 cups) whole-milk or part-skim ricotta cheese, drained if necessary*

4 large eggs

1 teaspoon vanilla extract

¼ teaspoon lemon oil, or 1 tablespoon grated lemon rind

CRUST   Roll the dough into a 13- to 14-inch circle. Roll from the center out in firm strokes; don't overwork the dough. Transfer dough to a 9-inch removable-bottom cheesecake pan, or 9- or 10-inch springform pan. The dough is fragile, so you will probably have to patch up holes and tears that occurred as you were trying to get it into the pan. Don't worry; these won't show. Press the dough all the way up the sides of the pan. Place pan in refrigerator to chill while you make filling.

Preheat the oven to 350°F.

FILLING   In a large mixing bowl, combine flour, sugar, ricotta cheese, eggs, vanilla, and lemon oil. Mix slowly but thoroughly; you don't want to beat air into the filling, but you do want to combine the ingredients well.

Remove chilled crust from refrigerator and brush with a bit of milk on bottom and sides. This will help prevent crust from becoming soggy. Pour filling into crust. Place pie on the bottom rack of the oven and bake for 1 hour. Turn oven off and leave pie in oven an additional 30 minutes. Remove from oven and place on a wire rack to cool completely. When cool, remove from pan and dust with confectioners' sugar. Serve pie at room temperature, or refrigerate if you wish to serve it later.

*Ricotta cheese made with part skim milk is much closer to true Italian ricotta cheese than is whole-milk ricotta. Whole-milk ricotta cheese tends to be "looser" than skim-milk ricotta and should be drained before using, in a yogurt strainer or in a cheesecloth bag, for several hours in the refrigerator.

nutrition information per serving   **1 slice, 143g**

347 cal | 19g fat | 14g protein | 13g complex carbohydrates | 15g sugar | 175mg cholesterol | 192mg sodium | 132mg potassium | 1mg iron | 208mg calcium | 181mg phosphorus

Savory Pies

Savory pies have been gradually eclipsed by their sweet brethren over the years, but that's no reason to discount them entirely. The faint chill of a fall day or the definite cold of a winter night demands something lusty, a meal that will stick to your ribs. A slice of savory pie (pair it with a healthy salad, if you must) fills this particular bill just fine.

Pepper Steak Pie

ONE 9-INCH PIE, 10 SERVINGS

This nontraditional filling is just as popular as the following French-Canadian one.

One 9-inch double piecrust

1 pound ground or cubed beef

1½ cups thinly sliced onions (6 to 8 ounces, 1½ medium onions)

3 cups (8 ounces) sliced mushrooms

2 large (10 to 12 ounces) green or red peppers

1 teaspoon salt

1 teaspoon black pepper

1½ cups (6 ounces) cubed or grated Swiss cheese

Prepare pastry as directed in the tourtière recipe (next page) and chill it while you make the filling. Brown the meat, then drain off the fat. Add the onions, mushrooms, and peppers and cook until most of the moisture has evaporated, 5 to 10 minutes. Stir in the salt and pepper. Cool the mixture to lukewarm, then stir in the cheese. Follow assembly and baking instructions in the following recipe.

nutrition information per serving   **1 serving, 189g**

459 cal | 32g fat | 16g protein | 25g complex carbohydrates | 2g dietary fiber | 69mg cholesterol | 470mg sodium | 330mg potassium | 61RE vitamin A | 28mg vitamin C | 3mg iron | 217mg calcium | 238mg phosphorus

Tourtière
(French-Canadian Meat Pie)

ONE 9-INCH PIE, 10 SERVINGS

This traditional wintertime staple, often eaten with ketchup or tomato chutney and a green salad, will yield kudos from friends and families. Feel free to use your favorite double-crust pie recipe, or try the one that follows. It's not a flaky crust, but it's very tender and easy to work with.

CRUST

¾ cup (6 ounces) lard or ¾ cup (4⅞ ounces) vegetable shortening

⅓ cup (2⅞ ounces) boiling water

2¼ cups (9½ ounces) unbleached all-purpose flour

1½ teaspoons baking powder

½ teaspoon salt

FILLING

1 to 1½ teaspoons salt

2 cups (16 ounces) water

2½ cups peeled potatoes cut into ½-inch dice (12 to 14 ounces, 1 large potato)

½ pound ground beef*

½ pound ground pork*

1 cup chopped onion (4 to 5 ounces, 1 large onion)

1 cup chopped celery (3 to 4 ounces, 1 to 2 celery stalks)

2 garlic cloves (more to taste), peeled and minced

¼ teaspoon ground cloves

1 teaspoon ground thyme

½ teaspoon ground sage

1 teaspoon ground black pepper

CRUST Place the lard or shortening in a bowl. Add the boiling water, then stir well to melt the fat. Add the flour, baking powder, and salt and mix with a spoon or electric mixer to make a smooth dough. Scrape half the dough out of the bowl onto a piece of plastic wrap, form it into a disk, and wrap well. Repeat with the remaining dough and refrigerate both dough disks while preparing the filling.

FILLING Put the salt, water, and potatoes in a medium saucepan and bring the mixture to a boil over medium heat. Boil until the potatoes are fork-tender, then drain them, saving the water.

In a large frying pan, brown the meat, draining off any excess fat when finished. Add the onion, celery, garlic, spices, and potato water to the meat. Bring to a boil, then lower the heat to a simmer. Stirring occasionally, continue simmering the mixture for 30 minutes or longer, until the liquid has evaporated and the vegetables are tender.

Mash about half of the potato chunks and add them to the meat. Gently stir in the remaining chunks of potato. Remove the mixture from the heat and let it cool to room temperature.

ASSEMBLY Preheat the oven to 450°F. Take one piece of dough out of the refrigerator, unwrap it, and dust both sides with flour. Roll it out to about ¼ inch thick (or less if you prefer a thinner crust). Line a 9-inch pie pan with the dough, and fill it with the cooled meat mixture. Roll out the remaining dough disk and place it over the filling. Trim the excess from the dough and crimp the edges together with a fork or your fingers.

Bake the pie for 15 minutes. Reduce the oven heat to 350°F and bake for an additional 30 minutes, until the pie is golden brown. Let the pie cool for 15 minutes or so to set up before slicing.

*Or use all ground pork, if desired.

nutrition information per serving   1 slice, 212g

415 cal | 26g fat | 13g protein | 30g complex carbohydrates | 2g dietary fiber | 55mg cholesterol | 440mg sodium | 396mg potassium | 3RE vitamin A | 7mg vitamin C | 3mg iron | 64mg calcium | 149mg phosphorus

Church Supper Chicken Pie

8 TO 12 SERVINGS

This recipe could just as easily be titled Grange Supper Chicken Pie, or American Legion Supper Chicken Pie, or B.P.O.E., or Odd Fellows, the volunteer fire department, or any number of organizations that have regular "suppers," fund-raising or just social. A good "church supper chicken pie" is one of the most comforting foods we know.

CHICKEN
One 5-pound roasting chicken, or 5 pounds of chicken parts, including light and dark meat*
1 large onion (7 ounces) cut into chunks
2 large carrots (7 ounces) cut into chunks
5 sprigs fresh parsley
½ teaspoon thyme
1 bay leaf
1 teaspoon salt
2 quarts (64 ounces) water

SAUCE
¼ cup (2 ounces) chicken fat (reserved from poaching liquid below)
2 tablespoons (1 ounce) butter

½ cup (2 ounces) unbleached all-purpose flour
1 teaspoon salt
3½ cups (28 ounces) chicken stock (prepared from poaching liquid, below)

BISCUITS
2 cups (8½ ounces) unbleached all-purpose flour
1 tablespoon sugar
4 teaspoons baking powder
½ teaspoon salt
½ cup (3¼ ounces) shortening
1 large egg
⅔ cup (5¼ ounces) milk

FILLING Place the chicken, onion, carrots, parsley, thyme, bay leaf, and salt in a deep stock pot. Add the water. Bring to a boil, skim off the foam, reduce the heat to low, and cover. Simmer the chicken and vegetables for about 1¼ hours (for a whole chicken) or 45 minutes to 1 hour (for chicken parts), until chicken is cooked through.

Remove the chicken and vegetables, discarding the vegetables and spreading the chicken on a platter to cool. Simmer the stock until it's reduced to 3½ cups; this will take about 30 minutes. If after 30 minutes there's more than 3½ cups of stock remaining, simply measure out 3½ cups and save or discard the rest. Alternatively, you can use 28 ounces of canned chicken broth.

SAUCE When the yellow fat has risen to the top of the stock—this should take about 40 minutes—skim off, strain, and reserve ¼ cup, discarding the rest. Place the fat in a saucepan with the butter, and heat over medium heat until butter has melted. Add the flour and salt (omit the salt if using canned broth) and stir to combine. Gradually pour in the stock, whisking constantly. Cook and stir the sauce over medium heat until it comes to a boil, then reduce the heat and simmer it for 5 minutes.

While the sauce is simmering, remove the skin and bones from the chicken, discard, and tear the meat into 1-inch pieces. Stir the chicken into the sauce. Add ground black pepper and additional salt to taste, if needed.

Spoon the chicken into a shallow 2- to 3-quart casserole dish or 9 x 13-inch pan.

BISCUITS In a mixing bowl, combine the flour, sugar, baking powder, and salt. Using a pastry blender, your fingers, or an electric mixer, cut in the shortening until the mixture is crumbly. Whisk together the egg and milk and stir into the dry ingredients, mixing just until fully combined. The dough will be very wet and sticky.

Preheat the oven to 450°F. Using a spoon or cookie (or ice cream) scoop, drop the batter in golf ball–sized rounds onto the chicken, spacing them evenly and leaving a bit of room in between for expansion. Place the chicken and biscuits in the oven and bake for 15 to 18 minutes, until the biscuits are golden brown. Remove from the oven and serve hot or warm.

*If you decide to use leftover cooked turkey or chicken, you'll need 2 to 2¼ pounds of boneless, skinless meat, which is between 6 and 7 cups of meat.

nutrition information per serving ¹⁄₁₂ **of pie, 181g**

413 cal | 24.9g fat | 25g protein | 18g complex carbohydrates | 1g sugar | 1g dietary fiber | 101mg cholesterol | 609mg sodium | 241mg potassium | 74RE vitamin A | 2mg iron | 152mg calcium | 216mg phosphorus

Pizza Rustica

ONE 10-INCH PIE, 8 SUBSTANTIAL SERVINGS

Pizza rustica is a savory, deep-dish pie, native to Italy, which bears little resemblance to the flat pizzas we're used to in this country. The traditional pizza rustica incorporates ham, cheese, eggs, and a white sauce in a rich pastry shell. However, there are as many variations on this dish as there are Italian bakers. This version, featuring a buttery crust and vegetable-cheese filling, has been a take-along favorite of ours for some years now. Sliced pepperoni is a nice addition to the filling. Bake it, enjoy some warm from the oven (not hot; let it cool a bit so the cheeses firm up), then refrigerate the remainder to pack for a picnic.

One 9-inch double piecrust

FILLING
5 large eggs
2 cups (1 pound) ricotta cheese, whole-milk* or part-skim
1 small onion (4 ounces), chopped
1 cup (3½ ounces) grated Parmesan cheese
1 tablespoon chopped parsley
½ teaspoon salt (more or less, to taste)
½ teaspoon coarsely ground black pepper

2 tablespoons (1 ounce) olive oil
4 large garlic cloves (about 1 tablespoon chopped)
2 cups (16 ounces) tomato sauce
1 tablespoon granulated sugar
½ teaspoon dried oregano
½ teaspoon dried basil
⅔ cup (2¼ ounces) sliced black olives
1 large green bell pepper (about 8 ounces)
2 cups (8 ounces) shredded mozzarella cheese

FILLING Beat the eggs and stir in the ricotta cheese, onion, Parmesan, parsley, salt and pepper. Set aside.

Heat the oil in a frying pan. Crush or dice the garlic and add it to the hot oil, frying until golden. Stir in the tomato sauce, sugar, oregano, and basil. Add the olives and simmer for 5 minutes.**

Preheat the oven to 425°F.

Core and seed the green pepper and slice into thin matchsticks.

Divide the crust into two pieces. Roll out the first piece and fit into a 10-inch deep-dish pie pan.*** Sprinkle a little milk (about 1 teaspoon) into the crust and spread it around with your fingers; this helps seal the crust and keeps it from becoming soggy.

Spread half the ricotta-Parmesan mixture on the crust. Sprinkle on half the mozzarella, then spread with half the sauce and top with half the green pepper. Repeat layers.

Roll out the top crust and place it over the filling, pinching all around to seal securely. Use a sharp knife to make three parallel slashes in the top crust.

Bake for 35 to 40 minutes, until the crust is golden and filling is bubbling. Remove from the oven and let stand at least 30 minutes before serving (if you don't wait, your filling ingredients will flow like lava as soon as you slice the pie). Store in the refrigerator; serve warm, at room temperature, or cold.

*If you're using whole-milk ricotta and it seems watery, drain it first in a very fine strainer or in cheesecloth. Using part-skim mozzarella cheese and part-skim ricotta cheese will lower fat to 36 grams.

**If you wish to skip all this, simply substitute a 16-ounce jar of spaghetti or pizza sauce for the oil, garlic, tomato sauce, sugar and spices.

***You can also use a 10-inch springform pan; if you do, make the first piece of dough slightly larger to go up the walls of the pan.

nutrition information per serving   1 serving, 292 g

607 cal | 42g fat | 25g protein | 30g complex carbohydrates | 2g sugar | 4g dietary fiber | 272mg cholesterol | 1327mg sodium | 450 mg potassium | 23mg vitamin C | 5mg iron | 519mg calcium | 394mg phosphorus

Winter Vegetable Pie

ONE 9-INCH PIE, 10 SERVINGS

This plain-sounding dish is greater than the sum of its parts. Does cooked cabbage bring to mind evil odors and bland flavor? Banish the thought! The shredded cabbage in this pie pairs pleasingly with mushrooms, onions, and herbs, and is enhanced by the smoothness of cream cheese and hard-boiled eggs. Though not exactly low-cal, this pie definitely warms the belly on a cold night.

One 9-inch double piecrust

FILLING

3 tablespoons (1½ ounces) butter

3 cups (11 ounces, ½ small head) coarsely shredded cabbage, lightly packed

1¼ cups (1 medium, 5½ ounces) chopped onion

1 teaspoon dried basil

1 teaspoon salt

½ teaspoon ground black pepper

3 cups (8 ounces) sliced mushrooms

½ cup (4 ounces) cream cheese, softened

4 large hard-boiled eggs, sliced ¼ inch thick

½ teaspoon dried dill weed

Melt 2 tablespoons of the butter in a large skillet. Add the cabbage and onions and sauté until the cabbage is wilted and the onions are soft. Stir in the basil, salt, and pepper. Spoon into a bowl.

Melt the remaining tablespoon of butter and sauté the mushrooms until they release their juices and shrink to about half their original size. Stir the mushrooms into the cabbage mixture.

Preheat the oven to 400°F.

Roll one pastry disk into an 11- to 12-inch circle and fit it into a 9-inch pie plate. Gently spread the softened cream cheese over the bottom, then layer on the sliced eggs. Sprinkle lightly with dill. Spoon the cabbage mixture on top. Roll out the remaining crust and place it over the filling. Seal and crimp the edges of the crust and slice a few vents in the top.

Bake the pie for 15 minutes, then lower the oven heat to 350°F and continue to bake for another 20 to 25 minutes, until the crust is lightly browned.

nutrition information per serving | **1 slice, 159g**

361 cal | 26g fat | 8g protein | 24g complex carbohydrates | 2g dietary fiber | 129mg cholesterol | 394mg sodium | 273mg potassium | 135RE vitamin A | 12mg vitamin C | 2mg iron | 47mg calcium | 118mg phosphorus

Quiche

What's the difference between pie and quiche (aside from the fact that Real Men Don't Eat Quiche, while one can assume they do deign to eat pie)? Both are round, rather flat pastry crusts filled with vegetables/fruits/dairy products in an array of varying combinations. Most often a pie is perceived as sweet, a quiche as savory; but then chicken pot pie comes along to throw off the equation.

We've come to the conclusion that pies can be either sweet or savory, while quiches are always savory. Pies are usually baked in pie pans, while quiches can be baked in either pie pans or wider, shallower tart pans. A quiche can be thought of as a savory custard tart. Originating in France's Alsace-Lorraine, quiche is nearly as boundless in its variety as fruit pie; meats and vegetables play an equal role in lending quiche its versatility.

Quiche usually contains cheese, and cheese is one of the interchangeable elements in this flexible dish. We like to team a mild cheese, such as Swiss, with more assertive vegetables, such as onions. On the other hand, a rather bland vegetable like zucchini teams well with a stronger-tasting cheese, such as sharp cheddar. You can use 2 cups of thick salsa in place of the vegetables and add Monterey Jack cheese. Top with a thin layer of milk-thinned sour cream and an additional sprinkling of Monterey Jack before baking, if desired.

Preparing Vegetables for Quiche

We find that cooking vegetables before using them in quiche results in better flavor; this is true of all vegetables except tomatoes, which can be used raw but do need to be seeded and squeezed fairly dry. Slice or dice vegetables, then sauté in a bit of olive oil until lightly browned, seasoning sparingly with salt and less sparingly with pepper. Drain, cool, and add to quiche custard.

Alternatively, you can "oven-sauté" vegetables. This is an ideal method for cooking lots of vegetables at once; use what you want in quiche, then save the rest for pasta sauce or as a tasty dish in themselves.

First, slice, dice, or cut vegetables into wedges. Carrots or other very hard vegetables should be cut into ¼-inch slices; zucchini, summer squash, and eggplant into thicker (½-inch) slices; onions and tomatoes can be cut in wedges, and small vegetables, such as cherry tomatoes and green beans, can be left whole. Coat a large cookie sheet (with sides) or other large pan with a thin layer of olive oil; place vegetables in a single layer in the pan. Drizzle additional olive oil over the vegetables. Bake at 400°F for about 1 hour, or in a cooler oven for a longer amount of time, until golden.

When the vegetables start piling up at the end of the summer, we like to throw a pan in the oven every time we bake something. When nothing else is in the oven, we cook vegetables at about 275°F for a couple of hours, then leave them in the turned-off oven for an hour or so. The point is, you want them to give up their moisture and become golden brown and slightly pliable, like dried apricots; preparing vegetables in this method really heightens their flavor and natural sweetness. Turn the vegetables with a spatula partway through their time in the oven. You'll find they will have shrunk considerably and can be moved into the center of the pan, away from the edges, where they tend to burn. When vegetables are done, remove from oven and store in the refrigerator.

Basic Vegetable Quiche

ONE 9-INCH QUICHE, 8 SERVINGS

One 9-inch single piecrust

1 cup (4 ounces) grated cheese, or more, if desired

1½ cups (12 ounces) buttermilk*

3 large eggs

3 tablespoons (¾ ounce) unbleached all-purpose flour

½ teaspoon salt

½ to 1 teaspoon dried, crumbled herbs (basil, Italian seasoning, oregano, marjoram)

1 teaspoon minced garlic (optional)

2 cups cut-up and sautéed vegetables

1 cup (4 ounces) additional grated cheese (optional)

Preheat the oven to 425°F.

Roll out piecrust and fit it into a 9-inch pie or 10-inch tart pan. Trim edges and crimp decoratively. Sprinkle with a thin layer of the cheese; this seals the crust, preventing it from becoming soggy. Set aside.

In a mixing bowl, combine buttermilk, eggs, flour, and salt. Beat until well mixed. Stir in herbs, garlic, vegetables, and cheese.

Pour vegetable mixture into prepared crust. Sprinkle with additional cheese, if desired. Bake on the bottom rack for 15 minutes, then reduce heat to 350°F and bake an additional 35 to 40 minutes, or until crust is golden brown. Remove from oven and cool completely on a wire rack. Store in the refrigerator.

*Buttermilk teams especially well with cheese, but you can use regular milk or cream, if you prefer.

nutrition information per serving   **1 slice, without extra cheese, 162g**

229 cal | 12g fat | 10g protein | 19g complex carbohydrates | 1g dietary fiber | 103mg cholesterol | 349mg sodium | 188mg potassium | 106RE vitamin A | 2mg vitamin C | 1mg iron | 209mg calcium | 186mg phosphorus

Quiche Lorraine

ONE 9- OR 10-INCH QUICHE, 6 SERVINGS

Quiche Lorraine, a rich, eggy cheese custard cradling bacon, eggs, ham, and chives in a golden crust, is another one of those dishes that made an elegant splash in the fifties. Like pizza, its popularity in this country sprang from returning World War II veterans, who'd enjoyed it in France—particularly Paris, once that city was liberated. The notion of quiche was attractive to American wives; back then everyone could make a pie, so it was no big deal to change the filling from sweet to savory.

Cold quiche makes a wonderful, elegant picnic dish served with a salad and with cookies or fresh fruit for dessert. You may choose to bring a whole quiche (keep it cool) and slice it just before serving, or prepare individual quiches in the cups of a muffin pan. Feel free to lighten it up by substituting milk for the cream, but why not just eat a smaller slice and enjoy it at its creamy best?

One 9-inch single piecrust

¼ pound bacon (about 5 slices), diced

½ large onion, diced (3 to 4 ounces, a generous ¾ cup)

¼ pound ham, diced (a generous ¾ cup)

1 cup (8 ounces) milk

1 cup (8 ounces) heavy cream

½ teaspoon salt

¼ teaspoon ground black pepper

3 large eggs

2 tablespoons (about ⅛ ounce) fresh or freeze-dried chives

1 cup (4 ounces) shredded Swiss, Gruyère, or sharp cheddar cheese

Roll out the pastry dough to a circle 2 to 3 inches larger than the pan you're using. Place the crust into a lightly greased 9-inch pie pan or 10-inch tart or quiche pan. Build up the edges of the crust by folding excess dough under and then crimping it. Prick the bottom with a fork every 2 inches. Brush with lightly beaten egg white; this will help the crust remain crisp. Using another pie pan or pie weights, partially blind-bake the crust in a preheated 425°F oven for 15 minutes. Set the crust aside. Turn the oven down to 350°F.

FILLING Sauté the bacon until crisp. Pour off as much fat as possible, then add the onion and cook until soft. Add the ham and brown slightly. Remove from the heat and set aside.

In a medium-sized saucepan, heat the milk and cream with the salt and pepper until the mixture is just below a simmer. Remove from the heat. Add some of the hot cream to the eggs, beat well, then stir the hot cream and egg mixture into the hot cream.

Layer the bacon mixture into the baked pie shell. Pour the egg and cream mixture into the shell, then sprinkle with chives and cheese.

Bake the quiche for 35 to 40 minutes. Be careful not to overbake it or it will be watery; the quiche is done when a knife inserted in the center comes out clean, though the center is still wobbly. The temperature should register 160°F to 165°F on an instant-read thermometer. Don't be tempted to turn up the oven if the quiche seems to be taking a long time; the time from not sufficiently cooked to overbaked is short. Allow the quiche to cool for 15 minutes before serving.

nutrition information per serving   **1 slice, 201g**

550 cal | 40g fat | 21g protein | 22g complex carbohydrates | 1g dietary fiber | 283mg cholesterol | 904mg sodium | 318mg potassium | 379RE vitamin A | 12mg vitamin C | 2mg iron | 223mg calcium | 302mg phosphorus

Quiche Bites

72 QUICHE BITES

Looking for perfect hors d'ouevres for that special party? These bites will be a huge hit. When making your pastry, remember to roll it out very thin and cut it into circles twice as wide as the bottom of the muffin cup you are using. Keep chilled until ready to use. These can be made up to a month ahead, and frozen (well-wrapped) until needed.

2 batches Cream Cheese Pastry Dough (p. 459) or Favorite Tender Crust (p. 418) cut into 2½-inch circles, or a 9-inch double piecrust

2 tablespoons (1 ounce) butter

3 cups (12 ounces) thinly sliced leeks, well washed and drained

½ to ¾ pound smoked trout or smoked salmon

6 large eggs

1 quart (32 ounces) half-and-half

½ teaspoon Worcestershire sauce

½ teaspoon freshly ground black pepper

4 cups (1 pound) grated cheddar cheese

Preheat the oven to 375°F.

In a large sauté pan over medium heat, melt the butter and add the leeks. Cook for 4 to 5 minutes, until they are soft and bright green in color. Set them aside to cool. Break the smoked fish into bite-sized pieces. Grease either regular or mini-sized muffin tins, then line with circles of pastry dough using your favorite recipe. (For a tip on technique, see illustrations on p. 459). Put in the freezer to chill for 5 minutes.

Gently whisk together the eggs, half-and-half, Worcestershire, and ground pepper. Take pastry out of freezer and put a bit of the leeks and trout in each cup. Top with a small bit of cheese and fill to top of pastry with egg mixture.

Bake for 15 to 20 minutes, slightly longer for the larger quiches, until the custard is puffy and slightly browned. Remove from pan to cool. Serve warm or chilled.

nutrition information per serving   **1 mini-quiche, 35g**

80 cal | 6g fat | 3g protein | 3g complex carbohydrates | 30mg cholesterol | 106mg sodium | 42mg potassium | 42RE vitamin A | 65 mg calcium | 62mg phosphorus

Spinach Quiche

ONE 9-INCH QUICHE, 8 SERVINGS

This vegetarian-friendly quiche, enriched with two types of cheese and topped with a sumptuous layer of sour cream, is a meal in itself. Add a salad and some warm bread and you'll hardly mind that it's snowing yet again.

One 9-inch single piecrust

1 medium onion, diced (about 5 ounces, 1 cup)

2 cups (1 pound) whole-milk* or part-skim ricotta cheese

½ teaspoon salt

Pinch of thyme

3 large eggs, beaten

One 10-ounce box frozen chopped spinach, thawed and thoroughly squeezed dry

3 tablespoons (¾ ounce) unbleached all-purpose flour

1 cup (4 ounces) grated Swiss or Gruyère cheese

Dash of nutmeg

TOPPING

1 cup (8 ounces) sour cream

Paprika (optional)

Preheat the oven to 375°F.

Sauté the onion in 2 tablespoons butter until it's soft and golden brown. Remove it from the heat and combine with the remaining filling ingredients, stirring until well combined.

Spoon the filling into the unbaked piecrust. Spread evenly with the sour cream. Sprinkle with paprika, if desired.

Bake the quiche for 50 to 55 minutes, until it appears set almost all the way into the center. Remove from the oven and serve warm.

*If you use whole-milk ricotta and it seems watery, drain it in a fine sieve or cheesecloth before using.

nutrition information per serving   1 slice, 186g

329 cal | 22g fat | 15g protein | 18g complex carbohydrates | 1g dietary fiber | 130mg cholesterol | 467mg sodium | 280mg potassium | 401RE vitamin A | 4mg vitamin C | 2mg iron | 339mg calcium | 287mg phosphorus

Pastry and Viennoiserie

The Coupe du Monde de la Boulangerie, a worldwide competition involving a dozen national baking teams from a variety of countries, is held every three years in Paris. "The bread-baking Olympics," as it's termed, is an event that attracts the world's most ardent bread aficionados, professional and amateur alike. If you love homemade bread—particularly artisan European-style bread, bread made with natural leavens, given time to develop flavor, and lovingly shaped by hand—the Coupe is your Nirvana. The competition, presided over by a panel of well-known bread-baker judges, encompasses baguettes, that most basic of French breads; viennoiserie, which includes croissants, Danish, and other sweet yeast-raised pastries; and bread sculpture, for which each country completes a display piece—a sculpture or other work of art—from bread dough. Breads and pastries are meticulously graded on the basis of appearance, taste, volume, and weight, so the bakers are clearly vying to produce the absolute perfect loaf, a creation of Olympian properties.

The competition is held in conjunction with a massive baking trade show and occupies one corner of a large hall on the outskirts of Paris. Three large booth/stages, each equipped with identical equipment—mixers and workbenches and ovens—are arrayed side by side. Each booth features a team from a different country, twelve teams in all; each team has eight hours to produce a wide variety of breads within the three classes of competition. Bleachers in front of the booths allow spectators to sit and watch; each national team has its own group of followers filling the bleachers.

It's strangely reminiscent of a ball game to sit in the stands and watch the competition. The fans include the competitors' spouses, many of whom are mirrors of the baseball wives shown on TV, starry-eyed and nervous; and, in many cases, their proud parents as well. Then there are the "bread groupies"—people vying with one another to determine whose knowledge of bread is the most detailed, who knows the most "name" bread bakers, and who's had private tours of which bakeries. As a particularly artful finishing touch is put on an element of the bread sculpture, or as golden brown loaves are pulled crackling hot from the oven, the fans cheer—not unlike baseball fans celebrating a home run. At the end of the competition, silver loving cups are awarded to the top three teams; the bakers stand on stage, basking in the wild applause, conquering heroes of the world of bread.

While many home bakers have happily spent hours reading about and trying to reproduce the perfect baguette, there are very, very few of us who've ever tried our hands at bread sculpture. As for viennoiserie and its sibling, puff pastry (and its cousin, pâte à choux), there are those among us who've made croissants by hand—and those who read about the process, feel absolutely daunted, and buy croissants at the bakery. The following recipes aren't exactly dauntless, but neither are they daunting: if you're a dedicated bread baker, you'll thoroughly enjoy the long (though not particularly difficult) process involved in producing puff pastry, puff dough, and the incredibly flaky, delicate treats made from them.

Pâte Feuilletée: Classic Puff Pastry

Classic puff pastry, the dough used to create the ultimate in French butter pastries, uses essentially the same ingredients (though a bit more butter) as piecrust; it's the way these ingredients are combined that make this dough special.

The French call it pâte feuilletée, (pronounced paht foy yuh TAY), which means "pastry made leaflike." In fact, it has so many "leaves" that it's also called millefeuille (meel FWEE), meaning "a thousand leaves." Each of these leaves consists of a layer of flour separated by a layer of butter. The expansion (puff) occurs because the butter layers create steam when exposed to the heat of an oven, expanding the space between the flour layers. Ultimately, in classic puff pastry, you want to create 729 layers of folded dough—not quite one thousand but, like the millipede (which really doesn't have a thousand legs), the effect is there.

And how do you go about creating 729 layers of folded dough? It's not as challenging as it sounds. As with piecrust, you start by rolling out the dough (into a square, not a circle); but, unlike piecrust, you don't stop there. You add a layer of butter, fold the dough in thirds, roll it into a long rectangle, and fold it in thirds again. You've now completed two "turns"; classic puff pastry is made with six turns, usually with stints in the refrigerator to solidify the butter and relax the flour's gluten. So you see, it's not a difficult process; just somewhat time-consuming.

The thing that's wonderful about puff pastry is that once it's put together and in your refrigerator, it can be made into something elegant and delicious reasonably quickly. A great way to share the joy of baking is to give a friend a block of chilled puff pastry with instructions for shaping and baking it; a gift of both heart and hands.

Classic Puff Pastry: A Primer

2¾ POUNDS OF DOUGH, ENOUGH FOR 24 CROISSANTS

Anyone who can fold a letter in thirds and hold a rolling pin can make puff pastry. We think you'll be surprised at how satisfying it is to create more layers and a more ethereal product with every fold. The first surprise is how malleable butter can be. After that, remember to pay attention to the temperature of both your work area and the butter; give the dough regular time-outs in the refrigerator; and line up your edges as neatly as you can. We'll give you plenty of hints and pictures along the way.

Step 1: Making the Dough

3½ cups (14¾ ounces) unbleached all-purpose flour*

4 tablespoons (½ stick, 2 ounces) chilled butter

1½ teaspoons salt

1¼ cups (10 ounces) cold water

Place the flour in a mixing bowl and combine it with the chilled butter until the mixture resembles cornmeal. Add the salt to the water, stir well, then add to the flour. Mix gently with a fork or a dough whisk (see Tools, p. 595) until you have a rough dough that pulls away from the sides of the bowl. If you need to add more water, do so a tablespoon at a time until the dough holds together. Turn out the dough onto a lightly floured surface and knead until it's smooth and a bit springy, 2 to 3 minutes. Pat it into a square, wrap it in plastic wrap, or place in a large plastic bag and refrigerate for at least 30 minutes.

*You may substitute 1 cup unbleached pastry flour or ½ cup cornstarch for an equal amount of all-purpose flour for a more tender final product.

Step 2: Preparing the Butter

½ cup (2 ounces) unbleached all-purpose flour

1¾ cups (3½ sticks, 14 ounces) butter, softened but still cool to the touch

Using a mixer, a food processor, or a spoon, combine the flour and butter until they are smooth and well blended. Lightly flour a piece of plastic wrap or waxed paper, and on it shape the butter-flour mixture into an 8-inch square. Cover the butter and place it on a flat surface in the refrigerator for at least 30 minutes. Adding flour to the butter helps to stabilize it, so it won't "flow" out the seams when it is being rolled.

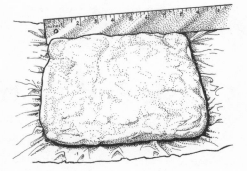

Combine the chilled butter and flour until smooth, then form it into an 8-inch square on a piece of lightly floured plastic wrap. It will be about ¾-inch thick.

Step 3: Rolling and Folding

Have on hand:
flour for dusting
rolling pin

yardstick or tape measure
pastry brush

Remove the dough from the refrigerator and put it on a lightly floured surface. Gently roll it into a square about 12 inches across. Put the butter square in the center of the dough, at a 45-degree angle, so it looks like a diamond in the square.

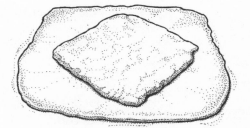

Place the butter on the dough so it's rotated 45 degrees. It will look like a diamond in the square.

Fold the flaps of the dough over the edges of the butter until they meet in the middle. Pinch and seal the edges of the dough together; moisten your fingers with a little water, if necessary. Dust the top with flour, then turn the dough over and tap it gently with the rolling pin into a rectangular shape. Make sure the dough isn't sticking underneath, and roll it from the center out into a larger rectangle, 20 x 10 inches. (The barrel of most standard sized rolling pins is 10 inches long, so when width of the rectangle matches the pin, you're in good shape. You'll need a yardstick to check the rectangle's length.)

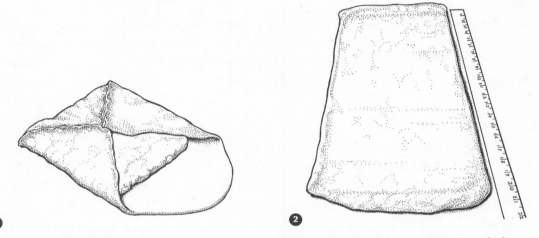

1. Bring the flaps of dough up and over the butter, and pinch the seams to seal them together. Use a little water on your fingers to ensure a tight seal if necessary, and try not to capture any air bubbles inside. **2.** Roll the dough/butter package from the center out into a rectangle 20 x 10 inch rectangle.

When the dough is the right size, lightly sweep off any excess flour from the top with your pastry brush, then fold the bottom third up to the center, and the top third over (like a business letter). Line the edges up on top of each other and even up the corners so they're directly atop one another. Turn the dough package 90 degrees to the right so it looks like a book ready to be opened. It's okay to use a little water to stick the corners together so they don't shift. If the dough is still cool to the touch and relaxed, do another rolling and turning the same way.

If you've successfully rolled out the dough and folded it twice, you've com-

Dusting, dusting . . .

As you work, keep the dough, work surface, and rolling pin well dusted with flour. Turn over the dough from time to time. As you roll you tend to expand the top layers more than the bottom. By flipping it over, you'll even it out. Before folding the dough over on itself, use your pastry brush to sweep off the excess flour. This will help the dough stick to itself when you roll it again, so the layers don't slide around.

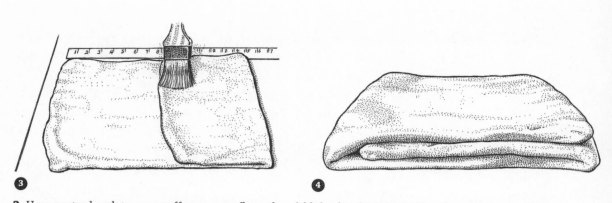

3. Use a pastry brush to sweep off any excess flour, then fold the dough in thirds, like a business letter. Take care to line the outside edges up directly over each other. **4.** Turn the folded dough 90 degrees to the right, so it looks like a book ready to be opened. Be sure the corners are directly lined up over each other. Use a little water to help them stick on top of each other if necessary.

pleted two turns. Make a note of how many folds you've completed and the time, and then put the dough back in the refrigerator. Classic puff pastry gets six turns before being formed into finished shapes and should rest, chilled, for at least 30 minutes between every two turns.

Repeat the above folding and turning process two more times. When all six turns have been completed, wrap the dough well and refrigerate it for at least an hour (preferably overnight) before using. This recipe makes enough for twenty-four 4 x 6-inch pieces of dough, so you may want to take a portion of the folded pastry and freeze it for later. It will keep for 3 to 6 months, as long as it's tightly wrapped and no air gets to its surface in the freezer.

Bubbles and Leaks

It's not unusual to have air trapped inside your laminated dough (dough layered with butter), making an awkward bubble. If this happens, simply pop the bubble with a toothpick and press down the dough with your fingers so it lies flat again. If you find yourself with a bare spot where butter is coming through, dust the leak with flour, pressing down lightly so the flour sticks, and continue on with the fold. Refrigerate the dough as soon as the fold is complete, to firm up the dough and the butter.

Croissants de Pâtissier

12 CROISSANTS

Puff pastry croissants are called "croissants de pâtissier" because they're made by a pastry chef rather than a baker, who would make yeast-based "croissants de boulanger" (see p. 494). Any puff pastry needs to be baked at a high temperature to create the steam that separates the layers of dough. All of that moisture takes some time to cook out, so make sure you don't take your croissants out of the oven until they're a deep golden brown. If they come out of the oven too soon, the centers will still be damp and underdone.

½ recipe Classic Puff Pastry (p. 477)   1 egg beaten with 1 tablespoon water, to glaze

TO SHAPE THE CROISSANTS On a lightly floured surface, roll the dough to a 12 x 18-inch rectangle. Trim the edges of the dough all the way around by using a ruler and cutting straight down with a very sharp knife or a pizza wheel. This cuts off the folded edges that would inhibit the "puff."

Cut the dough in thirds lengthwise and in half through the middle. This will give you six 4 x 9-inch pieces. Cut these pieces in half diagonally and arrange them so the points of the triangles are facing away from you. It's okay to stretch them out slightly to elongate them when you do this. Cut a ½-inch notch in the short edge of the triangle.

If you wish, put a dollop (no more than a heaping teaspoon) of filling (see Fillings, p. 505) in the center. Then roll up each triangle starting with the notched edge, work-

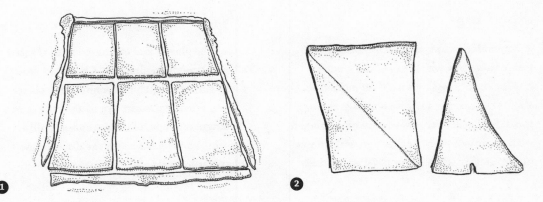

1. Roll the dough to a 12 x 18-inch rectangle, trim the edges with a sharp knife or pizza cutter. Cut the dough in thirds lengthwise, and in half across the middle. **2.** After cutting each piece of dough into two triangles, cut a half-inch notch in the center of the short side, closest to you.

After rolling the croissant, bend the two ends toward the spot where the tip of the dough is tucked under.

ing toward the tip. Make sure the point is tucked under the bottom of the croissant—if you have to stretch the dough a little to do so, that's okay. Form the crescent by bending the two ends toward the place where the dough's tip is tucked under the roll.

Place the croissants on a lightly greased or parchment-lined baking sheet. Cover and chill for at least 30 minutes. During that time, preheat the oven to 425°F.

TO BAKE THE CROISSANTS Take the croissants out of the refrigerator, uncover them, and brush the tops with the beaten egg. Bake for 15 minutes; reduce the heat to 350°F and bake for another 10 to 15 minutes. The croissants should be a deep golden brown, even where the dough overlaps itself. Remove from the oven and cool completely on a wire rack.

nutrition information per serving | 1 unfilled croissant, 52g

205 cal | 15g fat | 2g protein | 15g complex carbohydrates | 1g dietary fiber | 41mg cholesterol | 136mg sodium | 30mg potassium | 143RE vitamin A | 1mg iron | 5mg calcium | 22mg phosphorus

Finishing

When making croissants, it's traditional to finish them in a way that signals what's inside. Plain croissants need no more than the shine they acquire in the oven from the egg wash. Fruit-filled croissants are often glazed with sugar or honey, or drizzled with confectioners' sugar icing. Almond-filled pastries should be glazed and sprinkled with toasted sliced or chopped almonds. Chocolate croissants get a thin stripe of melted chocolate. Savory filled croissants are usually made in a rectangular shape, with just enough filling showing at the ends to let the diner know what waits inside.

Napoleons

16 PASTRIES

Most people assume this delightful combination of crisp pastry layers and creamy filling is in some way connected with Monsieur Bonaparte. Au contraire. The name is a French derivation of the word Neapolitan; this style of pastry was originally made in Naples. It can be made with Classic Puff Pastry or a blitz dough. For filling, any flavored pastry creams will do nicely.

½ recipe Classic Puff Pastry, page 477, or 1 recipe Blitz Puff Pastry, page 486

1 recipe Pastry Cream, page 398

Fresh berries, optional

GLAZE

2 cups (8 ounces) confectioners' sugar

¼ cup (2 ounces) heavy cream or milk

1 teaspoon corn syrup

½ ounce melted unsweetened chocolate

On a lightly floured surface, roll out one half of the dough to a 14-inch square, ⅛ inch thick. Halfway through this process, transfer the dough to a piece of parchment paper, since it's difficult to move once it's been rolled very thin. Transfer the parchment and dough to a flat baking sheet. Prick the dough all over with a fork or a dough docker (see Tools, p. 604), cover with a second sheet of parchment, and let it rest in the refrigerator for at least 30 minutes. Repeat this process with the other half of the dough.

Preheat the oven to 375°F.

After its rest, remove the dough from the refrigerator and place another flat-bottomed baking sheet on top of the parchment. Bake the dough sandwiched between the two pans for 20 minutes. Remove the top sheet pan and the paper underneath it, then return the uncovered pastry to the oven to continue baking for another 10 minutes, until the dough is a deep golden brown and baked all the way through. Remove from the oven and cool the pastry on a rack.

FOR THE GLAZE Place the confectioners' sugar in a bowl and stir in the cream and corn syrup. Remove ¼ cup of the mixture and, in a separate bowl, stir it into the melted chocolate.

TO ASSEMBLE Trim the edges of the cooked dough pieces with a serrated knife using gentle sawing motions, to make two 12-inch squares. Cut each square into thirds, to make a total of six 4-inch-wide strips. Select the two best looking strips of pastry and place them snugged up against each other on a piece of parchment or waxed paper. Pour the white glaze over the top to cover them completely. Smooth the glaze with an icing spatula. Pipe the chocolate glaze in narrow parallel lines across the top. With a toothpick or the tip of a paring knife, draw alternating lines perpendicularly through the chocolate stripes to pull them into a pattern. Carefully place tops on a rack to dry.

Take half of the chilled pastry cream and spread on two of the remaining strips of pastry; it should be about ¾ inch thick. If you're using berries, push them down into this layer, then top with another strip of pastry. Repeat the process for the second layer, then put the iced strips on the top. Put the pastries in the refrigerator for half an hour to set up.

To slice, use a serrated knife to cut the strips into bars 1½ inches wide.

Cover the baked pastry sheets with an even layer of confectioners' sugar glaze. Pipe chocolate glaze in horizontal stripes, ¾-inch apart. With a toothpick or the point of a pairing knife, draw lines in alternating directions through the icing to pull the lines into points, as shown.

nutrition information per serving   **1 napoleon, 96g**

225 cal | 13g fat | 3g protein | 4g complex carbohydrates | 21g sugar | 93mg cholesterol | 69mg sodium | 99mg potassium | 143RE vitamin A | 1mg vitamin C | 73 mg calcium | 79mg phosphorus | 1mg caffeine

Why Take the Puff out of the Pastry?

Why go to all the effort of making puff pastry, only to bake it under the weight of another baking sheet? By limiting the vertical expansion of the layers while baking, they form themselves into an incredibly crisp pastry sheet that can carry the weight of the rich pastry cream on top. Covered baking also allows for slow caramelizing of the dough, yielding a deep, rich flavor. Napoleons are an excellent way to use scraps and trimmings from puff pastry dough, since there's no concern about the dough rising evenly.

Puff Pastry Turnovers

6 TURNOVERS

These turnovers can be assembled with any filling you can think of (see the fillings section of this chapter on p. 505 for some ideas), as long as it's not too loose.

½ recipe Classic Puff Pastry, page 477
¾ cup thick filling of your choice

1 egg beaten with 1 tablespoon water, for glaze

TO SHAPE On a lightly floured surface, roll the dough to a 12 x 18-inch rectangle. Trim it all the way around by pressing straight down with a very sharp knife or a bench knife. Cut the dough in half from top to bottom and in thirds from side to side. This should give you six 6 x 6-inch squares.

TO FILL Put 2 tablespoons of your favorite filling in the center of the dough. Moisten the edges with a bit of water and fold the dough in half diagonally. Press the edges to seal, and make a couple of small cuts in the top crust (to vent steam). Place turnovers on a lightly greased baking sheet, cover, and chill for at least 30 minutes.

Preheat the oven to 425°F.

Before baking, brush the turnovers with the egg glaze. Bake for 15 minutes. Reduce the heat to 350°F and bake for another 15 to 20 minutes, until the turnovers are golden brown. Remove from the oven and cool completely on a rack.

nutrition information per serving   1 turnover, made with apple filling, 53g

140 cal | 9g fat | 2g protein | 10g complex carbohydrates | 3g sugar | 1g dietary fiber | 63mg cholesterol | 97mg sodium | 49mg potassium | 91RE vitamin A | 1mg vitamin C | 1mg iron | 9mg calcium | 31mg phosphorus

Pâte Feuilletée Rapide (Blitz Puff Pastry) and Faux Puff Pastry

As with any process that's time-consuming, someone is bound to come up with a way to save some of that time. Pâte feuilletée rapide—blitz puff pastry—is made with puff pastry ingredients, but the butter is cut into small pieces and added to the dough at the outset. Up to this point, it's much like a buttery piecrust; it strays off the piecrust path when the baker gives it a couple of folds, refrigerates it for 30 minutes or so, then gives it two more folds. The pastry is ready to use after another hour in the fridge. The "blitz" comes from adding the butter right to the dough and leaving out two of classic puff pastry's six turns.

If you don't want to bother with any turns at all, faux puff pastry is the way to go. Flour and chunks of butter are mixed roughly, then held together by sour cream (which also serves to tenderize the flour's gluten). Baking powder gives this dough some added oomph in the oven. While it's nontraditional, and will yield pastry that's not quite as flaky or tender, it's a wonderful boon for the busy baker.

Blitz Puff Pastry

ENOUGH FOR 24 CROISSANTS

As the name implies, this is a quicker way to make very flaky pastry dough. It's a perfectly good dough to use if you want to make napoleons or turnovers, without going through quite as much preparation time as with a classic puff pastry.

3 cups (12¾ ounces) bread flour	1 cup (8 ounces) cold water
1½ cups (3 sticks, 12 ounces) butter, chilled, cut into ½-inch pieces	2 teaspoons salt

Using an electric mixer with the paddle attachment, mix the flour and cold butter in a medium-sized bowl, on low speed, until the mixture forms large chunks. Combine the water and salt and add to the flour-butter mixture. Mix on low speed, just until the dough begins to come together into a shaggy mass. Turn out the dough onto a floured surface and fold it over on itself until it comes together (a bench knife can be helpful with gathering the dough at this point). Form the dough into a block. Wrap in plastic wrap or put in a large plastic bag and refrigerate for 30 minutes. After this rest, remove from the refrigerator and give four letter folds, with rolling, as described on page 478. After the last fold, chill the dough for 30 minutes before using.

Faux Puff Pastry

TWELVE 4-INCH SQUARES OF PASTRY

This pastry is very quick to put together and mimics the flakiness of classic puff pastry. The sour cream gives this dough a markedly tender texture. Be sure to have the butter well chilled before starting.

1½ cups (6¼ ounces) unbleached all-purpose flour

¼ teaspoon salt

½ teaspoon baking powder

1 cup (2 sticks, 8 ounces) cold butter

½ cup (4 ounces) sour cream

In a medium-sized bowl, whisk together the flour, salt, and baking powder. Cut in the butter, leaving it in pea-sized bits, larger than you would for a normal piecrust. If you have a food processor, a few quick pulses is all it takes. Stir in the sour cream; the dough won't be cohesive at this point. Turn it out onto a floured work surface and bring it together with a few quick kneads.

Pat the dough into a square and roll it into an 8 x 10-inch rectangle. Dust both sides of the dough with plenty of flour, fold in three (like a business letter), flip the dough over and give it a 90-degree turn, and repeat the process. Chill the dough in the refrigerator for 30 minutes. Use for turnovers, tart shells, or pastry crusts.

Cheese Twists

ABOUT 3 DOZEN 12- TO 14-INCH TWISTS

Don't you just love it when you discover a recipe that's easy to make, yet yields something that's not only delicious, but gives the appearance of having been difficult to execute? The showman in all of us must want people to "oooh and ahhh," otherwise why the quest for a beautifully decorated cake, a pie topped with intricate pastry cutouts, or a dessert plate garnished with drizzles of raspberry syrup and a delicate sprinkle of powdered sugar? Surely the cake or pie or dessert would taste as good without the decoration, but the overall impression would certainly be lacking.

PASTRY
2 recipes Faux Puff Pastry, above, or
1 recipe Blitz Puff Pastry, page 486

FILLING
1½ cups (5¼ ounces) grated Parmesan cheese

2 teaspoons paprika
¼ teaspoon cayenne, or to taste*

EGG WASH
2 large eggs
2 tablespoons (1 ounce) water

FOR THE FILLING Combine the Parmesan, paprika, and cayenne and set aside.

FOR THE EGG WASH Beat the eggs with the water in a small bowl, and set aside.

Preheat the oven to 400°F.

ASSEMBLY Divide the dough into two pieces. Working with one piece at a time, roll it out to a 12 x 24-inch rectangle ⅛ inch thick. Brush the entire surface with egg wash. Sprinkle half of the filling evenly over half of the dough. Fold the dough without filling on it over to make a 12-inch square, and roll it lengthwise, until the two halves stick together. You should have a rectangle of dough about 12 x 13 inches. Repeat this process with the second piece of dough.

Using a rolling pizza cutter or a sharp knife, cut the dough crosswise into ¾-inch-wide strips, so that you have about 17 strips. Pick up a dough strip and twist the ends in opposite directions until the dough is a spiraled cylinder. Place the twists on a lightly greased or parchment-lined baking sheet and repeat with the remaining dough. Brush the tops lightly with egg wash, then sprinkle with salt. Bake the twists for 15 to 18 minutes, until they're golden brown. Remove from the oven and cool them on a wire rack. Serve in a long bread basket or arrayed upright in a tall, thin glass canister or vase.

*This amount yields a twist that is noticeably but not assertively hot. Reduce or increase the amount of cayenne as you see fit.

nutrition information per serving   **1 twist, 34g**

153 cal | 13g fat | 2g protein | 8g complex carbohydrates | 46mg cholesterol | 40mg sodium | 31mg potassium |
131RE vitamin A | 12mg calcium | 23RE phosphorus

Mini Elephant Ears

48 SMALL PASTRIES

These flat, crunchy, sweet pastry spirals are a delicious accompaniment to fresh berries.

2¼ cups (9½ ounces) unbleached all-purpose flour

1 tablespoon dough relaxer (optional, but very helpful)

¼ teaspoon salt

½ teaspoon baking powder

¾ cup (1½ sticks, 6 ounces) unsalted butter, cut into ¼-inch dice and frozen for 30 minutes

¾ cup (6 ounces) sour cream

½ to ¾ cup (3½ to 5¼ ounces) sugar

In a medium-sized bowl, combine the flour, dough relaxer, salt, and baking powder, then cut in the frozen butter, mixing until even crumbs form. Stir in the sour cream and gather the dough into a ball. Divide it in half, then cover and refrigerate for at least 1 hour, or overnight.

Remove one piece of the dough from the refrigerator, sprinkle your work surface heavily with sugar, and roll the dough into a 12 x 10-inch rectangle. Sprinkle more sugar over the dough and gently press it in with a rolling pin. Starting with the long sides, roll the edges of the pastry toward each other until they meet in the center, like a scroll. Repeat with remaining dough, wrap the scrolls, and refrigerate for at least 1 hour.

Preheat the oven to 425°F.

Using a serrated knife, gently cut each scroll into ⅓-inch-thick slices and lay the slices on parchment-lined or lightly greased baking sheets.

Bake the pastries for 9 to 10 minutes, until the sugar on the bottom has begun to brown. Turn them over and bake for an additional 3 to 5 minutes, until the sugar is lightly browned on the other side. Watch closely—these go from golden brown to scorched in nothing flat. Remove the pastries from the oven and cool completely on a rack.

nutrition information per serving | 2 mini ears, 30g

124 cal | 7g fat | 1g protein | 8g complex carbohydrates | 5g sugar | 19mg cholesterol | 38mg sodium | 30mg potassium | 70RE vitamin A | 1mg iron | 18mg calcium | 22mg phosphorus

Kringle

THREE 10-INCH-DIAMETER KRINGLES, 16 SLICES EACH

In the Midwest, and particularly in Wisconsin (and especially in Racine, Wisconsin), kringle is a staple item in many bakeries. It's a festive confection, comprised of a dinner-plate-sized ring of flaky sweet dough enclosing any of a variety of filling flavors. There are all kinds of recipes for this pastry. Some are based on yeast doughs, some have a quick-bread base, and another uses sour cream and butter to make a very flaky, tender pastry. This is the recipe we like the best.

You can experiment with different fillings (raspberry jam and caramel are two that are often used). Since this recipe makes three kringles, you can have two very impressive gifts to give away, with a third kringle for your own family to enjoy. The dough is very simple to put together, but requires gentle handling and thorough chilling, as it's quite soft. Kringles originally came from Denmark and were formed into a pretzel shape, which has since evolved to a more simple wreath shape. In some places you'll find kringle in an oblong form more like a stollen. No matter what shape it comes in, it's a welcome sight around the holiday table.

DOUGH

2 cups (8½ ounces) unbleached all-purpose flour, sifted

½ teaspoon salt

1 cup (2 sticks, 8 ounces) butter

1 cup (8 ounces) sour cream

NUT FILLING

(enough for one kringle)*

4 tablespoons (½ stick, 2 ounces) butter

½ cup (4 ounces) light brown sugar

¼ cup (1 ounce) flour

½ cup (2 ounces) walnuts or pecans

½ cup (3 ounces) raisins (optional)

TOPPING (ENOUGH FOR ALL THREE KRINGLES)

1 egg white

½ cup (3¾ ounces) Demerara or coarse white sugar

½ cup (2 ounces) finely chopped nuts (pulse in food processor)

FOR THE DOUGH In a medium-sized bowl, whisk together the flour and salt. Cut in the butter until the mixture resembles coarse crumbs. Stir in the sour cream to create a soft dough. Wrap well and refrigerate overnight.

FOR THE FILLING Bring the butter to room temperature, then mix with the remaining ingredients. Cover and refrigerate until you're ready to assemble the kringles. Bring the filling back to room temperature before using it, or it will tear the dough when you try to shape it.

Preheat the oven to 375°F.

TO ASSEMBLE Take the kringle dough out of the refrigerator and divide it in thirds (each piece should weigh about 9½ ounces). Put two pieces back in the refrigerator. Take a 24-inch long piece of parchment and lightly flour the surface. Put the dough on the paper and lightly sprinkle it and your hands with flour. Roll the dough into a long,

5 x 26-inch strip (it helps to go diagonally on your sheet of parchment; the strip will hang over the ends by an inch or so, but that's okay). Be sure to pick up the dough from time to time and sprinkle more flour underneath as necessary to keep it from sticking. With a dry pastry brush, carefully sweep any excess flour off the surface of the dough. Place the filling down the center of the dough, in a strip about an inch wide. Gently take the edge closest to you (a bowl scraper or bench knife can help you here) and fold it up and over the filling. Brush the edge of the dough farthest away from you with egg white. Next, fold that edge to overlap the first, making a slightly flat, filled tube of dough. Brush off any excess flour, then carefully shape the dough into a circle. Seal the open ends together and brush the kringle with lightly beaten egg white. Sprinkle the top with the mixture of sugar and chopped nuts. Trim off excess parchment, and slide the kringle, riding on the parchment, onto a baking sheet. Repeat the process with the other two pieces of dough, varying the fillings as you like.

Bake for 25 minutes, or until evenly golden brown. Remove from the oven and cool on a rack. If desired, dust with confectioners' sugar before serving.

*Fill the others with preserves of your choice and/or Raisin or Nut Cinnamon Filling (see p. 506).

nutrition information per serving   nut filling ,1 slice, 29g

137 cal | 10g fat | 1g protein | 5g complex carbohydrates | 7g sugar | 19mg cholesterol | 26mg sodium | 57mg potassium | 68RE vitamin A | 1mg iron | 15mg calcium | 24mg phosphorus

Puff Dough
(laminated yeast dough)

ENOUGH FOR 24 CROISSANTS OR 2 COFFEECAKES

This is the version of puff pastry found in France at the boulangerie, or bakery, as opposed to the classic puff pastry made at the pâtisserie (pastry shop). Sometimes it's sweet; sometimes it's not. But it, too, has many layers of butter rolled into it—not quite as many as puff pastry, but enough so that it's yeast dough at its most elegant. Yeasted puff dough is incredibly light, but has more body than classic puff pastry. It can be made into Danish pastries, croissants, coffeecakes, or any number of pastries. The great advantage of this kind of dough is that once it's made, you can keep it for several days in the refrigerator, or you can even freeze it until the right occasion inspires you. It's easy to roll out, fill, and bake into a breakfast fit for the gods.

DOUGH

2 large eggs plus enough warm water to make 2 cups liquid (16 ounces)

¼ cup (1¾ ounces) sugar

5½ to 6 cups (23¼ to 25½ ounces) unbleached all-purpose flour

2¼ teaspoons instant yeast

½ cup (2½ ounces) nonfat dry milk (optional, but will make a mellower, richer dough)

1 scant tablespoon salt

1 teaspoon vanilla extract (if making sweet pastry)

2 tablespoons (1 ounce) butter, melted

BUTTER

1¾ cups (3¾ sticks, 14 ounces) chilled butter

½ cup (2⅛ ounces) unbleached all-purpose flour

Flour for sprinkling

FOR THE DOUGH Make a sponge by cracking the eggs into a 2-cup liquid measure and adding enough warm water to equal 2 cups. Beat until blended and pour into a large mixing bowl or the bowl of your electric mixer. Add 1 tablespoon of the sugar, 3 cups of the flour, and the yeast. Mix until well blended. Cover and set aside at room temperature.

In a separate mixing bowl, blend together 2½ cups of the remaining flour, the dry milk, and the salt. Set it aside.

FOR THE BUTTER Mix the butter and ½ cup flour until they're smooth and well blended. You can do this with a mixer, a food processor, or with a spoon, by hand. Lightly flour a piece of plastic wrap or parchment, place the butter-flour mixture on it, and pat it into an 8-inch square (see illustration, p. 478). Cover the butter and place it in the refrigerator on a flat surface for at least 30 minutes. Adding flour to the butter helps to stabilize it so it won't "flow" out the seams when it's being rolled.

Turn your attention back to the dough. The yeast should have gotten to work and made the sponge bubbly and expanded by now. Give it a stir and blend in the vanilla and the melted butter. Stir in the flour-milk-salt mixture, mixing until you have a soft but kneadable dough.

Sprinkle flour on your kneading surface, turn out the dough, and knead for 8 to 10 minutes, until it's bouncy and elastic. Wrap loosely and refrigerate for 30 minutes. You can also knead this dough in an electric mixer or in a bread machine.

MAKING THE TURNS Follow the procedure for Classic Puff Pastry, page 477, giving a total of four turns to the dough. Wrap the dough loosely after its last turn, since the yeast will cause it to expand. Refrigerate for at least 2 hours, but preferably overnight.

Use to make croissants (see Croissants de Boulanger, p. 494) or a filled coffeecake.

nutrition information per serving | **1 plain croissant, 61g**

223 cal | 16g fat | 3g protein | 15g complex carbohydrates | 2g sugar | 1g dietary fiber | 68mg cholesterol | 277mg sodium | 43mg potassium | 155RE vitamin A | 1mg vitamin C | 1mg iron | 8 mg calcium | 37mg phosphorus

Filled Coffeecake

1 COFFEECAKE, 16 SERVINGS

½ recipe Puff Dough (see p. 491)

1 recipe filling of your choice (see fillings, p. 505)

Egg wash made from 1 large egg beaten with 1 tablespoon milk

Sugar for topping (optional)

Remove the dough from the refrigerator and roll it into an 8 x 22-inch rectangle. Spread the filling over the dough, leaving ½ inch of dough uncovered on the long sides of the rectangle, but spreading it all the way up to the short ends.

Starting with the long edge with filling, roll the dough into a tube. Shape it into a circle, and place on a piece of parchment. Bring the ends together and tuck one inside the other, pinching the dough together to seal it.

With kitchen shears or a sharp knife, cut through the ring, leaving the inside inch around the center intact. Turn the slices on their sides, overlapping them. Place the coffeecake on a baking sheet or into a greased 9 x 2-inch round pan. Cover and let rise at room temperature for 1 to 1½ hours, until the dough is puffy. Don't worry if it hasn't doubled; it will rise quite a bit during baking.

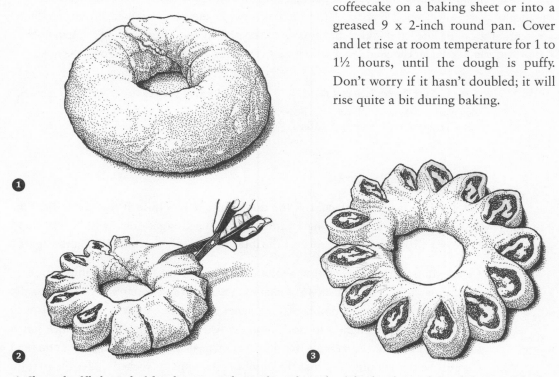

1. Shape the filled spiral of dough into a circle, pinching the ends of the dough together tightly to seal them. Use a little water on your fingers to help, if needed. **2.** Cut through the dough every 1½ inches, leaving a 1-inch strip of dough intact at the center. **3.** Twist the slices to lie on their sides, overlapping them to form a pinwheel shape.

Preheat the oven to 375°F.

After the dough has risen, brush the top with egg wash and sprinkle with sugar. Bake for 30 to 35 minutes, until the top is evenly browned and the internal temperature of the dough has reached 190°F.

nutrition information per serving   1 slice, made with cinnamon raisin or nut filling, 36g

150 cal | 4g fat | 1g protein | 10g complex carbohydrates | 13g sugar | 1mg fiber | 19mg cholesterol | 83mg sodium | 132mg potassium | 62RE vitamin A | 21mg calcium | 18mg phosphorus

Croissants de Boulanger

24 CURVED OR 18 RECTANGULAR CROISSANTS

The croissants found at bread bakers' shops in France are made with laminated yeast dough. Their texture is a bit sturdier and more flexible than those made from puff pastry, which is so flaky it practically shatters when pulled apart. The bread baker's croissant can be shaped into the familiar crescent, or it can be filled and folded into a rectangle before baking. These rectangles often hold a bar of chocolate (pain au chocolat), and wear a zebra stripe of chocolate drizzled over the top.

1 recipe Puff Dough (see p. 491)
Egg wash made from 2 large eggs beaten with 2 tablespoons (1 ounce) water

Fillings of your choice (see fillings section, p. 505)

Preheat the oven to 400°F.

On a lightly floured surface, roll the dough into a 12 x18-inch rectangle. Trim the edges all the way around using a yardstick, cutting straight down with a very sharp knife or a pizza wheel. This cuts off the folded edges, which would inhibit the "puff."

Cut the dough in thirds lengthwise and in half across the middle (see illustration, p. 481). This should give you six 4 x 9-inch squares. Cut these squares in half diagonally and arrange them so the points of the triangles are facing away from you. It's okay to stretch them out slightly to elongate them when you do this. Cut a ½-inch notch in the short edge of the triangle (see illustration, p. 481). Roll the dough from this end toward the tip, making sure that the point of the dough is tucked under the bottom of the croissant. Push the outside edges toward the center to form the crescent shape.

PROOFING AND BAKING Place the croissants on a parchment-lined baking sheet, use a proof cover or greased plastic wrap to cover them, and let rise until almost doubled in size.

Preheat the oven to 400°F. When fully proofed (20 to 30 minutes), brush the croissants with egg wash, then bake for 18 to 22 minutes, until they're a deep golden brown, even where the layers of dough overlap; if underdone, they'll have moist and spongy centers. An instant-read thermometer should read about 190°F when inserted into the center of one.

---

nutrition information per serving   1 plain croissant, 61g

223 cal | 16g fat | 3g protein | 15g complex carbohydrates | 2g sugar | 1g dietary fiber | 68mg cholesterol | 277mg sodium | 43mg potassium | 155RE vitamin A | 1mg vitamin C | 1mg iron | 8 mg calcium | 37mg phosphorus

Variation   ALMOND CROISSANTS: Roll Almond Filling (p. 505) into a log about ¾ inch in diameter and 3 inches long. Place across the wide part of the triangle and with gentle pressure roll it up. Make sure the point of the pastry ends up on the bottom. Gently curve the ends toward the point of the croissant and transfer it to the baking sheet.

FILLED CROISSANTS: This shape can also be filled with jam or preserves (2 teaspoons per pastry), or raisin, nut, or cinnamon filling (see Raisin or Nut Cinnamon Filling, p. 506).

FILLED SQUARE CROISSANTS: Roll half the dough into a 12 x 18-inch rectangle. Cut in thirds both lengthwise and across its width, to make nine 4 x 6-inch rectangles. Place 2 tablespoons filling on the lower third of each rectangle (see illustration at left). Roll the dough so that the edges stay lined up and the seam is centered underneath. Press down the dough gently.

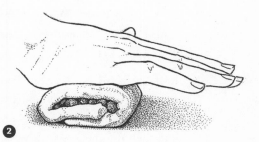

1. Place 2 tablespoons of filling or chocolate on the lower third of the rectangle. **2.** Press the folded croissant to flatten it slightly and keep it from unwinding during baking.

Fillings   CHOCOLATE: Place 1 ounce of chocolate chips or chopped chocolate on the bottom third of the dough before rolling.

FRUIT AND CHEESE: Place a ½-inch strip of jam and another ½-inch strip of cheese filling (p. 215) next to it at the bottom of the rectangle. Shape as directed above.

HAM AND CHEESE: Trim a slice of ham to fit just inside the shape of the rectangle. Cut a slice of cheese to stack two pieces on the lower third of the rectangle. Shape as directed above.

Traditional Danish Pastries

24 DANISH PASTRIES

If there's one pastry that's familiar to just about any American coffee drinker, it's Danish. The version you'll make here is richer, fresher-tasting, and flakier than any but those made by the most traditionally skilled bakeshop bakers.

Make the recipe for Puff Dough, page 491, and include the following spices with the second addition of flour:

½ teaspoon cardamom   ⅛ teaspoon cloves
¼ teaspoon nutmeg

Danish pastry fillings are a matter of personal preference. Two of the most popular are raspberry and cheese. The filling for the raspberry cream cheese braid will work perfectly, see page 215. Other fillings are on pages 505 to 506.

Roll in the butter and give the dough four folds, as demonstrated on pages 478 to 479. Let the dough rest overnight.

Roll one-third of the dough to an 8 x 16-inch rectangle. With a pizza wheel or sharp knife, cut it in half lengthwise and then in quarters widthwise, so you have eight 4-inch squares. For bite-sized pastries, cut each square into four miniature squares.

TO MAKE POCKETS OR ENVELOPES Take the 4-inch squares, egg wash the edges, and place 2 teaspoons of filling in the center. (Be conservative with the amount of filling

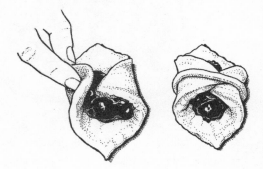

POCKETS Place a spoonful of filling in the center of the dough square. Bring opposite points of the square together to form a pocket shape. Use a strip of scrap dough to "tie" the pocket together.

you place on these small pieces of dough, since it tends to occupy more space than you would think.) For pockets, take the opposite corners and bring them into the center and press them together. Take a scrap piece of dough and wrap around the overlap like a belt to keep it together while it bakes (see illustration, p. 496). For an envelope, bring all four corners of the square to the center and press down to seal. You can put a little more filling on top of the center once the pastry is formed.

TO MAKE PINWHEELS 1. Starting from each corner of the square, make four cuts into the center, stopping about ½ inch from the center itself. **2.** Take the left (or right) side of each corner (make sure it's the same side all the way around), and press it into the center. **3.** After the pastry has risen, brush the top with egg wash, then fill the center with jam or cheese filling just before putting in the oven.

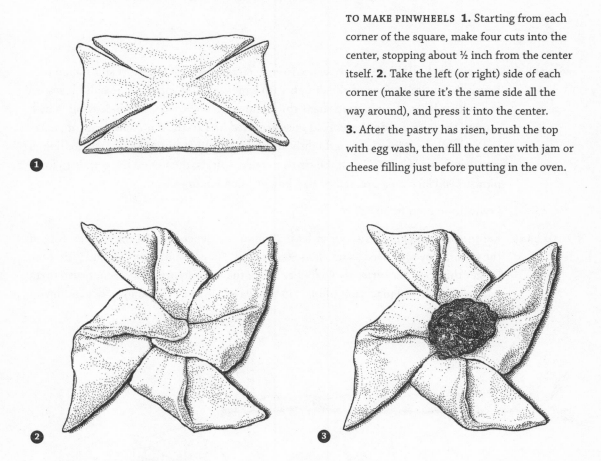

TO MAKE BEAR CLAWS OR COCKSCOMBS (See illustration on next page.) Instead of cutting squares, keep the dough in 4-inch strips. Roll a ½-inch diameter log of Almond Filling, page 505, and place it on the farthest edge of the strip. Egg wash the edge closest to you, roll the dough over the filling toward you, and press the edge together tightly. Roll the tube toward you a quarter turn, to make sure the seam is centered on the bottom, and press the tube flat with your fingers. With a sharp knife or a pair of kitchen scissors, make cuts through the dough every ½ inch or so, stopping where the dough begins to bulge out around the filling. Cut the strip into 4-inch pieces. Place on a baking sheet and bend slightly into a crescent to open the cuts.

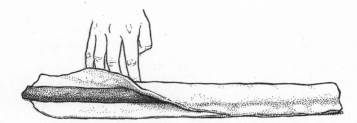

BEAR CLAWS Cut the filled strip of dough with scissors, leaving a ½-inch strip intact along the edge.

TO MAKE FILLED ROUNDS Roll the dough to an 8 x 16-inch rectangle, with the short side facing you. Brush the entire surface of the dough with egg wash and sprinkle the half closest to you with a layer of cinnamon sugar thick enough to cover the dough, leaving ½ inch around the outside edge bare. Fold the uncovered half of the dough toward you, making sure all the edges line up. Lightly roll with a rolling pin to seal. Cut the dough into 1-inch-wide strips. Twist the strips to make spirals, then wind the spirals to form pinwheels. Place on a greased or parchment-lined baking sheet.

Preheat the oven to 400°F.

TO BAKE Let the formed Danish rise for at least 20 minutes; depending on the temperature of the room, they may need as much as 90 minutes. They should look full and puffy; the longer they rise, the airier they will be. When the pastries are fully risen, brush them with egg wash and place any fillings on top. Bake for 18 to 22 minutes, depending on

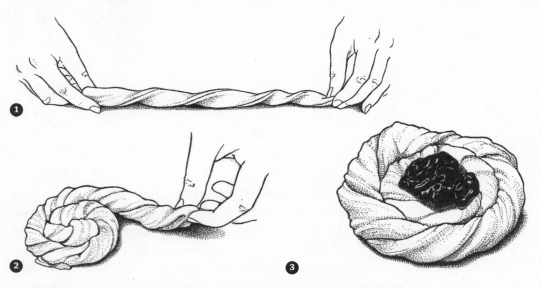

FILLED ROUNDS **1.** Twist the ends of each strip of dough in opposite directions to form a spiral. **2.** Wind the twisted dough around itself like a snail, to form a round Danish. **3.** Place a tablespoon of jam or filling in the center after the dough has risen, just before baking.

the shapes you've chosen. The Danish should be a deep golden brown all over. Remove from the oven, cool on a rack, and glaze or frost as you like (see p. 507).

(see p. 507)

nutrition information per serving   **1 Danish, filled with raspberry jam, 81g**

277 cal | 16g fat | 3g protein | 16g complex carbohydrates | 12g sugar | 1g dietary fiber | 68mg cholesterol | 277mg sodium | 62mg potassium | 155RE vitamin A | 1mg iron | 9mg calcium | 39mg phosphorus

Pâte à Choux: Cream Puff Pastry

3 CUPS, ENOUGH FOR 12 ÉCLAIRS OR 16 CREAM PUFFS

Pâte à choux (paht ah SHOO), which means literally cabbage paste (and refers to the similarity in shape between cream puffs and small cabbages), is also called choux paste, but is most familiarly known to Americans as cream puff pastry. It's a cousin to popover batter, in that both baked products are leavened by steam, which expands them quickly and leaves large holes in their middles, ready to hold your choice of sweet fillings.

Pâte à choux is the basis for cream puffs (filled with whipped cream), éclairs (filled with pastry cream), and profiteroles (filled with ice cream). It's a pastry beloved by dessert-bakers. And of all the pastry recipes explored here, it ranks right up there with faux puff pastry as the easiest to make.

1 cup (8 ounces) water
8 tablespoons (1 stick, 4 ounces) butter
¼ teaspoon salt

1¼ cups (5¼ ounces) unbleached all-purpose flour
4 large eggs

Preheat the oven to 425°F.

Put the water, butter, and salt in a saucepan and bring the mixture to a rolling boil. Remove it from the heat and add the flour all at once. Stir vigorously. Return the pan to the burner and cook over medium heat, stirring all the while, until the mixture forms a ball; this should take only about a minute. Remove the pan from the heat and let the mixture cool for 5 to 10 minutes, to 140°F. It will still feel hot, but you should be able to hold a finger in it for a few seconds. Transfer the dough to a mixer and beat in the eggs one at a time; the mixture will become fluffy. Beat for at least 2 minutes after adding the last egg.

Form the choux paste into whatever shape you desire, using a spoon, or by putting the dough into a pastry bag and piping it.

Bake for 15 minutes, then reduce the oven temperature to 375°F and bake for an additional 15 minutes. Turn off the oven, open the door a crack, and leave the pastry inside to cool for 30 minutes. Remove from the oven to cool completely. Carefully split the pastry, fill, and frost as desired.

nutrition information per serving   **1 unfilled éclair, 40g**

105 cal | 8g fat | 1g protein | 7g complex carbohydrates | 22mg cholesterol | 46mg sodium | 15mg potassium | 75RE vitamin A | 1mg iron | 3mg calcium | 11mg phosphorus

If the Choux Fits

The principle behind choux paste is very simple: a hot oven creates steam, which lifts the dough high before it sets. What you might not know is that the ratio of liquid to flour to eggs is very flexible and can be adjusted depending on the texture you want. You can use amounts ranging from 1 part liquid to 2 parts flour to equal amounts of flour and liquid (all by volume). Using a higher percentage of flour will make a sturdier, more crisp puff, more suitable for a heavy or wet filling. You can also increase crispness by using two egg whites in place of one of the whole eggs.

If you're seeking a tender, ethereal pastry that will be eaten soon after it's filled, use the higher amount of liquid. Our basic choux paste recipe is on this end of the spectrum.

Cream Puffs and Éclairs

16 CREAM PUFFS AND 12 ÉCLAIRS

What is more delightful than these confections composed of crisp choux paste shells and cool, smooth custardy fillings? They're not nearly so difficult to prepare as their appearance might suggest. For best results, assemble these as close in time as you can to serving them, and store them and any leftovers in the refrigerator.

1 recipe prepared Choux Paste (p. 499)

½ recipe Pastry Cream (p. 398)

CHOCOLATE GLAZE FOR ÉCLAIRS

1 tablespoon (½ ounce) butter

1 ounce unsweetened baking chocolate

1 tablespoon (½ ounce) hot water

½ cup (2 ounces) confectioners' sugar

Preheat the oven to 450°F.

To make cream puffs, drop the choux paste by rounded tablespoonfuls (or use the large round tip of a pastry bag to form 1½-inch rounds) on a waxed paper or parchment-lined baking sheet, leaving a bit of space between them. For éclairs, use the large round tip of a pastry bag to shape 3½ x 1-inch fingers on the baking sheet, also leaving a bit of space between them.

Bake the pastries for 15 minutes, then lower the heat to 350°F and bake until the sides are set, about 20 minutes more. Make a small slit in the end of all the pastries and return them to the oven for 5 minutes, for the steam to escape. Cool on racks while you prepare the pastry cream.

When the pastry cream has cooled, cut each cream puff or éclair in half, fill the bottom halves with cream, and replace the top halves.

FOR THE ÉCLAIR GLAZE Melt the butter with the chocolate in a microwave oven or in the top of a double boiler set over simmering water. Remove from the heat. Stir in the water and sugar. Beat with a spoon or fork until the glaze is smooth and soft enough to pour, then drizzle it onto the éclairs.

FOR PROFITEROLES Just before serving, slice cream puffs in half, then fill with a scoop of your favorite ice cream. Replace the top, then drizzle with your favorite chocolate sauce.

nutrition information per serving   **1 cream puff with vanilla pastry cream, 32g**

63 cal | 4g fat | 2g protein | 3g complex carbohydrates | 1g sugar | 52mg cholesterol | 32mg sodium | 27mg potassium | 45RE vitamin A | 21mg calcium | 25mg phosphorus

Spicy Cheese Puffs

60 SMALL PUFFS

These tiny puffs are based on gougère, a French choux-type pastry that's typically flavored with Gruyère cheese, baked in a large ring, and served in slices as an appetizer. Our version makes individual light-as-air puffs; serve them plain, gild the lily by filling them with tiny bits of cream cheese or chicken, ham, tuna, or egg salad, or make them into savory cheese sticks. They're a delightful appetizer, and also go well with soup or salad.

1 recipe Choux Paste (p. 499)

1 teaspoon dry mustard

¼ teaspoon ground cayenne

1 teaspoon ground black pepper

1 teaspoon paprika

1½ cups (6 ounces) grated sharp cheddar cheese

¼ cup (1 ounce) grated Parmesan cheese

Preheat the oven to 425°F.

Prepare choux paste as directed in the recipe, increasing the salt to 1 teaspoon and combining the spices above with the flour. Once the eggs are beaten in, beat in the cheeses. Use a small (teaspoon-size) cookie scoop or a pastry bag to drop or pipe cherry-sized mounds of dough onto a lightly greased or parchment-lined baking sheet. For cheese sticks, fit a pastry bag with an open star tip with a ⅛- to ¼-inch opening. Pipe sticks the length of your choice; long sticks across a bowl of soup (about 8 inches long) are impressive.

Bake the puffs for 15 minutes, reduce the oven temperature to 350°F, and continue to bake for an additional 10 to 15 minutes, until the puffs are golden brown. Turn off the oven, crack open the door, and let the puffs cool in the oven slowly; they'll dry out as they cool, which is the desired outcome.

If you're making sticks, bake them for a total of 14 minutes at the higher oven temperature, then turn off the oven, crack the door open, and let them cool in the oven for 5 minutes before taking them out and allowing them to cool completely on a rack. Store the puffs or sticks in an airtight container. If they become soft or soggy, reheat them in a preheated 400°F oven for 5 minutes.

nutrition information per serving   **1 puff, 15g**

39 cal | 3g fat | 1g protein | 2g complex carbohydrates | 22mg cholesterol | 66mg sodium | 11mg potassium | 33RE vitamin A 27mg calcium | 26mg phosphorus

Paris–Brest Framboise

ONE PARIS-BREST, 16 SERVINGS

This variation on a classic French pastry, one of France's most common uses for choux paste, is shaped in a wheel to commemorate an 1891 bicycle race from Paris to Brest.

1 recipe Choux Paste (p. 499)

1 recipe Raspberry Mousse Filling (p. 385)

½ pint (4 ounces) fresh raspberries

1 cup (8 ounces) heavy cream

¼ cup (1 ounce) confectioners' sugar

½ teaspoon vanilla extract

Mint leaves for garnish, optional

Preheat the oven to 450°F.

To get a perfect pastry ring, trace around a dinner plate (an 8-inch circle is the right size) on parchment, then turn over the paper (you don't want to bake on top of your ink or pencil) and place it on a baking sheet. You can pipe the choux around the inside edge of the circle, or use a scoop and drop mounds, just barely touching one another, around the circle. Bake for 15 minutes. Turn down the oven to 350°F and bake for another 5 to 10 minutes. Turn off the oven and let the pastry cool for 10 minutes, with the oven door propped open. Remove and let cool completely. Slice in half horizontally.

Fill the bottom half of the pastry ring with the raspberry mousse filling. Top the filling with half of the raspberries, then place the top half of the ring over them.

Whip the cream until it holds a medium peak, then add the confectioners' sugar and vanilla. Place the whipped cream in a pastry bag with a star tip and pipe cream rosettes on top. Decorate with fresh raspberries and mint leaves. Chill for 30 minutes or up to several hours (or longer) before serving. (The raspberry cream will hold its shape for several days if kept refrigerated, though the choux will lose its crispness over time.)

nutrition information per serving   1 slice, 54g

142 cal | 12g fat | 1g protein | 7g complex carbohydrates | 2g sugar | 1g dietary fiber | 37mg cholesterol | 40mg sodium | 34mg potassium | 121RE vitamin A | 2mg vitamin C | 13mg calcium | 18mg phosphorus

Fruit and Custard Tart

ONE 12-INCH TART, 16 SERVINGS

The inspiration for this dessert came from a pastry called Gâteau St. Honoré, named after the patron saint of bakers. The base of this cake is a "shortcut" puff paste, topped by pâte à choux (cream puff dough) piped in petal shapes. The baked base is crowned with custard or whipped cream, then topped with fresh berries to create a stunning, delicious, elegant dessert that really doesn't take much time to prepare. You could make true puff pastry, but faux puff pastry is much easier, and nearly as good.

    The recipe that follows includes cooked pastry cream, but a worthy substitute is instant vanilla pudding mixed with 1½ cups light or whipping cream (instead of milk) and 1 teaspoon vanilla extract.

PASTRY
1 recipe Faux Puff Pastry (p. 487)
1 recipe Choux Paste (p. 499)

FILLING
1 cup (8 ounces) whipping or light cream
1 teaspoon almond extract (optional)

1 recipe Pastry Cream (p. 449)

TOPPING
2 cups (1 pint, 12 to 16 ounces) berries (a mixture of strawberries and blueberries is delicious)

Roll the chilled puff pastry dough into a 12-inch circle, ¼ to ⅓ inch thick, trimming the edges with a sharp knife to make a perfect circle. (If you have a large dinner plate, you can invert it on top of the dough and run the knife around the edge.) Place the dough on an ungreased baking sheet and chill while making the choux paste.

Preheat the oven to 425°F.

Take the chilled puff dough from the refrigerator and set it on a lightly greased or parchment-lined baking sheet. Using a pastry bag, a cookie scoop, or 2 teaspoons, place mounds of choux around the edge of the pastry about 1¼ inches from the perimeter, leaving about 1 inch between each puff to allow for expansion. (If you have a pastry bag and star tip, pipe a solid strip around the circle, about 1¼ inches from the edge.) Pipe strips of choux across the pastry, dividing it into six wedge-shaped "petals"; or just make a small mound of choux in the center.

Bake the pastry for 15 minutes, then reduce the oven heat to 375°F and bake for an additional 15 minutes. Turn off the oven, open the door a crack, and leave the pastry inside to cool for 30 minutes. Remove it from the oven to cool completely.

FILLING AND ASSEMBLY Whip the cream until it holds a peak. Stir in the extract and fold the whipped cream into the cold pastry cream, filling the inside of the tart with the mixture (either the six sections or around the middle). Top with berries. Serve immediately, to keep the crust crisp. All the components may be made a day ahead and assembled just before serving. If the weather is humid, refresh the pastry by heating it for 5 minutes in a hot oven. Let cool completely before assembly.

nutrition information per serving | 1 slice, 90g

262 cal | 22g fat | 3g protein | 12g complex carbohydrates | 3g sugar | 1g dietary fiber | 76mg cholesterol | 90mg sodium | 90mg potassium | 225RE vitamin A | 1mg iron | 43mg calcium | 51mg phosphorus

Fillings, Washes, and Glazes

Part of the fun of creating these wonderful confections is filling them with your favorite filling and finishing them with a glaze of your choice. We suggest you mix and match the following recipes as your palate dictates.

Almond Filling

2 CUPS

This filling is pliable enough to be spread inside a coffeecake, and thick enough to be rolled into shapes. It's a traditional filling for sweet croissants.

¼ cup (2¼ ounces) almond paste	½ teaspoon salt
¼ cup (1¾ ounces) sugar	¾ cup (2¼ ounces) sliced almonds
1 large egg	1 cup (5 ounces) cake crumbs*
2 teaspoons brandy, rum, or almond syrup	

Place the almond paste, sugar, egg, brandy, and salt in a food processor and purée until smooth. Pour the mixture into a mixing bowl and stir in the almonds and the cake crumbs. Refrigerate mixture until ready to use.

*To make cake crumbs, place six ½-inch slices of pound cake on an ungreased baking sheet and bake for 10 minutes at 300°F. Turn over, bake 10 minutes more, then cool. Process the slices in a food processor to make crumbs.

nutrition information per serving | 2 tablespoons, 26g

108 cal | 6g fat | 3g protein | 4g complex carbohydrates | 6g sugar | 1g dietary fiber | 23mg cholesterol | 96mg sodium | 82mg potassium | 18RE vitamin A | 1mg iron | 27mg calcium | 65mg phosphorus

Apple Filling

2 CUPS

This filling is good for turnovers, Danishes, or coffeecakes. You can dress up the apples with any dried fruit you like, or add chopped nuts.

12 ounces cooking apples,* peeled, cored, thinly sliced, then cut into ½-inch pieces (3 cups)

1 tablespoon (½ ounce) lemon juice

½ cup (3½ ounces) sugar

½ teaspoon cinnamon

¼ teaspoon allspice

⅛ teaspoon nutmeg

¼ teaspoon salt

1 tablespoon cornstarch

¼ cup (2 ounces) cold water

⅓ cup (2 ounces) raisins, dried fruit, or nuts (optional)

Place the apple slices in a medium-sized saucepan with the lemon juice, sugar, spices, and salt. Cover and bring to a simmer over medium heat; cook for 5 minutes. Meanwhile, mix the cornstarch with the cold water until smooth. Pour this mixture over the simmering apples and return to a simmer, cooking until the filling thickens and bubbles in the center, about 30 seconds. Remove from the heat and, if you're using any optional ingredients, stir them in. Cool before using.

*A firm apple is best for this, such as Granny Smith, Braeburn, Northern Spy, or Rome.

nutrition information per serving   1 tablespoon, 17g

23 cal | 3g complex carbohydrates | 3g sugar | 22mg sodium | 22mg potassium | 1mg vitamin C | 2mg calcium | 2mg phosphorus

Raisin or Nut Cinnamon Filling

2 CUPS

If you don't like raisins, this filling can be made with any dried fruit, such as apricots or cranberries.

8 tablespoons (1 stick, 4 ounces) soft butter

¼ cup (1 ounce) unbleached all-purpose flour

1 cup (8 ounces) light brown sugar

2 teaspoons cinnamon

½ teaspoon salt

1 cup (6 ounces) raisins, or 1 cup (4 ounces) chopped nuts

Combine all ingredients except the raisins in a mixer at low speed until smooth. Add the raisins or nuts, mix until combined, then refrigerate until ready to use.

nutrition information per serving   2 tablespoons, 17g

72 cal | 3g fat | 5g complex carbohydrates | 7g sugar | 8mg cholesterol | 37mg sodium | 65mg potassium | 28RE vitamin A | 11mg calcium | 8mg phosphorus

Egg wash

This homely mixture is the key to well-shaped pastries that literally glisten. It's used to help edges stay together and fillings stay put. When used to coat your pastry, it keeps the surface from drying out during proofing, as well as lending a gorgeous golden color and shine to the finished product.

1 large egg	**2 to 3 teaspoons water or milk**

Beat either the whole egg, the white, or the yolk with 2 to 3 teaspoons of water or milk. Just the white makes a transparent but shiny crust; the yolk makes a bronzed crust; the whole egg makes something in between. Before baking the pastry, brush on the wash with a goose feather or a pastry brush.

Glazes

The shine that makes individual pastries in the bakery case sparkle like jewels comes from two sources: the egg wash that's applied before baking, and the glaze that's often brushed over afterward, to help seal the top and keep the filling from drying out.

Here are a few of the many glazing options available:

Sugar glaze

In a small saucepan, combine 1 cup (4 ounces) confectioners' sugar and 2 tablespoons liquid (water, milk, or lemon juice). Bring to a simmer over medium heat, cooking until the mixture becomes translucent. Brush this on the baked pastry with a goose feather or pastry brush.

Honey glaze

Heat ¼ to ½ cup (3 to 6 ounces) honey until it's liquid. Blend with 1 to 2 teaspoons lemon juice. This can go on the pastry just as it comes out of the oven, or after it's cooled.

Jelly glaze

This is traditionally an apricot or currant glaze, but your favorite jam will work just fine. Melt the jam or preserve, in a microwave or in a saucepan set over low heat, and thin it with enough water to give it a consistency that will allow you to spread it with a pastry brush. Strain the jam if there are chunks of fruit or seeds in it. Use to brush over cooled, filled pastry.

Ingredients

The key to a baking masterpiece is in its inception: choosing the ingredients. A fine hand and a quick mind are key attributes of the home baker, but knowledge and creativity won't make up for the wrong ingredients.

An old advertisement hangs in our offices at King Arthur Flour. It features a '50s mom serving what she thought was going to be a beautiful cake, with her family gathered around in grateful anticipation. But the cake is a disappointment, and her unhappiness is clear; she saved 10 cents buying a lesser-quality flour, but wasted hours of her precious time creating a failure, all because she used the wrong ingredient. Hyperbole? We don't think so. This chapter is devoted to giving you an objective review of most of the ingredients you'll encounter as a baker.

Knowing what type of flour, fat, sweetener, liquid, salt, leavener and other ingredients works best in the recipe you've chosen is not just important, it's imperative. Not all chocolate is created equal. Granulated sugar and powdered sugar are vastly different. Want to know more? Read on.

Flour

Wheat

The most fundamental ingredient for the baker is flour. The single most important thing for the baker to understand about flour is that all flour is *not* created equal. Knowing which flour will do what in the kitchen will allow you to be both creative and successful with your baking because you'll find yourself, as they say, using the right tool for the right job.

In order to better understand flour, we need to gain insight into some basics and some history. When we think of flour we generally think of flour made from wheat. There's a reason for that. While flour can be ground from a number of different grains, it is only the flour milled from wheat that has certain unique characteristics we associate with the word *flour*.

Wheat flour contains two proteins called glutenin and gliadin. When a flour that contains these proteins is mixed with a liquid, a substance called gluten is produced. Like a rubber band, gluten will stretch. Unlike a rubber band, which snaps back to its original form, gluten will eventually stop trying to go back to its original shape and will stay put in its new configuration. This combination of cohesion and elasticity allows a bread dough to capture, expand, and contain the carbon dioxide bubbles produced by yeast. In short, gluten is the magic substance that allows a dough to rise. This ability to leaven dough is what has made wheat flour synonymous with baking.

Different flours produce different amounts of gluten. The amount of gluten is determined by the protein level of the flour. Protein levels of the wheat from which flour is milled can vary from crop to crop, season to season. But there are even more significant variations in different types of wheat.

The Major Classifications of Modern Wheat

After eons of isolating and encouraging the genetic development of more "user-friendly" characteristics, there are more than thirty thousand varieties of wheat today, each with its own merits. To bring some order to this, in the United States wheat is grouped into six classes: hard red winter, hard red spring, hard white, soft red winter, soft white, and durum. These all have origins in seeds that were carried to the United States by people emigrating from Europe. As more wheat varieties are emerging from breeding facilities, those classifications will probably have some additions. For example, a relatively new type of wheat that is beginning to appear in the American market is hard white wheat. Like hard red wheat, it too can be grown as a winter or spring crop even though the preceding classifications don't yet acknowledge that. To make wheat types easier to understand, we'll look at current wheat varieties as some combination of the following: hard or soft, red or white, winter or spring.

Hard Wheats

Hard wheats are the high-protein wheats that contain more gluten-producing proteins than soft wheats and thus produce more gluten, that elastic component of a dough that can capture and hold carbon dioxide. Hard wheats, because they can produce more gluten, are therefore best for yeast-leavened goods. Physically, a hard wheat berry tends to be longer and more bullet-shaped than soft wheat berries, which are plumper. There are many more acres planted to hard wheats than soft wheats in this hemisphere.

Hard wheat berries can be either red or white, the color of the pigment in the bran. Most of the hard wheat in this country is red, but there is a growing percentage of white wheat that is being grown every year. Hard wheats, both red and white, can be either winter or spring varieties.

Winter wheat is grown from Texas north through Kansas, which is the largest wheat state, into mid-Nebraska. It is planted in the fall, grows until it's about five

The Story of Wheat

Approximately 10,000 years ago, along the eastern shore of the Mediterranean and east to the valley of the Tigris and Euphrates, people stopped searching for randomly growing patches of wild wheat and started to gather it where it had been purposely sown. Although this "domesticated" wheat was still essentially wild, the fact that it was consciously "contained" was of great significance. The next step was even more momentous.

Like dandelions, stalks of wild wheat at their peak of maturity release their seeds, or berries, and commit them to the winds. For the wheat, this ensured another crop, but totally at the will of the wind. For the early wheat farmers, it meant the possibility of not having another crop where they wanted it in addition to missing the food value of the current one.

What eventually became clear was that a few kernels of wheat in those crops of wild wheat weren't released. By collecting and planting those wheat berries, people found that the next crop would produce more of the same. Thus very slowly began the human manipulation of the genetic codes of wild wheat and the beginnings of real wheat husbandry and domestication.

Turkey Red is the wheat that is the ancestor of almost all our American hard red winter wheats. Its essence is in King Arthur's unbleached all-purpose flour. Turkey Red was not an indigenous grass in the United States, and it hasn't been here very long in the grand scheme of things. In some ways we have the increasing repression in Russia during the latter part of the nineteenth century to thank for it. The following came to us several years ago from Mark Nightengale, a friend from Heartland Mill, a cooperative in Marienthal, Kansas. It was a prelude to the story of his

(continued)

own grandfather who came to Kansas from Kiev. It's the fascinating story of Turkey Red.

"During the time of religious reformation in Europe, a group of Mennonites left the European lowlands [Holland], and at the invitation of Katherine the Great, headed for Russia. In their travels, they passed through the Crimea, a peninsula jutting into the Black Sea across from Turkey. It was here that they discovered and acquired a prized wheat known as Turkey Red. From this point they traveled to the Ukraine, settled, and began to farm. They planted their Turkey Red and started to develop it genetically.

As time went by, a change in the political wind began to blow across Russia. Many of the Mennonites became restless and began to look toward America as an opportunity for the freedoms that they were beginning to lose. In 1874, a wave of Mennonite emigrants crossed the Atlantic, bringing with them seeds from their prized Turkey Red wheat. This particular type of wheat was completely new to Americans, as they had been used to spring wheats, those planted in the spring and harvested in late summer. The Mennonites planted their wheat in the fall and it immediately began to grow. At the first hard frost it stopped growing, and through the long winter lay as if dead. But the next spring, it began to grow again. Upon completion of the harvest, millers discovered a quality of wheat they had never known before. And bakers discovered its excellent baking qualities. From this point in history, the heartland of America became known as 'the bread basket of the world.' Today's premium milling and baking wheats are strains of the original Turkey Red brought to this country by those Mennonites in search of new beginnings."

inches tall, and then with the onset of winter and cold weather, it becomes dormant under a good snow cover (vernalization). It resumes growing the following spring and is harvested in late spring and early summer. The protein of hard winter wheat ranges between 10 and 12 percent protein, the right amount for artisan and home bread baking, which is done primarily by hand.

Spring wheat is grown primarily in the Dakotas, Minnesota, and Montana into Canada, where the climate is more severe. It is planted in the spring and harvested in late summer and early fall. Spring wheat flours range between 12 percent and 14 percent protein, high enough levels that they are better developed by machine. Spring wheats are also a good choice when you're adding nonwheat (i.e., nongluten-producing) ingredients to your dough.

Durum wheat is the hardest of the hard wheats, but it is in a category by itself. It is a more primitive wheat and, as such, its protein has very different characteristics. It doesn't create the elastic gluten that is characteristic of more modern hard wheats. It is usually milled into semolina (a golden-colored granulated flour with the consistency of Cream of Wheat), which is used primarily for pasta. It can also be milled into a finer golden flour that can be used for the same purpose, or in conjunction with other types of wheat in breads, cakes, and so on.

Soft Wheats

Soft wheats are the plump ones; they have a larger percentage of carbohydrates, meaning less protein, and thus less gluten-forming ability. These are used for baked goods that don't need a highly developed matrix of gluten strands, such as cakes, biscuits, pastry, etc. These are almost all winter wheats, that is, they are planted in the fall and winter over in a state of dormancy to begin growing the following spring. Soft winter wheats are grown primarily east of the Mississippi, from Missouri and Illinois east to Virginia and the Carolinas in the South, and New York State in the North. There are also important crops of soft white wheat in the northern Pacific states.

Soft white flour has a greater absorption rate than soft red flour, that is, it has slightly more protein. Its protein is also more tolerant, meaning it retains its elastic characteristics during manipulation for a significantly longer period than does soft red. Soft whites are usually used for pastry flours. Soft reds are used for cake flour, which is bleached, chemically creating a "tougher" flour that can contain large amounts of fat and sugar but still produce a light cake.

From Wheat to Flour

Look at a wheat berry itself. In simplest terms, it is composed of the following:

• **Bran,** the outside coating that holds the wheat berry together and protects it

• **Germ,** the embryo of a new wheat seedling were it to germinate

• **Endosperm** ("that which is within the seed"), the remaining part of the wheat berry that is the food or nutritive source for the growing wheat seedling

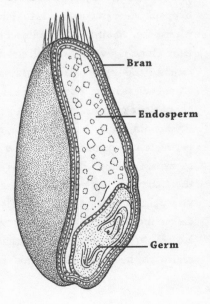

While many espouse the use of whole grains for their nutritional value, there are some benefits to flours that don't contain the germ or bran. The most obvious is that the gluten-producing proteins are in the endosperm, not the germ or the bran. A bread dough made from flour ground from just the endosperm—white flour—will enjoy the greatest expansion and create the lightest loaf since there is nothing to interfere with the development of the gluten. The bran, no matter how finely ground, has sharp edges that tend to shred the strands of gluten that have been developed in a dough. When the gluten matrix is torn, some of the carbon dioxide bubbles created by the yeast escape, resulting in a denser loaf.

Second, the oil-rich germ, like any other vegetable oil, will eventually become rancid. Before the development of the refrigerator or freezer, storage of whole grains for any period of time was a real problem. Flour that doesn't contain the germ, if kept cool and dry and free of infestation, will keep almost indefinitely, with no loss in performance or nutritional value. All of these considerations made white flour very desirable.

Milling

Once the wheat berries are cleaned and tempered (soaking the wheat berries to bring them all to a common level of moisture) they're passed through the first steel rollers,

Storing Flours and Grains

Flours that don't contain the germ, for example, all-purpose bleached or unbleached, bread, white rye, and so forth, can be stored where it's cool and dry for an indefinite period of time. Whole grains are a different story. Once you rupture the oily germ of the berry, which happens when you grind it into flour or meal, it's exposed to air and thus subject to oxidation. This simply means it will slowly become rancid. Freshly ground whole grains, if they're stored where it's cool and dry, will keep for about three months. If they're stored in an airtight container in the refrigerator, this time period can be extended for another three months. Freezing will prolong this even further, particularly if your freezer has a stable internal temperature, that is, if it is non-self-defrosting. But freezing will not stop oxidation entirely. When you're dealing with whole grains, the best bet is to buy small amounts often and use them up in something wonderful while they still taste that way.

All grains are subject to insect infestation. Grains that are milled at large mills are passed through an entoletor. This is a clever bit of technology that mechanically destroys (not chemically) any potential insect visitor, in either adult or egg form. This means that flours bagged at mills that have these machines will be subject to infestation only from external sources. But grain and grain products are appealing foods for mealworms and millers (flour moths), which are fairly ubiquitous creatures. If you're going to have flour around at room temperature for any length of time, tuck in a bay leaf to discourage any "visitors." If you're going to be gone for any length of time, particularly over the summer, use all your flour or freeze it. Storage in an airtight container is advisable.

the "first break." These rollers are corrugated and designed to break the berry into its constituent parts so the chunks of endosperm can begin to be separated from the bran and germ. With each successive pass through increasingly smooth rollers, the small chunks of endosperm are ground into flour and passed through a series of sieves, with mesh of various sizes, resulting in several "streams" of flour. The first stream produces what's known as "patent" flour, that which contains the least amount of insoluble material. This can be equated with the earliest runs of maple sap that produce the fanciest syrup, the first cold-pressing of olives that produce extra virgin olive oil, or the first pressing of wine grapes that produces the highest quality wines.

With each successive rolling and sifting, streams of increasing mineral content are removed. The next major stream to come off is known as "First Clear Flour." This is significantly darker relative to patent flour. It is used often in making rye breads to add gluten-producing characteristics. "Second Clear Flour" follows "First," and contains an even greater level of non-endosperm (i.e., bran) material. The last is the lowest flour grade of all, often referred to as Red Dog. Along with the bran and germ that has been removed from the other flour streams, it is generally used as animal feed. When all the streams of endosperm are blended together, except for the "Clears" and "Red Dog," you have what is known as "straight" flour.

Additives

Once a flour has emerged from the milling process, a number of things can be added to it. As required by a U.S. Government mandate, today's "enriched" flours have small amounts of iron, niacin, thiamin, and riboflavin added. All-purpose flour usually has malted flour added to enhance its performance for yeast baking. In some instances, flour is treated with other additives to produce certain characteristics. History and tradition have created a desire for white flour. Because it was difficult for medieval millers to separate the germ and the bran from the flour they milled, the small amounts of white flour produced were saved for the lord of the manor. Thus began the association of white flour with the upper classes. Until the current century, an enterprising though unethical miller accomplished this "whitening" by adding a whole variety of things to his flour: ground lime, chalk, alum, bone. In 1757 the English Parliament passed a law banning the addition of alum or anything else to flour, although it was generally ignored.

Contemporary millers are still in the business of making white flour. The first step in accomplishing this is to eliminate the bran and germ through the milling process itself. The next step is to "whiten" the remaining flour. This can happen a couple of ways. Time and exposure to air will slowly oxidize and whiten it. This rest period, which should be around two weeks in the summer and up to a month in the winter, also changes its chemistry so that it will create a dough that is more responsive and elastic. However, rather than using time as an agent as King Arthur Flour does, most millers use chemicals to make this happen almost instantly. So as the flour comes off the line, bleaching and oxidizing chemicals are added in order to quicken or actually replace this aging time.

Chlorine dioxide, benzoyl peroxide, and chlorine gas, all of which whiten and/or oxidize flour, are currently permissible additives. Benzoyl peroxide leaves benzoic acid, which, although it has an FDA GRAS (general recognition of safety) status, can be mildly toxic to the skin, eyes, and mucous membranes. This can be detected as a bitter aftertaste by people with an acute sense of taste. Benzoyl peroxide whitens flour but does not appreciably change the baking qualities. Chlorine gas leaves hydrochloric acid, a colorless toxic agent. It has been linked to respiratory problems in mills where it is used. In baked goods where other ingredients do not mask it, it imparts a detectable flavor to people with sensitive palates.

The most controversial additive at present is potassium bromate, which is still in use both as an oxidizer and a conditioner in many commercially available flours. It has come under scrutiny, however, as tests with it have indicated that it is carcinogenic in animals and probably in humans. Since 1991, flour sold in California containing potassium bromate has had to carry a warning label. It is banned in Canada, Europe, and Japan. Although there are scientists who claim that there is no harmful residue left in bromated flour, we are guessing that potassium bromate will ultimately also be retired as an additive.

King Arthur Flours

In the late nineteenth century, when the effects of the roller milling process were really beginning to be felt, a lot of people wanted to get into the flour business. It looked like a burgeoning industry and a promising way to make money. Unfortunately, there were no federal standards or guidelines for milling flour. As a result, a lot of inconsistently milled and low-grade flour was produced, which was then "improved" with chemicals.

Messrs. Sands, Taylor, and Wood, the three who introduced the King Arthur brand of flour back in the 1890s (prior to that the company had distributed but not milled its own flour), decided to take another approach. Rather than produce a flour of minimal quality, they developed a formula for a flour of the highest quality. Quality in flour is something very specific and is measurable. If, as we have learned, protein level and its quality is what determines how a flour will behave in a recipe, a higher quality flour is one that is utterly consistent in its protein level; it will always perform in the same way. No other flour purveyor has more rigorous standards for the wheat from which its flour is milled, or a more consistently performing flour, than King Arthur.

This decision, to be purveyors of the finest flour possible, has stood us in good stead. King Arthur Flour has stood the test of time, the vagaries of the market, the decline in home baking, and remains the finest flour available. Flour has been central to our business for more than two hundred years; it is the one ingredient on which we stake our reputation and around which the rest of our business is built.

In order to take full advantage of the predictable performance of our fine flours, you will need to have an understanding of each of them.

KING ARTHUR UNBLEACHED ALL-PURPOSE FLOUR is a patent flour milled from hard red wheat with a protein level, after milling, of about 11.7 percent. The protein level of our flour is clearly higher than that in other all-purpose flours. In fact, because New Englanders are bread bakers by tradition and it was formulated back in 1896 with them in mind, it is as high as can be adequately kneaded by hand. Because it is not bleached, that is, the protein has not been "strengthened" or toughened through the bleaching process, it is "mellow" enough that, handled correctly, it will make wonderful quick breads, biscuits, cookies, pastry, and so on. The protein in our King Arthur all-purpose flour also has great "tolerance." This means the gluten can be manipulated for a long time before it begins to break down. As far as the bread baker is concerned, it's a very forgiving flour. You can make a dough, punch it down several times or just ignore it all day, and it will still have enough strength to produce a wonderful loaf of bread. In fact, it will be a better bread because, as a result of such a long fermentation, the flavor will be more complex and satisfying. We've found, not unexpectedly, that our all-purpose flour is also an excellent flour for the bread machine.

SIR GALAHAD is the institutional equivalent of our signature flour, King Arthur unbleached all-purpose flour. It is used by commercial bakers who make artisan breads.

ROUND TABLE PASTRY FLOUR is an unbleached patent grade of soft white New York state wheat with a protein level of about 9 percent. It can be used as is to make tender cakes and pastry (because it is not bleached, cakes made from this flour won't rise quite as high and the texture won't be as light). It can be used in conjunction with our unbleached all-purpose flour to make French-type breads that have the characteristics of both flours. By combining the two in various proportions, you can create a protein that will produce the kind of texture you want in whatever you are baking. Our pastry flour is available institutionally or, for the home baker, only through *The Baker's Catalogue* (see Where to Find It, p. 609).

QUEEN GUINEVERE CAKE FLOUR is milled from soft red wheat and is about 8 percent protein. Cake flours are by definition heavily bleached both with dry bleaches and with chlorine gas. These substantially change the nature of the wheat starch, allowing it to absorb more liquid. This means that a batter made with a bleached cake flour will be able to support the large amounts of sugar and fat that are usually part of cake formulations. Bleaching also makes the flour more acidic. The greater acidity ensures that the starch gelatinizes and becomes "set" in the oven more quickly. These things combined produce a lighter result than will an unbleached flour. Cakes made with unbleached flour have more body, which some people prefer. High-quality pastry flour is never bleached, as untreated gluten is more tender and, handled gently, will produce a more tender and flaky result. Good bread flour also should not be bleached as this interferes with the development of gluten in a dough. Cake flour is the only one of our flours that is treated with bleach, and only to give the flour characteristics desired by many bakers.

KING ARTHUR BREAD FLOUR is milled from hard red spring wheat and has a higher protein level than our all-purpose, about 12.7 percent. It is designed for yeast baking and its high protein is most adequately developed by machine. It works well in the bread machine particularly in conjunction with nongluten-producing flours and meals such as rye, barley, corn, oat, and the like. It is available both institutionally and at retail.

SIR LANCELOT HIGH-GLUTEN FLOUR is our highest protein flour, 14.2 percent. It is used primarily to make ultra-chewy bagels, or to lighten rye breads and for some pizza doughs. It is most effectively developed by machine. It is available institutionally and through *The Baker's Catalogue.*

KING ARTHUR TRADITIONAL WHOLE WHEAT FLOUR is ground from the whole grain of hard red spring wheat with a protein level of about 15 percent. The protein level here is misleading, as a percentage of it is located in the germ and the bran and is not gluten. In extrapolating (for practical baking purposes) the amount of gluten-producing protein in whole grain flours, take about 75 percent of the amount given. This brings the level of gluten-producing protein to about 11.25 percent, an appropriate amount for yeast baking and kneading by hand.

KING ARTHUR WHITE WHOLE WHEAT FLOUR In the early 1990s, we were sent a sample of a new strain of whole wheat flour from a consortium of farmers in Kansas (now known as Farmer Direct Foods, Inc.) who had been working for some time with Kansas State University's breeding program. After we had baked with it we knew that we had something really exciting.

Some people find that traditional whole wheat flour has a flavor that is a little off-putting. This new whole wheat flour seemed to be the answer to this. In baking with it we found we could substitute it 100 percent for white flour in many breads with not a whisper of resistance from our loving children and spouses. What was the magic in it that made it taste so good? As we mentioned earlier, hard wheats in this country are almost always high-protein red wheats. This new wheat is also a hard, high-protein wheat and is effectively the same strain as our red wheat. Its baking characteristics are similar. It has the same nutritional value. But the red is not there. In red wheat, the red is created by an element related to tannins known as phenolic acid. You'll find a similar pigment in tea. The taste is bitter and astringent and sort of sets your teeth on edge. This is the flavor in red whole wheat that some people just don't like. And it's what is not in white whole wheat that makes its flavor so much less intrusive and claimed by some to be even sweet.

White wheat flour is still whole wheat flour. It contains the bran and the germ, a fact you need to keep in mind both for baking quality and for storage. With the exception of certain types of cakes and delicate pastries, you can substitute white wheat flour 100 percent for white flour in almost everything and no one will be the wiser. It makes wonderful (and is best hidden in) quick breads and muffins, cookies and bars. If you don't want to go 100 percent to begin with, try 50 percent so you know that your family won't object.

KING ARTHUR'S EURO-STYLE FLOURS We are always experimenting with creating new specialty flours. Here is a sampling.

- **Artisan bread flour** is a combination of an 11.7 percent unbleached winter wheat flour, some organic whole wheat flour, and a touch of ascorbic acid.

- **Italian-style flour** is an equivalent of Italian 00, an unbleached short-patent flour with a protein level of approximately 9.2 percent.

- **French-style flour,** an 11.5 percent higher ash (.70) flour milled from hard white winter wheat. (Ash is a miller's measurement used to determine how much and what part of the wheat berry's endosperm was used to mill the flour. The higher the ash, the greater—and farther out from the center of the berry—the endosperm used.)

- **Irish-style "wholemeal" flour,** a coarsely ground soft red whole wheat flour.

SPECIALTY BLENDS

- **Pasta flour** blended from durum semolina, durum flour, and all-purpose flour.

- **Pizza flour** blended from durum and all-purpose flours, all-natural dough conditioner, and baking powder.

- **Mellow Pastry Blend,** a combination of unbleached all-purpose and pastry flours resulting in a 10.3 percent protein, combining the strength of all-purpose flour with the tenderness of pastry flour.

Other Wheat Products

We've focused primarily on wheat as a flour. Here are some other options.

WHEAT BERRIES, any kind, can be used intact if they are soaked long enough (start with boiling water) to render them chewable. It is also possible to sprout them and add them to a bread dough, or you can even sprout them, dry them slowly, and grind them into flour to make your own diastatic malt (see p. 525).

CRACKED WHEAT is the whole wheat berry cracked into pieces. It can be soaked just liked wheat berries to add texture to bread. It can also be cooked into a delicious cereal to be eaten as such or to be added to bread. Cracked wheat won't sprout.

BULGUR wheat is cracked wheat that's been steamed (partially cooked) and dried before it's cracked. It can be added to bread doughs after a shorter soaking period. It also makes a very tasty substitute for rice.

WHEAT FLAKES are the wheat equivalent of oatmeal or oat flakes. They can be added straight to a bread dough for texture, or try substituting them for oats in a granola recipe.

WHEAT BRAN AND WHEAT GERM, available separately, can be added to whatever you're baking to increase the attributes of each or both in a final baked product.

VITAL WHEAT GLUTEN (or gluten flour) is flour that has been wet to activate the gluten-producing proteins, washed to remove the starchy part of the flour, and then dried and milled back to a flourlike consistency. This is not the same as high-gluten flour (see Sir Lancelot, p. 518). It can be added, about a tablespoon per loaf, to bread doughs that contain low protein flours or meals (ryes, oats, corn, etc.) or a lot of extras (such as cheese, onions, dried fruit or nuts) to produce lighter loaves.

Rye

Rye flours are associated with northern Europe and Scandinavia, primarily because rye is the grain that grows most successfully in those climates. In fact it was the backbone of most bread made during the Middle Ages. Today rye is produced around the world, but most of the world's supplies are produced in northeastern Europe: Russia, Germany, Poland, Ukraine, and Belarus. Much of the rye we use in the United States comes from Canada.

Like wheat berries, rye berries contain an endosperm (the food source for a sprouting rye seedling), the bran (the outer coat of the berry), and the germ (the embryo that would produce a rye seedling if the berry were planted). Rye contains more minerals than wheat (iron, phosphorus, and potassium), but almost no gluten-producing protein. To make a loaf of rye bread that isn't as solid as a brick, you need to incorporate some wheat in your dough or to understand a little of the chemistry of a rye dough.

Rye comes as "flour," "meal," or "chops." Rye flour is ground just from the endosperm of the rye berry and, like white wheat flour, does not contain the bran or the germ. Rye flour comes in a whole array of colors.

RYE FLOUR ground from the center of the endosperm is "white rye." Rye flour ground from a larger percentage of the endosperm, moving nearer the seed coat, is called "cream rye." Rye flour ground from the outside of the endosperm, after the white and cream ryes have been removed, is "dark rye." It is dark because it contains the greatest amount of ash, not because it is a whole-grain flour. "Medium rye" is ground from the entire endosperm.

RYE MEAL is a coarser flour ground from the entire rye berry and is equivalent to whole wheat flour. Rye meal is available in three grinds—fine, medium, or coarse. Coarse rye meal is commonly called "pumpernickel flour." Pumpernickel is an affectionate German name given in fun, both to the meal and the hearty breads made with it, to describe their effect on the digestive system. (*Pumpern* is the German word for "intestinal wind" and *nickel* is a word for "demon" or "sprite.")

RYE CHOPS is the equivalent of cracked wheat and can add the same crunch to bread. **RYE FLAKES,** berries that are steamed, then rolled, are like rolled oats; they add a slightly less intrusive texture. And the berries can be used whole in bread handled like wheat berries.

Rye Bread

Rye bread, the kind that you associate with northern Europe, is a totally different creature from the wheat breads with which most of us have grown up. If you are using rye as an addition to a wheat bread dough, or if you are adding significant amounts of wheat flour to lighten a rye dough, you are still essentially making a wheat bread (see the recipe for a lighter rye bread on p. 204). When you use nothing but rye, you have to throw out everything you know about making bread. Creating bread out of rye flour is another science that we'll touch a bit on here. There is a traditional dense-rye bread recipe in the sourdough chapter (see p. 288).

Although rye contains about the same amount of protein as wheat does, it doesn't behave the same way in a dough. When it's mixed with water it doesn't form gluten. For a loaf of bread made completely with rye flour, to attain some volume, you have to look elsewhere for help. A component in rye flour is the pentosan, a kind of sugar. The molecules of pentosan contain 5 carbon atoms (as opposed to the 6-carbon-atom sugars we are familiar with as sweeteners). These pentosans, located in the cell walls of the endosperm, can absorb a great deal of water and become glutinous or gummy, which helps create the structure in an all-rye bread.

But along with pentosans, rye flour contains an enzyme, amylase, that very happily turns endosperm (starch) molecules into sugars. In a dough made with wheat, these enzymes are rendered inactive before the dough, or protein structure, "sets." In rye, however, the structure created by the pentosans continues to be attacked by those enzymes even after it has "set," which can create an unfortunate end product. The water contained by the pentosans is released, the structure begins to fail, and you wind up with something pretty heavy and soggy.

But if you change the pH of the dough, lower it and make it "sour," you can slow down those enzymes and make them stop their destructive work. That way you wind up with the familiar flavor of the quintessential rye bread, slightly acidic, full of flavor (as well as being more digestible), and as full of volume as a rye bread can be. It also keeps exceptionally well.

Corn

Most of the major classes of corn that we use today had been developed by Native Americans before the colonists arrived, with the exception of a hybrid that produced the dent corns that are the predominant and most productive corns we grow today. These we know more commonly as "field corn." With this hybrid, the American

Corn Belt (Illinois, Iowa, and Nebraska) has become one of the most productive in the world, akin to the granary of the Kansas wheat fields.

Dent or field corn gets its name because of the dent that forms in the kernel as moisture evaporates from the endosperm. This is the type of corn developed by colonists that has become the powerhouse of the Corn Belt. Sixty percent is used for feed, but you'll also find it in cornmeals, sugars, syrups, cornstarch, vegetable substitutes for lard and butter, whiskey, and a myriad of nonfeed items; dyes, paints, oilcloth, oil for soaps, cellulose in press boards, insulating materials, ethanol fuel, and sundry chemicals.

CORNMEAL is the most common form of this grain that we use in baking. Most of the cornmeal you find on the grocer's shelf is made in large mills and is degermed and hulled, which means it will keep pretty indefinitely. There are a number of gristmills around the United States that still mill the whole kernel, including the germ. As with whole wheat flour, the oils in the germ are subject to rancidity so need to be consumed fairly quickly. Needless to say, these whole kernel meals are much more interesting and have much more flavor and texture than the large production ones.

Cornmeal comes in fine, medium, and coarse grinds, as well as in several colors, yellow being the most common. White is grown in the South and blue in the Southwest. Nutritionally the yellow comes out on top as it contains beta-carotene, which translates to an additional 630 IU of vitamin A per cup.

Like any nonwheat grain, it contains no gluten so needs some wheat to hold it together in a bread or muffin or cake. The early New England colonists used cornmeal in making Indian pudding, cornmeal mush, Johnny cake, and Anadama bread.

CORN FLOUR is a more finely ground version of cornmeal.

CORNSTARCH is a more refined part of the starchy endosperm of the corn kernel, milled until it's essentially a powder. It is used primarily as a thickening agent, although a small amount can be added to wheat flour to temper its gluten producing ability (essentially lower its protein).

HOMINY tastes distinctly different from corn. In order to eat dent corn, you need to either mill it (cornmeal) or remove the outer covering of the kernel. You just can't cook it until it's soft. To remove the kernels' armor, you need to soak them in an alkaline solution. This makes the endosperm swell, which cracks the case and releases the inside. This is then consumed as hominy or hominy grits.

Corn contains a lot of niacin, but it isn't nutritionally available in its untreated form. Soaking the kernels in water that's soaked in wood ashes (which is how Native Americans did it) not only frees the kernel, but also frees the niacin so it can be absorbed.

MASA HARINA is hominy that has been dried and ground, then used to make tortillas and tamales. It's already nutritionally superior to regular cornmeal, but traditionally these flatbreads were eaten with some kind of beans, the beans containing amino acids that complete those in the cornmeal and thus create a whole protein.

POLENTA is made from a coarse (or fine) whole cornmeal, preferably ground at a small gristmill, and cooked with water or, preferably, chicken stock. This Italian staple used to be eaten with beans but now appears in all sorts of company.

Oats

Unlike wheat berries, oats are harvested with hulls or husks that constitute about 25 percent of their weight. Before milling, these hulls need to be removed, not an easy task. Once the hulls are off, the remaining berries are called groats and look very similar to wheat berries. Nutritionally, oats contain a higher percentage of fat than wheat, about 7 percent versus 2 percent. (This means that about 17 percent of calories from whole oats come from fat, an amount that anyone on a diet would be proud to own up to.) Oats contain more protein as well, although it is not gluten producing. Oat bran is rich in water-soluble fiber, which current thinking suggests helps reduce blood cholesterol. Oats also contain more iron, B-vitamins, calcium, and calories than wheat.

To make old-fashioned rolled oats—their most familiar form—the oat groats, with the hulls removed, are first steamed to make them pliable, and then passed through rollers that flatten them. To make quick-cooking oats, the groats are first cut, then steamed and rolled to produce flakes that are thinner and consequently more quickly cooked. There are also "instant" flakes that are even thinner than the quick-cooking variety. These are so thin, however, that they tend to lose their identity when they're cooked and wind up pretty much as mush.

To make steel-cut or Irish oats (what the Scots call pinhead oats), whole oat groats are passed over steel drums perforated with holes large enough for the groats to fall into, but small enough so that they're held there about half-exposed. As the drum turns, a stationary blade cuts the groats in half as they pass by. Steel-cut oats are available in some specialty stores (and through *The Baker's Catalogue*). They make a wonderful, nutty cooked cereal as well as a great addition, both for flavor and texture, to breads.

Oat flour is produced as a by-product of the cutting and flaking operations and is being used more and more in cereals, as an addition to breads and other baked goods, and in baby foods, as it's easy to digest. Except on breads, try substituting about 25 percent oat flour (either manufactured, or ground in your food processor from rolled oats) for the same amount of wheat flour, to create the typical nutty oat flavor. Because oats in any form are not gluten-producing you'll have to use them in conjunction with wheat in bread making, probably not more than 15 percent of the flour used. In other baking, the percentage can be higher.

Amaranth

Amaranth, also known as Inca wheat, is probably one of America's oldest crops. It was used as a food crop by both the Incas and Aztecs and was as prevalent as corn before the arrival of the Spanish. Amaranth disappeared because of its use in sacrificial ceremonies and the belief by the Spanish Church that by eliminating it the ceremonies would disappear as well. But it managed to survive wild in the mountainous regions of western South America and is now experiencing somewhat of a comeback because of its versatility and nutrition.

Amaranth is not a true grain. It is related to pigweed, also known as lamb's-quarters, which you often find as a volunteer in your garden. As a crop, it grows very quickly, is extremely hardy, and can survive where a lot of other "grain" crops will not. It is also useful in that the whole plant can be consumed. The "grain" itself is actually not much bigger than a poppy seed, but it occurs in huge numbers. These seeds also contain more of the amino acid lysine, which boosts its usable protein significantly more than grass-crops grains. Like oats it also contains much soluble fiber.

Amaranth can be cooked and eaten as a cereal; it can be popped like popcorn; it can be ground into flour. Because it contains no gluten, it needs to be mixed with wheat flours for yeast-bread baking in similar amounts (about 15 percent) as soy flour. You can use it in much greater amounts in making pancakes or flatbreads. Amaranth can be found in health food stores.

Barley

Barley, another wild grass, with a nutrition profile similar to other grasses, has a history that is as old as wheat. Remnants have been found in a swath between North Africa all the way to Afghanistan. In ancient times, and even in modern historic times in Europe, barley played a much greater role than it does today, even greater than that of wheat. It was easier to grow in many places and, as a choice of grain for malting (beer and ale were consumed much the way we consume water today), it was felt to be the best choice. But as people discovered the gluten-producing properties of wheat protein, and what it meant for bread made with it, barley began to lose favor. It did persist as the grain used most by the lower classes and as a feed for animals. And it has persisted as the best grain for malting. In fact, the word for barley is a derivative of an old English word for beer.

In its heyday, the length of a barley grain became the foundation of our linear measurement system. Three of them laid end to end equaled an Anglo-Saxon ynce (later inch). The weight of a barley "grain" eventually became the "gram," the foundation of the metric system. But as the foundation of our human food system, barley lost its place to wheat.

Although barley is available in several forms (pearled barley, scotch barley, barley grits), what the baker will most likely use is barley flour. This is roasted barley that has been ground into a nutty-flavored flour. Like wheat flour it can be used for thickening.

You can include it in any baked product by substituting it for wheat flour. Because it is not gluten producing, you probably don't want to use more than a couple of tablespoons per cup of wheat flour. Barley flour adds its own flavor to whatever you bake.

MALT is used primarily to make beers and ales. In Scotland, malt is strongly identified with whisky (in Ireland, whiskey). Although other grains can be malted, long periods of experience and experimenting have led people to believe that barley produces the best result.

Malt making used to be a much more visible process. In the Middle Ages, women were responsible for this task. Later, you would find a malt house in almost every village. Now malting is done at an industrial level so most of us don't even know what the process is or why it's done. To understand why one would make malt, first we should understand what it is and what it does.

DIASTATIC MALT is grain that has been sprouted, slowly dried at relatively low temperatures, and then ground into a powder. When grain begins to sprout, there is a rise in the level of enzyme activity that begins to break down the starch in the endosperm into simple sugars that the new seedling can feed on. This is primarily maltose, thus the name "malt." By allowing the grain to begin to sprout, then drying at it low temperatures, and finally grinding it, the enzymes are not destroyed. Once the enzymes are in some kind of wet medium, they become active again and continue to turn available starch to sugar. This sugar, intended for a new grain seedling, can also create a fine food for yeast, which in turn can be used for making either beer or bread. If you look on a bag of all-purpose flour, you'll see that there is a tiny amount of malt added. Wheat flour has its own enzymes, but often not enough to create a flour that will make good bread. So the level of enzyme activity is corrected by adding a bit of diastatic barley malt.

Is My Malted Milkshake Really Just a Glass of Beer?

No. The classic malt flavor comes from non-diastatic malt, a malt powder that has been dried at temperatures high enough so the enzymes are destroyed and no longer active. This powder is used as a sweetener with its associated malt flavor.

Malt for baking is dried slowly and at a very low heat. Malt for beer is also dried slowly, but after the berries have reached about 10 percent moisture and the enzymes are stabilized, the heat is increased and the berries are then allowed to develop some color the lighter colors are for pale ales, the darker colors for stronger flavored porters or stouts. As the color gets darker (and the flavors more pronounced), the enzyme activity becomes more and more compromised.

NON-DIASTATIC MALT is a malt powder that has been dried at temperatures high enough so the enzymes are destroyed and no longer active. This powder can be used simply as a sweetener with its associated malt flavor.

MALT SYRUP is made from barley berries that have sprouted and are thus full of maltose, the sugar that gives malt its name. It can be either diastatic or non-diastatic. To make malt syrup, sprouted barley berries are soaked in water to allow the now-available sugars to dissolve. The water is strained off from the spent grain and then cooked down until it is a sweet syrup. Malt syrup is not quite as sweet as honey and not as strongly flavored as molasses. It has a characteristic malt flavor and can be used in baking like honey or molasses. If you want to replace sugar with it, you have to reduce the amount of liquid in your recipe by ¼ cup for every cup of malt syrup used.

Buckwheat

Buckwheat is not a grass like most of the other grains with which we bake (wheat, corn, rice, rye, oats). It's actually related to rhubarb and burdock and grows as vigorously as the latter. It probably originated in China, although some claim Russia, and is a minor crop in the United States. Because it blooms continuously throughout the summer, it is a good bee crop and makes a unique honey. Its hulls make great mulch as well as pillow filling. Buckwheat flour is nongluten producing and has an assertive flavor all its own that is somewhat of an acquired taste. It is used most familiarly in Russian pancakes (blini), particularly right before Lent, when they are served with almost anything, caviar being traditional, but also salmon, sour cream, jam, whatever tempts the baker.

Chickpea Flour

Chickpeas, also known as garbanzos, are a legume like soybeans, that nitrogen-fixing group of plants that can enrich the soil. They grow well in warm climates and historically were found in Egypt and the Levant, those countries that border the eastern coast of the Mediterranean. From there they found their way around the Mediterranean to Spain and east to India, where they found a receptive home. Chickpeas have always been a poor man's food. But just as we are discovering the nutritional value of a lot of "lesser" grains, so we have with chickpeas. Nutritionally, chickpeas have a higher fat content than other legumes, but they are rich in calcium and iron and are a good source of fiber.

In India, chickpeas are ground into a flour called "besan," which is used for fillings for chapatis, for dumplings, noodles, as a thickener, and in batter for deep-fried foods. In southwestern France and in northwestern Italy, you'll find a street food that is a very thin pizza, a chickpea pancake fried in olive oil on a griddle. In Nice it's called "socca." Across the border it's called "farinata."

Millet

A native of Africa and Asia, millet has the ability to deal with arid climates and nutritionally deficient soils, which is why it has long been seen as a poor man's crop. But in addition to its ability to grow in harsh conditions, millet has other benefits. It's nutritionally similar to wheat but has a greater number of amino acids (the components in protein) than wheat and most of the other grains found in this country. Most millet grown today in the United States is used for animal and bird feed, but we can benefit from millet too. Think of it like rice or bulgur. Try adding some to your next loaf of bread; it will give it lovely gold flecks and some delightful crunch. Just as we've learned to share oats with horses, we need to learn to share millet with the birds.

Quinoa

Quinoa ("keen-wah") is native to this hemisphere and was a staple of (and considered sacred by) the Incas. It self-seeds, and it too grows in extremes of temperature and altitude. Though technically not a grain, quinoa has more complete protein, iron, and vitamins B_1 and B_2 than the traditional grains that we consume, and can be a valuable addition to our culinary repertoires. When it's cooked it looks like a collection of tiny Saturns, the planet with the rings around it. It, too, can be used like millet, bulgur, rice, and so on. Whole quinoa as well as quinoa flour, available at health food stores, can be added like soy flour, at about 15 percent, to any baked goods to enhance their nutritional value.

Rice

Rice is another grass that has adapted itself to almost every geographical area and climate. But unlike wheat, which began its geographical journey from the Middle East, and corn, which did the same in the Western Hemisphere, rice is an Eastern grass. It is said that it reached Europe with Alexander the Great about 300 BCE so it has a much shorter history in the Western world. But like wheat and corn, it feeds an enormous percentage of the world's population, more than half of it in fact, although it is still culturally Eastern.

Rice flour is not a large part of our baking heritage although it is often added to shortbread and other cookie recipes to make a sandier texture. It is a boon for people who have wheat (gluten) allergies as it can be combined with other ingredients to make fairly acceptable baked goods.

Soy

Soybeans are a wonder plant. Unlike the Chinese who have been growing and eating them for thousands of years, our relationship with them is just a bit over a century old. Today however, you will find soy products in all kinds of surprising places: in candy, pies, doughnuts, cakes and rolls, pasta, pancake mixes, frozen desserts.
For humans, soybeans provide myriad benefits. Unlike most other beans, they contain all the amino acids that make up complete proteins, similar to those found in meat, fowl, or fish. They are also high in calcium, iron, vitamin A and the B vitamins. In addition, and unlike animal proteins, soybeans contain no cholesterol and very little saturated fat.

Because it adds moisture to baked products, soy flour can also be used as a cholesterol-free egg substitute. In some recipes, where egg isn't used as a leavening agent, you can replace an egg with 1 tablespoon of soy flour and 1 tablespoon water. Again, remember that you're also substituting the flavor of soy for the flavor of egg.

Soy flour is ground from roasted soybeans and is available either as full-fat soy flour, which contains the natural oils that are found in the soybean, or defatted soy flour, which has the oils removed during processing. Because the important nutrients in soybeans are not found in the oil, defatted soy flour is more nutritionally concentrated. Soy flour does increase moistness in baked products and gives them a longer shelf life. So, in addition to its nutritional benefits, it has others as well. Full-fat soy flour, like any whole grain, will become rancid, so if this is the flour you wish to use, we suggest buying it in small quantities and either using it quickly or storing it in the freezer.

Baking with Soy

Like baked products that contain honey, baked products containing soy flour tend to brown more quickly, so lower your oven temperature by 25°F or shorten the baking time. In fried foods, like doughnuts, soy flour reduces the amount of fat that is absorbed by the dough.

Like most flours, soy flour tends to settle in a container, so always stir or sift it before measuring. Because the protein in soy flour is not gluten producing, it works best when it is combined with wheat flour. A general rule when using soy flour in yeast breads is to replace about 15 percent of wheat flour with soy. This can be done by sprinkling 2 tablespoons of soy flour in a measuring cup and filling the remainder with wheat flour. If you want to accentuate the flavor of the soy flour in your bread, toast it on a baking sheet in a medium oven for a few minutes, stirring it occasionally, before you add it to your dry ingredients.

Because quick breads don't depend on the gluten-producing properties of wheat flour, soy flour works particularly well in quick breads, muffins, pancakes, waffles, brownies, and other bars. You can use up to twice as much soy flour in these as you do in yeasted breads, or ¼ cup soy to ¾ cup wheat flour (1 ounce to 3 ounces), again with the introduction of soy overtones in the flavor.

Teff

Teff, a tiny milletlike grain, is grown in Ethiopia and Eritrea and has been that region's primary cereal grain for thousands of years. Its name is an ancient Ethiopian, or Amharic, word meaning "lost" because it is, in fact, so easily lost in harvesting. Like amaranth, it has elevated levels of lysine making its protein more complete and more valuable for human consumption than that of other grass grains.

It is also an excellent source of fiber and iron and has many times the amount of calcium and potassium found in other grains.

Teff is used to make injera, a fermented, foot-and-a-half-wide sour-tasting pancake that is a mainstay in Ethiopia, both as a food and as an implement for eating. The fermenting process, which takes two or three days, gives the resulting pancake, which is cooked just on one side, a spongy surface with a lot of "eyes." (You'll recognize those from cooking wheat-based pancakes.) The pancake itself is used as scoop and/or a container for their spicy stews and finally eaten itself soaked with the remaining juices.

Triticale

Triticale is a hybrid of wheat and rye, the first successful new grain crop created by combining species from two distinct genera. In the cereal world, this is very new on the scene. It was originally developed in Sweden in the late nineteenth century but didn't appear as "triticale" in the United States until just before World War II. In the Americas, it is grown primarily in northern United States and in Canada. Its primary use is for feed, but there are hopes for its future as a cereal crop for human consumption.

The thinking that stimulated the effort behind production of triticale is that this hybrid would have some of the hardiness of rye combined with the high-yield potential and baking characteristics of wheat. But it is still a work in progress. Some experimentation is being done with durum wheat, which seems to produce a better result. Triticale does contain more lysine than wheat does, which is the limiting amino acid in wheat. Because of this triticale is a slightly better source of complete protein. In combination with wheat, it can increase the nutritional value of many baked goods. In bread making it functions somewhere between rye and wheat flours. It is recommended that you use it in conjunction with wheat flour in making bread. Triticale is available in health food stores.

Milk, Cream, Cheese, and Eggs

Milk is a given in much of baking, along with flour, sugar, butter, and eggs. Somehow we feel reasonably comfortable substituting one form of milk for another in what we bake, just as we do on our cereal. It seems a matter of taste, preference, or dietary concern. Once we're beyond different types of fresh milk and into more esoteric forms, such as dry milk, evaporated milk, condensed milk, buttermilk, or sour milk, then questions begin to arise. There is also an interesting continuum between fresh and fermented dairy products. While we have found ways to extend the shelf life of milk by heating it enough to kill organisms in it that would cause it to spoil, other cultures have used those very organisms to create signature dairy products that would also be much less perishable than the original, the "cultures" of other cultures. These have identities quite beyond their original forms, and have taken on lives and culinary momentum of their own independent of their food of origin. We know several of them as sour milk, sour cream, buttermilk, yogurt, crème fraîche, clotted cream, and most cheeses. Even European butter has been made from cream that has been allowed to develop character through the activity of its inherent bacteria.

Milk

Nutritionally, milk is an excellent source of complete protein, along with calcium, magnesium and phosphorus and a good dose of vitamins A, B_1, B_2, and riboflavin. In addition, it's usually fortified with vitamin D. Fresh milk is available in a fairly wide range of options, from whole milk, containing 8 grams of fat per cup, to skim milk, with almost none, to options with various levels of fat in between. When it's combined with grains, you wind up with all the amino acids that create complete proteins. Just from a nutritional point of view, milk is a good alternative to water as the liquid to choose for baking

But what, beyond nutrition, does milk contribute to baked goods?

Bread made with milk that contains at least some fat will have a lighter, softer texture than the same made with water. Milk also acts as a "conditioner," making a dough easier to handle and shape. The fat in the milk slows down fermentation somewhat so it makes the proofing process more flexible, that is, it allows a bread dough to retain gas better so elongates the period of peak proof. Better gas retention also means that the resulting loaf will have greater volume than one made with water. The presence of milk sugar (lactose) and albumin (a protein found in milk), changes the crust of the bread as it goes through the Maillard Reaction (see sidebar). From a sensory point of view, this means a more richly browned crust as well as flavors and aromas that are unique to milk breads.

As for the bread itself, milk deepens flavor and creates a more tender crumb and a finer grain, which makes it easier

A Golden Brown Crust

The Maillard Reaction is the caramelization that produces the lovely golden brown color of bread's crust as it bakes. The long fermentation of the yeast in bread breaks down complex carbohydrates from the starches in flour to simple sugars. These simple sugars will caramelize at lower temperatures than sugar alone.

Lactose, unlike sucrose (table sugar), does not ferment, that is, yeast will not feed on it so it remains intact throughout mixing and baking. It is not a substitute for a sugar, which can be used to stimulate the growth of yeast, but it will contribute to the Maillard Reaction.

to slice. And, as long as the milk you're using contains some fat, your bread will also stay fresher longer.

In quick breads, muffins, and cakes, milk can increase body and enhance the impact of other flavors.

In a piecrust, as in a bread crust, the Maillard Reaction (see sidebar on previous page) also plays a part in browning both the top and bottom crusts. Milk also makes the crust more tender and less apt to get soggy.

MILK WARNING: In non-yeasted baked goods, you can use whatever fresh milk you choose. If you're baking with yeast, read on.

Fresh milk contains an enzyme that enables yeast to break starch into the simple sugars that the yeast can digest. But there is enough of this enzyme (protease) in flour itself to perform the above functions admirably. When you add milk with its own protease, you're faced with protease overload, which means that the yeast can work too quickly, rendering the gluten too mellow or slack. Here are several ways to have the benefits of milk in a yeast dough without its liabilities.

SCALDING: Milk was originally scalded to eliminate harmful bacteria, which is now done through pasteurization. As mentioned above, there are certain enzymes in fresh milk that can interfere with the growth of yeast. Not everyone agrees on how to handle this. Some feel that pasteurization disables them; others feel that milk needs to be scalded. Ultrapasteurization is likely to make them inoperative; and UHT (ultra-high temperature) milk most certainly won't interfere with yeast production.

To scald milk, bring it to just short of a boil in a heavy saucepan. Look for bubbles just beginning to appear around the edge of the milk with a skim of coagulated protein covering the surface. Don't bring it to a full boil. Remove from the heat and cool.

PASTEURIZATION: This is a process that heats milk to 145°F to 150°F for about half an hour, or to 161°F for 15 seconds. This does change the flavor of the original milk, the longer and/or the hotter the process the more undesirable the flavor changes. But it does disable certain bacteria and enzymes that can cause it to spoil. When pasteurized milk is refrigerated, it has a shelf life of about two weeks.

ULTRAPASTEURIZATION: This is an even more intense heat treatment (280°F for 2 seconds) that kills virtually all natural bacteria and renders the milk refrigerator-safe for one to three months. The flavor changes in this milk are more pronounced than that in pasteurized milk. Although this process is more common with cream, ultrapasteurized milk is beginning to show up more frequently. Once milk is opened, pasteurized or ultrapasteurized, it's best consumed within a week.

UHT MILK: This is a process used most frequently in Europe. UHT milk is heated to 282°F, held for several seconds, then cooled to 70 degrees in a pressurized system. Then it's packaged aseptically, that is, sealed from any outside contamination in a container that doesn't allow light through it. The benefit of treating milk this way is that it has a room-temperature shelf life of about nine months, which means it can be transported long distances without refrigeration. Once it has been opened it will spoil like any milk, and must be refrigerated, which will give it one to two weeks.

DRY MILK is available in two versions, one that dissolves easily in water and a second that needs to be added to dry ingredients. The latter is processed with higher heat, which disables the protease enzymes that can interfere with the growth of yeast. The water-soluble type is most often available at grocery stores. The other is available in *The Baker's Catalogue* (see Where to Find It, p. 609) or can be bought in health food stores.

EVAPORATED MILK, either whole or skim, is milk that has had about half the water removed from it. It was developed during the nineteenth century, before refrigerators, as a way to deal with milk's propensity to "go off." Before refrigeration or pasteurization, milk had to be consumed very quickly because, in its raw state, it is quickly perishable. The high-heat process used in evaporating milk gives it a different flavor than fresh milk, though not necessarily unpleasing. It also is slightly darker in color. Because it's concentrated, the nutrients and the calories are concentrated as well. As a result, it adds richness to baked goods and can, in some instances, be substituted for cream. Evaporated whole milk has 340 calories and 20 grams fat per cup, while evaporated skim milk has just 200 calories and less than 1 gram fat per cup. Which to use is up to you. It depends on what you're trying to accomplish. Both contain significantly less fat than cream.

SWEETENED CONDENSED MILK is simply evaporated milk that has sugar added to it, about 50 percent of the total volume. This was done as a preservative since such a sugar-saturated environment is lethal to most bacteria. Like evaporated milk, its nutrients and calories are also concentrated. The addition of sugar makes it even richer.

When mixed with an acidic ingredient, sweetened condensed milk does something almost magical. Its consistency changes from something that can only be described as gloppy, to something that has some kind of integrity, a loose solid that doesn't flow. This property, combined with the juxtaposition of the sweet with the acidic making a compelling flavor, is found most famously in Key Lime Pie. You can also drizzle condensed milk over fruit as a topping. Unopened cans of condensed milk can be stored at room temperature for many months. You'll find that milk in an older can may be darker in color, but will be still be fine to use.

Cream

Creams, like milk, are pasteurized and it's getting harder to find them not ultrapasteurized. The least processed cream will have better flavor and will whip more easily.

AMERICAN CREAMS go from "light" (20.6 percent fat), to "whipping" (31.3 percent fat), to "heavy" (about 37.6 percent fat). Then there is half-and-half (12 percent fat), nondairy creamer, and cream whips, which really don't count as cream at all. Cream is usually used as a garnish, but there are some recipes for baked products that call for cream as the liquid with no added, or substantially reduced, butter or other fat. Because cream is halfway between milk and butter, it endows baked goods with the attributes of both: richness, tenderness, and wonderful flavor.

FRENCH CRÈME CHANTILLY (or, in English, chantilly cream) is essentially lightly whipped cream enhanced with some kind of flavor—vanilla or other extract, brandy, citrus zest, and so forth. This is used primarily as a garnish.

The British embrace cream more warmly than do we. A single cream (minimum 18 percent fat) is essentially like our light cream; from there, they move up to whipping cream (minimum 35 percent fat), which is closer to our heavy cream and where we stop in the cream department. They then go on to double cream (minimum 48 percent fat), and finally soar to clotted cream, which can come in between 55 percent and 60 percent fat. (Butter in either country is about 81 percent fat.) In both countries there is ultrapasteurized cream that is extra-high-heat treated so its shelf life is longer. Because heat destroys the native bacteria and enzymes in the cream that will naturally ferment them, they can never develop the flavors that untreated creams can. This makes them safe but not nearly as interesting.

Hint for Whipping Cream

Whipped cream is simply cream with lots of air incorporated into it. At warm temperatures, the fat in the cream will more easily coalesce and turn to butter. To prevent this, keep the cream chilled, and if you think of it, chill the bowl and beaters as well. In hot weather, whip it over a bowl of ice. To avoid turning cream to butter, beat at high speed with an electric mixer until the cream begins to thicken, then lower the speed to medium and watch it carefully. Err on the side of leaving it too slack rather than almost butter. If you think you've gone a bit too far, beat in two or more tablespoons of milk or cream, which should rescue it. Finally, by using confectioners' sugar as a sweetener, the cornstarch that it contains will act as a stabilizer and help the whipped cream hold its shape. Whipped cream that is to be used as a filling needs to be beaten more stiffly than that which is to be used as a garnish.

For a lower-calorie garnish, try this: whip ⅓ cup heavy cream until stiff. Stir in ⅔ cup nonfat plain or vanilla yogurt. If you find this too tart, try it at ½ cup cream and ½ cup yogurt.

Fermented Milk Products

Fresh cow's milk, which we Americans take so much for granted, does not exist in many cultures, and if it does, only ephemerally. Our commitment to fresh milk has caused us to take a different tack to preserve it as we described earlier, that of eliminating the naturally occurring bacteria found in raw milk by heating it in order to preserve its "freshness."

Another probable reason for the significant presence of fresh milk in our groceries is the fact that a large part of our population can still digest it. Strangely enough, this ability, which is characteristic of almost all western Europeans, is absent in three-fourths of the people from Eastern Europe, the Middle East and the Far East. For reasons about which scientists are still speculating, these people stop producing lactase, the enzyme that allows them to digest lactose (milk sugar) before adulthood.

Many of these cultures, probably without really understanding the biological process they were implementing, allowed naturally occurring bacteria to ferment their native milks until they had undergone some inherent changes. This process of fermentation gave milk a texture and taste (as well as a natural shelf life) of its own. This is due to fermentation's by-product, lactic acid, a substance that precludes or greatly retards the growth of many pathogens that are potentially harmful to humans (i.e., typhoid and typhus, tuberculosis, etc.). The bacteria involved in fermentation also "predigest" the lactose, which make the resulting products easier to digest for people with lactose intolerance. Nutritionally, fermented milk does have benefits beyond those of the milk that it was made from. Modern science is slowly confirming many of these claims.

Because each geographic area has its own native bacteria that are adapted to its particular climate, fermented milk products, like sourdough breads, have their own regionally influenced characteristics. Warmer climates and the bacteria congenial to them produce a firmer, more acidic ferment; cooler climates produce a milder, looser product. Another important factor playing a part in the final product is the type of milk that is being fermented. Where the cow isn't part of a local agriculture, you'll find people using milk from sheep, goats, horses, water buffalo, and so on. Each has its own identity.

For Tender Texture, Increase Acidity

Yogurt, buttermilk, sour milk, and sour cream can be used interchangeably pretty successfully in baking. All three products will produce rich and tender baked goods, because of their acidity. Just be aware that each will produce a slightly different flavor and texture.

The resulting fermented milks and milk products are used in multiple ways; they can be liquid, solid, savory, or sweet. But however you find them, in the cultures that developed them centuries ago, they've become an integral part of their culinary traditions. All of these have quite a long life in the refrigerator, significantly longer than fresh milk.

Following are the soured milk products and soft, fresh cheeses that are meant to be eaten quickly. In most cultures there is cottage cheese, or a local variety of the same. In the United States, we have cream cheese as well; in Italy, ricotta, mozzarella, and mascarpone; in France, fromage blanc; in Germany, quark. These are the cheeses that are primarily used in baking although you will find some recipes that contain grated hard cheeses.

Sour milk used to happen naturally as a result of the indigenous bacteria present in the milk. Now you can sour milk easily by adding a tablespoon of lemon juice or vinegar to a cup of fresh milk and letting it sit for 5 minutes.

BUTTERMILK, which used to be the by-product of butter making, is made nowadays by treating low-fat or nonfat milk with special bacteria. It's thinner than sour cream but thicker than sour milk. It's usually quite low in fat, but its thickness and slight acidity make it taste much richer than it is.

COTTAGE CHEESE is made from low-fat pasteurized milk that has been treated with a bacterial starter that increases its acidity and precipitates the milk proteins and fats from the whey. The resulting curds are drained to produce the loose solid we know as cottage cheese, available with a variety of fat contents, but none greater than that of whole milk. If the cheese is drained longer, the result is firmer and is called pot cheese. Pressed of the remaining moisture, so it becomes drier and crumbly, it's called farmer cheese. There is also a version of this that is aged and thus more flavorful.

RICOTTA, an Italian cheese, was traditionally made from the whey that is separated from the curds of sheep's milk that are used in the production of pecorino cheese. Whey contains a protein that can be coagulated by heating it. These "curds" are collected, placed in shallow conical baskets (fiscelle), and left to drain for twelve to fourteen hours. This is the low-fat version. There are now richer ricottas available that have been fortified with more milk and butterfat. Ricotta can be used very much the way cottage cheese is used, and it can also be smoothed in a blender to make a cream cheese substitute. In Italy it is used in fillings for pastas, pizzas, and cannoli. And it can be the major ingredient in delicious cheesecakes.

AMERICAN CREAM CHEESE is made from cream with at least 33 percent butterfat and treated with a live culture to separate the curds from the whey. Once the whey has been removed, the resulting cheese is 90 percent fat in terms of calories. In some brands there are other ingredients added to stabilize it and increase its shelf life. There is a "light" cream cheese version that has about half the amount of calories as standard cream cheese. There is also a whipped version that can't be substituted for the original because it contains a large percentage of air. Neufchatel cheese, which comes in the traditional cream cheese block, is made from a lighter cream with about 25 percent butterfat. Nonfat cream cheese is a final option and is a better choice to use on something baked rather than in it.

ITALIAN MASCARPONE is made from a combination of cream and milk. It is treated with an acidic ingredient to separate the curds from the whey and, because there are no added stabilizers, tends to be softer than cream cheese. The two can be used fairly interchangeably, although you may want to add a few tablespoons of cream and/or sour cream to cream cheese to loosen it and make the texture a bit lighter. For a lower calorie version, you can use ricotta or cottage cheese whipped until smooth.

YOGURT has become familiar to Americans only in the later part of the last century. Being accustomed to drinking milk fresh, we have been introduced to yogurt primarily as a sweet, artificially solidified (i.e., with something other than what's in the milk itself—check the labels) "health food." It is available as almost a liquid, or thick like a pudding that can be substituted for sour cream in many recipes, and as yogurt cheese that has been drained of its whey. You can use yogurt cheese in just about any way you'd use cream cheese. It's a lower fat, tart substitute. Liquid yogurts can be substituted for sour milk or buttermilk. Yogurt is easy to make at home. If you want a thick yogurt, use a whole milk, also scald it in a nonreactive saucepan. Let it cool to room temperature, remove about a half cup and stir in a couple of tablespoons of yogurt that contains active cultures. Stir this back into the main body of milk, cover, keep warm and let sit for about six hours. Do not stir. Chill.

CRÈME FRAÎCHE is a delicious French version of sour cream. It is a naturally cultured cream (containing active cultures) that becomes thick and develops a wonderful flavor, delicious on fresh fruit as it's used in France. It is also called for in some cream pie recipes. Though now usually available at the market, crème fraîche is easy to make at home. Pour 2 cups of heavy cream (not ultrapasteurized) into a saucepan and add 1 tablespoon of buttermilk that contains an active culture. Pour the cream mixture into a jar. Cover loosely with foil or waxed paper and set aside at room temperature (60°F to 85°F) for 8 to 24 hours, until the mixture becomes thick. Store in the refrigerator for up to one week.

SOUR CREAM was traditionally made by allowing the bacteria present in the cream to do their own work naturally. Because there is some risk in this (sometimes a bacteria will grow that is not pleasant tasting or is unsafe to eat), commercial sour cream is first pasteurized and then re-inoculated with a culture that will allow it to sour safely. Then it is often repasteurized to stop the process so there are no active cultures in many commercial sour creams. This makes it quite stable at refrigerator temperatures. Most of them also contain thickening agents such as guar gum and modified food starch. If you have access to a local dairy that makes sour cream, or an organic sour cream, you may find a version that has much better flavor. It can be used as you would crème fraîche.

What Is Whey?

There aren't many of us today who've had much experience with curds and whey except as children, when we recited that nursery rhyme. We do eat curds (cottage and other cheeses), but in this country we don't consume much whey in a form that anyone would recognize. For the most part, we consider it a waste product of cheese making. Large amounts of it have been dumped in waterways, creating general havoc with their ecosystems. So we've missed the boat with whey in a couple of ways, both environmentally and nutritionally.

Whey is milk minus the fat and the milk solids. It contains almost all the calcium and potassium found in whole milk. One cup of whey contains a third of the calcium you need on a daily basis and a sixth of the potassium, almost as much as in a banana. Finally, whey contains about 25 percent of the protein in whole milk and is fat-free. Because almost all the calcium found in milk is in the whey, the cheese products contain only about 15 percent of the calcium found in a whole milk product. This doesn't mean they are nutritionally empty, but it does mean that these particular products are not good sources of calcium.

If the whey has been removed after milk has been fermented slightly (as in making yogurt and some cheeses), it's slightly tart, like buttermilk. If you take it another step and remove the water from it, you're left with a powder similar to powdered milk or buttermilk, with the concentrated nutrition of whey. Whey, both liquid and dried, can add significant nutrition to your diet.

Its benefits in baking are several. Wherever you might have used water, whey is a more nutritional substitute. But it has other interesting benefits as well. Whey acts like salt by accentuating and enhancing flavor. It also improves the color and texture of most baked goods and helps them retain moisture. And, because it's acidic, it can be used with baking soda as a leavening agent.

Liquid whey can be substituted for water or milk in baking on a 1 to 1 basis. Dried whey can be stored at room temperature for an unlimited time if it's kept cool and dry.

A general rule of thumb is to use about 1 tablespoon of dried whey per cup of flour in sweet baking. Just add it directly to dry ingredients.

- **Breads** (white, whole grain, and other variety breads, plus sourdough): In these, the addition of whey intensifies and deepens flavor as well as improves the softness of the crumb and the color of the crust. In sourdoughs, it helps develop the sour flavor.

- **Cakes:** Here, whey improves tenderness and moisture-retention, making it possible to reduce the amount of fat and get a good result. Start with about 25 percent reduction of fat and experiment until you produce a combination you're happy with. It also intensifies the flavor of chocolate and spices.

Liquids in Baking

Water, milk products, fruit juices, potato water, wine or beer, each will contribute in a different way to the personality of a baked product. In yeast baking, liquids make the development of gluten possible. They also facilitate the gelatinization of starch, which contributes to bread's structure as well as the crispness of the crust.

Liquids act as a solvent, allowing the chemistry of leavening to take place. Liquids also help disperse ingredients throughout a batter or dough. Depending on the type, liquids may also act as a leavening agent in concert with other ingredients. Milk, because of its sugar content, can contribute to browning.

- **Cookies and bars:** Whey will make cookies and bars softer and chewier by improving moisture retention. (Don't use it in crisp cookies.) As in cakes, it will intensify the flavor of spices and chocolate.

- **Crackers, pretzels, and other small savories:** Whey will intensify the flavor of herbs and cheese and improve browning.

Eggs

Eggs went from being considered a health food in the forties and fifties, something that should be consumed at least once a day, to being shunned as a cause of heart disease in the eighties. Today, in the new millennium, the pendulum has swung back again. Yes, eggs contain cholesterol, about 213 milligrams per large egg. But this cholesterol really isn't the villain for people with cholesterol problems; rather, the problem is the cholesterol created by your own body, which is more easily controlled through the kinds of fats we eat. In one egg there are 4.5 grams of fat, of which only 1.5 grams are saturated. Eggs actually contain nutrients that can help lower the risk of heart disease, including protein, vitamins B_{12} and D, riboflavin, and folate. So eggs three or four times a week are probably relatively good nutrition. (People with diabetes or those who have cholesterol problems should check with their doctors before they go on an egg-rich diet.) Eggs in baking shouldn't be much of an issue, since most baked goods call for only one or two for a recipe that makes several servings.

Since eggs are easy to separate into their three components—shell, white, and yolk—let's break down one large egg nutritionally and see what falls where (the shell falling immediately into the compost heap):

	LARGE WHOLE EGG	EGG YOLK	EGG WHITE
CALORIES	79	63	16
FAT	5.6g	5.6g	0.0g
PROTEIN	6.5g	3.0g	3.5g
CHOLESTEROL	274mg	274mg	0mg
SODIUM	58.0mg	8.0mg	50.0mg
CALCIUM	28.0mg	26.0mg	2.0mg
VITAMIN A	313RE	313RE	0RE

Hmmm, this looks like an easy choice. Aside from sodium, calcium, and vitamin A, why don't we just eat the white and throw the yolk (cooked) to the dog or cat? In some cases, this is perfectly okay and even a good idea. But because the egg yolk contains lots of good vitamin A, and its fat is what gives baked goods their wonderful tenderness and keeping qualities, we won't advocate doing that most of the time. We do try different methods of cutting down on the fat in our baking here at King

Arthur. For instance, you can substitute 1½ egg whites for each whole egg called for in a recipe to cut down on cholesterol, but there is a corresponding decrease in tenderness. So, substituting egg whites for whole eggs isn't something that we recommend as a general practice. (The same goes for substituting applesauce, low-fat yogurt, or prune butter for eggs; these alternatives work better when you substitute them for the oil in your recipe, not the egg.)

Baking with Eggs

There's just something about whole eggs that's key to baking. Muffins, quick breads, or cakes made with only egg whites are usually tough, rubbery, chewy, and potentially dry. Handled right, those characteristics, in a modified sense, are appropriate in an angel food cake, but not in many other places. It is interesting that hearth breads also have some of those characteristics and some feel an added egg white in the dough is an asset. But most traditional hearth-bread recipes depend on appropriate gluten development in the flour to create chewiness.

Considering that you usually use only a couple or three eggs in a recipe, and said recipe probably provides between 10 and 12 servings, you're getting only about 1 gram of fat per serving. That's not too much to worry about if the rest of your diet is balanced. And, if you've gotten beyond cholesterol concerns and want a very yellow, rich, tender cake, you can substitute 2 egg yolks for each whole egg called for, a practice that works particularly well with that cake at the other end of the spectrum, the pound cake.

Egg Size, Storage, and Handling

Our recipes call for large eggs, which weigh just over 2 ounces apiece. Five eggs will yield just about 1 cup by volume measurement. If you use medium-sized eggs, you'll need almost 1½ eggs for each large egg called for. If you need half an egg, beat the egg then measure out about 2 tablespoons.

Use only clean, uncracked grade A eggs. Store eggs in their original container in the refrigerator; it's a good insulator and will prevent the porous-shelled eggs from picking up off-flavors. Don't wash eggs except directly before use, as eggs have a thin coating on the shell that helps protect them from drying out and bacteria from getting in.

Eggs, like butter, need to be at room temperature when you begin to put a recipe together. If you add cold eggs to butter that you've just beaten until light, the butter cells will turn solid and actually break, releasing all of the air that you've just beaten into them. If a recipe calls for separated eggs, separate the yolks and whites as soon as you take the eggs out of the refrigerator. If you try to separate a room-temperature egg, you're likely to end up with egg yolk in the whites.

Salmonella

The F.D.A. discourages eating eggs that haven't either been pasteurized or completely cooked. So, no more sunny side up eggs, no raw egg yolk in Caesar salad or mayonnaise, and no Italian or other meringue that won't be completely cooked. As we understand it, no egg is considered safe unless it's been brought to 140°F and held at that temperature for 3 minutes, or brought to 160°F and held for 1 minute. Aside from the above uses, this is a problem in making meringues that include uncooked egg whites, as well as some butter-creams and pie fillings that include uncooked egg yolks. Most professional chefs we've talked to use pasteurized powdered or liquid eggs in any dish that won't meet the afore-mentioned safety conditions.

Even though most experts will tell you that the incidence of getting salmonella directly from contaminated eggs is low and that cross-contamination or bad food handling can be equally a problem, eating raw eggs is still a hazard, especially for the very old, very young, or those with any auto-immune disease. If you buy your eggs from a small, independent farmer whose flock is healthy, the eggs are probably free from con-tamination; but there are no guarantees. Probably the safest way to handle these guide-lines is to use powdered egg products when cooking for other people. (What you decide to do for yourself is your own business. We'll probably continue to lick egg beaters and eat an occasional bite of raw cookie dough.) We've successfully used powdered whites in the meringues and frostings used in the recipes in this book. It's up to you.

Eggs in a Dough or Batter

So let's look at what each part of the egg contributes. The egg white is a stabilizer and, because you can incorporate so much air into it (it has the ability to increase in volume six to eight times), it opens and lightens the texture of whatever you're bak-ing. The air that's beaten into them also is a primary leavener in sponge and angel food cakes. The yolk is an emulsifier and tenderizer. Taken altogether, an egg colors, binds, leavens, lightens, tenderizes, and in recipes where the gluten in the flour is not developed (such as quick breads, cakes, muffins, or certain cookies), eggs become an integral part of the structure.

Some recipes call for adding beaten eggs to butter that has been creamed with sugar. As you dribble in the eggs, the batter may start to separate and curdle. Stop adding the eggs for a few moments and keep beating until the batter has re-emulsified.

Eggs in Yeast Breads

In yeast breads, eggs also bring the same attributes as described above. But because they interfere somewhat with gluten development, the resulting texture of an egg bread is more cakelike. If you are looking for a chewy hearth bread, don't include eggs.

Eggs in Piecrust Dough

Whole eggs add protein, water, and fat to piecrust dough, along with color and flavor. Adding a lightly beaten egg will enhance browning and texture. If you use just the yolk, you add mostly fat, which will enhance tenderness and color.

Eggs in Custard

Quiche, flan, crème anglaise, and caramel custard all use eggs as a primary ingredient and also as a binder or thickener. One large egg (or 2 yolks) will soft set or gel 1 cup of milk or cream. Custards can either be baked, or cooked on the stovetop. The difference between a custard that's baked and one that's cooked on the stovetop while being stirred, is that the stovetop version will never coalesce further than the sauce stage; it can't gel as solidly as a baked custard, because the protein molecules, while they are being agitated by a spoon, aren't able to form as strong bonds as those baked in an oven.

To successfully make a custard on the stovetop you need to cook it slowly over low heat. Once the proteins in an egg start to bind at a molecular level, the rate at which they bind increases geometrically with each degree the temperature rises. At high heat the proteins are binding so quickly they're difficult to control, and you'll end up with a product that's been overcooked and "weeping" fluid. So keep the water at a simmer; don't let it boil.

To successfully bake a custard in a dish or cup, set it in a water bath with the water just at or below a simmer. This water will act as an insulator, keeping the temperature of the custard appropriately low as it cooks. On the other hand, if you're baking a quiche or custard pie, skip the water bath; the crust is insulation enough. A custard is done when a knife inserted in the middle comes out relatively clean. It should be wobbly, as it will continue to cook as it cools. If you have an instant-read thermometer, make sure the internal temperature of the custard does not go above 165°F. This is the point at which those proteins will begin to bind too quickly and the custard will begin to curdle and become tough.

Curdling

When a custard becomes watery, it's a signal that the eggs have been overcooked. Egg protein has the capacity to hold only a specific amount of water. As it cooks, the proteins bind tighter together and hold less water. Think of a sponge; it can hold a lot of water, but when it's squeezed, the water is forced out. This is what happens when something curdles. The water that was bound between the protein molecules is forced out as the proteins pull more tightly together as they cook.

Egg Whites

Another incredible property of the egg is the white's ability to foam and retain air. This is what allows you to make meringue (or lighter cake batter). It's important to beat egg whites to their full volume, but not beyond. Overwhipping causes the whites to dry out and break down. The easy way to eliminate this problem is to beat them in a copper bowl, or if that's not available, to add something acidic to accomplish the same thing. The rule of thumb is ⅛ teaspoon of cream of tartar per egg white. The acid keeps the outer layer of the egg-white cells flexible. Without it, the cell walls can be become "brittle" and when you try to fold them into a batter, they will "shatter" and release all that air you beat into them.

When beating egg whites, make sure your bowl is clean and that there's absolutely no yolk attached to the whites. Just the tiniest amount of fat in the yolk will prevent the whites from expanding fully. Egg whites at room temperature will beat up more quickly, so you save a bit of time.

The Problem of Weeping and Shrinking Meringue

The meringue on top of a piecrust may shrink and collect beads of moisture on its surface ("weep") as the pie cools, or when it's stored in the refrigerator. Sometimes, due to atmospheric conditions, this is inevitable; but sometimes it can be prevented. When spreading meringue on your pie prior to baking, make sure the meringue extends all the way onto the crust all around the edge of the pie, i.e., make sure all of the filling is well covered with meringue. This can help prevent the dreaded weeping and shrinking.

Leavens

The word *leaven,* as applied to baking, means to lighten dough (i.e., cause it to rise), either physically or chemically, or biologically. There are three types of leavening in baking. First, the unsung leavens: These are the leavening agents inherent in the ingredients themselves, and in how they maximize trapped air when they're combined. Next are the biological leavens: yeast, both wild (sourdough), and domesticated. Finally, chemical leavens include baking powder, baking soda, and their chemical siblings.

The Unsung Leavens

The most basic leaven is simply the air that is captured in a dough or batter. This air is created and trapped by a number of different processes while dough is being mixed.

BEATING AND CREAMING: Don't minimize the importance of these steps; give them the time that's required. Electric mixers have greatly simplified the task of beating sugar, butter, and eggs into a light and creamy emulsion for cake, or of making egg whites into meringue. When a recipe calls for ten minutes of beating—do it!

FLOUR: Fluff up your flour before sprinkling it into a measuring cup. Aerated flour will get whatever you're baking off to a much lighter start. (One of the first things a King Arthur employee learns when taking our basic bread-baking class is to take a flour scoop and fluff up the first several inches of flour in its container.)

FATS: The way you incorporate fat into a dough or batter also increases the amount of air you add. Creaming butter and sugar together incorporates air, both through the action of the beaters and because jagged sugar crystals "grab" air as they come to the surface. Vegetable oil will produce a heavier product because it just doesn't contain as much air as butter. Also, the water in butter, when heated in the oven, expands and turns to steam; this also helps create a lighter baked good.

EGGS: Most recipes calling for eggs have them beaten until they're light and lemon-colored; that's the signal that they've incorporated an appropriate amount of air. Egg whites can be beaten until they've ballooned with air and become meringue. And if you beat eggs together with fat (e.g., creaming eggs and butter), you produce an emulsion that can hold more air than either alone.

LIQUIDS: Cool liquids have more oxygen than warm ones. We're not advocating cold necessarily, but use cooler (cool tap water, milk from the refrigerator) rather than warmer, unless directed otherwise.

SWEETENERS: Dry sugars will capture more air in a batter or dough than liquid sweeteners. This isn't to say you shouldn't use honey or molasses or maple syrup; when liquid sweeteners are used, the recipe calls for another type of leavening to raise the batter sufficiently.

Biological Leavens

WILD YEAST is a ubiquitous part of nature; a small, one-celled plant, it lives on many growing things, including grapes (where it manifests itself as the powdery sheen on a ripe grape), and grains. See the Sourdough chapter for more complete information on wild yeast and how to use it in bread baking.

Domestic Yeast

Domestic yeast is wild yeast that's been captured and "domesticated" by a yeast manufacturer. Each yeast manufacturer works with basically the same strain of yeast, *Saccharomyces cerevisiae;* but how each cultivates the yeast to produce a final product is what differentiates the different yeasts produced by different companies.

Manufacturers identify certain characteristics that they decide are desirable, isolate them, and then replicate them. The resulting yeast is given a "training" diet to make it replicate, then the cells, now in high density, are filtered, dried, measured into appropriate sizes, packaged, and sent off to the market.

There are several types of yeast available to home bakers today. Here's how to make sense of the ones most of us have probably heard of.

CAKE OR COMPRESSED YEAST: This was the original "domestic yeast," moist, mushroom-colored, claylike in texture and reasonably perishable. It's what our mothers and grandmothers used, and what most commercial bakers use today. Cake yeast will keep, refrigerated, in an airtight container for about a week. If your recipe calls for cake or compressed yeast, you may substitute ¼ ounce (2¼ teaspoons) dry yeast for every ounce (cake) of compressed yeast.

ACTIVE DRY YEAST is live yeast that's been dried, a process that kills up to 70 percent of the yeast cells. These dead cells surround the live cells, acting as a cocoon to protect them. For this reason, you must "proof" active dry yeast—dissolve it in water, to expose the live cells—before baking with it. Yeast in this form was developed just before World War II to provide fresh bread for American troops: fresh yeast wouldn't survive long-distance shipping and remain viable. Active dry yeast is much more stable than cake yeast and will keep, in an airtight container, almost indefinitely in the freezer (above 0°F), or for several weeks refrigerated. It is most often found in packets in the dairy products section at your grocery store. One packet = ¼ ounce = 2¼ teaspoons. To substitute active dry yeast for cake yeast, use about 40 percent by weight.

INSTANT YEAST is also live yeast, but it's been dried at a much lower temperature, and using a different process. Only about 30 percent of the cells are dead, and therefore it begins to work much faster than active dry yeast (though active dry yeast will eventually catch up over the course of several hours' fermentation). Mix instant yeast with your dry ingredients; there's no need to proof it first. While the instructions say you can use less, we never bother to make the conversion, just use whatever amount the recipe calls for. Instant yeast is particularly favored by bread machine users and is often identified as "bread machine yeast." It, too, can be kept for long periods in the freezer. Following are three types of instant yeast.

REGULAR INSTANT YEAST: This strain has been developed for general baking. Its tolerance is fairly wide but it may not be appropriate for very sweet doughs, where it can overdose itself on sugar and burn itself out early.

INSTANT YEAST for high sugar or sourdough breads: This strain was developed to deal with sweet and more acid doughs. It's more circumspect about its eating habits and will grow in these situations at a slower, more even rate.

RAPID RISE YEAST is designed to work fast and die fast. It was created more as a marketing device for bakers in a hurry than to make good bread. As bread develops its wonderful flavor over a long, slow period of fermentation, we don't recommend short-circuiting the process by using this type of yeast.

Chemical Leavens

Most chemical leavens are fairly modern, having been developed in the past two hundred years. They were seen as a more "controllable" substitute for yeast, and it was originally thought that chemical leavens would completely replace yeast. But instead they've created a baking category of their own, leaving yeast to continue the good work it's been doing for so long.

Chemical leavens work by first being mixed into the batter, where it dissolves and begins its work. Triggered by moisture, heat, or both, the leaven begins to release carbon dioxide, which then dissolves in the batter's liquid. Once it saturates the liquid, it begins to devolve into the bubbles of air captured in the batter. The carbon dioxide inside the air bubbles causes them to expand and, as they heat in the oven, they continue to expand until the batter around them bakes into a firm structure. That's how chemically leavened baked goods rise.

Each of the following commonly used chemical leaveners has its own characteristics, some desirable, some not.

AMMONIUM CARBONATE OR AMMONIUM BICARBONATE, which we know as baker's ammonia, is an old-fashioned leavener not usually available in stores, although it can be found in some pharmacies, baking supply companies, or catalogues. The positive attribute of baker's ammonia is that, unlike modern baking powders, it leaves absolutely no chemical residue in finished baked goods, neither smell, taste, nor color. It has a fast reaction time and while the release of gases (as a result of the chemical itself, plus heat, plus liquid) produces a telltale ammonia smell, this odor disappears once baking is complete, producing wonderfully crisp cookies and crackers. Baker's ammonia is used mainly in thin cookies and crackers, and sometimes in cream puffs and éclairs. It shouldn't be used in cakes or thick and/or moist cookies, as the ammonia won't have time to evaporate. Due to the unfamiliarity most bakers have with it, and its somewhat tricky nature, baker's ammonia should be used only in recipes calling for it.

BAKING SODA (sodium bicarbonate, or sodium acid carbonate) is a natural alkaline ingredient derived from an ore called trona. The bulk of it is mined in the Green River Basin in Wyoming by Church and Dwight Co., makers of Arm and Hammer Baking Soda.

A finished product made with baking soda usually is associated with a slightly coarse or shaggy texture. Baking soda works by reacting with the naturally acidic ingredients in a dough or batter (e.g., buttermilk, sour cream, whey, citrus juice or, less obvious, brown sugar, chocolate, or molasses). It releases most of its gas immediately when combined with an acid and moisture, and a bit more when heated. Try to get a baking soda dough into the oven as quickly as you can, as it begins losing its leavening ability as soon as it's mixed. If all the baking soda isn't neutralized, meaning there's not enough acid to balance it, the final baked product will have a slightly soapy taste and a brownish-yellow cast. To balance baking soda, use ½ teaspoon baking soda with the following: 1 cup yogurt, buttermilk, whey, sour milk, or citrus juice; or ¾ cup honey or brown sugar; or ½ cup natural cocoa.

CREAM OF TARTAR is another natural ingredient, a fruit acid that accumulates on the inside of wine casks as the wine matures. It's one of the ingredients that, along with baking soda, goes into baking powder. Cream of tartar is often used to stabilize meringue, as its acid helps strengthen the proteins in the egg white, allowing them to trap more air as they're beaten.

BAKEWELL CREAM®, a proprietary chemical equivalent of cream of tartar produced by Maine's Apple Ledge Company, is beloved by New England bakers, particularly for the biscuits it produces in conjunction with baking soda.

DOUBLE-ACTING BAKING POWDER (most baking powder on the market today is double-acting) means that its reaction occurs in two stages, using two different acids. One acid reacts very quickly and, when combined with a liquid, helps to aerate the batter. The second acid is slower acting, and begins to release carbon dioxide only when heated. This one-two kick is an advantage for several reasons. It gives the baker more timing flexibility; items such as baking powder biscuits may be made ahead, then refrigerated before being baked, and still have some chemical kick left by the time they go into the oven. Since double-acting baking powder includes a perfectly balanced amount of acid and soda, you don't need to worry about a soapy aftertaste (as long as the baking powder is evenly distributed).

Substitutions

When a recipe calls for baking soda, you can always choose to use baking powder instead. However, since the baking powder possesses an inherent acid/base balance, any acidic ingredient in the dough won't be neutralized, and will therefore have a more prominent flavor. If you like the slightly acidic flavor of buttermilk, and your recipe calls for baking soda to neutralize it, try using baking powder instead, which will allow the flavor of the buttermilk to be more assertive.

In general terms, up to 1 teaspoon of baking powder or ¼ teaspoon baking soda is sufficient to leaven 1 cup of flour in any given recipe. If you want to use baking powder as a substitute for baking soda, you'll need about four times the amount of baking powder as baking soda called for in the recipe: for example, ½ teaspoon baking soda = 2 teaspoons baking powder, plus an acidic ingredient in the recipe.

Substituting baking soda for baking powder is a bit trickier. You can make the substitution successfully only if there's enough acid present to react with it; don't substitute baking soda for baking powder in a recipe without some clearly acidic ingredients.

To make your own self-rising flour, add 1½ teaspoons baking powder and ¼ teaspoon salt to 1 cup all-purpose flour. This equals one cup of self-rising flour.

Fats

Regardless of all the emotional baggage we have about fat, let's start off on the right foot and think of it as a baker's ally.

Fat is understood to be that which "shortens" or tenderizes. The term *shortening* refers to any fat used in baking—butter, margarine, vegetable oil, lard, and vegetable shortening. Shortening takes its name from the fact that fat coats the protein molecules in flour, making it difficult for them to combine and create that stretchy material called gluten. Any gluten strands that do form are shortened, (rather than lengthened, as is the goal with fat-free hearth breads). When you use fats with flour in a recipe, you have the tender, fine-grained texture of a cake, rather than the chewy, open texture of low-fat hearth breads.

There are other ingredients that can do some of this work that fall under the dairy category, ingredients such as milk, cream, and eggs. And in discussing fats, you have more options for those that you put "on" your baked goods as opposed to "in." In other words, there are some types of fat substitutes that are fine as spreads, but can't be substituted for "real" fats in baking without damage to your recipe.

Fat is nature's clever way to store energy. Animals have it; so do plants. Most animal fats are solid at room temperature; most vegetable fats are liquid. Fat is a more compact storage unit than is a carbohydrate. A gram of fat provides more than twice as much energy as a gram of carbohydrates (or a gram of protein for that matter).

Our general philosophical position about fat in baking is to use as much of the appropriate one as optimizes whatever you're making. The trick with deciding how much to eat of the delicious thing you've created is to remember that you're not out loping over the tundra looking for the next mastodon to put on your plate, you're only ambling across the kitchen to the refrigerator a few times. Or, perhaps more realistically, the trick is to pick a fat that balances both your health needs and the particular recipe you're making.

Fats in Baking

Certain baked goods, such as most piecrusts and cookies, have to be made with a solid fat to attain their distinctive texture. Even solid fats vary in their melting points enough that you'll see a difference in texture between cookies made with shortening and those made with butter; since butter has a lower melting point, it will produce a softer, flatter cookie than shortening. Lard will produce a different result in a piecrust than will butter. And butter cannot be substituted for suet in a steamed pudding without changing the results.

So why use vegetable shortening instead of butter, or margarine instead of shortening? Each has a slightly different melting point and taste, and each will yield a slightly different final product. Become familiar with the following information, which should help you decide what fat to use or how to substitute one for another.

The Solid Fats

BUTTER, a by-product of milk, is 80 percent fat with the remainder water and milk solids. Butter can be salted or sweet, meaning without salt, which is prized for its delicate flavor and is the type we call for in our recipes. Like other dairy products, and unlike most other fats, butter contains a significant natural nutritional boost in the form of vitamin A. Although whipped butter is still butter, it's had air beaten into it so it is expanded and can't be used successfully in most recipes with volume measurements.

Butter is made up of several types of fats; slightly more than half is saturated, a bit more than a quarter is monounsaturated, and the remainder is polyunsaturated. It also contains some cholesterol, some calcium, potassium, and lots of vitamin A. The melting point of butter is just about at body temperature, which is why it has such a wonderful "mouth feel." Because of the milk solids in it, it begins to burn at a lower temperature than vegetable oil.

Butter has another attribute that is key in baking—it tastes wonderful. When you do use it in baking, buy the best. All butter is not the same. Good butter is very firm, which means it will hold more air in creaming which will help to leaven cakes, and it will create a flakier result in a pastry.

Butter, with its lower melting point, is often used in conjunction with shortening in making piecrusts, providing wonderful flavor and enhancing browning of the crust. It is a more brittle fat than lard or vegetable shortening, harder when cold, and softer when warmed to room temperature. When working with butter in piecrusts, biscuits, laminated doughs, anything where butter must be rubbed into the flour, everything must be kept cool. If the butter is overworked and warm, too much will melt into the flour, changing the texture of whatever you're baking. Since it is also about 80 percent fat, with the rest mostly water, you may need to use more butter and less water if substituting butter for lard or vegetable shortening in a recipe.

Salted butter will keep almost six months if stored where it is dark and not subject to a lot of temperature fluctuation, say in the freezer, or a backup refrigerator. Unsalted butter has a shorter shelf life, about three months. It's what our recipes are written for and the one we prefer. But either way, it's best to buy what you need and use it up fairly quickly.

EUROPEAN-STYLE "CULTURED" BUTTERS are beginning to be found on some of our supermarket shelves. They are higher in butterfat, anywhere from 84 percent to 88 percent, and are traditionally made from cream that has been allowed to develop some flavor through the activity of its inherent bacteria before being churned into butter. Their flavors are more complex and intense. In baked goods where butter is a primary ingredient, such as shortbread or butter cookies, this butter not only adds its flavor but it will make these baked goods crisper.

CLARIFIED BUTTER is butter that has had the water and milk solids removed so it is 100 percent fat. As a result it has a much longer shelf life and a much higher smoke point than regular butter. While it can be used to fry things without smoking, it is missing the flavor components that the milk solids provide. But it does have its uses. Clarified butter is wonderful for sautéing, in sauces such as hollandaise and béarnaise, and in baked goods where you don't need to cream the butter (such as genoise).

Clarifying Butter

It's easy to clarify butter. Remember that the result will be between 20 percent and 25 percent less than the original amount. First, melt a pound of unsalted butter in a saucepan. Keep it over medium heat until the milk solids on the bottom just begin to brown (this adds a delicious nutty flavor). Remove the butter from the heat, skim any remaining foam off the top, and chill. After it has become solid, loosen the butter from the pot by placing it on the heat just momentarily. Turn it out onto a shallow dish upside down. Scrape off the milk solids that will have settled to the bottom (now the top). The remaining butter is now clarified, and if stored properly covered, will keep for many months in the refrigerator.

MARGARINE has been around for well over a century. It was first developed in 1869 by a French food research chemist, responding to a directive by Napoleon to find a substitute for butter, presumably because it would be cheaper to make than the original. The original margarine contained a lot of animal fats combined with some vegetable oils. As we acquired the ability to hydrogenate liquid vegetable oils to make them solid, the percentage of vegetable fats increased as the animal fats decreased.

For many years, margarine was considered a healthy substitute for butter because of its lower percentage of saturated fats; then its reputation began to deteriorate because of the discovery of the negative health implications of transfatty acids, a byproduct of hydrogenation. However, there are now some margarines and/or margarine butter-blends on the shelf that are considered "heart healthy," with reduced and even no transfatty acids.

Most margarines are made almost entirely from vegetable oils, with added skim milk or whey solids (derived from milk) in some brands. And, like butter, they must be, as mandated by the USDA, at least 80 percent fat to mimic butter. They also must be fortified with vitamin A. "Diet" or "light" margarine is simply margarine that has had air and/or water whipped into it. Like whipped butter, it can't be used successfully as a solid-fat substitute in baking.

With so many margarine products on the shelf, it's hard to figure out how they differ and what to use when you're baking. Two key things to look for are the number of calories per tablespoon (for a solid, block margarine, it will be 100) and/or that it contain at least 60 percent fat. Other products may be fine as spreads but will not fare well as a baking ingredient. In general, we don't like to use margarine in baking; it seems an inferior compromise between butter and vegetable shortening, with flavor not matching butter's, and a melting point not as favorable as shortening's.

LARD was the primary baking fat available to our ancestors. It is significantly lower in saturated fat and cholesterol than butter, made up of about 40 percent saturated, 50 percent monounsaturated, and 10 percent polyunsaturated fatty acids. The best lard is known as "leaf" lard, which comes from the fat around the kidneys of a pig. But most lard is rendered (melted and clarified) from pork trimmings. This is likely the kind you'll find at the grocery store. It tends to be milder in flavor and more homogenous in texture. Both are 100 percent fat and are softer and oilier than other solid fats. Because of its large crystalline structure, it works exceptionally well in biscuits and piecrusts, but won't create as fine a grain in cakes as butter, margarine, or shortening. And you can't find anything better for frying doughnuts. (If you fry doughnuts correctly, they'll absorb only about a teaspoon of lard each, and they'll have that flavor that your taste buds will immediately identify as doughnut.)

Lard is somewhat soft even when cold, so when making a pie dough, some of the fat coats the flour, inhibiting much of the gluten development. The remaining fat, which stays in larger flakes, melts at a slightly higher temperature than butter, keeping the layers of flour and water separate. This also allows what little water is in the dough to turn to steam and separate the layers further, which is what creates a piecrust's flakiness.

Because of its characteristic structure, lard makes the flakiest crust possible. If you're considering making an old-fashioned pie, try making it with the crust it grew up with. Just make sure the lard is fresh, and keep your serving moderate. Lard will develop an off-flavor fairly quickly, so try to buy it fresh and use it soon.

SUET is the equivalent of leaf lard but comes from the area around the kidneys of cows and sheep. Many supermarkets will give you "suet" that really isn't suet, but fat from other parts of the beast, for feeding birds. Make sure to let your butcher know what you're using it for so you get the appropriate version.

Suet is used primarily in steamed puddings. Because it has a higher melting point than butter, it creates a very different texture in a finished pudding than will butter. If you try to substitute butter for suet, it will melt before the pudding has a chance to set, which results in something quite heavy and greasy. Suet doesn't melt until the batter has begun to set, so as it melts into its surroundings it leaves tiny holes that make the pudding light. If you feel you just can't use suet, vegetable shortening with its similar melting point is the best substitution. However, it will definitely change the flavor and character of your product.

VEGETABLE SHORTENING is made from vegetable oils and is thus 100 percent fat. To make this fat solid at room temperature, these oils have been hydrogenated, chemically treated to change some of their polyunsaturated fatty acids to saturated fatty acids. This also gives it baking qualities necessary for many recipes as well as to prolong its shelf life. Unfortunately, hydrogenating the vegetable oils transforms something that was nutritionally a "good" fat into one that's not.

But unlike the vegetable oil it was made from, and like butter, it can be creamed (i.e., because it's a solid, it can be beaten until its malleable to contain air, which helps with leavening). As a result it can be used for such things as butter cream icings. Because it is all fat, this makes these icings more stable than those made with butter, which can begin to separate at warm temperatures. But you trade stability for flavor.

And shortening does make piecrusts that are almost as flaky as those made with lard. In a piecrust dough in which the pieces of fat are layered into the flour, shortening serves as a buffer between flour and any liquid that is added to hold it all together. As the crust bakes, the water turns to steam, forcing the flour/shortening layers apart and holding them apart until it melts, by which time the crust is set. This produces the classic tender, flaky piecrust.

High-sugar cookies tend to spread as they bake; but if you use shortening rather than butter, its higher melting point will force the cookies to keep their structure long enough for the other ingredients to set, thus preventing spreading.

The Liquid Fats

These are oils that come primarily from plants: seeds, nuts, and vegetables. They all contain the same amount of total fat per tablespoon. But they vary greatly in percentage of saturated fat, with coconut oil checking in at 92 percent saturated fat, while canola oil contains only 7.6 percent saturated fat. Choose an oil that has a high percentage of polyunsaturated and/or monounsaturated fats (olive oil is the highest in monounsaturated fat, but its flavor usually isn't suitable for baking, except in the case of bread). They are used in baking where you don't need to cream or beat air into a fat. They moisten, tenderize, and help retain freshness. Liquid fats won't provide any structure in your cookie, cake, or pie; but it does a good job of "shortening" gluten strands, so it's fine for enhancing the texture of sandwich breads, muffins, quick breads, or other baked goods that don't depend on solid shortening for their structure. The type of oil best suited for most baking should have a light and unobtrusive flavor. Stronger flavored oils, such as extra virgin olive, peanut, or sesame, are best used for other purposes. It's important to store them in an airtight container where it's dark and cool to prevent rancidity.

Melting Points and Smoke Points

Knowing the points at which a fat becomes liquid and when it will begin to smoke as you heat it on the stove are of value in deciding what types of fat are best for any given purpose. Listed below are some of the fats you will most likely be using in baking and, where appropriate, their melting points and their smoke points. The melting points of most oils are not present as they are liquid at room temperature. And the smoke points of those fats you would not use for high-heat cooking are also not included. The presence of salt lowers the melting point of both butter and margarine.

	SMOKE POINT	MELTING POINT
BUTTER	up to 350°F	98.6°F
CLARIFIED BUTTER	350–365°F	
MARGARINE	356–370°F	94–98°F
LARD	360–375°F	95–113°F
SUET		115–122°F
VEGETABLE SHORTENING	325–375°F	115–119°F
COCOA BUTTER		96.8°F
CANOLA OIL	460°F	
CORN OIL	450–460°F	
OLIVE OIL	375–400°F	
PEANUT OIL	440–450°F	
SAFFLOWER OIL	510°F	
SESAME OIL	420°F	

It's fairly clear that animal fats and those that are solid at room temperature have much lower smoke points and are mostly not appropriate for frying doughnuts. But as most general rules in the kitchen have anomalies, you'll find a lot of old-time doughnut makers who wouldn't use anything but lard for frying doughnuts, in spite of its low smoke point. Fresh lard produces a flavor all its own and, if it is truly fresh and you keep the temperature of the fat where it should be, very compelling. (These are also the people who wouldn't use anything but lard for making piecrusts; and they have a point. There isn't anything that can approach a piecrust made with lard for flakiness and tenderness. That's because, when lard cools, it solidifies into very large crystals, which accentuates the flakiness of a piecrust.)

Faux Fats

CUTTING DOWN ON FAT We think the best way to reduce fat in baking is simply to cut down on it. If a recipe calls for ½ cup vegetable oil, try it with ¼ cup and see if you can tell the difference. You may also substitute low-fat ingredients for high-fat in many cases, such as using skim milk in place of whole, or low-fat yogurt in place of sour cream. In some cases, the fat is important to the structure; don't try using non-fat sour cream in a cake recipe where that is the only fat. Then there are "faux fats" that can be used in conjunction with real fats. You probably don't want to replace all the fat called for with one of these, but again, experiment and find a compromise that works for you.

There are a number of these on the market based on different concepts. Some are based on protein, some are carbohydrate based, some are fat based and some are fruit based. An overview can be found at the following website: www.caloriecontrol.org/frgloss.html.

We've had experience with the following, but we tend to use them only as partial replacements for whatever fat is called for in a recipe.

BETA-TRIM is a hydrolyzed oat flour, which is a carbohydrate-based product. Beta-Trim is a water-soluble form of enzyme-treated oat flour containing beta-glucan soluble fiber and is used as a fat replacer, and texturizing ingredient. We've had a long history with this particular fat replacer. By replacing half the fat in a recipe with this, you can produce a fairly respectable result.

FRUIT PURÉES won't produce a crisp cookie. And because fat carries flavors in baking, a fruit purée just isn't going to help here either. Sunkist makes a product that includes a mix of puréed plum and apple as well as pectin to thicken it and some sweeteners. It's essentially a jam but can be used in place of an equal amount of fat in some baked goods. There is also Fruit Sweet, a blend of pear and unsweetened pineapple and peach syrups, which is used mostly as a sugar substitute, although the company maintains that you can use less fat when baking with it because it's so rich tasting and the sugars help retain moisture in the finished good. They suggest adding half as much syrup as the amount of fat called for (so ½ cup of syrup instead of 1 cup of oil). We suggest eliminating or substituting for only half the fat so you don't lose all its positive properties.

LECITHIN is a fatty substance naturally found in soybeans, egg yolks, and wheat. It's a very good emulsifier, meaning it's expert at bringing together disparate ingredients in a recipe. In its easy-to-use granular form, which we prefer, lecithin contains about 4 grams of fat per tablespoon. In liquid form, it's extremely sticky and very hard to wash off measuring utensils; spraying the measuring spoon or cup with a nonstick baking spray is helpful. Granular lecithin is not water-soluble, but it is dispersible. Mixing lecithin with liquids or oil before adding to dough ingredients helps it to mix in uniformly.

In baking bread, lecithin may be used in place of fat in recipes calling for 1 to 2 tablespoons of fat per 3 to 4 cups of flour. The lecithin will help the bread stay soft and tender. In recipes calling for large amounts of fat, substituting 1 or 2 tablespoons of lecithin for an equal amount of fat is fine; you can't, however, use a cup of lecithin in place of a cup of butter—the texture and taste of the final product will suffer.

So when can you substitute lecithin for fat, and how much? In places where it's used for its softening effect, for example, when just a couple or so tablespoons of fat are called for in the recipe, use either fat or lecithin. If, as in the case of brioche or cake, the fat is a major structure builder, lecithin can be used in addition to the fat or to replace a small portion of the fat, but not in place of it. Using a small amount of lecithin along with the called-for fat in bread and cake recipes will give breads and cakes a finer texture, and bread crusts will stay softer.

Large manufacturers use lecithin to help control shrinkage in piecrusts and pizza dough. It's often added to commercially made waffles to help them release from the waffle iron and to increase the crispness of the waffle. Feel free to experiment within the parameters here, and see if you notice a difference in your baked goods.

Weighty Conclusions

There's a lot of magic in fat. Animals have it. Plants have it. It's the most efficient container of calories (that measure of those fuels that allow us to live) in nature's emporium of nutrients. For human beings, at the dawn of civilization, fat in our bodies was a storage of fuel that helped us to seek yet more fuel, and it was a hedge against hard times. On our bodies it kept us warm. But now in the age of easy access to fat calories, and overindulgence in the same, the magic has paled a bit—as does the value of anything when available in excess. But fat still has a critical place in our diets; we just need to know how to use it. And in most baked goods, it's invaluable. The venerable baguette is perhaps the most obvious exception. But even then, we tend to anoint it with some kind of fat when we eat it.

In baked goods, solid fats can be persuaded to contain a lot of air to lighten, it can be a buffer to tenderize, it can be incorporated in small or large sheets to create flakiness; it moisturizes; it crisps. All fats can contain more heat than water and are thus an efficient cooking medium. Some fats add flavor components of their own. And some just provide the assist for other flavors. Unfortunately, the English word for "fat" is difficult. It doesn't roll off the tongue easily; it stops dead and just sits there right in the middle of the mouth. Perhaps if we could use the French *(grasse)* or Italian *(grasso)*, it would flow more easily and allow us to live with it more comfortably, as they seem to do.

Sweeteners

Sugar, in its myriad forms, is a critical component of most baked goods. It flavors both directly and indirectly, and it exacts its own chemistry on the other ingredients with which it's partnering. There are many myths about various forms of sugar, including the argument that some forms of sugar are better for you than others; that, as with grains, less refining means more nutrition. But all sweeteners are equal as far as energy is concerned; they contain about 4 calories of energy per gram. Although there are arguments that some sweeteners are better for you because they contain trace minerals and vitamins, or come from organic sources, all of them, with insignificant exceptions, are essentially empty nutritionally aside from the energy they produce.

Our bodies break down all carbohydrates, the simple kind (sugars) and the complex kind (fruits, vegetables, and grains) into glucose molecules so we can metabolize them to create energy. Your body can't tell whether the broken down glucose came from fruit, vegetable, bread, straight from the hive, a maple tree, or from a bowl of sugar.

Dry Sugars

Granulated white sugar is the most common sugar, the least expensive, the easiest to use, and imparts the least amount of flavor (other than sweetness). This is the sugar most commonly used in baking and on the table. It's the one we use as a benchmark for measuring the sweetness and baking characteristics of other sugars. Because it's the least assertive sweetener, it allows flavors of other ingredients to dominate. Some combinations:

CINNAMON SUGAR: 1 cup granulated sugar combined with 2 tablespoons cinnamon.

CITRUS SUGAR: 1 cup granulated sugar blended with 1 tablespoon lemon or orange peel, or ¼ teaspoon lemon or orange oil.

VANILLA SUGAR: 1 cup granulated sugar infused for several days with 1 or 2 chopped vanilla beans.

SUPERFINE, ULTRAFINE, OR BAR SUGAR is the finest of the granulated sugars. It's ideal for extra-fine-textured cakes and meringues and it dissolves easily, making it perfect for sweetening beverages. It's known as castor sugar in England, for the silver castors it is kept and served in.

CONFECTIONERS' OR ICING SUGAR is a powdered white sugar with about 3 percent cornstarch added to prevent clumping. Because of its added cornstarch, don't bake with it unless the recipe calls for it. It can't be substituted in most baked goods for granulated sugars, either white or brown. In this country there are three grades of confectioners' sugar, with only the finest (10X) available in supermarkets; the other coarser grades are used by institutional bakeries. Confectioners' sugar is used in icings, confections, and whipped cream. Glazing sugar is finer than confectioners' sugar, with maltodextrin added as an anti-caking agent. It can be directly substituted for confectioners' sugar.

COARSE AND SANDING SUGARS are white sugars in large crystals. They're more stable than granulated sugar at baking temperatures, and thus can be used to deco-

Caveat Emptor

There's a sugar product in the sugar section at the grocery store that looks like granulated sugar but isn't. It's a combination of glucose (dextrose) and granulated sugar, and doesn't work well in some baked goods, particularly brownies and meringues. In fact, the fine print on the back of the bag tells you not to use it in brownies or meringues, and adds that it may affect the texture of cakes, as well. So, read the label; granulated sugar will say simply "granulated sugar."

rate cookies or other pastries before baking. Since they don't melt at the same temperature as granulated sugar, they shouldn't be used as a substitute.

BROWN SUGAR is granulated sugar with some molasses mixed in to darken and deepen its flavor and texture. Light brown sugar has less added molasses (and less assertive flavor) than dark brown sugar; they can be used interchangeably, depending on personal preference. Dark brown sugar can be substituted for white granulated sugar measure for measure; it will alter the flavor just as you would expect, and will create a moister end product. If you're out of brown sugar and want to substitute white sugar, add a bit of molasses to approximate the flavor, 1 tablespoon of molasses per cup for light brown sugar and 2 tablespoons for dark.

Brownulated sugar is granulated brown sugar and can be substituted for either white or traditional brown sugars, with the same kinds of differences as you would discern between white and brown sugars.

TURBINADO SUGAR is what most people imagine brown sugar is: granulated sugar that hasn't yet been refined. Unrefined sugar still has molasses in it. While brown sugar has molasses added back in, turbinado never had it taken out; it's a less-processed form of granulated sugar. Turbinado behaves the way brown sugar does, but at a higher price.

DEMERARA SUGAR, an English version of turbinado sugar, has larger crystals; it's often used in tea or on hot cereals, and can be used like coarse sugar to decorate pastries. The name denotes where this sugar originally came from, the Demerara district of British Guyana on the South American mainland.

SUCANAT is a brand name referring to a "natural," organic sugar made from pressed and evaporated sugarcane juice. It contains some nutrients, but in such small amounts that it can't be claimed to be a source for them.

Demerara, turbinado, and Sucanat sugars can all be substituted for granulated sugar, but will have a brown-sugar flavor.

RAW SUGAR isn't legally available in the United States because, like unpasteurized milk, it can contain bacteria and other foreign matter. "Sugar in the Raw" is a version of turbinado sugar.

MAPLE SUGAR is maple syrup cooked down and then beaten into a crystallized form. Maple sugar has flavor overtones that result from its unique mineral content and the fact that the maple flavor is developed as the sap boils and the sugar caramelizes. This is not a good substitute for any other sugar; it is best appreciated as a garnish.

Rescuing Rock-Hard Sugar

If your brown sugar has gotten rock hard, place it in a plastic bag with a slice of apple. It will soften in a day. For a quick fix, heat the sugar in a 250°F oven for a few minutes, or microwave on low for one to two minutes. Use it immediately before it seizes up. Better yet, store your brown sugar with a sugar softener or sugar bear (see Tools, p. 608) to keep it moist all the time.

MALT is a powder made from barley that has been sprouted and dried. Not long ago there was interest in sprouting grains to add an inexpensive nutritional wallop to one's diet. Malting takes this one step further. There are two types of dry malt—diastatic and non-diastatic.

As barley (or any grain berry) gets closer and closer to sprouting, it develops diastatic enzymes that will break down its starch into the simple sugars, maltose and dextrin, that become the food source for an emerging seedling. This is the food it uses while it develops its own independent feeding system. We can capture those enzymes by allowing barley or other grain berries to sprout. When their activity is at its greatest, the berries are dried at a relatively low temperature (not over 170°F) that doesn't damage the enzymes. They are then ground into a slightly sweet flour.

If you read the ingredient statement of most bags of all-purpose flour in this country, you'll find that a small amount of malted barley flour has been added as a natural yeast food. It has also long been used as a yeast food in Europe. When a tiny amount of malted barley flour is added to wheat flour in a dough, it breaks the wheat starch into sugars for yeast to feed on, and gives the dough a real boost.

Non-diastatic malt is made the same way, but dried at higher temperatures that destroy the ability of the enzymes to act on the starch.

Malt is an unsung health food that has been around for years. Diastatic malt, used in small amounts, enhances the appearance, flavor, and texture of bread; non-diastatic malt, in larger amounts, adds a familiar malt flavor, but is only one-third as sweet as granulated sugar.

Liquid Sugars

There are several liquid sweeteners (syrups) that are made from sources that define their flavor, color, and some baking characteristics. Some pure syrups include molasses (sugarcane), honey (bees), maple syrup (the sugar maple tree), and sorghum (sweet sorghum grass). There are others that are blends, in some cases with other flavors added. The base for several of these is corn syrup (or high-fructose corn syrup) because it has little flavor of its own and combines well with stronger flavored syrups. Dark corn syrup is an example of this, as is King's syrup. The most commonly used syrups are listed first.

CORN SYRUP (KARO SYRUP) is a sweetener that's become increasingly important, as corn is a relatively inexpensive and easy crop to grow. Corn syrup, the kind available in the grocery for the home baker, is about 25 percent water. The remainder is glucose, high-fructose corn syrup, salt, and vanilla. Glucose is hygroscopic, or moisture retaining; baked goods made with corn syrup will stay moist longer.

DARK KARO SYRUP is made from dark corn syrup, refiner's (cane) syrup, caramel flavor, salt, caramel color, and a preservative. Its flavor is stronger than light Karo syrup.

HONEY is probably our oldest sweetener. It's unique as a sweetener because it only needs to be removed from the hive. Once out and strained of bits of comb, it's ready to eat. It was used extensively by the Greeks and Romans and was the primary sweetener in Europe until the sixteenth century, when cane sugar became more easily available.

Honey is made by bees rather than humans. It's perceived as sweeter than sugar and it has different browning characteristics so you need to bake with it at a lower temperature. Honey is more hygroscopic than table sugar and will help keep baked goods moist. It also has a unique flavor that's an important part of many traditional baked goods, like lebkuchen and baklava.

MAPLE SYRUP is another sweetener that, in its natural state, is as pure a source for sugar as is honey (unlike cane syrup, which has a lot of undesirable stuff in it that needs to be removed).

There are very few areas in the world where the sugar maple grows well and, fortunately for us, one of them is the northeastern United States (and Canada just to the north of us). Native Americans were making syrup long before Europeans came on the scene, but with Europeans came equipment and technology that has made the process somewhat easier.

Maple sugar and syrup were the sweeteners of choice for early Colonial cooks. Before the Revolution, sugar from the West Indies was heavily taxed so was too expensive for general use. Later on as our distaste for slavery grew, our distaste for sugar produced by slave labor grew as well. So maple sugar managed to sustain our needs for sweetening for quite some time. By the end of the nineteenth century, sugar from sugar beets began to be available and that, plus the fact that cane sugar had become much less expensive, meant that the maple was no longer used as a major sugar source. Maple syrup is still produced by hardy Northeasterners who can't yet get into their fields to plant and who somehow can't let the sugar season go by without a "go at it."

Maple sap tastes like water with a faint echo of sweetness. The sugar season begins in early spring when nights are still below freezing but days soar to heady temperatures of 45° to 50°F, preferably with no wind and lots of sun. Then the trees are tapped to release the sap (a slow, drip, drip, drip kind of process). After the sap is collected, it is poured into an evaporator placed over a wood- or oil-fired "arch."

To make a gallon of syrup, you need to boil down 35 to 50 gallons of sap. Early season sap is lighter flavored than later season sap, when bacterial activity begins to work on the sucrose and break it down into a larger glucose/fructose component. Thus early season sap makes grade A (light amber) syrup, while grades B and C (dark) syrup come from the later sap. Some people prefer dark syrup for its assertiveness in baking. Others love the ethereal taste of the first-run syrup as a condiment, on pancakes, waffles, and hot cereal.

MOLASSES is what's left after the juice of the sugarcane has been boiled and concentrated and all the available sucrose has crystallized. Because molasses making is done in three stages, there are three resulting grades. "First" molasses is lighter in color and flavor than "second" and "third" (blackstrap) molasses. With each boiling and extraction, the remaining liquid becomes more and more caramelized (darker), the minerals and other "impurities" become more and more concentrated, and the sugar content becomes lower. Blackstrap molasses contains only about 50 percent sugar components, with the result that its flavor is too strong to use in any but small amounts. In baking, use it in combination with other, lighter flavored sweeteners. "First" molasses produces the most pleasing flavor. It has a signature flavor that combines well with ginger and other spices in cookies and cakes, particularly gingerbread.

Molasses and maple syrup usually are interchangeable in a recipe, especially if there is not a lot of it used. Most other liquid sugars can be substituted for each other too, except barley malt syrup, corn syrup, and rice syrup. These are much less sweet than their counterparts. Be aware that some have a higher water content than others and they all behave slightly differently. Experiment with them, but not when you've got special guests arriving.

GOLDEN SYRUP is an English sweetener (the Australians and New Zealanders have their versions, too). An ultrathick, smooth syrup that tastes like a caramelized version of our corn syrup, golden syrup has much more flavor and is much more interesting. It's often drizzled onto scones or hot cereal, or into tea.

TREACLE, another English sweetener, is essentially the same as molasses, although technically more refined. It can be used in place of molasses.

MALT SYRUP (barley malt syrup) is made from malted barley that is ground and then briefly treated with an acid to dissolve the enzymes, sugars, and vitamins. It is then heated with water to form the mildly sweet, concentrated liquid we know as malt syrup. Although dark-colored like molasses, its flavor is much milder. To create a moist and chewy bagel with a shiny shell, commercial bagel bakers add a small amount of malted barley syrup in place of ordinary sweetener.

SORGHUM is a classic Southern and Midwestern American sweetener extracted from an Old World grass. Its slightly molasses flavor complements a range of muffins, pancakes, cereals, and quick breads.

KING'S SYRUP is a mainstay of the Amish in Pennsylvania, an important ingredient in shoofly pie. It is a mixture of corn syrup and refiner's (cane) syrup, the same ingredients as Dark Karo syrup but with its own flavor profile.

Substitutions

We don't recommend substituting liquid sweeteners for granulated or brown sugars in recipes in which the fat is creamed with the sweetener. Liquid sweeteners can't induce fats to contain air because they don't have a crystalline structure. The result will be a dense, heavy product.

One potential substitution, honey for table sugar, can be done with some adjustments. It is sweeter than table sugar, so for 1 cup of sugar, use a generous ¾ cup of honey and decrease the liquid in the recipe by 3 to 4 tablespoons. If the recipe contains no additional liquid, increase the flour by 3 tablespoons. Don't use honey in recipes that need to be cooked at over 350°F because it scorches.

If a recipe calls for honey and you're out, you can substitute 1¼ cups of granulated sugar or brown sugar plus ¼ cup of water.

How Sugars Affect What We Bake

Certain breads are definitely superior with no added sweetener, but can you imagine a cake, cookie, quick bread, or pie without any sweetening? So sugar's most important attribute is easy to understand. It's sweet and we just like it.

But sugar's chemistry in baking is a more important consideration. Because it's hygroscopic (it attracts and absorbs water), it competes with the protein (gluten) in flour for liquids in a batter. By not allowing the flour to have all the liquid, it slows down the development of the gluten, which means that your cakes, quick breads, and cookies will be tender. And by slowing down the rate at which the flour can absorb the liquid in a batter, it allows a cake or quick bread to expand (rise) for a longer time. The same cake made without sugar not only will taste pretty bad, but will be tough as well as flat. This is why, when you make quick breads or biscuits that contain small amounts of sugar (or none at all), it's really important to do minimal mixing (20 seconds) because there's no sugar there to interfere with the development of the gluten.

When you cream granulated sugar (remember it is in crystals so it has a lot of edges and sides) with butter in making a cake, air gets trapped on its surface to make this combination light and fluffy. When the rest of the ingredients are mixed in and the resulting batter is baked, the air bubbles expand and make the cake rise.

In angel food cakes, sugar, along with cream of tartar, helps stiffen and stabilize the egg white (protein), which means it can, like wheat protein (gluten), trap air and carbon dioxide bubbles. This makes these cakes bake up almost lighter than air. Another way in which sugar makes these cakes light is that, during the baking process, the sugar molecules get in the way of the egg whites' protein molecules, so they have to work harder and take longer to form bonds with each other (to "cook"). Because they take longer to cook, they can continue to expand longer, making the cake lighter. It also makes the cake tender.

At 350–375°F, granulated sugar caramelizes or, really, begins to burn slightly. It becomes golden in color and develops a flavor that most of us find very pleasing. This helps the surface of cakes and cookies brown and become a bit crisp. The bonds that caramelized sugar form on the surface keep moisture inside your baked good. The higher the sugar content, the more browning will occur.

This caramelizing on the surface of cookies creates a "cracked" surface, golden brown color, and great flavor. Sugar's at work on the inside of the cookie, too; after a cookie dough is mixed, about half the sugar is still undissolved. As the cookie bakes, the sugar finally dissolves and allows the cookie to spread. The less sugar, the less spread.

All sugars are hygroscopic. But it's good to remember some are more hygroscopic than others; when you bake with honey, corn syrup, or another liquid sweetener, you'll have a moister end product. Cookies made with granulated sugar will be hard and crisp when they cool. Cookies made with corn syrup or honey will brown more easily and will become soft when they cool.

In a piecrust dough, sugar also will interfere with gluten formation, making a more tender crust. Piecrusts with a lot of sugar will have a sandy texture and not enough gluten development to be easily rolled out. There are some recipes where this is a good thing and some where it's not. For more information, see the Pies, Tarts, and Quiches chapter.

Even when no sugar is added to a bread recipe, sugar is at work. When a bread dough is rising, yeast is growing by converting the wheat starch into sugars. It is these sugars that create that lovely golden surface on a well-baked loaf of bread.

Each sweetener has its own signature flavor that can create or change the personality of whatever you're baking. We don't recommend substituting one for another, as substituting sweeteners often changes the chemical balance in a recipe enough that it won't work right. Use your common sense; it's okay to substitute Golden syrup for Karo syrup, or light brown sugar for dark brown, but don't stray too far from the recipe's original sweetener or you may find yourself in trouble.

Sugar Substitutes

Refined sugar is 99 percent sucrose and is a simple carbohydrate. There are many additional types of sugars that have "natural" sources. You'll recognize some of them on product labels because their chemical names also end in "-ose." Included are glucose (also called dextrose), fructose (also called levulose), lactose, and maltose. Additionally there are sugar alcohols, which are actually neither sugar nor alcohol. They are mostly found in candies and processed foods. You can identify them because most of them end in "-ol," maltitol, sorbitol, xylitol, and mennitol.

GRANULATED FRUCTOSE is a sucrose look-alike and can be found often with traditional sugars in the grocery store. It has the same caloric value as regular sugar, but is perceived as sweeter; therefore you can use about one-third less of it and thus decrease your intake of calories. But beware, it doesn't behave exactly like granulated sugar in baking. Because fructose is more hygroscopic than sucrose, fructose-sweetened products tend to be moister and darker than if they were made with white sugar.

FRUIT JUICE CONCENTRATES (apple, orange, or white grape) also can be substituted for sugar. To use them in baking, use ¾ cup for every cup of white sugar and decrease the amount of liquid by 3 tablespoons. Start by substituting for only half the sugar called for in a recipe.

FRUIT SWEET is a brand of fruit concentrate that's marketed to be used as a sugar substitute. Its primary product is a blend of pear, unsweetened pineapple, and peach syrups that contain all three fruit sugars. If you want to eliminate all the white sugar

Sugar's Colorful Past

The production of granulated white sugar, the most common baking sugar, is a complex and labor intensive job. Although the juice of sugarcane is almost 13 percent sucrose, it contains a lot of other stuff that makes it unpalatable in its natural state. This has to be removed (no easy task), and the remainder has to undergo a number of other processes to leave a crystalline structure that can be used for food consumption.

Sugarcane presumably originated in the South Pacific and then, with human migration, traveled west to Asia. It had reached the Indian subcontinent sometime before the Christian era and was used there to make a kind of raw sugar for sweetening. It continued traveling west with the Persians and then with the Arabians who conquered them. The Crusades made the connection between the Middle East and Europe during the Middle Ages. Venice was to become the conduit for Eastern sugar flowing to Europe during that period, although it didn't reach England until early in the fourteenth century.

Over the next several hundred years, as Europeans developed a real taste for cane sugar, it was clear that the potential market for this sweetener was vast. So, in spite of the obstacles, the sugar industry was aggressively developed. This precipitated one of the ugliest periods in European and American history and had an enormous impact on how the Western Hemisphere was colonized and exploited, as well as how Africa was exploited and de-colonized.

In their search for an appropriate climate to grow sugarcane and to break their dependence on Middle Eastern sugar, Europeans found their way to the West Indies. To facilitate the production of sugar, hundreds of thousands of slaves were brought there from Africa. Thus began that infamous trade of slaves, molasses and sugar, and rum that created enormous fortunes, new and thriving ports, and a social blight that eventually led to our own Civil War.

The hideous conditions that sugar-producing slaves had to endure finally induced the European countries to outlaw the importation of West Indian sugar. As a result, this eventually allowed the development of another sugar source, the sugar beet. Because sugar beets can be grown in cooler climates in a recipe, use ⅔ cup Fruit Sweet for each cup of sugar and reduce the liquid in the recipe by a little less than ¼ cup.

Artificial Sweeteners

The following four artificial sweeteners have been approved by the FDA and can be purchased for home use. There are a number of others in the FDA pipeline, so this is not the last word on the subject.

Artificial sweeteners provide sweetness but not the other characteristics one than sugarcane, it has become a thriving crop in the United States, Europe, and Russia. The world's sugar consumption is now divided pretty evenly between cane and beet sugars, although the United States is now using a form of corn sugar, fructose, in many manufactured products such as soft drinks.

Up until the early part of the twentieth century, some cane sugar still arrived in Europe and North America in "loaves." In the early years of West Indian sugar production the loaves were cones that were approximately a foot or more in diameter at the base and 3 feet high. A cone of sugar this size weighed about 30 pounds and lasted a very long time. As time went on, smaller and more manageable "loaves" became available in 14-pound and 8- or 9-pound sizes. To remove usable sugar from these loaves, the housewife had a special sugar cutter to cut off chunks that were kept in sugar drawers or boxes. When one wanted sugar for cooking, it was then pounded into granules.

The conical shape of the sugar helps explain molasses production. To make granulated or crystallized sugar, the cane was first crushed, then cleared of impurities and finally cooked until almost all the water had boiled off. It was then poured into cone-shaped clay molds to crystallize and harden. There was a hole in the tip so during this crystallization period, which lasted several days, any liquid residue (molasses) ran out the hole into a collection vessel. Often this meant that there were several grades of sugar in the cone. It was clearest and whitest at the wide (top) end and grew increasingly dark and more like what we think of as brown sugar toward the tip.

Europe's first reaction to sugar was to use it as a spice and a flavoring. This perhaps explains the Medieval taste for dishes that were both savory and sweet, the remnants of which we have today in plum puddings and mincemeat pies, which were originally composed of much meat and some fruit. One of the earliest confections that could be considered simply a candy were almonds coated with sugar. These evolved into marzipan, a paste made of almonds and sugar ground together, which has become an integral part of European confection making and baking.

expects from sugar, such as bulk and flavor. If you are going to use these, we recommend using them as a substitute for only some of the sugar in a recipe.

ASPARTAME was discovered in 1965 and is 160 to 220 times sweeter than sucrose. The FDA approved aspartame in 1981, making it the first low-calorie sweetener approved by the FDA in more than twenty-five years (since Saccharin). It is sold under trade names such as NutraSweet and Equal.

Aspartame sweeteners are heat-sensitive. They are not appropriate for recipes that are cooked more than twenty minutes because the chemical compounds break down and lose their sweetening power. Thus they aren't recommended for use in sweet yeast breads, quick breads, or cakes. You might want to experiment with short-bake cookies. It is best added to noncooked items such as fillings for no-bake pies or to puddings after they have been removed from the heat and are partially cooled. It is also marketed as "Equal for Recipes" and "Equal Spoonfuls," but while the packaging states that they can be used in "practically any recipe where sugar functions primarily as a sweetener," the label goes on to say, "In recipes where sugar also provides structure and volume [and other baking characteristics], some modifications may be required for best results." It takes 7¼ teaspoons of Equal to equal 1 cup of table sugar.

People with a rare condition called phenylketonuria (PKU) should avoid aspartame. **ACESULFAME POTASSIUM OR "ACESULFAME K"** was discovered in 1967 and was brought to market in 1988. It is about two hundred times sweeter than table sugar and sold under the brand names Sunett and Sweet One. It is heat stable so it can be used in baking and cooking, and it's suggested that you use acesulfame K in combination with granulated sugar when baking. Substitute 6 (1-gram) packets for each ¼ cup sugar.

SACCHARIN, up to seven hundred times sweeter than sugar, is named after the Latin word for sugar *(saccharum)* and has the longest history of all the sugar substitutes. It was discovered in 1879 and was used during both world wars to compensate for sugar shortages and rationing. Saccharin is sold under the trade names of Sweet'N Low, Sucaryl, Sugar Twin, Sweet Magic, and Zero-Cal. It has a long shelf life and is stable at high temperatures so is appropriate for use in baked goods. But as is stated on the Sweet'N Low container, "Many recipes require some sugar for proper volume, texture, and browning. We suggest replacing half the sugar your recipe calls for with an equivalent amount of Sweet'N Low." Some people with sensitive palates can detect an aftertaste. Because saccharin can pass from a mother to an unborn child, pregnant women may want to check with their obstetricians about the use of saccharin.

SUCRALOSE is the only noncaloric sweetener actually made from sucrose (table sugar) and was approved for public use by the FDA in 1998. To create it, three atoms of chlorine are substituted for three hydroxyl groups on the sugar molecule, a change that produces a sweetener that has no effective calories. It is six hundred times sweeter than the sugar from which it was created, yet still tastes like it. Unlike aspartame-based sweeteners, it does not deteriorate at high temperatures so it can be used in cooking and baking. It measures and pours like sugar. It is sold under the brand name Splenda.

Splenda can be used whenever you use sugar in cooking and baking. However, it works best in recipes where sugar is used primarily for sweetening, like fruit fillings, custards, sauces, and marinades. It also works well in quick breads, muffins, cookies, and pies. In recipes where sugar provides bulk structure to the product, such as yellow or chocolate cakes, you'll need to make a few changes in your recipe for best results. In recipes where the amount of sugar is quite high, such as meringues, caramel, pecan pies, and angel food or pound cakes, complete substitution for the entire sweetener called for may not yield the best results.

Other Ingredients

Flour, sugar, butter, water, milk, yeast—these are the workhorses of the baking world. But other key ingredients add such wonderful finesse to baked goods. What would the world be without chocolate? Without vanilla? How these and other baking accoutrements are chosen and used can be the defining element in your finished good.

Chocolate

Chocolate, *theobroma cacao,* "food of the gods," is one of those significant discoveries from the New World that has changed the lives (for better and worse) of all those who have come in contact with it. The cacao tree originated in the river valleys of South America. Sometime in the fifth century, the tree's seeds, or beans, were carried into what is now Mexico by the Mayas. When Columbus arrived in the New World he took seeds from the cacao tree back to Spain. As with many things ahead of their time, so was chocolate, at least in Europe. Spain wasn't interested. So it took another generation and another explorer to make the chocolate connection between new world and old. The rest, as they say, is history (see p. 570). It became such a prized ingredient that we still think of it as special.

Cocoa

NATURAL COCOA: Cocoa sold in the United States contains between 11 percent and 24 percent cocoa butter, with most supermarket cocoas falling in the 12 to 16 percent range. In Britain, cocoa must contain a minimum of 20 percent fat (the British know and like their fats). But they may know something else as well. Because fats are carriers of flavor, cocoa that has had most of the cocoa butter removed from it loses its flavor fairly quickly. Natural cocoa is light brown and has, because of its acidity, a slight edge to it. Because natural cocoa is acidic, you most often use baking soda, rather than baking powder, when you bake with it. The chemical reaction between the two creates carbon dioxide bubbles, which leaven the batter. At the same time, the baking soda neutralizes the acidity of the cocoa and the cocoa color darkens. Because of its lighter color and unique flavor, natural cocoa is used to make the beverage itself, as well as frosting, chocolate sauce, and fudge.

DUTCH-PROCESS (DUTCHED) COCOA: Dutch-process cocoa is either neutral or slightly alkaline. When you bake with it, you'll most often use baking powder rather than baking soda. Baking powder contains the acid that's needed for leavening that's been removed from the cocoa. Dutched cocoas are best in cakes and cookies.

If you have some cocoa and don't know whether it's natural or Dutch-process, stir some into a little warm water. Add a pinch of baking soda. If the cocoa fizzes and becomes a deeper color, you have natural cocoa. If it doesn't fizz, it's been Dutched.

BLACK COCOA: This is cocoa that has been severely Dutched, which intensifies the darkening and also the flavor. Use 1 or 2 tablespoons in conjunction with regular Dutch-process cocoa. This is the cocoa that makes Oreo cookies so dark.

From Tree to Table

For the past twenty-five years, most of the chocolate that's consumed worldwide, more than half a million tons a year, comes from Ghana in Africa. But the world's "chocolate belt" encircles the globe, located in those tropical countries within about 20 degrees south and north of the equator (the areas known as the tropic of Capricorn and tropic of Cancer, respectively). Some of the finest varieties come from this hemisphere.

The cacao tree produces buds, blossoms, and fruit on an ongoing basis. The pods (fruit), which are 9 or 10 inches in length and 4 or 5 inches in diameter, look a bit like large acorn squash, with ridges more rounded than sharp. As the pods become ripe, they're gathered, split open with a machete, and allowed to dry for twenty-four hours. The seeds within the pulp are then removed and thrown into boxes, where they begin to ferment. This is called "sweating," which goes on for several days. During fermentation, the juice of the pulp in which the seeds (or beans) are embedded drains away, the germ within the bean dies, the beans themselves develop a reddish tint, their bitterness is tempered and their flavor developed.

After the fermenting period, the beans are spread out in the sun or in a kiln, where their moisture is reduced from about 33 percent to 6 or 7 percent. The flavor continues to develop and become less acidic. At this point the beans are bagged (it takes twenty to thirty beans to make a pound) and sent to a chocolate processing plant.

The bean itself consists of the husk or shell (14 percent) and the interior kernel or "nib" (86 percent). The nibs are about 50 percent fat (the cocoa butter), 17 percent protein, and 30 percent various types of complex carbohydrates.

They're particularly rich in potassium, calcium, phosphorus, and, of course, caffeine (although not as much as one might think—certainly less than coffee or even tea).

At the processing plant the beans are cleaned and roasted, allowing the chocolate flavor and color to emerge. The nibs pull away from the shells, making them easier to remove. Once the shells have been cracked open and winnowed away, just the nibs are left, and the process of making chocolate can begin. The nibs are screened by size, then mixed with others from other plantations to create blends that will suit different needs and tastes. Then they're ground. During the grinding process, the beans are heated, melting the fatty part (the cocoa butter) and creating a fairly liquid mass that we know as "chocolate liquor" (which has nothing at all to do with alcohol). Chocolate liquor is a combination of about 47 percent chocolate solids and 53 percent cocoa butter.

Chocolate liquor is processed in three ways. If it's to be made into bitter (or unsweetened baking) chocolate, the pure liquor itself is molded into cakes and chilled. If it's to be made into eating chocolate, additional cocoa butter and sugar are added and then it's conched, a kneading/rolling process taking four to seventy-two hours, which aerates, mellows, and creates that famous silky consistency of the best chocolate. After conching, it's molded into bars or blocks and cooled.

If it's to be made into cocoa, the liquor is pressed hydraulically to remove a certain percent of the fat or cocoa butter (which goes into eating chocolate or is made into "white" chocolate). The remaining solids are pulverized into a powder or "cocoa."

Solid Chocolate

BITTER (UNSWEETENED) BAKING CHOCOLATE: Baking chocolate is essentially pure chocolate liquor—the ground cacao bean itself, chocolate solids, and cocoa butter. It contains no sugar. This is the only chocolate that's fairly straightforward.

SWEET CHOCOLATE: This ranges from bittersweet to semisweet. There are different varieties and grades but in the United States they must contain a minimum of 35 percent chocolate liquor. The best bittersweet varieties contain 65 to 70 percent; in general, the higher the percentage of chocolate liquor, the darker and stronger the chocolate. Also included is sugar, additional cocoa butter, and such flavorings as vanilla beans (the whole bean), vanillin (just the chemical essence), salt, and/or spices (cinnamon, cloves, etc.). If a chocolate contains 70 percent chocolate liquor, what is the rest? Ideally, just sugar, vanilla, and milk powder if it's a milk chocolate. Because cocoa butter is expensive, some eating chocolates contain other vegetable fats to keep their price down.

BITTERSWEET CHOCOLATE: Used often in baking, bittersweet chocolate has a stronger chocolate flavor than semisweet chocolate because it contains less sugar. But because the amount of sugar is not regulated, what one manufacturer calls bittersweet may be called semisweet by another manufacturer, so what you use is a matter of choice and taste.

MILK CHOCOLATE: This contains 15 to 20 percent milk solids substituted for a portion of the chocolate liquor. Although this is America's favorite eating chocolate, it's not used often in baking.

"WHITE" CHOCOLATE: We all know there's no such thing; to be "chocolate" there must be chocolate solids present. The best white chocolate is made from cocoa butter, with sugar and milk solids added.

COATING CHOCOLATE (COUVERTURE): The best contains no other fat than cocoa butter, which is tempered to behave in a certain way. Because tempering is a bit tricky, there are other coating chocolates that contain other vegetable fats that aren't so heat-sensitive and don't require tempering. But these lack the texture, shine, and flavor of chocolate made solely with cocoa butter. Coating chocolate is not the same as chocolate coating.

Cocoa Substitutions

If a recipe calls for natural cocoa and baking soda and you want to use Dutch-process cocoa, substitute an equal amount of Dutch-process cocoa but replace the soda with twice the amount of baking powder. If the recipe calls for Dutch-process cocoa and baking powder, substitute the same amount of natural cocoa but replace the baking powder with half the amount of baking soda. To substitute for a 1-ounce square of bitter baking chocolate, use 3 tablespoons of cocoa and 1 tablespoon of vegetable shortening, oil, or butter. To substitute cocoa for 1 ounce of semisweet chocolate, use the above formula, and add 3 tablespoons granulated sugar.

Tempering Chocolate

Cocoa butter, also known as theobroma oil, is a very stable fat. It contains natural antioxidants that discourage rancidity and allows chocolate to be stored for two to five years. For chocolate aficionados, it's most valued for the way it behaves in the mouth. While it remains brittle at room temperature or lower, it begins to melt just below body temperature, which creates the silky, sensuous "mouth feel" of high-quality chocolate.

You can only temper chocolate that contains cocoa butter, no other kind of fat. Cocoa butter is actually not just one fat, but a variety of structurally different components. Some of them melt at a higher temperature than others. When chocolate has been heated and begins to cool, the high-melt-point fats solidify first. These are the ones that give high-quality chocolate its shine and snap.

The object of tempering is to create an evenly distributed, very fine fat-crystal structure which will yield chocolate that remains shiny as it hardens. Because the high-melt-point fats solidify (crystallize) first, you're trying to "seed" the chocolate with these crystals, so the others fats will build their structure upon them as they cool and begin to set.

The easiest way to temper chocolate is with a chocolate tempering machine, available to the home baker through some catalogues, or at gourmet stores. To temper chocolate without a machine, place it in a double boiler (rather than over direct heat, because it can burn so easily). Heat it to between 115°F and 118°F to make sure all the fats are melted. These temperatures are approximate because each chocolate has its own appropriate melting point. Some high-quality Swiss chocolate needs to be heated to 122°F. The manufacturer should be able to give you information on whatever chocolate you want to temper.

It's important not to let any moisture infiltrate the chocolate, or it will seize (become grainy). Allow the chocolate to melt uncovered to allow any steam generated to dissipate. Seizing is essentially a chaotic crystallization of all the fats around the point where the water en-

HYBRID CHOCOLATE: Hybrid chocolates are those that contain fats in addition to cocoa butter. Due to the difference in melting points, some hybrid chocolates can have a waxy texture as a result. Brands that contain only cocoa butter are regarded as higher quality. But even the "best" need to be judged based on personal taste and inclination.

CHOCOLATE CHIPS: Most are usually hybrid chocolate and should be used where they are called for, for example, they should not be substituted for other baking chocolate made only with cocoa butter, because they won't behave the same way. There are some chips made for the professional baker that are made just with cocoa butter. Make sure you check the label.

CHOCOLATE EXTRACT: This is a natural extract from a special blend of cocoa beans that enhances the chocolate flavoring in baked goods. It's available through specialty shops and catalogues.

tered; it's characterized by chocolate that has turned into a lumpy, grainy, unfortunate mass.

Once the chocolate is melted, remove two-thirds of it from the heat, set it in a cool place, and stir constantly until it reaches a temperature of 78°F. At this point, fine fat crystals have formed and the chocolate is thick and pasty. Many chocolate manufacturers recommend slow cooling with constant stirring in order to produce the best texture, but there are a number of pastry chefs who prefer to speed things up by stirring the chocolate over cold water or by pouring it onto a marble slab and working it with a bench knife until it's cool. (This process can be compared to the beating you give fudge after it's cooked and cooled to create the ultrasmooth texture and flavor of good fudge. When the chocolate has reached 78°F, stir it back into the hot chocolate. The temperature should then be about 88°F. At this point, the chocolate is tempered.

After the tempered chocolate has cooled and crystallized appropriately, it's too thick for dipping, molding, or anything else and must be warmed slightly before it can be used. Again using a double boiler, it should be reheated to 86°F to 88°F, where it's liquid enough to use. Don't let it get warmer than this, or the fat crystals will melt and come "out of temper." If that happens, it will take a long time to set and when it finally does, the texture won't be as good. In addition, some of the cocoa butter tends to precipitate to the surface, causing the chocolate to "bloom."

There are two types of chocolate bloom, both the result of storage conditions. Fat bloom happens when chocolate has been stored where it's too warm. The low-melt-point fat crystals melt and recrystallize in larger crystals, which migrate to the surface of the chocolate. This makes the chocolate look as if it had been dusted with a gray or white powder. While it might look moldy, it's not; it can still be used for baking and/or the crystals can be recrystallized to assume their original form by tempering.

Sugar bloom happens when chocolate has been stored where it's damp. Because sugar is hygroscopic, moisture can condense on the surface of the chocolate and will slowly dissolve the sugars it comes in contact with. As it evaporates, it will leave small sugar crystals on the surface, which we experience as roughness.

Vanilla

This is a "new world" flavor from an orchid that grew only in central America until the middle of the nineteenth century. The Aztecs used it for flavor in conjunction with cacao. From here it made its way to the Philippines and, in 1846, to Tahiti. But the orchid wouldn't produce a bean just anywhere. In Mexico, a specific type of bee and hummingbird were responsible for its pollination and the subsequent bean. Finally, in Madagascar, in what used to be known as the Bourbon Islands (from the name of the royal French family) off the southeast coast of Africa it was discovered that the flowers could be pollinated by hand. Thus began the successful pursuit of the commercial growing of vanilla beans, the "Bourbon vanilla" which is about 75 percent of the vanilla that we use today.

A Bit of Chocolate History

For early Meso-Americans, the cacao tree played an important role. The beans formed a basis for currency. For the appropriate quantity, one could buy everything from food to slaves (a fairly good slave for about 100 beans). The beans were also the source of an unsweetened drink, xocoatl, made by pounding them and mixing them with boiling water. Xocoatl was drunk and cacao beans offered to the deities that presided over every important ritual during their lives.

At court, Spanish explorer Hernán Cortés was ceremoniously served xocoatl, this beverage of the gods, the name coming from an Aztec word meaning "bitter water." Bitter it was. Not long after this congenial welcome, Cortés, in the name of Spain, took Montezuma prisoner and slaughtered hundreds of his people. Montezuma died while in captivity and the ascendancy of the Aztec nation came to a halt. Two years later, the Aztec capital, Tenochtitlán (now Mexico City), was under Spanish control.

Cortés returned to Spain by way of Africa, planting some of his Mexican cacao beans there. This agrarian impulse enabled Spain, which ultimately acknowledged the value of the cacao bean, to monopolize the trade in chocolate for the next century. Today the bulk of the world's chocolate is supplied by trees that are the descendants of those that Cortés took to Africa.

The Spanish treated chocolate differently than had the Meso-Americans. They sweetened it with honey and flavored it with cinnamon and vanilla. Served hot as a restorative, this new incarnation of the cacao tree remained a Spanish secret for close to a century before it found its way over the border to France. The French acquired chocolate when Jews were expelled from Spain and subsequently settled in the region of Bayonne, just over the Spanish border. The French initially considered the bitter paste made from the cacao bean to be noxious, so its production was forced outside the town limits. As many perceptions are changed from the top down, Spanish nobility who married into the French court helped illuminate their countrymen about the virtues of chocolate. Ultimately, Bayonne chocolate was celebrated by its citizens.

Once chocolate became the darling of the aristocrats, its movement into other markets began to happen more quickly. In the early seventeenth century a recipe found its way into Italy. In 1657, a Frenchman opened a shop in London called the Coffee Mill and Tobacco Roll, from which he sold this bitter chocolate paste to be used for beverage making. This initial appearance of chocolate in England was so expensive (it cost more than half its weight in gold because of excessively high import duties on cacao beans) that again, only the wealthy could afford to buy and use it.

Wherever it went, people experimented with flavorings. Vanilla, the one favored by the Aztecs, has survived to become the flavor most frequently paired with chocolate, although many others have been tried. Chocolate flavored with cloves was popular in the seventeenth century. Anise, ginger, pepper, and chilies have also been used. Today you'll find chocolate flavored with honey, as well as coffee, almond, hazelnuts, and in Spain and Mexico, almost always, cinnamon. And in today's desserts, chocolate is paired with oranges, raspberries, strawberries, and other fruits.

Because so much ritual grows up around those things we perceive to be valuable and available only to a select few, there appeared in London, Amsterdam, and other European capitals fashionable chocolate houses where the wealthy would gather to savor this esoteric "restorative" drink. It wasn't until the mid-nineteenth century, when the duty on cacao beans was lowered to a rate of a penny a pound, that chocolate ceased being a luxury and began its ascendancy into popular culture.

In 1828 a Dutchman, C. J. Van Houten, found that by treating the cacao nibs with an alkali, he could make them release their fat (cocoa butter) more easily, the flavor was improved and the color darkened. This process has come to be known as "Dutching." Once chocolate liquor could be separated into its constituents, a great many opportunities for the evolution of chocolate presented themselves. The flavor of the chocolate was not contained in the fat, but in the separated solids. These solids, pulverized into a powder we now know as cocoa, was a much more intensely flavored chocolate product. And the ability to handle cocoa butter separately made possible the next important incarnation of chocolate.

As the nineteenth century progressed, many of the names that we now associate with chocolate began their creative borrowings and building on each other's developments and discoveries. In England, first Fry and Sons and, two years later, Cadbury, found that by adding sugar and additional cocoa butter to chocolate liquor they could create a solid chocolate that could be eaten out of hand. Although we think of the Swiss as the originators or keepers of some the most successful recipes for making chocolate, they were actually slow to get to it. The Italians dominated the manufacture of chocolate in the eighteenth century. At the end of the eighteenth century, the Swiss began to become serious about chocolate, and some of the most famous names in the field began to emerge. In 1819 the first Swiss chocolate factory was opened by François-Louis Cailler. Philippe Suchard opened a factory in the 1850s. Jean Tobler, of Toblerone fame, didn't make his appearance until the beginning of the twentieth century.

Because we also associate dairy products with the Swiss, it wasn't an accident that the Swiss developed another chocolate incarnation: milk chocolate. Earlier in the century, Henri Nestlé, a Swiss chemist, developed a process to make what we now know as condensed milk. In 1875 a Swiss chocolate manufacturer named Daniel Peter (who married into the Cailler chocolate dynasty) combined Henri Nestlé's condensed milk with his chocolate product. And so milk chocolate was born. Another significant contribution made by the Swiss was that of Rodolphe Lindt, who developed "conching," a kneading/rolling process that both improved flavor and removed the grittiness that had been associated with solid chocolate.

Chocolate finally made its way back across the Atlantic, north of its original origins, to the America colonies in the eighteenth century. Because the colonists were entranced by it, New England sea captains began bringing home cacao beans from their trading voyages to the West Indies. So Americans became seriously involved in the story of chocolate at just about the same time as the Europeans.

The manufacture of chocolate started in America in 1765 in Milton Lower Falls, near Dorchester, Massachusetts. James Baker financed the first water-powered chocolate mill. Since then, other American companies have become involved in the manufacture of chocolate. Although there's a sense that the best chocolate comes from Europe, there are today a number of American manufacturers that produce extremely high-quality chocolate.

The process of creating vanilla is intensive and long so it is still an expensive flavoring. After the flowers are pollinated, bean pods begin to form, and take about a month and a half to reach full size, somewhere between 6 and 10 inches in length. They are picked before they are ripe, heated quickly to stop the ripening process, and then placed in the sun to dry. For several days, they dry in the sun during the day and are wrapped up to sweat at night. Then they are laid out to dry completely in the shade. Finally they are sorted and placed in containers to continue to age, during which time flavor and character are developed.

Today Mexican vanilla is relatively scarce because its habitat has been reduced. But Mexican vanilla is considered, by some, to be the best in the world because of its complex and desirable flavor. Make sure you buy Mexican vanilla from a reliable source as sometimes it's cut with other (potentially dangerous) ingredients. Tahitian vanilla is preferred by some for its flowery mellow aroma and flavor. Indonesian vanilla has the simplest flavor. Madagascar vanilla is the most widely used and is also preferred by many.

Vanilla is available as a whole bean (from which you can flavor any number of things, including sugar). It is also available ground to a powder, wonderful in custard, cookies, ice cream, or whipped cream, anywhere that you want an intense vanilla flavor and the visibility of bean flecks. Because the flavor of the powder doesn't evaporate when heated (vanilla extract loses some of its flavor in heating), it's well suited for baked goods. Vanilla extract, the essential oil of the vanilla bean dissolved in alcohol, is more widely available. There are double- and triple-strength vanilla extracts, as well as a vanilla essence so strong that only a drop or two is needed. These are available through special suppliers by mail order. To minimize the evaporation of vanilla extract when making cookies or cakes, always add it to the butter and sugar when you cream them. The butter acts as a buffer and protects it from the heat, resulting in more flavor. Vanilla paste can be used measure-for-measure in place of vanilla extract but with the addition of flecks of vanilla bean that are evident in the end product. One tablespoon of vanilla paste equals one vanilla bean.

Make Your Own Vanilla

You can make your own vanilla extract by combining a vanilla bean, slit lengthwise and cut into 3 pieces, with 1 cup unflavored vodka or brandy. Put the mixture in a nonreactive container (glass is ideal) and let it steep for 2 to 8 weeks, or longer. The longer it steeps, the stronger the vanilla will be. Though this won't have the complexity of flavor of professionally manufactured vanilla extract, it's eminently suitable for recipes where vanilla plays a minor, rather than starring, role.

Almonds and Almond Flavoring

Next to vanilla, almond extract is probably the baker's most frequently used flavoring. Almonds, too, are an important ingredient in many baked goods. Almonds grow on flowering twenty- to thirty-foot tall trees, beautiful enough that in some areas they are grown just for their aesthetic characteristics. The almond belongs to the same genus as apricots, cherries, plums, and peaches, but its fruit is not equivalently succulent; what we eat is the seed.

Trees that are grown for the almonds that they produce are found in a fairly narrow band around the world where conditions are frost-free but not tropical. Although you will find producing almond trees in most Mediterranean countries, today California supplies more than half of the world's supply.

There are two types of almond, bitter and sweet.

SWEET ALMONDS are the ones we eat, with or without skins, unblanched or blanched. The skins are edible but can sometimes be bitter. If they're not too bitter (the taste test will determine this), don't bother blanching them because the skin adds positive flavor notes to whatever you're making.

Almonds have a mild flavor. You can find them in most groceries whole, sliced, slivered, and sometimes as meal or flour. Almond meal doesn't maintain its flavor very long so you may opt to make your own by grinding whole, blanched almonds in a blender or food processor. Almond paste and marzipan are made of blanched sweet almonds that have been ground with sugar and almond extract added to sweeten and intensify the flavor. Almond paste has less sugar than marzipan and is more coarsely ground.

BITTER ALMONDS, cousins of the sweet almond, contain prussic acid, which is highly toxic. It makes the nuts so unpleasant to the taste that it is unlikely that anyone would eat enough (fifty or so can be lethal) to do any harm. It is these almonds from which oil is extracted—the prussic acid is destroyed during processing—and blended with ethyl alcohol to make almond extract, probably the most common baking extract after vanilla. Bitter almond oil is also sold without the addition of alcohol; it's extremely strong and should be used by the drop, rather than by the teaspoon.

Like any nuts that contain oil, almonds will eventually become rancid. Packaged natural almonds can be stored in unopened packages in a cool dark place up to two years. Unopened roasted almonds can be stored under the same conditions up to one year. Both will last even longer if refrigerated. Almond paste can be stored in the refrigerator up to two years. A hot pantry will hasten rancidity. Once packaged almonds are opened, be sure to store in an airtight container or sealed plastic bag with air squeezed out in a cool, dry, dark place (ideally in the refrigerator) and use within three months. Avoid exposing nuts to humidity for maximum shelf life.

Other Extracts, Oils, and Flavors

EXTRACTS are made from the essential oils and/or flavoring components of natural ingredients dissolved in alcohol. There is a great array available, including those from fruit, nuts, and seeds and such things as mint and coffee. If you don't want to use an alcohol-based extract, which is the most common form, there are also glycerin-based extracts available from specialty shops and catalogues that perform the same way with the same intensity of flavor.

OTHER ESSENTIAL OILS available include orange, lemon, and lime. These are very powerful and very little is needed to add flavor to any baked good. The oil comes from the skin of the fruit (the zest), where there is an intensity of flavor. Zest from both oranges and lemons is available although it's easy to create your own.

FLOWER WATERS are other flavoring agents. The ones most commonly available are made from the essential oils of rose petals and orange flower petals. They are more subtle than oils but add lovely overtones to lightly flavored confections, whipped cream, ice cream, sponge cake, and angel food cake.

BUTTERSCOTCH and caramel are often confused with each other. Today it is usually accepted that the flavor of butterscotch is that of brown sugar cooked with butter. To make butterscotch candy, according to F. Marian McNeill in *The Scots Kitchen,* you cook a combination of 1 pound of brown sugar with ¼ pound of butter to the soft-crack stage. Then you remove it from the heat, flavor it with a touch of ginger and a bit of lemon zest, beat it with a fork for a few minutes and pour it on a slab to cool. Crack off pieces with the back of a knife.

CARAMEL is produced by cooking granulated sugar in a heavy pan until it melts and caramelizes, that is, becomes liquid and essentially begins to burn. This is what gives it its unique flavor. Caramel can range in color from light to deep brown by cooking it somewhere between 320°F to 350°F. You'll also find caramelized sugar on crème brulée which is done with a small culinary blowtorch or with a caramelizing iron. If caramel is cooked until it's very dark, it can be used as coloring in a variety of things from breads (usually rye) to gravy.

Spices and Herbs

ALLSPICE: This New World spice is from a tree in the myrtle family and was thought by Columbus to be pepper, which he was hoping to find at the end of his voyage, and which the allspice berry resembles. Today, most of the world's supply is grown in Jamaica and Jamaican allspice is coveted. Although it has its own personality, allspice is suggestive of a combination of other aromatic spices, particularly cinnamon and cloves but with a hint of nutmeg and black pepper. Allspice berries can be used whole in marinades or in pickling. Ground allspice is available in most groceries or you can grind your own. A touch is wonderful in applesauce and it can also be used with other spices in fruit desserts, steamed puddings, pies, and cakes. As a substitute, try ground cloves, about one-quarter the amount of allspice called for, and a touch of nutmeg.

ANISE: This self-seeding annual, related to parsley, dill, and caraway, comes from countries bordering the eastern Mediterranean. It tastes like a sweet licorice and is used, as a seed, to flavor a variety of European breads, but it is also used to flavor other baked goods and desserts. As a substitute, try fennel.

STAR ANISE: This has some of the same flavor components and can also be used in baked goods. It is native to China and comes from an evergreen related to the magnolia.

CARDAMOM: A member of the ginger family, cardamom, after vanilla and saffron, is the third most expensive spice in the world. It grows as a perennial herb in South India and Sri Lanka, and also in Guatemala. The pods, which are about the size of a plump raisin, encapsulate three small compartments that contain tiny seeds. The pods should be either green or white (not brown or black, which is not true cardamom and of less interest to the baker). It is used to flavor teas and certain traditional baked goods from Germany and Scandinavia. The crushed seeds (a rolling pin does this nicely) produce the strongest flavor, although they can be bought already ground. If you have no cardamom, try substituting ginger.

CARAWAY: This plant is related to anise (their aromas are faintly similar), parsley, and dill. It is most frequently used as a seed rather than ground into a powder and as such is used to flavor many German and northern European breads as well as some Irish soda breads. You will also find it in some cheeses. Caraway is used most frequently in savory goods, but it can also be an interesting counterpoint in sweet goods, particularly paired with citrus or, in the case of soda breads, raisins. Caraway is not easily substituted. A caraway-flavored thyme comes close but is not easily available unless you grow your own. Fennel is another option.

CINNAMON: This spice comes from the dried bark of a tree native to Sri Lanka. It grows only there and in India and is the only true cinnamon recognized in Britain. But there are two types of "cinnamon" acknowledged in the United States and a number of other countries as well. The second is the one with which we are probably most familiar. This is cassia cinnamon, which is a member of the same family as true cinnamon, a type of laurel. This cinnamon is native to Southeast Asia, southern China, northern Vietnam, and Indonesia. Both are harvested from the bark of a tree. You can tell the difference between sticks of the former and the latter by the way they roll. Sticks of the Ceylon cinnamon curl just in one direction looking like rolled up paper. Sticks of cassia curl inward from both sides to resemble a scroll. Both types are available ground as well. The color as well as the flavor of Ceylon cinnamon is lighter. Cassia cinnamon is darker, redder, and more intense. Most of the cinnamon we buy at the grocery store is cassia cinnamon. But there are commercial cinnamons that are a blend of the two. If you buy ground cinnamon, buy it in small quantities as the flavor deteriorates with time. If you are out of cinnamon, you can substitute allspice with maybe a touch of ginger and nutmeg but use about a quarter as much.

Try sprinkling some cinnamon on French toast as you cook it before you turn it over.

CLOVES: This perennial evergreen shrub native to the Moluccas in East Indonesia belongs to the myrtle family. The unopened flower bud, picked by hand and then dried, becomes the little nail-like seed container that we know as cloves. In fact the name "clove" evolved through a number of Latin-based languages and was ultimately incorporated into Middle English as "clowe," meaning nail shaped. Cloves are used commonly to flavor both savory and sweet foods. But, as has been stated by an astute culinarian, "the flavor is best when kept below the level of recognition." Cloves are available whole or ground. The most appropriate substitute is allspice.

GINGER: Not known as a wild plant, ginger probably originally came from Southeast Asia. It's been in use for several thousand years both for culinary as well as medicinal purposes. It reached Europe via Rome. When Rome fell, it was reintroduced to the West by Marco Polo. In medieval times, ginger as a flavoring became very common in England, and in fact ginger and pepper were two of the most frequently used spices. It was at that point that gingerbread became part of culinary history. Ginger and gingerbread were for medieval England what chocolate is for us today. In pre-twentieth-century cookbooks, you'll find numerous "receipts" for ginger-based cakes.

Today half the world's ginger comes from India, but it is also grown in China, Hawaii, Africa, and some parts of the Middle East. Australia has become a new player and is the source of some of the best crystallized ginger. In the Orient, ginger is used widely to flavor savory foods. In Europe and the United States it is used most frequently in sweet baked goods. But we also experience it in ginger ale. For the baker, ginger is available as the whole root, the mature root dried and powdered, the young root crystallized, and in ginger syrup or extract. Powdered ginger is quite different from fresh or crystallized ginger and isn't an appropriate substitute when the former are called for. If you are out of powdered ginger, you might try allspice with a little cinnamon or mace.

LAVENDER: Historically, lavender was used by the Greeks and Romans as a bath perfume. It was introduced into Britain in 1568, and English gardeners started an immediate love affair with the plant. Pillows and sachets were stuffed with dried lavender flowers, and lavender "washing water" came into use. The culinary use of the flower was noted as early as the reign of Queen Elizabeth I. Powdered lavender was served as a condiment, and the Queen so enjoyed conserve of lavender that it was always on her table. In this country, the Shakers use lavender in cooking, in their famous lemon pies and lemon breads. Its penetrating, sunny taste marries surprisingly well with the flavors of both butter and vanilla. Long having been overlooked as an edible flower, lavender makes a delightful contribution to baked goods. The pleasures of lavender transcend the garden when the flower is dried and used in baking. Anticipate the essence of summer by using lavender in pound cakes, cookies, and bread.

NUTMEG AND MACE: These spirits come from the same tree, native to the Moluccas in Indonesia, although it's grown today in the West Indian island of Grenada. After the fruit is removed (the fruit itself is dried with palm sugar and eaten as a snack food in Indonesia), you'll find a thin, lacy, leathery reddish tissue on the outside of the pit.

This is called mace, and is removed and dried and is sold either whole, as "blade mace," or ground. Mace has a faint aroma of nutmeg, but you'll also smell undertones of cinnamon, maybe cloves and ginger. You can substitute any or a combination of those if you don't have any at hand.

After the mace has been removed and the nutmeg pit dried, the shell is cracked and the nutmeg removed to be sold whole or as powder. Nutmeg has a flavor all its own, which belongs in eggnog, but you'll also find a touch in savory dishes as well, such as quiche and béchamel sauce. Nutmeg's flavor makes it difficult to find a substitute, but try a little cinnamon, ginger, or mace.

MINT: A great addition to a baker's kitchen, mint comes in a whole array of flavors. Apple, chocolate, orange, peppermint, spearmint, pineapple, all can be used to flavor syrups, frostings, candy, and chocolate.

PEPPER: True pepper, or *piper nigrum*, grows on a tropical vine native to the Tranvancore and Malabar Coast of India (the southwestern tip). Although one of the finest kinds still comes from that part of India, it is now cultivated near the equator around the globe.

Like many other spices, pepper has played an important role in the power struggles throughout our history. It was valued so highly that it spurred new trade routes between the east and west. Like salt, it was used during the Middle Ages as money.

Black pepper is dried from still green but-about-to-be-ripe peppercorns. White peppercorns are dried from the hulled version of the same fruit after it has reached maturity. By changing the time of picking and drying you can make black, white, red, and green pepper from the same plant. Tellicherry (a district on the Malabar coast of India) pepper is dried from peppercorns that have been allowed to ripen beyond green to a yellow-orange. Because pickers wait until just this point to harvest them, this pepper has particularly rich flavor. This method is used only in India. Tellicherry peppercorns are larger than typical black peppercorns and their color is a dark, warm brown. They are slightly more expensive than regular black pepper because it's riskier to wait to pick until that precise point of ripeness. Another equally good type is the Lampong pepper (from the Lampong district of southeastern Sumatra, the second largest of the Indonesian islands). These two are considered the best varieties of black pepper.

Black pepper enhances savory dishes but it can also be used to enhance and give a little extra "spice" to spice mixes for certain sweet goods such as gingerbread, steamed puddings, and spice cakes. White pepper is missing the outer skin of black pepper, which contains some of the flavor components. Although it's more expensive than black pepper because it takes more work to produce, white pepper is used primarily where the black flecks of black pepper are not wanted.

SAFFRON: The costliest of all the spices, real saffron is the dried stigma of a crocus-like flour that originated probably in Persia but today is grown from Spain to Kashmir. It was of great importance in medieval Europe where it was used as both a flavoring and also a dye.

The dried stigmas look like red threads and, when soaked in a liquid, emit a bright yellow color. One hundred fifty thousand flowers are needed for one kilogram of dried saffron. Less expensive varieties are often adulterated with the yellow stamen of the flower, which has the right color but no flavor of its own. Spain and Iran are the largest producers, accounting for more than 80 percent of the world's production.

Saffron has long flavored a cake unique to the west country of England, called Saffron Cake. It's also important in a Swedish bread (Lussekatter or St. Lucia's cats) that is made for the festival of Santa Lucia. You'll find it also as a dominant flavor in Provençal bouillabaisse. The flavor of saffron is not easily duplicated, although turmeric is an option for producing a yellow color.

Spice Blends

APPLE PIE SPICE can be any number of combinations, including whatever you decide you like. Here are a couple of commercial ones: cinnamon with a touch of cloves and nutmeg; or a more ambitious version is a blend of cinnamon, fenugreek (an herb that has the aroma of curry and is used in same), lemon peel, ginger, cloves, and nutmeg.

Pumpkin pie spice is multiple combinations, but usually includes cinnamon, ginger, cloves, and nutmeg.

You can use these spice blends to season any apple or pumpkin (or squash) dish, or any other dish you think would benefit from these particular blends of spices. Simply substitute the spice blend for the same amount, combined, of other spices called for in the recipe (excluding salt). For example, if a recipe calls for 1 teaspoon of cinnamon, ¼ teaspoon of cloves, and ¼ teaspoon of allspice, substitute 1½ teaspoons apple pie spice. Use pumpkin pie spice in a similar manner. You can also sprinkle a little pumpkin pie spice over a dish of baked or mashed squash; or try a dash of apple pie spice on ice cream, or over hot applesauce.

ENGLISH MIXED SPICE is available in some specialty stores. This is a traditional English combination of several spices ground together. Most versions contain allspice, cloves, coriander, mace, and nutmeg, with sometimes a bit of cinnamon. Use it as described above.

Salt

Salt has become fashionable and fun. Like bed linens that used to be white, salt now comes in a variety of shapes and colors, from white to gray to red, and physically as small solid cubes to lovely pyramid-shaped crystals. There are some that are less refined with more minerals in them creating, as many are convinced, subtle and unique flavors. And, of course, there are now the flavored "boutique" salts, garlic, chili, lavender, rosemary, and so on.

In baking, when any of these salts are allowed to dissolve, their impact in a baked product will be hard to differentiate (aside from the flavored ones). But when you use them as accoutrements, there may be flavor differentiations that are more discernable. And there are some that physically will "stick" better and will melt more quickly (or not so quickly) on your tongue.

Most fascinating are the cultures and history that they evoke. All salt comes from the sea, mined from old seabeds deep in the earth, or from salt deposits on the surface, or actively evaporated from the sea.

Salt intensifies and enhances flavors in all baked goods. Because it is hygroscopic, it attracts moisture. This is good in some situations, and not in others (bread crusts for instance). In yeast baking, salt strengthens dough and tightens its structure, which increases the time needed to sufficiently develop the gluten. It also slows fermentation. Bread without salt is insipid. Even the Tuscans' bread, which is traditionally unsalted, is eaten with salty foods. One of the most appealing ways to eat bread is to spread a slice of pain de campagne with sweet butter and sprinkle it with a bit of fleur de sel, a French sea salt.

There isn't anything that you can substitute for salt. In most baked goods it's there in quantities that are small enough not to be a problem. But if you need to reduce your salt intake, try cutting it in half before you eliminate it entirely.

Herbs

These flavorful little leaves are usually used fresh and are delightful in all manner of breads. Some actually have flavors that blend well with sweet goods, such as lemon thyme and caraway.

BASIL has an almost licorice or aniselike flavor when it is fresh, which is when it should be used. It is best used on top of flatbreads such as pizza or focaccia, and of course it is the linchpin in pesto or Provençal pistou, both of which are delicious on bread.

DILL flavor can be found in either its flowers or its seeds. Dill seeds are wonderful in breads, particularly soda breads, where you can substitute them for caraway.

GARLIC is also best on, rather than in, a bread. Minced raw, it can flavor butter or olive oil, or you can bake it until it is soft and sweet and use as a condiment. To bake garlic, break a head into individual cloves, spread on a baking sheet, sprinkle with olive oil and a bit of salt, and bake for about 30 minutes. Then squeeze the cloves out of their skins with your fingers and mash.

OREGANO AND MARJORAM are similar in aroma and flavor, with oregano being the more assertive of the two. They can be used in savory quick or yeast breads along with, or in place of thyme.

ROSEMARY has a very appealing and assertive flavor that is wonderful with roasted potatoes and lamb, in potato and cheese breads, and paired with ginger in some sweet goods.

TARRAGON is also anise-flavored but different from anise and fennel. You can infuse milk with it to use in sweet breads, or use it in a savory quick bread.

THYME, like mint, comes in many flavors—lemon, oregano, caraway, and traditional English. Lemon thyme can flavor sweet baked goods, but some of the others are wonderful in savory quick or yeast breads. Thyme is fun to grow and is probably the best way to come by some of the less common versions.

Nuts

Nuts are a wonderful addition to baked goods, adding flavor and texture. Almonds, pecans, and walnuts all seem to have a sweeter and deeper flavor if they are lightly toasted. Because nuts contain a significant amount of oil, you need to buy them fresh. If you buy them in bulk, keep them in the freezer. They'll keep nicely for up to a year.

To toast, spread nuts on a baking sheet and bake them at 350°F for 8 to 10 minutes. Keep an eye on them because they can burn quickly.

The easiest, fastest way to chop nuts is to put the required amount in a plastic bag, close the bag loosely, and whack nuts with the flat end of a meat mallet or other heavy object. A few whacks will give you coarsely chopped nuts; more whacks, and you'll get finely chopped, almost ground nuts. To make nut meal, pulse them in a food processor until they are as fine as you want.

ALMONDS (see p. 573)

CHESTNUTS have had a long history in Europe as a food staple. Chestnut flour was even used to make bread and was the basis of Italian polenta before cornmeal, or maize, was introduced from the Americas. Nowadays it is more of a condiment. Chestnuts are often eaten roasted but chestnut flour, ground from dried chestnuts, can be used in many baked goods.

COCONUT, from the coconut palm tree, is almost always used flaked or shredded by bakers. Sometimes it is sweetened as well. It is used to flavor baked goods and sprinkled on top of frosted cakes as decoration, flavor, and for texture.

HAZELNUTS, or filberts, are grown in this country in Oregon and farther north, in British Columbia. They are delicious buttery nuts that are wonderful alone, but are particularly wonderful with chocolate. They have a light, crunchy texture and can be used in cakes, breads, cookies, quick breads, and candy, anywhere you want the flavor and texture of nuts. Hazelnuts can also be purchased as a flour.

Here's an easy way to skin them. Most methods call for you to toast whole hazelnuts, and then to rub them between two towels to release their skins. We've found an easier method is to toast the hazelnuts for about 10 minutes (until they begin to brown) in a 350°F oven. Remove the nuts from the oven and let cool for 2 minutes. Put the nuts into a food processor equipped with the plastic dough blade and pulse until the nuts have shed most of their skins. Some of the nuts will crack, but this is quick and very effective. Pick the nuts out of the pile of skins, and you're ready to roll.

PECANS are a North American nut and probably one of the more frequently used, particularly in the South, where they are native. They are delicious raw and even more so toasted. You can purchase them whole, in pieces, or as meal, although it's easy to chop your own. You can easily create pecan meal in a food processor. Because of their oil content, they can become bitter fairly quickly, so use them up or keep them in the freezer. They can be used anywhere walnuts (or most other nuts) are called for.

PINE NUTS, or pignoli, are the rich, sweet, small seeds from the pinecones of certain pine trees, which are found in several parts of the world, including the Southwest. These trees are not easily cultivated and are happier living wild where all kinds of creatures vie for the nuts. The Hopi, Navajo, and other Southwestern tribes have used them as a staple for thousands of years, eaten in every form, whole, ground and baked into cakes, or pounded into a paste. Today, the most common pine nuts in our groceries are from a tree of the northern coastline of the Mediterranean, from Portugal and Spain in the west to Lebanon in the east. Pine nuts are essential in pesto, but after you've nibbled a few, you'll find you'll want to put them in other baked goods from quick breads to cookies.

PISTACHIOS, those lovely pale green nuts that are hard to stop eating, have been enjoyed by Middle Easterners for several thousand years. They grow on a small tree native to Turkey and the area around the Caspian Sea. There were formerly forests of pistachio trees from Lebanon, across Syria and eastward through and beyond northern Iraq. There is a variety raised in California. Pistachios are wonderful in ice cream, but you can use them in almost any baked good where you want the texture and flavor of nuts.

WALNUTS come from a tree that grows in temperate climates found wild from southeastern Europe all the way to China. Today they grow in abundance in California, especially in the Sacramento Valley, making the United States the largest walnut producer in the world.

Walnuts are related to the pecan. Also related are the American butternut (or American white walnut) and the black walnut, both of which grow in the east and whose nuts both have a slightly stronger flavor. In baking, all of these can be used interchangeably although there are some flavor differences.

Seeds

Seeds add flavor and texture to baked goods. Because they contain a lot of oil, like nuts, they are subject to rancidity. Freezing will extend the life of many seeds, but they're best when fresh.

FLAX SEED, the slightly larger bronze brothers of sesame seeds, can be sprinkled on the outside of bread. But because they are almost useless nutritionally unless the seed coat is cracked, it's best to use cracked or milled flax seeds in bread. They add a pleasing nutty flavor and their oil makes adding additional fat or oil unnecessary. Buy them often and use them fresh, as they will become rancid over time.

POPPY SEEDS are sprinkled on top of many baked goods and add a delicious flavor to coffeecakes and other quick breads. They can also be crushed and used with almonds, sugar, and a touch of lemon in pastry fillings. Toasting can bring out their flavor quite nicely. Buy just enough to use, or freeze what you don't use.

PUMPKIN SEEDS, or pepitas, are too large to be used on rolls or breads, but they can certainly be used in them, or in cookies or quick breads. They are enhanced with a bit of toasting.

SESAME SEEDS, also called benne seeds, are found in Southern cookies called Benne wafers (see p. 163). They have a lovely, nutty flavor that toasting will bring out. You can use them on breads, rolls, and other baked goods, as well as in them. Sesame seeds are also ground into a paste called tahini or sesame butter. Tahini has a nutty flavor that can be used as a dip on its own or mixed with chickpeas, lemon juice, and garlic to make hummus. Sesame seeds mixed with honey are used to make halvah, a Middle Eastern confection.

SUNFLOWER SEEDS are our own native seeds. Unhulled they make wonderful bird food (because birds can do their own hulling). Hulled, they taste great plain and, like small nuts, can be used in many baked goods as well as on them. They are very tasty raw or toasted. And sunflowers are enough to make anyone smile.

Tools

Baking can be a simple matter of using your imagination, a
spoon, and a bowl to create everything from brownies to bread. On the other
hand, the journey from recipe to oven-hot goodies can involve any number
of specialized tools and pans. There is almost no end to the array of tools
(some say "toys") that a baker can accumulate. But knowing how to select the
best tools for your baking, and also what attributes those tools should have,
can save you a lot of time and money. Our test kitchens work with hundreds
of tools every year, poking, dropping, and trying to scratch, break, or
otherwise abuse just about every tool in the marketplace. Here's what we've
learned from using all those funny whisks, trying every shape and surface
imaginable for a mixing bowl, and baking in every pan—assessing it for
size, durability, and ease of release—that comes our way.

Pans

Baking pans are typically made from aluminum (an excellent heat conductor), or an aluminum-steel combination. Less common are stainless-steel pans; while easy to clean and nonreactive, they don't conduct heat as well as aluminum. A wonderful hybrid pan combines a core of aluminum between thin top and bottom layers of stainless steel, giving the baker the best of both worlds—good heat conduction and easy cleanup. Some newer pans are made from soft silicone, a naturally nonstick material whose flexibility assists the baker in getting baked goods out of the pan undamaged. We've found silicone pans to be best for sweet baked goods, whose sugar helps them brown; baked goods low in sugar or fat (e.g., hearth breads) baked in a silicone pan don't brown well.

Other common materials for baking pans include glass, ceramic, or stoneware. On the plus side, these pans are often lovely to look at, and a clear glass pan allows you to see how well the crust is browning as the product bakes. On the minus side, ceramic or stoneware doesn't conduct heat as quickly as metal pans. If you're baking something where precise temperature isn't critical (bread pudding or pie), they're a perfectly acceptable choice. Because clear glass conducts heat almost too quickly compared to aluminum, it's recommended that you reduce the oven temperature 25°F when using a glass pan.

Baking pans are often coated with a nonstick surface. This is usually helpful, but also means you shouldn't cut baked goods in the pan unless you use a special nonstick-safe knife or server. Angel food pans should not have a nonstick surface, as the baking batter actually needs to climb up the wall of the pan in order for the cake to rise.

Look for pans that are sturdy, but not so heavy that they're hard to handle. When a recipe calls for a 9-inch round pan, it means the top inside measurement should be 9 inches. Many manufacturers cut corners and make their pans 9 inches from edge to edge, but only 8¾ inches (or less) inside. This makes a difference, particularly with pies, in whether the pan can hold a recipe comfortably.

Yeast Bread Pans

LOAF PANS: Just as the baguette is France's signature loaf, pan bread—the familiar sandwich loaf—must surely be America's. To make a sandwich loaf using a recipe calling for 3 to 3½ cups flour, use a pan that measures 8½ x 4½ x 2½ inches. For a recipe calling for 4 cups of flour, use a 9 x 5 x 2½-inch pan. Using the proper size pan will give you a nicely domed loaf; using a pan that's too big will yield a loaf that's flat across the top.

Standard loaf pan

A pain de mie or Pullman pan, usually 13 x 4 x 4 inches, is a straight-sided loaf pan with a flat sliding cover. Holding a recipe made with about 4½ cups of flour, it will produce a very fine-textured, flat-topped bread, perfect for sandwiches. If you have a pain de mie pan, try the White Bread 101 recipe on page 198, increasing the amount of all of the ingredients (except the yeast) by 50 percent.

When making sweet breads, use a light-colored pan, to keep the bread's crust from burning. When making bread without a significant amount of sugar (1½ tablespoons of sugar or less per cup of flour), use a dark-colored pan to promote good browning.

Pain de mie pan

COVERED STONE BAKERS: For extra-crisp hearth-style loaves, choose a covered stone baker. Shaped to hold round or baguette loaves, a covered stone baker will draw moisture from the bread as it bakes, producing a crunchy bottom crust. In addition, while that moisture is drawn off during the initial part of baking, it collects as steam inside the covered pan, keeping the bread's upper crust soft, so that it can rise to its fullest. Once the steam has dissipated into the oven, the upper crust becomes crisp as well.

Stoneware

SHAPED PANS: There are a variety of pans on the market designed to shape and hold particular loaves. Included in this group are pans for baguettes (double and triple); Italian loaves (usually double); breadsticks; and Italian sandwich rolls (4 to 5 rolls). These pans are usually perforated, allowing for air circulation for a crisp crust. Other shapes include pans for hot dog and hamburger buns; brioche; panettone; and sticky buns or cinnamon rolls. These pans aren't perforated, as the goal is a soft crust and, in the case of sticky buns, no leaks!

Brioche pans

PIZZA PANS: Whether your choice is Sicilian-style (rectangular thick-crust), Neapolitan (round thin-crust), deep-dish, or free-form, there's a pizza pan to fill your need. Pizza pans are usually made of dark metal, either anodized aluminum or, less common, blue steel. Both of these materials transfer heat quickly and thoroughly, and if there's one thing every pizza needs, it's high heat delivered quickly. An exception to this is porous (unglazed) stoneware pans. Because of their ability to draw moisture from the dough, they'll make pizza crust every bit as crisp as a dark metal pan, with less chance of burning the crust. For this reason some folks prefer unglazed stoneware to metal. Another alternative is to cook pizza directly on a preheated baking stone.

Pizza pans are available in 12- and 14-inch round size, both deep-dish and thin-crust versions; in individual deep-dish pans (about 6½ inches wide, usually sold in a set of four); and in 13 x 18-inch rectangular. You can find them perforated or solid bottom; we prefer a perforated pan, which we set directly on a preheated baking stone. Don't purchase a nonstick pizza pan; you're sure to injure the finish eventually by cutting in the pan. Instead, make sure there's a good film of olive oil in the bottom of the pan before you add the dough.

Unless you're making a Chicago-style deep-dish pizza, which requires a 12- to 14-inch round pan at least 2 inches deep, your pizza pan doesn't need to be very deep. In fact, a flat, rimless, perforated pizza disk is the top choice for some, as it allows the oven's heat to reach all parts of the pizza.

A typical pizza crust recipe calling for 3 cups of flour will make two thin-crust 12-inch pizzas; or a thick-crust 14-inch round or 13 x 18-inch (half-sheet pan) rectangular pizza; or four medium-crust 6½- to 8-inch individual pizzas.

Cookie Pans

COOKIE SHEETS: Flat metal sheets designed to hold rows of baking cookies come in a variety of sizes and finishes. Purchase a cookie sheet that optimizes the size of your oven. For best heat circulation, it should have a 2-inch clearance on all sides when set on the oven rack. Make sure the sheet is substantial enough that it won't warp or buckle at high heat, or develop hot spots.

Light-colored shiny cookie sheets will produce cookies much less likely to burn. Nonstick sheets are often black, and for this reason we don't recommend nonstick cookie sheets, unless their coating is no darker than light gray to gray. (If you already have a dark-colored nonstick cookie sheet and it tends to burn the bottoms of your cookies, reduce the oven temperature by 25°F.) If you have trouble with cookies sticking (and many cookies don't stick even on an ungreased pan, due to their high fat content), we recommend using parchment or a pan liner (see page 595).

Insulated cookie pans make it very hard to burn the bottom of your cookies. However, since they are very poor heat conductors, they also make it hard to bake your cookies at all; cookies baked on insulated pans tend to bake so long before browning that they dry out.

Cookie sheet (above)
Silicone lining (below)

SHAPED COOKIE MOLDS: Many traditional European cookies, including shortbread, require molds. Molds to make shortbread, a simple butter, sugar, and flour

Shortbread pan

cookie, are made of stoneware, 7 to 8 inches square, or octagonal; their insides feature a raised design that will be transferred to the cookies as they bake. Baked cookies are turned out of the pan and cut along the marks left by the pan prior to serving.

There is a pan made specifically for biscotti's first bake, a shallow aluminum loaf pan, 12 x 5½ x 2 inches. While not entirely necessary, it helps shape the dough into a log, prior to cutting it into slices and baking it again.

Quick Bread Pans

QUICK LOAF PANS: Most quick loaf recipes (banana bread, zucchini bread) are written for 9 x 5 x 2¾-inch pans, a traditionally shaped loaf pan that's just slightly larger than a yeast bread loaf pan. Caveat emptor: Using a yeast loaf pan for a quick bread recipe may result in batter overflowing the pan. Likewise, using a quick bread pan for a yeast loaf recipe may result in a loaf that doesn't dome. These pans, though similar in size and shape, are not interchangeable. Quick loaves also can be baked in a longer, narrower pan (about 12 x 4 x 2½ inches).

Quick bread loaf pans

Since quick loaves bake for a long time (close to an hour, or more), feel free to use a stoneware, glass, or ceramic pan, as the quick transfer of heat a metal pan gives isn't as essential as it is with other baked goods, such as cookies.

SCONE PANS: While scones are often made free-form by cutting a circular round of dough into wedges, or cut with a biscuit cutter, the scone pan, with its eight wedge-shaped wells, forms beautifully shaped scones. Unless scones are very sweet (not generally the case), a dark pan will give them a lovely brown crust during the very short time they spend in the oven.

POPOVER PANS: Popovers do well in a pan with specially shaped cups in order to attain their full height. Sized in regular (to make 6 large popovers) or mini (to make 12 smaller ones), popover pans feature deep, narrow wells, which force the baking batter to rise up and then out (rather than flatten), producing the typical popover shape. Popover pans made of dark metal will produce the best crust.

Mini popover pan

MUFFIN PANS: Muffins range from mini to maxi, and pans come in a variety of shapes and sizes. A standard muffin pan has 12 wells, each measuring about 2½ inches wide at

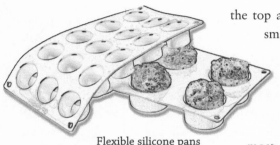
Flexible silicone pans

the top and 1½ inches deep. A pan with wells significantly smaller than that won't hold a standard-size muffin recipe. A mini-muffin pan includes 24 wells, each about 1¾ inches wide and 1 inch deep; it will hold a standard muffin recipe, as will a jumbo muffin pan, with 6 wells about 3¾ x 2 inches deep.

Muffin pans are traditionally made of metal, most commonly aluminum, but also can be found in stoneware and, most recently, flexible silicone. We've found the stoneware pans don't brown muffins as well as metal as they're too slow to absorb heat. Silicone pans are naturally nonstick (but we still recommend greasing them), and their flexibility allows you to gently pop muffins out of the pan without damaging them. This type of flexible pan must be set on a cookie or baking sheet before being put into the oven.

PUDDING STEAMERS: Also known as pudding molds, these aluminum or tinned steel tube pans often come with a clip-on lid to keep the baking pudding moist. The pan, which comes in 1-quart or 2-quart sizes, is filled with the batter for a steamed bread (Boston brown bread) or pudding (Christmas pudding). The lid is clamped on and the pan is set on a rack in a kettle of simmering water a couple of inches deep, where the bread or pudding steams for 1 to 3 hours, until it's cooked through.

Pudding steamer

CRÊPE PANS: A shallow, flat-sided sauté pan is helpful in making crêpes. Most crêpe pans are made of cast iron, heavy aluminum, or carbon steel, as these metals heat evenly and quickly without hot spots. Crêpe pans can be nonstick, but it isn't crucial; crêpes cook in a film of butter and slide out of whatever pan you choose. Sizes range from about 4 inches to 10 inches, with the smaller crêpes suitable for dessert, the larger ones perfect for entrées.

Cake Pans

Nearly all cake pans are made from light-colored aluminum, as cakes need quick, steady heat to rise correctly. Some cakes (pineapple upside-down cake, cobbler) were traditionally baked in a cast iron "spider," a round, medium-depth skillet. Cast iron is still a useful way to make any type of cake that includes a melted or cooked layer atop which batter is poured; cast iron is very happy to go from stovetop to oven, unlike many types of cookware.

LAYER CAKE PANS: You'll want a set of round layer cake pans if you're baking a birthday or wedding cake. Our material of choice is light-colored aluminum. Layer cake recipes nearly always call for 8- or 9-inch pans; to assure batter won't overflow, choose pans that are at least 2 inches deep and fill them with no more than 5 to 6 cups of batter.

SHEET CAKE PANS: When you choose to bake a single layer sheet cake, you'll nearly always use a 9 x 13-inch pan. Some smaller cake recipes call for a 9 x 9-inch pan. Again, either one should be at least 2 inches deep. For best cleanup, look for pans whose inside corners are slightly rounded to avoid trapping crumbs in crevices. A 9 x 13 x 2-inch pan shouldn't be filled with any more than 12 cups of batter; 10 cups is safer, though you can go to 12 with dense cakes that don't rise much.

A typical cake recipe will fill two 9-inch round pans; two (thick layers) or three (thin layers) 8-inch round pans; a 9 x 13-inch pan; or make 24 standard-size cupcakes. If you've got a collection of odd-sized pans and don't know how they match up to these standards, just do your math. A 7 x 11-inch pan (77 square inches) or 10-inch round pan (79 square inches) are both roughly equivalent to a 9 x 9-inch pan (81 square inches), assuming all are the same depth.

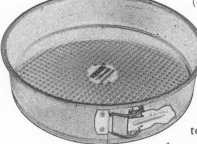

Sheet cake pan (above)

Springform cake pan (below)

SPRINGFORM PANS: For delicate tortes and cheesecakes, streusel-topped cakes, or any time you want to remove a cake from its pan to serve (but not upend it in the process), the springform pan is your best solution. They are usually round and available in lots of sizes, from about 4½ inches in diameter to 12 inches. The flat bottom is surrounded by a 2½- to 3-inch tall removable locking sidewall. Less expensive springform pans are prone to leaks. When purchasing one, examine how tightly the walls lock onto the base when fastened into position.

BUNDT-STYLE, TUBE, AND ANGEL FOOD PANS: These pans are the choice for angel food cake, or to bake a cake that looks fancier than a layer or sheet cake. Generally 8½ to 10 inches in diameter and featuring an 8- to 12-cup capacity, bundt-style pans are usually nonstick aluminum or aluminum-steel, with the occasional glass or tinned steel pan available as well. For single-serving cakes, plaques featuring 4 or 6 small bundt-style wells are available. The similarly sized tube pan has plain (rather than embossed) slightly flaring sides.

An angel food pan is a tube pan with some special features: it should not be non-stick; and it should include either "feet" (small posts attached to the top rim; be sure they're at least 2 inches long), or a tube wide enough to fit comfortably over the top of a glass bottle, such as a wine bottle. Angel food cakes attain their maximum height by cooling upside down, either on the shoulders of a bottle or resting on the pan's feet. While not as intricately shaped as bundt-style pans, these pans come in various shapes, including round, square, and flower. Choose one that's at least 4 inches deep, 9 to 10 inches wide, and has a minimum 10-cup capacity.

SPECIALTY CAKE PANS: If you want to bake an Easter lamb or bunny, a jack-o'-lantern, or Santa, these shapes and many more are available as cake pans. While classic two-piece Easter lamb or rabbit pans are made of heavy cast aluminum, without a nonstick coating, most other specialty pans are lightweight aluminum; the more intricately designed they are, the more you'll appreciate them having a nonstick coating.

To make filled tunnel cakes, use a set of pans specifically designed for that purpose. These come in various shapes, usually round.

Pie and Tart Pans

For variations in size, shape, and composition in the world of baking pans, there's not much that beats the pie pan. From tiny tartlets to mega-pies (think four and twenty blackbirds), from aluminum, tinned steel, or handpainted ceramic to unglazed stoneware, clear glass, or flexible silicone, pie pans cover a lot of ground.

TRADITIONAL PIE PANS: Most pie recipes are written to fit a 9- or 10-inch wide, 1½-inch deep pie. Beware of pie pans that are much shallower than 1½ inches; while 1¼ inches is barely acceptable, a 1-inch-deep pie pan will not hold a typical pie filling. For deep-dish pies, choose a pan that's 1½ inches to 2 inches deep, with 2 inches the preferred depth. A 9-inch pie pan should hold 4 to 10 cups of filling. Why the wide variation? Because while 4 cups of pumpkin filling will expand just a bit, 10 cups of raspberries will shrink enormously. Both amounts (or anything in between) can make a nice-looking pie.

Smaller diameter pans (4¾ to 5 inches) are ideal for individual servings or savory pot pies. Pot pie pans, usually ceramic, have more gently sloped walls than individual pie pans (usually made of aluminum, and sold in sets of 4), which flare from bottom to top quite dramatically. The straighter walls of the pan give pot pies a greater ratio of filling to crust.

Deep dish ceramic pie pan (above)
Metal pie pan (below)

Dark-colored metal pie pans tend to become hotter, and transfer heat better, than ceramic pans, and for that reason brown crust more quickly, a plus in pie-baking (where a pale, soggy bottom crust is the inexperienced baker's nemesis). However, most pie pans will brown a crust thoroughly, given enough time; and in the case of many pies (e.g., fruit pies), extending baking time beyond what the recipe says isn't a problem, so long as you cover the pie's exposed edges with a crust shield to prevent burning. We've forgotten pies in the oven sometimes, and even after 2 hours they've emerged happily bubbling and beautifully browned.

The advantage of stoneware or ceramic dishes (pans) is their beauty. Thanksgiving, a dinner party, or anytime you're seeking a fancier touch, choose a handsome colored or painted ceramic pie dish instead of utilitarian metal. Clear glass dishes allow you to see when the bottom crust is sufficiently browned.

NESTING PANS FOR BLIND-BAKING: Use these pans for blind-baking (prebaking a crust without filling). Available most commonly in standard 9 x 1½-inch aluminum, each set includes a solid-bottom pan and a perforated pan that nests inside the solid pan. Crust is fitted into the solid pan, the perforated pan is nested on top to weigh it down, and the crust is baked.

TART PANS AND QUICHE DISHES: Tart pans, usually fluted, shiny tinplate, shaped round, square, or rectangular, often feature a removable bottom, very handy for removing the tart from the pan without harming the appearance of the crust. Because they're usually only 1 inch deep, tarts will have a greater ratio of crust to filling, an appropriate balance considering tart fillings often include pastry cream or some other very rich confection.

Mini-tarts or mini-quiches are easy to make with a tartlet plaque, akin to a muffin pan but with 1- to 3-inch shallow wells, sometimes fluted. Pastry is pushed into the wells with a tart tamper (a wooden dowel with a flattened ball at one end), then filling is added. Some tartlet plaques are made of flexible silicone, which is a big help in turning out the tartlets, but the pastry doesn't brown as nicely as it does in a metal pan.

Large round tart pan

The classic French quiche dish is usually round, ceramic, and 10 to 11 inches in diameter, 1 to 1½ inches deep. Most quiche dishes have fluted sides, and unlike pie pans, the sides are straight, not slanted.

Yeast Bread Tools

While you can make yeast bread dough using nothing more than a bowl, measuring cup, and your hands, there are a number of tools to make your life much easier. Choose the ones you feel will help you the most.

KNEADING MAT: The nonstick surface of a silicone kneading mat makes dough-kneading easy and cleanup a snap. Mats range from 8 x 11 inches to about 16 x 24 inches; the larger the mat, the more room you have to let the flour fly. Be sure to use only a plastic dough scraper on these mats, as metal will cut their surface.

Bench knife

BAKER'S BENCH KNIFE: Use a bench knife, a 6-inch long rectangle of stainless steel with a handle across the top, to divide dough into pieces, or to scrape bits of dried dough from your countertop.

SHAPING BASKETS AND COUCHE: European-style hearth loaves are traditionally given their second rise in shaping baskets, before being turned out onto an oven stone to bake. The French banneton, a willow basket lined with linen or canvas, comes in the same shapes as French breads, including boule, batard, and baguette. The cloth lining, which is floured before use, draws moisture from the dough as it rises, making the baked bread's crust chewy. Most times, when making baguettes French bakers let their shaped loaves rise in a linen couche, a rectangular piece of cloth that can cradle multiple rising baguettes in its folds.

The German brotform, made of a coil of wood, gives German bread its classic beehive shape; the basket is heavily floured, and when the risen loaf is turned out onto a stone or pan, it retains the circular marks of the flour.

Brotform

Banneton

RISING BUCKETS: Often bakers let dough rise in a lidded rising bucket, a 2- to 6-quart acrylic or plastic bucket with measurements on the side, making it easy to judge when the dough has doubled or tripled in size. The lid keeps the dough moist, allowing it to rise fully.

PROOF COVER: A clear acrylic proof cover, designed to cover your pan of rising rolls or loaves, obviates the need for plastic wrap or a wet towel, both of which may stick to the dough and deflate it. We recommend a cover large enough to fit over a half-sheet pan (13 x 18 inches) and at least 5 inches tall; this size is perfect for just about any rising loaves other than sandwich loaves, which ultimately require more height.

LAME: A curved razor blade set into a handle is called a lame *(lahm),* and French bakers use it to slash the top crust of risen country loaves (most famously, baguettes). The slash allows the bread to expand fully to its proper shape as it bakes. A small, very sharp paring or serrated knife can be substituted.

KAISER ROLL CUTTER: The swirl-topped hard rolls called kaiser rolls are most easily created with the aid of a kaiser roll cutter. Use this tool to cut nearly all the way through balls of dough, then let them rise cut side down before turning them over just before baking.

Lame

BAKER'S PEEL: Also known as a pizza peel, this beveled-edge square of flat wood with a handle (or square of aluminum, with a wooden handle) transfers large, flat loaves or pizzas from work surface to hot baking stone. If your dough sticks to the peel, put a piece of parchment on the peel, place the dough on the parchment, then slide both parchment and dough onto the stone; the parchment won't undermine the stone's ability to produce a crisp crust.

BAKING STONE: A baking stone, placed on the bottom shelf of your oven, is a wonderful surface for baking pizzas and hearth breads. The porous stone draws moisture away from the crust as it bakes, yielding a crisp, crunchy crust. The immediate contact between dough and hot surface helps bread with its oven spring. Select a baking stone that's at least ½ inch thick; thinner stones may crack. The stone's dimensions should mirror your oven rack's, leaving 2 inches of clearance on all sides for heat circulation.

Gadgets, Utensils, and Tools

PIZZA WHEEL: Also known as a rolling pizza cutter, this sharp wheel, with handle, makes short work of cutting bread sticks from a rectangle of unbaked dough. It's also useful for cutting crackers, the strips of pastry for a lattice piecrust, fettuccine from fresh pasta dough or, of course, slices of pizza.

Pizza wheel

TONGS: Choose heat-safe metal tongs, with a heatproof handle, that lock closed, so they're easier to store. If you're turning bagels or doughnuts in boiling water or hot oil, choose tongs with a flat, smooth underside; many tongs are manufactured in a folding process that leaves a perfect channel for water or oil to funnel through. When you lift this type of tongs, boiling oil or water is delivered directly to your wrist.

Tongs

FLOUR TOOLS: Sifting aerates flour, giving many types of cake a head start, and making the measuring process more accurate. When a recipe calls for "sifted flour," it's important to sift the flour before measuring it. When "flour, sifted" is called for, the flour should be measured first, then sifted.

Canister flour sifters, the most familiar kind, come in a variety of types and materials, including crank, shake, and electric, and aluminum, stainless steel, and plastic. Since sifters don't need to be washed—any spills or smears on the outside can be easily wiped off—there's no need to worry about dishwasher safeness. Choose a flour sifter with a minimum 3-cup capacity; any less than that and all but the smallest amount of flour will tend to overflow when you start to sift it.

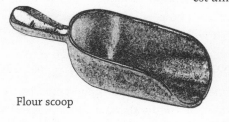

Flour scoop

Another type of sifter, called a tamis or drum sieve, consists of a 2- to 3-inch deep round wooden frame, usually about 9 inches in diameter, with a metal or nylon mesh screen stretched across the bottom. Flour is simply shaken through the screen to sift it. The advantage of a tamis is its large capacity and speed; the disadvantage is its lack of focus: you need to sift into a large bowl (at least 12 inches in diameter), or onto a large sheet of parchment.

Many bakers no longer bother to sift flour. But even though the flour bag says "pre-sifted," that doesn't mean the flour shouldn't be aerated before using. Flour in the bag has settled during shipment, and to measure correctly it needs to be fluffed up. A flour scoop—cast aluminum, wood, stainless steel, or plastic—is used to stir and fluff the flour, then gently sprinkle it into a measuring cup. Choose a flour scoop with a straight edge long enough to sweep the excess flour off the top of your dry measuring cup in one even motion.

POTHOLDERS AND OVEN MITTS: When you're pulling hot cookie sheets and cake pans out of the oven, it's critical to protect your hands. Don't rely on a handy dishtowel, because at some point you'll pick up a wet towel, grab a hot pan, and drop the pan on the floor as soon as the water in the towel turns to scalding steam.

Many bakers find long baker's mitts—mitts that cover your hands and part of your arms—useful in preventing burns on the tender under part of your forearms. However, if you're careful to stay away from the hot oven rack when loading and unloading pans, shorter mitts are sufficient. Potholders are fine if you're adept enough to use them successfully with your own collection of pans. Pans lacking good grabbing spots are more easily handled with mitts.

Potholders or mitts are made from quilted cotton (least protection), suede, or thick terrycloth (better protection), or a pricey combination of heatproof fabrics, with or without steam-proof liners (best protection). Flexible silicone mitts and holders are also available; they're a snap to wash and their protection is comparable to that of terrycloth. But don't think because they're waterproof you can plunge your hand into boiling water and leave it there; it's okay to snatch a simmering bagel or steaming ear of corn out of the pot, but prolonged exposure to boiling liquid will heat the silicone (and your hand) to uncomfortable levels.

HEAT DIFFUSERS: For simmering soup, cooking custard, melting chocolate, or any time even your burner's lowest flame isn't low enough (or, with gas stoves, if the flame keeps going out) a cast aluminum heat diffuser is a good solution. Heat diffusers (burner covers) with a lip on the underside are sized to cover your burners (6 or 8 inches); or choose a large, flat diffuser that simply sits atop the burner.

SPATULAS: Spatulas are used to scrape cake batter off the sides of the mixing bowl, spread filling onto cinnamon bun dough, or any number of baking tasks. They are made of heat-resistant silicone so they also can be used to stir custard, scramble eggs, or turn doughnuts in a deep-fat fryer. Spatulas come in a variety of sizes; our favorite features a flat blade that's about 2 inches wide, 3½ inches long. Some spatulas are a solid piece of silicone; some feature a silicone blade attached to a wooden, plastic, or stainless steel handle. If you choose a spatula that's not all one piece, try to pull the blade off the handle; if it comes off without using a gargantuan amount of effort, choose another type. Eventually a blade that's not well-fastened will fall off, usually just as you're scraping cake batter into a pan.

A spoonula is simply a spatula whose blade has been made spoon-shaped; not only can it be used as a spatula, it can also be used as a spoon, to beat batter, or scoop (rather than scrape) it into a pan.

Spatulas

DOUGH OR BOWL SCRAPER: With one straight edge and one curved (it looks like a squared-off circle), a flexible plastic bowl scraper is useful for everything from sweeping all of the batter out of the bowl in one scoop or cutting cinnamon bun dough to scraping bits of piecrust off the counter, crumbs into the wastebasket—or ice off your car wind-

Bowl scraper

shield. Choose one that's flexible enough to curve easily to the shape of your bowl.

WHISKS: One way to aerate flour, besides sifting or fluffing, is to beat it gently with a wire whisk, a series of looped wires fastened into a handle. Whisks come in various sizes; we have whisks as small as 3 inches and as large as a small person. They're most commonly made of stainless steel, though copper, plastic, and wooden whisks are also available; we find stainless to be the easiest to clean.

From top to bottom:
All-purpose whisk,
Danish dough whisk,
cake whisk

Whisks are distinguished by their size, the strength of their wires (the stronger the wires, the heavier the task the whisk can perform), and the shape those wires form. A balloon whisk, whose wires form a nearly round ball, is the choice for whipping egg whites and cream, as it whips more air into a mixture than any other design. A standard whisk has a more elongated head and can be used to whip batter, combine eggs and milk, in place of a mixer. A flat or roux whisk is shaped particularly for making custard, white sauce, or other thickened sauces made in a saucepan.

We find two other whisks useful. A dough whisk, also known as a *brodpisker*, is a long, wooden handled, stainless steel whisk ideal for mixing bread dough, even stiff ones. A cake whisk has a flow-through blade that beats a lot of air into cake batter but can also be used for mixing muffins just enough to moisten the batter.

Whisks are like spoons: choose one that feels comfortable in your hand. Our favorite all-purpose whisk is a standard one 10 to 12 inches long, with thin, flexible (rather than thick, stiff) wires.

Rotary whisks that rotate when you push down on the handle are a good choice for blending liquids in confined spaces (e.g., an egg and cup of milk in a 2-cup measuring cup), but not useful at all for whisking dry ingredients.

PASTRY BRUSHES: These are essential for brushing a loaf of hot bread with crust-softening butter, egg wash onto breadsticks or bagels, egg white onto the edges of turnovers, or milk onto a piecrust. Choose a natural bristle brush; natural (boar) bristles are much less likely to become spiky and bent with use. The bristles should be sealed into the handle with a plastic sealant; the brush will be easier to clean and the bristles won't fall out.

Our favorite all-purpose pastry brushes are 1 to 1½ inches wide with fairly long, flexible bristles; the more flexible the bristles, the gentler you can be, a major point when brushing risen bread dough. For extra-fine work, a goose feather brush is the best choice; unfortunately, these are not easy to find.

PARCHMENT AND PAN LINERS: To avoid the aggravation of cookies glued to the cookie sheet or cakes that stick to the pan and crumble, use a pan liner. Pan liners negate the need to grease your baking pan; however, in recipes calling for a pan to be both greased and floured, if you use parchment you should grease the pan, then add the parchment, then grease the parchment (no flour necessary).

Parchment is the traditional pan liner; made of silicone or vegetable-oil coated paper, it's greaseproof and nonstick. It can be used more than once, but isn't as long-lasting as silicone or flexible fiberglass pan liners, which can be washed and reused hundreds of times (see p. 586). Parchment comes in sheets sized for half-sheet (13 x 18-inch) and full-sheet (18 x 26-inch) baking pans; in rolls; and in sizes and shapes for particular pans, such as 9-inch rounds for layer cake pans, or rectangles for loaf pans. Pan liners come in fewer sizes and shapes.

Parchment also comes precut in triangles to make pastry cones, used for piping decorations onto cakes.

COOLING RACKS: If fresh-from-the-oven baked goods are cooled on or in a pan, their crust can become soggy, due to condensation. Racks prevent this and are also helpful when you're drizzling icing or chocolate atop pastries and don't want them to end up in a sweet puddle.

Racks are available in round (various diameters), perfect for layer cakes; and square or rectangular, also in varying sizes, good for cookies and pastries. Our favorite racks feature a grid design, rather than just parallel strips of wire; the grid supports soft pastries and keeps them from drooping. Nonstick racks are available, but not necessary. If something is so sticky it'll stick to a regular rack, it also sticks to a nonstick rack.

Handy innovations include racks that fold for storage, and tiered racks, set atop one another, which save counter space.

BOWLS: The baker's most constant friend is a bowl. Bowls range from tiny, 1-tablespoon ingredient bowls, to 2-gallon (or larger) bowls perfect for mixing up a triple yeast bread recipe or holiday fruitcakes.

Consider a variety of factors when choosing bowls. If you'll be melting butter or warming milk in a microwave, choose a microwave-safe bowl. Whipping cream in a chilled bowl? Choose stainless steel or copper (copper is especially good for whipping egg whites into meringue). Making a lot of yeast bread? Choose a crockery bowl, which will stay warm as the dough rises.

Another factor to consider is bowl shape. Sure, they're almost all round; but deep, narrow bowls are best for beating batters, whipped cream, or for other loose mixtures that splatter. Wider bowls are best for mixing solid ingredients, like the fruits for a fruitcake or apples for a pie. A bowl that's neither particularly narrow nor wide is ideal for dough, such as biscuits or piecrust, as it keeps the ingredients confined (and thus promotes cohesion), but also lets you get your hands into the bowl to work.

Some bowls come with a nonskid ring or coating on the bottom to keep them from slipping on the counter as you beat. This is a nice option, but not necessary, unless you do some fairly physical, vigorous mixing. Some bowls come with a spout (batter bowls), which makes them a good choice for pancake batter, melted chocolate, or anything else you'll be pouring.

A final factor to consider is weight. Extra-large crockery bowls are very attractive and are usually oven-safe (lovely for baking a stew), but before purchasing decide whether you're strong enough, and have a good enough grip, to maneuver them around the kitchen. Acrylic bowls come in fun colors and they're lightweight and easy to handle, but some aren't microwave-safe. Stainless steel bowls are a good all-around choice, but if they're lightweight enough to handle easily, they'll also dent just as easily. Whatever material you choose, a set of bowls—approximately 2-, 4-, and 6-quart—is most useful. Add a larger bowl, if you like, for the occasional big baking job.

KNIVES AND SLICING GUIDES: A good bread knife should be a part of every bread baker's arsenal of tools. A bread knife should be serrated, preferably with a "wave" serration, as this is the most versatile style, and will work best on anything from a chewy-crusted hearth loaf to soft white sandwich bread. The blade should be 8 to 10 inches long, made of high-carbon stainless steel (which sharpens better than regular stainless steel), and should feel balanced and comfortable in your hand. To preserve the knife's blade, hand-washing is a good choice; particularly if the knife has a wooden handle, drying it after washing is also good practice.

An offset bread knife, shaped like an offset spatula with the blade set below rather than even with the handle, allows you to slice all the way to the bottom of the loaf without rapping your knuckles on the breadboard. While not critical, it's a handy design feature.

Offset bread knife

A bread slicing guide, consisting of two rows of upright wooden or plastic posts on opposite sides of a bread board, is a useful tool for cutting even slices of bread. If you bake bread in a bread machine, be sure to get a slicing guide that's wide enough to fit the size of loaf you bake. The loaf is inserted between the posts and they're used as a guide for the knife as the bread is cut.

To cut pie, cake, or other pastries, a triangular-blade cake or pie server, serrated on one edge for cutting, combines two tools in one. The serrations for cake or pie knives are generally smaller than those on a bread knife, to better deal with those pastries' tender crusts.

If you have nonstick bakeware and you bake things that are cut right in the pan, you'll need an acrylic or plastic serrated knife. These work well; even though they won't cut your hand or bakeware, they do a fine job slicing through brownies or a pizza. So put your prejudices about plastic aside and buy one.

CAKE TESTER: Remember Mom pulling a straw out of the kitchen broom to poke into the center of her baking cake? If the straw came out clean, the cake was ready. That old-fashioned tool hasn't changed much; now you can buy a small "broom" made just for plucking cake-testing straws from, or sharpened wooden testers about the diameter of cooked spaghetti, or thin metal cake testers. Choose one that's thick enough that you can easily see whether or not it's coated with batter after withdrawing it from the cake, but not so thick it leaves a noticeable hole.

Cake tester

TURNERS: For flipping flapjacks or transferring cookies from pan to cooling rack, a good turner is essential. Choose one with a wide enough blade to handle your favorite size of pancake on the griddle, but not so wide that it's not maneuverable around cookies lined up on a cookie sheet; around 3 inches is a good compromise. A turner that's safe on nonstick surfaces is useful if you have a lot of nonstick pans. A bevel on the end of the blade is useful for getting underneath thin cookies. Press the turner down on the counter to flex the blade; it should flex willingly, but not be so flimsy that it can't do the hard work of getting the first brownie out of the pan.

MORTAR AND PESTLE: The easiest way to crush cardamom or any type of seeds is with a mortar and pestle, a small, heavy bowl (mortar) and round-headed crusher with handle (pestle) that fits inside the bowl. Marble is a common material for both mortar and pestle; the heaviness of the stone does much of the work for you. Make sure the pestle and inside of the mortar are unglazed; a rough surface is essential for best crushing.

Spice grinder

Mortar and pestle

Some mortars and pestles, called spice grinders, are shaped specifically for crushing whole spices and seeds; the mortar has a much shallower bowl (more surface area), and the pestle a head that fits the bowl exactly, so no spices can escape as you work.

GRATERS: Looking very much like a wood rasp (in fact, that's the design they're based on), the plane grater does an excellent all-around job on cheese, chocolate, garlic, citrus peel, or anything else you can grip and grate. Ranging from long, thin, fine-blade graters to wider graters with blades ranging from extra-fine to coarse, these graters are easy to use, sharp and efficient, and easy to clean. We prefer them to the standard box grater.

Another option is the rotary grater, a rotating drum gripped inside two handles. Just insert bits of chocolate, cheese, or nuts and crank. The advantage of this grater is its safety and speed; the disadvantage is its small capacity.

ZESTER: When you need just a teaspoon or two of fresh citrus zest, use a zester, a simple stainless steel rod with a series of sharpened holes across one end. Simply scrape the zester across the orange or lemon with the same motion you'd use with a paring knife.

Plane grater

Measuring

Baking, while considered an art, is equal parts science. Accurate measuring is always important, and sometimes essential, to baking success. Thus it's important that you invest in some good quality (accurate) measuring tools.

MEASURING SPOONS: It used to be measuring spoons came in a simple set of four round spoons: ¼ and ½ teaspoon, 1 teaspoon, and 1 tablespoon. Now, that basic set has expanded to include ⅛, ¾, and 1½ teaspoon measures; and the spoons themselves may be oblong-shaped, to fit easily into spice cans, or given a handle with a bent end, to balance them securely on the counter when filled with salt or vanilla.

While it's difficult to ascertain the accuracy of measuring spoons, one check you can make is that the parts add up to the whole: 3 teaspoons should equal a tablespoon, two ½-teaspoons a teaspoon, and so on. If these measurements don't add up, the overall accuracy of the spoons should be questioned.

Our favorite measuring spoons are stainless steel, with the size of each imprinted on its handle. They hold their shape through the heat of the dishwasher, unlike some plastic spoons. If you're willing to wash plastic spoons by hand, however, they're a good low-cost alternative. And, if they're color-coded (red = 1 teaspoon, etc.), they're ideal for those dealing with vision problems.

MEASURING CUPS: There are two basic types of measuring cup: liquid, and dry. A liquid measure should have a pouring spout and be made of clear glass or plastic, with clear markings on the side; markings should include as many in-between volumes as possible (e.g., ⅔, ¾, etc.). While some liquid measuring cups include all kinds of markings besides straight American volume and metric (fluid ounces, etc.), we find these extraneous. Most American recipes are written using American volume measurements; these are the markings you need.

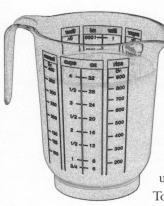

Liquid
measure

Some newer measuring cups allow you to look straight down into the cup at its markings; this is handy, as leaving the cup on the counter steadies the liquid, making it easy to measure.

Our favorite liquid measure size is 2 cups; we also appreciate a measure that's microwave-safe, for warming milk and melting butter.

To accurately read a traditional measuring cup, set it on a flat surface and crouch down to where you can see the top of the liquid at eye level. You'll see two very thin lines atop the surface of the liquid. This is the meniscus—you learned this in high school physics, right? Read the level at the base (bottom) of the meniscus.

Dry measures come in sets; a complete set will include ⅛-, ¼-, ⅓-, ½-, ⅔-, ¾-, and 1-cup measures. Add 1½-, 2-, and 3-cup measures, if you like. These measures shouldn't have spouts; a dry measure needs to be filled right up to the top to be accurate, and shouldn't be used for measuring liquids. While usually made of stainless steel, they also come in plastic. Each cup's size should be imprinted on its handle; some measuring cups also print the size on the outside base of the cup, so you can read it when the cup is hanging on a pegboard, a handy feature. It's also useful if the cups nest nicely, so you can stow them in a drawer if you don't want to hang them.

Another kind of measuring cup, consisting of a clear, round sleeve with a sliding solid base set within, is wonderful for measuring shortening, peanut butter, molasses, and other sticky ingredients. One common brand name is Wonder Cup.

If you have what you believe to be an accurate scale, you can check the accuracy of your measuring cups by measuring out 1 cup of water and weighing it; it should weigh 8 ounces (if you live close to sea level). Check smaller and larger amounts, as well.

Wonder Cup

THERMOMETERS: Instant-read thermometers (those that register a final temperature within 15 seconds or so) are an essential baking tool. Rather than guessing, it's nice to know the temperature of a fully cooked custard pie (165°F), a loaf of baked bread (190°F to 210°F), or yeast dough at its optimum rising temperature (76°F to 78°F). Why choose instant-read, rather than standard? Because standing with the oven door open waiting for a standard thermometer to work is unpleasant for you, and not helpful to your baked goods.

Instant-read thermometer

Thermometers are made of a sharpened, stainless-steel probe attached to a measuring dial or window. The better thermometers will read temperature in the final ⅛-inch of the probe; lower-quality thermometers need to be inserted deeper in order to work, not helpful when you're trying to take the temperature of a shallow custard-based tart. The greater the temperature range of the thermometer, the more expensive it will be. It's helpful to have a thermometer that reads to at least 370°F, as that's the oil temperature required by many fried doughs. At the other end, yeast does well dissolved in water that's about 105°F, so choose a thermometer that goes that low.

A nice innovation is a thermometer whose probe is attached to the measuring dial via a long, thin metal cord. The probe can be inserted into your partially baked loaf of bread, the oven door closed, and when the bread's reached 190°F (or whatever temperature you program it for), the thermometer will beep to let you know.

Probe thermometer

Instant-read thermometers come in both digital and mechanical versions.

Digital thermometers are generally easier to read and may be more accurate; however, they also require a battery. Mechanical thermometers are less expensive.

An oven thermometer is also useful. One that can both hang from the oven rack, or stand on its own is handy; move it around the oven to check for any hot spots. Oven thermometers are always mechanical, never digital; while mercury oven thermometers are a bit more accurate, we hesitate to use them due to the slight possibility they could break and spill their mercury in the oven.

SCALE: You'll notice that all of the recipes in this book include weight as well as volume measurements; this is because weight measurements are more accurate, and it's usually easier to scale a recipe up or down (i.e., increase or decrease the yield) dealing with weight, not volume.

The two main types of scale are digital and mechanical. Digital scales are much more accurate, and, unless expense is a real issue, we suggest spending the money for a battery-powered digital scale. Here are some things to consider when purchasing a digital scale. First, make sure the measuring platform fits your favorite bowls; we suggest buying a scale with a flat platform rather than a detachable bowl. Second, ascertain that it measures in both American pounds and ounces, and metric grams, and that it's easy to switch from one to the other; the switch should be located on the front of the scale, not its bottom.

Scale

Third, assess the scale's capacity. In general, scales weigh up to about 4 pounds, in ⅛-ounce or 2g (sometimes 1g) increments; up to about 11 pounds, in ¼-ounce or 5g (sometimes 2g) increments; or a combination (the smaller increments at the lower weights). If you are baking small to standard quantities and have lightweight bowls, choose the smaller-capacity scale. If your bowls are heavy, or you like to double or triple recipes, choose the larger-capacity scale. Fourth, make sure the scale has a "tare" feature—this allows you to measure one ingredient into your mixing bowl, then reset the scale to zero in order to measure the next ingredient. Finally, check the scale's automatic shut-off; our favorite scales will remain on during at least 5 minutes of inactivity (something that happens frequently when we're distracted by the phone ringing, the dog barking to be let out, or kids asking questions). A scale that shuts off after 1 minute is annoying; if you were partway through measuring flour into the bowl, you need to start over (unless you can remember how much was in the bowl before it shut off).

TIMERS: Like scales and thermometers, timers come in both mechanical and battery-powered digital versions. We prefer digital timers; not just because they're more accurate, but because we've never found a mechanical timer with a ring longer than about 8 seconds, and that's not long enough for the busy baker who might have stepped out of the kitchen for 10 seconds.

A popular digital timer is a small, lightweight version that hangs around your neck; there's never a chance of burning your cookies because you're out in the garden or upstairs reading. Most digital timers are magnetized to attach to your refrigerator or oven; some also include a fold-out stand and/or clip to attach to a belt or pocket. Important features to assess include loudness and length of ring (1 minute is a good standard); size of numerals (¾ inch is helpful for older eyes); and range. Some timers count down by seconds, and their range is up to 9 hours, 99 minutes, 99 seconds. Some timers don't count by seconds, but their range is much higher. If you don't need second-by-second timing, choose the timer with the greater range; we prefer timers that measure by seconds, as often we're beating whipped cream or doing some other chore we like to measure in 30- or 90-second intervals.

Storage

BREAD BAGS: Storing bread at room temperature is best; refrigeration stales bread quickly. A plastic bag sized to fit your loaf is most efficient and works best. For bread with a crisp crust, try to purchase perforated plastic bags; they protect the bread while letting it breathe. Plastic-lined cloth bread bags are attractive and reusable.

INGREDIENT STORAGE: Flour and sugar are usually stored in lidded canisters. While flour and sugar canisters—made of ceramic, stainless steel, or clear glass— don't need to be airtight, that's an option if you're particularly troubled by moth infestations or ants. Choose canisters with an opening wide enough to dip a scoop into, and to hold a cup over to sweep off the excess.

Other ingredients do best in containers with tighter lids, as they gradually deteriorate when exposed to air. Yeast, baking powder, and baking soda, the big three of leavening, do well in gasketed canisters with snap-tight lids. Olive oil and liquid flavors and extracts deteriorate in light, as well as air and heat, so keep them in dark or opaque, tightly closed containers, away from the stove.

Flour canister

Whole grains should be stored in the freezer for best shelf life. Plastic jars with screw-on lids are a good option here; be sure to mark the jar with what's inside, or someday you'll find yourself trying to identify something brown and grainy by looks alone.

Yeast canist with spoon

Cutters

COOKIE CUTTERS, STAMPS, AND MOLDS: Christmas and, increasingly, holidays such as Thanksgiving, Halloween, and July Fourth are marked by shaped cookies ranging from angels and trees to shooting stars, turkeys, and black cats. These cookies are made by rolling out cookie dough (sugar or gingerbread are the traditional flavors), then cutting it with a shaped cutter.

Most cookie cutters are made of tin, plastic, copper, or copper-plated aluminum. All work equally well, though the tin ones, if particularly flimsy, will bend out of shape easily. Many bakers keep their copper cutters on display in the kitchen when not in use. Be sure any cutters you purchase are at least ½ inch deep, and that they have a sharp side (for cutting), and a dull side (for holding).

Pastry cutters are similar to cookie cutters in all respects except one: they're usually very small, ranging from ¾ to 2 inches in size. They're used to cut shapes from piecrust (leaves and stars are typical) to decorate the top and edges of a pie.

Cookie stamps, often made of terra-cotta, are used to stamp designs into the top of shortbread-type cookies. The dough is rolled into a ball, then flattened with the stamp, whose impression remains after the cookie is baked. One caveat: you must choose a recipe without leavening, as stamped cookies won't hold their design if the cookie rises.

Ceramic cookie molds are a combination cookie stamp and cookie cutter. Cookie dough (again, unleavened is best) is pressed into the mold, where it acquires its shape and design; it's turned out of the mold onto a pan, and baked. Springerle molds, native to Germany, were traditionally made of wood, but now are usually made of a wood-and-resin composite. Very intricately carved, these molds (or a springerle rolling pin) shape a traditional anise-scented dough that's turned onto baking sheets and dried overnight before baking—producing one tough cookie! Some folks enjoy springerle, but many feel they're better as Christmas tree ornaments than something you'd eat.

COOKIE PRESS: A cookie press, either manual or electric, is a necessity when making all manner of extruded cookies. Cookie dough is loaded into a hollow cylinder and pressed out through a shaped opening to create various fanciful designs. A key point to ensure cookie press success is to use the right cookie recipe; too stiff, and the press is difficult to work; too soft, and the cookies won't hold their shape. Also, pay attention to the temperature of the dough as mentioned in the recipe.

BISCUIT CUTTERS: Biscuit cutters are key to producing high-rising biscuits; biscuits cut with a dull cutter won't rise well, as their sidewalls have been compacted rather than cleanly cut. Round biscuit cutters, made of tin, stainless steel, or plastic, usually come in nesting sets ranging from 1½ to 2¾ inches in diameter. Be sure they're at least 1 inch deep, in order to cut through your thickest biscuit dough. Biscuit cutters (which also come in linked hexagons) can double as cookie cutters. In addition, we like to use biscuit cutters to cut small rounds out of a sheet cake, which we then ice and decorate to make tiny individual cakes.

Biscuit cutters

DOUGHNUT OR BAGEL CUTTER: A circular cutter with a smaller cutter in the center, the doughnut (bagel) cutter is used to cut standard-size (3½-inch) doughnuts or bagels. Make sure the cutters are aligned; when you press the cutter down on the dough, both should cut all the way through. Less expensive cutters may be out of alignment, making them frustrating to use.

CAKE SLICER: When you want to cut a cake layer through the middle to make two thinner layers, try a cake slicer, an adjustable-height, thin wire stretched tautly between two posts (similar to a jigsaw). Gently saw the wire back and forth through the cake; if you keep the metal feet at the bottom of the posts flush with the counter, you'll make a nice, straight, even cut.

Doughnut cutter

Pastry Tools

CAKE COMB: The distinctive thin, parallel lines decorating the sides of a fancy iced layer cake are made with a cake comb, which features numerous thin, sharp sawlike teeth. The baker holds the comb in place against the side of the cake, then turns the turntable (below) to make lines.

CAKE TURNTABLE: For easiest cake decorating, invest in a turntable (akin to a lazy susan). Turntables come in expensive cast aluminum or less expensive plastic. Some are elevated, some nearly flush with the counter; the elevated turntable raises the cake so it's easier to work with. An important thing to check before purchasing a turntable is whether it turns without wobbling. Crouch down so you're eye level with the top of the turntable and give it a spin; it should spin smoothly, without moving out of line at all.

Cookie scoops

COOKIE SCOOP: Also known as a disher or depositor, the cookie scoop is simply an ice cream scoop sized to deposit a traditional (1 teaspoon or 1 tablespoon) ball of dough onto a cookie sheet, quickly and cleanly. While neither the 1-teaspoon nor 1-tablespoon scoop portions out that exact measurement of dough, the amount it scoops is what recipes have traditionally called for: the amount a rounded teaspoon or tablespoon—the kind you eat with, not the measuring kind—would spoon out. The teaspoon scoop will make cookies that are about 1½ inches in diameter; the tablespoon scoop will make 2½-inch cookies.

Choose a cookie scoop that's easy for you to squeeze; it will keep your hand and wrist from tiring when you're making lots of cookies. If dough starts to stick in the scoop, simply wipe the interior clean, spray with a nonstick baking spray, and continue.

DOUGH DOCKER: Looking like a very small (3- to 4-inch) spiked rolling pin, the dough docker cuts even rows of holes into cracker dough, or thoroughly pricks the bottom of a tart or pie shell in a few

Dough docker

easy swipes. Unless you're very particular about how your
pastry looks, or you're doing lots of pastry that needs
docking, a fork can easily substitute for the docker.

Flour wand

FLOUR WAND OR SHAKER: This old-fashioned tool is used to
dust a work surface (or the top of pastry or bread dough) with flour.
A ball of coiled metal is filled with flour, then the handle is squeezed to
let just a bit of the flour sift out, exactly where you direct it. It's perfect
when you want just a dusting, rather than scattered handfuls, of flour.

GIANT SPATULA: This 10 x 10-inch aluminum blade, affixed in a plastic handle, easily moves a rolled-out piecrust into its pan, transfers a small pizza or risen
loaf of bread onto a hot baking stone, shovels crackers onto a baking sheet in two
easy swipes, or moves cookies from cookie sheet to cooling rack. (See illustration, p.
606.) Two used in tandem will move even the biggest, most fragile filled braid with ease.

ICING SPATULA: For icing cakes, use an icing spatula, a long, narrow, flexible stainless-steel turner, one that follows the curve of the cake as it smoothes frosting around
the sides, or can bend to create artful swirls on top. Icing spatulas are available
straight or offset, in an array of lengths; rounded on the end or tapering to a narrow point (for fine work). Choose a medium-sized spatula
that feels comfortable in your hand.

Offset spatula

MAGI-CAKE STRIP: This 30-inch strip of
heat-resistant coated cotton is first
soaked in water, then fastened around
the circumference of a round layer cake
pan to insulate its sides, preventing the edges
from setting before the center of the cake, and thus keeping the
cake's top surface flat.

Magi-Cake Strip

MUFFIN SCOOP: Big brother to the cookie or ice cream scoop, a muffin scoop dishes
out ¼ cup of muffin, cupcake, or pancake batter—easily, evenly, and quickly. Cupcakes
or muffins will have smoother, rounder tops (and pancakes will be evenly sized) when
they're deposited into the pan with a muffin scoop.

OVEN GUARD: A doughnut-shaped ring of easy-clean nonstick aluminum, an oven
guard is designed to catch any spills from your bubbling fruit pies before they hit the
oven floor and make a sticky black mess. Setting your pie pan on a baking sheet lined
with parchment or a nonstick mat will accomplish the same purpose.

PASTRY BAG AND TIPS: To shape the dough for éclairs or cream puffs, or to decorate a cake, use a pastry bag, a cone made of plastic-lined canvas, or single-use
parchment or plastic. Batter or icing is spooned into the bag, then squeezed out
through a decorative chrome-plated or stainless-steel metal tip. Tips come in a huge
array of designs and sizes; the beginning cake decorator does well to purchase a basic
kit, which will include a bag and about a dozen different tips and accompanying
paraphernalia (couplers, cleaners, etc.).

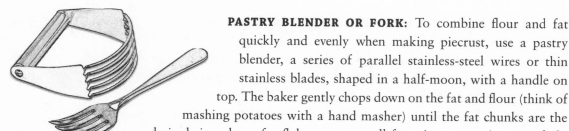

Pastry blender and fork

PASTRY BLENDER OR FORK: To combine flour and fat quickly and evenly when making piecrust, use a pastry blender, a series of parallel stainless-steel wires or thin stainless blades, shaped in a half-moon, with a handle on top. The baker gently chops down on the fat and flour (think of mashing potatoes with a hand masher) until the fat chunks are the desired size—large for flaky pastry, small for crisp pastry. A pastry fork, which resembles an oversized dinner fork with larger, thicker, wider-spaced tines, performs the same function.

PASTRY BOARD: Rather than roll pastry or piecrust dough on a counter, some bakers prefer to use a cloth-covered wooden pastry board or canvas pastry frame. Flour is sprinkled onto the board or frame, and once the crust is rolled out, the board can easily be taken outside to shake off excess flour, or to the sink to wash. Sometimes these boards or frames are marked with measured circles, templates for rolling dough to the perfect circumference for various pie sizes. Make sure any board or frame you purchase is a minimum of 14 inches wide; a 9-inch pie demands at least a 12-inch crust.

Giant spatula
and pastry board

A new design of pastry boards features an adjustable-height board set inside a frame, which allows the baker to determine ahead of time exactly how thick the crust should be, then roll it to a perfectly even thickness. This is useful in recipes calling for a specific crust thickness.

PASTRY WHEEL: A pastry wheel is used to cut strips of pie pastry for a lattice-top crust, cut circles of turnover dough, or for any kind of dough-cutting chore. A standard pastry wheel resembles a miniature pizza wheel, with a circular blade that's only 1½ to 2 inches in diameter. A deckle-edge wheel lends a zigzag pattern to the edges of cut pastry dough. A sealing pastry wheel (also called a ravioli cutter) is designed to both seal and cut dough in one motion, useful for making ravioli or turnovers.

Pastry wheel

PIE CHAIN AND PIE WEIGHTS: When blind-baking a piecrust (baking it prior to adding the filling), it's necessary to prevent it puffing up by adding weight. The old-fashioned solution, and one that still works, is to line the crust with parchment or waxed paper, then fill it with dried beans or uncooked rice. The beans or rice can be replaced by reusable pie weights, pea-sized ceramic or aluminum balls, which don't require that the crust be lined with parchment. However, ceramic weights should be washed regularly, as they tend to absorb some of the crust's fat.

The stainless-steel pie chain, a beaded chain designed to be coiled onto the crust, is an easy solution. When crust is baked, simply lift the chain out with a pair of tongs; no worrying about hot beans or pie weights spilling all over the counter. While most pie chains on the market are 6 feet long, that's not really long enough to cover the crust; the 10-foot version is preferable.

PIECRUST MOLDS (RINGS): "Roll crust to a 13-inch round"—how many times have you read those directions, tried to follow them, and ended up with a raggedy crust that's 14 inches wide one way, 10 inches the other? Piecrust molds—flat plastic 1-inch-wide rings—provide the boundaries you need to roll the perfect ⅛-inch thick, evenly round crust. Three different rings allow you to roll an 11-, 12-, or 13-inch diameter crust, sufficient to completely line the bottom of an 8-, 9-, or 10-inch pie pan.

PIECRUST SHIELD: The bottom and top crusts of your baking pie are insulated by the filling, and are nigh impossible to overbake. The edge of the crust, however, is a different story—thin and unprotected by steamy filling, it's liable to burn if left in the oven too long. A piecrust shield—a round, flat piece of lightweight aluminum—replaces the crumpled strips of foil our mothers used to shield their piecrusts. Sized to fit a standard 9-inch pie, the shield sits very gently atop any fancy fluted edges; just be sure not to put it on until the edge has had a chance to set, 20 minutes or so into the baking time. Also, don't wait until the edge of the crust is perfectly browned before adding the shield; even with the shield it will continue to brown, albeit slowly, so add the shield while the crust is still a light golden brown.

ROLLING PINS: The rolling pin is a critical tool for shaping all kinds of baked goods, so it's important to have one that works well and that you enjoy using.

Some folks scoff at the need for a rolling pin, saying they get along just fine using an empty bottle. Yes, a bottle will work; so does a washboard, so why bother to buy a washing machine? The efficient, effective, easy way a rolling pin flattens dough is unmatched by any substitute.

Rolling pins come in a variety of types, ranging from 20-inch, one-piece hardwood pins tapered at both ends (a "French pin"), to 2-inch-long pastry pins, with lots of styles and sizes in between. Let's start with the pastry pin. Set between two rods attached to a central handle, this tiny, agile pin is a good choice when you're rolling dough in a pan and need to get into the corners.

A good all-around size, for rolling dough on a counter or board, is a pin with a 10-inch barrel. The wider the diameter of the barrel, the fewer strokes you'll need to take, and the more tender your pastry will be, as the gluten won't become overworked. Larger pins are fine, but anything smaller than a 10-inch barrel is inefficient.

Long pins, like the aforementioned French pin, are useful for rolling strudel or pasta dough, or other large sheets of dough; in addition, some bakers claim they have a better "feel" for the dough with this narrow-diameter pin. But if you're simply making standard recipes, an all-purpose pin is a better choice.

The most important part of a rolling pin is its barrel. Barrels are made from stainless steel, marble, nonstick aluminum, nylon, wood, composite, or even glass (an empty glass pin, designed to be filled with chilled water). Our favorites are heavy wood or stainless steel; the weight of either takes much of the effort out of rolling.

Nonstick is a gimmick; we've never tried a nonstick pin that worked any better than a stainless-steel pin. A pin that can be chilled before using (e.g., a marble or metal pin) will help keep the fat in piecrust and puff pastry from melting as you roll.

Another factor to consider is the pin's rolling mechanism. In some pins, the barrel simply rotates on a thin rod inserted through the center; on others, ball bearings help the rolling motion along.

When you've decided on the style and composition of your rolling pin, see if you can find a few to test before buying. Some will feel great under your hands; others, you just won't connect with. Roll the pin across a flat surface to make sure it rolls smoothly, with no catches; see if it's the best weight for your strength. A good rolling pin should last you a lifetime, so it's worth it to take some time to find the right one.

SUGAR SOFTENER: Also known as a sugar bear for its traditional shape, this small (2- to 3-inch), flat piece of porous terra-cotta is soaked in water, then added to a bag or canister of hard brown sugar. Within a day or two (depending on the quantity of sugar), the sugar will be soft again.

Sugar softener

Appliances

BREAD MACHINE: For kneading bread dough, nothing beats the efficiency and skill of a good bread machine. In side-by-side tests we've done, dough kneaded in a bread machine produced a higher-rising loaf of bread than dough kneaded by hand, electric mixer, or food processor. Look for a machine whose pan is a nice loaf shape, for those times you want to bake in the machine; and if you're a seasoned bread baker, you'll appreciate a programmable machine, one into which you can program your own kneading and rising times. There are a lot of bread machines on the market and many share the same features, so quality is what distinguishes one from another. Keep in mind that the lower the price, the less likely it is to be a quality machine.

MIXERS AND BEATERS: Unless you're really committed to doing everything the old-fashioned way, an electric mixer—either hand or stand—is a tool you should own.

When purchasing an electric hand mixer, look for one whose beaters are made from rounded wires (like the type found in a whisk), rather than flat metal bars. The whisk-type beaters do a better job and are easier to clean. When shopping for one, pick up the mixer and hold it as if you were using it. Is it comfortable? Not too heavy? Can you reach the controls easily, with one hand? Some hand mixers aren't sized for smaller hands. Is the cord long enough to let you maneuver around the counter a bit? Does the mixer have an extra-slow first speed, so flour and cocoa won't fly out of the mixing bowl? Check out what attachments come with the mixer. Does it have dough hooks? Perhaps a balloon whisk, for egg whites and whipped cream? What size is its motor compared to other mixers? The higher-power the motor, the more and stiffer dough the mixer will be able to handle.

The stand mixer—an electric mixer attached to a stand, with a removable bowl—should go through an examination similar to that given a hand mixer. Are the controls conveniently located? Are the bowl and/or beating attachments easy to take off and put back on? Does the bowl have a handle? (This is a real selling point when you're trying to spoon a double batch of brownie batter out of a heavy, often greasy bowl.) What's the bowl's capacity? (We prefer 5 quarts or greater.) Check the lowest speed; is it sufficiently slow to allow dry ingredients to be added without poofing? What attachments come with the mixer? (A dough hook or hooks, flat beater, and whisk should all be included.) What about extras, such as a pouring shield, extra bowl, a cover, or an interesting recipe book? What kinds of attachments would you be interested in purchasing in the future (pasta extruder? juicer?), and are they available for the model you're examining? How powerful is the motor? Does the machine appear sturdy enough to remain steady on the counter, even while dealing with a double batch of stiff bagel dough? If you take the time to answer all of these questions to your satisfaction before purchasing, you'll be much more pleased with the mixer you choose.

FOOD PROCESSOR: Most food processors include instructions for kneading bread dough. While it's not our favorite method to knead dough—we feel a food processor overheats and "beats up" the dough more than necessary—it does a satisfactory job. The processor does well with cookie dough or muffin batter, though you do need to watch carefully when adding chocolate chips, dried fruit, or other ingredients, so that you don't accidentally purée them. The processor's best baking uses, in our opinion, are chopping nuts (anything from a coarse dice, to nut flour); chopping chocolate; whipping ganache; making piecrust; shredding cheese and slicing vegetables, for pizza or focaccia; making bread crumbs from a stale loaf; or slicing fruit for pies.

When choosing a food processor, make sure the feed tube is conveniently located and sufficiently large that you don't need to do too much pre-chopping of ingredients. We prefer a machine with a medium-sized (11- to 14-cup capacity) workbowl. The machine should be heavy enough to sit securely on the counter.

Where to Find It

Most of the ingredients in the recipes in this book are available from King Arthur Flour's wholly owned subsidiary, *The Baker's Catalogue*, a catalogue of fine tools, ingredients, and recipes for the home baker. Many are also available in grocery and gourmet stores throughout the United States. Some of the tools mentioned in this section are available at quality kitchen accessory stores; all can be purchased from *The Baker's Catalogue*. If you would like a copy of the catalogue, call 1-800-777-4434, or log on to www.bakerscatalogue.com. For more recipes, visit our web site, www.kingarthurflour.com. When you're in Vermont, stop by The Baker's Store here in Norwich, which carries everything in the catalogue, and more. Feel free to ask an employee-owner to sign your book!

Index